What you need to know about this book.

- Student Online Companion takes students to the Web for additional work.

- ExamView testing software gives you the option of generating a printed test, LAN-based test, or test over the Internet.

- New Perspectives Labs provide students with self-paced practice on computer-related topics.

- All tutorial cases are NEW to this edition!

- Contemporary case stories draw on the latest high-tech scenarios, including a network consulting business and an electronic graphic design firm. Other case stories involve more traditional businesses (such as a landscape design company) that have adapted to modern business demands.

- Students will appreciate how the concepts of desktop publishing are presented and compared to Web page design.

- Our coverage of mail merge explains how to complete the merge using both the new Mail Merge Task Pane and the toolbar buttons.

- The tutorial on sharing documents begins by having students compare and merge three documents. The tutorial clearly explains the issues related to sharing documents in printed form, via e-mail, and as a Web page.

- Students master automation techniques so they can work more efficiently. Students create their own macros and even edit macro code in the VBA editor. They also learn how to use the new Smart Tag feature.

- The tutorial on managing long documents includes extensive coverage of many advanced features, such as master documents, versions, routing, revision tracking, digital signatures, indexes, tables of contents, and tables of figures.

- This book is certified at the MOUS Expert level for Word 2002!

CASE	TROUBLE?	SESSION 1.1	QUICK CHECK	RW
Tutorial Case Each tutorial begins with a problem presented in a case that is meaningful to students. The case sets the scene to help students understand what they will do in the tutorial.	**TROUBLE? Paragraphs** These paragraphs anticipate the mistakes or problems that students may have and help them continue with the tutorial.	**Sessions** Each tutorial is divided into sessions designed to be completed in about 45 minutes each. Students should take as much time as they need and take a break between sessions.	**Quick Check Questions** Each session concludes with conceptual Quick Check questions that test students' understanding of what they learned in the session.	**Reference Windows** Reference Windows are succinct summaries of the most important tasks covered in a tutorial. They preview actions students will perform in the steps to follow.

www.course.com/NewPerspectives

APPROVED COURSEWARE

What does this logo mean?

It means this courseware has been approved by the Microsoft® Office User Specialist Program to be among the finest available for learning Microsoft Word 2002. It also means that upon completion of this courseware, you may be prepared to become a Microsoft Office User Specialist.

What is a Microsoft Office User Specialist?

A Microsoft Office User Specialist is an individual who has certified his or her skills in one or more of the Microsoft Office desktop applications of Microsoft Word, Microsoft Excel, Microsoft PowerPoint®, Microsoft Outlook®, or Microsoft Access, or in Microsoft Project. The Microsoft Office User Specialist Program typically offers certification exams at the "Core" and "Expert" skill levels. * The Microsoft Office User Specialist Program is the only Microsoft approved program in the world for certifying proficiency in Microsoft Office desktop applications and Microsoft Project. This certification can be a valuable asset in any job search or career advancement.

More Information:

To learn more about becoming a Microsoft Office User Specialist, visit www.mous.net

To purchase a Microsoft Office User Specialist certification exam, visit www.DesktopIQ.com

To learn about other Microsoft Office User Specialist approved courseware from Course Technology, visit www.course.com/NewPerspectives/TeachersLounge/mous.cfm

---

BRIEF CONTENTS

BRIEF CONTENTS

New Perspectives on

MICROSOFT® WORD 2002

Comprehensive

S. SCOTT ZIMMERMAN
Brigham Young University

BEVERLY B. ZIMMERMAN
Brigham Young University

ANN SHAFFER

COURSE
TECHNOLOGY
———*———
™
THOMSON LEARNING   Australia • Canada • Mexico • Singapore • Spain • United Kingdom • United States

COURSE TECHNOLOGY

THOMSON LEARNING

New Perspectives on Microsoft® Word 2002—Comprehensive
is published by Course Technology.

Managing Editor:
Greg Donald

Technology Product Manager:
Amanda Young

Production Editor:
Elena Montillo

Senior Editor:
Donna Gridley

Editorial Assistant:
Jessica Engstrom

Composition:
GEX Publishing Services

Senior Product Manager:
Kathy Finnegan

Marketing Manager:
Sean Teare

Text Designer:
Meral Dabcovich

Product Manager:
Melissa Hathaway

Developmental Editors:
Lisa Ruffolo, Ann Shaffer

Cover Designer:
Efrat Reis

Preface

Course Technology is the world leader in information technology education. The New Perspectives Series is an integral part of Course Technology's success. Visit our Web site to see a whole new perspective on teaching and learning solutions.

New Perspectives—Building Computer Skills Has Never Been This Real

Why New Perspectives will work for you.

Critical thinking and problem solving—without them, computer skills are learned but soon forgotten. With its case-based approach, the New Perspectives Series challenges students to apply what they've learned to real-life situations. Become a member of the New Perspectives community and watch your students not only master computer skills, but also retain and carry this knowledge into the world.

New Perspectives catalog
Our online catalog is never out of date! Go to the Catalog button on our Web site to check out our available titles, request a desk copy, download a book preview, or locate online files.

Complete system of offerings
Whether you're looking for a Brief book, an Advanced book, or something in between, we've got you covered. Go to the Catalog button on our Web site to find the level of coverage that's right for you.

Instructor materials
We have all the tools you need—data files, solution files, figure files, a sample syllabus, and ExamView, our powerful testing software package.

How well do your students know Microsoft Office?
Find out with performance-based testing software that measures your students' proficiency in the application. Click the Tech Center button to learn more.

Get certified
If you want to get certified, we have the titles for you. Find out more by clicking the Teacher's Lounge button.

Interested in online learning?
Enhance your course with any one of our online learning platforms. Go to the Teacher's Lounge to find the platform that's right for you.

Your link to the future is at
www.course.com/NewPerspectives

TABLE OF CONTENTS

Microsoft Office XP   OFF 1

Read This Before You Begin   OFF 2

Tutorial 1   OFF 3

Introducing Microsoft Office XP

Preparing Promotional Materials for Delmar Office Supplies

Microsoft Word 2002—
Level I Tutorials   WD 1.01
Read This Before You Begin   WD 1.02

Tutorial 1   WD 1.03

Creating a Document

Writing a Business Letter for Art4U Inc.

SESSION 1.1   **WD 1.04**

SESSION 1.2   **WD 1.14**

Acknowledgments

I'm extremely grateful to the following reviewers for their detailed comments and suggestions, which were very helpful. Reviewing a manuscript is hard work, and they did a great job: Anne Burchardt, Jackson Community College; Michael Feiler, Merritt College; Eric Johnston, Vatterott College; Carol Milliken, Kellogg Community College; and Barbara Williams, Wisconsin Indianhead Technical College.

Many thanks to the following members of the Quality Assurance team at Course Technology for verifying the technical accuracy of every step: John Bosco, Quality Assurance Project Leader; Marianne Broughey, Quality Assurance Tester; and Harris Bierhoff, Quality Assurance Tester.

Thank you to the smart, friendly, helpful people on the New Perspectives Team, including Greg Donald, Donna Gridley, Jessica Engstrom, and Rachel Crapser. Special thanks to Kathy Finnegan, Senior Product Manager, who cheerfully kept track of a thousand details and deadlines and who always managed to provide encouragement at exactly the right moment. Sincere thanks to the amazing Lisa Ruffolo, of The Software Resource; a writer couldn't hope for a better editor or a kinder friend. Thank you, also, to Elena Montillo, Production Editor, for patiently managing a very complicated production process, transforming the manuscript into a published book. I owe a great debt to Beverly and Scott Zimmerman, writers and teachers extraordinaire, for giving me the opportunity to be a part of their team. Finally, this book is dedicated to Dean, Joe, and Jerome, three of the nicest wise guys I could ever hope to meet.

Ann Shaffer

We likewise want to thank all those who made this book possible. We specifically thank Ann Shaffer, our co-author, for her hard work and creative talents in bringing this new edition to fruition.

Beverly and Scott
Zimmerman

New Perspectives on

MICROSOFT®

WINDOWS® 2000

PROFESSIONAL

Read This Before You Begin

To the Student

Make Data Disk Program

To complete the Level I tutorials, Review Assignments, and Projects, you need three Data Disks. Your instructor will either provide you with Data Disks or ask you to make your own.

If you are making your own Data Disks you will need three blank, formatted high-density disks and access to the Make Data Disk program. If you want to install the Make Data Disk program to your home computer, you can obtain it from your instructor or from the Web. To download the Make Data Disk program from the Web, go to www.course.com, click Data Disks, and follow the instructions on the screen.

To install the Make Data Disk program, select and click the file you just downloaded from www.course.com, 6548-9.exe. Follow the onscreen instructions to complete the installation. If you have any trouble obtaining or installing the Make Data Disk program, ask your instructor or technical support person for assistance.

Once you have obtained and installed the Make Data Disk program, you can use it to create your Data Disks according to the steps in the tutorials.

Course Labs

The Level I tutorials in this book feature three interactive Course Labs to help you understand Using a Keyboard, Using a Mouse, and Using Files concepts. There are Lab Assignments at the end of Tutorials 1 and 2 that relate to these Labs. To start a Lab, click the **Start** button on the Windows 2000 taskbar, point to **Programs**, point to

Course Labs, point to **New Perspectives Course Labs**, and click the name of the Lab you want to use.

Using Your Own Computer

If you are going to work through this book using your own computer, you need:

- ■ **Computer System** Microsoft Windows 2000 Professional must be installed on a local hard drive or on a network drive. This book is about Windows 2000 Professional—for those who have Windows 2000 Millennium, you might notice some differences.

- ■ **Data Disks** You will not be able to complete the tutorials or exercises in this book using your own computer until you have your Data Disks. See "Make Data Disk Program" above for details on obtaining your Data Disks.

- ■ **Course Labs** See your instructor or technical support person to obtain the Course Lab software for use on your own computer.

Visit Our World Wide Web Site

Additional materials designed especially for you are available on the World Wide Web. Go to http://www.course.com.

To the Instructor

The Make Data Disk Program and Course Labs for this title are available in the Instructor's Resource Kit for this title. Follow the instructions in the Help file on the CD-ROM to install the programs to your network or standalone computer. For information on using the Make Data Disk Program or the Course Labs, see the "To the Student" section above. Students will be switching the default installation settings to Web style in Tutorial 2. You are granted a license to copy the Data Files and Course Labs to any computer or computer network used by students who have purchased this book.

OBJECTIVES

In this tutorial you will:

- Start and shut down Windows 2000

- Identify the objects on the Windows 2000 desktop

- Practice mouse functions

- Run software programs, switch between them, and close them

- Identify and use the controls in a window

- Use Windows 2000 controls such as menus, toolbars, list boxes, scroll bars, option buttons, tabs, and check boxes

- Explore the Windows 2000 Help system

LABS

Using a Keyboard   **Using a Mouse**

EXPLORING THE BASICS

Investigating the Windows 2000 Operating System

CASE

Your First Day on the Computer

You walk into the computer lab and sit down at a desk. There's a computer in front of you, and you find yourself staring dubiously at the screen. Where to start? As if in answer to your question, your friend Steve Laslow appears.

"You start with the operating system," says Steve. Noticing your puzzled look, Steve explains that the **operating system** is software that helps the computer carry out operating tasks such as displaying information on the computer screen and saving data on your disks. (Software refers to the **programs**, or **applications**, that a computer uses to perform tasks.) Your computer uses the **Microsoft Windows 2000 Professional** operating system—Windows 2000, for short.

Steve explains that much of the software available for Windows 2000 has a standard graphical user interface. This means that once you have learned how to use one Windows program, such as Microsoft Word word-processing software, you are well on your way to understanding how to use other Windows software. Windows 2000 lets you use more than one program at a time, so you can easily switch between them—between your word-processing software and your appointment book software, for example. Finally, Windows 2000 makes it very easy to access the **Internet**, the worldwide collection of computers connected to one another to enable communication. All in all, Windows 2000 makes your computer effective and easy to use.

Steve recommends that you get started right away by starting Microsoft Windows 2000 and practicing some basic skills.

SESSION 1.1

In this session, in addition to learning basic Windows terminology, you will learn how to use a pointing device, how to start and close a program, and how to use more than one program at a time.

Starting Windows 2000

Using a Keyboard

Windows 2000 automatically starts when you turn on the computer. Depending on the way your computer is set up, you might be asked to enter your username and password.

To start Windows 2000:

1. Turn on your computer.

TROUBLE? If you are asked to select an operating system, do not take action. Windows 2000 will start automatically after a designated number of seconds. If it does not, ask your technical support person for help.

TROUBLE? If prompted to do so, type your assigned username and press the Tab key. Then type your password and press the Enter key to continue.

TROUBLE? If this is the first time you have started your computer with Windows 2000, messages might appear on your screen informing you that Windows is setting up components of your computer. If the Getting Started with Windows 2000 box appears, press and hold down the Alt key on your keyboard and then, while you hold down the Alt key, press the F4 key. The box closes.

After a moment, Windows 2000 starts. Windows 2000 has a **graphical user interface** (**GUI,** pronounced "gooey"), which uses **icons,** or pictures of familiar objects, such as file folders and documents, to represent items in your computer such as programs or files. Microsoft Windows 2000 gets its name from the rectangular work areas, called "windows," that appear on your screen as you work (although no windows should be open right now).

The Windows 2000 Desktop

In Windows terminology, the area displayed on your screen when Windows 2000 starts represents a **desktop**—a workspace for projects and the tools needed to manipulate those projects. When you first start a computer, it uses **default** settings, those preset by the operating system. The default desktop, for example, has a plain blue background. However, Microsoft designed Windows 2000 so that you can easily change the appearance of the desktop. You can, for example, add color, patterns, images, and text to the desktop background.

Many institutions design customized desktops for their computers. Figure 1-1 shows the default Windows 2000 desktop and two other examples of desktops, one designed for a business, North Pole Novelties, and one designed for a school, the University of Colorado. Although your desktop might not look exactly like any of the examples in Figure 1-1, you should be able to locate objects on your screen similar to those in Figure 1-1. Look at your screen and locate the objects labeled in Figure 1-1. The objects on your screen might appear larger or smaller than those in Figure 1-1, depending on your monitor's settings.

| Figure 1-1 | THE WINDOWS 2000 DESKTOP |

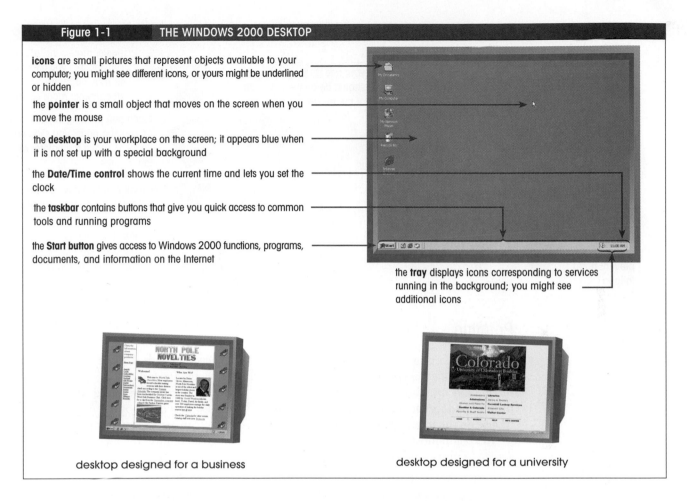

icons are small pictures that represent objects available to your computer; you might see different icons, or yours might be underlined or hidden

the **pointer** is a small object that moves on the screen when you move the mouse

the **desktop** is your workplace on the screen; it appears blue when it is not set up with a special background

the **Date/Time control** shows the current time and lets you set the clock

the **taskbar** contains buttons that give you quick access to common tools and running programs

the **Start button** gives access to Windows 2000 functions, programs, documents, and information on the Internet

the **tray** displays icons corresponding to services running in the background; you might see additional icons

desktop designed for a business

desktop designed for a university

If the screen goes blank or starts to display a moving design, press any key to restore the Windows 2000 desktop.

Using a Pointing Device

Using a Mouse

A **pointing device** helps you interact with objects on the screen. Pointing devices come in many shapes and sizes; some are designed to ensure that your hand won't suffer fatigue while using them. Some are directly attached to your computer via a cable, whereas others function like a TV remote control and allow you to access your computer without being right next to it. Figure 1-2 shows examples of common pointing devices.

The most common pointing device is called a **mouse**, so this book uses that term. If you are using a different pointing device, such as a trackball, substitute that device whenever you see the term "mouse." Because Windows 2000 uses a graphical user interface, you need to know how to use the mouse to manipulate the objects on the screen. In this session you will learn about pointing and clicking. In Session 1.2 you will learn how to use the mouse to drag objects.

You can also interact with objects by using the keyboard; however, the mouse is more convenient for most tasks, so the tutorials in this book assume you are using one.

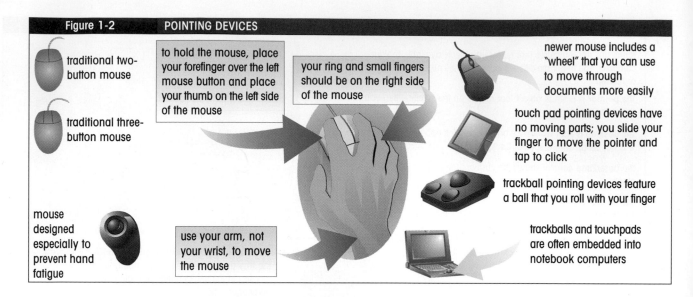

Figure 1-2 POINTING DEVICES

traditional two-button mouse

traditional three-button mouse

to hold the mouse, place your forefinger over the left mouse button and place your thumb on the left side of the mouse

your ring and small fingers should be on the right side of the mouse

newer mouse includes a "wheel" that you can use to move through documents more easily

touch pad pointing devices have no moving parts; you slide your finger to move the pointer and tap to click

trackball pointing devices feature a ball that you roll with your finger

mouse designed especially to prevent hand fatigue

use your arm, not your wrist, to move the mouse

trackballs and touchpads are often embedded into notebook computers

Pointing

You use a pointing device to move the pointer over objects on the desktop. The pointer is usually shaped like an arrow ⇖ , although it can change shape depending on where it is on the screen and on what tasks you are performing. Most computer users place the mouse on a **mouse pad**, a flat piece of rubber that helps the mouse move smoothly. As you move the mouse on the mouse pad, the pointer on the screen moves in a corresponding direction.

You begin most Windows operations by positioning the pointer over a specific part of the screen. This is called **pointing**.

To move the pointer:

1. Position your right index finger over the left mouse button, as shown in Figure 1-2, but don't click yet. Lightly grasp the sides of the mouse with your thumb and little fingers.

   TROUBLE? If you want to use the mouse with your left hand, ask your instructor or technical support person to help you use the Control Panel to swap the functions of the left and right mouse buttons. Be sure to find out how to change back to the right-handed mouse setting, so that you can reset the mouse each time you are finished in the lab.

2. Place the mouse on the mouse pad and then move the mouse. Watch the movement of the pointer.

   TROUBLE? If you run out of room to move your mouse, lift the mouse and place it in the middle of the mouse pad. Notice that the pointer does not move when the mouse is not in contact with the mouse pad.

When you position the mouse pointer over certain objects, such as the objects on the taskbar, a "tip" appears. These "tips" are called **ScreenTips**, and they tell you the purpose or function of an object.

To view ScreenTips:

1. Use the mouse to point to the **Start** button ![Start], but don't click it. After a few seconds, you see the tip "Click here to begin," as shown in Figure 1-3.

TROUBLE? If the Start button and taskbar don't appear, point to the bottom of the screen. They will then appear.

Figure 1-3	VIEWING SCREENTIPS

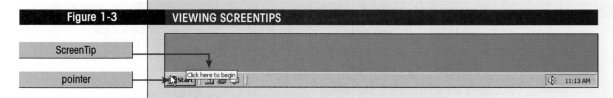

ScreenTip

pointer

2. Point to the time on the right end of the taskbar. Notice that today's date (or the date to which your computer's time clock is set) appears.

Clicking

Clicking is when you press a mouse button and immediately release it. Clicking sends a signal to your computer that you want to perform an action on the object you click. In Windows 2000 most actions are performed using the left mouse button. If you are told to click an object, click it with the left mouse button, unless instructed otherwise.

When you click the Start button, the Start menu appears. A **menu** is a list of options that you use to complete tasks. The **Start menu** provides you with access to programs, documents, and much more. Try clicking the Start button to open the Start menu.

To open the Start menu:

1. Point to the **Start** button ![Start].

2. Click the left mouse button. An arrow ▶ following an option on the Start menu indicates that you can view additional choices by navigating a **submenu**, a menu extending from the main menu. See Figure 1-4.

Figure 1-4	START MENU

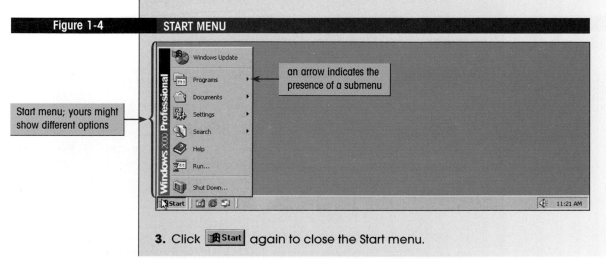

an arrow indicates the presence of a submenu

Start menu; yours might show different options

3. Click ![Start] again to close the Start menu.

Next you'll learn how to select items on a submenu.

Selecting

In Windows 2000, pointing and clicking are often used to **select** an object, in other words, to choose it as the object you want to work with. Windows 2000 shows you which object is selected by highlighting it, usually by changing the object's color, putting a box around it, or making the object appear to be pushed in, as shown in Figure 1-5.

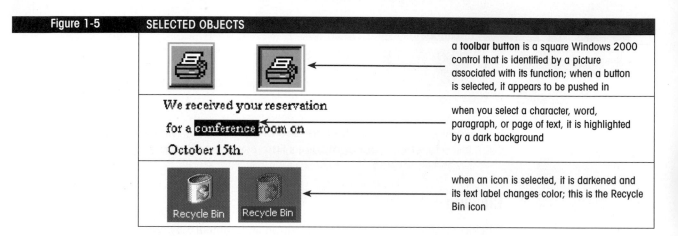

Figure 1-5   SELECTED OBJECTS

a **toolbar button** is a square Windows 2000 control that is identified by a picture associated with its function; when a button is selected, it appears to be pushed in

We received your reservation for a conference room on October 15th.

when you select a character, word, paragraph, or page of text, it is highlighted by a dark background

when an icon is selected, it is darkened and its text label changes color; this is the Recycle Bin icon

In Windows 2000, depending on your computer's settings, some objects are selected when you simply point to them, others when you click them. Practice selecting the Programs option on the Start menu to open the Programs submenu.

To select an option on a menu:

1. Click the **Start** button 🔳Start and notice how it appears to be pushed in, indicating it is selected.

2. Point to (but don't click) the **Programs** option. After a short pause, the Programs submenu opens, and the Programs option is highlighted to indicate it is selected. See Figure 1-6.

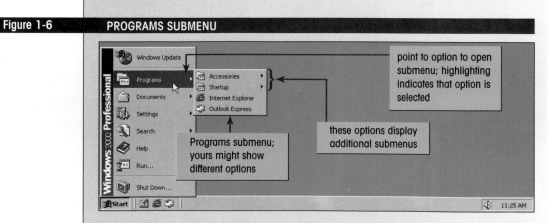

Figure 1-6   PROGRAMS SUBMENU

point to option to open submenu; highlighting indicates that option is selected

these options display additional submenus

Programs submenu; yours might show different options

TROUBLE? If a submenu other than the Programs menu opens, you selected the wrong option. Move the mouse so that the pointer points to Programs.

> TROUBLE? If the Programs option doesn't appear, your Start menu might have too many options to fit on the screen. If that is the case, a double arrow ⌄ appears at the top or bottom of the Start menu. Click first the top and then the bottom arrow to view additional Start menu options until you locate the Programs menu option, and then point to it.
>
> **3.** Now close the Start menu by clicking **Start** again.

You return to the desktop.

Right-Clicking

Pointing devices were originally designed with a single button, so the term "clicking" had only one meaning: you pressed that button. Innovations in technology, however, led to the addition of a second and even a third button (and more recently, options such as a wheel) that expanded the pointing device's capability. More recent software—especially that designed for Windows 2000—takes advantage of the additional buttons, especially the right button. However, the term "clicking" continues to refer to the left button; clicking an object with the *right* button is called **right-clicking**.

In Windows 2000, right-clicking both selects an object and opens its **shortcut menu**, a list of options directly related to the object you right-clicked. You can right-click practically any object—the Start button, a desktop icon, the taskbar, and even the desktop itself—to view options associated with that object. For example, the first desktop shown in Figure 1-7 illustrates what happens when you click the Start button with the left mouse button to open the Start menu. Clicking the Start button with the right button, however, opens the Start button's shortcut menu, as shown in the second desktop.

| Figure 1-7 | CLICKING WITH THE LEFT AND RIGHT MOUSE BUTTONS |

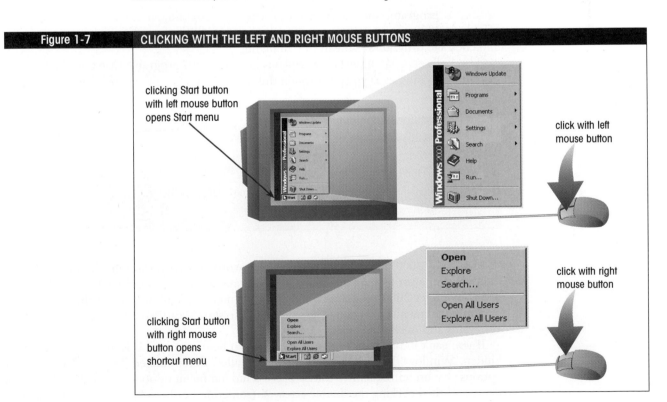

Try using right-clicking to open the shortcut menu for the Start button.

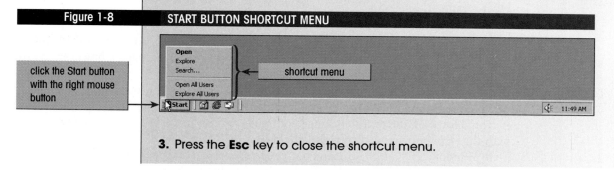

To right-click an object:

1. Position the pointer over the Start button.

2. Right-click the **Start** button [Start]. The shortcut menu that opens offers a list of options available to the Start button.

TROUBLE? If you are using a trackball or a mouse with three buttons or a wheel, make sure you click the button on the far right, not the one in the middle.

TROUBLE? If your menu looks slightly different from the one in Figure 1-8, don't worry. Different systems will have different options.

| Figure 1-8 | START BUTTON SHORTCUT MENU |

click the Start button with the right mouse button

Open
Explore
Search...

Open All Users
Explore All Users

shortcut menu

Start   11:49 AM

3. Press the **Esc** key to close the shortcut menu.

You again return to the desktop.

Starting **and Closing a Program**

To use a program, such as a word-processing program, you must first start it. With Windows 2000 you usually start a program by clicking the Start button and then you locate and click the program's name in the submenus.

The Reference Window below explains how to start a program. Don't do the steps in the Reference Windows as you go through the tutorials; they are for your later reference.

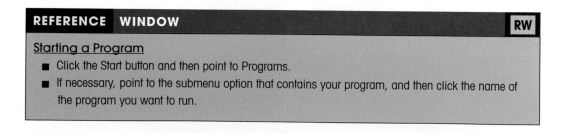

REFERENCE WINDOW   **RW**

Starting a Program
- Click the Start button and then point to Programs.
- If necessary, point to the submenu option that contains your program, and then click the name of the program you want to run.

Windows 2000 includes an easy-to-use word-processing program called WordPad. Suppose you want to start the WordPad program and use it to write a letter or report. You open Windows 2000 programs from the Start menu. Programs are usually located on the Programs submenu or on one of its submenus. To start WordPad, for example, you select the Programs and Accessories submenus.

If you can't locate an item that is supposed to be on a menu, it is most likely temporarily hidden. Windows 2000 menus use a feature called **Personalized Menus** that hides menu options you use infrequently. You can access hidden menu options by pointing to the menu name and then clicking the double arrow ⬇ (sometimes called a "chevron") at the bottom of the menu. You can also access the hidden options by holding the pointer over the menu name.

To start the WordPad program from the Start menu:

1. Click the **Start** button [Start] to open the Start menu.

2. Point to **Programs**. The Programs submenu appears.

3. Point to **Accessories**. The Accessories submenu appears. Figure 1-9 shows the open menus.

TROUBLE? If a different menu opens, you might have moved the mouse diagonally so that a different submenu opened. Move the pointer to the right across the Programs option, and then move it up or down to point to Accessories. Once you're more comfortable moving the mouse, you'll find that you can eliminate this problem by moving the mouse quickly.

TROUBLE? If WordPad doesn't appear on the Accessories submenu, continue to point to Accessories until WordPad appears.

| Figure 1-9 | START MENU |

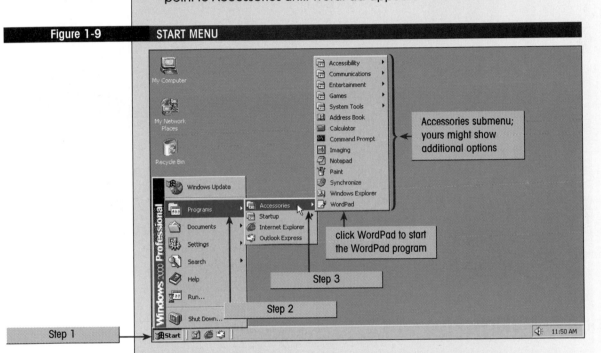

4. Click **WordPad**. The WordPad program opens, as shown in Figure 1-10. If the WordPad window fills the entire screen, don't worry. You will learn how to manipulate windows in Session 1.2.

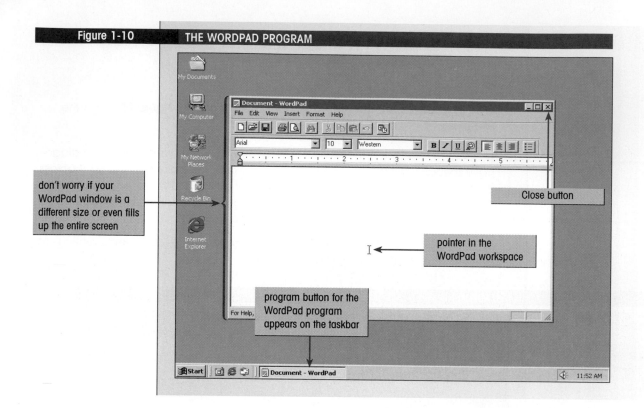

Figure 1-10   THE WORDPAD PROGRAM

don't worry if your WordPad window is a different size or even fills up the entire screen

Close button

pointer in the WordPad workspace

program button for the WordPad program appears on the taskbar

When a program is started, it is said to be **open** or **running**. A **program button** appears on the taskbar for each open program. You click program buttons to switch between open programs. When you are finished using a program, click the Close button ☒.

To exit the WordPad program:

1. Click the **Close** button ☒. See Figure 1-10. You return to the Windows 2000 desktop.

Running **Multiple Programs**

One of the most useful features of Windows 2000 is its ability to run multiple programs at the same time. This feature, known as **multitasking**, allows you to work on more than one project at a time and to switch quickly between projects. For example, you can start WordPad and leave it running while you then start the Paint program.

To run WordPad and Paint at the same time:

1. Start WordPad again and then click the **Start** button 🏁 Start again.

2. Point to **Programs** and then point to **Accessories**.

3. Click **Paint**. The Paint program opens, as shown in Figure 1-11. Now two programs are running at the same time.

   TROUBLE? If the Paint program fills the entire screen, don't worry. You will learn how to manipulate windows in Session 1.2.

Figure 1-11 | **THE PAINT PROGRAM**

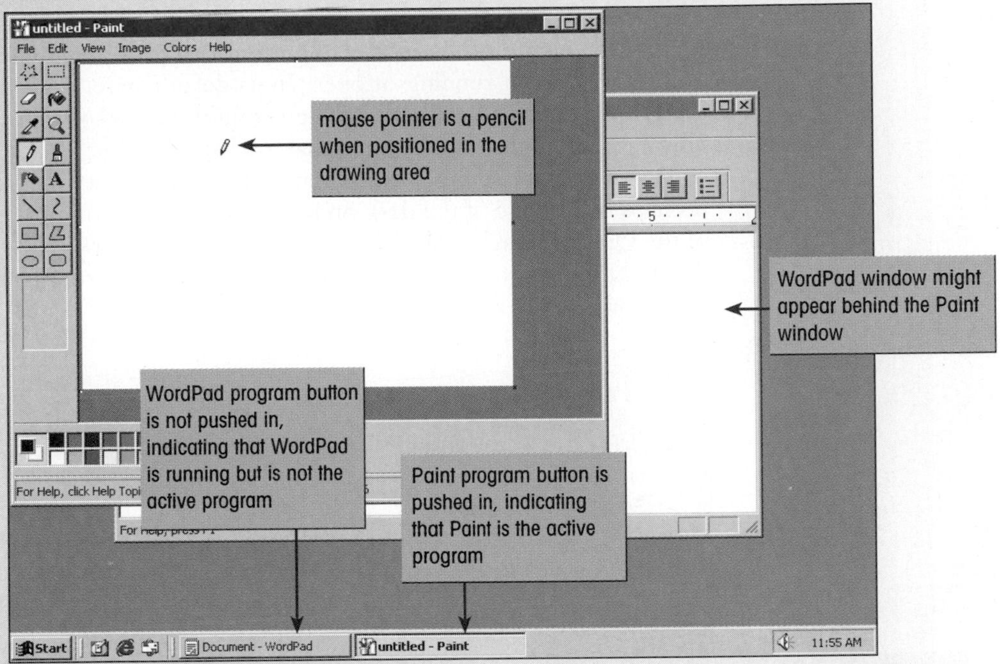

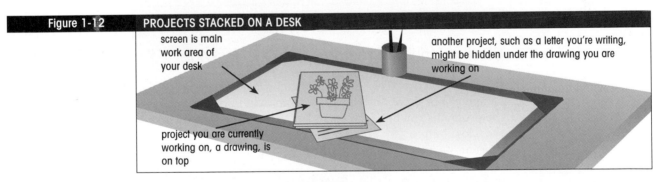

What happened to WordPad? The WordPad program button is still on the taskbar, so even if you can't see it, WordPad is still running. You can imagine that it is stacked behind the Paint program, as shown in Figure 1-12. Paint is the active program because it is the one with which you are currently working.

Figure 1-12 | **PROJECTS STACKED ON A DESK**

screen is main work area of your desk

another project, such as a letter you're writing, might be hidden under the drawing you are working on

project you are currently working on, a drawing, is on top

Switching Between Programs

The easiest way to switch between programs is to use the buttons on the taskbar.

To switch between WordPad and Paint:

1. Click the button labeled **Document - WordPad** on the taskbar. The Document - WordPad button now looks as if it has been pushed in, to indicate that it is the active program, and WordPad moves to the front.
2. Next, click the button labeled **untitled - Paint** on the taskbar to switch to the Paint program.

The Paint program is again the active program.

Accessing the Desktop from the Quick Launch Toolbar

The Windows 2000 taskbar, as you've seen, displays buttons for programs currently running. It also can contain **toolbars**, sets of buttons that give single-click access to programs or documents that aren't running or open. In its default state, the Windows 2000 taskbar displays the **Quick Launch toolbar**, which gives quick access to Web programs and to the desktop. Your taskbar might contain additional toolbars, or none at all.

When you are running more than one program but you want to return to the desktop, perhaps to use one of the desktop icons such as My Computer, you can do so by using one of the Quick Launch toolbar buttons. Clicking the Show Desktop button returns you to the desktop. The open programs are not closed; they are simply made inactive and reduced to buttons on the taskbar.

To return to the desktop:

1. Click the **Show Desktop** button on the Quick Launch toolbar. The desktop appears, and both the Paint and WordPad programs are temporarily inactive. See Figure 1-13.

   TROUBLE? If the Quick Launch toolbar doesn't appear on your taskbar, right-click the taskbar, point to Toolbars, and then click Quick Launch and try Step 1 again.

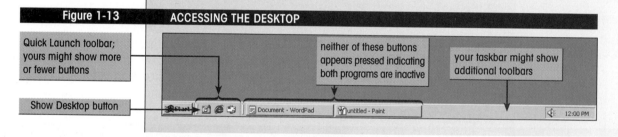

Figure 1-13   ACCESSING THE DESKTOP

Quick Launch toolbar; yours might show more or fewer buttons

Show Desktop button

neither of these buttons appears pressed indicating both programs are inactive

your taskbar might show additional toolbars

Start | Document - WordPad | untitled - Paint | 12:00 PM

Closing Inactive Programs from the Taskbar

It is good practice to close each program when you are finished using it. Each program uses computer resources, such as memory, so Windows 2000 works more efficiently when only the programs you need are open. You've already seen how to close an open program using the Close button. You can also close a program, whether active or inactive, by using the shortcut menu associated with the program button on the taskbar.

To close WordPad and Paint using the program button shortcut menus:

1. Right-click the **untitled – Paint** button on the taskbar. To right-click something, remember that you click it with the right mouse button. The shortcut menu for that program button opens. See Figure 1-14.

2. Click **Close**. The button labeled "untitled – Paint" disappears from the taskbar, indicating that the Paint program is closed.

3. Right-click the **Document – WordPad** button on the taskbar, and then click **Close**. The WordPad button disappears from the taskbar.

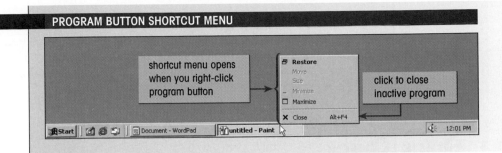

| Figure 1-14 | PROGRAM BUTTON SHORTCUT MENU |

Shutting Down Windows 2000

It is very important to shut down Windows 2000 before you turn off the computer. If you turn off your computer without correctly shutting down, you might lose data and damage your files.

You should typically use the "Shut Down" option when you want to turn off your computer. However, your school might prefer that you select the Log Off option in the Shut Down Windows dialog box. This option logs you out of Windows 2000, leaves the computer turned on, and allows another user to log on without restarting the computer. Check with your instructor or technical support person for the preferred method at your lab.

To shut down Windows 2000:

1. Click the **Start** button ▓Start on the taskbar to display the Start menu.

2. Click the **Shut Down** menu option. A box titled "Shut Down Windows" opens.

   TROUBLE? If you can't see the Shut Down menu option, your Start menu has more options than your screen can display. A double arrow ☰ appears at the bottom of the Start menu. Click this button until the Shut Down menu option appears, and then click Shut Down.

   TROUBLE? If you are supposed to log off rather than shut down, click the Log Off option instead and follow your school's logoff procedure.

3. Make sure the **Shut Down** option appears in the box shown in Figure 1-15.

   TROUBLE? If "Shut down" does not appear, click the arrow to the right of the box. A list of options appears. Click Shut Down.

| Figure 1-15 | SHUTTING DOWN |

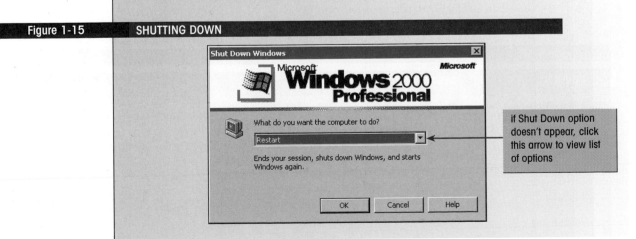

4. Click the **OK** button.

5. Wait until you see a message indicating it is safe to turn off your computer. If your lab staff has requested you to switch off your computer after shutting down, do so now. Otherwise leave the computer running. Some computers turn themselves off automatically.

Session 1.1 QUICK CHECK

1. What is the purpose of the taskbar?

2. The _____ feature of Windows 2000 allows you to run more than one program at a time.

3. The _____ is a list of options that provides you with access to programs, documents, submenus, and more.

4. What should you do if you are trying to move the pointer to the left edge of your screen, but your mouse bumps into the keyboard?

5. Even if you can't see an open program on your desktop, the program might be running. How can you tell if a program is running?

6. Why is it good practice to close each program when you are finished using it?

7. Why should you shut down Windows 2000 before you turn off your computer?

SESSION 1.2

In this session you will learn how to use many of the Windows 2000 controls to manipulate windows and programs. You will also learn how to change the size and shape of a window; how to move a window; and how to use menus, dialog boxes, tabs, buttons, and lists to specify how you want a program to carry out a task.

Anatomy of a Window

When you run a program in Windows 2000, it appears in a window. A **window** is a rectangular area of the screen that contains a program or data. Windows, spelled with an uppercase "W," is the name of the Microsoft operating system. The word "window" with a lowercase "w" refers to one of the rectangular areas on the screen. A window also contains controls for manipulating the window and for using the program. Figure 1-16 describes the controls you are likely to see in most windows.

Figure 1-16	WINDOW CONTROLS
CONTROL	**DESCRIPTION**
Menu bar	Contains the titles of menus, such as File, Edit, and Help
Sizing buttons	Let you enlarge, shrink, or close a window
Status bar	Provides you with messages relevant to the task you are performing
Title bar	Contains the window title and basic window control buttons
Toolbar	Contains buttons that provide you with shortcuts to common menu commands
Window title	Identifies the program and document contained in the window
Workspace	Part of the window you use to enter your work—to enter text, draw pictures, set up calculations, and so on

WordPad is a good example of a typical window, so try starting WordPad and identifying these controls in the WordPad window.

To look at window controls:

1. Make sure Windows 2000 is running and you are at the Windows 2000 desktop.

2. Start WordPad.

   TROUBLE? To start WordPad, click the Start button, point to Programs, point to Accessories, and then click WordPad.

3. On your screen, identify the controls labeled in Figure 1-17. Don't worry if your window fills the entire screen or is a different size. You'll learn to change window size shortly.

Figure 1-17 | WORDPAD WINDOW CONTROLS

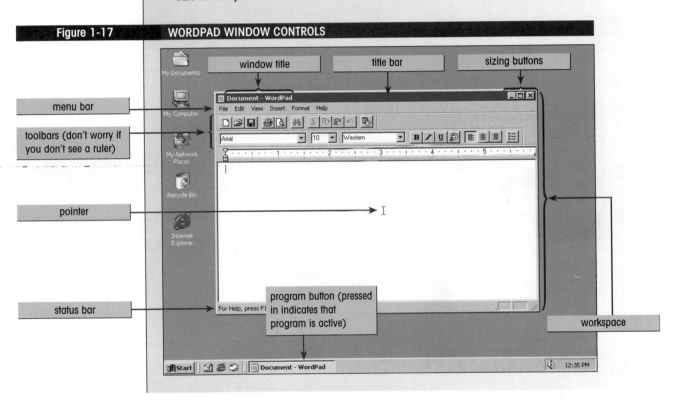

Manipulating a Window

There are three buttons located on the right side of the title bar. You are already familiar with the Close button. The Minimize button ▬ hides the window so that only its program button is visible on the taskbar. The other button changes name and function depending on the status of the window (it either maximizes the window or restores it to a predefined size). Figure 1-18 shows how these buttons work.

Minimizing a Window

The Minimize button hides a window so that only the button on the taskbar remains visible. You can use the Minimize button when you want to temporarily hide a window but keep the program running.

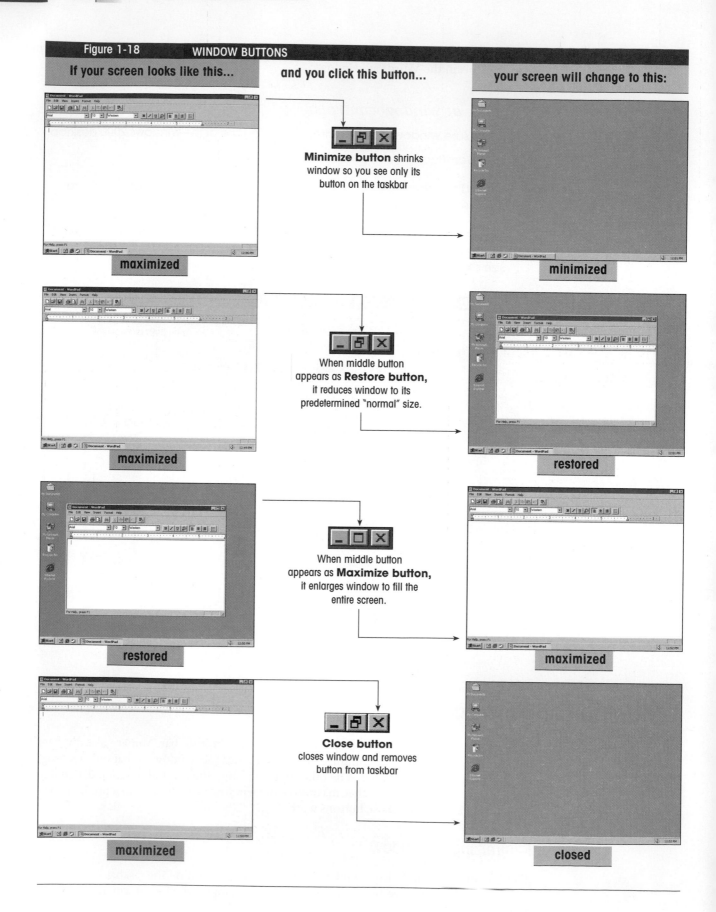

Figure 1-18   WINDOW BUTTONS

If your screen looks like this...   **and you click this button...**   **your screen will change to this:**

maximized

Minimize button shrinks window so you see only its button on the taskbar

minimized

maximized

When middle button appears as **Restore button,** it reduces window to its predetermined "normal" size.

restored

restored

When middle button appears as **Maximize button,** it enlarges window to fill the entire screen.

maximized

maximized

Close button closes window and removes button from taskbar

closed

To minimize the WordPad window:

1. Click the **Minimize** button ☐. The WordPad window shrinks so that only the Document - WordPad button on the taskbar is visible.

   TROUBLE? If you accidentally clicked the Close button and closed the window, use the Start button to start WordPad again.

Redisplaying a Window

You can redisplay a minimized window by clicking the program's button on the taskbar. When you redisplay a window, it becomes the active window.

To redisplay the WordPad window:

1. Click the **Document - WordPad** button on the taskbar. The WordPad window is restored to its previous size. The Document - WordPad button looks pushed in as a visual clue that WordPad is now the active window.

2. The taskbar button provides another means of switching a window between its minimized and active state: Click the **Document - WordPad** button on the taskbar again to minimize the window.

3. Click the **Document - WordPad** button once more to redisplay the window.

Maximizing a Window

The Maximize button enlarges a window so that it fills the entire screen. You will probably do most of your work using maximized windows because they allow you to see more of your program and data.

To maximize the WordPad window:

1. Click the **Maximize** button ☐ on the WordPad title bar.

   TROUBLE? If the window is already maximized, it will fill the entire screen, and the Maximize button won't appear. Instead, you'll see the Restore button ☐. Skip Step 1.

Restoring a Window

The Restore button ☐ reduces the window so it is smaller than the entire screen. This is useful if you want to see more than one window at a time. Also, because of its smaller size, you can drag the window to another location on the screen or change its dimensions.

To restore a window:

1. Click the **Restore** button ☐ on the WordPad title bar. Notice that once a window is restored, ☐ changes to the Maximize button ☐.

Moving a Window

You can use the mouse to move a window to a new position on the screen. When you click an object and hold down the mouse button while moving the mouse, you are said to be **dragging** the object. You can move objects on the screen by dragging them to a new location. If you want to move a window, you drag its title bar. You cannot move a maximized window.

To drag the WordPad window to a new location:

1. Position the mouse pointer on the WordPad window title bar.

2. While you hold down the left mouse button, move the mouse to drag the window. A rectangle representing the window moves as you move the mouse.

3. Position the rectangle anywhere on the screen, then release the left mouse button. The WordPad window appears in the new location.

4. Now drag the WordPad window to the upper-left corner of the screen.

Changing the Size of a Window

You can also use the mouse to change the size of a window. Notice the sizing handle at the lower-right corner of the window. The **sizing handle** provides a visible control for changing the size of a window.

To change the size of the WordPad window:

1. Position the pointer over the sizing handle . The pointer changes to a diagonal arrow .

2. While holding down the mouse button, drag the sizing handle down and to the right.

3. Release the mouse button. Now the window is larger.

4. Practice using the sizing handle to make the WordPad window larger or smaller, and then maximize the WordPad window.

You can also drag the window borders left, right, up, or down to change a window's size.

Using **Program Menus**

Most Windows programs use menus to organize the program's menu options. The menu bar is typically located at the top of the program window and shows the titles of menus such as File, Edit, and Help.

Windows menus are relatively standardized—most Windows programs include similar menu options. It's easy to learn new programs, because you can make a pretty good guess about which menu contains the option you want.

Selecting Options from a Menu

When you click any menu title, choices for that menu appear below the menu bar. These choices are referred to as **menu options** or **commands**. To select a menu option, you click it. For example, the File menu is a standard feature in most Windows programs and contains the options typically related to working with a file: creating, opening, saving, and printing a file or document.

To select the Print Preview menu option on the File menu:

1. Click **File** on the WordPad menu bar to display the File menu. See Figure 1-19.

   TROUBLE? If you open a menu but decide not to select any of the menu options, you can close the menu by clicking its title again.

Figure 1-19	FILE MENU

don't worry if your menu shows additional options →

Print Preview option →

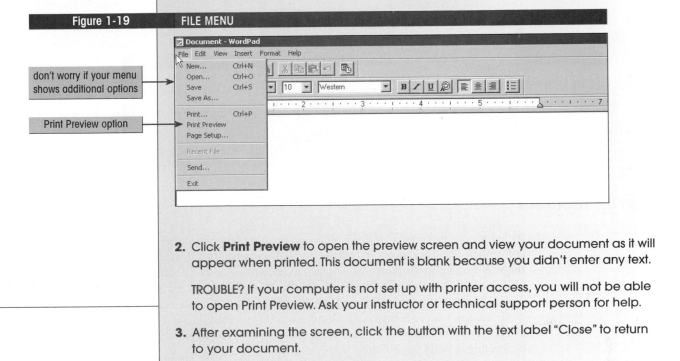

2. Click **Print Preview** to open the preview screen and view your document as it will appear when printed. This document is blank because you didn't enter any text.

   TROUBLE? If your computer is not set up with printer access, you will not be able to open Print Preview. Ask your instructor or technical support person for help.

3. After examining the screen, click the button with the text label "Close" to return to your document.

   TROUBLE? If you close WordPad by mistake, restart it.

Not all menu options immediately carry out an action—some show submenus or ask you for more information about what you want to do. The menu gives you hints about what to expect when you select an option. These hints are sometimes referred to as **menu conventions**. Figure 1-20 describes the Windows 2000 menu conventions.

Figure 1-20	MENU CONVENTIONS
CONVENTION	**DESCRIPTION**
Check mark	Indicates a toggle, or "on-off" switch (like a light switch) that is either checked (turned on) or not checked (turned off)
Ellipsis	Three dots that indicate you must make additional selections after you select that option. Options without dots do not require additional choices—they take effect as soon as you click them. If an option is followed by an ellipsis, a dialog box opens that allows you to enter specifications for how you want a task carried out.
Triangular arrow	Indicates the presence of a submenu. When you point at a menu option that has a triangular arrow, a submenu automatically appears.
Grayed-out option	Option that is not available. For example, a graphics program might display the Text Toolbar option in gray if there is no text in the graphic to work with.
Keyboard shortcut	A key or combination of keys that you can press to activate the menu option without actually opening the menu
Double arrow	Indicates that additional menu options are available; click the double arrow to access them

Figure 1-21 shows examples of these menu conventions.

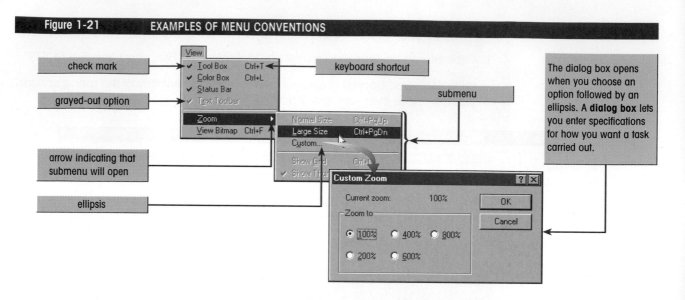

Figure 1-21   EXAMPLES OF MENU CONVENTIONS

Using Toolbars

Although you can usually perform all program commands using menus, toolbar buttons provide convenient one-click access to frequently used commands. For most Windows 2000 functions, there is usually more than one way to accomplish a task. To simplify your introduction to Windows 2000 in this tutorial, we will usually show you only one method for performing a task. As you become more accomplished at using Windows 2000, you can explore alternate methods.

In Session 1.1 you learned that Windows 2000 programs include ScreenTips, which indicate the purpose and function of a tool. Now is a good time to explore the WordPad toolbar buttons by looking at their ScreenTips.

To find out a toolbar button's function:

1. Position the pointer over any button on the toolbar, such as the Print Preview button. After a short pause, the name of the button appears in a box near the button, and a description of the button appears in the status bar just above the Start button. See Figure 1-22.

Figure 1-22   TOOLBAR BUTTON AIDS

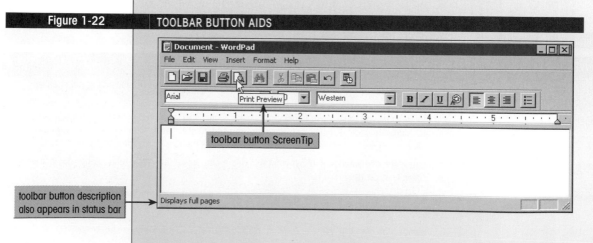

2. Move the pointer over each button on the toolbar to see its name and purpose.

You select a toolbar button by clicking it.

To select the Print Preview toolbar button:

1. Click the **Print Preview** button ⬚. The Print Preview screen appears. This is the same screen that appeared when you selected Print Preview from the File menu.

2. After examining the screen, click the button with the text label "Close" to return to your document.

Using **List Boxes and Scroll Bars**

As you might guess from the name, a **list box** displays a list of choices. In WordPad, date and time formats are shown in the Date/Time list box. List box controls usually include arrow buttons, a scroll bar, and a scroll box, as shown in Figure 1-23.

To use the Date/Time list box:

1. Click the **Date/Time** button ⬚ to display the Date and Time dialog box. See Figure 1-23.

Figure 1-23	LIST BOX

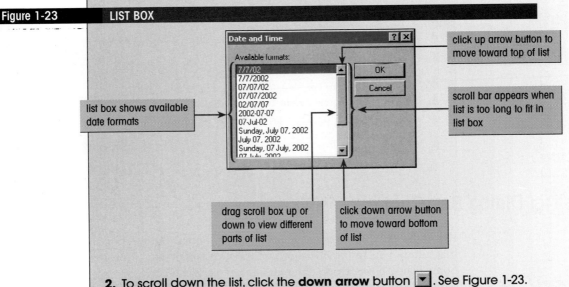

list box shows available date formats

click up arrow button to move toward top of list

scroll bar appears when list is too long to fit in list box

drag scroll box up or down to view different parts of list

click down arrow button to move toward bottom of list

2. To scroll down the list, click the **down arrow** button ▼. See Figure 1-23.

3. Find the scroll box on your screen. See Figure 1-23.

4. Drag the **scroll box** to the top of the scroll bar. Notice how the list scrolls back to the beginning.

TROUBLE? You learned how to drag when you learned to move a window. To drag the scroll box up, point to the scroll box, press and hold down the mouse button, and then move the mouse up.

5. Find a date in the format "July 07, 2002." Click that date format to select it.

6. Click the **OK** button to close the Date and Time dialog box. This inserts the current date in your document.

You can access some list boxes directly from the toolbar. When a list box is on the toolbar, only the current option appears in the list box. A **list arrow** appears on the right of the box and you can click it to view additional options.

To use the Font Size list box:

1. Click the **Font Size** list arrow, as shown in Figure 1-24.

Figure 1-24	FONT SIZE LIST ARROW

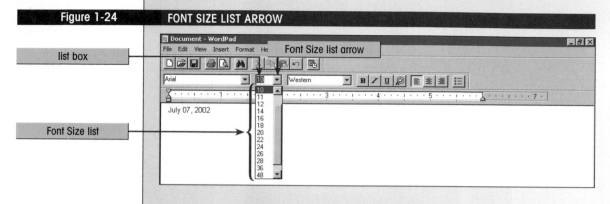

2. Click **18**. The list disappears, and the font size you selected appears in the list box.

3. Type a few characters to test the new font size.

4. Click the **Font Size** list arrow again.

5. Click **12**.

6. Type a few characters to test this type size.

7. Click the **Close** button ☒ to close WordPad.

8. When you see the message "Save changes to Document?" click the **No** button.

Using Dialog Box Controls

Recall that when you select a menu option or button followed by an ellipsis, a dialog box opens that allows you to provide more information about how a program should carry out a task. Some dialog boxes group different kinds of information into bordered rectangular areas called **panes**. Within these panes, you will usually find tabs, option buttons, check boxes, and other controls that the program uses to collect information about how you want it to perform a task. Figure 1-25 describes common dialog box controls.

Figure 1-25	DIALOG BOX CONTROLS
CONTROL	**DESCRIPTION**
Tabs	Modeled after the tabs on file folders, tab controls are often used as containers for other Windows 2000 controls such as list boxes, radio buttons, and check boxes. Click the appropriate tabs to view different pages of information or choices.
Option buttons	Also called **radio buttons**, option buttons allow you to select a single option from among one or more options.
Check boxes	Click a check box to select or deselect it; when it is selected, a check mark appears, indicating that the option is turned on; when deselected, the check box is blank and the option is off. When check boxes appear in groups, you can select or deselect as many as you want; they are not mutually exclusive, as option buttons are.
Spin boxes	Allow you to scroll easily through a set of numbers to choose the setting you want
Text boxes	Boxes into which you type additional information

Figure 1-26 displays examples of these controls.

Figure 1-26   EXAMPLES OF DIALOG BOX CONTROLS

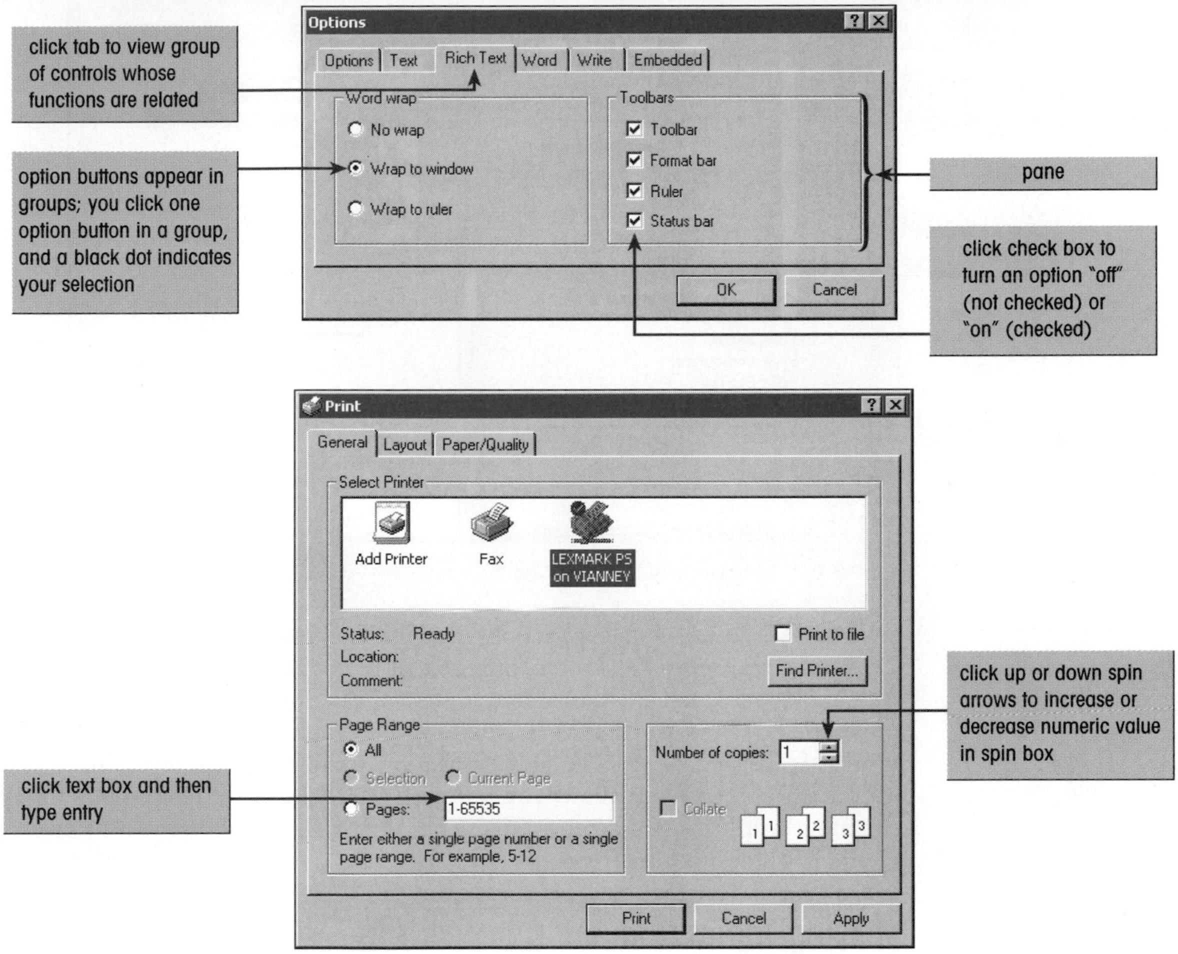

click tab to view group of controls whose functions are related

option buttons appear in groups; you click one option button in a group, and a black dot indicates your selection

pane

click check box to turn an option "off" (not checked) or "on" (checked)

click up or down spin arrows to increase or decrease numeric value in spin box

click text box and then type entry

Using Help

Windows 2000 **Help** provides on-screen information about the program you are using. Help for the Windows 2000 operating system is available by clicking the Start button on the taskbar, then selecting Help from the Start menu. If you want Help for a program, such as WordPad, you must first start the program, then click Help on the menu bar.

When you start Help, a Windows Help window opens, which gives you access to help files stored on your computer as well as help information stored on Microsoft's Web site. If you are not connected to the Web, you have access only to the help files stored on your computer.

To start Windows 2000 Help:

1. Click the **Start** button.

2. Click **Help**. The Windows 2000 window opens to the Contents tab. See Figure 1-27.

   TROUBLE? If the Contents tab is not in front, click the Contents tab to view the table of contents.

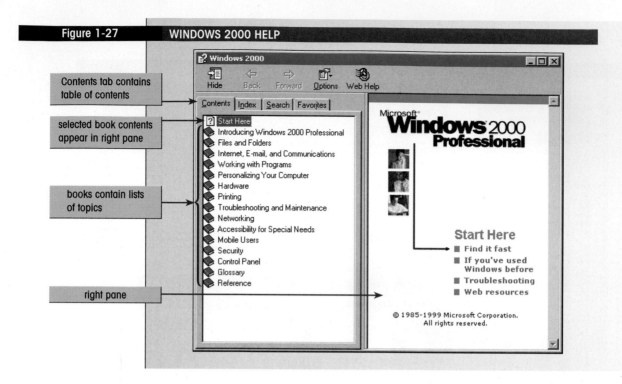

Figure 1-27 **WINDOWS 2000 HELP**

Contents tab contains table of contents

selected book contents appear in right pane

books contain lists of topics

right pane

Help uses tabs for the four sections of Help: Contents, Index, Search, and Favorites. The **Contents tab** groups Help topics into a series of books. You select a book 📖 by clicking it. The book opens, and a list of related topics appears from which you can choose. Individual topics are designated with the [?] icon. Overview topics are designated with the 📖 icon.

The **Index tab** displays an alphabetical list of all the Help topics from which you can choose. The **Search tab** allows you to search the entire set of Help topics for all topics that contain a word or words you specify. The **Favorites tab** allows you to save your favorite Help topics for quick reference.

Viewing Topics from the Contents Tab

You know that Windows 2000 gives you easy access to the Internet. Suppose you're wondering how to connect to the Internet from your computer. You can use the Contents tab to find more information on a specific topic.

To use the Contents tab:

1. Click the **Internet, E-mail, and Communications** book icon 📖. A list of topics and an overview appear below the book title.

2. Click the **Connect to the Internet** topic icon [?]. Information about connecting to the Internet appears in the right pane. See Figure 1-28.

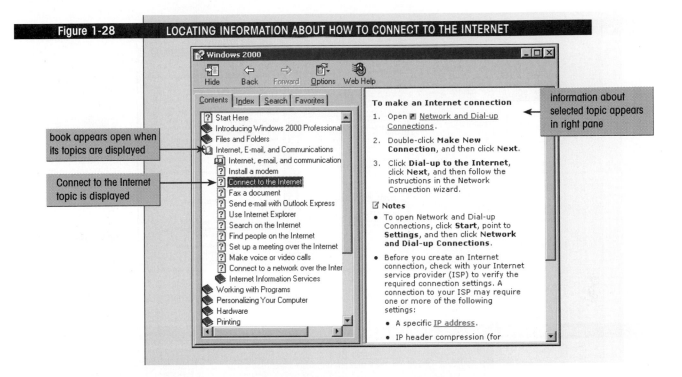

Figure 1-28   LOCATING INFORMATION ABOUT HOW TO CONNECT TO THE INTERNET

Selecting a Topic from the Index

The Index tab allows you to jump to a Help topic by selecting a topic from an indexed list. For example, you can use the Index tab to learn more about the Internet.

To find a Help topic using the Index tab:

1. Click the **Index** tab. A long list of indexed Help topics appears.

   TROUBLE? If this is the first time you've used Help on your computer, Windows 2000 needs to set up the Index. This takes just a few moments. Wait until you see the list of index entries in the left pane, and then proceed to Step 2.

2. Drag the scroll box down to view additional topics.

3. You can quickly jump to any part of the list by typing the first few characters of a word or phrase in the box above the Index list. Click the box and then type **Internet**.

4. Click the topic **searching the Internet** (you might have to scroll to see it) and then click the **Display** button. When there is just one topic, it appears immediately in the right pane; otherwise, the Topics Found window opens, listing all topics indexed under the entry you're interested in. In this case, there are four choices.

5. Click **Using Internet Explorer** and then click the **Display** button. The information you requested appears in the right pane. See Figure 1-29. Notice in this topic that there are a few underlined words. You can click underlined words to view definitions or additional information.

Figure 1-29   USING THE INDEX TO LOCATE INFORMATION

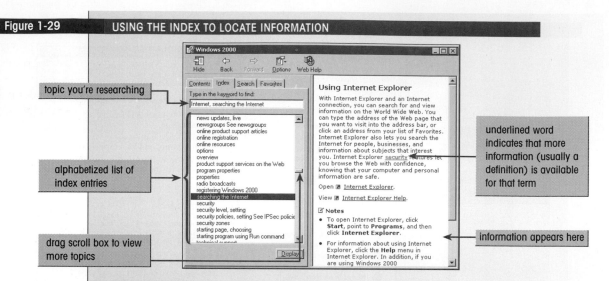

6. Click **security**. A small box appears that defines the term "security." See Figure 1-30.

Figure 1-30   VIEWING ADDITIONAL INFORMATION

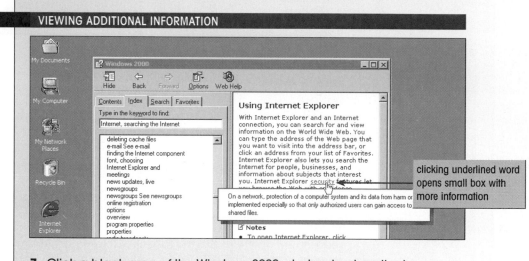

7. Click a blank area of the Windows 2000 window to close the box.

The third tab, the Search tab, works similarly to the Index tab, except that you type a word, and then the Help system searches for topics containing that word. You'll get a chance to experiment with the Search and Favorites tabs in the Review Assignments.

Returning to a Previous Help Topic

You've looked at a few topics now. Suppose you want to return to the one you just saw. The Help window includes a toolbar of buttons that help you navigate the Help system. One of these buttons is the **Back** button, which returns you to topics you've already viewed. Try returning to the help topic on connecting to the Internet.

To return to a Help topic:

1. Click the **Back** button. The Internet topic appears.
2. Click the **Close** button ❌ to close the Windows 2000 window.
3. Log off or shut down Windows 2000, depending on your lab's requirements.

Now that you know how Windows 2000 Help works, don't forget to use it! Use Help when you need to perform a new task or when you forget how to complete a procedure.

You've finished the tutorial, and as you shut down Windows 2000, Steve Laslow returns from class. You take a moment to tell him all you've learned: you know how to start and close programs and how to use multiple programs at the same time. You have learned how to work with windows and the controls they employ. Finally, you've learned how to get help when you need it. Steve is pleased that you are well on your way to mastering the fundamentals of using the Windows 2000 operating system.

Session 1.2 QUICK CHECK

1. What is the difference between the title bar and a toolbar?

2. Provide the name and purpose of each button:
   a. ☐   b. ☐   c. ☐   d. ☒

3. Describe what is indicated by each of the following menu conventions:
   a. Ellipsis...   b. Grayed-out   c. ▶   d. ✔

4. A(n) _____ consists of a group of buttons, each of which provides one-click access to important program functions.

5. What is the purpose of the scroll bar? What is the purpose of the scroll box?

6. Option buttons allow you to select _____ option(s) at a time.

7. It is a good idea to use _____ when you need to learn how to perform new tasks.

REVIEW ASSIGNMENTS

1. **Running Two Programs and Switching Between Them** In this tutorial you learned how to run more than one program at a time, using WordPad and Paint. You can run other programs at the same time, too. Complete the following steps and write out your answers to questions b through f:
   a. Start the computer. Enter your username and password if prompted to do so.
   b. Click the Start button. How many menu options are on the Start menu?
   c. Run the Calculator program located on the Accessories menu. How many program buttons are now on the taskbar (don't count toolbar buttons or items in the tray)?
   d. Run the Paint program and maximize the Paint window. How many programs are running now?
   e. Switch to Calculator. What are two visual clues that tell you that Calculator is the active program?
   f. Multiply 576 by 1457 using the Calculator accessory. What is the result?
   g. Close Calculator, then close Paint.

Explore

2. **WordPad Help** In Tutorial 1 you learned how to use Windows 2000 Help. Almost every Windows 2000 program has a Help feature. Many users can learn to use a program just by using Help. To use Help, start the program, then click the Help menu at the top of the screen. Try using WordPad Help:
   a. Start WordPad.
   b. Click Help on the WordPad menu bar, and then click Help Topics.
   c. Using WordPad Help, write out your answers to questions 1 through 4.
      1. How do you create a bulleted list?
      2. How do you set the margins in a document?
      3. How do you undo a mistake?
      4. How do you change the font style of a block of text?
   d. Close WordPad.

Explore 3. **The Search Tab** In addition to the Contents and Index tabs you worked with in this tutorial, Windows 2000 Help also includes a Search tab. Windows 2000 makes it possible to use a microphone to record sound on your computer. You could browse through the Contents tab, although you might not know where to find information about microphones. You could also use the Index tab to search through the indexed entry. Or you could use the Search tab to find all Help topics that mention microphones.

   a. Start Windows 2000 Help and use the Index tab to find information about microphones. How many topics are listed?

   b. Now use the Search tab to find information about microphones. Type "microphone" in the box on the Search tab, and then click the List Topics button.

   c. Write a paragraph comparing the two lists of topics. You don't have to view them all, but indicate which tab seems to yield more information, and why. Close Help.

4. **Getting Started** Windows 2000 includes Getting Started, an online "book" that helps you discover more about your computer and the Windows 2000 operating system. You can use this book to review what you learned in this tutorial and pick up some tips for using Windows 2000. Complete the following steps and write out your answers to questions d–j.

   a. Start Help, click the Contents tab, click Introducing Windows 2000 Professional, and then click Getting Started online book. Read the information and then click Windows 2000 Professional Getting Started.

   b. In the right pane, click New to Windows? Notice the book icons in the upper-right and upper-left corners of the right pane.

   c. Read each screen, and then click the right book icon to proceed through the Help topics. Alternately, you can view specific Getting Started Help topics by clicking them on the Contents tab. To answer the following questions, locate the information on the relevant Help topic. All the information for these questions is located in Chapter 4—"Windows Basics." When you are done, close Help.

   d. If your computer's desktop style uses the single-click option, how do you select a file? How do you open a file?

   e. What features are almost always available on your desktop, regardless of how many windows you have open?

   f. How can you get information about a dialog box or an area of the dialog box?

   g. How does the Getting Started online book define the word "disk"?

   h. If your computer is connected to a network, what Windows 2000 feature can you use to browse network resources?

   i. Why shouldn't you turn off your computer without shutting it down properly?

5. **Favorite Help Topics** You learned in this tutorial that you can save a list of your favorite Help topics on the Favorites tab. Try adding a topic to your list of favorites.

   a. Open a Help topic in the Help system. For this assignment, click the Contents tab, click Personalizing Your Computer, and then click Personalizing your workspace overview.

   b. Click the Favorites tab. The topic you selected appears on the right, and the topic name appears in the lower-left corner.

   c. Click the Add button. The topic appears in the box on the Favorites tab. This provides you an easy way to return to this topic.

   d. Click the Remove button to remove the topic from the Favorites list.

PROJECTS

1. There are many types of pointing devices on the market today. Go to the library and research the types of devices available. Consider what devices are appropriate for these situations: desktop or laptop computers, connected or remote devices, and ergonomic or standard designs (look up the word "ergonomic").

Use up-to-date computer books, trade computer magazines such as *PC Computing* and *PC Magazine*, or the Internet (if you know how) to locate information. Your instructor might suggest specific resources you can use. Write a one-page report describing the types of devices available, the differing needs of users, special features that make pointing devices more useful, price comparisons, and what you would choose if you needed to buy a pointing device.

2. Using the resources available to you, either through your library or the Internet (if you know how), locate information about the release of Windows 2000. Computing trade magazines are an excellent source of information about software. Read several articles about Windows 2000 and then write a one-page essay that discusses the features that are most important to the people who evaluated the software. If you find reviews of the software, mention the features that reviewers had the strongest reaction to, pro or con.

3. Upgrading is the process of placing a more recent version of a product onto your computer. When Windows 2000 first came out, people had to decide whether or not they wanted to upgrade to Windows 2000. Interview several people you know who are well-informed Windows computer users. Ask them whether they are using Windows 2000 or an older version of Windows. If they are using an older version, ask why they have chosen not to upgrade. If they are using Windows 2000, ask them why they chose to upgrade. Ask such questions as:
   a. What features convinced you to upgrade or made you decide to wait?
   b. What role did the price of the upgrade play?
   c. Would you have had (or did you have) to purchase new hardware to make the upgrade? How did this affect your decision?
   d. If you did upgrade, are you happy with that decision? If you didn't, do you intend to upgrade in the near future? Why, or why not?

   Write a single-page essay summarizing what you learned from these interviews.

4. Choose a topic to research using the Windows 2000 online Help system. Look for information on your topic using three tabs: the Contents tab, the Index tab, and the Search tab. Once you've found all the information you can, compare the three methods (Contents, Index, Search) of looking for information. Write a paragraph that discusses which tab proved the most useful. Did you reach the same information topics using all three methods? In a second paragraph, summarize what you learned about your topic. Finally, in a third paragraph, indicate under what circumstances you'd use which tab.

LAB ASSIGNMENTS

Using a Keyboard

Using a Keyboard To become an effective computer user, you must be familiar with your primary input device—the keyboard. See the Read This Before You Begin page for information on installing and starting the lab.

1. The Steps for the Using a Keyboard Lab provide you with a structured introduction to the keyboard layout and the function of special computer keys. Click the Steps button and begin the Steps. As you work through the Steps, answer all of the Quick Check questions that appear. When you complete the Steps, you will see a Summary Report that summarizes your performance on the Quick Checks. Follow the directions on the screen to print the Summary Report.

2. In Explore, start the typing tutor. You can develop your typing skills using the typing tutor in Explore. Take the typing test and print out your results.

3. In Explore, try to improve your typing speed by 10 words per minute. For example, if you currently type 20 words per minute, your goal will be 30 words per minute. Practice each typing lesson until you see a message that indicates that you can proceed to the next lesson.

Create a Practice Record, as shown here, to keep track of how much you practice. When you have reached your goal, print out the results of a typing test to verify your results.

Practice Record
Name:
Section:
Start Date: Start Typing Speed: wpm
End Date: End Typing Speed: wpm
Lesson #:   Date Practiced/Time Practiced

Using a Mouse A mouse is a standard input device on most of today's computers. You need to know how to use a mouse to manipulate graphical user interfaces and to use the rest of the Labs. See the Read This Before You Begin page for information on installing and starting the lab.

1. The Steps for the Using a Mouse Lab show you how to click, double-click, and drag objects using the mouse. Click the Steps button and begin the Steps. As you work through the Steps, answer all of the Quick Check questions that appear. When you complete the Steps, you will see a Summary Report that summarizes your performance on the Quick Checks. Follow the directions on the screen to print the Summary Report.

2. In Explore, create a poster to demonstrate your ability to use a mouse and to control a Windows program. To create a poster for an upcoming sports event, select a graphic, type the caption for the poster, then select a font, font styles, and a border. Print your completed poster.

QUICK CHECK ANSWERS

Session 1.1

1. The taskbar contains buttons that give you access to tools and programs.
2. multitasking
3. Start menu
4. Lift the mouse up and move it to the right.
5. Its button appears on the taskbar.
6. To conserve computer resources such as memory.
7. To ensure you don't lose data and damage your files.

Session 1.2

1. The title bar identifies the window and contains window controls; toolbars contain buttons that provide you with shortcuts to common menu commands.
2. a. Minimize button shrinks window so you see button on taskbar
   b. Maximize button enlarges window to fill entire screen
   c. Restore button reduces window to predetermined size
   d. Close button closes window and removes button from taskbar
3. a. ellipsis indicates a dialog box will open
   b. grayed-out indicates option is not currently available
   c. arrow indicates a submenu will open
   d. check mark indicates a toggle option
4. toolbar
5. Scroll bars appear when the contents of a box or window are too long to fit; you drag the scroll box to view different parts of the contents.
6. one
7. online Help

In this tutorial you will:

- Format a disk

- Enter, select, insert, and delete text

- Create and save a file

- Open, edit, and print a file

- Create and make a copy of your Data Disk

- View the list of files on your disk and change view options

- Move, copy, delete, and rename a file

- Navigate a hierarchy of folders

LABS

Using Files

WORKING WITH FILES

Creating, Saving, and Managing Files

CASE

Distance Education

You recently purchased a computer in order to gain new skills so you can stay competitive in the job market. You hope to use the computer to enroll in a few distance education courses. **Distance education** is formalized learning that typically takes place using a computer and the Internet, replacing normal classroom interaction with modern communications technology. Distance education teachers often make their course material available on the **World Wide Web**, a popular service on the Internet that makes information readily accessible.

Your computer came loaded with Windows 2000. Your friend Shannon suggests that before you enroll in any online courses, you should get more comfortable with your computer and with Windows 2000. Knowing how to save, locate, and organize your files will make your time spent at the computer much more productive. A **file**, often referred to as a **document**, is a collection of data that has a name and is stored in a computer. Once you create a file, you can open it, edit its contents, print it, and save it again—usually using the same program you used to create it.

Shannon suggests that you become familiar with how to perform these tasks in Windows 2000 programs. Then she'll show you how to choose different ways of viewing information on your computer. Finally, you'll spend time learning how to organize your files.

SESSION 2.1

In Session 2.1, you will learn how to format a disk so it can store files. You will create, save, open, and print a file. You will find out how the insertion point differs from the mouse pointer, and you will learn the basic skills for Windows 2000 text entry, such as entering, selecting, inserting, and deleting. For the steps of this tutorial you will need two blank 3½-inch disks.

Formatting a Disk

Before you can save files on a floppy disk, the disk must be formatted. When the computer **formats** a disk, the magnetic particles on the disk surface are arranged so that data can be stored on the disk. Today, many disks are sold preformatted and can be used right out of the box. However, if you purchase an unformatted disk, or if you have an old disk you want to completely erase and reuse, you can format the disk using the Windows 2000 Format command. This command is available through the **My Computer window**, a feature of Windows 2000 that you use to view, organize, and access the programs, files, drives and folders on your computer. You open My Computer by using its icon on the desktop. You'll learn more about the My Computer window later in this tutorial.

The following steps tell you how to format a 3½-inch high-density disk, using drive A. Your instructor will tell you how to revise the instructions given in these steps if the procedure is different for your lab.

Make sure you are using a blank disk (or one that contains data you no longer need) before you perform these steps.

To format a disk:

1. Start Windows 2000, if necessary.

2. Write your name on the label of a 3½-inch disk and insert your disk in drive A. See Figure 2-1.

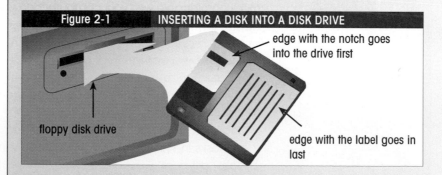

Figure 2-1   INSERTING A DISK INTO A DISK DRIVE

edge with the notch goes into the drive first

floppy disk drive

edge with the label goes in last

TROUBLE? If your disk does not fit in drive A, put it in drive B and substitute drive B for drive A in all of the steps for the rest of the tutorial.

3. Click the **My Computer** icon on the desktop. The icon is selected. Figure 2-2 shows this icon on your desktop.

TROUBLE? If the My Computer window opens, skip Step 4. Your computer is using different settings, which you'll learn to change in Session 2.2.

4. Press the **Enter** key to open the My Computer window. See Figure 2-2 (don't worry if your window opens maximized).

TROUBLE? If you see a list of items instead of icons like those in Figure 2-2, click View, and then click Large Icons. Don't worry if your toolbars don't exactly match those in Figure 2-2.

TROUBLE? If you see additional information or a graphic image on the left side of the My Computer window, Web view is enabled on your computer. Don't worry. You will learn how to return to the default Windows 2000 settings in Session 2.2.

| Figure 2-2 | MY COMPUTER WINDOW |

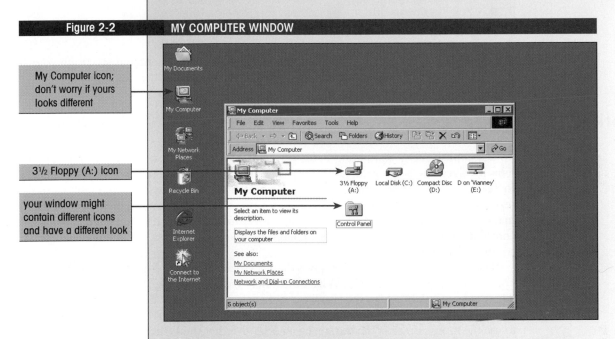

My Computer icon; don't worry if yours looks different

3½ Floppy (A:) icon

your window might contain different icons and have a different look

5. Right-click the **3½ Floppy (A:)** icon to open its shortcut menu, and then click **Format**. The Format dialog box opens.

6. Make sure the dialog box settings on your screen match those in Figure 2-3.

| Figure 2-3 | FORMATTING A FLOPPY DISK |

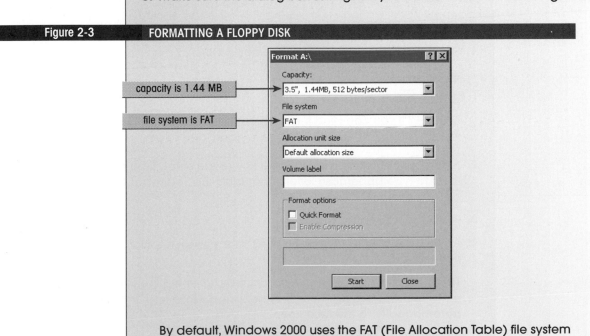

capacity is 1.44 MB

file system is FAT

By default, Windows 2000 uses the FAT (File Allocation Table) file system for floppy disks. A **file system** is the way files are organized on the disk. Windows 2000 supports other file systems such as FAT32 and NTFS, but this is a more advanced topic.

7. Click the **Start** button to start formatting the disk.

8. Click the **OK** button to confirm that you want to format the disk (the actual formatting will take a minute to perform). Click the **OK** button again when the formatting is complete.

9. Click the **Close** button.

10. Click the **Close** button ⊠ to close the My Computer window.

Now that you have a formatted disk, you can create a document and save it on your disk. First you need to learn how to enter text into a document.

Working with Text

To accomplish many computing tasks, you need to enter text in documents and text boxes. This involves learning how to move the pointer so the text will appear where you want it, how to insert new text between existing words or sentences, how to select text, and how to delete text. When you type sentences of text, do not press the Enter key when you reach the right margin of the page. Most software contains a feature called **word wrap**, which automatically continues your text on the next line. Therefore, you should press Enter only when you have completed a paragraph.

If you type the wrong character, press the Backspace key to back up and delete the character. You can also use the Delete key. What's the difference between the Backspace and Delete keys? The **Backspace** key deletes the character to the left, while the **Delete** key deletes the character to the right. If you want to delete text that is not next to where you are currently typing, you need to use the mouse to select the text; then you can use either the Delete key or the Backspace key.

Now you will type some text, using WordPad, to practice text entry. When you first start WordPad, notice the flashing vertical bar, called the **insertion point**, in the upper-left corner of the document window. The insertion point indicates where the characters you type will appear.

To type text in WordPad:

1. Start WordPad and locate the insertion point.

TROUBLE? If the WordPad window does not fill the screen, click the Maximize button ▢.

TROUBLE? If you can't find the insertion point, click in the WordPad **document window**, the white area below the toolbars and ruler.

2. Type your name, pressing the Shift key at the same time as the appropriate letter to type uppercase letters and using the Spacebar to type spaces, just as on a typewriter.

3. Press the **Enter** key to move the insertion point down to the next line.

4. As you type the following sentences, watch what happens when the insertion point reaches the right edge of the page:

This is a sample typed in WordPad. See what happens when the insertion point reaches the right edge of the page. Note how the text wraps automatically to the next line.

TROUBLE? If you make a mistake, delete the incorrect character(s) by pressing the Backspace key on your keyboard. Then type the correct character(s).

TROUBLE? If your text doesn't wrap, your screen might be set up to display more information than the screen used for the figures in this tutorial, or your WordPad program might not be set to use Word Wrap. Click View, click Options, make sure the Rich Text tab is selected, click the Wrap to window option button, and then click the OK button.

The Insertion Point Versus the Pointer

The insertion point is not the same as the mouse pointer. When the mouse pointer is in the text-entry area, it is called the **I-beam pointer** and looks like I. Figure 2-4 explains the difference between the insertion point and the I-beam pointer.

Figure 2-4	THE INSERTION POINT VS. THE POINTER

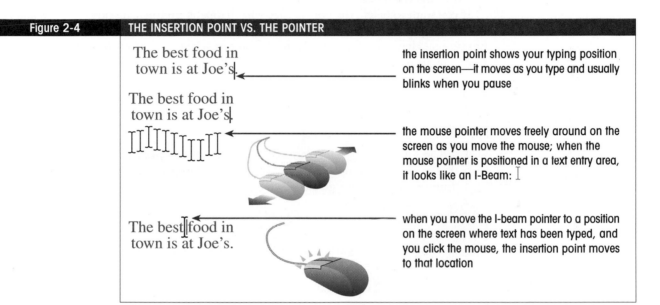

When you enter text, the insertion point moves as you type. If you want to enter text in a location other than where the mouse pointer is currently positioned, you move the I-beam pointer to the location where you want to type, and then click. The insertion point jumps to the location you clicked. In most programs, the insertion point blinks, making it easier for you to locate it on a screen filled with text.

To move the insertion point:

1. Check the locations of the insertion point and the I-beam pointer. The insertion point should be at the end of the sentence you typed in the last set of steps. The easiest way to locate the I-beam pointer is to move your mouse gently until you see the pointer. Remember that it will look like ⃕ until you move the pointer into the document window.

2. Use the mouse to move the I-beam pointer just to the left of the word "sample" and then click the mouse button. The insertion point should be just to the left of the "s."

   TROUBLE? If you have trouble clicking just to the left of the "s," try clicking in the word and then using the arrow keys to move the insertion point one character at a time.

3. Move the I-beam pointer to a blank area near the bottom of the workspace and then click. Notice the insertion point does not jump to the location of the I-beam pointer. Instead the insertion point jumps to the end of the last sentence or to the point in the bottom line directly above where you clicked. The insertion point can move only within existing text. It cannot be moved out of the existing text area.

Selecting Text

Many text operations are performed on a **block** of text, which is one or more consecutive characters, words, sentences, or paragraphs. Once you select a block of text, you can delete it, move it, replace it, underline it, and so on. To deselect a block of text, click anywhere outside the selected block.

If you want to delete the phrase "See what happens" in the text you just typed and replace it with the phrase "You can watch word wrap in action," you do not have to delete the first phrase one character at a time. Instead, you can select the entire phrase and then type the replacement phrase.

To select and replace a block of text:

1. Move the I-beam pointer just to the left of the word "See."

2. While holding down the mouse button, drag the I-beam pointer over the text to the end of the word "happens." The phrase "See what happens" should now be highlighted. See Figure 2-5.

TROUBLE? If the space to the right of the word "happens" is also selected, don't worry. Your computer is set up to select spaces in addition to words. After completing Step 4, simply press the Spacebar to type an extra space if required.

| Figure 2-5 | SELECTING TEXT |

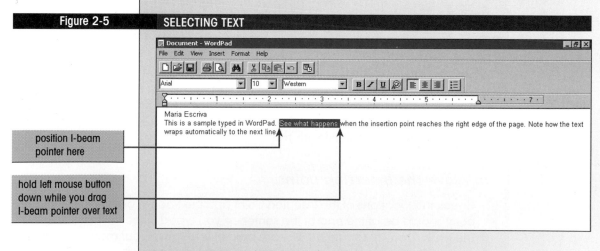

position I-beam pointer here

hold left mouse button down while you drag I-beam pointer over text

3. Release the mouse button.

TROUBLE? If the phrase is not highlighted correctly, repeat Steps 1 through 3.

4. Type **You can watch word wrap in action**

The text you typed replaces the highlighted text. Notice that you did not need to delete the selected text before you typed the replacement text.

Inserting a Character

Windows 2000 programs usually operate in **insert mode**—when you type a new character, all characters to the right of the insertion point are pushed over to make room.

Suppose you want to insert the word "page" before the word "typed" in your practice sentences.

To insert text:

1. Move the I-beam pointer just before the word "typed" and then click to position the insertion point.

2. Type **page**

3. Press the **Spacebar**.

Notice how the letters in the first line are pushed to the right to make room for the new characters. When a word gets pushed past the right margin, the word-wrap feature moves it down to the beginning of the next line.

Saving a File

As you type text, it is held temporarily in the computer's memory, which is erased when you turn off the computer. For permanent storage, you need to save your work on a disk. In the computer lab, you will probably save your work on a floppy disk in drive A.

When you save a file, you must give it a name, called a **filename**. Windows 2000 allows you to use up to 255 characters in a filename—this gives you plenty of room to name your file accurately enough so that you'll know the contents of the file by just looking at the filename. You may use spaces and certain punctuation symbols in your filenames. You cannot use the symbols \ / ? : * " < > | in a filename, because Windows uses those for designating the location and type of the file, but other symbols such as & ; - and $ are allowed.

Another thing to consider is whether you might use your files on a computer running older programs. Programs designed for the Windows 3.1 and DOS operating systems (which were created before 1995) require that files be eight characters or less with no spaces. Thus when you save a file with a long filename in Windows 2000, Windows 2000 also creates an eight-character filename that can be used by older programs. The eight-character filename is created from the first six nonspace characters in the long filename, with the addition of a tilde (~) and a number. For example, the filename Car Sales for 1999 would be converted to Carsal~1.

Most filenames have an extension. An **extension** (a set of no more than three characters at the end of a filename, separated from the filename by a period) is used by the operating system to identify and categorize the file. In the filename Car Sales for 1999.doc, for example, the file extension "doc" identifies the file as one created with Microsoft Word. You might also have a file called Car Sales for 1999.xls—"xls" identifies the file as one created with Microsoft Excel, a spreadsheet program. When pronouncing filenames with extensions, say "dot" for the period, so that the file Resume.doc is pronounced "Resume dot doc."

You usually do not need to add extensions to your filenames because the program you use to create the file does this automatically. Also, Windows 2000 keeps track of file extensions, but not all computers are set to display them. The steps in these tutorials refer to files by using the filename without its extension. So if you see the filename Practice Text in the steps, but "Practice Text.doc" appears on your screen, don't worry—these refer to the same file. Also don't worry if you don't use consistent lowercase and uppercase letters when saving files. Usually the operating system doesn't distinguish between them. Be aware, however, that some programs are "case-sensitive"—they check for case in filenames.

Now you can save the WordPad document you typed.

To start saving a document:

1. Click the **Save** button 🖫 on the toolbar. The Save As dialog box opens, as shown in Figure 2-6.

| Figure 2-6 | SAVING A FILE |

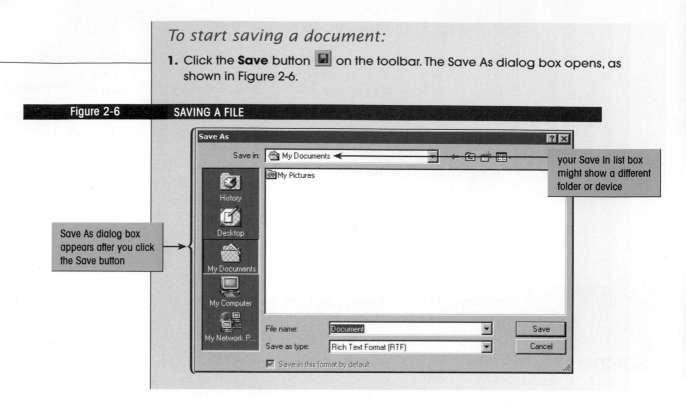

Save As dialog box appears after you click the Save button

your Save In list box might show a different folder or device

You use the Save As dialog box to specify where you want to save your file (on the hard drive or on a floppy disk, in a folder or not, and so on). Before going further with the process of saving a file, let's examine some of the features of the Save As dialog box so that you learn to save your files exactly where you want them.

Specifying the File Location

In the Save As dialog box, Windows 2000 provides the **Places Bar**, a list of important locations on your computer. When you click the different icons in the Places Bar, the contents of those locations will be displayed in the white area of the Save As dialog box. You can then save your document directly to those locations. Figure 2-7 displays the icons in the Places Bar and gives their function.

| Figure 2-7 | ICONS IN THE PLACES BAR |

ICON	DESCRIPTION
History	Displays a list of recently opened files, folders, and objects
Desktop	Displays a list of files, folders, and objects on the Windows 2000 desktop
My Documents	Displays a list of files, folders, and objects in the My Documents folder
My Computer	Displays a list of files, folders, and objects in the My Computer window
My Network P...	Displays a list of computers and folders available on the network

To see this in action, try displaying different locations in the dialog box.

To use the Places Bar:

1. Click the **Desktop** icon in the Places Bar.

2. The Save As dialog box now displays the contents of the Windows 2000 desktop. See Figure 2-8.

Figure 2-8	USING THE PLACES BAR

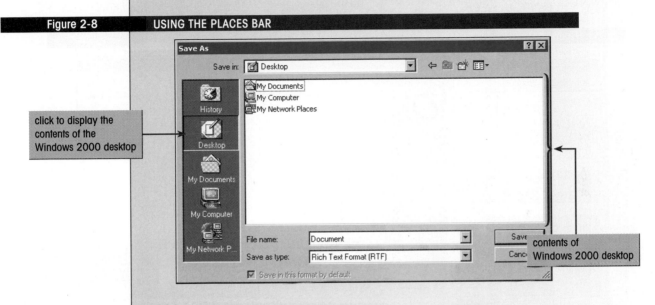

click to display the contents of the Windows 2000 desktop

contents of Windows 2000 desktop

3. Click the **My Documents** icon to display the contents of the My Documents folder.

Once you've clicked an icon in the Places Bar, you can open any file displayed in that location, and you can save a file into that location. The Places Bar doesn't have an icon for every location on your computer, however. The **Save in** list box (located at the top of the dialog box) does. Use the Save in list box now to save your document to your floppy disk.

To use the Save in list box:

1. Click the **Save in** list arrow to display a list of drives.

2. Click **3½ Floppy (A:)**.

   Now that you've specified where you want to save your file, you can specify a name and type for the file.

Specifying the File Name and Type

After choosing the location for your document, you have to specify the name of the file. You should also specify (or at least check) the file's format. A file's **format** determines what type of information you can place in the document, the document's appearance, and what kind of programs can work with the document. There are five file formats available in WordPad: Word for Windows 6.0, Rich Text Format (RTF), Text, Text for MS-DOS, and Unicode Text. The Word and RTF formats allow you to create documents with text that can use bold-faced or italicized fonts as well as documents containing graphic images and scanned photos. However, only word-processing programs like WordPad or Microsoft Word can work with those files. The three text formats allow only simple text with no graphics or special formatting, but such documents are readable by a wider range of programs. The default format for WordPad documents is RTF, but you can change that, as you'll see shortly.

   Continue saving the document, using the name "Practice Text" and the file type Word 6.0.

To finish saving your document:

1. Select the text **Document** in the File name text box and then type **Practice Text** in the File name text box. The new text replaces "Document."

2. Click the **Save as type** list arrow and then click **Word for Windows 6.0** in the list. See Figure 2-9.

Figure 2-9	COMPLETED SAVE AS DIALOG BOX

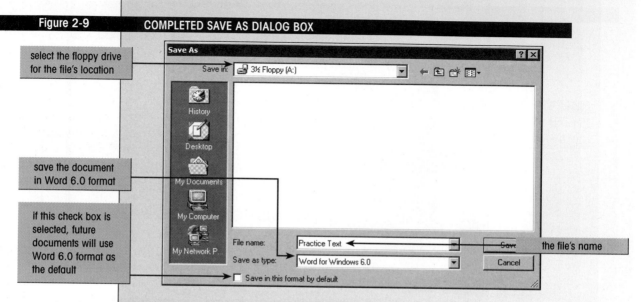

select the floppy drive for the file's location

save the document in Word 6.0 format

if this check box is selected, future documents will use Word 6.0 format as the default

the file's name

Note that if you want all future documents saved by WordPad to use the Word 6.0 format as the default format rather than RTF, you can select the Save in this format by default check box. If you select it, the next time you save a document in WordPad, this format will be the initial choice, so you won't have to specify it.

3. Click the **Save** button in the lower-right corner of the dialog box.

4. If you are asked whether you are sure that you want to save the document in this format, click the **Yes** button.

Your file is saved on your Data Disk, and the document title, "Practice Text," appears on the WordPad title bar.

Note that after you save the file the document appears a little different. What has changed? By saving the document in Word 6.0 format rather than RTF, you've changed the format of the document slightly. One change is that the text is wrapped differently in Word 6.0 format. A Word 6.0 file will use the right margin and, in this case, limit the length of a single line of text to 6 inches.

What if you try to close WordPad before you save your file? Windows 2000 will display a message—"Save changes to Document?" If you answer "Yes," Windows will display the Save As dialog box so you can give the document a name. If you answer "No," Windows 2000 will close WordPad without saving the document. Any changes you made to the document will be lost, so when you are asked if you want to save a file, answer "Yes," unless you are absolutely sure you don't need to keep the work you just did.

After you save a file, you can work on another document or close WordPad. Since you have already saved your Practice Text document, you'll continue this tutorial by closing WordPad.

To close WordPad:

1. Click the **Close** button ❌ to close the WordPad window.

Opening a File

Suppose you save and close the Practice Text file, then later you want to revise it. To revise a file you must first open it. When you open a file, its contents are copied into the computer's memory. If you revise the file, you need to save the changes before you close the program. If you close a revised file without saving your changes, you will lose them.

There are several methods to open a file. You can select the file from the Documents list (available through the Start menu) if you have opened the file recently, since the Documents list contains the 15 most recently opened documents. This list is very handy to use on your own computer, but in a lab, other student's files quickly replace your own. You can also locate the file in the My Computer window (or in **Windows Explorer**, another file management tool) and then open it. And finally, you can start a program and then use the Open button within that program to locate and open the file. Each method has advantages and disadvantages.

The first two methods for opening the Practice Text file simply require you to select the file from the Documents list or locate and select it from My Computer or Windows Explorer. With these methods the document, not the program, is central to the task; hence, this method is sometimes referred to as **document-centric**. You need only to remember the name of your file—you do not need to remember which program you used to create it.

Opening a File from the My Computer Window

If your file is not in the Documents list, you can open the file by selecting it from the My Computer window. Either way, Windows 2000 uses the file extension (whether it is displayed or not) to determine which program to start so you can manipulate the file. It starts the program, and then automatically opens the file. The advantage of both methods is simplicity. The disadvantage is that Windows 2000 might not start the program you expect. For example, when you select Practice Text, you might expect Windows 2000 to start WordPad because you used WordPad to create it. Depending on the programs installed on your computer system, however, Windows 2000 might start Microsoft Word instead. Usually this is not a problem. Although the program might not be the one you expect, you can still use it to revise your file.

To open the Practice Text file by selecting it from My Computer:

1. Open the **My Computer** window, located on the desktop.

2. Click the **3½ Floppy (A:)** icon in the My Computer window.

   TROUBLE? If the 3½ Floppy (A:) window opens, skip Step 3.

3. Press the **Enter** key. The 3½ Floppy (A:) window opens.

4. Click the **Practice Text** file icon.

   TROUBLE? If the Practice Text document opens, skip Step 5.

5. Press the **Enter** key. Windows 2000 starts a program, and then automatically opens the Practice Text file. You could make revisions to the document at this point, but instead, you'll close all the windows on your desktop so you can try the other method for opening files.

   TROUBLE? If Windows 2000 starts Microsoft Word or another word-processing program instead of WordPad, don't worry. You can use Microsoft Word to revise the Practice Text document.

6. Close all open windows on the desktop.

Opening a File from Within a Program

The third method for opening the Practice Text file requires you to open WordPad, and then use the Open button to select the Practice Text file. The advantage of this method is that you can specify the program you want to use—WordPad, in this case. This method, however, involves more steps than the method you tried previously.

You can take advantage of the Places Bar to reduce the number of steps it takes to open a file from within a program. Recall that one of the icons in the Places Bar is the History icon, which displays a list of recently opened files or objects. One of the most recently opened files was the Practice Text file, so it should appear in the list.

To start WordPad and open the Practice Text file:

1. Start **WordPad** and, if necessary, maximize the WordPad window.

2. Click the **Open** button 🖻 on the toolbar.

3. Click **History** in the Places Bar.

The Practice Text file doesn't appear in the list. Why not? Look at the Files of Type list box. The selected entry is "Rich Text Format (*.rtf)". What this means is that the Open dialog box will display only RTF files (as well as drives). This frees you from having to deal with the clutter of unwanted or irrelevant files. The downside is that unless you're aware of how the Open dialog box will filter the list of files, you may mistakenly think that the file you're looking for doesn't exist. You can change how the Open dialog box filters this file list. Try this now by changing the filter to show only Word documents.

To change the types of files displayed:

1. Click the **Files of type** list arrow and then click **Word for Windows (*.doc)**

   The Practice Text file now appears in the list.

2. Click **Practice Text** in the list of files. See Figure 2-10.

| Figure 2-10 | THE OPEN DIALOG BOX |

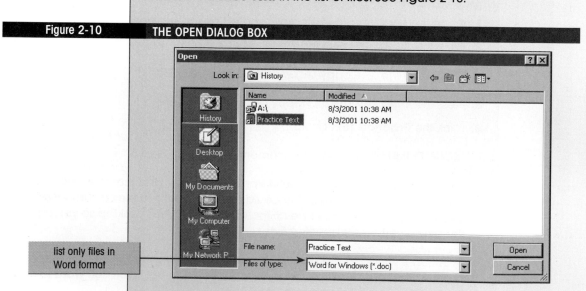

list only files in Word format

3. Click the **Open** button. The document should once again appear in the WordPad window.

Now that the Practice Text file is open, you can print it.

Printing a File

Windows 2000 provides easy access to your printer or printers. You can choose which printer to use, you can control how the document is printed, and you can control the order in which documents will be printed.

Previewing your Document Before Printing

It is a good idea to use Print Preview before you send your document to the printer. **Print Preview** shows on the screen exactly how your document will appear on paper. You can check your page layout so that you don't waste time and paper printing a document that is not quite the way you want it. Your instructor might supply you with additional instructions for printing in your school's computer lab.

To preview, then print, the Practice Text file:

1. Click the **Print Preview** button 🔍 on the toolbar.

   TROUBLE? If an error message appears, printing capabilities might not be set up on your computer. Ask your instructor or technical support person for help, or skip this set of steps.

2. Look at your document in the Print Preview window. Before you print the document, you should make sure the font, margins, and other document features look the way you want them to.

   TROUBLE? If you can't read the document text on screen, click the Zoom In button as many times as needed to view the text.

3. Click the **Close** button to close Print Preview and return to the document.

Now that you've verified that the document looks the way you want, you can print it.

Sending the Document to the Printer

There are three ways to send your document to the printer. The first approach is to print the document directly from the Print Preview window by clicking the Print button. Thus once you are satisfied with the document's appearance, you can quickly move to printing it.

Another way is to click the Print button 🖨 on your program's toolbar. This method will send the document directly to your printer without any further action on your part. It's the quickest and easiest way to print a document, but it does not allow you to change settings such as margins and layout. What if you have access to more than one printer? In that case, Windows 2000 sends the document to the default printer, the printer that has been set up to handle most print jobs.

If you want to select a different printer, or if you want to control how the printer prints your document, you can opt for a third method—selecting the Print command from the File menu. Using this approach, your program will open the Print dialog box, allowing you to choose which printer to use and how that printer will operate. Note that clicking the Print button from within the Print Preview window will also open the Print dialog box so you can verify or change settings.

To open the Print dialog box:

1. Click **File** on the WordPad menu bar and then click **Print**.

2. The Print dialog box opens, as displayed in Figure 2-11. Familiarize yourself with the controls in the Print dialog box.

Figure 2-11   **THE PRINT DIALOG BOX**

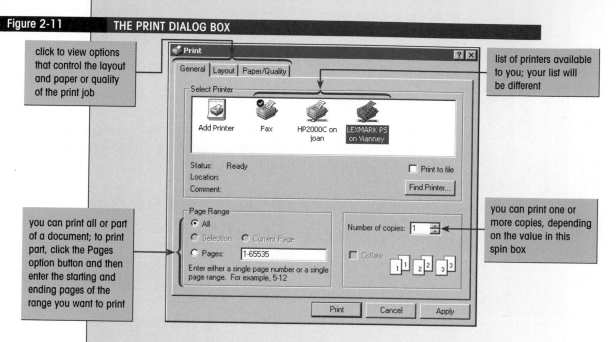

click to view options that control the layout and paper or quality of the print job

list of printers available to you; your list will be different

you can print all or part of a document; to print part, click the Pages option button and then enter the starting and ending pages of the range you want to print

you can print one or more copies, depending on the value in this spin box

3. Make sure your Print dialog box shows the Print range set to "All" and the Number of copies set to "1."

4. Select one of the printers in the list (your instructor may indicate which one you should select) and then click the **Print** button. The document is printed.

5. Close WordPad.

TROUBLE? If you see the message "Save changes to Document?" click the No button.

You've now learned how to create, save, open, and print word-processed files—essential skills for students in distance education courses that rely on word-processed reports transmitted across the Internet. Shannon assures you that the techniques you've just learned apply to most Windows 2000 programs.

Session 2.1 QUICK CHECK

1. A(n) _____ is a collection of data that has a name and is stored on a disk or other storage medium.

2. _____ erases all the data on a disk and arranges the magnetic particles on the disk surface so that the disk can store data.

3. True or False: When you move the mouse pointer over a text entry area, the pointer shape changes to an I-beam.

4. What indicates where each character you type will appear?

5. What does the History icon in the Places Bar display?

6. A file that you saved does not appear in the Open dialog box. Assuming that the file is still in the same location, what could be the reason that the Open dialog box doesn't display it?

7. What are the three ways to print from within a Windows 2000 application? If you want to print multiple copies of your document, which method(s) should you use and why?

SESSION 2.2

In this session, you will learn how to change settings in the My Computer window to control its appearance and the appearance of desktop objects. You will then learn how to use My Computer to manage the files on your disk; view information about the files on your disk; organize the files into folders; and move, delete, copy, and rename files. For this session you will use a second blank 3½-inch disk.

Creating Your Data Disk

Starting with this session, you must create a Data Disk that contains some practice files. You can use the disk you formatted in the previous session.

If you are using your own computer, the NP on Microsoft Windows 2000 menu option will not be available. Before you proceed, you must go to your school's computer lab and find a computer that has the NP on Microsoft Windows 2000 program installed. If you cannot get the files from the lab, ask your instructor or technical support person for help. Once you have made your own Data Disk, you can use it to complete this tutorial on any computer running Windows 2000.

To add the practice files to your Data Disk:

1. Write "Disk 1 - Windows 2000 Tutorial 2 Data Disk" on the label of your formatted disk (the same disk you used to save your Practice Text file).

2. Place the disk in drive A.

3. Click the **Start** button ![Start].

4. Point to **Programs**.

5. Point to **NP on Microsoft Windows 2000 – Level I**.

   TROUBLE? If NP on Microsoft Windows 2000 - Level I is not listed, ask your instructor or technical support person for help.

6. Click **Disk 1 (Tutorial 2)**. A message box opens, asking you to place your disk in drive A (which you already did, in Step 2).

7. Click the **OK** button. Wait while the program copies the practice files to your formatted disk. When all the files have been copied, the program closes.

Your Data Disk now contains practice files you'll use throughout the rest of this tutorial.

My Computer

The My Computer icon, as you have seen, represents your computer, with its storage devices, printers, and other objects. The My Computer icon opens into the My Computer window, which contains an icon for each of the storage devices on your computer. My Computer also gives you access to the **Control Panel**, a feature of Windows 2000 that controls the behavior of other devices and programs installed on your computer. Figure 2-12 shows how the My Computer window relates to your computer's hardware.

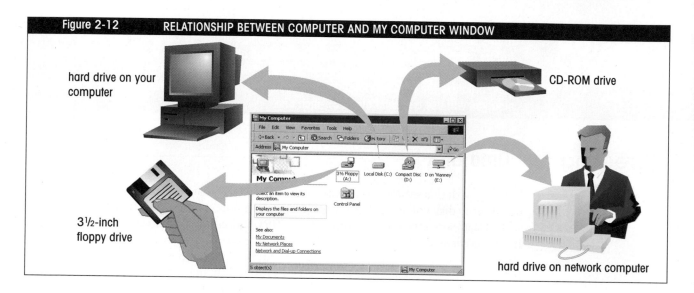

Figure 2-12 RELATIONSHIP BETWEEN COMPUTER AND MY COMPUTER WINDOW

Each storage device that you have access to has a letter associated with it. The first floppy drive on a computer is usually designated as drive A (if you add a second floppy drive, it is usually designated as drive B), and the first hard drive is usually designated drive C. Additional hard drives will have letters D, E, F and so forth. If you have a CD-ROM drive, it will usually have the next letter in the alphabetic sequence. If you have access to hard drives located on other computers on a network, those drives will sometimes (though not always) have letters associated with them. In the example shown in Figure 2-12, the network drive has the drive letter E.

You can use the My Computer window to organize your files. In this section of the tutorial, you'll use the My Computer window to move and delete files on your Data Disk, which is assumed to be in drive A. If you use your own computer at home or work, you will probably store your files on drive C instead of drive A. In a school lab environment, you can't always save your files to drive C, so you need to carry your files with you on a floppy disk. Most of what you learn about working on the floppy drive will also work on your home or work computer when you use drive C (or other hard drives).

Now you'll open the My Computer window.

To open the My Computer window and explore the contents of your Data Disk:

1. Open the My Computer window.

2. Click the **3½ Floppy (A:)** icon and then press the **Enter** key. A window appears showing the contents of drive A; maximize this window if necessary. See Figure 2-13.

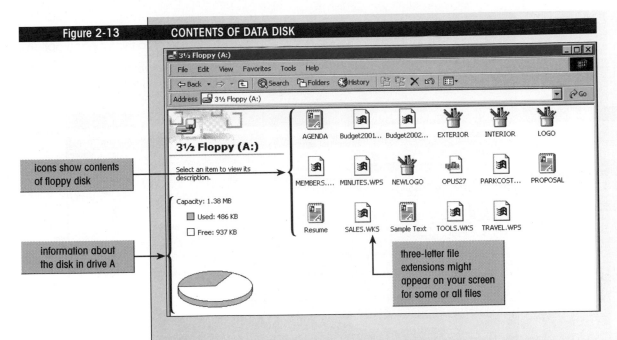

Figure 2-13   CONTENTS OF DATA DISK

icons show contents of floppy disk

information about the disk in drive A

three-letter file extensions might appear on your screen for some or all files

TROUBLE? If the window appears before you press the Enter key, don't worry. Windows 2000 can be configured to use different keyboard and mouse combinations to open windows. You'll learn about these configuration issues shortly.

TROUBLE? If you see a list of filenames instead of icons, click View on the menu bar and then click Large Icons on the menu.

Changing the Appearance of the My Computer Window

Windows 2000 offers several different options that control how toolbars, icons, and buttons appear in the My Computer window. To make the My Computer window look the same as it does in the figures in this book, you need to ensure three things: that only the Address and Standard toolbars are visible, that files and other objects are displayed using large icons, and that the configuration of Windows 2000 uses the default setting. Setting your computer to match the figures will make it easier for you to follow the steps.

Controlling the Toolbar Display

The My Computer window, in addition to displaying a Standard toolbar, allows you to display the same toolbars that can appear on the Windows 2000 taskbar, such as the Address toolbar or the Links toolbar. These toolbars make it easy to access the Web from the My Computer window. In this tutorial, however, you need to see only the Address and Standard toolbars.

To display only the Address and Standard toolbars:

1. Click **View**, point to **Toolbars**, and then examine the Toolbars submenu. The Standard Buttons and Address Bar options should be preceded by a check mark. The Links and Radio options should not be checked. Follow the steps below to ensure that you have check marks next to the correct options.

2. If the Standard Buttons and Address Bar options *are not checked*, then click them to select them (you will have to repeat Step 1 to view the Toolbars submenu to do this for each option).

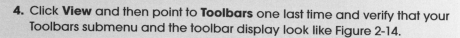

3. If the Links or Radio options *are checked*, then click them to deselect them (you will have to repeat Step 1 to view the Toolbars submenu to do this for each option).

4. Click **View** and then point to **Toolbars** one last time and verify that your Toolbars submenu and the toolbar display look like Figure 2-14.

Figure 2-14   CHECKING VIEW OPTIONS

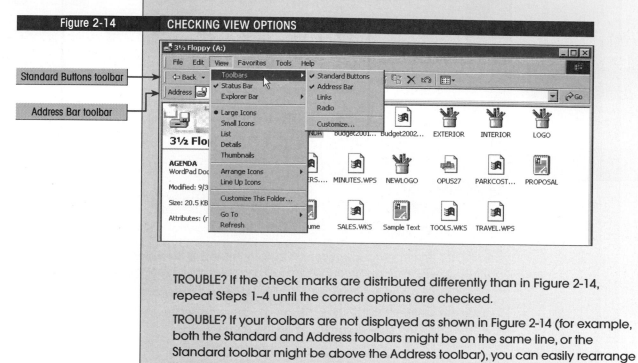

TROUBLE? If the check marks are distributed differently than in Figure 2-14, repeat Steps 1–4 until the correct options are checked.

TROUBLE? If your toolbars are not displayed as shown in Figure 2-14 (for example, both the Standard and Address toolbars might be on the same line, or the Standard toolbar might be above the Address toolbar), you can easily rearrange them. To move a toolbar, drag the vertical bar at the far left of the toolbar. By dragging that vertical bar, you can drag the toolbar left, right, up, or down.

Changing the Icon Display

Windows 2000 provides five ways to view the contents of a disk—Large Icons, Small Icons, List, Details, and Thumbnails. Figure 2-15 shows examples of these five styles.

Figure 2-15   VIEWING STYLES

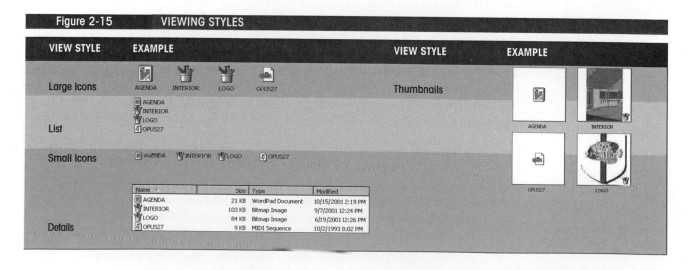

The default view, **Large Icons view**, displays a large icon and title for each file. The icon provides a visual cue to the type of the file, as Figure 2-16 illustrates. You can also get this same information with the smaller icons displayed in the **Small Icons** and **List** views, but in less screen space. In Small Icons and List views, you can see more files and folders at one time, which is helpful when you have many files in one location.

Figure 2-16	TYPICAL ICONS IN WINDOWS 2000

FILE AND FOLDER ICONS	
	Text documents that you can open using the Notepad accessory are represented by notepad icons.
	Graphic image documents that you can open using the Paint accessory are represented by drawing instruments.
	Word-processed documents that you can open using the WordPad accessory are represented by a formatted notepad icon, unless your computer designates a different word-processing program to open files created with WordPad.
	Word-processed documents that you can open using a program such as Microsoft Word are represented by formatted document icons.
	Files created by programs that Windows does not recognize are represented by the Windows logo.
	A folder icon represents folders.
	Certain folders created by Windows 2000 have a special icon design related to the folder's purpose.

PROGRAM ICONS	
	Icons for programs usually depict an object related to the function of the program. For example, an icon that looks like a calculator represents the Calculator accessory.
	Non-Windows programs are represented by the icon of a blank window.

All of the three icon views (Large Icons, Small Icons, and List) help you quickly identify a file and its type, but what if you want more information about a set of files? **Details view** shows more information than the Large Icon, Small Icon, and List views. Details view shows the file icon, the filename, the file size, the program you used to create the file, and the date and time the file was created or last modified.

Finally, if you have graphic files, you may want to use **Thumbnails view**, which displays a small "preview" image of the graphic, so that you can quickly see not only the filename, but also which picture or drawing the file contains. Thumbnails view is great for browsing a large collection of graphic files, but switching to this view can be time-consuming, since Windows 2000 has to create all of the preview images.

To see how easy it is to switch from one view to another, try displaying the contents of drive A in Details view.

To view a detailed list of files:

1. Click **View** and then click **Details** to display details for the files on your disk, as shown in Figure 2-17. Your files might be listed in a different order.

Figure 2-17

DETAILS VIEW

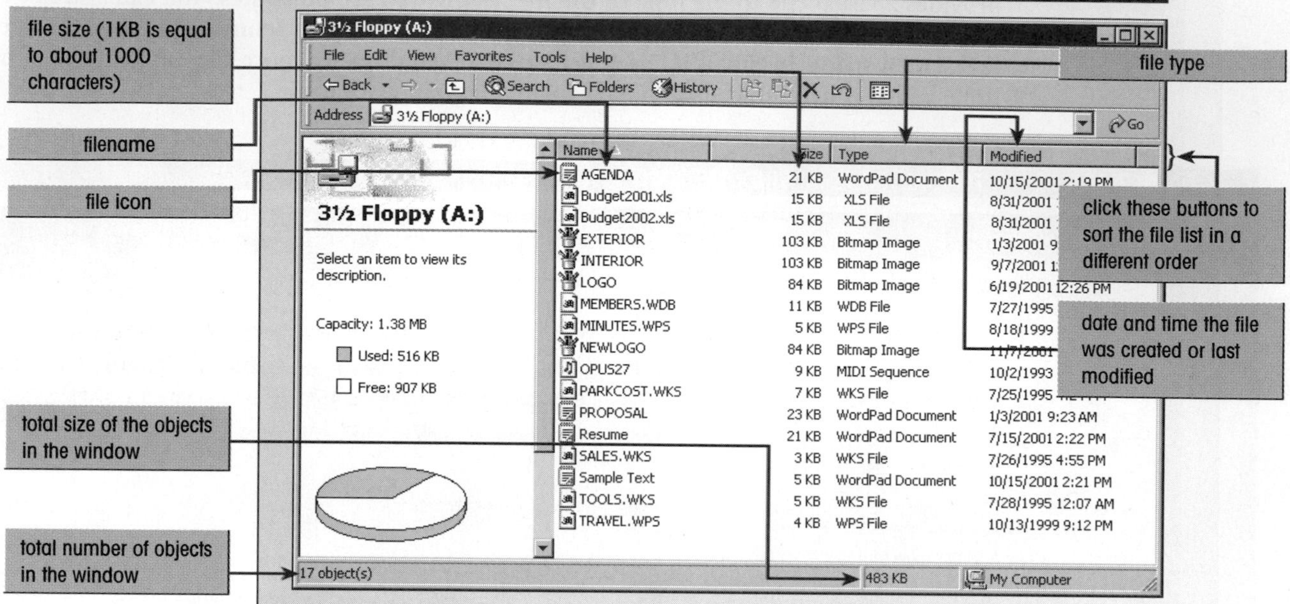

file size (1KB is equal to about 1000 characters)

filename

file icon

file type

3½ Floppy (A:)

File Edit View Favorites Tools Help

← Back ▾ → ▾ 🔁 🔍 Search 📁 Folders 🕘 History ⬚ ⬚ ✕ ↻ ▦ ▾

Address 🖫 3½ Floppy (A:)   ▾ ⟳ Go

3½ Floppy (A:)

Select an item to view its description.

Capacity: 1.38 MB

🟦 Used: 516 KB

⬜ Free: 907 KB

Name	Size	Type	Modified
AGENDA	21 KB	WordPad Document	10/15/2001 2:19 PM
Budget2001.xls	15 KB	XLS File	8/31/2001
Budget2002.xls	15 KB	XLS File	8/31/2001
EXTERIOR	103 KB	Bitmap Image	1/3/2001 9
INTERIOR	103 KB	Bitmap Image	9/7/2001 1
LOGO	84 KB	Bitmap Image	6/19/2001 12:26 PM
MEMBERS.WDB	11 KB	WDB File	7/27/1995
MINUTES.WPS	5 KB	WPS File	8/18/1999
NEWLOGO	84 KB	Bitmap Image	11/7/2001
OPUS27	9 KB	MIDI Sequence	10/2/1993
PARKCOST.WKS	7 KB	WKS File	7/25/1995
PROPOSAL	23 KB	WordPad Document	1/3/2001 9:23 AM
Resume	21 KB	WordPad Document	7/15/2001 2:22 PM
SALES.WKS	3 KB	WKS File	7/26/1995 4:55 PM
Sample Text	5 KB	WordPad Document	10/15/2001 2:21 PM
TOOLS.WKS	5 KB	WKS File	7/28/1995 12:07 AM
TRAVEL.WPS	4 KB	WPS File	10/13/1999 9:12 PM

click these buttons to sort the file list in a different order

date and time the file was created or last modified

total size of the objects in the window

total number of objects in the window

17 object(s)   483 KB   🖳 My Computer

2. Look at the file sizes. Do you see that Exterior and Interior are the largest files?

3. Look at the dates and times the files were modified. Which is the oldest file?

One of the advantages that Details view has over other views is that you can sort the file list by filename, size, type, or the date the file was last modified. This helps if you're working with a large file list and you're trying to locate a specific file.

To sort the file list by type:

1. Click the **Type** button at the top of the list of files.

The files are now sorted in alphabetical order by type, starting with the "Bitmap Image" files and ending with the "XLS File" files. This would be useful if, for example, you were looking for all the .doc files (those created with Microsoft Word), because they would all be grouped together under "M" for "Microsoft Word."

2. Click the **Type** button again.

The sort order is reversed with the "XLS File" files now at the top of the list.

3. Click the **Name** button at the top of the file list.

The files are now sorted in alphabetical order by filename.

Now that you have looked at the file details, switch back to Large Icon view.

To switch to Large Icon view:

1. Click **View** and then click **Large Icons** to return to the large icon display.

Restoring the My Computer Default Settings

Windows 2000 provides other options in working with your files and windows. These options fall into two general categories: Classic style and Web style. **Classic style** is a mode of working with windows and files that resembles earlier versions of the Windows operating system. **Web style** allows you to work with your windows and files in the same way you work with Web pages on the World Wide Web. For example, to open a file in Classic style, you can double-click the file icon (a **double-click** is clicking the left mouse button twice quickly) or click the file icon once and press the Enter key. To open a file in Web style, you would simply click the file icon once, and the file would open. You could also create your own style, choosing elements of both the Classic and Web styles, and add in a few customized features of your own.

In order to simplify matters, this book will assume that you're working in the Default style, that is the configuration that Windows 2000 uses when it is initially installed. No matter what changes you make to the configuration of Windows 2000, you can always revert back to the Default style. Try switching back to Default style now.

To switch to the Default style:

1. Click **Tools** and then click **Folder Options** on the menu.

2. If it is not already selected, click the **General** tab.

   The General sheet displays general options for working with files and windows. Take some time to look over the list of options available.

3. Click the **Restore Defaults** button.

4. Click the **View** tab.

   The View sheet displays options that control the appearance of files and other objects. You should set these options to their default values as well.

5. Click the **Restore Defaults** button.

6. Click the **OK** button to close the Folder Options dialog box.

Working with Folders and Directories

Up to now, you've done a little work with files and windows, but before going further you should look at some of the terminology used to describe these tasks. Any location where you can store files on a computer is referred to as a **directory**. The main directory of a disk is sometimes called the **root directory**, or the **top-level directory**. All of the files on your Data Disk are currently in the root directory of your floppy disk.

If too many files are stored in a directory, the list of files becomes very long and difficult to manage. You can divide a directory into **subdirectories,** also called **folders**. The number of files for each folder then becomes much fewer and easier to manage. A folder within a folder is called a **subfolder**. The folder that contains another folder is called the **parent folder**.

All of these objects exist in a **hierarchy**, which begins with your desktop and extends down to each subfolder. Figure 2-18 shows part of a typical hierarchy of Windows 2000 objects.

Figure 2-18 | PART OF A TYPICAL HIERARCHY OF WINDOWS 2000 OBJECTS

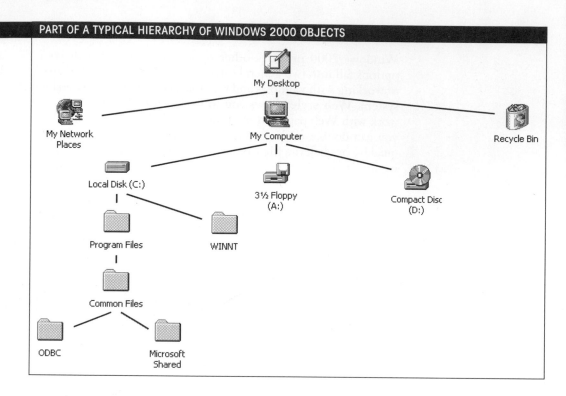

Creating a Folder

You've already seen folder icons in the various windows you've previously opened. Now, you'll create your own folder called Practice to hold your documents.

To create a Practice folder:

1. Click **File** and then point to **New** to display the submenu.

2. Click **Folder**. A folder icon with the label "New Folder" appears.

3. Type **Practice** as the name of the folder.

   TROUBLE? If nothing happens when you type the folder name, it's possible that the folder name is no longer selected. Right-click the Practice folder, click Rename, and then repeat Step 3.

4. Press the **Enter** key.

   The folder is now named "Practice" and is the selected item on your Data Disk.

5. Click a blank area next to the Practice folder to deselect it.

Navigating Through the Windows 2000 Hierarchy

Now that you've created a subfolder, how do you move into it? You've seen that to view the contents of a file, you open it. To move into a subfolder, you open it in the same way.

> ### To view the contents of the Practice folder:
>
> 1. Click the **Practice** folder and press the **Enter** key.
>
> 2. The Practice folder opens. Because there are no files in the folder, there are no items to display. You'll change that shortly.

You've seen that to navigate through the devices and folders on your computer, you open My Computer and then click the icons representing the objects you want to explore. But what if you want to move back to the root directory? The Standard toolbar, which stays the same regardless of which folder or object is open, includes buttons that help you navigate through the hierarchy of drives, directories, folders, subfolders and other objects in your computer. Figure 2-19 summarizes the navigation buttons on the Standard toolbar.

Figure 2-19		NAVIGATION BUTTONS
BUTTON	**ICON**	**DESCRIPTION**
Back	←	Returns you to the folder, drive, directory, or object you were most recently viewing. The button is active only when you have viewed more than one window in the current session.
Forward	→	Reverses the effect of the Back button.
Up	⬆	Moves you up one level in the hierarchy of directories, drives, folders, and other objects on your computer.

You can return to your floppy's root directory by using the Back or the Up button. Try both of these techniques now.

> ### To move up to the root directory:
>
> 1. Click the **Back** button ←.
>
>   Windows 2000 moves you back to the previous window, in this case the root directory of your Data Disk.
>
> 2. Click the **Forward** button →.
>
>   The Forward button reverses the effect of the Back button and takes you to the Practice folder.
>
> 3. Click the **Up** button ⬆.
>
>   You move up one level in hierarchy of Windows 2000 objects, going to the root directory of the Data Disk.

Another way of moving around in the Windows 2000 hierarchy is through the Address toolbar. By clicking the Address list arrow, you can view a list of the objects in the top part of the Windows 2000 hierarchy (see Figure 2-20). This gives you a quick way of moving to the top without having to navigate through the intermediate levels.

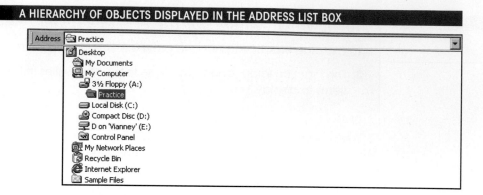

Figure 2-20   A HIERARCHY OF OBJECTS DISPLAYED IN THE ADDRESS LIST BOX

Now that you know how to move among the folders and devices on your computer, you can practice manipulating files. The better you are at working with the hierarchy of files and folders on your computer, the more organized the hierarchy will be, and the easier it will be to find the files you need.

Working with Files

As you've seen, the Practice folder doesn't contain any files. In the next set of steps, you will place a file from the root directory into it.

Moving and Copying a File

If you want to place a file into a folder from another location, you can either move the file or copy it. **Moving** a file takes it out of its current location and places it in the new location. **Copying** places the file in both locations. Windows 2000 provides several different techniques for moving and copying files. One way is to make sure that both the current and the new location are visible on your screen and then hold down the right mouse button and drag the file from the old location to the new location. A menu will then appear, and you can then select whether you want to move the file to the new location or make a copy in the new location. The advantage of this technique is that you are never confused as to whether you copied the file or merely moved it. Try this technique now by placing a copy of the Agenda file in the Practice folder.

To copy the Agenda file:

1. Point to the **Agenda** file in the root directory of your Data Disk and press the *right* mouse button.

2. With the right mouse button still pressed down, drag the **Agenda** file icon to the **Practice** folder icon; when the Practice folder icon turns blue, release the button.

3. A menu appears, as shown in Figure 2-21. Click **Copy Here**.

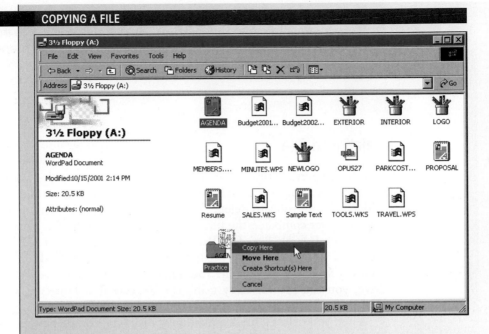

Figure 2-21 | COPYING A FILE

TROUBLE? If you release the mouse button by mistake before dragging the Agenda icon to the Practice folder, the Agenda shortcut menu opens. Press the Esc key and then repeat Steps 1 and 2.

4. Double-click the **Practice** folder.

The Agenda file should now appear in the Practice folder.

Note that the "Move Here" command was also part of the menu. In fact, the command was in boldface, indicating that it is the default command whenever you drag a document from one location to another on the same drive. This means that if you were to drag a file from one location to another on the same drive using the left mouse button (instead of the right), the file would be moved and not copied.

Renaming a File

You will often find that you want to change the name of files as you change their content or as you create other files. You can easily rename a file by using the Rename option on the file's shortcut menu or by using the file's label.

Practice using this feature by renaming the Agenda file "Practice Agenda," since it is now in the Practice folder.

To rename the Agenda file:

1. Right-click the **Agenda** icon.

2. Click **Rename**. After a moment the filename is highlighted and a box appears around it.

3. Type **Practice Agenda** and press the **Enter** key.

> TROUBLE? If you make a mistake while typing and you haven't pressed the Enter key yet, you can press the Backspace key until you delete the mistake, then complete Step 3. If you've already pressed the Enter key, repeat Steps 1-3 to rename the file a second time.
>
> The file appears with a new name.

Deleting a File

You should periodically delete files you no longer need so that your folders and disks don't get cluttered. You delete a file or folder by deleting its icon. Be careful when you delete a folder, because you also delete all the files it contains! When you delete a file from a hard drive on your computer, the filename is deleted from the directory but the file contents are held in the Recycle Bin. The Recycle Bin is an area on your hard drive that holds deleted files until you remove them permanently; an icon on the desktop allows you easy access to the Recycle Bin. If you change your mind and want to retrieve a file deleted from your hard drive, you can recover it by using the Recycle Bin. However, once you've emptied the Recycle Bin, you can no longer recover the files that were in it.

When you delete a file from a floppy disk or a disk that exists on another computer on your network, it does not go into the Recycle Bin. Instead, it is deleted as soon as its icon disappears—and you can't recover it.

Try deleting the Practice Agenda file from your Data Disk. Because this file is on a floppy disk and not on the hard disk, it will not go into the Recycle Bin, and if you change your mind you won't be able to get it back.

To delete the Practice Agenda file:

1. Right-click the icon for the Practice Agenda file.

2. Click **Delete** on the menu that appears.

3. Windows 2000 asks if you're sure that you want to delete this file. Click the **Yes** button.

4. Click the **Close** button ⊠ to close the My Computer window.

If you like using your mouse, another way of deleting a file is to drag its icon to the Recycle Bin on the desktop. Be aware that if you're dragging a file from your floppy disk or a network disk, the file will *not* be placed in the Recycle Bin—it will still be permanently deleted.

Other Copying and Moving Techniques

As was noted earlier, there are several ways of moving and copying. As you become more familiar with Windows 2000, you will no doubt settle on the technique you like best. Figure 2-22 describes some of the other ways of moving and copying files.

Figure 2-22	METHODS FOR MOVING AND COPYING FILES	
METHOD	**TO MOVE**	**TO COPY**
Cut, copy, and paste	Select the file icon. Click **Edit** on the menu bar and **Cut** on the menu bar. Move to the new location. Click **Edit** and **Paste**.	Select the file icon. Click **Edit** on the menu bar and **Copy** on the menu bar. Move to the new location. Click **Edit** and **Paste**.
Drag and drop	Click the file icon. Drag and drop the icon in the new location.	Click the file icon. Hold down the Ctrl key and drag and drop the icon in the new location.
Right-click, drag and drop	With the right mouse button pressed down, drag the file icon to the new location. Release the mouse button and click **Move Here** on the menu.	With the right mouse button pressed down, drag the file icon to the new location. Release the mouse button and click **Copy Here** on the menu.
Move to folder and copy to folder	Click the file icon. Click **Edit** on the menu bar and **Move to Folder** on the menu bar. Select the new location in the Browse for Folder dialog box.	Click the file icon. Click **Edit** on the menu bar and **Copy to Folder** on the menu bar. Select the new location in the Browse for Folder dialog box.

The techniques shown in Figure 2-22 are primarily for document files. Because a program might not work correctly if moved into a new location, the techniques for moving program files are slightly different. See the Windows 2000 online Help for more information on moving or copying a program file.

Copying **an Entire Floppy Disk**

You can have trouble accessing the data on your floppy disk if the disk is damaged, is exposed to magnetic fields, or picks up a computer virus. To avoid losing all your data, it is a good idea to make a copy of your floppy disk.

If you wanted to make a copy of an audiocassette, your cassette player would need two cassette drives. You might wonder, therefore, how your computer can make a copy of your disk if you have only one floppy disk drive. Figure 2-23 illustrates how the computer uses only one disk drive to make a copy of a disk.

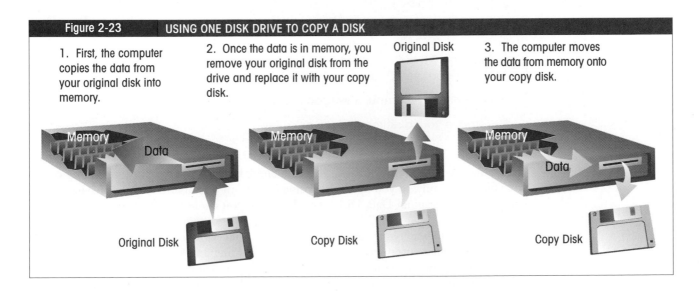

Figure 2-23	USING ONE DISK DRIVE TO COPY A DISK

1. First, the computer copies the data from your original disk into memory.

2. Once the data is in memory, you remove your original disk from the drive and replace it with your copy disk.

Original Disk

3. The computer moves the data from memory onto your copy disk.

Memory

Data

Memory

Memory

Data

Original Disk

Copy Disk

Copy Disk

REFERENCE WINDOW **RW**

Copying a Disk

- Insert the disk you want to copy in drive A.
- In My Computer, right-click the 3½ Floppy (A:) icon, and then click Copy Disk.
- Click Start to begin the copy process.
- When prompted, remove the disk you want to copy, place your second disk in drive A, and then click OK.

If you have an extra floppy disk, you can make a copy of your Data Disk now. Make sure you copy the disk regularly so that as you work through the tutorials in this book it will stay updated.

To copy your Data Disk:

1. Write your name and "Windows 2000 Disk 1 Data Disk Copy" on the label of your second disk. Make sure the disk is blank and formatted.

   TROUBLE? If you aren't sure if the disk is blank, place it in the disk drive and open the 3½ Floppy (A:) window to view its contents. If the disk contains files you need, get a different disk. If it contains files you don't need, you could format the disk now, using the steps you learned at the beginning of this tutorial.

2. Make sure your original Data Disk is in drive A and the My Computer window is open.

3. Right-click the **3½ Floppy (A:)** icon, and then click **Copy Disk**. The Copy Disk dialog box opens.

4. Click the **Start** button and then the **OK** button to begin the copy process.

5. When the message "Insert the disk you want to copy to (destination disk)..." appears, remove your Data Disk and insert your Windows 2000 Disk 1 Data Disk Copy in drive A.

6. Click the **OK** button. When the copy is complete, you will see the message "Copy completed successfully." Click the **Close** button.

7. Close the My Computer window.

8. Remove your disk from the drive.

As you finish copying your disk, Shannon emphasizes the importance of making copies of your files frequently, so you won't risk losing important documents for your distance learning course. If your original Data Disk were damaged, you could use the copy you just made to access the files.

Keeping copies of your files is so important that Windows 2000 includes a program called Backup that automates the process of duplicating and storing data. In the Projects at the end of the tutorial you'll have an opportunity to explore the difference between what you just did in copying a disk and the way in which a program such as the Windows 2000 Backup program helps you safeguard data.

Session 2.2 Quick Check

1. If you want to find out about the storage devices and printers connected to your computer, what window could you open?

2. If you have only one floppy disk drive on your computer, it is usually identified by the letter _____ .

3. The letter C is typically used for the _____ drive of a computer.

4. What information does Details view supply about a list of folders and files?

5. The main directory of a disk is referred to as the _____ directory.

6. What is the topmost object in the hierarchy of Windows 2000 objects?

7. If you have one floppy disk drive, but you have two disks, can you copy the files on one floppy disk to the other?

REVIEW ASSIGNMENTS

1. **Opening, Editing, and Printing a Document** In this tutorial you learned how to create a document using WordPad. You also learned how to save, open, and print a document. Practice these skills by copying the document called **Resume** into the Practice folder on your Data Disk. Rename the file **Woods Resume**. This document is a resume for Jamie Woods. Make the changes shown in Figure 2-24. Save your revisions in Word for Windows 6.0 format, preview, and then print the document. Close WordPad.

Figure 2-24

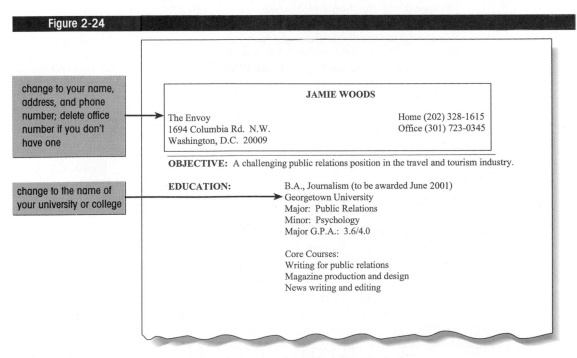

change to your name, address, and phone number; delete office number if you don't have one

change to the name of your university or college

JAMIE WOODS

The Envoy
1694 Columbia Rd. N.W.
Washington, D.C. 20009

Home (202) 328-1615
Office (301) 723-0345

OBJECTIVE: A challenging public relations position in the travel and tourism industry.

EDUCATION:

B.A., Journalism (to be awarded June 2001)
Georgetown University
Major: Public Relations
Minor: Psychology
Major G.P.A.: 3.6/4.0

Core Courses:
Writing for public relations
Magazine production and design
News writing and editing

2. **Creating, Saving, and Printing a Letter** Use WordPad to write a one-page letter to a relative or a friend. Save the document in the Practice folder on your Data Disk with the name **Letter**. Use the Print Preview feature to look at the format of your finished letter, then print it, and be sure to sign it. Close WordPad.

3. **Managing Files and Folders** Using the copy of the disk you made at the end of the tutorial, complete steps a through f below to practice your file-management skills, and then answer the questions below.

   a. Create a folder called Spreadsheets on your Data Disk.
   b. Move the files **Parkcost**, **Budget2001**, **Budget2002**, and **Sales** into the Spreadsheets folder.
   c. Create a folder called Park Project.
   d. Move the files **Proposal**, **Members**, **Tools**, **Logo**, and **Newlogo** into the Park Project folder.
   e. Delete the file called **Travel**.
   f. Switch to the Details view and write out your answers to Questions 1 through 5:
      1. What is the largest file or files in the Park Project folder?
      2. What is the newest file or files in the Spreadsheets folder?
      3. How many files (don't include folders) are in the root directory of your Data Disk?
      4. How are the Opus and Exterior icons different? Judging from the appearance of the icons, what would you guess these two files contain?
      5. Which file in the root directory has the most recent date?

4. **More Practice with Files and Folders** For this assignment, you need a third blank disk. Complete steps a through g below to practice your file-management skills.

   a. Write "Windows 2000 Tutorial 2 Assignment 4" on the label of the blank disk, and then format the disk if necessary.
   b. Create another copy of your original Data Disk, using the Assignment 4 disk. Refer to the section "Creating Your Data Disk" in Session 2.2.
   c. Create three folders on the Assignment 4 Data Disk you just created: Documents, Budgets, and Graphics.
   d. Move the files **Interior**, **Exterior**, **Logo**, and **Newlogo** to the Graphics folder.
   e. Move the files **Travel**, **Members**, and **Minutes** to the Documents folder.
   f. Move **Budget2001** and **Budget2002** to the Budgets folder.
   g. Switch to Details view and write out your answers to Questions 1 through 6:
      1. What is the largest file or files in the Graphics folder?
      2. How many word-processed documents are in the root directory? *Hint*: These documents will appear with the WordPad, Microsoft Word, or some other word-processing icon, depending on what software you have installed.
      3. What is the newest file or files in the root directory (don't include folders)?
      4. How many files in all folders are 5 KB in size?
      5. How many files in the root directory are WKS files? *Hint*: Look in the Type column to identify WKS files.
      6. Do all the files in the Graphics folder have the same icon? What type are they?

5. **Searching for a File** Windows 2000 Help includes a topic that discusses how to search for files on a disk without looking through all the folders. Start Windows Help, then locate this topic, and answer Questions a through c:

   a. To display the Search dialog box, you must click the _____ button, then point to _____ on the menu, and finally click _____ on the submenu.
   b. Do you need to type in the entire filename to find the file?
   c. How do you perform a case-sensitive search?

6. **Help with Files and Folders** In Tutorial 2 you learned how to work with Windows 2000 files and folders. What additional information on this topic does Windows 2000 Help provide? Use the Start button to access Help. Use the Index tab to locate topics related to files and folders. Find at least two tips or procedures for working with files and folders that were not covered in the tutorial. Write out the tip in your own words and include the title of the Help screen that contains the information.

7. **Formatting Text** You can use a word processor such as WordPad to format text, that is, to give it a specific look and feel by using bold, italics, and different fonts, and by applying other features. Using WordPad, type the title and words to one of your favorite songs and

then save the document on your Data Disk (make sure you use your original Data Disk) with the filename Song.

a. Select the title, and then click the Center ▤, Bold **B**, and Italic *I* buttons on the toolbar.
b. Click the Font list arrow and select a different font. Repeat this step several times with different fonts until you locate a font that is appropriate for the song.
c. Experiment with other formatting options until you find a look you like for your document. Save and print the final version.

PROJECTS

1. Formatting a floppy disk removes all the data on a disk. Answer the following questions using full sentences:

    a. What other method did you learn in this tutorial for removing data from a disk?
    b. If you wanted to remove all data from a disk, which method would you use? Why?
    c. What method would you use if you wanted to remove only one file? Why?

2. A friend who is new to computers is trying to learn how to enter text into WordPad. She has just finished typing her first paragraph when she notices a mistake in the first sentence. She can't remember how to fix a mistake, so she asks you for help. Write the set of steps she should try.

3. Computer users usually develop habits about how they access their files and programs. Follow the steps below to practice methods of opening a file, and then evaluate which method you would be likely to use and why.

    a. Using WordPad, create a document containing the words to a favorite poem, and save it on your Data Disk with the name Poem.
    b. Close WordPad and return to the desktop.
    c. Open the document using a document-centric approach.
    d. After a successful completion of step c, close the program and reopen the same document using another approach.
    e. Write the steps you used to complete steps c and d of this assignment. Then write a paragraph discussing which approach is most convenient when you are starting from the desktop, and indicate what habits you would develop if you owned your own computer and used it regularly.

Explore 4. The My Computer window gives you access to the objects on your computer. In this tutorial you used My Computer to access your floppy drive so you could view the contents of your Data Disk. The My Computer window gives you access to other objects too. Open My Computer and write a list of the objects you see, including folders. Then open each icon and write a two-sentence description of the contents of each window that opens.

Explore 5. In this tutorial you learned how to copy a disk to protect yourself in the event of data loss. If you had your own computer with an 80 MB hard drive that was being used to capacity, it would take many 1.44 MB floppy disks to copy the contents of the entire hard drive. Is copying to floppy disks a reasonable method to use for protecting the data on your hard disk? Why, or why not?

    a. As mentioned at the end of the tutorial, Windows 2000 also includes an accessory called Backup that helps you safeguard your data. Backup doesn't just copy the data—it organizes it so that it takes up much less space than if you simply copied it. This program might not be installed on your computer, but if it is, try starting it (click the Start button, point to Programs, point to Accessories, point to System Tools, and then click Backup) and opening the Help files to learn what you can about how it functions. If it is not installed, skip Part a.
    b. Look up the topic of backups in a computer concepts textbook or in computer trade magazines. You could also interview experienced computer owners to find out which method they use to protect their data. When you have finished researching the concept of the backup, write a single-page essay that explains the difference between copying and backing up files, and evaluates which method is preferable for backing up large amounts of data, and why.

LAB ASSIGNMENTS

Using Files In this Lab you manipulate a simulated computer to view what happens in memory and on disk when you create, save, open, revise, and delete files. Understanding what goes on "inside the box" will help you quickly grasp how to perform basic file operations with most application software. See the Read This Before You Begin page for instructions on starting the Using Files Course Lab.

1. Click the Steps button to learn how to use the simulated computer to view the contents of memory and disk when you perform basic file operations. As you proceed through the Steps, answer all of the Quick Check questions that appear. After you complete the Steps, you will see a Quick Check Summary Report. Follow the instructions on the screen to print this report.

2. Click the Explore button and use the simulated computer to perform the following tasks:
    a. Create a document containing your name and the city in which you were born. Save this document as NAME.
    b. Create another document containing two of your favorite foods. Save this document as FOODS.
    c. Create another file containing your two favorite classes. Call this file CLASSES.
    d. Open the FOOD file and add another one of your favorite foods. Save this file without changing its name.
    e. Open the NAME file. Change this document so that it contains your name and the name of your school. Save this as a new document called SCHOOL.
    f. Write down how many files are on the simulated disk and the exact contents of each file.
    g. Delete all the files.

3. In Explore, use the simulated computer to perform the following tasks.
    a. Create a file called MUSIC that contains the name of your favorite CD.
    b. Create another document that contains eight numbers and call this file LOTTERY.
    c. You didn't win the lottery this week. Revise the contents of the LOTTERY file, but save the revision as LOTTERY2.
    d. Revise the MUSIC file so that it also contains the name of your favorite musician or composer, and save this file as MUSIC2.
    e. Delete the MUSIC file.
    f. Write down how many files are on the simulated disk and the exact contents of each file.

QUICK CHECK ANSWERS

Session 2.1
1. file
2. Formatting
3. True
4. insertion point
5. a list of recently opened files and objects
6. The Files of Type list box could be set to display files of a different type than the one you're looking for.
7. From the Print Preview window, using the Print button on the toolbar, and using the Print command from the File menu. If you want to print multiple copies of a file, use either the Print button from the Print Preview window or the Print command from the File menu—both of these techniques will display the Print dialog box containing the options you need to set.

Session 2.2
1. My Computer
2. A
3. hard
4. filename, size, type, and date modified
5. root or top-level
6. the Desktop
7. yes

New Perspectives on

MICROSOFT®
OFFICE XP

Read This Before You Begin

To the Student

Data Disks

To complete this tutorial and the Review Assignments, you need one Data Disk. Your instructor will either provide you with the Data Disk or ask you to make your own.

If you are making your own Data Disk, you will need **one** blank, formatted high-density disk. You will need to copy a set of files and/or folders from a file server, standalone computer, or the Web onto your disk. Your instructor will tell you which computer, drive letter, and folder contain the files you need. You could also download the files by going to www.course.com and following the instructions on the screen.

The information below shows you which folder goes on your disk, so that you will have enough disk space to complete the tutorial and Review Assignments:

Data Disk 1

Write this on the disk label:
Data Disk 1: Introducing Office XP

Put this folder on the disk:
Tutorial.01

When you begin the tutorial, be sure you are using the correct Data Disk. Refer to the "File Finder" chart at the back of this text for more detailed information on which files are used in the tutorial. See the inside front or inside back cover of this book for more information on Data Disk files, or ask your instructor or technical support person for assistance.

Using Your Own Computer

If you are going to work through this tutorial using your own computer, you need:

- ■ **Computer System** Microsoft Windows 98, NT, 2000 Professional, or higher must be installed on your computer. This book assumes a typical installation of Microsoft Office XP.

- ■ **Data Disk** You will not be able to complete this tutorial or Review Assignments using your own computer until you have your Data Disk.

Visit Our World Wide Web Site

Additional materials designed especially for you are available on the World Wide Web.
Go to www.course.com/NewPerspectives.

To the Instructor

The Data Disk Files are available on the Instructor's Resource Kit for this title. Follow the instructions in the Help file on the CD-ROM to install the programs to your network or standalone computer. For information on creating the Data Disk, see the "To the Student" section above.

You are granted a license to copy the Data Disk Files to any computer or computer network used by students who have purchased this book.

In this tutorial you will:

- Explore the programs that comprise Microsoft Office

- Explore the benefits of integrating data between programs

- Start programs and switch between them

- Use personalized menus and toolbars

- Save and close a file

- Open an existing file

- Print a file

- Get Help

- Close files and exit programs

INTRODUCING MICROSOFT OFFICE XP

Preparing Promotional Materials for Delmar Office Supplies

CASE

Delmar Office Supplies

Delmar Office Supplies, a company in Wisconsin founded by Nicole Delmar in 1996, sells recycled office supplies to businesses and home-based offices around the world. The demand for quality recycled papers, reconditioned toner cartridges, and renovated office furniture has been growing each year. Nicole and all her employees use Microsoft Office XP, which provides everyone in the company the power and flexibility to store a variety of information, create consistent documents, and share data. In this tutorial, you'll review some of the latest documents the company's employees have created using Microsoft Office XP.

Exploring Microsoft Office XP

Microsoft Office XP, or simply **Office**, is a collection of the most popular Microsoft programs: Word, Excel, PowerPoint, Access, and Outlook. Each Office program contains valuable tools to help you accomplish many tasks, such as composing reports, analyzing data, preparing presentations, and compiling information.

Microsoft Word 2002, or simply **Word**, is a **word processing program** you use to create text documents. The files you create in Word are called **documents**. Word offers many special features that help you compose and update all types of documents, ranging from letters and newsletters to reports, fliers, faxes, and even books—all in attractive and readable formats. You also can use Word to create, insert, and position figures, tables, and other graphics to enhance the look of your documents. Figure 1 shows a business letter that a sales representative composed with Word.

Figure 1 LETTER COMPOSED IN A WORD DOCUMENT

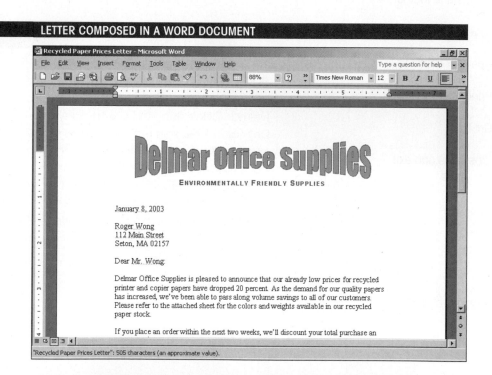

Microsoft Excel 2002, or simply **Excel**, is a **spreadsheet program** you use to display, organize, and analyze numerical information. You can do some of this in Word with tables, but Excel provides many more tools for performing calculations than Word does. Its graphics capabilities also enable you to display data visually. You might, for example, generate a pie chart or bar chart to help readers quickly see the significance of and the connections between information. The files you create in Excel are called **workbooks**. Figure 2 shows an Excel workbook with a line chart that the Operations Department uses to track the company's financial performance.

Figure 2   FINANCIAL DATA IN AN EXCEL WORKBOOK

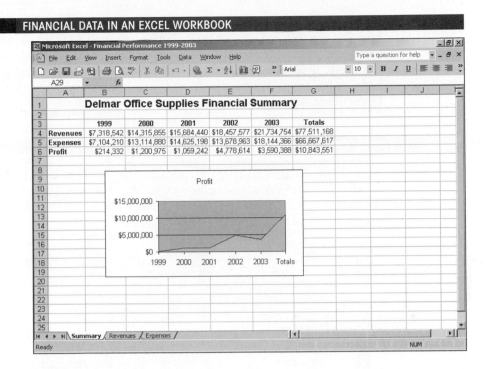

Microsoft **PowerPoint 2002**, or simply **PowerPoint**, is a **presentation graphics program** you use to create a collection of "slides" that can contain text, charts, pictures, and so on. The files you create in PowerPoint are called **presentations**. You can show these presentations on your computer monitor, project them onto a screen as a slide show, print them, share them over the Internet, or display them on the World Wide Web. You also can use PowerPoint to generate presentation-related documents such as audience handouts, outlines, and speakers' notes. Figure 3 shows an effective slide presentation the Sales Department created with PowerPoint to promote the latest product line.

Figure 3   SLIDE PRESENTATION CREATED IN POWERPOINT

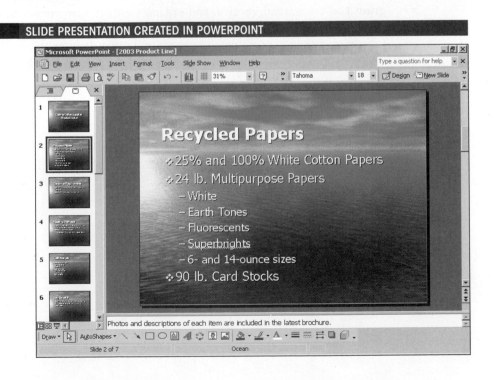

Microsoft Access 2002, or simply **Access**, is a **database program** you use to enter, organize, display, and retrieve related information. The files you create in Access are called **databases**. With Access you can create data entry forms to make data entry easier, and you can create professional reports to improve the readability of your data. Figure 4 shows a table in an Access database with customer names and addresses compiled by the Sales Department.

Figure 4	CUSTOMER ADDRESSES COMPILED IN AN ACCESS DATABASE

Microsoft Outlook 2002, or simply **Outlook**, is an **information management program** you use to send, receive, and organize e-mail; plan your schedule; arrange meetings; organize contacts; create a to-do list; and jot down notes. You also can use Outlook to print schedules, task lists, or phone directories and other documents. Figure 5 shows how Nicole Delmar uses Outlook to plan her schedule and create a to-do list.

Figure 5   **CALENDAR AND TASKS IN OUTLOOK**

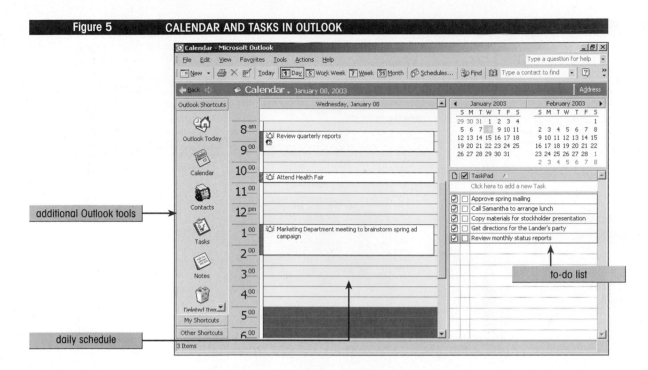

additional Outlook tools

to-do list

daily schedule

Although each Office program individually is a strong tool, their potential is even greater when used together.

Integrating Programs

One of the main advantages of Office is **integration**, the ability to share information between programs. Integration ensures consistency and accuracy, and it saves time because you don't have to re-enter the same information in several Office programs. The staff at Delmar Office Supplies uses the integration features of Office daily, including the following examples:

■ The Accounting Department created an Excel bar chart on the last two years' fourth-quarter results, which they inserted into the quarterly financial report, created in Word. They added a hyperlink to the Word report that employees can click to open the Excel workbook and view the original data. See Figure 6.

| Figure 6 | WORD DOCUMENT WITH AN EXCEL CHART |

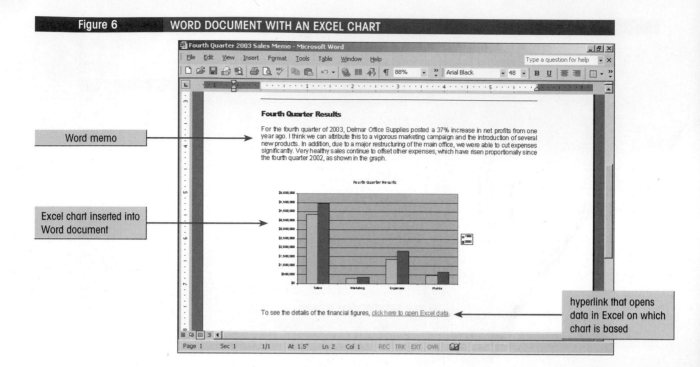

Word memo

Excel chart inserted into Word document

hyperlink that opens data in Excel on which chart is based

■ An Excel pie chart of sales percentages by divisions of Delmar Office Supplies can be duplicated on a PowerPoint slide. The slide is part of the Operations Department's presentation to stockholders. See Figure 7.

| Figure 7 | POWERPOINT PRESENTATION WITH AN EXCEL CHART |

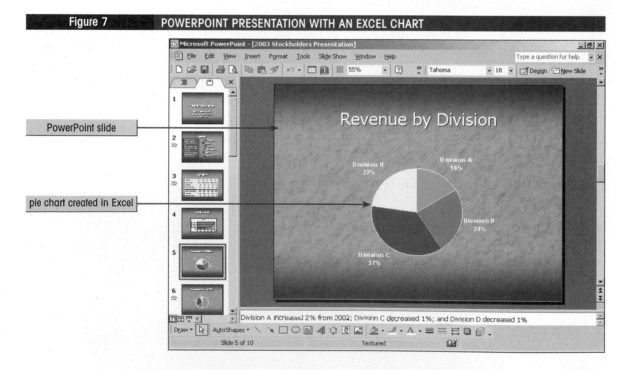

PowerPoint slide

pie chart created in Excel

■ An Access database or an Outlook contact list that stores the names and addresses of customers can be combined with a form letter that the Marketing Department created in Word, to produce a mailing promoting the company's newest products. See Figure 8.

Figure 8	WORD LETTER WITH ACCESS OR OUTLOOK DATA

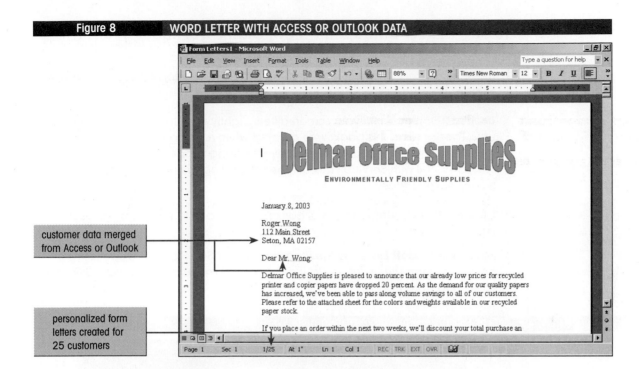

customer data merged from Access or Outlook

personalized form letters created for 25 customers

These are just a few examples of how you can take information from one Office program and integrate it into another.

Starting Office Programs

All Office programs start the same way—from the Programs menu on the Start button. You select the program you want, and then the program starts so you can immediately begin to create new files or work with existing ones.

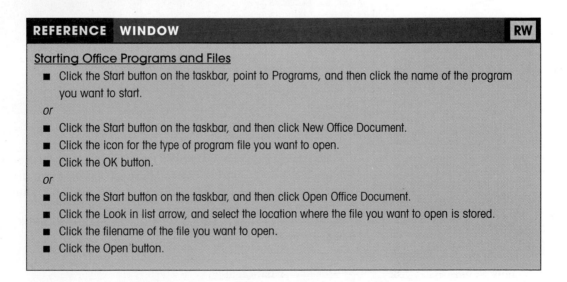

REFERENCE WINDOW   RW

Starting Office Programs and Files
- Click the Start button on the taskbar, point to Programs, and then click the name of the program you want to start.

or

- Click the Start button on the taskbar, and then click New Office Document.
- Click the icon for the type of program file you want to open.
- Click the OK button.

or

- Click the Start button on the taskbar, and then click Open Office Document.
- Click the Look in list arrow, and select the location where the file you want to open is stored.
- Click the filename of the file you want to open.
- Click the Open button.

You'll start Excel using the Start button.

To start Excel and open a new, blank workbook from the Start menu:

1. Make sure your computer is on and the Windows desktop appears on your screen.

   TROUBLE? Don't worry if your screen differs slightly from those shown in the figures. The figures in this book were created while running Windows 2000 in its default settings, but Office runs equally well using Windows 98 or later or Windows NT 4 with Service Pack 5. These operating systems share the same basic user interface.

2. Click the **Start** button on the taskbar, and then point to **Programs** to display the Programs menu.

3. Point to **Microsoft Excel** on the Programs menu. See Figure 9. Depending on how your computer is set up, your desktop and menu might contain different icons and commands.

Figure 9	START MENU WITH PROGRAMS MENU DISPLAYED

other ways to open Office programs and files

click to start Excel

Office programs

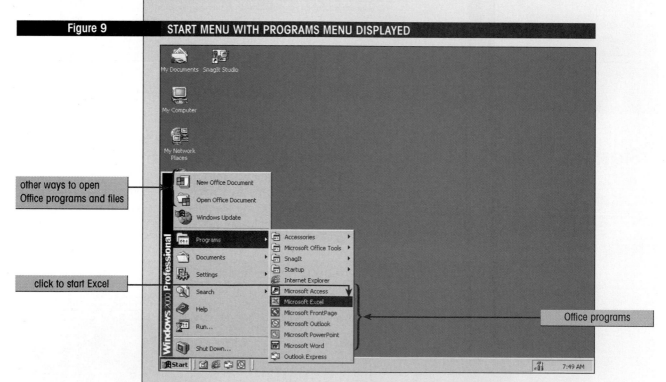

   TROUBLE? If you don't see Microsoft Excel on the Programs menu, point to Microsoft Office, and then point to Microsoft Excel. If you still don't see Microsoft Excel, ask your instructor or technical support person for help.

4. Click **Microsoft Excel** to start Excel and open a new, blank workbook. See Figure 10.

| Figure 10 | NEW, BLANK EXCEL WORKBOOK |

title bar

menu bar

Standard toolbar

Formatting toolbar

New Workbook
Task Pane

click to close file

click to close program

An alternate method for starting programs with a blank file is to click the New Office Document command on the Start menu; the kind of file you choose determines which program opens. You'll use this method to start Word and open a new, blank document.

To start Word and open a new, blank document with the New Office Document command:

1. Leaving Excel open, click the **Start** button on the taskbar, and then click **New Office Document**. The New Office Document dialog box opens, providing another way to start Office programs. See Figure 11.

| Figure 11 | NEW OFFICE DOCUMENT DIALOG BOX |

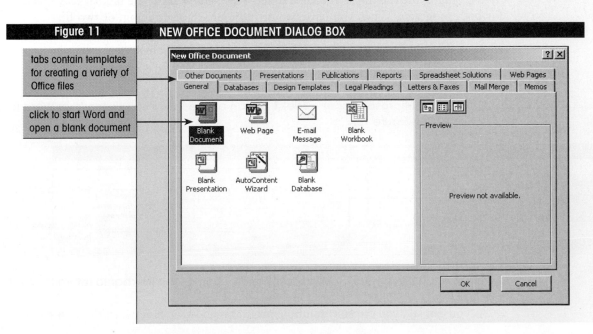

tabs contain templates for creating a variety of Office files

click to start Word and open a blank document

2. If necessary, click the **General** tab, click the **Blank Document** icon, and then click the **OK** button. Word opens with a new, blank document. See Figure 12.

| Figure 12 | NEW, BLANK DOCUMENT IN WORD |

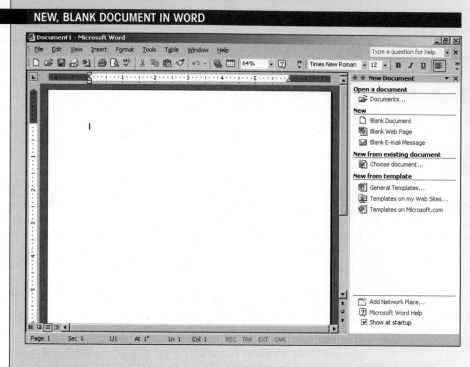

TROUBLE? If you don't see the New Document Task Pane, click File on the Word menu bar, and then click New.

You've tried two ways to start a program. There are several methods for performing most tasks in Office. This flexibility enables you to use Office in the way that fits how you like to work.

Switching Between Open Programs and Files

Two programs are running at the same time—Excel and Word. The taskbar contains buttons for both programs. When you have two or more programs running, or two files within the same program open, you can use the taskbar buttons to switch from one program or file to another. The employees at Delmar Office Supplies often work in several programs at once.

To switch between Word and Excel:

1. Click the **Microsoft Excel – Book1** button on the taskbar to switch from Word to Excel. See Figure 13.

| Figure 13 | EXCEL AND WORD PROGRAMS OPENED |

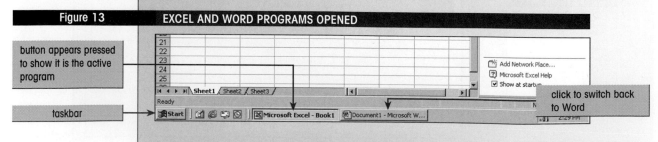

button appears pressed to show it is the active program

taskbar

click to switch back to Word

2. Click the **Document1 – Microsoft Word** button on the taskbar to return to Word.

As you can see, you can start multiple programs and switch between them in seconds.

The Office programs also share many features, so once you've learned one program, it's easy to learn the others. One of the most visible similarities among all the programs is the "personalized" menus and toolbars.

Using Personalized Menus and Toolbars

In each Office program, you perform tasks using a menu command, a toolbar button, or a keyboard shortcut. A **menu command** is a word on a menu that you click to execute a task; a **menu** is a group of related commands. For example, the File menu contains commands for managing files, such as the Open command and the Save command. A **toolbar** is a collection of **buttons** that correspond to commonly used menu commands. For example, the Standard toolbar contains an Open button and a Save button. **Keyboard shortcuts** are combinations of keys you press to perform a command. For example, Ctrl+S is the keyboard shortcut for the Save command (you hold down the Ctrl key while you press the S key). Keyboard shortcuts are displayed to the right of many menu commands.

When you first use a newly installed Office program, the menus and toolbars display only the basic and most commonly used commands and buttons, streamlining the program window. The other commands and buttons are available, but you have to click an extra button to see them (the double-arrow button on a menu and the Toolbar Options button on a toolbar). As you select commands and click buttons, the ones you use often are put on the short, personalized menu and on the visible part of the toolbars. The ones you don't use remain available on the full menus and toolbars. This means that the Office menus and toolbars might display different commands and buttons on each person's computer.

To view a personalized and full menu:

1. Click **Insert** on the Word menu bar to display the short, personalized menu. See Figure 14. The Bookmark command, for example, does not appear on the short menu.

| Figure 14 | SHORT, PERSONALIZED MENU |

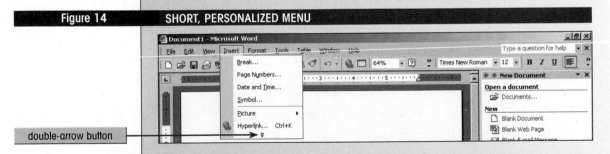

double-arrow button

TROUBLE? If the Insert menu displays different commands than shown in Figure 14, you need to reset the menus. Click Tools on the menu bar, click Customize (you might need to pause until the full menu appears to see that command), and then click the Options tab in the Customize dialog box. Click the Always show full menus check box to remove the check mark if necessary, and then click the Show full menus after a short delay check box to insert a check mark if necessary. Click the Reset my usage data button, and then click the Yes button to confirm that you want to reset the commands. Click the Close button. Repeat Step 1.

You can display the full menu in one of three ways: (1) pause until the full menu appears, which might happen as you read this; (2) click the double-arrow button at the bottom of the menu; or (3) double-click the menu name on the menu bar.

2. Pause until the full Insert menu appears, as shown in Figure 15. The Bookmark command and other commands are now visible.

Figure 15   EXPANDED, FULL MENU

commands with light border appear on short menu

commands with dark border appear only on full menu

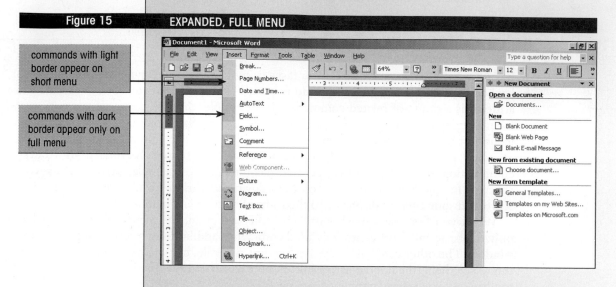

3. Click the **Bookmark** command. A dialog box opens when you click a command whose name is followed by an ellipsis (...). In this case, the Bookmark dialog box opens.

4. Click the **Cancel** button to close the Bookmark dialog box.

5. Click **Insert** on the menu bar again to display the short, personalized menu. The Bookmark command appears on the short, personalized menu because you used it.

6. Press the **Esc** key to close the menu.

As you can see, the menu changed based on your actions. Over time, only the commands you use frequently will appear on the personalized menu. The toolbars work similarly.

To use the personalized toolbars:

1. Observe that the Standard and Formatting toolbars appear side by side below the menu bar.

TROUBLE? If the toolbars appear on two rows, you need to reset them. Click Tools on the menu bar, click Customize, and then click the Options tab in the Customize dialog box. Click the Show Standard and Formatting toolbars on two rows check box to remove the check mark. Click the Reset my data usage button, and then click the Yes button to confirm you want to reset the commands. Click the Close button. Repeat Step 1.

The Formatting toolbar sits to the right of the Standard toolbar. You can see most of the Standard toolbar buttons, but only a few Formatting toolbar buttons.

2. Click the **Toolbar Options** button 》 at the right side of the Standard toolbar. See Figure 16.

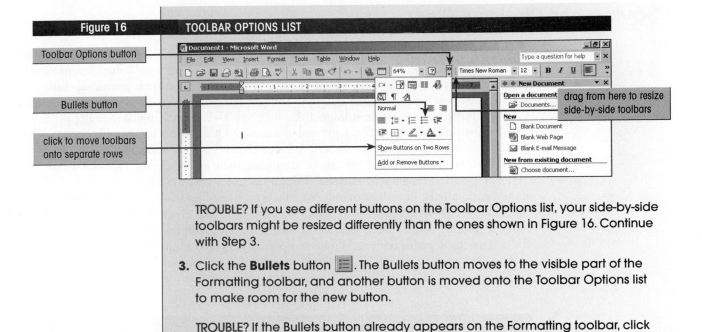

Figure 16   TOOLBAR OPTIONS LIST

Toolbar Options button

Bullets button

click to move toolbars onto separate rows

drag from here to resize side-by-side toolbars

TROUBLE? If you see different buttons on the Toolbar Options list, your side-by-side toolbars might be resized differently than the ones shown in Figure 16. Continue with Step 3.

3. Click the **Bullets** button 📋. The Bullets button moves to the visible part of the Formatting toolbar, and another button is moved onto the Toolbar Options list to make room for the new button.

   TROUBLE? If the Bullets button already appears on the Formatting toolbar, click another button on the Toolbar Options list. Then click that same button again in Step 4 to turn off that formatting.

4. Click 📋 again to turn off the Bullets formatting.

Some people like that the menus and toolbars change to meet their work habits. Others prefer to see all the menu commands or to display the toolbars on different rows so that all the buttons are always visible. You'll change the toolbar setting now.

To turn off the personalized toolbars:

1. Click the **Toolbar Options** button 📋 at the right side of the Standard toolbar.

2. Click the **Show Buttons on Two Rows command**. The toolbars move to separate rows (the Standard toolbar on top) and you can see all the buttons on each toolbar.

You can easily access any button on the toolbars with one mouse click. The drawback is that the toolbars take up more space in the program window.

Using Speech Recognition

Another way to perform tasks in Office is with your voice. Office's **speech recognition technology** enables you to say the names of the toolbar buttons, menus, menu commands, dialog box items, and so forth, rather than clicking the mouse or pressing keys to select them. The Language toolbar includes the Speech Balloon, which displays the voice command equivalents of a selected button or command. If you switch from Voice mode to Dictation mode, you can dictate the contents of your files rather than typing the text or numbers. For better accuracy, complete the Training Wizard, which helps Office learn your vocal quality, rate of talking, and speech patterns. To start using speech recognition, click Tools on the menu bar in any Office program, and then click Speech. The first time you start this feature, the Training Wizard guides you through the setup process.

Saving and Closing a File

As you create and modify Office files, your work is stored only in the computer's temporary memory, not on disk. If you were to exit the programs, turn off your computer, or experience a power failure, your work would be lost. To prevent losing work, frequently save your file to a disk—at least every ten minutes. You can save files to the hard disk located inside your computer or to portable storage disks, such as CD-ROMs, Zip disks, or floppy disks.

The first time you save a file, you need to name it. This name is called a **filename**. When you choose a filename, select a descriptive one that accurately reflects the content of the document, workbook, presentation, or database, such as "Shipping Options Letter" or "Fourth Quarter Financial Analysis." Filenames can include a maximum of 255 letters, numbers, hyphens, or spaces in any combination. Office appends a **file extension** to the filename, which identifies the program in which that file was created. The file extensions are .doc for Word, .xls for Excel, .ppt for PowerPoint, and .mdb for Access. Whether you see file extensions depends on how Windows is set up for your computer.

You also need to decide where you'll save the file—on which disk and in what folder. Choose a logical location that you'll remember whenever you want to use the file again.

REFERENCE WINDOW — RW

Saving a File

- Click the Save button on the Standard toolbar (*or* click File on the menu bar, and then click Save or Save As).
- Click the Save in list arrow, and then select the location where you want to save the file.
- Type a filename in the File name text box.
- Click the Save button.
- To resave the named file to the same location, click the Save button on the Standard toolbar (*or* click File on the menu bar, and then click Save).

Nicole has asked you to start working on the agenda for the stockholder meeting. You enter text in a Word document by typing. After you type some text, you'll save the file.

To enter text in a document:

1. Type **Delmar Office Supplies**, and then press the **Enter** key. The text you typed appears on one line in the Word document.

   TROUBLE? If you make a typing error, press the Backspace key to delete the incorrect letters, and then retype the text.

2. Type **Stockholder Meeting Agenda**, and then press the **Enter** key. The text you typed appears on the second line.

The two lines of text you typed are not yet saved on disk. You'll do that now.

To save a file for the first time:

1. Insert your Data Disk in the appropriate drive.

   TROUBLE? If you don't have a Data Disk, you need to get one before you can proceed. Your instructor or technical support person will either give you one or ask you to make your own by following the instructions on the "Read This Before You Begin" page at the beginning of this tutorial. See your instructor or technical support person for more information.

2. Click the **Save** button 🖫 on the Standard toolbar. The Save As dialog box opens. See Figure 17. The first few words of the first line appear in the File name text box, as a suggested filename. You'll replace this with a more descriptive filename.

| Figure 17 | SAVE AS DIALOG BOX |

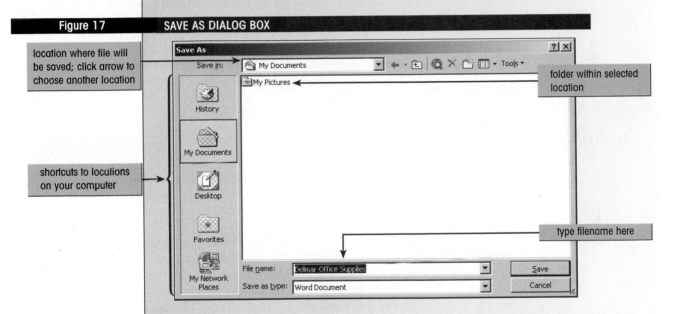

location where file will be saved; click arrow to choose another location

folder within selected location

shortcuts to locations on your computer

type filename here

TROUBLE? If the .doc file extension appears after the filename, then your computer is configured to show file extensions. Just continue with Step 3.

3. Type **Stockholder Meeting Agenda** in the File name text box.

4. Click the **Save in** list arrow, and then click the drive that contains your Data Disk.

5. Double-click the **Tutorial.01** folder in the list box, and then double-click the **Tutorial** folder. This is the location where you want to save the document.

6. Click the **Save** button. The Save As dialog box closes, and the name of your file appears in the program window title bar.

The saved file includes everything in the document at the time you saved. Any edits or additions you then make to the document exist only in the computer's memory and are not saved in the file on the disk. As you work, remember to save frequently so that the file is updated to reflect the latest content of the document.

Because you already named the document and selected a storage location, the second and subsequent times you save, the Save As dialog box doesn't open. If you wanted to save a copy of the file with a different filename or to a different location, you would reopen the Save As dialog box by clicking File on the menu bar, and then clicking Save As. The previous version of the file remains on your disk as well.

You need to add your name to the agenda. Then you'll save your changes and close the file. You can close a file by clicking the Close command on the File menu or by clicking the Close Window button in the upper-right corner of the menu bar.

> ### To modify, save, and close a file:
>
> **1.** Type your name, and then press the **Enter** key. The text you typed appears on the next line.
>
> **2.** Click the **Save** button 🖫 on the Standard toolbar.
>
> The updated document is saved to the file. When you're done with a file, you can close it. Although you can keep multiple files open at one time, you should close any file you are no longer working on to conserve system resources.
>
> **3.** Click the **Close Window** button ☒ on the Word menu bar to close the document. Word is still running, but no documents are open.
>
> TROUBLE? If a dialog box opens and asks whether you want to save the changes you made to the document, you modified the document since you last saved. Click the Yes button to save the current version and close it.

Opening a File

Once you have a program open, you can create additional new files for the open programs or you can open previously created and saved files. You can do both of these from the New Task Pane. The New Task Pane enables you to create new files and open existing ones. The name of the Task Pane varies, depending on the program you are using: Word has the New Document Task Pane, Excel has the New Workbook Task Pane, PowerPoint has the New Presentation Task Pane, and Access has the New File Task Pane.

When you want to work on a previously created file, you must open it first. Opening a file transfers a copy of the file from the storage disk (either a hard disk or a portable disk) to the computer's memory and displays it on your screen. The file is then in your computer's memory and on the disk.

> **REFERENCE WINDOW**   **RW**
>
> <u>Opening an Existing or New File</u>
> - Click File on the menu bar, click New, and then (depending on the program) click the More documents, More workbooks, More presentations, or More files link in the New Task Pane (*or* click the Open button on the Standard toolbar *or* click File on the menu bar, and then click Open).
> - Click the Look in list arrow, and then select the storage location of the file you want to open.
> - Click the filename of the file you want to open.
> - Click the Open button.
> *or*
> - Click File on the menu bar, click New, and then (depending on the program) click the Blank Document, Blank Workbook, Blank Presentation, or Blank Database link in the New Task Pane (*or* click the New button on the Standard toolbar).

Nicole asks you to print the agenda. To do that, you'll reopen the file. Because Word is still open, you'll use the New Document Task Pane.

To open an existing file:

1. If necessary, click **File** on the menu bar, and then click **New** to display the New Document Task Pane. See Figure 18.

| Figure 18 | NEW DOCUMENT TASK PANE |

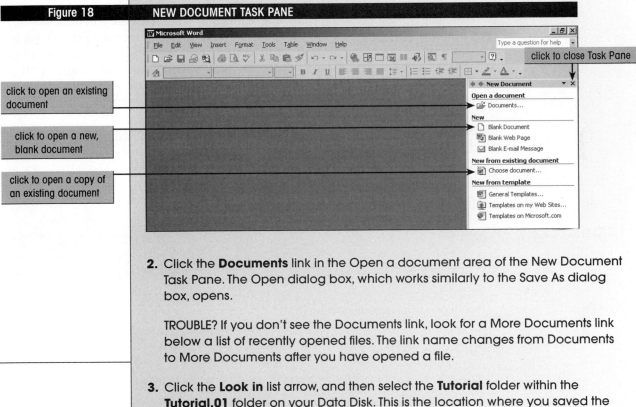

click to open an existing document

click to open a new, blank document

click to open a copy of an existing document

click to close Task Pane

2. Click the **Documents** link in the Open a document area of the New Document Task Pane. The Open dialog box, which works similarly to the Save As dialog box, opens.

   TROUBLE? If you don't see the Documents link, look for a More Documents link below a list of recently opened files. The link name changes from Documents to More Documents after you have opened a file.

3. Click the **Look in** list arrow, and then select the **Tutorial** folder within the **Tutorial.01** folder on your Data Disk. This is the location where you saved the agenda document.

4. Click **Stockholder Meeting Agenda** in the file list. See Figure 19.

| Figure 19 | OPEN DIALOG BOX |

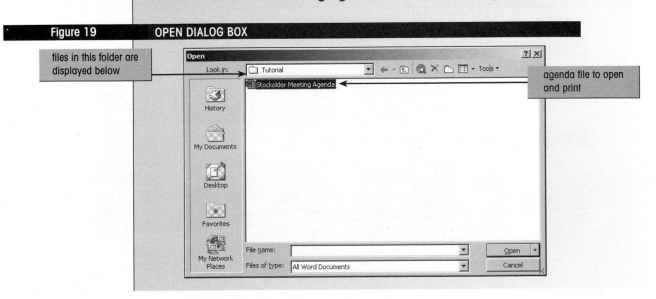

files in this folder are displayed below

agenda file to open and print

5. Click the **Open** button. The file you saved earlier reopens in the Word program window, and the New Document Task Pane closes.

After the file is open, you can view, edit, print, or resave it.

Printing a File

At times, you'll want a paper copy of your Office file. The first time you print during each computer session, you should use the Print menu command to open the Print dialog box so you can verify or adjust the printing settings. You can select a printer, the number of copies to print, the portion of the file to print, and so forth; the printing settings vary slightly from program to program. For subsequent print jobs you can use the Print button to print without opening the dialog box, if you want to use the same default settings.

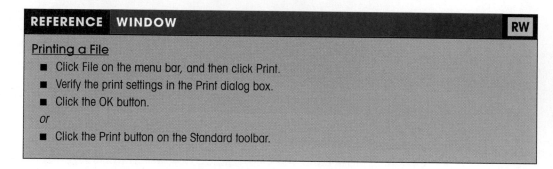

REFERENCE WINDOW | **RW**

Printing a File
- Click File on the menu bar, and then click Print.
- Verify the print settings in the Print dialog box.
- Click the OK button.

or

- Click the Print button on the Standard toolbar.

You'll print the agenda document.

To print a file:

1. Make sure your printer is turned on and contains paper.

2. Click **File** on the menu bar, and then click **Print**. The Print dialog box opens. See Figure 20.

Figure 20 | PRINT DIALOG BOX

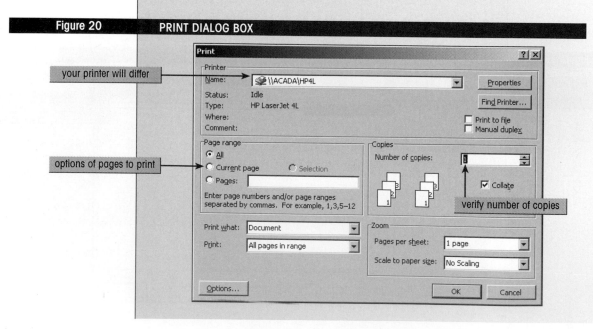

your printer will differ

options of pages to print

verify number of copies

3. Verify that the correct printer appears in the Name list box. If the wrong printer appears, click the **Name** list arrow, and then click the correct printer from the list of available printers.

4. Verify that **1** appears in the Number of copies text box.

5. Click the **OK** button to print the document. See Figure 21.

Figure 21	PRINTED STOCKHOLDER MEETING AGENDA DOCUMENT

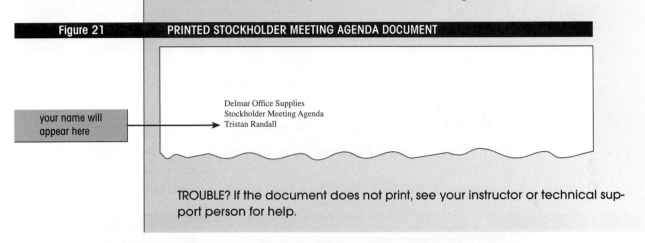

your name will appear here

Delmar Office Supplies
Stockholder Meeting Agenda
Tristan Randall

TROUBLE? If the document does not print, see your instructor or technical support person for help.

Another important aspect of Office is the ability to get help right from your computer.

Getting Help

If you don't know how to perform a task or want more information about a feature, you can turn to Office itself for information on how to use it. This information, referred to simply as **Help**, is like a huge encyclopedia stored on your computer. You can access it in a variety of ways.

There are two fast and simple methods you can use to get Help about objects you see on the screen. First, you can position the mouse pointer over a toolbar button to view its **ScreenTip**, a yellow box with the button's name. Second, you can click the **What's This?** command on the Help menu to change the pointer to ▷?, which you can click on any toolbar button, menu command, dialog box option, worksheet cell, or anything else you can see on your screen to view a brief description of that item.

For more in-depth help, you can use the **Ask a Question** box, located on the menu bar of every Office program, to find information in the Help system. You simply type a question using everyday language about a task you want to perform or a topic you need help with, and then press the Enter key to search the Help system. The Ask a Question box expands to show Help topics related to your query. You click a topic to open a Help window with step-by-step instructions that guide you through a specific procedure and explanations of difficult concepts in clear, easy-to-understand language. For example, you might ask how to format a cell in an Excel worksheet; a list of Help topics related to the words you typed will appear. The Help window also has Contents, Answer Wizard, and Index tabs, which you can use to look up information directly from the Help window.

If you prefer, you can ask questions of the **Office Assistant**, an interactive guide to finding information from the Help system. In addition, the Office Assistant can provide Help topics and tips on tasks as you work. For example, it might offer a tip when you select a menu command instead of clicking the corresponding toolbar button. You can turn on or off the tips, depending on your personal preference.

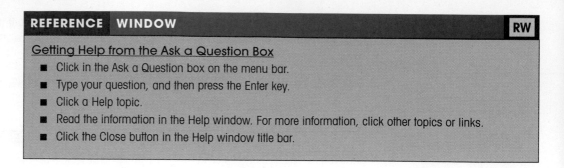

REFERENCE WINDOW   **RW**

<u>Getting Help from the Ask a Question Box</u>
- Click in the Ask a Question box on the menu bar.
- Type your question, and then press the Enter key.
- Click a Help topic.
- Read the information in the Help window. For more information, click other topics or links.
- Click the Close button in the Help window title bar.

You'll use the Ask a Question box to obtain more information about Help.

To use the Ask a Question box:

1. Click in the **Ask a Question** box on the menu bar, and then type **How do I search help?**.

2. Press the **Enter** key to retrieve a list of topics, as shown in Figure 22.

Figure 22	ASK A QUESTION BOX WITH HELP TOPICS

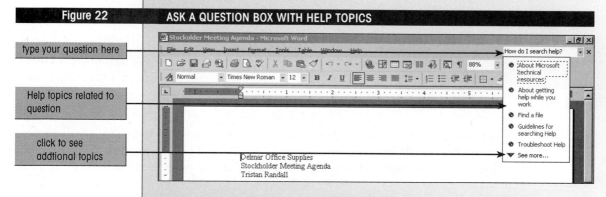

type your question here

Help topics related to question

click to see addtional topics

3. Click the **See more** link, review the additional Help topics, and then click the **See previous** link.

4. Click **About getting help while you work** to open the Help window and learn more about the various ways to obtain assistance in Office. See Figure 23.

Figure 23	HELP WINDOW

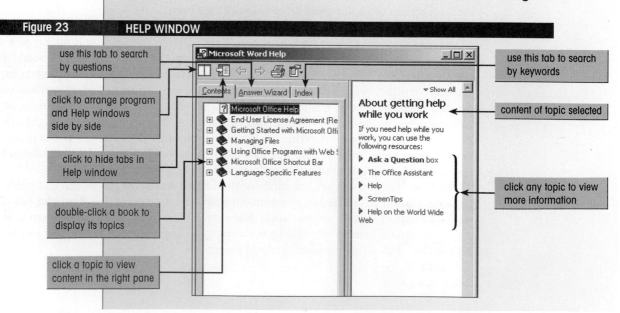

use this tab to search by questions

click to arrange program and Help windows side by side

click to hide tabs in Help window

double-click a book to display its topics

click a topic to view content in the right pane

use this tab to search by keywords

content of topic selected

click any topic to view more information

5. Click **Help** in the right pane to display information about that topic.

6. Click the other links about Help features and read the information.

7. When you're done, click the **Close** button ⊠ in the Help window title bar to return to the Word window.

The Help features enable the staff at Delmar Office Supplies to get answers to questions they have about any task or procedure when they need it. The more you practice getting information from the Help system, the more effective you will be at using Office to its full potential.

Exiting Programs

Whenever you finish working with a program, you should exit it. As with many other aspects of Office, you can exit programs with a button or from a menu. You'll use both methods to close Word and Excel.

To exit a program:

1. Click the **Close** button ⊠ in the upper-right corner of the screen to exit Word. Word exits, and the Excel window is visible again on your screen.

   TROUBLE? If a dialog box opens, asking whether you want to save the document, you may have inadvertently made a change to the document. Click the No button.

2. Click **File** on the menu bar, and then click **Exit**. The Excel program exits.

Exiting programs after you are done using them keeps your Windows desktop uncluttered for the next person using the computer, frees up your system's resources, and prevents data from being lost accidentally.

QUICK CHECK

1. Which Office program would you use to write a letter?
2. Which Office programs could you use to store customer names and addresses?
3. What is integration?
4. Explain the difference between Save As and Save.
5. What is the purpose of the New Task Pane?
6. When would you use the Ask a Question box?

REVIEW ASSIGNMENTS

Before the stockholders meeting at Delmar Office Supplies, you'll open and print documents for the upcoming presentation.

1. Start PowerPoint using the Start button and the Programs menu.

2. Use the Ask a Question box to learn how to change the toolbar buttons from small to large, and then do it. Use the same procedure to change the buttons back to regular size. Close the Help window when you're done.

3. Open a blank Excel workbook using the New Office Document command on the Start menu.

Explore ▶

4. Switch to the PowerPoint window using the taskbar, and then close the presentation but leave open the PowerPoint program. (*Hint:* Click the Close Window button in the menu bar.)

Explore ▶

5. Open a new, blank PowerPoint presentation from the New Presentation Task Pane. (*Hint:* Click Blank Presentation in the New area of the New Presentation Task Pane.)

6. Close the PowerPoint presentation and program using the Close button in the PowerPoint title bar; do not save changes if asked.

Explore ▶

7. Open a copy of the Excel **Finances** workbook located in the **Review** folder within the **Tutorial.01** folder on your Data Disk using the New Workbook Task Pane. (*Hint:* Click File on the Excel menu bar and then click New to open the Task Pane. Click Choose Workbook in the New from existing workbook area of the New Workbook Task Pane; the dialog box functions similarly to the Open dialog box.)

8. Type your name, and then press the Enter key to insert your name at the top of the worksheet.

9. Save the worksheet as **Delmar Finances** in the **Review** folder within the **Tutorial.01** folder on your Data Disk.

10. Print one copy of the worksheet using the Print command on the File menu.

11. Exit Excel using the File menu.

Explore ▶

12. Open the **Letter** document located in the **Review** folder within the **Tutorial.01** folder on your Data Disk using the Open Office Document command on the Start menu.

13. Use the Save As command to save the document with the filename **Delmar Letter** in the **Review** folder within the **Tutorial.01** folder on your Data Disk.

Explore ▶

14. Press and hold the Ctrl key, press the End key, and then release both keys to move the insertion point to the end of the letter, and then type your name.

15. Use the Save button on the Standard toolbar to save the change to the Delmar Letter document.

16. Print one copy of the document, and then close the document.

17. Exit the Word program using the Close button on the title bar.

QUICK | CHECK ANSWERS

1. Word
2. Access or Outlook
3. the ability to share information between programs
4. Save As enables you to change the filename and save location of a file. Save updates a file to reflect its latest contents using its current filename and location.
5. enables you to create new files and open existing files
6. when you don't know how to perform a task or want more information about a feature

New Perspectives on

MICROSOFT® WORD 2002

Read This Before You Begin

To the Student

Data Disks

To complete the Level I tutorials, Review Assignments, and Case Problems, you need one Data Disk. Your instructor will either provide you with the Data Disk or ask you to make your own.

If you are making your own Data Disk, you will need **one** blank, formatted high-density disk. You will need to copy a set of files and/or folders from a file server, standalone computer, or the Web onto your disk. Your instructor will tell you which computer, drive letter, and folders contain the files you need. You could also download the files by going to www.course.com and following the instructions on the screen.

The information below shows you which folders go on your disk, so that you will have enough disk space to complete all the tutorials, Review Assignments, and Case Problems:

Data Disk 1

Write this on the disk label:
Data Disk 1: Word 2002 Tutorials 1-4

Put these folders on the disk:
Tutorial.01, Tutorial.02, Tutorial.03, Tutorial.04

When you begin each tutorial, be sure you are using the correct Data Disk. Refer to the File Finder chart at the back of this text for more detailed information on which files are used in which tutorials. See the inside front or inside back cover of this book for more information on Data Disk files, or ask your instructor or technical support person for assistance.

Course Labs

The Word Level I tutorials feature an interactive Course Lab to help you understand word processing concepts.

There are Lab Assignments at the end of Tutorial 1 that relate to this Lab.

To start a Lab, click the **Start** button on the Windows taskbar, point to **Programs**, point to **Course Labs**, point to **New Perspectives Course Labs**, and then click the name of the Lab you want to use.

Using Your Own Computer

If you are going to work through this book using your own computer, you need:

- **Computer System** Microsoft Windows 98, NT, 2000 Professional, or higher must be installed on your computer. This book assumes a typical installation of Microsoft Word.

- **Data Disk** You will not be able to complete the tutorials or exercises in this book using your own computer until you have your Data Disk.

- **Course Labs** See your instructor or technical support person to obtain the Course Lab software for use on your own computer.

Visit Our World Wide Web Site

Additional materials designed especially for you are available on the World Wide Web.
Go to www.course.com/NewPerspectives.

To the Instructor

The Data Disk Files and Course Labs are available on the Instructor's Resource Kit for this title. Follow the instructions in the Help file on the CD-ROM to install the programs to your network or standalone computer. For information on creating Data Disks or the Course Labs, see the "To the Student" section above.

OBJECTIVES

In this tutorial you will:

- Plan a document

- Identify the components of the Word window

- Choose commands using toolbars and menus

- Create a new document

- Scroll a document

- Correct errors

- Save, preview, and print a document

- Enter the date with AutoComplete

- Remove Smart Tags

- Create an envelope

LAB

Word Processing

CREATING A DOCUMENT

Writing a Business Letter for Art4U Inc.

CASE

Creating a Contract Letter for Art4U Inc.

Megan Grahs is the owner and manager of Art4U Inc., a graphics design firm in Tucson, Arizona. When Megan founded Art4U in the early 1980s, the company drew most of its revenue from design projects for local magazines, newspapers, advertising circulars, and other print publications. The artists at Art4U laboriously created logos, diagrams, and other illustrations by hand, using watercolors, ink, pastels, and a variety of other media. Since the advent of the Internet, however, Art4U has become one of the Southwest's leading creators of electronic artwork. The firm's artists now work exclusively on computers, saving each piece of art as an electronic file that they can e-mail to a client in a matter of minutes.

Thanks to e-mail, Art4U is no longer limited to the local Tucson market. As a result, Art4U has nearly doubled in size over the past few years. Most of the increase in business has come from Web page designers, who continually need fresh and innovative graphics to use in their Web pages. In fact, Megan has just signed a contract with Web Time Productions agreeing to create a series of logos for a high-profile Web site. She needs to return the signed contract to Web Time's office in Chicago.

In this tutorial, you will create the cover letter that will accompany the contract. You will create the letter using Microsoft Word 2002, a popular word-processing program. Before you begin typing the letter, you will learn to start the Word program, identify and use the elements of the Word screen, and adjust some Word settings. Next you will create a new Word document, type the text of the cover letter, save the letter, and then print the letter for Megan. In the process of entering the text, you'll learn several ways to correct typing errors.

SESSION 1.1

In this session you will learn how to start Word, identify and use the parts of the Word window, and adjust some Word settings. With the skills you learn in this session, you'll be prepared to use Word to create a variety of documents, such as letters, reports, and memos.

Four Steps to a Professional Document

Word helps you produce quality work in minimal time. Not only can you type a document in Word, but you can also quickly make revisions and corrections, adjust margins and spacing, create columns and tables, and add graphics to your documents. The most efficient way to produce a document is to follow these four steps: (1) planning and creating, (2) editing, (3) formatting, and (4) printing.

In the long run, *planning* saves time and effort. First, you should determine what you want to say. State your purpose clearly and include enough information to achieve that purpose without overwhelming or boring your reader. Be sure to *organize* your ideas logically. Decide how you want your document to look as well. In this case, your letter to Web Time Productions will take the form of a standard business letter. It should be addressed to Web Time's president, Nicholas Brower. Megan has given you a handwritten note indicating what she would like you to say in the letter. This note is shown in Figure 1-1.

Figure 1-1	MEGAN'S NOTES FOR CONTRACT LETTER

Please write a cover letter for the Web Time Productions contract. In the letter please include the following questions:

- When will we receive a complete schedule for the project?
- How many preliminary designs do you require?
- Will you be available to discuss the project with our artists via a conference call next week?

Send the letter to Web Time's president, Nicholas Brower. The address is: 2210 West Sycamore Avenue, Chicago, IL 60025.

After you plan your document, you can go ahead and *create* it using Word. This generally means typing the text of your document. The next step, *editing*, consists of reading the document you've created, correcting your errors, and, finally, adding or deleting text to make the document easy to read.

Once your document is error-free, you can *format* it to make it visually appealing. Formatting features, such as adjusting margins to create white space (blank areas of a page), setting line spacing, and using boldface and italics, can help make your document easier to read. *Printing* is the final phase in creating an effective document. In this tutorial, you will preview your document before you spend time and resources to print it.

Exploring the Word Window

Before you can apply these four steps to produce a letter in Word, you need to start Word and learn about the general organization of the Word window. You'll do that now.

To start Microsoft Word:

1. Make sure Windows is running on your computer and that you can see the Windows desktop on your screen.

2. Click the **Start** button on the taskbar to display the Start menu, and then point to **Programs** to display the Programs menu.

3. Point to **Microsoft Word** on the Programs menu. Depending on how your computer is set up, you might see a small yellow box (called a ScreenTip) containing an explanation of some common uses for Microsoft Word. See Figure 1-2.

Figure 1-2	STARTING MICROSOFT WORD

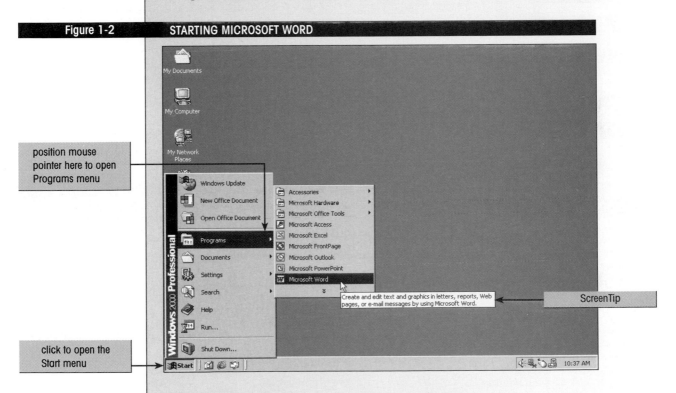

position mouse pointer here to open Programs menu

ScreenTip

click to open the Start menu

TROUBLE? Don't worry if your screen differs slightly from Figure 1-2. Although the figures in this book were created while running Windows 2000 in its default settings, Microsoft Word should run equally well using Windows 98, Windows 2000, Windows Millennium Edition, or Windows NT 4 (with Service Pack 6 installed).

TROUBLE? If you don't see the Microsoft Word option on the Programs menu, ask your instructor or technical support person for help.

TROUBLE? If the Office Shortcut Bar appears on your screen, your system is set up to display it. Because the Office Shortcut Bar is not required to complete these tutorials, it has been omitted from the figures in this text. You can close it or simply ignore it.

4. Click **Microsoft Word**. After a short pause, the Microsoft Word copyright information appears in a message box and remains on the screen until the Word program window opens. See Figure 1-3.

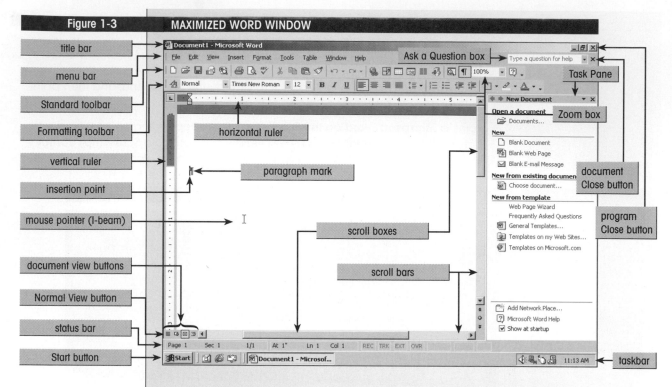

Figure 1-3   MAXIMIZED WORD WINDOW

- title bar
- menu bar
- Standard toolbar
- Formatting toolbar
- vertical ruler
- insertion point
- mouse pointer (I-beam)
- document view buttons
- Normal View button
- status bar
- Start button
- Ask a Question box
- Task Pane
- Zoom box
- document Close button
- program Close button
- horizontal ruler
- paragraph mark
- scroll boxes
- scroll bars
- taskbar

5. If the Word window does not fill the entire screen, click the **Maximize** button in the upper-right corner of the Word window. Your screen should now resemble Figure 1-3.

   TROUBLE? If your screen looks slightly different from Figure 1-3, just continue with the steps. You will learn how to change the appearance of the Word window shortly.

   TROUBLE? If you see the Language Bar (a toolbar with buttons such as correction and microphone), click its Minimize button, and then click OK.

   Word is now running and ready to use.

The Word window is made up of a number of elements which are described in Figure 1-4. You are already familiar with some of these elements, such as the menu bar, title bar, and status bar, because they are common to all Windows programs. Don't be concerned if you don't see everything shown in Figure 1-3. You'll learn how to adjust the appearance of the Word window soon.

Figure 1-4   PARTS OF THE WORD WINDOW

SCREEN ELEMENT	DESCRIPTION
Ask a Question box	Allows you to type a question for Word Help
Document Close button	Closes the current document
Document view buttons	Switches the document between four different views: Normal view, Web Layout view, Print Layout view, and Outline view
Document window	Area where you enter text and graphics
Formatting toolbar	Contains buttons to activate common font and paragraph formatting commands

Figure 1-4	PARTS OF THE WORD WINDOW (CONTINUED)
SCREEN ELEMENT	**DESCRIPTION**
Horizontal ruler	Adjusts margins, tabs, and column widths; vertical ruler appears in Print Layout view
Insertion point	Indicates location where characters will be inserted or deleted
Menu bar	Contains lists or menus of all the Word commands. When you first display a menu, you see a short list of the most frequently used commands. To see the full list of commands in the menu, you can either click the menu and then wait a few seconds for the remaining commands to appear, or click the menu and then click or point to the downward-facing double-arrow at the bottom of the menu.
Mouse pointer	Changes shape depending on its location on the screen (i.e., I-beam pointer in text area; arrow in nontext areas)
Paragraph mark	Marks the end of a paragraph
Program Close button	Closes the current document if more than one document is open; closes Word if one or no document is open
Scroll bars	Shift text vertically and horizontally on the screen so you can see different parts of the document
Scroll box	Helps you move quickly to other pages of your document
Standard toolbar	Contains buttons to activate frequently used commands
Start button	Starts a program, opens a document, provides quick access to Windows Help
Status bar	Provides information regarding the location of the insertion point
Taskbar	Shows programs that are running and allows you to switch quickly from one program to another
Task Pane	Contains buttons and options for common tasks
Title bar	Identifies the current application (i.e., Microsoft Word); shows the filename of the current document
Zoom box	Changes the document window magnification

If at any time you would like to check the name of a Word toolbar button, position the mouse pointer over the button without clicking. A **ScreenTip**, a small yellow box with the name of the button, will appear. (If you don't see ScreenTips on your computer, click Tools on the Word menu bar, click Options, click the View tab, click the ScreenTips check box to insert a check, and then click OK.)

Keep in mind that the commands on the menu bars initially display the commands that are used most frequently on your particular computer. When you leave the menu open for a few seconds or point to the double-arrow, a complete list of commands appears. Throughout these tutorials, you should point to the double-arrow on a menu if you do not see the command you need.

Setting Up the Window Before You Begin Each Tutorial

Word provides a set of standard settings, called **default settings**, that control how the screen is set up, and how a document looks when you first start typing. These settings are appropriate for most situations. However, these settings are easily changed, and most people begin a work session by adjusting Word to make sure it is set up the way they want it.

When you become more comfortable using Word, you will learn how to customize Word to suit your needs. But to make it easier to follow the steps in these tutorials, you should take care to arrange your window to match the tutorial figures. The rest of this section explains what your window should look like and how to make it match those in the tutorials. Depending on how many people use your computer (and how much they adjust Word's appearance), you might have to set up the window to match the figures each time you start Word.

Closing the Task Pane

The **Task Pane** is part of the Word window that you can use to perform common chores, such as sending e-mail. By default, the Task Pane appears on the right side of the Word window (as in Figure 1-5) when you start Word.

Figure 1-5   **TASK PANE IN THE WORD WINDOW**

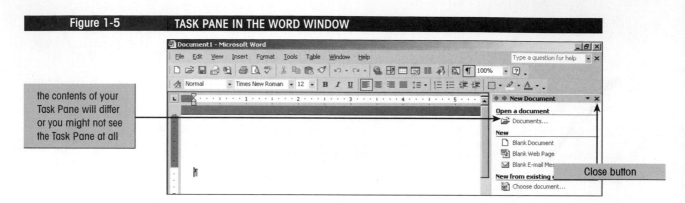

the contents of your Task Pane will differ or you might not see the Task Pane at all

Close button

Depending on how your computer is currently set up, your Task Pane might look different from the one in Figure 1-5, or you might not see the Task Pane at all. When you become a more experienced Word user, you will learn how to take advantage of the Task Pane to work more efficiently. But for now you will close it, using the Close button shown in Figure 1-5.

To close the Task Pane:

1. If the Task Pane is open on your computer, click its **Close** button ☒. The Document window expands to fill the space left by the Task Pane.

Setting the Document View to Normal

You can view your document in one of four ways—Normal, Web Layout, Print Layout, or Outline. **Web Layout view** and **Outline view** are designed for special situations that you don't need to worry about now. You will learn more about **Print Layout view**—which allows you to see a page's overall design and format—in later tutorials. In Print Layout view, Word displays both a horizontal ruler (below the toolbars) and a vertical ruler (along the left side of the Document window). For this tutorial you will use **Normal view**, which allows you to see more of the document than Print Layout view. By default, Word often displays the document in Print Layout view, just as it is in Figure 1-5. For this tutorial, you need to display the document in Normal view.

To make sure the Document window is in Normal view:

1. Click the **Normal View** button ☰ to the left of the horizontal scroll bar. See Figure 1-6. If your Document window was not in Normal view, it changes to Normal view now. The Normal View button is outlined, indicating that it is selected.

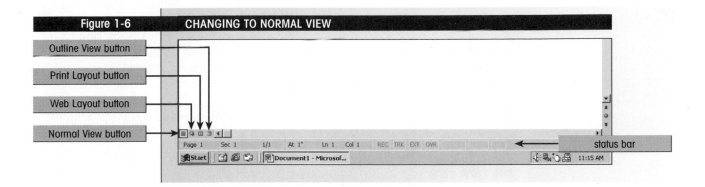

Figure 1-6   CHANGING TO NORMAL VIEW

Outline View button

Print Layout button

Web Layout button

Normal View button

status bar

Displaying the Toolbars and Ruler

The Word toolbars allow you to perform common tasks quickly by clicking a button. In the Word tutorials, you will most often use the Standard toolbar and the Formatting toolbar. While working through these tutorials, you should check to make sure that only the Formatting and Standard toolbars appear on your screen. The Standard toolbar should be positioned on top of the Formatting toolbar, just as they are in Figure 1-7.

Figure 1-7   STANDARD TOOLBAR ON TOP OF FORMATTING TOOLBAR

Standard toolbar

Formatting toolbar

Depending on the settings specified by the last person to use your computer, you may not see both toolbars or your toolbars may all appear on one row. You also may see additional toolbars, such as the Drawing toolbar. In the following steps, you will make sure that your Word window shows only the Standard and Formatting toolbars. Later you will make sure that they are stacked on top of each other.

To verify that your Word window shows the correct toolbars:

1. Position the pointer over any toolbar and click the right mouse button. A shortcut menu appears. The menu lists all available toolbars with a check mark next to those currently displayed. If the Standard and Formatting toolbars are currently displayed on your computer, you should see check marks next to their names.

   TROUBLE? If you don't see any toolbars on your screen, click Tools on the menu bar, click Customize, and then click the Toolbars tab. Click the Standard and Formatting check boxes to insert a check in each, and then click Close. To gain practice using a shortcut menu, begin again with Step 1, above.

2. Verify that you see a check mark next to the word "Standard" in the shortcut menu. If you do not see a check mark, click **Standard** now. (Clicking any item on the shortcut menu closes the menu, so you will need to re-open it in the next step.)

3. Redisplay the shortcut menu, if necessary, and look for a check mark next to the word "Formatting."

4. Redisplay the shortcut menu, if necessary. If any toolbars besides the Formatting and Standard toolbars have check marks, click each one to remove the check mark and hide the toolbar. When you are finished, only the Standard and Formatting toolbars should have check marks.

If the toolbars appear on one row, perform the next steps to arrange the toolbars on two rows.

To arrange the Standard toolbar and the Formatting toolbar on two rows:

1. Click **Tools** on the menu bar, and then click **Customize**. The Customize dialog box opens.

> **TROUBLE?** If you don't see the Customize command on the Tools menu, point to the double arrow, as explained earlier in this tutorial, to show the full list of commands.

2. Click the **Options** tab, and then click the **Show Standard and Formatting toolbars on two rows** check box to select it (that is, to insert a check).

3. Click **Close**. The Customize dialog box closes. The toolbars on your screen should now match those shown earlier in Figure 1-7.

Displaying the Horizontal Ruler

In Normal view, you can use the **Horizontal ruler** to position text on the page. As you complete these tutorials, the ruler should be visible to help you place items precisely. If the ruler is not displayed on your screen as it is in Figure 1-8, you need to perform the following steps.

| Figure 1-8 | HORIZONTAL RULER DISPLAYED IN NORMAL VIEW |

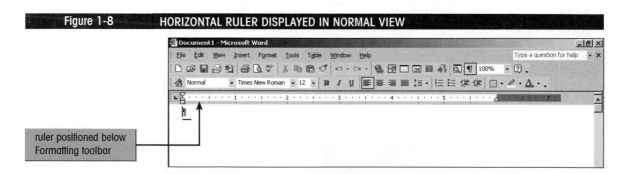

ruler positioned below
Formatting toolbar

To display the ruler:

1. Click **View** on the menu bar, and then point to the **double-arrow** at the bottom of the menu to display the hidden menu commands.

2. If "Ruler" does not have a check mark next to it, click **Ruler**. The horizontal ruler should now be displayed, as shown earlier in Figure 1-8.

Selecting a Zoom Setting

You can use the **Zoom box** on the Standard toolbar to change the magnification of the Document window. (The Zoom box is shown in Figure 1-9.) This is useful when you need a close-up view of a document—especially if you have difficulty reading small print on a computer screen. You will learn how to use the Zoom box later. For now you just need to know how to make the Zoom setting match the figures in these tutorials. By default, the Zoom setting is 100% when you first start Word (as it is in Figure 1-9). But the Zoom setting you see now depends on the setting used by the last person to work with Word on your computer. If your Zoom setting is not 100%, you need to perform the following steps.

Figure 1-9	ZOOM BOX IN STANDARD TOOLBAR

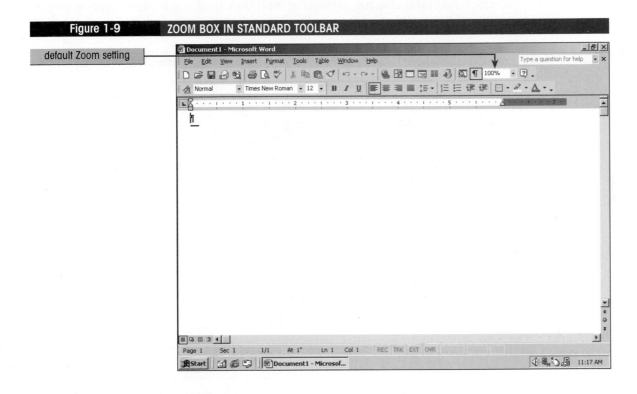

To adjust the Zoom setting:

1. Click the **list arrow** in the Zoom box. A list of settings appears.

2. Click **100%**. The list box closes, and 100% appears in the Zoom box, as shown in Figure 1-9.

Setting the Font and Font Size

A **font** is a set of characters that has a certain design, shape, and appearance. Each font has a name, such as Courier, Times New Roman, or Arial. The **font size** is the actual height of a character, measured in points, where one point equals 1/72 of an inch in height. You'll learn more about fonts and font sizes later, but for now keep in mind that most documents you create will use the Times New Roman font in a font size of 12 points. Word usually uses a default setting of Times New Roman 12 point, but someone else might have changed the setting after Word was installed on your computer. You can see your computer's current settings in the Font list box and the Font Size list box in the Formatting toolbar, as shown in Figure 1-10.

Figure 1-10	DEFAULT FONT AND FONT SIZE SETTINGS

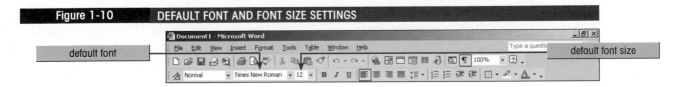

If your font setting is not Times New Roman 12 point, you should change the default setting now. You'll use the menu bar to choose the commands.

To change the default font and font size:

1. Click **Format** on the menu bar, and then click **Font**. The Font dialog box opens. If necessary, click the **Font** tab. See Figure 1-11.

Figure 1-11 FONT DIALOG BOX

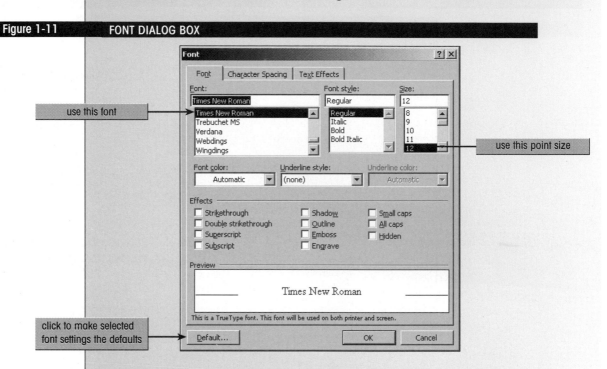

2. In the Font text box, click **Times New Roman**.

3. In the Size list box, click **12**.

4. Click the **Default** button to make Times New Roman and 12 point the default settings. Word displays a message asking you to verify that you want to make 12 point Times New Roman the default font.

5. Click **Yes**.

Displaying Nonprinting Characters

Nonprinting characters are symbols that can appear on the screen but do not show up when you print a document. You can display nonprinting characters when you are working on the appearance, or **format**, of your document. For example, one nonprinting character marks the end of a paragraph (¶), and another marks the space between words (•). It's helpful to display nonprinting characters so you can see whether you've typed an extra space, ended a paragraph, and so on.

Depending on how your computer is set up, nonprinting characters might have been displayed automatically when you started Word. In Figure 1-12, you can see the paragraph symbol (¶) in the blank Document window. Also, the Show/Hide ¶ button is outlined in the Standard toolbar. Both of these indicate that nonprinting characters are displayed. If they are not displayed on your screen, you need to perform the following steps.

Figure 1-12 | **NONPRINTING CHARACTERS DISPLAYED**

paragraph symbol

Show/Hide ¶ button

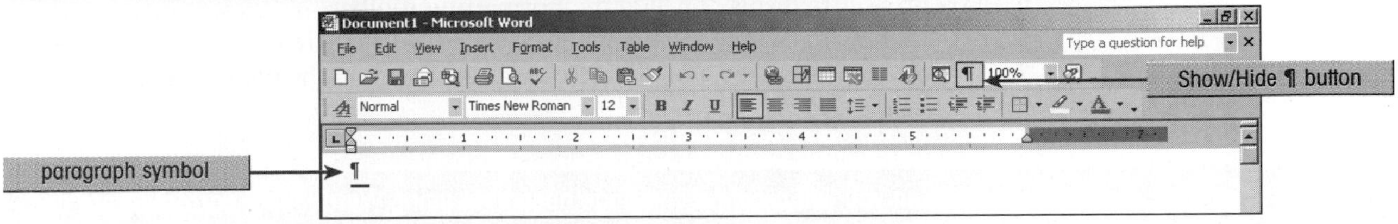

To display nonprinting characters:

1. Click the **Show/Hide ¶** button ¶ on the Standard toolbar. A paragraph mark (¶) appears at the top of the Document window. Your screen should now match Figure 1-12. To make sure your window always matches the figures in these tutorials, remember to complete the checklist in Figure 1-13 each time you sit down at the computer.

TROUBLE? If the Show/Hide ¶ button was already highlighted before you clicked it, you have now deactivated it. Click the Show/Hide ¶ button a second time to select it.

Figure 1-13 | **WORD WINDOW CHECKLIST**

SCREEN ELEMENT	SETTING	CHECK
Document view	Normal view	☐
Word window	Maximized	☐
Standard toolbar	Displayed, below the menu bar	☐
Formatting toolbar	Displayed, below the Standard toolbar	☐
Other toolbars	Hidden	☐
Nonprinting characters	Displayed	☐
Font	Times New Roman	☐
Point size	12 point	☐
Ruler	Displayed	☐
Task Pane	Closed	☐
Zoom box	100%	☐

Now that you have planned your letter, opened Word, identified screen elements, and adjusted settings, you are ready to begin typing a letter. In the next session, you will create Megan's letter to Web Time Productions.

Session 1.1 QUICK CHECK

1. In your own words, list the steps in creating a document.
2. How do you start Word from the Windows desktop?
3. Define each of the following in your own words:
   a. nonprinting characters
   b. document view buttons
   c. font size
   d. default settings

4. Explain how to change the default font size.
5. Explain how to display or hide the Formatting toolbar.
6. Explain how to change the document view to Normal view.
7. To close the Task Pane, you need to use a command on the menu bar. True or False?

SESSION 1.2

In this session you will create a one-page document using Word. You'll correct errors and scroll through your document. You'll also name, save, preview, and print the document. Finally, you will create an envelope for the letter.

Beginning a Letter

Word Processing

You're ready to begin typing Megan's letter to Nicholas Brower at Web Time Productions. Figure 1-14 shows the completed letter printed on company letterhead. You'll begin by opening a new blank page (in case you accidentally typed something in the current page). Then you'll move the insertion point to about 2.5 inches from the top margin of the paper to allow space for the Art4U letterhead.

Figure 1-14   COMPLETED LETTER

Art4U, Inc.
1921 Sedona Avenue
Tucson, AZ 85701
Art4U@WorldNet.com

February 21, 2003

Nicholas Brower, President
Web Time Productions
2210 West Sycamore Avenue
Chicago, IL 60025

Dear Nicholas:

Enclosed you will find the signed contract. As you can see, I am returning all three pages, with my signature on each.

Now that we have finalized the contract, I have a few questions: When will we receive a complete schedule for the project? Also, how many preliminary designs do you require? Finally, will you be available to discuss the project with our artists via a conference call some afternoon next week?

Thanks again for choosing Art4U. We look forward to working with you.

Sincerely yours,

Megan Grahs

To open a new document:

1. If you took a break after the previous session, make sure the Word program is running, that nonprinting characters are displayed, and that the font settings in the Formatting toolbar are set to 12 point Times New Roman. Also verify that the toolbars and the ruler are displayed. Currently, you have one document open in Word. This document is named Document1. If you have the taskbar displayed at the bottom of your screen, it should contain a button named Document1. If for some reason you need to switch between Word and another Windows program, you could click this taskbar button to redisplay the Word window. In the next steps, you'll try using this button, just for practice.

2. Click the **Minimize** button ▬ in the Word title bar. The Word window minimizes, revealing the Windows desktop. (If you couldn't see the taskbar earlier, you should see it now.)

3. Click the **Document1** button in the taskbar. The Word window maximizes again. Now you can open a new document where you can type Megan's letter.

4. Click the **New Blank Document** button ▢ on the Standard toolbar. A new document, named Document2, opens, as shown in Figure 1-15.

Figure 1-15	NEWLY OPENED DOCUMENT

name of new document

new taskbar button for Document 2

button for Document 1

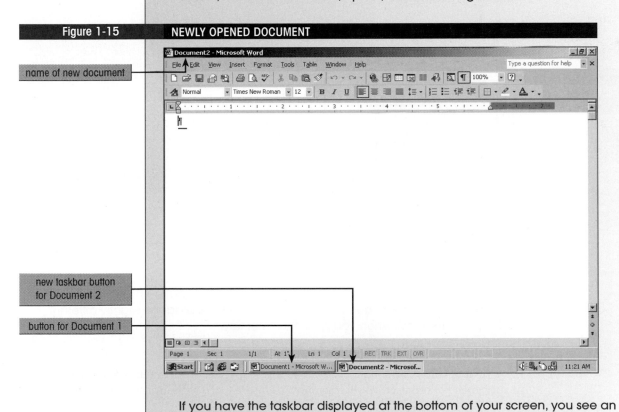

If you have the taskbar displayed at the bottom of your screen, you see an additional button for the new document. If you wanted to switch back to Document1, you could click its button on the taskbar.

Now that you have opened a new document, you need to insert some blank lines in the document so you leave enough room for the company letterhead.

To insert blank lines in the document:

1. Press the **Enter** key eight times. Each time you press the Enter key, a nonprinting paragraph mark appears. In the status bar (at the bottom of the Document window), you should see the setting "At 2.5"," indicating that the insertion point is approximately 2.5 inches from the top of the page. Another setting in the status bar should read "Ln 9," indicating the insertion point is in line 9 of the document. See Figure 1-16. (Your settings may be slightly different.)

Figure 1-16	DOCUMENT WINDOW AFTER INSERTING BLANK LINES

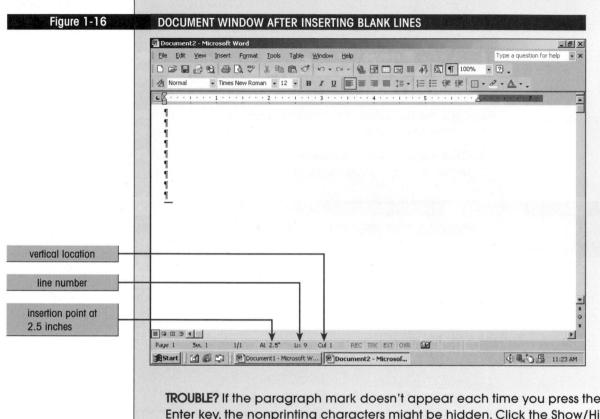

vertical location

line number

insertion point at 2.5 inches

TROUBLE? If the paragraph mark doesn't appear each time you press the Enter key, the nonprinting characters might be hidden. Click the Show/Hide ¶ button on the Standard toolbar.

TROUBLE? If you pressed the Enter key too many times, press the Backspace key to delete each extra line and paragraph mark. If you're on line 9 but the "At" number is not 2.5", don't worry. Different monitors produce slightly different measurements when you press the Enter key.

Pressing Enter is a simple, fast way to insert space in a document. When you are a more experienced Word user, you'll learn how to insert space without using the Enter key.

Entering Text

Normally, you begin typing a letter by entering the date. However, Megan tells you that she's not sure whether the contract will be ready to send today or tomorrow. So she asks you to skip the date for now and begin with the inside address. Making changes to documents is easy in Word, so you can easily add the date later.

In the following steps, you'll type the inside address (shown on Megan's note, in Figure 1-1). If you type a wrong character, press the Backspace key to delete the mistake and then retype the correct character.

To type the inside address:

1. Type **Nicholas Brower, President** and then press the **Enter** key. As you type, the nonprinting character (•) appears between words to indicate a space. Depending on how your computer is set up, you may also see a dotted underline beneath the name, Nicholas Brower, as shown in Figure 1-17. You'll learn the meaning of this underline later in this tutorial, when you type the date. For now you can just ignore it and concentrate on typing the letter.

Figure 1-17	FIRST LINE OF INSIDE ADDRESS

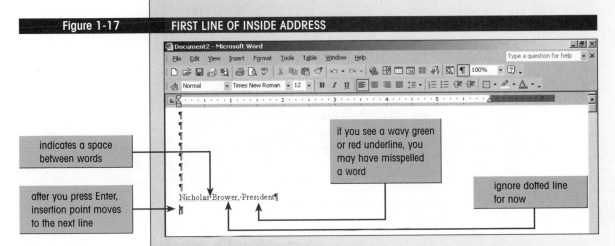

indicates a space between words

after you press Enter, insertion point moves to the next line

if you see a wavy green or red underline, you may have misspelled a word

ignore dotted line for now

Nicholas·Brower,·President¶

TROUBLE? If a wavy line (as opposed to a dotted line) appears beneath a word, check to make sure you typed the text correctly. If you did not, use the Backspace key to remove the error, and then retype the text correctly.

2. Type the following text, pressing the **Enter** key after each line to complete the inside address:
Web Time Productions
2210 West Sycamore Avenue
Chicago, IL 60025

Ignore the dotted underline below the street address. As mentioned earlier, you'll learn the meaning of this type of underline later in this tutorial.

3. Press the **Enter** key again to add a blank line after the inside address. (You should see a total of two paragraph marks below the inside address.) Now you can type the salutation.

4. Type **Dear Nicholas:** and press the **Enter** key twice to double space between the salutation and the body of the letter. When you press the Enter key the first time, the Office Assistant might appear, asking if you would like help writing your letter, as in Figure 1-18. (Depending on the settings on your computer, you might see a different Office Assistant.)

| Figure 1-18 | OFFICE ASSISTANT |

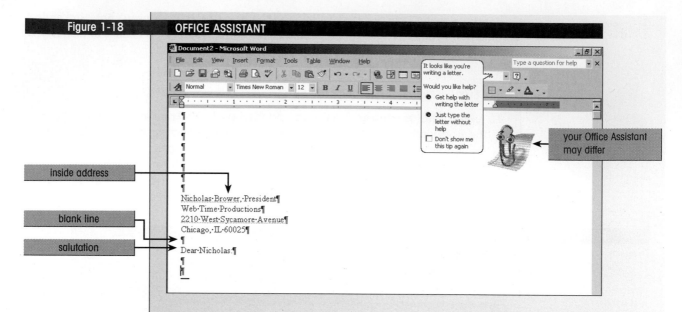

As you know, the Office Assistant is an interactive feature that sometimes appears to offer help on routine tasks. In this case, you could click "Get help with writing the letter" and have the Office Assistant lead you through a series of dialog boxes designed to set up the basic elements of a letter. For now, though, you'll close the Office Assistant and continue writing your letter.

5. Click **Just type the letter without help**. The Office Assistant closes.

   TROUBLE? If the Office Assistant remains open, right-click the Office Assistant, and then click Hide.

Before you continue with the rest of the letter, you should save what you have typed so far.

To save the document:

1. Place your Data Disk in the appropriate disk drive.

   TROUBLE? If you don't have a Data Disk, see the "Read This Before You Begin" page at the beginning of this tutorial.

2. Click the **Save** button 🔲 on the Standard toolbar. The Save As dialog box opens, similar to Figure 1-19. (Your Save As dialog box might be larger than the one shown in Figure 1-19.) Note that Word suggests using the first few words of the letter ("Nicholas Brower") as the filename. You will first replace the suggested filename with something more descriptive.

Figure 1-19	SAVE AS DIALOG BOX

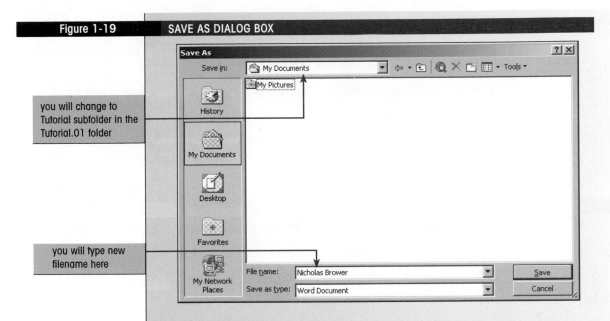

you will change to Tutorial subfolder in the Tutorial.01 folder

you will type new filename here

3. Type **Web Time Contract Letter** in the File name text box. Next, you need to tell Word where you want to save the document. In this case, you want to use the Tutorial subfolder in the Tutorial.01 folder on your Data Disk.

4. Click the **Save in** list arrow, click the drive containing your Data Disk, double-click the **Tutorial.01** folder, and then double-click the **Tutorial** folder. The word "Tutorial" is now displayed in the Save in box, indicating that the Tutorial folder is open and ready for you to save the document.

   TROUBLE? If Word automatically adds the .doc extension to your filename, your computer is configured to show filename extensions. Just continue with the tutorial.

5. Click the **Save** button in the Save As dialog box. The dialog box closes, and you return to the Document window. The new document name (Web Time Contract Letter) appears in the title bar.

Note that Word automatically appends the .doc extension to the filename to identify the file as a Microsoft Word document. However, unless your computer is set up to display file extensions, you won't see the .doc extension in any of the Word dialog boxes or in the title bar. These tutorials assume that filename extensions are hidden.

Taking **Advantage of Word Wrap**

Now that you have saved your document, you're ready to continue working on Megan's letter. As you type the body of the letter, you do not have to press the Enter key at the end of each line. Instead, when you type a word that extends into the right margin, both the insertion point and the word moves automatically to the next line. This automatic line breaking is called **word wrap**. You'll see how word wrap works as you type the body of the letter.

To observe word wrap while typing a paragraph:

1. Make sure the insertion point is at Ln 16 (according to the settings in the status bar). If it's not, move it to line 16 by pressing the arrow keys.

2. Type the following sentence: **Enclosed you will find the signed contract.**

3. Press the **spacebar**.

4. Type the following sentence: **As you can see, I am returning all three pages, with my signature on each.** Notice how Word moves the last few words to a new line when the preceding line is full. See Figure 1-20.

Figure 1-20	WORD WRAPPING TEXT

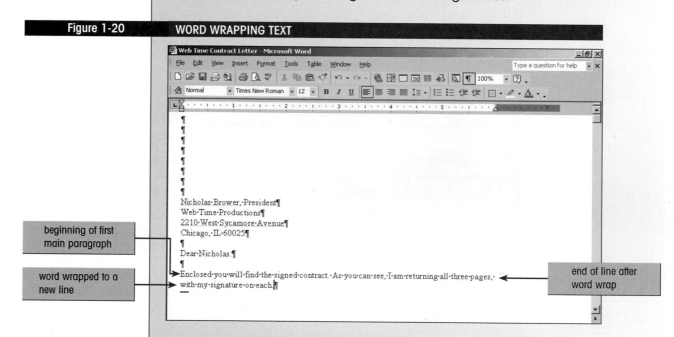

beginning of first main paragraph

word wrapped to a new line

end of line after word wrap

TROUBLE? If your screen does not match Figure 1-20 exactly, don't be concerned. The Times New Roman font can have varying letter widths and produce slightly different measurements on different monitors. As a result, the word or letter where the line wraps in your document might be different from the one shown in Figure 1-20. Continue with Step 5.

5. Press the **Enter** key to end the first paragraph, and then press the **Enter** key again to double space between the first and second paragraphs.

6. Type the following text:

   Now that we have finalized the contract, I have a few questions: When will we receive a complete schedule for the project? Also, how many preliminary designs do you require?

   When you are finished, your screen should look similar to Figure 1-21, although the line breaks on your screen might be slightly different.

Figure 1-21	BEGINNING OF SECOND MAIN PARAGRAPH

eight paragraph marks are currently visible

line breaks might be slightly different on your screen

insertion point

last line is line 20

Scrolling a Document

After you finish the last set of steps, the insertion point should be near the bottom of the Document window. It looks like there's not enough room to type the rest of Megan's letter. However, as you continue to add text at the end of your document, the text that you typed earlier will **scroll** (or shift up) and disappear from the top of the Document window. You'll see how scrolling works as you enter the rest of the second paragraph.

To observe scrolling while you're entering text:

1. Make sure the insertion point is positioned to the right of the question mark after the word "require" in the second main paragraph. In other words, the insertion point should be positioned at the end of line 20. (See Figure 1-21 above.)

   TROUBLE? If you are using a very large monitor, your insertion point may still be some distance from the bottom of the screen. In that case, you may not be able to perform the scrolling steps that follow. Read the steps to familiarize yourself with the process of scrolling. You'll have a chance to scroll longer documents later.

2. Press the **spacebar**, and then type the following text:

   Finally, will you be available to discuss the project with our artists via a conference call some afternoon next week?

   Notice that as you begin to type the text, Word moves the insertion point to a new line. Also, the first paragraph mark at the top of the letter scrolls off the top of the Document window to make room for the end of the question. When you are finished typing, your screen should look like Figure 1-22. (Don't worry if you make a mistake in your typing. You'll learn a number of ways to correct errors in the next section.)

Figure 1-22   **PARAGRAPH MARK SCROLLED OFF THE SCREEN**

first paragraph mark scrolled off the screen

now only seven paragraph marks are visible

[Screenshot of Microsoft Word window titled "Web Time Contract Letter - Microsoft Word"]

Nicholas·Brower,·President¶
Web·Time·Productions¶
2210·West·Sycamore·Avenue¶
Chicago,·IL·60025¶
¶
Dear·Nicholas:¶
¶
Enclosed·you·will·find·the·signed·contract.·As·you·can·see,·I·am·returning·all·three·pages,·with·my·signature·on·each.¶
¶
Now·that·we·have·finalized·the·contract,·I·have·a·few·questions:·When·will·we·receive·a·complete·schedule·for·the·project?·Also,·how·many·preliminary·designs·do·you·require?·Finally,·will·you·be·available·to·discuss·the·project·with·our·artists·via·a·conference·call·some·afternoon·next·week?¶

Page 1   Sec 1   1/1   At 5"   Ln 22   Col 26   REC   TRK   EXT   OVR

3. Press the **Enter** key twice. The document scrolls up to make room for the new lines at the bottom.

4. Type the following text:

   Thanks again for choosing Art4U. We look forward to working with you.

5. Press the **Enter** key twice.

6. Type **Sincerely yours,** (including the comma) to enter the complimentary closing.

7. Press the **Enter** key five times to allow space for a signature. Unless you have a very large monitor, part of the inside address scrolls off the top of the Document window.

8. Type **Megan Grahs**. If you see a wavy underline below Megan's name, ignore it for now. You'll learn the meaning of this underline in the next section. You've completed the letter, so you should save your work.

9. Click the **Save** button 🖫 on the Standard toolbar. Word saves your letter with the same name and to the same location you specified earlier. Your letter should look like Figure 1-23. Don't be concerned about any typing errors. You'll learn how to correct them in the next section.

Figure 1-23   **SIGNATURE PORTION OF LETTER**

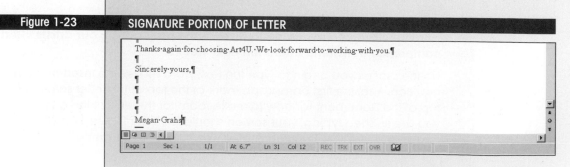

Thanks·again·for·choosing·Art4U.·We·look·forward·to·working·with·you.¶
¶
Sincerely·yours,¶
¶
¶
¶
¶
Megan·Grahs¶

Page 1   Sec 1   1/1   At 6.7"   Ln 31   Col 12   REC   TRK   EXT   OVR

In the last set of steps, you watched the text at the top of your document move off your screen. You can scroll this hidden text back into view so you can read the beginning of the letter. When you do, the text at the bottom of the screen will scroll out of view. To scroll the Document window, you can click the up or down arrows in the vertical scroll bar, click anywhere in the vertical scroll bar, or drag the scroll box. Figure 1-24 summarizes these options.

Figure 1-24   SCROLLING THE DOCUMENT WINDOW

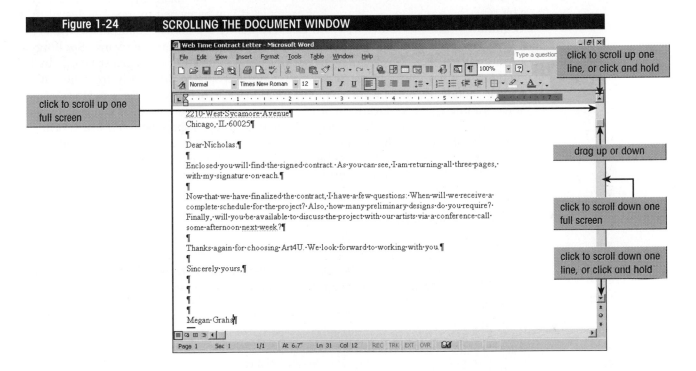

In the next set of steps, you will practice using the vertical scroll bar.

To scroll the document using the vertical scroll bar:

1. Position the mouse pointer on the up arrow at the top of the vertical scroll bar. Press and hold the mouse button to scroll the text. When the text stops scrolling, you have reached the top of the document and can see the beginning of the letter. Note that scrolling does not change the location of the insertion point in the document.

2. Click the down arrow on the vertical scroll bar. The document scrolls down one line.

3. Click anywhere in the vertical scroll bar, below the scroll box. The document scrolls down one full screen.

4. Drag the scroll box up until the first line of the inside address ("Nicholas Brower, President") is positioned at the top of the Document window.

Correcting Errors

If you discover a typing error as soon as you make it, you can press the Backspace key to erase the characters and spaces to the left of the insertion point one at a time. Backspacing erases both printing and nonprinting characters. After you erase the error, you can type the correct characters. (You can also press the Delete key to delete characters to the right of the insertion point.)

In many cases, however, Word's **AutoCorrect** feature will do the work for you. This helpful feature automatically corrects common typing errors, such as entering "adn" for "and." You might have noticed AutoCorrect at work if you forgot to capitalize the first letter in a sentence as you typed the letter. AutoCorrect automatically corrects this error as you type the rest of the sentence. For example, if you happened to type "enclosed" at the beginning of the first sentence, Word would capitalize the initial "e" automatically.

In the case of more complicated errors, you can take advantage of Word's **Spelling and Grammar** checker. This feature continually checks your document against Word's built-in dictionary and a set of grammar rules. If a word is spelled differently from how it is in Word's dictionary, or if a word isn't in the dictionary at all (for example, a person's name), a wavy *red* line appears beneath the word. A wavy red line also appears if you type duplicate words (such as "the the"). If you accidentally type an extra space between words or make a grammatical error (such as typing "He walk to the store." instead of "He walks to the store."), a wavy *green* line appears beneath the error. The easiest way to see how these features work is to make some intentional typing errors.

To correct intentional typing errors:

1. Click the **Document1** button in the taskbar.

   TROUBLE? If you closed Document1 earlier, click the New Blank Document button in the Standard toolbar to open a blank document.

2. Carefully and slowly type the following sentence exactly as it is shown, including the spelling errors and the extra space between the last two words: **microsoft Word corects teh commen typing misTakes you make.** Press the **Enter** key when you are finished typing. Notice that as you press the spacebar after the word "commen," a wavy red line appears beneath it, indicating that the word might be misspelled. Notice also that when you pressed the spacebar after the words "corects," "teh," and "misTakes," Word automatically corrected the spelling. After you pressed the Enter key, a wavy green line appeared under the last two words, alerting you to the extra space. See Figure 1-25.

| Figure 1-25 | DOCUMENT WITH INTENTIONAL TYPING ERRORS |

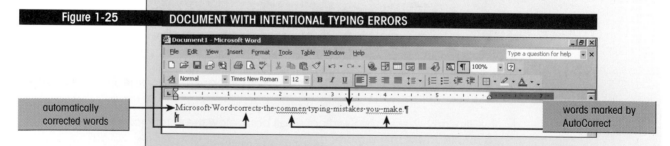

automatically corrected words

words marked by AutoCorrect

TROUBLE? If red and green wavy lines do not appear beneath mistakes, Word is probably not set to check spelling and grammar automatically as you type. Click Tools on the menu bar, and then click Options to open the Options dialog box. Click the Spelling & Grammar tab. If necessary, insert check marks in the "Check spelling as you type" and the "Check grammar as you type" check boxes, and click OK. If Word does not automatically correct the incorrect spelling of "the," click Tools on the menu bar, click AutoCorrect Options, and make sure that all seven boxes at the top of the AutoCorrect tab have check marks. Then scroll down the AutoCorrect list to make sure that there is an entry that changes "teh" to "the," and click OK.

Working with AutoCorrect

Whenever AutoCorrect makes a change, Word inserts an **AutoCorrect Options button** in the document. You can use this button to undo a change, or to prevent AutoCorrect from making the same change in the future. To see an AutoCorrect Options button, you position the mouse pointer over a word that has been changed by AutoCorrect.

To display the AutoCorrect Options buttons:

1. Position the mouse pointer over the word "corrects." A small blue rectangle appears below the first few letters of the word, as in Figure 1-26.

   TROUBLE? If you see a blue button with a lightning bolt, you pointed to the blue rectangle after it appeared. Move the pointer so that only the rectangle is visible, and continue with the next step.

| Figure 1-26 | WORD CHANGED BY AUTOCORRECT |

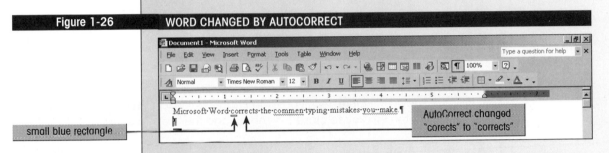

small blue rectangle

2. Point to the **blue rectangle** below "corrects". The blue rectangle is replaced by the AutoCorrect Options button.

3. Click the **AutoCorrect Options** button ![icon]. A menu with commands related to AutoCorrect appears. You could choose to change "corrects" back to "corects". You could also tell AutoCorrect to stop automatically correcting "corects".

4. Click anywhere in the document. The AutoCorrect menu closes.

Correcting Spelling and Grammar Errors

After you verify that AutoCorrect made changes you want, you should scan your document for wavy underlines. Again, the red underlines indicate potential spelling errors, while the green underlines indicate potential grammar or punctuation problems. In the following steps, you will learn a quick way to correct such errors.

To correct spelling and grammar errors:

1. Position the I-Beam pointer ⌶ over the word "commen" and click the right mouse button. A shortcut menu appears with suggested spellings. See Figure 1-27.

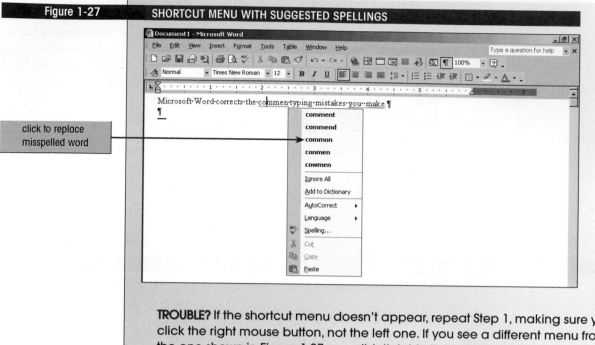

Figure 1-27   SHORTCUT MENU WITH SUGGESTED SPELLINGS

click to replace
misspelled word

TROUBLE? If the shortcut menu doesn't appear, repeat Step 1, making sure you click the right mouse button, not the left one. If you see a different menu from the one shown in Figure 1-27, you didn't right-click exactly on the underlined word. Press the Esc key to close the menu, and then repeat Step 1.

2. Click **common** in the shortcut menu. The menu disappears, and the correct spelling appears in your document. Notice that the wavy red line disappears after you correct the error.

3. Click to the right of the letter "u" in the word "you". Press the **Delete** key to delete the extra space.

You can see how quick and easy it is to correct common typing errors with AutoCorrect and the Spelling and Grammar checker. Remember, however, to thoroughly proofread each document you create. AutoCorrect will not catch words that are spelled correctly, but used improperly (such as "your" for "you're").

Proofreading the Letter

Before you can proofread your letter, you need to close the document with the practice sentence. You don't need to save this document, because you only created it to practice correcting errors.

To close the practice document:

1. Click the **Document Close** button [X] (on the right end of the menu bar). You see a dialog box asking if you want to save your changes to the document.

2. Click **No**. You return to the document named Web Time Contract Letter.

Now you can proofread the letter for any typos. You can also get rid of the wavy red underline below Megan's last name.

To respond to possible spelling errors:

1. Scroll down until the signature line is visible. Because Word doesn't recognize "Grahs" as a word, it marked it as a potential error. You need to tell Word to ignore this name wherever it occurs in the letter.

2. Right-click **Grahs**. A shortcut menu opens.

3. Click **Ignore All**. The wavy red underline disappears from below "Grahs".

4. Scroll up to the beginning of the letter, and proofread it for typos. If a word has a wavy red or green underline, right-click it and choose an option in the short-cut menu. To correct other errors, click to the right or left of the error, use the Backspace or Delete key to remove it, and then type a correction.

Inserting a Date with AutoComplete

The beauty of using a word processing program such as Microsoft Word is that you can eas-ily make changes to text you have already typed. In this case, you need to insert the current date at the beginning of the letter. Megan tells you that she wants to send the contract to Web Time Productions on February 21, so you need to insert that date into the letter now.

Before you can enter the date, you need to move the insertion point to the right loca-tion. In a standard business letter, the date belongs approximately 2.5 inches from the top. (As you recall, this is where you started the inside address earlier.) You also need to insert some blank lines to allow enough space between the date and the inside address.

To move the insertion point and add some blank lines:

1. Scroll up to display the top of the document.

2. Click to the left of the "N" in "Nicholas Brower," in the inside address. The status bar indicates that the insertion point is on line 9, 2.5 inches from the top. (Your status bar might show slightly different measurements.) You might see a square with a lowercase "i" displayed just above the name. Ignore this for now. You'll learn about this special button (called a Smart Tag Actions button) later in this tutorial.

3. Press **Enter** four times, and then press the ↑ key four times. Now the insertion point is positioned at line 9, with three blank lines between the inside address and the line where you will insert the date. See Figure 1-28.

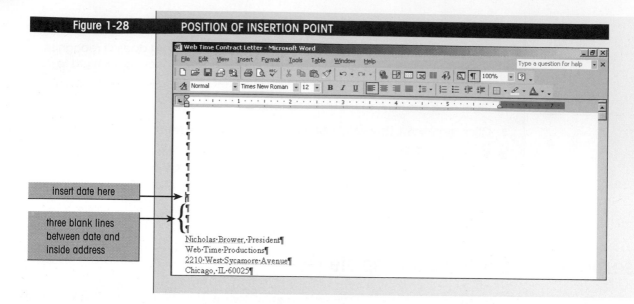

Figure 1-28   **POSITION OF INSERTION POINT**

insert date here

three blank lines between date and inside address

You're ready to insert the date. To do this you can take advantage of Word's **AutoComplete** feature, which automatically inserts dates and other regularly used items for you. In this case, you can type the first few characters of the month, and let Word insert the rest. (This only works for long month names like February.)

To insert the date:

1. Type **Febr** (the first four letters of February). A small yellow box, called an AutoComplete suggestion, appears above the line, as shown in Figure 1-29. If you wanted to type something other than February, you could continue typing to complete the word. In this case, though, you want to accept the AutoComplete tip, so you will press the Enter key in the next step.

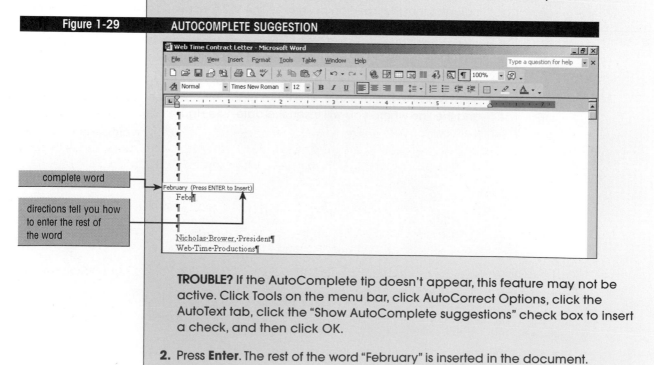

Figure 1-29   **AUTOCOMPLETE SUGGESTION**

complete word

directions tell you how to enter the rest of the word

TROUBLE? If the AutoComplete tip doesn't appear, this feature may not be active. Click Tools on the menu bar, click AutoCorrect Options, click the AutoText tab, click the "Show AutoComplete suggestions" check box to insert a check, and then click OK.

2. Press **Enter**. The rest of the word "February" is inserted in the document.

3. Press the **spacebar** and then type **21, 2003**.

   TROUBLE? If February happens to be the current month, you will see an AutoComplete suggestion displaying the current date after you press the spacebar. To accept that AutoComplete tip, press Enter. Otherwise type the rest of the date as instructed in Step 3.

4. Click one of the blank lines below the date. Depending on how your computer is set up, you may see a dotted underline below the date. (You will learn the meaning of this underline in the next section.) You have finished entering the date. See Figure 1-30.

Figure 1-30	DATE ENTERED IN THE DOCUMENT

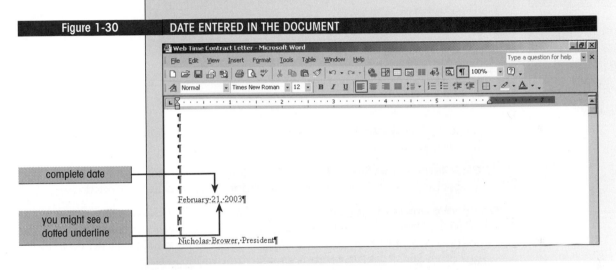

complete date

you might see a dotted underline

Removing Smart Tags

A dotted underline below a date, name, or address indicates that Word has inserted a Smart Tag in the document. A **Smart Tag** is a feature that that allows you to perform actions (such as sending e-mail or scheduling a meeting) that would normally require a completely different program. Word attaches Smart Tag Action buttons to certain kinds of text, including dates and names. You can click this button to open a menu (similar to a shortcut menu) where you can select commands related to that item. (For example, you might click a Smart Tag on a name to add that name to your e-mail address book.) You don't really need Smart Tags in this document, though, so you will delete them. (Your computer may not be set up to show Smart Tags at all, or it might show them on dates and addresses, but not names. If you do not see any Smart Tags in your document, simply read the following steps.)

> ### To remove the Smart Tags from the document:
>
> 1. If you see a dotted underline below the date, position the mouse pointer over the date. A Smart Tag icon ⓘ appears over the date.
>
> 2. Move the mouse pointer over the Smart Tag icon. The Smart Tag Actions button ⓘ▾ appears, as shown in Figure 1-31.

Figure 1-31 | **DISPLAYING THE SMART TAG ACTIONS BUTTON**

Smart Tag Actions button

these items may have also been marked with Smart Tags on your computer

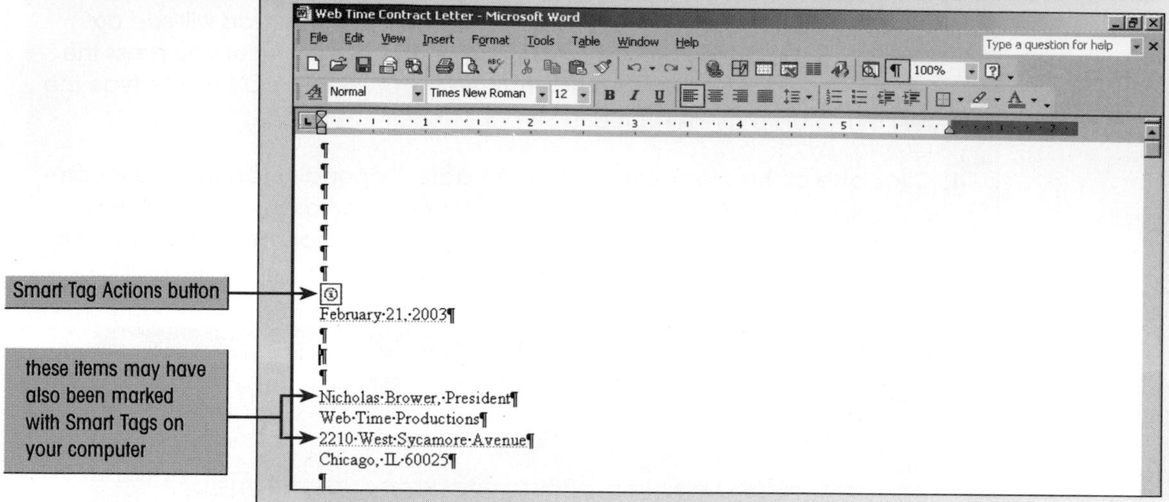

3. Click the **Smart Tag Actions** button. A menu of commands related to dates appears.

4. Click **Remove this Smart Tag**. The Smart Tag menu closes. The date is no longer underlined, indicating that the Smart Tag has been removed.

5. Remove any Smart Tags from the name and street address in the inside address. If necessary, remove the Smart Tag from the words "next week," in the second paragraph in the body of the letter, and from Megan's name in the signature line. If you notice any others, remove those also.

6. Click the **Save** button 🖫 on the Standard toolbar. Word saves your letter with the same name and to the same location you specified earlier.

Previewing and Printing a Document

Do you think the letter is ready to print? You could find out by clicking the Print button on the Standard toolbar and then reviewing the printed page. In doing so, however, you risk wasting paper and printer time. For example, if you failed to insert enough space for the company letterhead, you would have to add more space, and then print the letter all over again. To avoid wasting paper and time, you should first display the document in the Print Preview window. By default, the Print Preview window shows you the full page; there's no need to scroll through the document.

To preview the document:

1. Click the **Print Preview** button 🔍 on the Standard toolbar. The Print Preview window opens and displays a full-page version of your letter, as shown in Figure 1-32. This shows how the letter will fit on the printed page. The Print Preview toolbar includes a number of buttons that are useful for making changes that affect the way the printed page will look.

| Figure 1-32 | FULL PAGE DISPLAYED IN PRINT PREVIEW WINDOW |

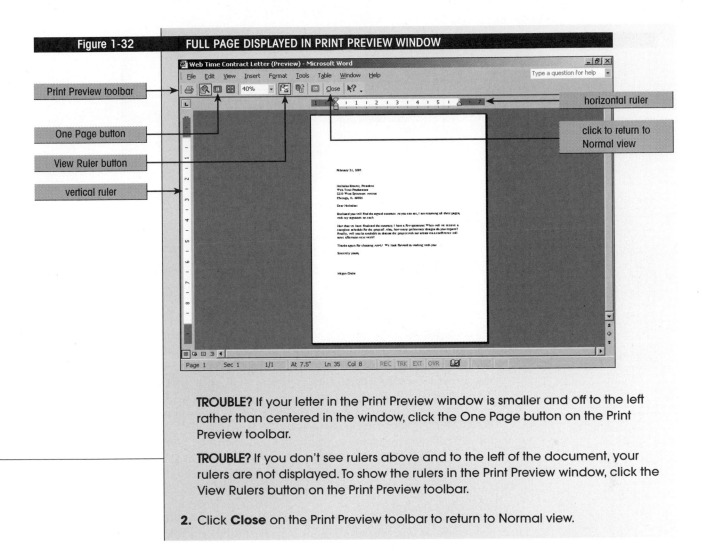

Print Preview toolbar

One Page button

View Ruler button

vertical ruler

horizontal ruler

click to return to Normal view

TROUBLE? If your letter in the Print Preview window is smaller and off to the left rather than centered in the window, click the One Page button on the Print Preview toolbar.

TROUBLE? If you don't see rulers above and to the left of the document, your rulers are not displayed. To show the rulers in the Print Preview window, click the View Rulers button on the Print Preview toolbar.

2. Click **Close** on the Print Preview toolbar to return to Normal view.

Note that it is especially important to preview documents if your computer is connected to a network so that you don't keep a shared printer tied up with unnecessary printing. In this case, the text looks well spaced and the letterhead will fit at the top of the page. You're ready to print the letter.

When printing a document, you have two choices. You can use the Print command on the File menu, which opens the Print dialog box in which you can adjust some printer settings. Or, if you prefer, you can use the Print button on the Standard toolbar, which prints the document using default settings, without opening a dialog box. In these tutorials, the first time you print from a shared computer, you should check the settings in the Print dialog box and make sure the number of copies is set to one. After that, you can use the Print button.

To print a document:

1. Make sure your printer is turned on and contains paper.

2. Click **File** on the menu bar, and then click **Print**. The Print dialog box opens. See Figure 1-33.

Figure 1-33 PRINT DIALOG BOX

name of printer (yours might differ)

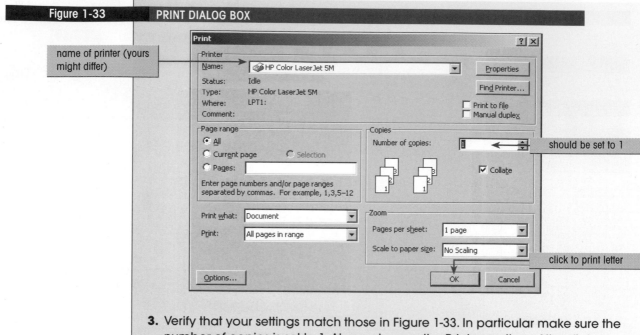

should be set to 1

click to print letter

3. Verify that your settings match those in Figure 1-33. In particular make sure the number of copies is set to 1. Also make sure the Printer section of the dialog box shows the correct printer. If you're not sure what the correct printer is, check with your instructor or technical support person.

TROUBLE? If the Print dialog box shows the wrong printer, click the Name list arrow, and then select the correct printer from the list of available printers.

4. Click **OK**. Assuming your computer is attached to a printer, the letter prints.

Your printed letter should look similar to Figure 1-14, but without the Art4U letterhead. The word wraps, or line breaks, might not appear in the same places on your letter because the size and spacing of characters vary slightly from one printer to the next.

Creating an Envelope

After you print the letter, Megan stops by your desk and asks you to print an envelope in which to mail the contracts. Creating an envelope is a simple process because Word automatically uses the inside address from the letter as the address on the envelope.

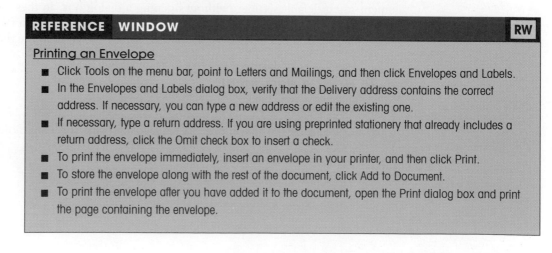

REFERENCE WINDOW RW

Printing an Envelope
- Click Tools on the menu bar, point to Letters and Mailings, and then click Envelopes and Labels.
- In the Envelopes and Labels dialog box, verify that the Delivery address contains the correct address. If necessary, you can type a new address or edit the existing one.
- If necessary, type a return address. If you are using preprinted stationery that already includes a return address, click the Omit check box to insert a check.
- To print the envelope immediately, insert an envelope in your printer, and then click Print.
- To store the envelope along with the rest of the document, click Add to Document.
- To print the envelope after you have added it to the document, open the Print dialog box and print the page containing the envelope.

Megan tells you that your printer is not currently stocked with envelopes. She asks you to create the envelope and add it to the document. Then she will print the envelope later, when she is ready to mail the contracts to Web Time Productions.

To create an envelope:

1. Click **Tools** on the menu bar, point to **Letters and Mailings,** and then click **Envelopes and Labels**. The Envelopes and Labels dialog box opens, as shown in Figure 1-34. By default, Word uses the inside address from the letter as the delivery address. Depending on how your computer is set up, you might see an address in the Return address box. Since you will be using Art4U's printed envelopes, you don't need to include a return address on this envelope.

Figure 1-34	ENVELOPES AND LABELS DIALOG BOX

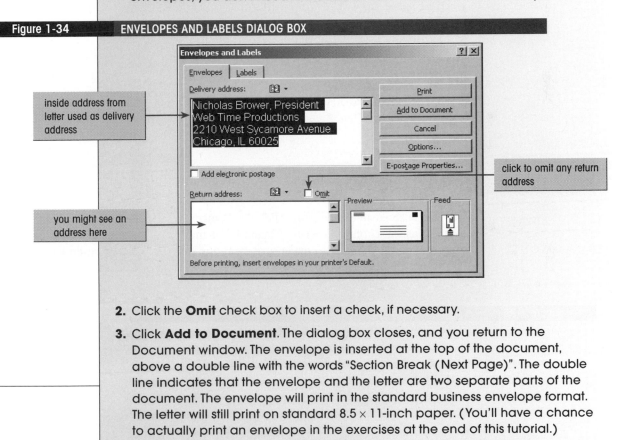

inside address from letter used as delivery address

you might see an address here

click to omit any return address

2. Click the **Omit** check box to insert a check, if necessary.

3. Click **Add to Document**. The dialog box closes, and you return to the Document window. The envelope is inserted at the top of the document, above a double line with the words "Section Break (Next Page)". The double line indicates that the envelope and the letter are two separate parts of the document. The envelope will print in the standard business envelope format. The letter will still print on standard 8.5 × 11-inch paper. (You'll have a chance to actually print an envelope in the exercises at the end of this tutorial.)

4. Click the **Save** button 🖫 on the Standard toolbar.

Congratulations on creating your first letter in Microsoft Word. Since you are finished with the letter and the envelope, you can close the document and exit Word.

To close the document and exit Word:

1. Click the **Close** button ⊠ in the menu bar. The Web Time Contract Letter closes.

   TROUBLE? If you see a dialog box with the message "Do you want to save the changes to 'Web Time Contract Letter?', you didn't save your most recent changes. Click Yes.

2. If necessary, close other open documents without saving them.

3. Click the **Close** button ❌ in the upper-right corner of the Word window. Word closes, and you return to the Windows desktop.

Session 1.2 QUICK CHECK

1. Explain how to save a document for the first time.
2. Explain how to enter the name of a month using AutoCorrect.
3. Explain how word wrap works in a Word document.
4. List the steps required to print an envelope.
5. In your own words, define each of the following:
   a. Scrolling
   b. AutoComplete
   c. AutoCorrect
   d. Print Preview
   e. Smart Tag

REVIEW ASSIGNMENTS

Megan received an e-mail from Nicholas Brower at Web Time Productions, confirming their plans for a conference call. Megan has e-mailed the graphic artists at Art4U, informing them about the call. To make sure everyone remembers, she would like you to post a memo on the bulletin board in the break room. Create the memo shown in Figure 1-35 by completing the following steps.

Figure 1-35

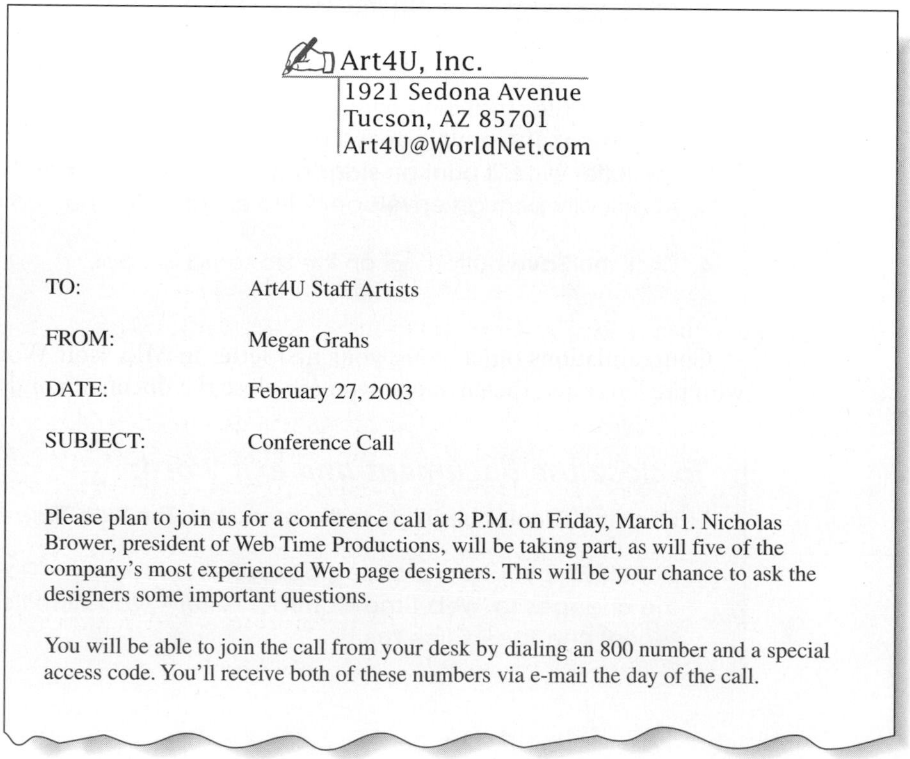

Art4U, Inc.
1921 Sedona Avenue
Tucson, AZ 85701
Art4U@WorldNet.com

TO: Art4U Staff Artists

FROM: Megan Grahs

DATE: February 27, 2003

SUBJECT: Conference Call

Please plan to join us for a conference call at 3 P.M. on Friday, March 1. Nicholas Brower, president of Web Time Productions, will be taking part, as will five of the company's most experienced Web page designers. This will be your chance to ask the designers some important questions.

You will be able to join the call from your desk by dialing an 800 number and a special access code. You'll receive both of these numbers via e-mail the day of the call.

1. If necessary, start Word and make sure your Data Disk is in the appropriate disk drive, and then check your screen to make sure your settings match those in the tutorials. In particular, make sure that nonprinting characters are displayed.

2. If the Office Assistant is open, hide it.

3. Click the New Blank Document button on the Standard toolbar to open a new document.

4. Press the Enter key eight times to insert enough space for the company letterhead.

5. Press the Caps Lock key, and then type "TO:" in capital letters.

Explore 6. You can use the Tab key to align text as a column. In this case, you want to align the To, From, Date, and Subject information. To begin, press the Tab key three times. Word inserts three nonprinting characters (right-pointing arrows), one for each time you pressed the Tab key.

7. Press the Caps Lock key to turn off capitalization, and then type "Art4U Staff Artists".

8. Press the Enter key twice, type "FROM:", press the Tab key twice, and then type your name in lowercase. Throughout the rest of this exercise, use the Caps Lock key as necessary to turn capitalization on and off.

9. Press the Enter key twice, type "DATE:", and then press the Tab key two times.

Explore 10. You can take advantage of AutoCorrect to type the current date. To try it now, type the name of the current month. If an AutoCorrect suggestion appears, press Enter to complete the name of the month; otherwise, continue typing. Press the spacebar. After you press the spacebar, an AutoCorrect suggestion appears with the current date. Press Enter to accept the suggestion.

11. Press the Enter key twice, type "SUBJECT:" and then press the Tab key two times. Type "Conference Call" and then press the Enter key twice.

12. Continue typing the rest of the memo as shown in Figure 1-35. (You will have a chance to correct any typing errors later.) Ignore any AutoCorrect suggestions that are not relevant to the text you are typing.

13. Save your work as **Conference Call Memo** in the Review folder for Tutorial 1.

14. Scroll to the beginning of the document and proofread your work.

15. Correct any misspelled words marked by wavy red lines. If the correct spelling of a word does not appear in the list box, press the Escape key to close the list, and then make the correction yourself. Remove any red wavy lines below words that are actually spelled correctly. Then correct any grammatical or other errors indicated by wavy green lines. Use the Backspace or Delete key to delete any extra words or spaces.

16. Remove any Smart Tags.

17. Save your most recent changes.

18. Preview and print the memo.

19. Close the document. Save any changes if necessary.

Explore 20. If you will be sending mail to someone regularly, it's helpful to add an envelope to a blank document, and then save the document, so that you can print the envelope in the future, whenever you need it. Open a new, blank document. Create an envelope for Nicholas Brower at Web Time Productions. Use the address you used as the inside address in the tutorial. For the return address, type your own address. Add the envelope to the document. If you are asked if you want to save the return address as the new default return address, click No. If your computer is connected to a printer that is stocked with envelopes, click File on the menu bar, click Print, click the Pages option button, type 1 in the Pages text box, and then click OK.

21. Save the document as **Web Time Envelope** in the Review folder for Tutorial 1.

22. Close any open documents and then exit Word.

CASE PROBLEMS

Case 1. Letter to Request Information about a Field Trip to Roaring Rapids Water Park
You are a teacher at Luis Sotelo Elementary School. Your students have been raising money all year for a trip to Roaring Rapids Water Park. Before you can plan the outing, you need to write for some information. Create the letter by doing the following:

1. If necessary, start Word, make sure your Data Disk is in the appropriate disk drive, and check your screen to make sure your settings match those in the tutorials.

2. Open a new blank document.

3. Type your name, press Enter, and then type the following address:

   Luis Sotelo Elementary School

   1521 First Avenue

   Durham, North Carolina 27701

Explore

4. Press the Enter key four times, and then type the name of the current month. (If an AutoCorrect suggestion appears, press Enter to complete the name of the month.) Press the spacebar. After you press the spacebar, an AutoCorrect suggestion appears with the current date. Press Enter to accept the suggestion.

5. Press the Enter key four times after the date, and, using the proper business letter format, type the inside address: "Scott Rowland, Roaring Rapids Water Park, 2344 West Prairie Street, Durham, North Carolina 27704".

6. Double space after the inside address (that is, press the Enter Key twice), type the salutation "Dear Mr. Rowland:" and then insert another blank line. Close the Office Assistant if it opens.

7. Type the first paragraph as follows: "I'd like some information about a class field trip to Roaring Rapids Water Park. Please answer the following questions:"

8. Save your work as **Water Park Information Letter** in the Cases folder for Tutorial 1.

9. Insert one blank line, and then type these questions on separate lines with one blank line between each:
   How much is a day pass for a 10-year-old child?
   How much is a day pass for an adult?
   Can you offer a discount for a group of 25 children and 5 adults?
   Are lockers available for storing clothes and other belongings?

10. Correct any typing errors indicated by wavy lines. (*Hint:* Because "Sotelo" is spelled correctly, click Ignore All on the shortcut menu to remove the wavy red line under the word "Sotelo" and prevent Word from marking the word as a misspelling.)

11. Insert another blank line at the end of the letter, and type the complimentary closing "Sincerely," (include the comma).

12. Press the Enter key four times to leave room for the signature, and type your full name. Then press the Enter key and type "Luis Sotelo Elementary School". Notice that "Sotelo" is not marked as a spelling error this time.

13. Scroll up to the beginning of the document, and then remove any Smart Tags in the letter.

14. Save your changes to the letter, and then preview it using the Print Preview button.

15. Print the letter, close the document, and exit Word.

Case 2. Letter to Confirm Food Service During the National Purchasing Management Association Conference As catering director for the Madison Convention and Visitors Bureau, you are responsible for managing food service at the city's convention center. The National Physical Therapy Association has scheduled a daily breakfast buffet during its annual convention (which runs July 6–10, 2003). You need to write a letter confirming plans for the daily buffet.

Create the letter using the skills you learned in the tutorial. Remember to include today's date, the inside address, the salutation, the date of the reservation, the complimentary closing, and your name and title. If the instructions show quotation marks around text you type, do not include the quotation marks in your letter. To complete the letter, do the following:

1. If necessary, start Word, make sure your Data Disk is in the appropriate disk drive, and check your screen to make sure your settings match those in the tutorials.

2. Open a new, blank document and press the Enter key until the insertion point is positioned about 2 inches from the top of the page. (Remember that you can see the exact position of the insertion point, in inches, in the status bar.)

3. Enter "June 6, 2003" as the date.

4. Press the Enter key four times after the date, and, using the proper business letter format, type the inside address: "Charles Quade, National Physical Therapy Association, 222 Sydney Street, Whitewater, WI 57332".

5. Double space after the inside address (that is, press the Enter key twice), type the salutation "Dear Mr. Quade:", and then double space again. If the Office Assistant opens, close it.

6. Write one paragraph confirming the daily breakfast buffets for July 6–10, 2003.

7. Insert a blank line and type the complimentary closing "Sincerely,".

8. Press the Enter key four times to leave room for the signature, and then type your name and title.

9. Save the letter as **Confirmation Letter** in the Cases folder for Tutorial 1.

10. Remove any Smart Tags. Reread your letter carefully, and correct any errors.

11. Save any new changes, and then preview and print the letter.

Explore 12. Create an envelope for the letter, and add it to the document. For the return address, type your own address. Add the envelope to the document. If you are asked if you want to save the return address as the new default return address, click No. If your computer is connected to a printer that is stocked with envelopes, click File on the menu bar, click Print, click the Pages option button, type 1 in the Pages text box, and then click OK.

13. Save your work and close the document, then exit Word.

Case 3. *Letter Congratulating a Professor* Liza Morgan, a professor of e-commerce at Kentucky State University, was recently honored by the Southern Business Council for her series of free public seminars on developing Web sites for nonprofit agencies. She also was recently named Teacher of the Year by a national organization called Woman in Technology. As one of her former students, you need to write a letter congratulating her on these honors. To write this letter, do the following:

1. If necessary, start Word, make sure your Data Disk is in the appropriate disk drive, and check your screen to make sure your settings match those in the tutorials.

2. Write a brief letter congratulating Professor Morgan on her awards. Remember to use the four-part planning process. You should plan the content, organization, and style of the letter, and use a standard letter format. For the inside address, use the following: Professor Liza Morgan, Department of Business Administration, Kentucky State University, 1010 College Drive, Frankfort, Kentucky 40601.

3. Save the document as **Liza Morgan Letter** in the Cases folder for Tutorial 1.

4. Correct any typing errors, remove any Smart Tags, and then preview and print the memo.

Explore 5. Create an envelope for the letter, and add it to the document. For the return address, type your own address. Add the envelope to the document. If you are asked if you want to save the return address as the new default return address, click No. If your computer is connected to a printer that is stocked with envelopes, click File on the menu bar, click Print, click the Pages option button, type 1 in the Pages text box, and then click OK.

6. Save the document and close it, and then exit Word.

Case 4. Memo Created With a Template You are the office manager for Head for the Hills, a small company that sells hiking equipment over the Internet. The company has just moved to a new building which requires a special security key card after hours. Some employees have had trouble getting the key cards to work properly. You decide to hold a meeting to explain the security policies for the new building and to demonstrate the key cards. But first you need to post a memo announcing the meeting. The recently ordered letterhead (with the company's new address) has not yet arrived, so you will use a Word template to create the memo. Word provides templates—that is, models with predefined formatting—to help you create complete documents (including a professional-looking letterhead) quickly. To create the memo, do the following:

1. If necessary, start Word, make sure your Data Disk is in the appropriate disk drive, and check your screen to make sure your settings match those in the tutorials.

Explore ▷ 2. If the Task Pane is not displayed, click View on the menu bar, and then click Task Pane. The Task Pane is displayed on the right side of the Word window. You see a number of options related to creating new documents.

Explore ▷ 3. Under "New from template," click General Templates. The Templates dialog box opens.

Explore ▷ 4. Click the Memos tab, click Professional Memo, and then click the OK button. A memo template opens containing generic, placeholder text that you can replace with your own information.

5. Make sure the template is displayed in Normal View. Click at the end of the line "Company Name Here" (at the top of the document), press Backspace to delete the text, and type "Head for the Hills".

6. Click the text "Click here and type name," and in the To: line, type "All Employees". After "From," replace the current text with your name.

7. Click after "CC:" and then press Delete to delete the placeholder text. Use the Backspace key to delete the entire "CC" line. Note that Word inserts the current date automatically after the heading "Date."

8. After "Re:" type "Meeting to discuss building security".

9. Delete the placeholder text in the body of the letter, and replace it with a paragraph announcing the meeting, which is scheduled for tomorrow at 2 P.M. in the Central Conference Room.

10. Save the letter as **Meeting Memo** (in the Cases folder for Tutorial 1).

Explore ▷ 11. The memo text is in a small font, which is hard to read. To make it easier to review your work, you can change the Zoom setting in Normal view. Click the Zoom list arrow in the Standard toolbar, and then click 150%.

12. Review the memo. Correct any typos and delete any Smart Tags. Save the memo again, preview it, and then print it.

13. Close the document and exit Word.

LAB ASSIGNMENTS

The New Perspectives Labs are designed to help you master some of the key computer concepts and skills presented in each chapter of the text. If you are using your school's lab computers, your instructor or technical support person should have installed the Labs software for you. If you want to use the Labs on your home computer, ask your instructor for the appropriate software. See the Read This Before You Begin page for more information on installing and starting the Lab.

Each Lab has two parts: Steps and Explore. Use Steps first to learn and review concepts. Read the information on each page and do the numbered steps. As you work through the Lab, you will be asked to answer Quick Check questions about what you have learned. At the end of the Lab, you will see a Summary Report of your answers to the Quick Checks. If your instructor wants you to turn in this Summary Report, click the Print button on the Summary Report screen.

When you have completed the Steps, you can click the Explore button to complete the Lab Assignments. You also can use Explore to practice the skills you learned and to explore concepts on your own.

Word Processing Word-processing software is the most popular computerized productivity tool. In this Lab you will learn how word-processing software works. When you have completed this Lab, you should be able to apply the general concepts you learned to any word-processing package you use at home, at work, or in your school lab.

1. Click the Steps button to learn how word-processing software works. As you proceed through the Steps, answer all of the Quick Check questions that appear. After you complete the Steps, you will see a Quick Check Summary Report. Follow the instructions on the screen to print this report.

2. Click the Explore button to begin. Click File, and then click Open to display the Open dialog box. Click the file **Timber.tex**, and then press the Enter key to open the letter to Northern Timber Company. Make the following modifications to the letter, and then print it. You do not need to save the letter.

    a. In the first and last lines of the letter, change "Jason Kidder" to your name.
    b. Change the date to today's date.
    c. The second paragraph begins "Your proposal did not include…". Move this paragraph so it is the last paragraph in the text of the letter.
    d. Change the cost of a permanent bridge to $20,000.
    e. Spell check the letter.

3. In Explore, open the file **Stars.tex**. Make the following modifications to the document and then print it. You do not need to save the document.

    a. Center and boldface the title.
    b. Change the title font to size —16-point Arial.
    c. Boldface the DATE, SHOWER, and LOCATION.
    d. Move the January 2–3 line to the top of the list.
    e. Double-space the entire document.

4. In Explore, compose a one-page double-spaced letter to your parents or to a friend. Make sure you date the letter and check your spelling. Print the letter and sign it. You do not need to save your letter.

INTERNET ASSIGNMENTS

Student Union

The purpose of the Internet Assignments is to challenge you to find information on the Internet that you can use to create effective documents. The actual assignments are updated and maintained on the Course Technology Web site. Log on to the Internet and use your Web browser to go to the Student Union on the New Perspectives Series site at **www.course.com/NewPerspectives/studentunion**. Click the Online Companions link, and then click the link for this text.

Quick Check answers

Session 1.1

1. (1) Plan the content, purpose, organization, and look of your document. (2) Create and then edit the document. (3) Format the document to make it visually appealing. (4) Preview and then print the document.

2. Click the Start button, point to Programs, and then click Microsoft Word.

3. a. symbols you can display on-screen but that don't print
   b. buttons to the left of the horizontal status bar that switch the document to Normal view, Web Layout view, Print Layout view, or Outline view
   c. actual height of a character measured in points
   d. standard settings

4. Click Format on the menu bar, click Font, select the font size in the Size list box, click the Default button, and then click Yes.

5. Right-click a toolbar, and then click Formatting on the shortcut menu.

6. Click the Normal View button.

7. False

Session 1.2

1. Click the Save button on the Standard toolbar, switch to the drive and folder where you want to save the document, enter a filename in the File name text box, and then click the Save button.

2. Type the first few characters of the month. When an AutoCorrect suggestion appears, press the Enter key.

3. When you type a word that extends into the right margin, Word moves that word and the insertion point to the next line.

4. Click Tools on the menu bar, point to Letters and Mailings, and then click Envelopes and Labels. In the Envelopes and Labels dialog box, verify that the Delivery address contains the correct address. If necessary, you can type a new address or edit the existing one. If necessary, type a return address. If you are using preprinted stationery that already includes a return address, click the Omit check box to insert a check. To print the envelope immediately, insert an envelope in your printer, and click Print. To store the envelope along with the rest of the document, click Add to Document. To print the envelope after you have added it to the document, open the Print dialog box and print the page containing the envelope.

5. a. The means by which text at the bottom of the document shifts out of view when you display the top of the document, and text at the top shifts out of view when you display the bottom of the document.
   b. A feature that automatically enters dates and other regularly used items.
   c. A feature that fixes common typing errors automatically.
   d. A window in which you can see how the document will look when printed.
   e. A feature that that allows you to perform actions (such as sending e-mail or scheduling a meeting) that would normally require a completely different program. Word attaches Smart Tag Action buttons to certain kinds of text, including dates and names.

OBJECTIVES

In this tutorial you will:

- Check spelling and grammar

- Move the insertion point around the document

- Select and delete text

- Reverse edits using the Undo and Redo buttons

- Move text within the document

- Find and replace text

- Change margins, line spacing, alignment, and paragraph indents

- Copy formatting with the Format Painter

- Change fonts and adjust font sizes

- Emphasize points with bullets, numbering, boldface, underlining, and italics

- Add a comment to a document

EDITING AND FORMATTING A DOCUMENT

Preparing a FAQ Document for Long Meadow Gardens

CASE

Long Meadow Gardens

Marilee Brigham is the owner of Long Meadow Gardens, a landscape and gardening supply company. The firm's large nursery provides shrubs and trees to professional landscape contractors throughout the Minneapolis/St. Paul area. At the same time, Long Meadow's retail store caters to home gardeners, who often call the store with questions about planting and caring for their purchases.

Marilee has noticed that retail customers tend to ask the same set of questions. To save time in answering these questions, she would like a series of handouts designed to answer these common questions. (Such a document is sometimes known as a FAQ—which is short for "frequently asked questions.") The company's chief horticulturist, Peter Chi, has just finished creating a FAQ containing information on planting trees. Now that Marilee has commented on and corrected the draft, Peter asks you to make the necessary changes and print the document.

In this tutorial, you will edit the FAQ according to Marilee's comments. You will open a draft of the document, resave it, and edit it. You will check the document's grammar and spelling, and then move text using two different methods. You will also find and replace one version of the company name with another.

Next, you will change the overall look of the document by changing margins and line spacing, indenting and justifying paragraphs, and copying formatting from one paragraph to another. You'll create a bulleted list to emphasize the species of water-tolerant trees and a numbered list for the steps involved in removing the burlap from around the base of a tree. Then you'll make the title more prominent by centering it, changing its font, and enlarging it. You'll add boldface to the questions to set them off from the rest of the text and underline an added note about how to get further information. Finally, you will add a comment, and then print the FAQ document.

In this session you will learn how to use the Spelling and Grammar checker to correct any errors in your document. You will also learn how to undo and redo changes in a document. Then you will edit the draft of the FAQ document by deleting words and moving text. Finally, you'll find and replace text throughout the document.

Reviewing the Document

Marilee's editing marks and notes on the first draft are shown in Figure 2-1. You'll begin by opening the first draft of the document, which has the filename FAQ.

| Figure 2-1 | DRAFT OF FAQ WITH MARILEE'S EDITS (PAGE 1) |

Figure 2-1	DRAFT OF FAQ WITH MARILEE'S EDITS (PAGE 2)

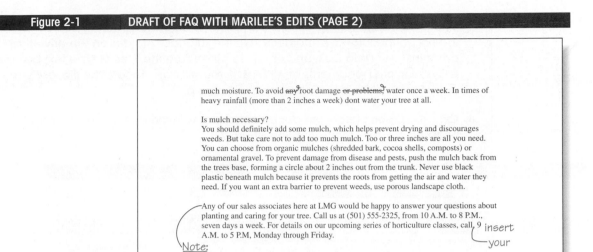

To open the document:

1. Place your Data Disk into the appropriate disk drive.

2. Start Word as usual.

3. Click the **Open** button ![open icon] on the Standard toolbar to display the Open dialog box, shown in Figure 2-2.

Figure 2-2	OPEN DIALOG BOX

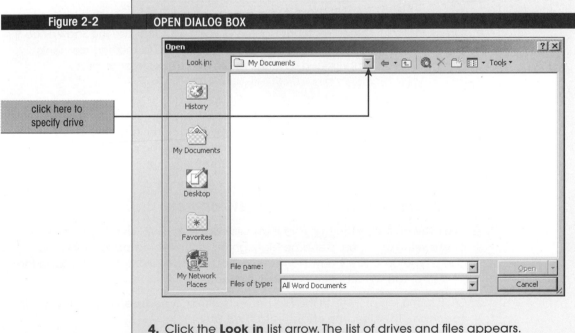

click here to specify drive

4. Click the **Look in** list arrow. The list of drives and files appears.

5. Click the drive that contains your Data Disk.

6. Double-click the **Tutorial.02** folder, and then double-click the **Tutorial** folder.

7. Click **FAQ** to select the file, if necessary.

TROUBLE? If you see "FAQ.doc" in the folder, Windows might be configured to display filename extensions. Click FAQ.doc and continue with Step 8. If you can't find the file with or without the filename extension, make sure you're looking in the Tutorial subfolder within the Tutorial.02 folder on the drive that contains your Data Disk, and check to make sure the Files of type text box displays All Word Documents or All Files. If you still can't locate the file, ask your instructor or technical support person for help.

8. Click the **Open** button. The document opens with the insertion point at the beginning of the document. See Figure 2-3.

| Figure 2-3 | OPEN DOCUMENT |

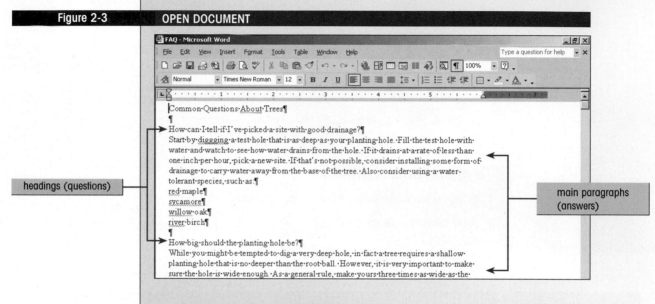

headings (questions)

main paragraphs (answers)

9. Check that your screen matches Figure 2-3. For this tutorial, use the Show/Hide ¶ button to display nonprinting characters. This will make formatting elements (tabs, paragraph marks, and so forth) visible and easier to change.

Now that you've opened the document, you can save it with a new name. To avoid altering the original file, FAQ, you will save the document using the filename Tree FAQ. Saving the document with another filename creates a copy of the file and leaves the original file unchanged in case you want to work through the tutorial again.

To save the document with a new name:

1. Click **File** on the menu bar, and then click **Save As**. The Save As dialog box opens with the current filename highlighted in the File name text box. You could type an entirely new filename, or you could edit the current one. In the next step, you will practice editing a filename.

2. Click to the left of "FAQ" in the File name text box, type **Tree**, and then press the **spacebar**. The filename changes to "Tree FAQ."

3. Verify that the Tutorial folder for Tutorial 2 is selected in the Save in box.

4. Click the **Save** button. The document is saved with the new filename.

Now you're ready to begin working with the document. First, you will check it for spelling and grammatical errors.

Using the Spelling and Grammar Checker

When typing a document, you can check for spelling and grammatical errors by looking for words underlined in red (for spelling errors) or green (for grammatical errors). But when you're working on a document that someone else typed, it's a good idea to start by using the Spelling and Grammar checker. This feature automatically checks a document word by word for a variety of errors. Among other things, the Spelling and Grammar checker can sometimes find words that, though spelled correctly, are not used properly. For example, it highlights the word "their" when it is mistakenly used instead of the word "there."

REFERENCE WINDOW   RW

Checking a Document for Spelling and Grammatical Errors

- Click at the beginning of the document, and then click the Spelling and Grammar button on the Standard toolbar.
- In the Spelling and Grammar dialog box, review any errors highlighted in color. Grammatical errors appear in green; spelling errors appear in red. Review the possible corrections in the Suggestions list box.
- To accept a suggested correction, click on it in the Suggestions list box. Then click Change to make the correction and continue searching the document for errors.
- Click Ignore Once to skip the current instance of the highlighted text and continue searching the document for errors.
- Click Ignore All to skip all instances of the highlighted text and continue searching the document for spelling errors. Click Ignore Rule to skip all instances of a particular grammatical error.
- To type your correction directly in the document, click outside the Spelling and Grammar dialog box, make the correction, and then click Resume in the Spelling and Grammar dialog box.

You'll see how the Spelling and Grammar checker works as you check the FAQ document for mistakes.

To check the FAQ document for spelling and grammatical errors:

1. Verify that the insertion point is located at the beginning of the document, to the left of the "C" in "Common Questions."

2. Click the **Spelling and Grammar** button [ABC✓] on the Standard toolbar. The Spelling and Grammar dialog box opens with the word "About" highlighted in green, indicating a possible grammatical error. The word "about" (with a lowercase "a") is suggested as a possible replacement. The line immediately under the title bar indicates the type of possible problem, in this case, Capitalization. See Figure 2-4. Normally, prepositions of fewer than six letters are not capitalized in titles. But Marilee prefers to keep this word capitalized because she thinks it makes the title look better.

   TROUBLE? If you see the word "diggging" selected instead of "About", your computer is not set up to check grammar. Click the Check grammar check box to insert a check, and then click Cancel to close the Spelling and Grammar dialog box. Next, click at the beginning of the document, and then repeat Step 2.

Figure 2-4   SPELLING AND GRAMMAR DIALOG BOX

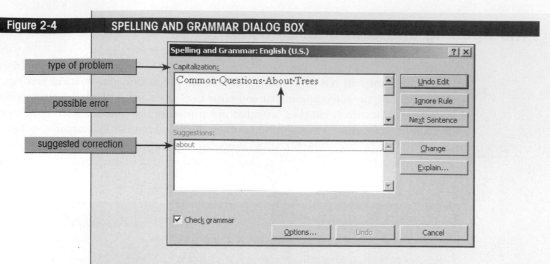

3. Click the **Ignore Rule** button. The word "diggging" is highlighted in red, with "digging" and "diggings" listed as possible corrections.

4. Verify that "digging" is highlighted in the Suggestions list box, and then click the **Change** button. "Digging" is inserted into the document.

At this point the word "composts" is highlighted in green, with "and composts" listed as a possible correction. It's not clear why Word suggests this change, so you need to request an explanation.

To ask the Spelling and Grammar Checker for an explanation:

1. Click the **Explain** button. The Office Assistant opens, showing an explanation of the rule in question.

2. Read the explanation, and then click the **Ignore Rule** button. The last sentence of the document is highlighted in green. The Office Assistant indicates that the highlighted text is a sentence fragment. In this case, Word is correct. The word "call" lacks a direct object—that is, you need to indicate whom the reader should call. You'll fix this problem later, when you insert your name in this sentence.

3. Click **Ignore Once**. The Office Assistant closes, and you see a message indicating that the spelling and grammar check is complete.

4. Click the **OK** button. The Spelling and Grammar dialog box and the Office Assistant close. You return to the FAQ document.

Although the Spelling and Grammar checker is a useful tool, remember that there is no substitute for careful proofreading. Always take the time to read through your document to check for errors the Spelling and Grammar checker might have missed. Keep in mind that the Spelling and Grammar checker probably won't catch *all* instances of words that are spelled correctly but used improperly. And of course, the Spelling and Grammar checker cannot pinpoint phrases that are confusing or inaccurate. To produce a professional document, you must read it carefully several times, and, if necessary, ask a co-worker to read it, too.

To proofread the FAQ document:

1. Scroll to the beginning of the document and begin proofreading. When you get near the bottom of the document, notice that the word "Too" is used instead of the word "Two" in the paragraph on mulch. See Figure 2-5. You will correct this error later in this tutorial, after you learn how to move the insertion point in a document.

| Figure 2-5 | WORD "TOO" USED INCORRECTLY |

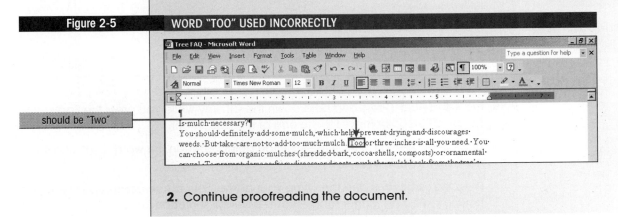

should be "Two"

2. Continue proofreading the document.

To make the proofreading corrections, and to make all of Marilee's changes, you need to learn how to move the insertion point quickly to any location in the document.

Moving the Insertion Point Around a Document

The arrow keys on your keyboard, ↑, ↓, ←, and →, allow you to move the insertion point one character at a time to the left or right, or one line at a time up or down. If you want to move more than one character or one line at a time, you can point and click in other parts of a line or the document. You also can press a combination of keys to move the insertion point. As you become more experienced with Word, you'll decide which method you prefer.

To see how quickly you can move through the document, you'll use keystrokes to move the insertion point to the beginning of the second page and to the end of the document.

To move the insertion point with keystrokes:

1. Press the **Ctrl** key and hold it down while you press the **Home** key. The insertion point moves to the beginning of the document.

2. Press the **Page Down** key to move the insertion point down to the next screen.

3. Press the **Page Down** key again to move the insertion point down to the next screen. Notice that the status bar indicates the location of the insertion point.

4. Press the ↑ or ↓ key to move the insertion point to just below the dotted line that spans the width of the page. The insertion point is now at the beginning of page 2, as shown in Figure 2-6. The dotted line is an **automatic page break** that Word inserts to mark the beginning of the new page. As you insert and delete text or change formatting in a document, the location of the automatic page breaks in your document continually adjust.

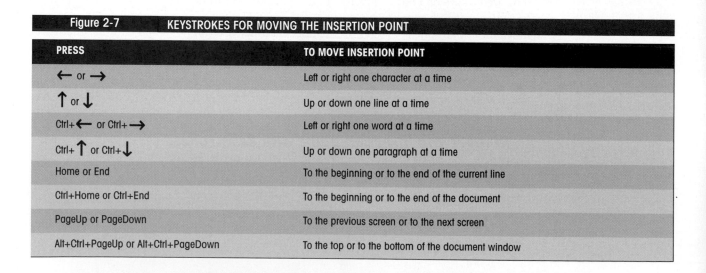

Figure 2-6   AUTOMATIC PAGE BREAK

automatic page break

insertion point at the beginning of page 2

5. Press **Ctrl+End**. (Press and hold down the Ctrl key while you press the End key.) The insertion point moves to the end of the document.

6. Use the ← key to position the insertion point between the word "call" and the comma that follows it.

7. Press the **spacebar** and then type your name. Your name completes the sentence and it is no longer marked as a possible sentence fragment.

8. Move the insertion point back to the beginning of the document.

Figure 2-7 summarizes the keystrokes you can use to move the insertion point around the document. When you simply need to display a part of a document, you'll probably want to use the vertical scroll bar. But when you actually need to move the insertion point to a specific spot, it's helpful to use these special keystrokes.

Figure 2-7   KEYSTROKES FOR MOVING THE INSERTION POINT

PRESS	TO MOVE INSERTION POINT
← or →	Left or right one character at a time
↑ or ↓	Up or down one line at a time
Ctrl+← or Ctrl+→	Left or right one word at a time
Ctrl+↑ or Ctrl+↓	Up or down one paragraph at a time
Home or End	To the beginning or to the end of the current line
Ctrl+Home or Ctrl+End	To the beginning or to the end of the document
PageUp or PageDown	To the previous screen or to the next screen
Alt+Ctrl+PageUp or Alt+Ctrl+PageDown	To the top or to the bottom of the document window

Selecting Parts of a Document

Before you can do anything to text (such as deleting, moving, or formatting it), you often need to highlight, or **select** it. You can select text by using the mouse or the keyboard, although the mouse is usually easier and more efficient. With the mouse you can quickly select a line or paragraph by clicking the **selection bar** (the blank space in the left margin area of the Document window). You can also select text using various combinations of keys.

Figure 2-8 summarizes methods for selecting text with the mouse and the keyboard. The notation "Ctrl+Shift" means you press and hold the two keys at the same time. Note that you will use the methods described in Figure 2-8 as you work on the FAQ document.

Figure 2-8	METHODS FOR SELECTING TEXT		
TO SELECT	**MOUSE**	**KEYBOARD**	**MOUSE AND KEYBOARD**
A word	Double-click the word.	Move the insertion point to the beginning of the word, hold down Ctrl+Shift, and then press ⟶.	
A line	Click in the selection bar next to the line.	Move the insertion point to the beginning of the line, hold down Ctrl+Shift, and then press ⟶ until the line is selected.	
A sentence			Press and hold down the Ctrl key, and click within the sentence.
Multiple lines	Click and drag in the selection bar next to the lines.	Move the insertion point to the beginning of the first line, hold down Ctrl+Shift, and then press ⟶ until all the lines are selected.	
A paragraph	Double-click in the selection bar next to the paragraph, or triple-click within the paragraph.	Move the insertion point to the beginning of the paragraph, hold down Ctrl+Shift, and then press ↓.	
Multiple paragraphs	Click and drag in the selection bar next to the paragraphs, or triple-click within the first paragraph and drag.	Move the insertion point to the beginning of the first paragraph, hold down Ctrl+Shift, and then press ↓ until all the paragraphs are selected.	
Entire document	Triple-click in the selection bar.	Press Ctrl+A.	Press and hold down the Ctrl key and click in the selection bar.
A block of text	Click at the beginning of the block, then drag the pointer until the entire block is selected.		Click at the beginning of the block, press and hold down the Shift key, and then click at the end of the block.
Multiple blocks of text	Press and hold the Ctrl key, then drag the mouse pointer to select multiple blocks of nonadjacent text.		

Deleting Text

When editing a document, you frequently need to delete text. You already have experience using the Backspace and Delete keys to delete a few characters. When you need to delete an entire word or multiple words, it's faster to select the text. After you select the text, you can either replace it with something else by typing over it, or by pressing the Delete key. You need to delete the word "Too" and replace it with "Two," so you'll use the first method now.

To replace "Too" with "Two":

1. Press **Ctrl+End**. The insertion point moves to the end of the document.

2. Press and hold the **Ctrl** key while you press ↑ three times. The insertion point is now positioned at the beginning of the paragraph that begins "You should definitely add some mulch." (The status bar indicates that this is line 5 of page 2.)

3. In the second line of the paragraph, double-click the word **Too**. The entire word is highlighted.

4. Type **Two**. The selected word is replaced with the correction. The sentence now correctly reads: "Two or three inches are all you need."

Next, Marilee wants you to delete the phrase "or problems" and the word "any" in the paragraph before the one you've just corrected. Peter explains that you can do this quickly by selecting multiple items and then pressing Delete. As you'll see in the following steps, selecting parts of a document by clicking and dragging takes a little practice, so don't be concerned if you don't get it right the first time. You can always try again.

To select and delete multiple items:

1. Press ↑ five times. As shown in Figure 2-9, the insertion point is now located in the sentence that begins "To avoid any root damage or problems." The status bar indicates that this is line 1 of page 2.

Figure 2-9	TEXT TO BE DELETED

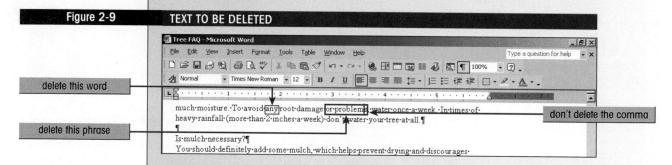

delete this word

delete this phrase

don't delete the comma

2. Double-click the word **any**. The word and the space following it are selected.

3. Press and hold the **Ctrl** key, and then click and drag to select the phrase "or problems." Do not select the comma after the word "problems". At this point the word "any" and the phrase "or problems" should be selected.

TROUBLE? If you don't get Step 3 right the first time (for instance, if you accidentally selected the word "damage"), click anywhere in the document and then repeat Steps 2 and 3.

4. Press the **Delete** key. The selected items disappear and the words around them move in to fill the space. As you can see in Figure 2-10, you need to delete the extra space before the comma.

TROUBLE? If you deleted the wrong text, click the Undo button (not the Redo button) on the Standard toolbar to reverse your mistake.

Figure 2-10	PARAGRAPH AFTER DELETING PHRASE

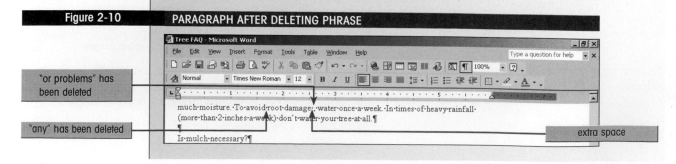

"or problems" has been deleted

"any" has been deleted

extra space

TROUBLE? If your screen looks slightly different than Figure 2-10, don't be concerned. The text may wrap differently on your monitor. Just make sure the text has been deleted.

5. Click to the right of the word "damage", and then press the **Delete** key. The extra space is removed.

After rereading the paragraph, Peter wonders if perhaps the text shouldn't have been deleted after all. You can retype the text, but there's an easier way to restore the phrase.

Using the Undo and Redo Commands

To undo (or reverse) the very last thing you did, click the **Undo button** on the Standard toolbar. If you want to restore your original change, the **Redo button** reverses the action of the Undo button (or redoes the undo). To undo more than your last action, you can click the Undo list arrow on the Standard toolbar. This list shows your most recent actions. Undo reverses the action only at its original location. You can't delete a word or phrase, move the surrounding text, and then undo the deletion at a different location.

You decide to undo the deletion to see how the sentence reads. Rather than retype the phrase, you will reverse the edit using the Undo button.

To undo the deletion:

1. Place the mouse pointer over the Undo button 🔄 on the Standard toolbar. The label "Undo Clear" appears in a ScreenTip, indicating that your most recent action involved deleting (or clearing) something from the document (in this case, a space).

2. Click the **Undo** button 🔄. The space after the word "damage" reappears.

TROUBLE? If the space doesn't reappear and something else changes in your document, you probably made another edit or change to the document between the deletion and the undo. Click the Undo button on the Standard toolbar until the space reappears in your document. If a list of possible changes appears under the Undo button, you clicked the list arrow next to the Undo button rather than the Undo button itself. Click the Undo button to restore the deleted phrase and close the list box.

3. Click 🔄 again. The deleted text reappears highlighted within the sentence.

4. Click in the paragraph to deselect the phrase.

As you read the sentence, you decide that it reads better without the word "any" and the phrase "or problems". Instead of deleting these items again, you'll redo the undo. As you place the pointer over the Redo button, notice that its ScreenTip indicates the action you want to redo.

5. Place the mouse pointer over the Redo button 🔁 on the Standard toolbar and observe the "Redo Clear" label.

6. Click the **Redo** button 🔁. The text disappears from the document again.

7. Click 🔁 again. The extra space after "damage" disappears again.

8. Click the **Save** button 💾 on the Standard toolbar to save your changes to the document.

You have edited the document by replacing "Too" with "Two", and by removing the text that Marilee marked for deletion. Now you are ready to make the rest of the edits she suggested.

Moving Text Within a Document

One of the most useful features of a word-processing program is the ability to move text. For example, Marilee wants to reorder the four points Peter made in the section "Do I have to do anything to the tree before planting?" on page 1 of his draft. You could reorder the list by deleting the item and then retyping it at a new location, but it's easier to select and then move the text. Word provides several ways to move text: drag and drop, cut and paste, and copy and paste.

Dragging and Dropping Text

One way to move text within a document is called drag and drop. With **drag and drop**, you select the text you want to move, press and hold down the mouse button while you drag the selected text to a new location, and then release the mouse button.

REFERENCE WINDOW   **RW**

Dragging and Dropping Text
- Select the text you want to move.
- Press and hold down the mouse button until the drag-and-drop pointer appears, and then drag the selected text to its new location.
- Use the dotted insertion point as a guide to determine exactly where the text will be inserted.
- Release the mouse button to drop the text at the insertion point.

Marilee wants you to change the order of the items in the list on page 1 of the document. You'll use the drag-and-drop method to reorder these items. At the same time, you'll practice using the selection bar to highlight a line of text.

To move text using drag and drop:

1. Scroll up until you see "Do I have to do anything to the tree before planting?" (line 29 of page 1). In the list of steps involved in planting a tree, Marilee wants you to move the third step ("Remove any tags from the trunk and branches.") to the top of the list.

2. Move the pointer to the selection bar to the left of the line "Remove any tags from the trunk and branches." The pointer changes from an I-beam I to a right-facing arrow ⌐∖.

3. Click to the left of the line "Remove any tags from the trunk and branches." The line is selected. Notice that the paragraph mark at the end of the line is also selected. See Figure 2-11.

Figure 2-11 | SELECTED TEXT TO DRAG AND DROP

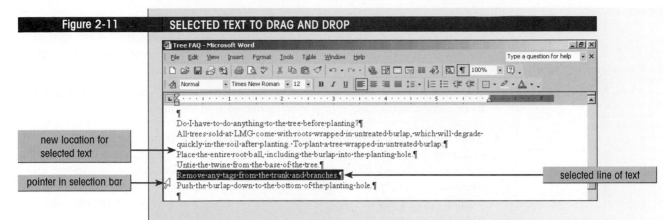

new location for selected text

pointer in selection bar

selected line of text

4. Position the pointer over the selected text. The pointer changes from a right-facing arrow to a left-facing arrow.

5. Press and hold down the mouse button until the drag-and-drop pointer appears. Note that a dotted insertion point appears within the selected text.

6. Drag the selected text up three lines until the dotted insertion point appears to the left of the word "Place". Make sure you use the dotted insertion point, rather than the mouse pointer, to guide the text to its new location. The dotted insertion point indicates exactly where the text will appear when you release the mouse button. See Figure 2-12.

Figure 2-12 | MOVING TEXT WITH THE DRAG-AND-DROP POINTER

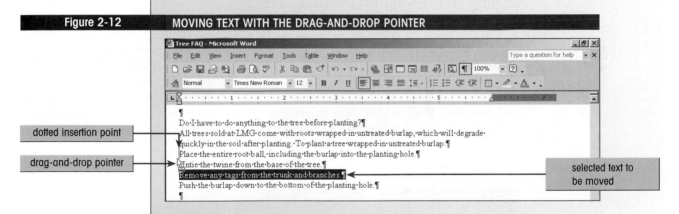

dotted insertion point

drag-and-drop pointer

selected text to be moved

7. Release the mouse button. The selected text moves to its new location as the first step in the list. A Paste Options button appears near the newly moved text, as shown in Figure 2-13.

Figure 2-13 | PASTE OPTIONS BUTTON

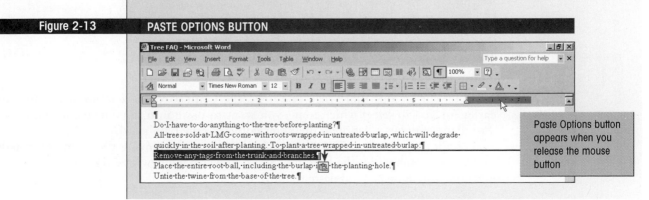

Paste Options button appears when you release the mouse button

TROUBLE? If the selected text moves to the wrong location, click the Undo button on the Standard toolbar, and then repeat Steps 2 through 7. Be sure you hold the mouse button until the dotted insertion point appears to the left of the word "Place".

TROUBLE? If you don't see the Paste Options button, your computer is not set up to display it. Read Step 7, and then continue with Step 8.

8. Click the **Paste Options** 📋 button. A menu of text-moving commands appears. These commands are useful when you are inserting text that looks different from the surrounding text. For instance, suppose you selected text formatted in Times New Roman and then dragged it to a paragraph formatted in Arial. You could then use the Match Destination Formatting command to format the moved text in Arial.

9. Deselect the highlighted text by clicking anywhere in the document. The Paste Options menu closes, but the button remains visible. It will disappear as soon as you perform another task.

Dragging and dropping works well if you're moving text a short distance in a document. However, Word provides another method, called cut and paste, that works well for moving text both long and short distances.

Cutting or Copying and Pasting Text

To **cut** means to remove text from the document and place it on the **Office Clipboard**, a feature that temporarily stores text or graphics until you need them later. To **paste** means to transfer a copy of the text from the Clipboard into the document at the insertion point. To perform a **cut-and-paste** action, you select the text you want to move, cut (or remove) it from the document, and then paste (or insert) it into the document in a new location. If you don't want to remove the text from its original location, you can copy it (rather than cutting it) and then paste the copy in a new location. This procedure is known as **copy and paste**.

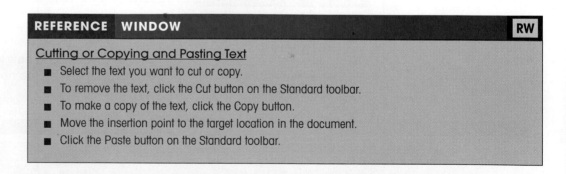

REFERENCE WINDOW   **RW**

Cutting or Copying and Pasting Text
- Select the text you want to cut or copy.
- To remove the text, click the Cut button on the Standard toolbar.
- To make a copy of the text, click the Copy button.
- Move the insertion point to the target location in the document.
- Click the Paste button on the Standard toolbar.

If you cut or copy more than one item, the **Clipboard Task Pane** opens, making it easier for you to select which items you want to paste into the document. This special Task Pane contains a list of all the items copied to the Clipboard.

As indicated earlier in Figure 2-1, Marilee suggested moving the word "thoroughly" (in the paragraph under the heading "Should I water my new tree right away?") to a new location. You'll use cut and paste to move this word.

To move text using cut and paste:

1. If necessary, scroll down until you can see the paragraph below the heading "Should I water my new tree right away?" near the bottom of page 1.

2. Double-click the word **thoroughly**. As you can see in Figure 2-14, you need to move this word to the end of the sentence.

Figure 2-14   **TEXT TO MOVE USING CUT AND PASTE**

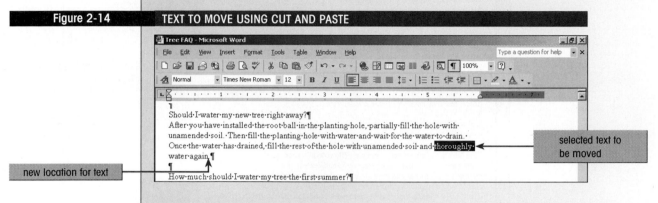

new location for text

selected text to be moved

---

3. Click the **Cut** button ✂ on the Standard toolbar to remove the selected text from the document.

4. If the Clipboard Task Pane opens, click its Close button ✕ for now. You'll have a chance to use the Clipboard Task Pane shortly.

5. Click between the "n" in "again" and the period that follows it. The insertion point marks the position where you want to move the text.

6. Click the **Paste** button 📋 on the Standard toolbar. The word "thoroughly" appears in its new location, along with a Paste Options button. Note that Word also included a space before the word, so that the end of the sentence reads: "and water again thoroughly." The Paste Options button that appeared earlier (when you dragged text to a new location) disappears.

   TROUBLE? If the Paste Options buttons on your computer do not behave exactly as described in these steps—for instance, if they do not disappear as described—ignore them.

Peter stops by your desk and mentions that he'll be using the paragraph on mulch and the paragraph on watering for the FAQ he plans to write on flowering shrubs. He asks you to copy that information and paste it in a new document that he can use as the basis for the new FAQ. You can do this using copy and paste. This technique is similar to cut and paste. In the process you'll have a chance to use the Clipboard Task Pane.

To copy and paste text:

1. Click **Edit** on the menu bar, and then click **Office Clipboard**. The Office Clipboard Task Pane opens on the right side of the Document window. It contains the message "Clipboard empty. Copy or cut to collect items." See Figure 2-15.

Figure 2-15   CLIPBOARD TASK PANE

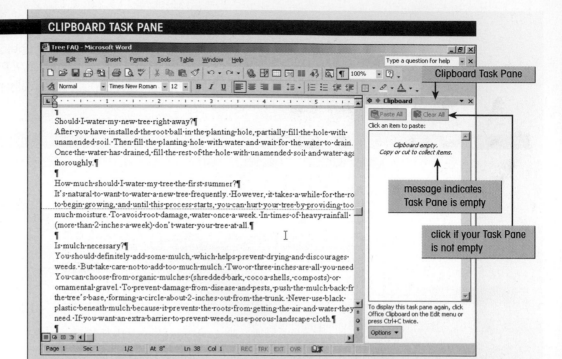

TROUBLE? If your Clipboard Task Pane does not show this message, click the Clear All button.

2. Move the mouse pointer to the selection bar and double-click next to the paragraph you edited in the last section (the paragraph that begins "After you have installed the root ball"). The entire paragraph is selected.

3. Click the **Copy** button 📋 on the Standard toolbar. The first part of the paragraph appears in the Task Pane.

4. If necessary, scroll down until you can see the paragraph below the heading "Is mulch necessary?"

5. Select the paragraph below the heading (the paragraph that begins "You should definitely add . . . ").

6. Click 📋 . The first part of the paragraph appears in the Task Pane, as shown in Figure 2-16. An icon appears in the Windows taskbar indicating that the Clipboard Task Pane is currently active.

Figure 2-16	ITEMS IN THE CLIPBOARD TASK PANE

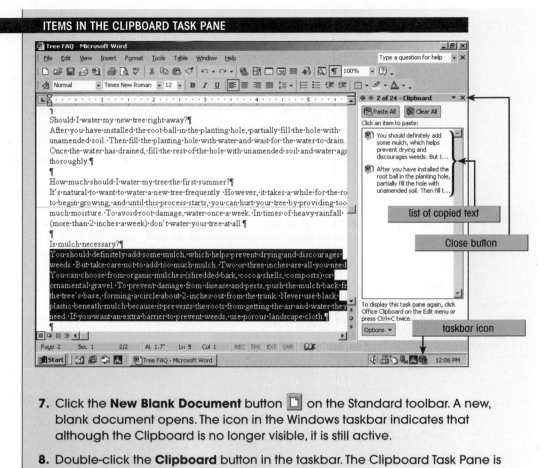

7. Click the **New Blank Document** button ☐ on the Standard toolbar. A new, blank document opens. The icon in the Windows taskbar indicates that although the Clipboard is no longer visible, it is still active.

8. Double-click the **Clipboard** button in the taskbar. The Clipboard Task Pane is now visible.

Now you can use the Clipboard Task Pane to insert the copied text into the new document.

To insert the copied text into the new document:

1. In the Clipboard Task Pane, click the item that begins "You should definitely add . . . " The text is inserted in the document.

2. Press **Enter** to insert a blank line, and then click the item that begins "After you have installed the root ball . . . " in the Task Pane. The text is inserted in the document.

3. Save the document as **Flowering Shrub FAQ** in the Tutorial folder for Tutorial 2, and then close the document. You return to the Tree FAQ document, where the Clipboard Task Pane is still open. You are finished using the Clipboard Task Pane, so you will delete its contents.

4. Click the **Clear All** button [Clear All] on the Clipboard Task Pane. The copied items are removed from the Clipboard Task Pane.

5. Click the **Close** button [X] on the Clipboard Task Pane. The Clipboard Task Pane disappears.

6. Click anywhere in the document to deselect the highlighted paragraph.

7. Save the document.

Finding and Replacing Text

When you're working with a longer document, the quickest and easiest way to locate a particular word or phrase is to use the **Find command**. If you want to replace characters or a phrase with something else, you can use the **Replace command**, which combines the Find command with a substitution feature. The Replace command searches through a document and substitutes the text you're searching for with the replacement text you specify. As you perform the search, Word stops and highlights each occurrence of the search text. You must determine whether or not to substitute the replacement text, and do so by clicking the Replace button.

If you want to substitute every occurrence of the search text with the replacement text, you can click the Replace All button. When using the Replace All button with single words, keep in mind that the search text might be found within other words. To prevent Word from making incorrect substitutions in such cases, it's a good idea to select the Find whole words only check box along with the Replace All button. For example, suppose you want to replace the word "figure" with "illustration". Unless you select the Find whole words only check box, Word would replace "configure" with "conillustration."

As you search through a document, you can search from the current location of the insertion point down to the end of the document, from the insertion point up to the beginning of the document, or throughout the document.

REFERENCE WINDOW	RW

Finding and Replacing Text
- Click Edit on the menu bar, and then click either Find or Replace.
- To find text, click the Find tab. To find and replace text, click the Replace tab.
- Click the More button to expand the dialog box to display additional options (including the Find whole words only option). If you see the Less button, the additional options are already displayed.
- In the Search list box, select Down if you want to search from the insertion point to the end of the document, select Up if you want to search from the insertion point to the beginning of the document, or select All to search the entire document.
- Type the characters you want to find in the Find what text box.
- If you are replacing text, type the replacement text in the Replace with text box.
- Click the Find whole words only check box to search for complete words.
- Click the Match case check box to insert the replacement text just as you specified in the Replace with text box.
- Click the Find Next button.
- Click the Replace button to substitute the found text with the replacement text and find the next occurrence.
- Click the Replace All button to substitute all occurrences of the found text with the replacement text.

Marilee wants the company initials, LMG, to be spelled out as "Long Meadow Gardens" each time they appear in the text.

To replace "LMG" with "Long Meadow Gardens":

1. Press **Ctrl+Home** to move the insertion point to the beginning of the document.

2. Click **Edit** on the menu bar, and then click **Replace**. The Find and Replace dialog box opens.

3. If you see a **More** button, click it to display the additional search options. (If you see a Less button, the additional options are already displayed.) Also, if necessary, click the **Search** list arrow, and then click **All**.

4. Click the **Find what** text box, type **LMG**, press the **Tab** key, and then type **Long Meadow Gardens** in the Replace with text box.

   TROUBLE? If you already see the text "LMG" and "Long Meadow Gardens" in your Find and Replace dialog box, someone has already performed these steps on your computer. Continue with Step 7.

5. Click the **Find whole words only** check box to insert a check.

6. Click the **Match case** check box to insert a check. This ensures that Word will insert the replacement text using initial capital letters, as you specified in the Replace with text box. Your Find and Replace dialog box should now look like Figure 2-17.

Figure 2-17   **FIND AND REPLACE DIALOG BOX**

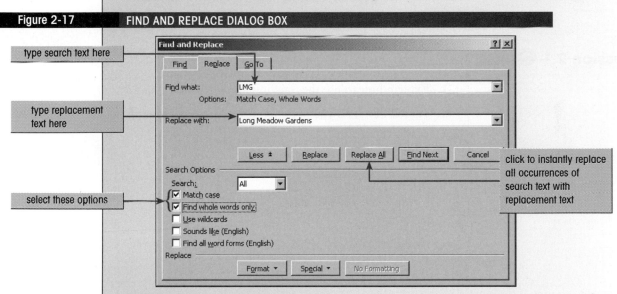

7. Click the **Replace All** button to replace all occurrences of the search text with the replacement text. When Word finishes making the replacements, you see a dialog box telling you that two replacements were made.

8. Click the **OK** button to close the dialog box, and then click the **Close** button in the Find and Replace dialog box to return to the document. The full company name has been inserted into the document, as shown in Figure 2-18. (You may have to scroll down to see this section.)

Figure 2-18   THE NAME "LONG MEADOW GARDENS" INSERTED INTO THE DOCUMENT

replacement text

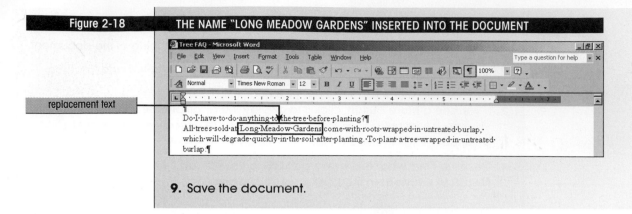

9. Save the document.

Note that you can also search for and replace formatting, such as bold, and special characters in the Find and Replace dialog box. Click in the Find what text box or the Replace with text box, enter any text if necessary, click the Format button, click Font to open the Font dialog box, and then select the formatting you want to find or replace. Complete the search or replace as usual.

You have completed the content changes Marilee requested. In the next session, you will make some changes that will affect the document's appearance.

Session 2.1 QUICK | CHECK

1. Explain how to use the Spelling and Grammar Checker.

2. Which key(s) do you press to move the insertion point to the following places:
   a. down one line
   b. to the end of the document
   c. to the next screen

3. Explain how to select the following items using the mouse:
   a. one word
   b. a block of text
   c. one paragraph

4. Define the following terms in your own words:
   a. selection bar
   b. Redo button
   c. drag and drop

5. Describe a situation in which you would use the Undo button and then the Redo button.

6. True or False: You can use the Redo command to restore deleted text at a new location in your document.

7. What is the difference between cut and paste, and copy and paste?

8. List the steps involved in finding and replacing text in a document.

SESSION 2.2

In this session you will make the formatting changes Marilee suggested. You'll use a variety of formatting commands to change the margins, line spacing, text alignment, and paragraph indents. You'll also learn how to use the Format Painter, how to create bulleted and numbered lists, and how to change fonts, font sizes, and emphasis. Finally, you will add a comment to the document.

Changing the Margins

In general, it's best to begin formatting by making the changes that affect the document's overall appearance. Then you can make changes that affect only selected text. In this case, you need to adjust the document's margin settings.

Word uses default margins of 1.25 inches for the left and right margins and 1 inch for the top and bottom margins. The numbers on the ruler (displayed below the Formatting toolbar) indicate the distance in inches from the left margin, not from the left edge of the paper. Unless you specify otherwise, changes you make to the margins affect the entire document, not just the current paragraph or page.

REFERENCE WINDOW   **RW**

<u>Changing Margins for the <u>Entire Document</u></u>
- With the insertion point anywhere in your document and no text selected, click File on the menu bar, and then click Page Setup.
- If necessary, click the Margins tab to display the margin settings.
- Use the arrows to change the settings in the Top, Bottom, Left, or Right text boxes, or type a new margin value in each text box.
- Make sure the Apply to list box displays Whole document.
- Click the OK button.

You need to change the top margin to 1.5 inches and the left margin to 1.75 inches, per Marilee's request. The left margin needs to be wider than usual to allow space for making holes so that the document can be inserted in a three-ring binder. In the next set of steps, you'll change the margins with the Page Setup command. You also can change margins in Print Layout view by dragging an icon on the horizontal ruler. You'll have a chance to practice this technique in the Review Assignments at the end of this tutorial.

To change the margins in the Tree FAQ document:

1. If you took a break after the previous session, make sure Word is running, the Tree FAQ document is open, and nonprinting characters are displayed.

2. Press **Ctrl+Home** to move the insertion point to the top of the document. This should also ensure that no text is selected in the document.

3. Click **File** on the menu bar, and then click **Page Setup** to open the Page Setup dialog box.

4. If necessary, click the **Margins** tab to display the margin settings. The Top margin setting is selected. See Figure 2-19. As you complete the following steps, keep an eye on the document preview, which will change to reflect any changes you make to the margins.

Figure 2-19   PAGE SETUP DIALOG BOX

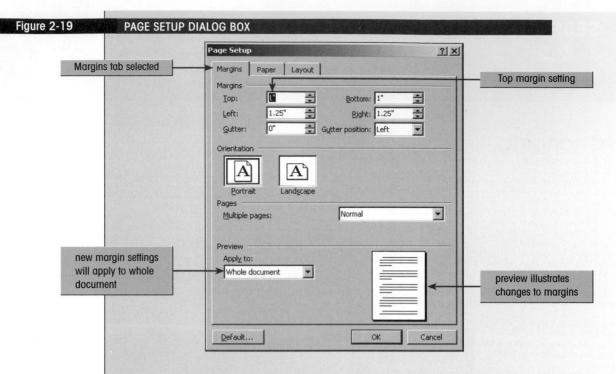

Margins tab selected

Top margin setting

new margin settings will apply to whole document

preview illustrates changes to margins

5. Type **1.5** to change the Top margin setting. (You do not have to type the inches symbol.)

6. Press the **Tab** key twice to select the Left text box and highlight the current margin setting. Notice how the text area in the Preview box moves down to reflect the larger top margin.

7. Type **1.75** and then press the **Tab** key. Watch the Preview box to see how the margin increases.

8. Make sure the **Whole document** option is selected in the Apply to list box, and then click the **OK** button to return to your document. Notice that the right margin on the ruler has changed to reflect the larger margins and the resulting reduced page area. The document text is now 5.5 inches wide. See Figure 2-20.

Figure 2-20   RULER AFTER SETTING LEFT MARGIN TO 1.75 INCHES

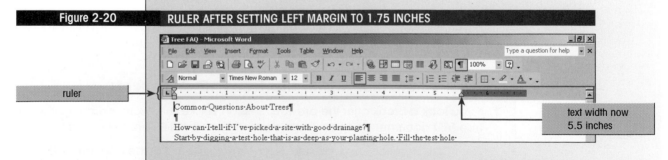

ruler

text width now 5.5 inches

TROUBLE? If a double dotted line and the words "Section Break" appear in your document, Whole document wasn't specified in the Apply to list box. If this occurs, click the Undo button on the Standard toolbar and then repeat Steps 1 through 8, making sure you select the Whole document option in the Apply to list box.

Next, you will change the amount of space between lines of text.

Changing Line Spacing

The line spacing in a document determines the amount of vertical space between lines of text. In most situations, you will want to choose from three basic types of line spacing: **single spacing** (which allows for the largest character in a particular line as well as a small amount of extra space); **1.5 line spacing** (which allows for one and one-half times the space of single spacing); and **double spacing** (which allows for twice the space of single spacing). The FAQ document is currently single-spaced because Word uses single spacing by default. Before changing the line-spacing setting, you should select the text you want to change. The easiest way to change line spacing is to use the Line Spacing button on the Formatting toolbar. You can also use the keyboard to apply single, double, and 1.5 line spacing.

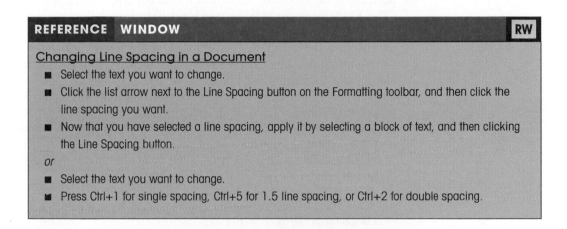

REFERENCE WINDOW   **RW**

<u>Changing Line Spacing in a Document</u>

- Select the text you want to change.
- Click the list arrow next to the Line Spacing button on the Formatting toolbar, and then click the line spacing you want.
- Now that you have selected a line spacing, apply it by selecting a block of text, and then clicking the Line Spacing button.

or

- Select the text you want to change.
- Press Ctrl+1 for single spacing, Ctrl+5 for 1.5 line spacing, or Ctrl+2 for double spacing.

Marilee has asked you to change the line spacing for the entire FAQ document to 1.5 line spacing. You will begin by selecting the entire document.

To change the document's line spacing:

1. Triple-click in the selection bar to select the entire document.

2. Move the mouse pointer over the Line Spacing button to display its ScreenTip. You see the text "Line Spacing (1)", indicating that single spacing is currently selected.

3. Click the **Line Spacing** list arrow. A list of line spacing options appears, as shown in Figure 2-21. To double-space the document, you click 2, while to triple-space it, you click 3. In this case, you need to apply 1.5 line spacing.

Figure 2-21	LINE SPACING LIST BOX

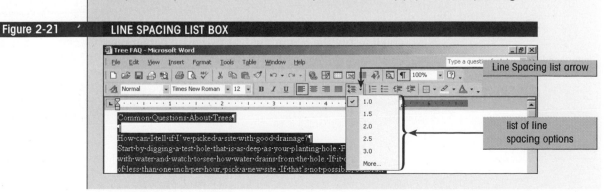

4. Click **1.5**. Notice the additional space between every line of text in the document.

5. Move the mouse pointer over 🔢 to display its ScreenTip. You see the text "Line Spacing (1.5)", indicating that 1.5 spacing is currently selected.

Now you are ready to make formatting changes that affect individual paragraphs.

Aligning Text

As you begin formatting individual paragraphs in the FAQ document, keep in mind that in Word, a **paragraph** is defined as any text that ends with a paragraph mark symbol (¶). A paragraph can also be blank, in which case you see a paragraph mark alone on a single line. (The FAQ document includes one blank paragraph before each question heading.)

The term **alignment** refers to how the text of a paragraph lines up horizontally between the margins. By default, text is aligned along the left margin but is **ragged**, or uneven, along the right margin. This is called **left alignment**. With **right alignment**, the text is aligned along the right margin and is ragged along the left margin. With **center alignment**, text is centered between the left and right margins. With **justified alignment**, full lines of text are spaced between or aligned along both the left and the right margins. The paragraph you are reading now is justified. The easiest way to apply alignment settings is by clicking buttons on the Formatting toolbar.

Marilee indicates that the title of the FAQ should be centered and that the main paragraphs should be justified. First, you'll center the title.

To center-align the title:

1. Click anywhere in the title "Common Questions About Trees" at the beginning of the document.

2. Click the **Center** button 🔳 on the Formatting toolbar. The text centers between the left and right margins. See Figure 2-22.

| Figure 2-22 | CENTERED TITLE |

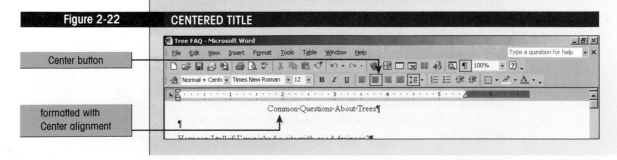

Center button

formatted with
Center alignment

Next, you'll justify the text in the first two main paragraphs.

To justify the first two paragraphs using the Formatting toolbar:

1. Click anywhere in the first main paragraph, which begins "Start by digging a test hole . . . "

2. Click the **Justify** button ▤ on the Formatting toolbar. The paragraph text spreads out, so that it lines up evenly along the left and right margins.

3. Move the insertion point to anywhere in the second main paragraph, which begins "While you might be tempted . . . "

4. Click ▤ again. The text is evenly spaced between the left and right margins. See Figure 2-23.

Figure 2-23	JUSTIFIED PARAGRAPHS

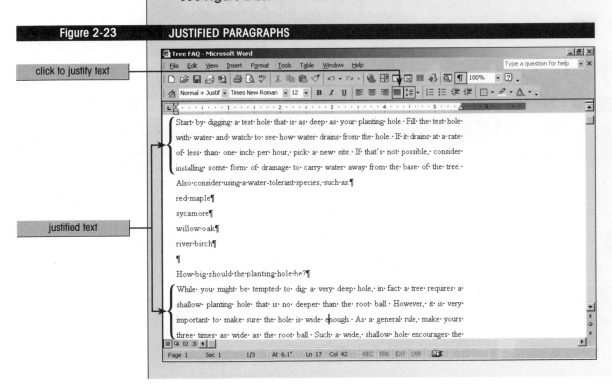

You'll justify the other paragraphs later. Now that you've learned how to change the paragraph alignment, you can turn your attention to indenting a paragraph.

Indenting a Paragraph

When you become a more experienced Word user, you might want to do some paragraph formatting, such as a **hanging indent** (where all lines except the first line of the paragraph are indented from the left margin) or a **right indent** (where all lines of the paragraph are indented from the right margin). You can select these types of indents on the Indents and Spacing tab of the Paragraph dialog box. (To open this dialog box, you click Format on the menu bar and then click Paragraph.)

In this document, though, you need to indent only the main paragraphs 0.5 inches from the left margin. This left indent is a simple paragraph indent, which requires only a quick click on the Formatting toolbar's Increase Indent button. According to Marilee's notes, you need to indent all of the main paragraphs.

To indent a paragraph using the Increase Indent button:

1. Click anywhere in the first main paragraph, which begins "Start by digging a test hole . . . "

2. Click the **Increase Indent** button 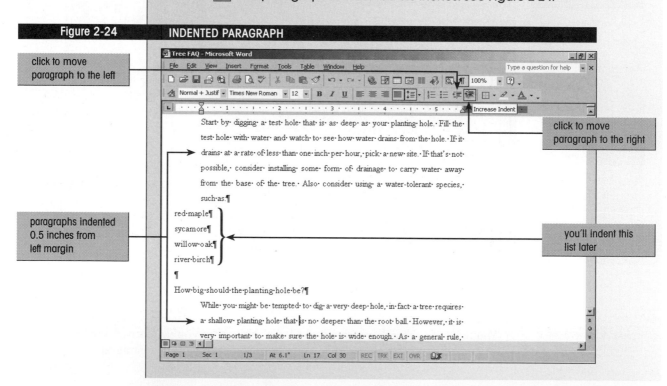 on the Formatting toolbar twice. (Don't click the Decrease Indent button by mistake.) The entire paragraph moves right 0.5 inches each time you click the Increase Indent button. The paragraph is indented 1 inch, 0.5 inches more than Marilee wants.

3. Click the **Decrease Indent** button on the Formatting toolbar to move the paragraph left 0.5 inches. The paragraph is now indented 0.5 inches from the left margin. Don't be concerned about the list of tree species. You will indent it later, when you format it as a bulleted list.

4. Move the insertion point to anywhere in the second main paragraph, which begins "While you might be tempted . . . "

5. Click . The paragraph is indented 0.5 inches. See Figure 2-24.

Figure 2-24	INDENTED PARAGRAPH

click to move paragraph to the left

paragraphs indented 0.5 inches from left margin

click to move paragraph to the right

you'll indent this list later

You can continue to indent and then justify each paragraph, or simply use the Format Painter command. The Format Painter allows you to copy both the indentation and alignment changes to all paragraphs in the document.

Using **Format Painter**

The **Format Painter** makes it easy to copy all the formatting features of one paragraph to other paragraphs. You can use this button to copy formatting to one or multiple items.

Using the Format Painter Button

- Select the item whose formatting you want to copy.
- To copy formatting to one item, click the Format Painter button and then drag the mouse pointer to select the item you want to format.
- To copy formatting to multiple items, double-click the Format Painter button and then drag the mouse pointer to each item you want to format. When you are finished, click the Format Painter button again to deselect it.

Use the Format Painter now to copy the formatting of the second paragraph to other main paragraphs. Begin by moving the insertion point to the paragraph whose format you want to copy.

To copy paragraph formatting with the Format Painter:

1. Verify that the insertion point is located in the second main paragraph, which begins "While you might be tempted . . ."

2. Double-click the **Format Painter** button 🖌 on the Standard toolbar. The Format Painter button will stay highlighted until you click the button again. When you move the pointer over text, the pointer changes to 🖌I to indicate that the format of the selected paragraph can be painted (or copied) onto another paragraph.

3. Scroll down, and then click anywhere in the third main paragraph, which begins "You may be accustomed . . ." The format of the third paragraph shifts to match the format of the first two main paragraphs. See Figure 2-25. Both paragraphs are now indented and justified. The Format Painter pointer is still visible.

| **Figure 2-25** | **FORMATS COPIED WITH FORMAT PAINTER** |

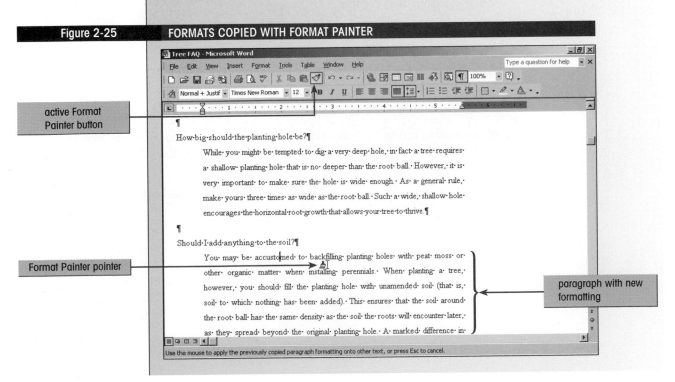

active Format Painter button

Format Painter pointer

paragraph with new formatting

4. Click the remaining paragraphs that are preceded by a question heading. Take care to click only the paragraphs below the question headings. Do not click the document title, the one-line questions, the lists, or the last paragraph in the document.

TROUBLE? If you click a paragraph and the formatting doesn't change to match the second paragraph, you single-clicked the Format Painter button rather than double-clicked it. Select a paragraph that has the desired format, double-click the Format Painter button, and then repeat Step 4.

TROUBLE? If you accidentally click a title or one line of a list, click the Undo button on the Standard toolbar to return the line to its original formatting. Then select a paragraph that has the desired format, double-click the Format Painter button, and finish copying the format to the desired paragraphs.

5. After you are finished formatting paragraphs with the Format Painter pointer, click ⟨⟩ to turn off the feature.

6. Save the document.

All the main paragraphs in the document are formatted with the correct indentation and alignment. Your next job is to make the lists easier to read by adding bullets and numbers.

Adding Bullets and Numbers

You can emphasize a list of items by adding a heavy dot, or **bullet**, before each item in the list. For consecutive items, you can use numbers instead of bullets. Marilee requests that you add bullets to the list of tree species on page 1 to make them stand out.

To apply bullets to a list of items:

1. Scroll to the top of the document until you see the list of tree species below the text "Also consider using a water-tolerant species such as:".

2. Select the four items in the list (from "red maple" to "river birch").

3. Click the **Bullets** button ⟨⟩ on the Formatting toolbar. A bullet, a dark circle, appears in front of each item. Each line indents to make room for the bullet.

4. In order to make the bullets align with the first paragraph, make sure the list is still selected, and then click the **Increase Indent** button ⟨⟩ on the Formatting toolbar. The bulleted list moves to the right.

5. Click anywhere within the document window to deselect the text. Figure 2-26 shows the indented bulleted list.

Figure 2-26	INDENTED BULLETED LIST

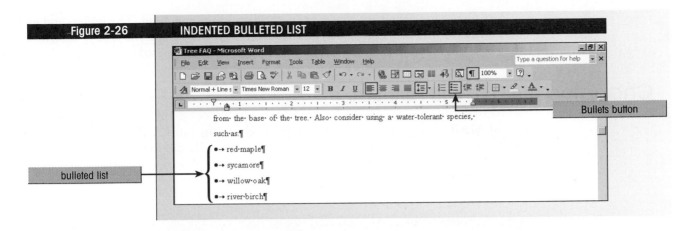

Next, you need to format the list of steps involved in planting a tree. Marilee asks you to format this information as a numbered list, an easy task thanks to the Numbering button, which automatically numbers selected paragraphs with consecutive numbers. If you insert a new paragraph, delete a paragraph, or reorder the paragraphs, Word automatically adjusts the numbers to make sure they remain consecutive.

To apply numbers to the list of items:

1. Scroll down until you see the list that begins "Remove any tags . . ." and ends with "of the planting hole."

2. Select the entire list.

3. Click the **Numbering** button 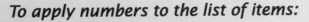 on the Formatting toolbar. Consecutive numbers appear in front of each item in the indented list. The list is indented, similar to the bulleted list. The list would look better if it was indented to align with the paragraph.

4. Click the **Increase Indent** button on the Formatting toolbar. The list moves to the right, so that the numbers align with the preceding paragraph.

5. Click anywhere in the document to deselect the text. Figure 2-27 shows the indented and numbered list.

Figure 2-27	INDENTED NUMBERED LIST

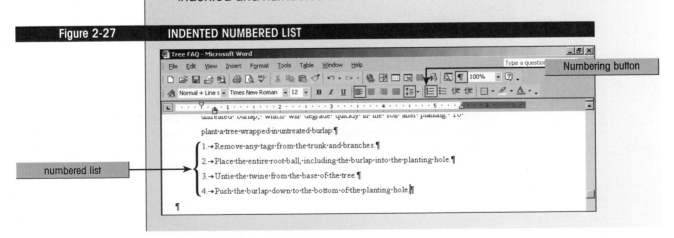

The text of the document is now properly aligned and indented. The bullets and numbers make the lists easy to read and give readers visual clues about the type of information they contain. Next, you need to adjust the formatting of individual words.

Changing the Font and Font Size

All of Marilee's remaining changes concern changing fonts, adjusting font sizes, and emphasizing text with font styles. The first step is to change the font of the title from 12-point Times New Roman to 14-point Arial. This will make the title stand out from the rest of the text.

REFERENCE WINDOW `RW`

Changing the Font and Font Size
- Select the text you want to change.
- Click the Font list arrow on the Formatting toolbar to display the list of fonts.
- Click the font you want to use.
- Click the Font Size list arrow, and click the font size you want to use.

or

- Select the text that you want to change.
- Click Format on the menu bar, and then click Font.
- In the Font tab of the Font dialog box, select the font and font size you want to use.
- Click the OK button.

Marilee wants you to change the font of the title as well as its size and style. To do this, you'll use the Formatting toolbar. Marilee wants you to use a **sans serif** font, which is a font that does not have the small horizontal lines (called serifs) at the tops and bottoms of the letters. Sans serif fonts are often used in titles so they contrast with the body text. Times New Roman is a serif font, and Arial is a sans serif font. The text you are reading now is a serif font, and the text in the following steps is a sans serif font.

To change the font of the title:

1. Press **Ctrl+Home** to move the insertion point to the beginning of the document, and then select the title **Common Questions About Trees**.

2. Click the **Font** list arrow on the Formatting toolbar. A list of available fonts appears in alphabetical order, with the name of the current font in the Font text box. See Figure 2-28. (Your list of fonts might be different from those shown.) Fonts that have been used recently might appear above a double line. Note that each name in the list is formatted with the relevant font. For example, "Arial" appears in the Arial font, and "Times New Roman" appears in the Times New Roman font.

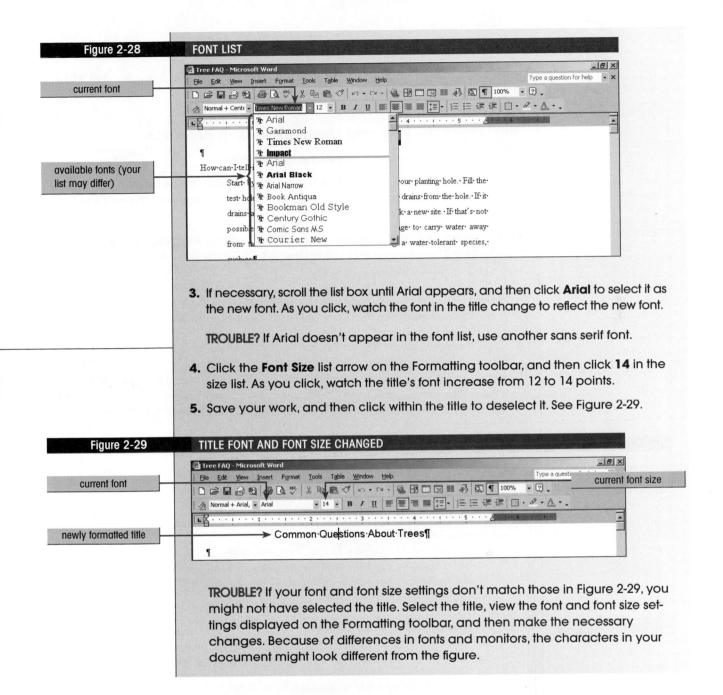

| Figure 2-28 | FONT LIST |

current font

available fonts (your list may differ)

3. If necessary, scroll the list box until Arial appears, and then click **Arial** to select it as the new font. As you click, watch the font in the title change to reflect the new font.

TROUBLE? If Arial doesn't appear in the font list, use another sans serif font.

4. Click the **Font Size** list arrow on the Formatting toolbar, and then click **14** in the size list. As you click, watch the title's font increase from 12 to 14 points.

5. Save your work, and then click within the title to deselect it. See Figure 2-29.

| Figure 2-29 | TITLE FONT AND FONT SIZE CHANGED |

current font

current font size

newly formatted title

Common Questions About Trees¶

TROUBLE? If your font and font size settings don't match those in Figure 2-29, you might not have selected the title. Select the title, view the font and font size settings displayed on the Formatting toolbar, and then make the necessary changes. Because of differences in fonts and monitors, the characters in your document might look different from the figure.

Emphasizing **Text with Boldface, Underlining, and Italics**

You can emphasize words in your document with boldface, underlining, or italics. These styles help make specific thoughts, ideas, words, or phrases stand out. (You can also add special effects such as shadows to characters.) Marilee marked a few words on the document draft (shown in Figure 2-1) that need this kind of special emphasis. You add boldface, underlining, or italics by using the relevant buttons on the Formatting toolbar. These buttons are **toggle buttons**, which means you can click them once to format the selected text, and then click again to remove the formatting from the selected text.

Bolding Text

Marilee wants to draw attention to the title and all of the question headings. You will do this by bolding them.

To format the title and the questions in boldface:

1. Select the title **Common Questions About Trees**.

2. Press and hold **Ctrl**, and then select the first question in the document ("How can I tell if I've picked a site with good drainage?"). Both the title and the first question are now selected.

3. Hold down **Ctrl** and select the remaining questions. To display more of the document, use the down arrow on the vertical scroll bar while you continue to hold down the Ctrl key.

   TROUBLE? If you accidentally select something other than a question, keep Ctrl pressed while you click the incorrect item. This should deselect the incorrect item.

4. Click the **Bold** button **B** on the Formatting toolbar, and then click anywhere in the document to deselect the text. The title and the questions appear in bold, as shown in Figure 2-30. After reviewing this change, you wonder if the title would look better without boldface. You can easily remove boldface by selecting the text and clicking the Bold button again to turn, or toggle, off boldfacing.

Figure 2-30   **TEXT IN BOLDFACE**

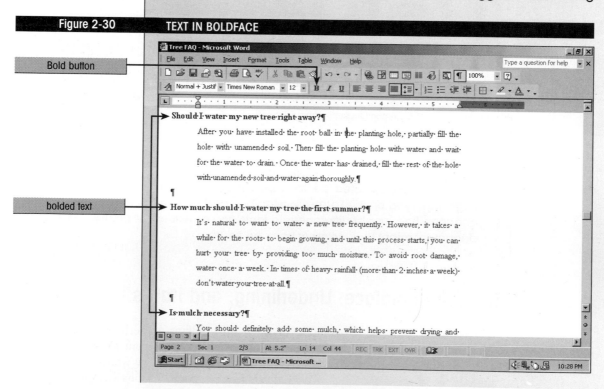

5. To remove the boldface, select the title, and then click **B**. The title now appears without boldface. You decide you prefer to emphasize the title with boldface after all.

6. Verify that the title is still selected, and then click **B**. The title appears in boldface again.

Underlining Text

The Underline button works in the same way as the Bold button. Marilee's edits indicate that the word "Note" should be inserted and underlined at the beginning of the final paragraph. Using the Underline button, you'll make both of these changes at the same time.

To underline text:

1. Press **Ctrl+End** to move the insertion point to the end of the document. Then move the insertion point to the left of the word "Any" in the first line of the final paragraph.

2. Click the **Underline** button **U** on the Formatting toolbar to turn on underlining. The Underline button remains highlighted. Whatever text you type now will be underlined on your screen and in your printed document.

3. Type **Note:** and then click **U** to turn off underlining. See how the Underline button is no longer pressed, and "Note:" is now underlined.

4. Press the **spacebar**. See Figure 2-31.

| Figure 2-31 | WORD TYPED WITH UNDERLINE |

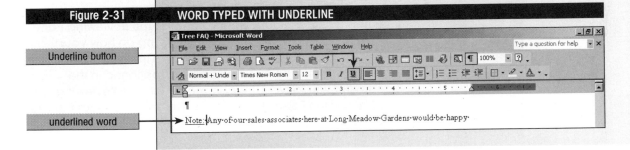

Italicizing Text

Next, you'll format each instance of "Long Meadow Gardens" in italics. This helps draw attention to the company name.

To italicize the company name:

1. Scroll up to the third to last question on the first page ("Do I have to do anything to the tree before planting?").

2. In the first line below the question, select **Long Meadow Gardens**.

3. Click the **Italic** button **I** on the Formatting toolbar. The company name changes from regular to italic text. In the next step, you'll learn a useful method for repeating the task you just performed.

4. Scroll down to the last paragraph of the document, select the company name, and then press the **F4** key. Keep in mind that you can use the F4 key to repeat your most recent action. It is especially helpful when formatting parts of a document.

5. Save the document.

Adding Comments

Peter stops by your desk to review your work. He's happy with the document's appearance, but wonders if he should add some information about fertilizing new trees. He asks you to insert a note to Marilee about this using Word's Comment feature. A **comment** is an electronic version of an adhesive note that you might attach to a piece of paper. To attach a comment to a Word document, select a block of text, click Comment on the Insert menu, and then type your comment in the Reviewing Pane. To display the comment, place the mouse pointer over text to which a comment has been attached. Comments are very useful when you are exchanging Word documents with co-workers electronically, either via e-mail or on floppies, because they allow you to make notes or queries without affecting the document itself.

You'll attach Peter's comment to the document title so that Marilee will be sure to see it as soon as she opens the document.

To attach a comment:

1. Scroll up to the top of the document, and then select the title **Common Questions About Trees**.

2. Click **Insert** on the menu bar, and then click **Comment**. The Reviewing Pane opens at the bottom of the document window. Depending on how your computer is set up, you might see your name, as well as the current date and time in the Reviewing Pane. The insertion point is positioned in the Reviewing Pane, ready for you to type the comment. Also, the Reviewing toolbar is displayed below the Formatting toolbar. Finally, notice that the title is enclosed in brackets. See Figure 2-32.

Figure 2-32   INSERTING A COMMENT

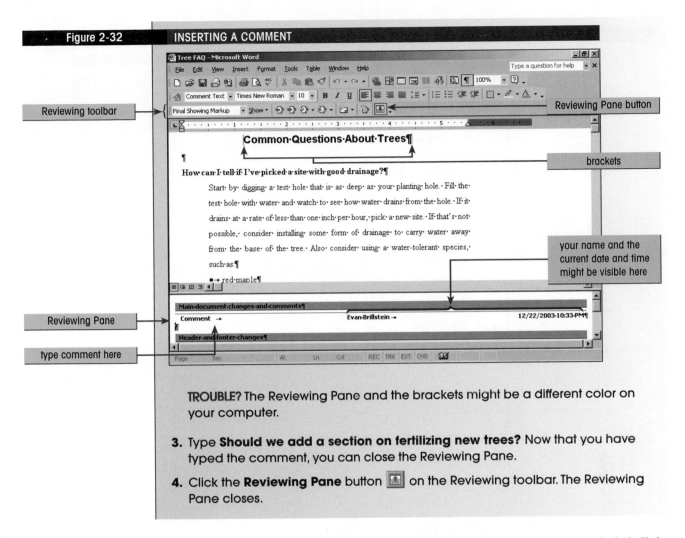

Reviewing toolbar

Reviewing Pane button

brackets

your name and the current date and time might be visible here

Reviewing Pane

type comment here

TROUBLE? The Reviewing Pane and the brackets might be a different color on your computer.

3. Type **Should we add a section on fertilizing new trees?** Now that you have typed the comment, you can close the Reviewing Pane.

4. Click the **Reviewing Pane** button on the Reviewing toolbar. The Reviewing Pane closes.

After you insert a comment, you should display it once to make sure you included all the necessary information.

To display a comment:

1. Move the mouse pointer over the title. The comment is displayed in a box over the title. Depending on how your computer is set up, you might see your name in the comment, as well as the date and time the comment was attached. See Figure 2-33.

Figure 2-33 | VIEWING A COMMENT

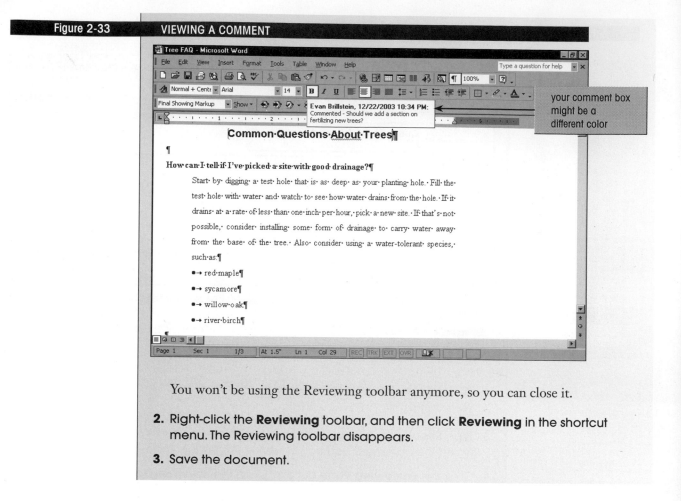

You won't be using the Reviewing toolbar anymore, so you can close it.

2. Right-click the **Reviewing** toolbar, and then click **Reviewing** in the shortcut menu. The Reviewing toolbar disappears.

3. Save the document.

Previewing Formatted Text

You have made all the editing and formatting changes that Marilee requested for the FAQ. It's helpful to preview a document after formatting it, because the Print Preview window makes it easy to spot text that is not aligned correctly.

To preview and print the document:

1. Click the **Print Preview** button on the Standard toolbar and examine the first page of the document. Notice the box in the right margin of the document, indicating that a comment has been attached to the document title. Use the vertical scroll bar to display the second page. (If you notice any formatting errors, click the Close button on the Print Preview toolbar, correct the errors in Normal view, save your changes, and then return to the Print Preview window.)

2. Click the **Print** button on the Print Preview toolbar. After a pause, the document prints. Note that the comment you inserted into the document earlier is not printed.

3. Click the **Close** button on the Print Preview toolbar.

4. Close the document and then close Word.

You now have a hard copy of the final FAQ, as shown in Figure 2-34.

Figure 2-34 FINAL VERSION OF TREE FAQ DOCUMENT

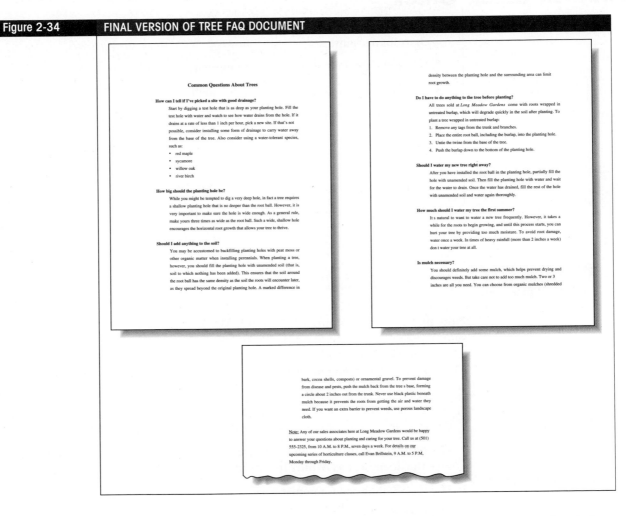

In this tutorial, you have helped Peter edit and format the FAQ that will be handed out to all customers purchasing a tree at Long Meadow Gardens. Peter will e-mail the file to Marilee later so that she can review your work and read the comment you attached.

Session 2.2 QUICK CHECK

1. What are Word's default margins for the left and right margins? For the top and bottom margins?

2. Describe the four types of text alignment.

3. Explain how to indent a paragraph 1 inch or more from the left margin.

4. Describe a situation in which you would use the Format Painter.

5. Explain how to add underlining to a word as you type it.

6. Explain how to transform a series of short paragraphs into a numbered list.

7. Explain how to format a title in 14-point Arial.

8. Describe the steps involved in changing the line spacing in a document.

REVIEW ASSIGNMENTS

Now that you have completed the FAQ, Marilee asks you to help her create a statement summarizing customer accounts for the Long Meadow Garden's wholesale nursery. She would also like you to create a document that contains contact information for Long Meadow Gardens. Remember to use the Undo and Redo buttons as you work to correct any errors.

1. If necessary, start Word, make sure your Data Disk is in the appropriate disk drive, and check your screen to make sure your settings match those in the tutorial.

2. Open the file **Statmnt** from the Review folder for Tutorial 2 on your Data Disk, and save the document as **Monthly Statement** in the same folder.

3. Use the Spelling and Grammar checker to correct any spelling or grammatical errors. If the Suggestions list box does not include the correct replacement, click outside the Spelling and Grammar dialog box, type the correction yourself, click Resume in the Spelling and Grammar dialog box, and continue checking the document.

4. Proofread the document carefully to check for any additional errors. Look for two words that are spelled correctly but used improperly.

5. Change the right margin to 2 inches using the Page Setup dialog box.

Explore

6. Change the left margin using the ruler in Print Layout view, as follows:
   a. Select the entire document.
   b. Position the pointer on the small gray square on the ruler at the left margin. A ScreenTip with the words "Left Indent" appears.
   c. Press and hold down the mouse button. A vertical dotted line appears in the document window, indicating the current left margin. Drag the margin left to the 0.5-inch mark on the ruler, and then release the mouse button.

7. Make all edits and formatting changes shown in Figure 2-35, and save your work.

Figure 2-35

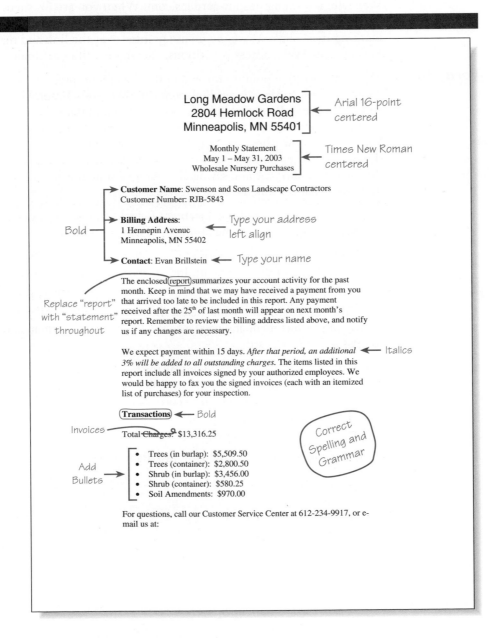

8. Remove any Smart Tags in the document.

Explore

9. When you type Web addresses or e-mail addresses in a document, Word automatically formats them as links. When you click a Web address formatted as a link, Windows automatically opens a Web browser (such as Microsoft Internet Explorer) and, if your computer is connected to the Internet, displays that Web page. If you click an e-mail address formatted as a link, Windows opens a program where you can type an e-mail message. The address you clicked is automatically included as the recipient of the e-mail. You'll see how this works as you add a Web address and e-mail address to the statement. In the address centered at the top of the document, click at the end of the ZIP code, add a new line, and then type the address for the company's Web site: www.longmeadowgardens.com. When you are finished, press Enter. Notice that as soon as you press Enter, Word formats the address in blue with an underline, marking it as a link. Move the mouse pointer over the link and read the ScreenTip. Because this Web address is fictitious, clicking it will not actually display a Web page.

Explore

10. Move the insertion point to the end of the document, press the spacebar, type long_meadow_gardens@worldlink.com and then press Enter. Word formats the e-mail address as a link. Press and hold the Ctrl button and then click the link. (If you see a message asking if you want to make Outlook Express your default mail client, click No.) You see a window where you could type an e-mail message to Long Meadow Gardens. (If your computer is not set up for e-mail, close any error messages that open.) Close the e-mail window without saving any changes. The link is now formatted in purple, indicating that the link has been clicked.

11 Move the last sentence of the document (which begins "For questions, call . . . ") to a new paragraph, just above the heading "Transactions".

12. Select the last Transactions portion of the document, from the heading "Transactions" down to the end of the document. Indent the selected text 1 inch by clicking the Increase Indent button twice.

13. Open the Clipboard Task Pane. Select the company name, address, and Web address at the top of the document and copy it to the Clipboard, and then copy the company e-mail address to the Clipboard.

Explore

14. Open a new, blank document and display the Clipboard Task Pane. In the Clipboard Task Pane, click the company address to insert this information at the top of the document. Insert two blank lines, type "Send all e-mail correspondence to YOUR NAME:" (replace YOUR NAME with your first and last name). Type a space and then, in the Clipboard Task Pane, click the company e-mail address. Type a period at the end of the e-mail address.

15. Clear the contents of the Clipboard Task Pane and then close the Task Pane.

Explore

16. If necessary, switch to Print Layout view. Then attach the following comment to the company name: "Marilee, please let me know how you want this document formatted." Notice that in Print Layout view you type the comment in a small comment window directly in the margin. Switch to Normal view, and display the comment by positioning the pointer over the company name.

17. Save the document as **LMG Contact Information** in the Review folder for Tutorial 2. Print and close the document.

18. Save the Monthly Statement document, preview and print it, and then close it. Also close the Clipboard Task Pane, if necessary. Then exit Word.

CASE PROBLEMS

Case 1. Authorization Form for Gygs and Bytes Melissa Martinez is the purchasing manager for Gygs and Bytes, a wholesale distributor of computer parts based in Portland, Oregon. Most of the company's business is conducted via catalog or through the company's Web site, but local customers sometimes drop by to pick up small orders. In the past Melissa has had problems determining which of her customers' employees were authorized to sign credit invoices. To avoid confusion, she has asked all local customers to complete a form listing employees who are authorized to sign invoices. She plans to place the completed forms in a binder at the main desk, so the receptionist at Gygs and Bytes can find the information quickly.

1. Open the file **Form** from the Cases folder for Tutorial 2 on your Data Disk, and save the file as **Authorization Form** in the same folder.

Explore

2. Correct any spelling or grammar errors. Ignore any words that are spelled correctly, but that are not included in Word's dictionary. When the Spelling and Grammar Checker highlights the word "sining", click the appropriate word in the Suggestions box, and then click Change.

Explore

3. If necessary, read Steps 9 and 10 in the Review Assignments to learn about adding Web addresses and e-mail addresses to a document. Below the company's mailing address, add the company Web address in all uppercase: WWW.G&B.NET.

4. Change the top and left margins to 1.5 inches.

5. Center the first five lines of the document (containing the form title and the company address).

6. Format the first line of the document (the form title) in 16-point Arial, with italics.

7. Format lines 2 through 5 (the address, including the Web address) in 12-point Arial.

Explore   8. Replace all instances of G&B, except the first one (in the Web address), with the complete company name, Gygs and Bytes. Use the Find Next button to skip an instance of the search text.

9. Format the blank ruled lines as a numbered list. Customers will use these blank lines to write in the names of authorized employees.

Explore   10. Format the entire document using 1.5 spacing. Then triple-space the numbered list (with the blank lines) and the Signature and Title lines as follows:
    a. Select the numbered list with the blank lines.
    b. Triple-space the selected text using the line spacing button on the Formatting toolbar.
    c. Select the "Signed:" and the "Title:" lines, and then press F4.

11. Save the document.

12. Drag "Customer Number:" up to position it above "Customer Name".

Explore   13. Select "Customer Name:", "Customer Number:", and "Address:". Press Ctrl+B to format the selected text in bold. Note that it is sometimes easier to use this keyboard shortcut instead of the Bold button on the Formatting toolbar.

14. Delete the phrase "all employees" and replace it with "all authorized personnel".

Explore   15. Select the phrase "all authorized personnel will be required to show a photo I.D." Press Ctrl+I to format the selected text in italics. It is sometimes easier to use this keyboard shortcut instead of the Italic button on the Formatting toolbar.

16. Insert your name in the form, in the "Customer Name:" line. Format your name without boldface, if necessary.

17. Insert your address, left aligned, without bold, below the heading "Address:".

18. Click the Print Preview button on the Standard toolbar to check your work.

Explore   19. Click the Shrink to Fit button on the Print Preview toolbar to reduce the entire document to one page. Word reduces the font sizes slightly in order to fit the entire form on one page. Close the Print Preview window and save your work.

Explore   20. Use the Print command on the File menu to open the Print dialog box. Print two copies of the document by changing the Number of copies setting in the Print dialog box.

Explore   21. You can find out the number of words in your documents by using the Word Count command on the Tools menu. Use this command to determine the number of words in the document, and then write that number in the upper-right corner of the printout.

22. Save and close the document, and then exit Word.

Case 2. Advertising Brochure for the CCW Web Site The *Carson College Weekly* is a student-run newspaper published through the Carson College Student Services Association. The newspaper is distributed around campus each Friday. The online version of the newspaper is posted on the CCW Web site on Thursdays. Local businesses have a long-established tradition of advertising in the print version of the newspaper, and the paper's advertising manager, Noah McCormick, would like to ensure that this same tradition carries over to the online newspaper. When he sends out the monthly statements to his print advertisers, he would like to include a one-page brochure encouraging them to purchase an online ad. He has copied the text of the brochure from the CCW Web site and saved it as unformatted text in a Word document.

1. Open the file **CCW** from the Cases folder for Tutorial 2 on your Data Disk, and save the file as **CCW Brochure** in the same folder.

2. Correct any spelling or grammar errors. Take time to make sure the right correction is selected in the Suggestions list box before you click Change. Proofread for any words that are spelled correctly but used incorrectly.

Explore 3. If necessary, read Steps 9 and 10 in the Review Assignments to learn about adding Web addresses and e-mail addresses to a document. Below *Carson College Weekly*, add the newspaper's Web address in all uppercase: WWW.CARSON.CCW.EDU, and then press Enter. At the end of the document, insert a space, type "advertising@carson.ccw.edu", (without the quotation marks), type a period, and then press Enter.

4. In the second to last sentence, replace "the CCW Advertising Office" with your name.

5. Change the right margin to 1.5 inches and the left margin to 2 inches.

6. Format the entire document in 12-point Times New Roman.

7. Format the four paragraphs below "Did you know?" as a bulleted list.

8. Drag the third bullet (which begins "You can include . . . ") up to the top of the bulleted list.

9. Format the first two lines of the document using a font, font size, and alignment of your choice. Use bold or italics for emphasis.

10. Format the entire document using 1.5 line spacing.

11. Add a comment to the first line (*Carson College Weekly*) asking Noah if he would like you to leave a printed copy of the brochure in his mailbox. Close the Reviewing Pane and the Reviewing toolbar when you are finished.

12. Save your work, preview the document, and then switch back to Normal view to make any changes you think necessary.

13. Print the document.

14. Save and close the document, and then exit Word.

Case 3. *Productivity Training Summary for UpTime* Matt Patterson is UpTime's marketing director for the Northeast region. The company provides productivity training for large companies across the country. Matt wants to provide interested clients with a one-page summary of UpTime's productivity training sessions.

1. If necessary, start Word, make sure your Data Disk is in the appropriate disk drive, and check your screen to make sure your settings match those in the tutorials.

2. Open the file **UpTime** from the Tutorial 2 Cases folder on your Data Disk, and save it as **UpTime Training Summary** in the same folder.

3. Change the title at the beginning of the document to a 16-point sans serif font. Be sure to pick a font that looks professional and is easy to read. (Remember to use the Undo and Redo buttons as you work to correct any editing mistakes.)

4. Center and bold the title and Web address.

5. Delete the word "general" from the second sentence of the first paragraph after the document title.

6. Convert the list of training components following the first paragraph to an indented, numbered list.

7. Under the heading "Personal Productivity Training Seminar," delete the last sentence from the first paragraph, the one beginning with "This seminar improves".

8. Under the heading "Personal Productivity Training Seminar," delete the phrase "at the seminar" from the first sentence in the second paragraph.

9. In the first paragraph under the heading "Management Productivity Training," move the first sentence (beginning with "UpTime provides management training") to the end of the paragraph.

10. Switch the order of the first and second paragraphs under the "Field Services Technology and Training" heading.

11. Search for the text "your name", and replace it with your first and last name. Use the Bold button and the Underline button on the Formatting toolbar to format your name in boldface, with an underline.

12. Change the top margin to 1.5 inches.

13. Change the left margin to 1.75 inches.

14. Bold and italicize the heading "Personal Productivity Training Seminar" and then use the Format Painter to copy this heading's format to the headings "Management Productivity Training" and "Field Services Technology and Training". Turn off the Format Painter when you're finished.

Explore

15. Select both occurrences of the word "free" in the second paragraph under the "Field Services Technology and Training" heading. Press Ctrl+I to format the selected text in italics.

16. Save and preview the document.

17. Print the document, and then close the file, and exit Word.

Case 4. _Product Description for Ridge Top_ Thomas McGee is vice president of sales and marketing at Ridge Top, an outdoor and sporting-gear store in Conshohocken, Pennsylvania. Each year Thomas and his staff mail a description of new products to Ridge Top's regular customers. Thomas has asked you to edit and format the first few pages of this year's new products' description.

1. If necessary, start Word, make sure your Data Disk is in the appropriate disk drive, and check your screen to make sure your settings match those in the tutorials.

2. Open the file **Ridge** from the Tutorial 2 Cases folder on your Data Disk, and save it as **RidgeTop Guide** in the same folder.

3. Use the Spelling and Grammar checker to correct any errors in the document. Because of the nature of this document, it contains some words that the Word dictionary on your computer may not recognize. It also contains headings that the Spelling and Grammar checker may consider sentence fragments. As you use the Spelling and Grammar checker, use the Ignore All button, if necessary, to skip over brand names.

4. Delete the phrase "a great deal" from the first sentence of the paragraph below the heading "Snuggle Up to These Prices." (Remember to use the Undo and Redo buttons to correct any editing mistakes as you work.)

5. Reverse the order of the first two paragraphs under the heading, "You'll Eat Up the Prices of This Camp Cooking Gear!"

6. Cut the last sentence of the first full paragraph ("Prices are good through . . . ") from the document. Then move the insertion point to the end of the document, press the Enter key twice, and insert the cut sentence as a new paragraph. Format it in 12-point Arial, and italicize it.

7. Format the Ridge Top tip items as a numbered list.

Explore 8. Reorder the items under the "Ridge Top Tips" heading by moving the fourth product idea and the following blank paragraph to the top of the list.

9. Search for the text "your name", and replace with your first and last name.

Explore 10. Experiment with two special paragraph alignment options: first line and hanging. First, select everything from the heading "Ridge Top Guarantees Warmth at Cool Prices" through the paragraph just before the heading "Ridge Top Tips". Next, click Format on the menu bar, click Paragraph, click the Indents and Spacing tab if necessary, click the Help button in the upper-right corner of the dialog box, click the Special list arrow, and review the information on the special alignment options. Experiment with both the First line and the Hanging options. When you are finished, return the document to its original format by choosing the none option.

11. Justify all the paragraphs in the document. (*Hint*: To select all paragraphs in the document at one time, click Edit on the menu bar, and then click Select All.)

12. Replace all occurrences of "RidgeTop" with "Ridge Top". (You may have already made this correction when you checked spelling in the document.)

13. Apply a 12-point, bold, sans serif font to each of the headings. Be sure to pick a font that looks professional and is easy to read. Use the Format Painter to copy the formatting after you apply it once using the Font list box.

14. Change the title's and subtitle's font to the same font you used for the headings, except set the size to 16 point.

15. Bold the title and subtitle.

16. Underline the names and prices for all of the brand name products.

17. Save and preview the document.

18. Print the document, and then close the file, and exit Word.

INTERNET ASSIGNMENTS

Student Union

The purpose of the Internet Assignments is to challenge you to find information on the Internet that you can use to create effective documents. The actual assignments are updated and maintained on the Course Technology Web site. Log on to the Internet and use your Web browser to go to the Student Union on the New Perspectives Series site at **www.course.com/NewPerspectives/studentunion**. Click the Online Companions link, and then click the link for this text.

QUICK CHECK ANSWERS

Session 2.1

1. Click at the beginning of the document, and then click the Spelling and Grammar button on the Standard toolbar. In the Spelling and Grammar dialog box, review any errors highlighted in color. Grammatical errors appear in green; spelling errors appear in red. Review the possible corrections in the Suggestions list box. To accept a suggested correction, click it in the Suggestions list box. Then click Change to make the correction and continue searching the document for errors.

2. (a) $\downarrow$; (b) Ctrl+End; (c) Page Down

3. (a) Double-click the word; (b) click at the beginning of the block, and then drag until the entire block is selected; (c) double-click in the selection bar next to the paragraph, or triple-click in the paragraph.

4. (a) the blank space in the left margin area of the Document window that allows you to easily select entire lines or large blocks of text; (b) the button on the Standard toolbar that redoes an action you previously reversed using the Undo button; (c) the process of moving text by first selecting the text, and then pressing and holding the mouse button while moving the text to its new location in the document, and finally releasing the mouse button

5. You might use the Undo button to remove the bold formatting you had just applied to a word. You could then use the Redo button to restore the bold formatting to the word.

6. False

7. Cut and paste removes the selected material from its original location and inserts it in a new location. Copy and paste makes a copy of the selected material and inserts the copy in a new location; the original material remains in its original location.

8. Click Edit on the menu bar, click Replace, type the search text in the Find what text box, type the replacement text in the Replace with text box, click Find Next or click Replace all.

Session 2.2

1. The default top and bottom margins are 1 inch. The default left and right margins are 1.25 inches.

2. Align-left: each line flush left, ragged right; Align-right: each line flush right, ragged left; Center: each line centered, ragged right and left.; Justify: each line flush left and flush right

4. You might use the Format Painter to copy the formatting of a heading to the other headings in the document.

5. Click the Underline button on the Formatting toolbar, type the word, and then click the Underline button again to turn off underlining.

6. Select the paragraphs, and then click the Numbering button on the Formatting toolbar.

7. Select the title, click the Font list arrow, and click Arial in the list of fonts. Then click the Font Size list arrow, and click 14.

8. Select the text you want to change, click the Line Spacing list arrow on the Formatting toolbar, and then click the line spacing option you want. Or select the text, and then press Ctrl+1 for single spacing, Ctrl+5 for 1.5 line spacing, or Ctrl+2 for double spacing.

In this tutorial you will:

- Set tab stops

- Divide a document into sections

- Change the vertical alignment of a section

- Center a page between the top and bottom margins

- Create a header with page numbers

- Create a table

- Sort the rows in a table

- Modify a table's structure

- Format a table

CREATING
A MULTIPLE-PAGE REPORT

Writing a Recommendation for Tyger Networks

CASE

Tyger Networks

Tyger Networks is a consulting company in Madison, Wisconsin that specializes in setting up computer networks for small businesses and organizations. Susan Launspach, the program director at New Hope Social Services, recently contacted Tyger Networks about linking the computer networks at New Hope's three main offices. The offices are scattered throughout southern Wisconsin in Madison, Janesville, and Milwaukee. Each office has its own self-contained computer network. To make it easier for a social worker in one office to access data stored on a computer in another office, Susan would like to establish some kind of connection between the three networks.

Caitilyn Waller, an account manager at Tyger Networks, is responsible for the New Hope account. In a phone call, she explained to Susan that connecting the three offices will create a new type of a network known as a wide area network (WAN). Because Susan is unfamiliar with networking terminology, Caitilyn offered to write a report that summarizes the options for creating this type of a network. Working with a task force of sales and technical personnel, Caitilyn compiled the necessary information in a multipage document. Now Caitilyn would like you to help her finish formatting the report. She also needs some help adding a table to the end of the report. Once the report is completed, Susan will present it to the board of directors at New Hope Social Services.

In this tutorial, you will format the report's title page so that it has a different layout from the rest of the report. The title page will contain only the title and subtitle and will not have page numbers like the rest of the report. You also will add a table to the report that summarizes the costs involved in creating a WAN.

SESSION 3.1

In this session you will review the task force's recommendation report. Then you will learn how to set tab stops, divide a document into sections, center a page between the top and bottom margins, create a header, and create a table.

Planning the Document

As head of the task force, Caitilyn divided the responsibility for the report among the members of the group. Each person gathered information about one topic and wrote the appropriate section of the report. Then Caitilyn compiled all the information into a coherent and unified report. In addition, she took care to follow the company's guidelines for content, organization, style, and format.

Because Caitilyn knows that some members of the New Hope board of directors will not have time to read the entire report, she began the report with an executive summary. The body of the report provides an in-depth explanation of the options for establishing a WAN. At the end of the report, she summarizes the costs of these options. The report's style follows established standards of business writing, and emphasizes clarity, simplicity, and directness.

In accordance with the company style guide, Caitilyn's report will begin with a title page, with the text centered between the top and bottom margins. Every page except the title page will include a line of text at the top, giving a descriptive name for the report, as well as the page number. The text and headings will be formatted to match all reports created at Tyger Networks, and will follow company guidelines for layout and text style.

Opening the Report

Caitilyn already has combined the individual sections into one document. She also has begun formatting the report by changing the font size of headings, adding elements such as bold and italics, and by indenting paragraphs. You'll open the document and perform the remaining formatting tasks on page 1, as indicated in Figure 3-1.

Figure 3-1	INITIAL DRAFT OF REPORT (PAGE 1)

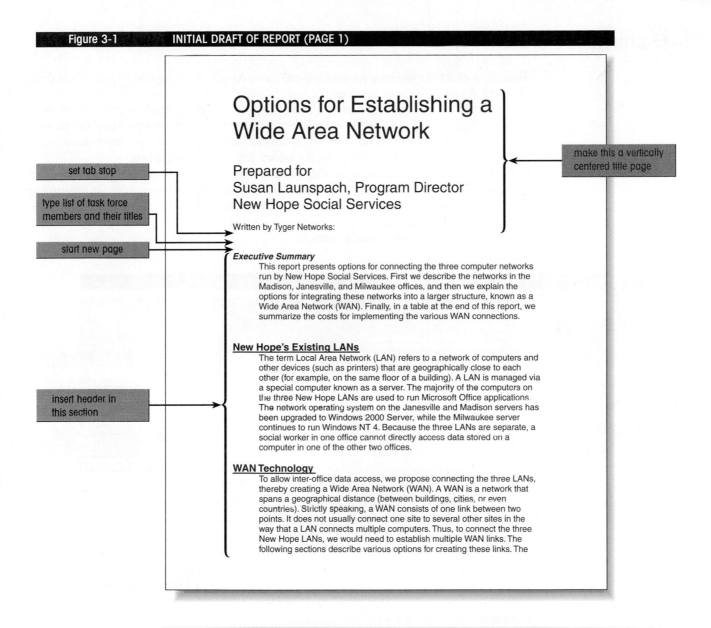

To open the document:

1. Start Word, and place your Data Disk in the appropriate drive.

2. Open the file **WAN** from the Tutorial folder in the Tutorial.03 folder on your Data Disk.

3. To avoid altering the original file, save the document as **New Hope WAN Report** in the Tutorial folder in the Tutorial.03 folder on your Data Disk.

4. Make sure your screen matches the figures in this tutorial. In particular, be sure to display the nonprinting characters and switch to Normal view if necessary.

Setting Tab Stops

Tabs are useful for indenting paragraphs and for vertically aligning text or numerical data in columns. A **tab** adds space between the margin and text in a column or between text in one column and text in another column. A **tab stop** is the location where text moves when you press the Tab key. When the Show/Hide button ¶ is pressed, the nonprinting tab character appears wherever you press the Tab key. A tab character is just like any other character you type; you can delete it by pressing the Backspace key or the Delete key.

Word provides several **tab-stop alignment styles**. The five major styles are left, center, right, decimal, and bar, as shown in Figure 3-2. The first three tab-stop styles position text in a similar way to the Align Left, Center, and Align Right buttons on the Formatting toolbar. The difference is that with a tab, you determine line by line precisely where the left, center, or right alignment should occur.

Figure 3-2	TAB STOP ALIGNMENT STYLES

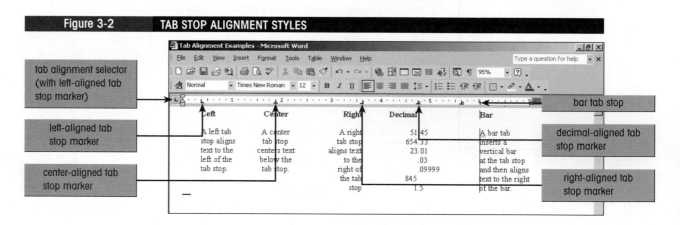

The default tab stops on the ruler are **Left tabs,** which position the left edge of text at the tab stop and extend the text to the right. **Center tabs** position text so that it's centered evenly on both sides of the tab stop. **Right tabs** position the right edge of text at the tab stop and extend the text to the left. **Decimal tabs** position numbers so that their decimal points are aligned at the tab stop. **Bar tabs** insert a vertical bar at the tab stop and then align text to the right of the bar. In addition, you also can use a **First Line Indent tab,** which indents the first line of a paragraph, and the **Hanging Indent tab,** which indents every line of a paragraph *except* the first line.

REFERENCE WINDOW **RW**

Setting Tab Stops

- To change tab stops for existing text, select the text for which you want to change the tab alignment, click the tab alignment selector on the far left of the horizontal ruler until the appropriate tab-stop alignment style appears, and then click the horizontal ruler where you want to set the tab stop.
- To set tab stops before typing text, move the insertion point to the part of the document where you want to change tab stops, click the tab alignment selector on the far left of the horizontal ruler until the appropriate tab-stop alignment style appears, click the horizontal ruler where you want to set the tab stop, and then type the text, pressing the Tab key to move from one tab stop to another.
- To remove a tab stop, click it and drag it off the horizontal ruler.

The Word default tab-stop settings are every one-half inch, as indicated by the small gray tick marks at the bottom of the ruler shown in Figure 3-3. You set a new tab stop by selecting a tab-stop alignment style (from the tab alignment selector at the left end of the horizontal ruler) and then clicking the horizontal ruler to insert the tab stop. You can remove a tab stop from the ruler by clicking it and dragging the tab stop off the ruler.

Figure 3-3	RULER WITH TAB STOPS

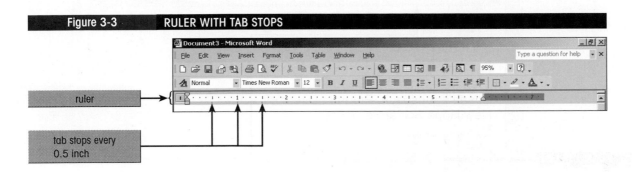

ruler

tab stops every 0.5 inch

You should never try to align columns of text by adding extra spaces with the spacebar. Although the text might seem precisely aligned in the document window, it might not be aligned when you print the document. Furthermore, if you edit the text, the extra spaces might disturb the alignment. However, if you edit text aligned with tabs, the alignment remains intact. If you want to align a lot of text in many columns, it is better to use a table, as described later in this tutorial.

To align columns using tabs, you can type some text, and press the Tab key. The insertion point then moves to the next tab stop to the right, where you can type more text. You can continue in this way until you type the first row of each column. Then you can press the Enter key, and begin typing the next row of each column. However, sometimes you'll find that text in a column stretches beyond the next default tab stop, and as a result the columns fail to line up evenly.

In the Tyger Networks report, you need to type the list of task force members and their titles. As you type, you'll discover whether Word's default tab stops are appropriate for this document, or whether you need to add a new tab stop.

To enter the task force list using tabs:

1. Verify that nonprinting characters are displayed, and then move the insertion point to the line below the text "Written by Tyger Networks:."

2. Type **Caitlyn Waller** and then press the **Tab** key. A tab character appears, and the insertion point moves to the first tab stop after the *r* in "Waller." This tab stop is located at the 1.5-inch mark on the horizontal ruler. See Figure 3-4.

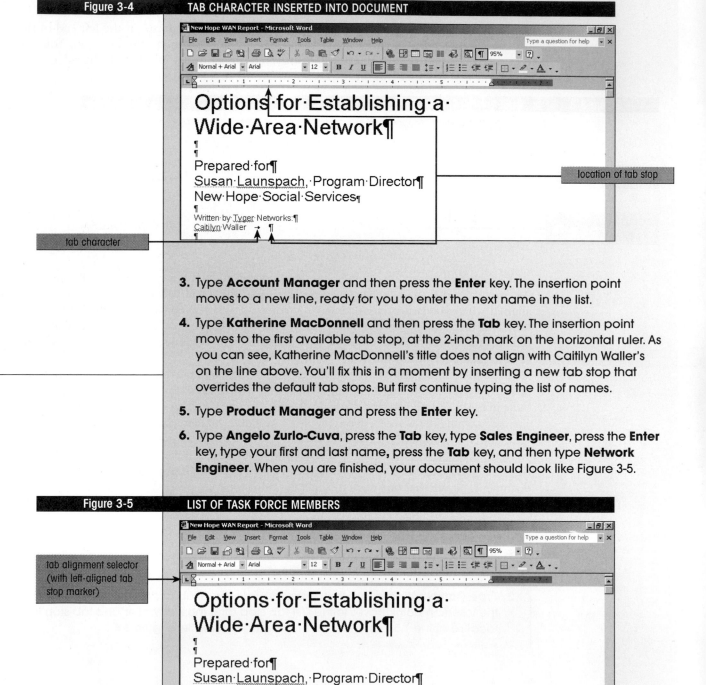

Figure 3-4 TAB CHARACTER INSERTED INTO DOCUMENT

location of tab stop

tab character

3. Type **Account Manager** and then press the **Enter** key. The insertion point moves to a new line, ready for you to enter the next name in the list.

4. Type **Katherine MacDonnell** and then press the **Tab** key. The insertion point moves to the first available tab stop, at the 2-inch mark on the horizontal ruler. As you can see, Katherine MacDonnell's title does not align with Caitlyn Waller's on the line above. You'll fix this in a moment by inserting a new tab stop that overrides the default tab stops. But first continue typing the list of names.

5. Type **Product Manager** and press the **Enter** key.

6. Type **Angelo Zurlo-Cuva**, press the **Tab** key, type **Sales Engineer**, press the **Enter** key, type your first and last name, press the **Tab** key, and then type **Network Engineer**. When you are finished, your document should look like Figure 3-5.

Figure 3-5 LIST OF TASK FORCE MEMBERS

tab alignment selector (with left-aligned tab stop marker)

your first and last name should appear here

titles do not align neatly

The list of names and titles is not aligned properly. You'll fix this by inserting a new tab stop.

To add a new tab stop to the horizontal ruler:

1. Click and drag the mouse pointer to select the list of task force members and titles.

2. Make sure the current tab-stop alignment style is left tab [L], as shown in Figure 3-5. If [L] is not selected, click the **tab alignment selector** one or more times until [L] appears.

3. Click the **tick mark** on the ruler that occurs at 2.5 inches. Word automatically inserts a left tab stop at that location and removes the tick marks to its left. The column of titles shifts to the new tab stop.

4. Deselect the highlighted text and then move the insertion point anywhere in the list of names and titles. See Figure 3-6.

Figure 3-6	LEFT TAB STOP ON RULER

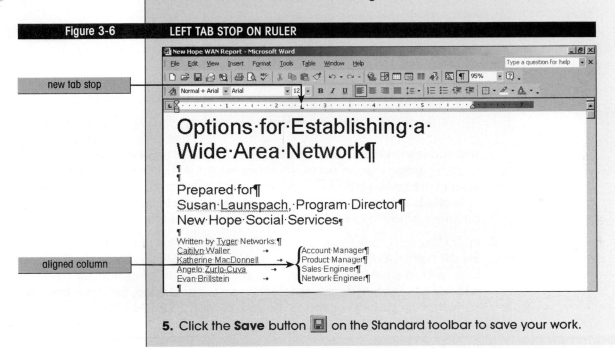

new tab stop

aligned column

5. Click the **Save** button on the Standard toolbar to save your work.

The two columns of information are now aligned, as Caitilyn requested. Notice that Word changed the tab stops only for the selected paragraphs, not for all the paragraphs in the document. Next, you need to change the layout of the title page.

Formatting the Document in Sections

According to the company guidelines, the title page of the report should be centered between the top and bottom margins of the page. To format the title page differently from the rest of the report, you need to divide the document into sections. A **section** is a unit or part of a document that can have its own page orientation, margins, headers, footers, and vertical alignment. Each section, in other words, is like a mini-document within a document.

To divide a document into sections, you insert a **section break** (a dotted line with the words "Section Break") that marks the point at which one section ends and another begins. Sections can start on a new page or continue on the same page. You can insert a section break with the Break command on the Insert menu.

To insert a section break after the title:

1. Position the insertion point immediately to the left of the "E" in the heading "Executive Summary." You want the text above this heading to be on a separate title page and the executive summary to begin on the second page of the report.

2. Click **Insert** on the menu bar, and then click **Break** to open the Break dialog box. See Figure 3-7.

Figure 3-7	BREAK DIALOG BOX

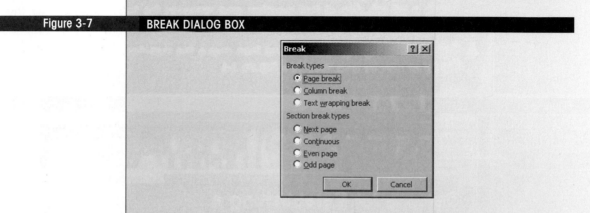

You can use this dialog box to insert several types of breaks into your document, including a **page break**, which moves the text after it onto a new page. Instead of inserting a page break, however, you will insert a section break that indicates both a new section and a new page. Later in this session, you will use another method to insert a page break into the document.

3. Under "Section break types" click the **Next page** option button, and then click the **OK** button. A double-dotted line and the words "Section Break (Next Page)" appear before the heading "Executive Summary," indicating that you have inserted a break that starts a new section on the next page. The status bar indicates that the insertion point is on page 2, section 2. See Figure 3-8.

Figure 3-8	SECTION BREAK

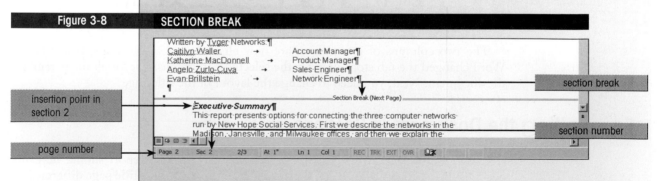

TROUBLE? If you see a single dotted line and the words "Page Break", you inserted a page break rather than a section break. Click the Undo button on the Standard toolbar, and then repeat Steps 1 through 3.

Now that the title page is a separate section and page from the rest of the report, you can make changes affecting only that section, leaving the rest of the document unchanged.

Changing the Vertical Alignment of a Section

You're ready to center the text of page 1 vertically on the page. But first you will switch to the Print Preview window, so you can more easily observe your changes to page 1.

To see the document in Print Preview:

1. Click the **Print Preview** button 🔎 on the Standard toolbar to open the Print Preview window.

2. Click the **Multiple Pages** button ▦ on the Print Preview toolbar, and then click and drag across the top three pages in the list box to select "1 × 3 Pages." The three pages of the report are reduced in size and appear side by side. See Figure 3-9. Although you cannot read the text on the pages, you can see the general layout.

Figure 3-9	REPORT IN PRINT PREVIEW WINDOW

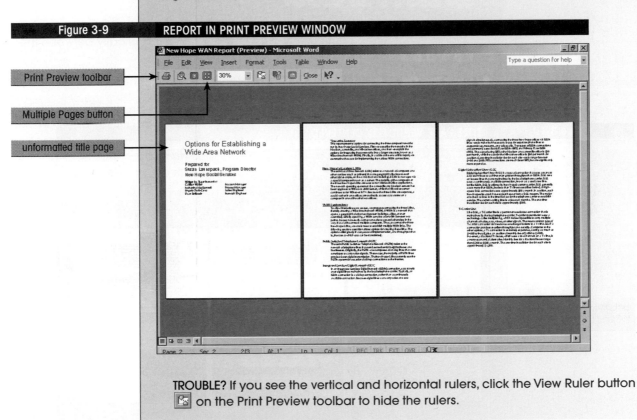

Print Preview toolbar

Multiple Pages button

unformatted title page

TROUBLE? If you see the vertical and horizontal rulers, click the View Ruler button 📇 on the Print Preview toolbar to hide the rulers.

Now you can change the vertical alignment to center the lines of text between the top and bottom margins. The **vertical alignment** specifies how a page of text is positioned on the page between the top and bottom margins—flush at the top, flush at the bottom, or centered between the top and bottom margins.

You'll center the title page text from within the Print Preview window.

To change the vertical alignment of the title page:

1. Click the **Magnifier** button 🔍 on the Print Preview toolbar once to deselect it.

2. Click the **leftmost page** in the Print Preview window to move the insertion point to page 1 (the title page). The status bar indicates that page 1 is the current page.

   TROUBLE? If the size of page 1 increases when you click it, you selected the Magnifier button in Step 1 instead of deselecting it. Click the Multiple Pages button on the Print Preview toolbar, drag to select "1 × 3 Pages," and then repeat Step 1.

3. Click **File** on the menu bar, and then click **Page Setup**. The Page Setup dialog box opens.

4. Click the **Layout** tab. In the Apply to list box, select **This section** (if it is not already selected) so that the layout change affects only the first section, not both sections, of your document.

5. Click the **Vertical alignment** list arrow, and then click **Center** to center the pages of the current section—in this case, just page 1—vertically between the top and bottom margins.

6. Click the **OK** button to return to the Print Preview window. The text of the title page is centered vertically, as shown in Figure 3-10.

Figure 3-10	TITLE PAGE VERTICALLY CENTERED

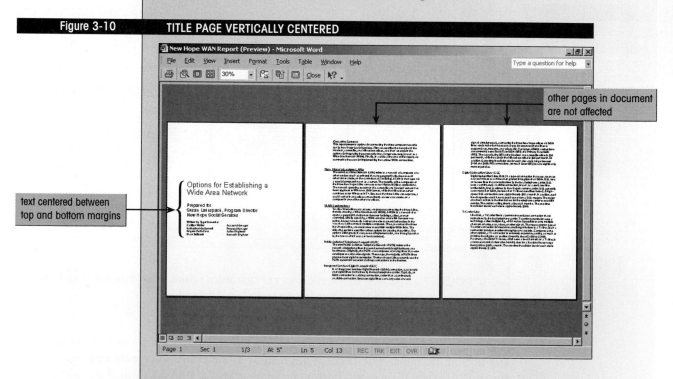

other pages in document are not affected

text centered between top and bottom margins

7. Click the **Close** button on the Print Preview toolbar to return to Normal view.

You have successfully centered the title page text. Next, you turn your attention to inserting a descriptive name for the report and the page number at the top of every page.

Adding Headers

The report guidelines at Tyger Networks require a short report title and the page number to be printed at the top of every page except the title page. Text that is printed at the top of every page is called a **header**. For example, the page number, tutorial number, and tutorial name printed at the top of the page you are reading is a header. Similarly, a **footer** is text that is printed at the bottom of every page. (You'll have a chance to work with footers in the Review Assignments at the end of this tutorial.)

When you insert a header or footer into a document, you switch to Header and Footer view. The Header and Footer toolbar is displayed, and the insertion point moves to the top of the document, where the header will appear. The main text is dimmed, indicating that it cannot be edited until you return to Normal or Print Layout view.

You'll create a header for the main body of the report (section 2) that prints "Options for Establishing a Wide Area Network" at the left margin and the page number at the right margin.

To insert a header for section 2:

1. Click anywhere after the section break, so that the insertion point is located in section 2 and not in section 1.

2. Click **View** on the menu bar, and then click **Header and Footer**. The Word window changes to Header and Footer view, and the Header and Footer toolbar appears in the document window. The header area appears in the top margin of your document surrounded by a dashed line and displays the words "Header -Section 2-". See Figure 3-11. (If the Header and Footer toolbar covers the header area, drag the toolbar below the header area, similar to its position in Figure 3-11.)

Figure 3-11	CREATING A HEADER

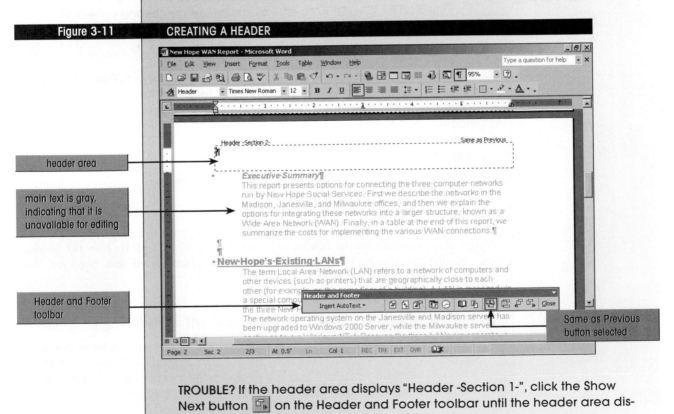

TROUBLE? If the header area displays "Header -Section 1-", click the Show Next button on the Header and Footer toolbar until the header area displays "Header -Section 2-".

TROUBLE? If the main text of the document doesn't appear on the screen, click the Show/Hide Document Text button 🖳 on the Header and Footer toolbar, and continue with Step 3.

3. Click the **Same as Previous** button 🖳 on the Header and Footer toolbar so that the button is *not* selected. When Same as Previous is selected, Word automatically inserts the same header text as for the previous section. You deselected it to ensure that the text of the current header applies only to the current section (section 2), and not to the previous section (section 1).

4. Type **Options for Establishing a Wide Area Network**. The title is automatically aligned on the left. See Figure 3-12.

Figure 3-12	HEADER TEXT

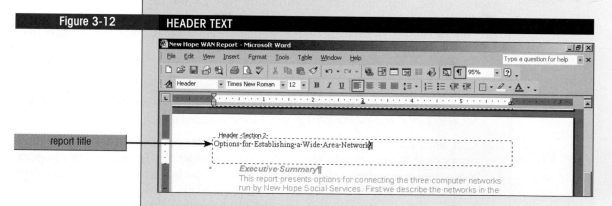

report title → Options·for·Establishing·a·Wide·Area·Network¶

5. Press the **Tab** key to move the insertion point to the right margin of the header area. (Notice that by default the header contains center and right-align tab stops.)

6. Type the word **Page** and press the **spacebar** once.

7. Click the **Insert Page Number** button 🔲 on the Header and Footer toolbar. The page number "2" appears at the right-aligned tab. The page number in the header looks like you simply typed the number 2, but you actually inserted a special instruction telling Word to insert the correct page number on each page. Now consecutive page numbers will print on each page of the header within this section.

8. Click the **Close** button on the Header and Footer toolbar to return to Normal view, and then save your changes.

Notice that you can't see the header in Normal view. To see exactly how the header will appear on the printed page, you will switch to the Print Preview window. *Note:* you can also use Print Layout view.

To view the header and margins in Print Preview:

1. Click the **Print Preview button** 🔍 on the Standard toolbar. The three pages of the document are displayed as they were earlier in the Print Preview window, although this time you can see a line of text at the top of pages 2 and 3. To read the header text, you need to increase the magnification.

2. If necessary, click the **Magnifier** button 🔍 on the Print Preview toolbar to select it.

3. Move the pointer over the second page of the document and then click the header text at the top of the page. The Print Preview window zooms in on the header text for page 2, as shown in Figure 3-13.

Figure 3-13	HEADER TEXT FOR PAGE 2 IN PRINT PREVIEW

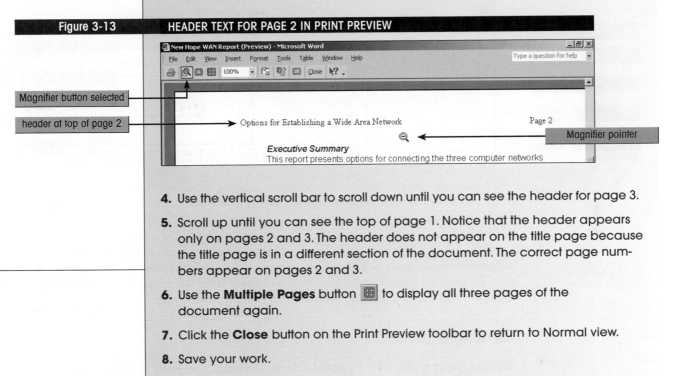

4. Use the vertical scroll bar to scroll down until you can see the header for page 3.

5. Scroll up until you can see the top of page 1. Notice that the header appears only on pages 2 and 3. The header does not appear on the title page because the title page is in a different section of the document. The correct page numbers appear on pages 2 and 3.

6. Use the **Multiple Pages** button to display all three pages of the document again.

7. Click the **Close** button on the Print Preview toolbar to return to Normal view.

8. Save your work.

The report now has the required header. You have formatted Caitilyn's report so that the results are professional-looking, clearly presented, and easy to read. Next, you will add a table that summarizes the costs of the various WAN options.

Inserting Tables

Using Word, you can quickly organize data and arrange text in an easy-to-read table format. A **table** is information arranged in horizontal rows and vertical columns. As shown in Figure 3-14, table rows are commonly referred to by number (row 1, row 2, and so forth), while columns are commonly referred to by letter (column A on the far left, then column B and so forth). However, you do not see row and column numbers on the screen. The area where a row and column intersect is called a **cell**. Each cell is identified by a column and row label. For example, the cell in the upper-left corner of a table is cell A1 (column A, row 1), the cell to the right of that is cell B1, the cell below cell A1 is A2, and so forth. The table's structure is shown by **gridlines**, which are light gray lines that define the rows and columns. By default, gridlines do not appear on the printed page. You can emphasize specific parts of a table on the printed page by adding a **border** (a line the prints along the side of a table cell).

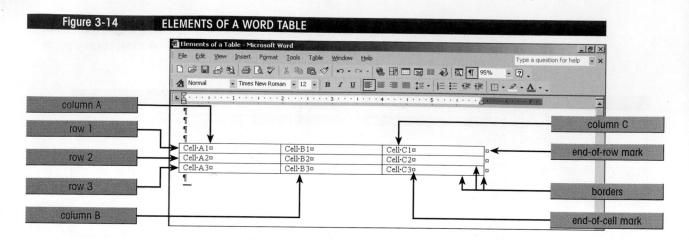

Figure 3-14 ELEMENTS OF A WORD TABLE

Depending on your needs, you can create a blank table and then insert information into it (as you'll do next), or you can convert existing text into a table (as you'll do in the Case Problems at the end of this tutorial).

You may be wondering why you can't use tabs to align text in columns. Tabs work well for smaller amounts of information, such as two columns with three or four rows, but tabs and columns become tedious and difficult to work with when you need to organize a larger amount of more complex information. The Word Table feature allows you to quickly organize data and to place text and graphics in a more legible format.

Creating a Table

You can create a table with equal column widths quickly by using the Insert Table button on the Standard toolbar. (You will use this technique to create the table Caitilyn requested.) You also can create a table by dragging the Draw Table pointer to draw the table structure you want. (You'll practice this method in the Case Problems.) However you create a table, you can modify it by using commands on the Table menu or the buttons on the Tables and Borders toolbar.

Caitilyn wants you to create a table that summarizes information in the Tyger Networks report. Figure 3-15 shows a sketch of what Caitilyn wants the table to look like. The table will allow the members of the New Hope board of directors to see at a glance the cost of each option. The top row of the table, called the **heading row**, identifies the type of information in each column.

Figure 3-15 TABLE SKETCH

Type of Connection	Monthly Charge
ISDN	$50 to $60
DSL	$80
T1	$1000 to $2000

Inserting a Page Break

Before you begin creating the table, you need to insert a page break so that the table will appear on a separate page.

Explore ▷

2. Select the entire document, click Table on the menu bar, point to Convert, and then click Text to Table. In the Convert Text to Table dialog box, make sure the settings indicate that the table should have three columns and that the text is separated by commas. Also, select the "AutoFit to contents" option button, to ensure that columns are sized appropriately, and then click the OK button. Word converts the list into a table.

3. Replace the name "Christian Brook" with your first and last name.

4. Insert a new row at the top of the table and insert some appropriate headings.

Explore ▷

5. When you need to format a table quickly, you can allow Word's AutoFormat command to do the work for you. Click anywhere in the table, click Table on the menu bar, and then click Table AutoFormat to open the Table AutoFormat dialog box. Scroll down the Table styles list box to see the available options. Click options that interest you, and observe the sample tables in the Preview box. Note that you can deselect the checkboxes in the "Apply special formats to" section to remove boldface or shading from columns or rows that don't require it. Select a table style that you think is appropriate for the Contacts table, deselect check boxes as you see fit, and then click the Apply button.

6. Sort the table alphabetically by column A.

Explore ▷

7. Place the pointer over the Table Resize handle, just outside the lower-right corner of the table. Drag the double-arrow pointer to increase the height and width of each cell to a size of your choice. Notice that all the parts of the table increase proportionally.

8. Save your work. Preview the table and then print it.

9. Close the document, and then exit Word.

Case 4. Brochure for Camp Winnemac Angela Freedman is the publicity director for Camp Winnemac, a sleep-away camp for girls located in Northern Michigan. She asks you to create an informational flier announcing the dates for Camp Winnemac's two summer sessions. She gives you a sketch, similar to the one shown in Figure 3-35. You decide to take advantage of the Word table features to structure the information in the sketch.

Figure 3-35

	Summer Sessions for Girls Ages 8 to 12	
Ultimate Sports Rock climbing, kayaking and white water rafting June 6 through July 2	**Equestrian Skills** Western and English style, for new and experienced riders July 6 through August 15	

Camp Winnemac

Camp Winnemac is located in Michigan's Northern Peninsula, and boasts over 140 acres of forests, streams, and trails. The campgrounds include a heated pool, a modern stable, eight log cabin dormitories, and a full-sized dining hall and kitchen. For information, contact Angela Freedman at 456-818-0000.

1. Open a new, blank document and save it as **Camp Winnemac** in the Cases folder for Tutorial 3.

2. If necessary, switch to Print Layout view and display rulers and the Tables and Borders toolbar.

3. Click the Draw Table button on the Tables and Borders toolbar, if necessary, to select the button and change the pointer to a pencil shape (the Draw Table pointer).

4. Select a single-line line style, with a line weight of 1½ points.

Explore 5. Click in the upper-left corner of the document (near the paragraph mark), and then drag down and to the right to draw a rectangle about 6 inches wide and 3.5 inches high.

Explore 6. Continue to use the Draw Table pointer to draw the columns and rows shown in Figure 3-35. For example, to draw the column border for the "Camp Winnemac" column, click at the top of the rectangle, where you want the column to begin, and drag down to the bottom of the rectangle. Use the same technique to draw rows. If you make a mistake, use the Undo button. To delete a border, click the Eraser button on the Tables and Borders toolbar, click the border you want to erase, and then click the Eraser button again to turn it off. Don't expect to draw the table perfectly the first time. You may have to practice awhile until you become comfortable with the Draw Table pointer, but once you can use it well, you will find it a helpful tool for creating complex tables. Click the Draw Table button on the toolbar again to turn it off.

Explore 7. In the left column, type the text "Camp Winnemac". With the pointer still in that cell, click the Change Text Direction button (on the Tables and Borders toolbar) twice to position the text vertically. Format the text in 26-point Times New Roman, and then center it in the cell using the Align Center option on the Tables and Borders toolbar. (*Hint*: You will probably have to adjust and readjust the row and column borders throughout this project, until all the elements of the table are positioned properly.)

8. Type the remaining text, as shown in Figure 3-35. Replace the name "Angela Freedman" with your own name. Use bold and italic as shown in Figure 3-35 to draw attention to key elements. Use the font styles, font sizes, and alignment options you think appropriate.

Explore

9. Click the Drawing button on the Standard toolbar to display the Drawing toolbar. Now you can insert the Camp Winnemac logo in the upper-right cell, using one of the tools on the Drawing toolbar. Click the upper-right cell, which at this point should be blank. Click the AutoShapes button on the Drawing toolbar, point to Basic Shapes, click the Sun shape. A box appears in the cell with the text "Create your drawing here." Click anywhere within the upper-right cell. The sun shape is inserted in the cell or somewhere nearby. The sun is selected, as indicated by the small circles, called selection handles, that surround it. If necessary, drag the sun to position it neatly within the cell. If the sun is not the right shape, click the lower-right selection handle, and drag up or down to adjust the size of the sun so that it fits within the cell borders more precisely. With the sun still selected, click the Fill Color list arrow on the Drawing toolbar, and then click a light pink square in the color palette.

10. Adjust column widths and row heights so that the table is attractive and easy to read.

Explore

11. Now that you have organized the information using the Word table tools, you can remove the borders so that the printed flier doesn't look like a table. Click the Table Move handle to select the entire table, click Table on the menu bar, click Table Properties, click the Table tab, click the Borders and Shading button, and then click the Borders tab, click the None option, click the OK button, and then click the OK button again. The borders are removed from the flier, leaving only the underlying gridlines, which will not appear on the printed page.

12. Save your work, preview the flier, make any necessary adjustments, print it, and then close the document and exit Word.

INTERNET ASSIGNMENTS

Student Union

The purpose of the Internet Assignments is to challenge you to find information on the Internet that you can use to create effective documents. The actual assignments are updated and maintained on the Course Technology Web site. Log on to the Internet and use your Web browser to go to the Student Union on the New Perspectives Series site at **www.course.com/NewPerspectives/studentunion**. Click the Online Companions link, and then click the link for this text.

QUICK | CHECK ANSWERS

Session 3.1

1. **a.** the location where text moves when you press the Tab key
   b. the intersection of a row and a column in a table
   c. information arranged in horizontal rows and vertical columns
   d. a tab stop that aligns numerical data on the decimal point
   e. a unit or part of a document that can have its own page orientation, margins, headers, footers, and vertical alignment

2. Insert a section break, move the insertion point within the section you want to align, click File, click Page Setup, click the Layout tab, select Center in the Vertical alignment list box, make sure "This section" is selected in the Apply to list box, and then click OK.

3. A header appears at the top of a page, whereas a footer appears at the bottom of a page.

4. Move the insertion point to the location where you want the table to appear. Click the Insert Table button on the Standard toolbar. In the grid, click and drag to select four columns and six rows, and then release the mouse button.

5. If the insertion point is in the cell at the far right in a row, press the Tab key. Otherwise, press the ↓ key.

6. Click View on the menu bar, click Header and Footer, verify that the insertion point is located in the Header area, press Tab to move the insertion point to where you want the page number to appear, and then click the Insert Page Number button on the Header and Footer toolbar.

7. Select the text whose tab alignment you want to change, click the tab alignment selector on the far left of the horizontal ruler until the appropriate tab stop alignment style appears, and then click in the horizontal ruler where you want to set the new tab stop.

8. You may want to divide a document into sections if you wanted to center only part of the document between the top and bottom margins.

9. It's better to use a table rather than tab stops when you need to organize more than a few columns of information.

10. Click the Table Move handle.

Session 3.2

1. Drag the right border of each column to a new position.

2. Select the row. Click the Line Style list arrow on the Tables and Borders toolbar and select a line style. Click the Line Weight list arrow on the Tables and Borders toolbar and select a line weight. Click the Borders list arrow on the Tables and Borders toolbar and then click the Bottom Border option.

3. a. the thickness of the line used to create a border

   b. the style of the line used to create a border

   c. the outline of a row, cell, column, or table

   d. a gray or colored background used to highlight parts of a table

4. Click the cell at the far right in the bottom row of the table, and then press the Tab key.

5. Double-click the column's right-hand border.

6. 10, 25, 45, 75

7. Click anywhere in the table, click Table on the menu bar, click Table Properties, click the Table tab, click Center, and then click OK.

OBJECTIVES

In this tutorial you will:

- Identify desktop-publishing features
- Create a title with WordArt
- Work with hyperlinks
- Create newspaper-style columns
- Insert and edit graphics
- Wrap text around a graphic
- Incorporate drop caps
- Use symbols and special typographic characters
- Add a page border

DESKTOP PUBLISHING A NEWSLETTER

Creating a Newsletter for Wide World Travel

CASE

Wide World Travel, Inc.

Wide World Travel, Inc. hosts international tours for travelers of all ages. Recently, the company has expanded its business by selling clothes and shoes specifically designed for the frequent traveler. Max Stephenson, one of the Wide World tour guides, has taken on the job of managing this new retail venture. In order to generate business, he wants to include an informational newsletter with each set of airline tickets mailed from the main office. He has asked you to help him create the newsletter.

Max has already written the text of the newsletter, which describes some of the most popular items sold by Wide World Travel. Now Max wants you to transform this text into an eye-catching publication that is neat, organized, and professional looking. He would like the newsletter to contain headings (so the customers can scan it quickly for interesting items) as well as a headline that will give the newsletter a memorable look. He wants you to include a picture that will reinforce the newsletter content.

In this tutorial, you'll plan the layout of the newsletter and then add some information about the Wide World Travel Web site. Then you'll get acquainted with the desktop-publishing features and elements you'll need to use to create the newsletter. Also, you'll learn how desktop publishing differs from other word-processing tasks and from Web page design. You'll format the title using an eye-catching design and divide the document into newspaper-style columns to make it easier to read. To add interest and focus to the text, you'll include a piece of art. You'll then fine-tune the newsletter layout, give it a more professional appearance with typographic characters, and put a border around the page to give the newsletter a finished look.

SESSION 4.1

In this session you will see how Max planned his newsletter and learn about desktop-publishing features and elements. Then you will add and remove a hyperlink, create the newsletter title using WordArt, modify the title's appearance, and format the text of the newsletter into newspaper-style columns.

Planning the Document

The newsletter will provide a brief overview of some popular items sold by Wide World Travel. Like most newsletters, it will be written in an informal style that conveys information quickly. The newsletter title will be eye-catching and will help readers quickly identify the document. Newsletter text will be split into two columns to make it easier to read, and headings will help readers scan the information quickly. A picture will add interest and illustrate the newsletter's content. Drop caps and other desktop-publishing elements will help draw readers' attention to certain information and make the newsletter design attractive and professional.

Elements of Desktop Publishing

Desktop publishing is the production of commercial-quality printed material using a desktop computer system from which you can enter and edit text, create graphics, compose or lay out pages, and print documents. In addition to newsletters, you can desktop publish brochures, posters, and other documents that include text and graphics. In the Case Problems, you'll have to create a brochure. The following elements are commonly associated with desktop publishing:

- High-quality printing. A laser printer or high-resolution inkjet printer produces final output.
- Multiple fonts. Two or three font types and sizes provide visual interest, guide the reader through the text, and convey the tone of the document.
- Graphics. Graphics, such as horizontal or vertical lines (called rules), boxes, electronic art, and digitized photographs help illustrate a concept or product, draw a reader's attention to the document, and make the text visually appealing.
- Typographic characters. Typographic characters such as typographic long dashes, called em dashes (—), in place of double hyphens (--), separate dependent clauses; typographic medium-width dashes, called en dashes (–), are used in place of hyphens (-) as minus signs and in ranges of numbers; and typographic bullets (•) signal items in a list.
- Columns and other formatting features. Columns of text, pull quotes (small portions of text pulled out of the main text and enlarged), page borders, and other special formatting features that you don't frequently see in letters and other documents distinguish desktop-published documents.

You'll incorporate many of these desktop-publishing elements into the Wide World Travel newsletter for Max.

Word's Desktop-Publishing Features

Successful desktop publishing requires that you first know what elements professionals use to desktop publish a document. Figure 4-1 defines some of the desktop-publishing features included in Word. Max wants you to use these features to produce the final newsletter shown in Figure 4-2. The newsletter includes some of the typical desktop-publishing elements that you can add to a document using Word.

Figure 4-1	WORD DESKTOP PUBLISHING FEATURES
ELEMENT	**DESCRIPTION**
Columns	Two or more vertical blocks of text that fit on one page
WordArt	Text modified with special effects, such as rotated, curved, bent, shadowed, or shaded letters
Clip art	Prepared graphic images that are ready to be inserted into a document
Drop cap	Oversized first letter of word beginning a paragraph that extends vertically into two or more lines of the paragraph
Typographic symbols	Special characters that are not part of the standard keyboard, such as em dashes (—), copy-right symbols (©), or curly quotation marks (")

Figure 4-2	WIDE WORLD TRAVEL NEWSLETTER

Travel in Style!

Wide World Tours

After countless trips abroad, our tour leaders have mastered the art of traveling light. The secret, they explain, is to pack a few well-made, light-weight items that you can wash in a sink and dry overnight on a line. Unless you lived in a large city with numerous specialty stores, finding good traveling clothes used to be nearly impossible. But now you can purchase everything you need for a fast-paced Wide World tour at the Wide World Web site. This newsletter describes a few of our most popular items. To learn more about other Wide World products, call us at 283-333-9010 or visit our Web site at www.wideworldtravel.com.

Easy Moving Knitware

Unbelievably versatile, these knit garments are so adaptable that you can wear them from the train station to the outdoor market to the theater with just a change of accessories. They combine the softness of cotton with the suppleness of Flexistyle®, a wrinkle-resistant synthetic fabric.

The cardigan has side vents for a graceful drape and looks great layered over the knit shell. The pants have comfortable elasticized waistbands and side-seam pockets. Available in Midnight Black, Azure, and Coffee. Sizes: XS, S, M, L, and XL.

Resilient Straw Hat

If you're planning a trip to sunny climes, bring along this eminently packable broad-brimmed hat. Crunch it in a ball and stuff it into your suitcase. When you unpack, the hat will spring back to its original, elegant shape—guaranteed! Available in Cream and Taupe. Sizes: S, M, L, and XL.

Comfort Trekkers

These amazingly supportive walking shoes combine the comfort of hiking boots with the style of light-weight athletic shoes, giving your feet both stability and support. Wear them to explore a mysterious medieval city in the morning, and then hike a mountain trail after lunch. Available in Antique Black and Desert Brown, in whole and half sizes.

Desktop Publishing Versus Web Page Design

In many ways, desktop-published documents are similar to another kind of document known as a Web page. As you probably know, a **Web page** is a document that can contain specially formatted text, graphics, video, and audio. A Web page is stored on a computer as a collection of electronic files and is designed to be viewed in a special program called a **browser**. You probably have experience using a browser such as Microsoft Internet Explorer to explore Web pages on the Internet.

Like desktop-published documents, Web pages often include drop caps, multiple fonts, and graphics. However, you must use these elements differently when designing a Web page than when desktop publishing a document. Figure 4-3 summarizes some basic distinctions between desktop publishing and Web page design.

Figure 4-3	DESKTOP-PUBLISHED DOCUMENTS COMPARED TO WEB PAGES
DESKTOP PUBLISHING	**WEB PAGE DESIGN**
Reader sees the entire page at one time. Large areas of white space or uneven columns are therefore very noticeable in a desktop-published document.	Reader sees only the portion of the Web page that is displayed in the browser window.
Use of color increases printing costs. For this reason, many desktop-published documents are designed to be printed on a black and white printer.	The use of color does not affect the cost of producing the Web page.
The quality of the printer greatly affects the appearance of graphics in the printed page. Thus, desktop publishers usually prefer simple graphics that print well on laser printers.	The quality of graphics is most affected by the type of electronic file in which the graphic is stored.
The page is static. The only devices that can be used to catch the reader's attention are desktop-publishing elements, such as headlines, columns, and graphics.	Parts of the page can be animated, or include video. Also, Web pages often convey information or attract the reader's attention by using sound.
The reader cannot interact with a desktop-published document.	The reader can interact with a Web page by clicking links that display other Web pages or by entering information into a form on the Web page.

Now that you are familiar with some basic concepts related to desktop publishing, you can begin work on Max's newsletter. Your first task is to insert some information about the Wide World Travel Web site in the first section. To do this, you need to understand how to work with specially formatted text called hyperlinks.

Working with Hyperlinks

As mentioned in Figure 4-3, Web pages often include special text called **hyperlinks** (or simply **links**) that you can click to display other Web pages. You can also use hyperlinks in Word documents that will be read **online** (that is, on a computer).

For example, if you type an e-mail address and then press Enter, Word will automatically format the e-mail address as a hyperlink. (Hyperlink text is usually formatted in blue with an underline.) When you press Ctrl and click an e-mail hyperlink, an e-mail program opens automatically, ready for you to type a message. (If you completed the Review Assignments for Tutorial 2, you already have experience using e-mail hyperlinks.)

In the same way, Word will automatically format a Web page address, or **URL**, as a hyperlink. (One example of a Web address is www.microsoft.com.) When you press Ctrl and click a Web page address that has been formatted as a hyperlink, your computer's browser opens automatically and attempts to display that Web page. (The browser may not actually be able to display the Web page if your computer is not currently connected to the Internet, or if the Web page is unavailable for some other reason.)

Including hyperlinks in a Word document is very useful when you plan to distribute it via e-mail and have others read it online. For instance, if you include your e-mail address in a memo to a potential customer, the customer can click the e-mail address to begin typing an e-mail message to you in reply. However, when you know that your document will only be distributed on paper, it's a good idea to remove any hyperlinks so that the e-mail address or Web address is formatted the same as the rest of the document. This helps ensure that a desktop-published document has a uniform look. To remove a hyperlink, right-click the hyperlink and then click Remove Hyperlink in the shortcut menu. Once you remove the hyperlink, the Web address or e-mail address remains in the document, but is no longer formatted in blue with an underline.

Max would like you to complete the newsletter text by adding a reference to the Wide World Travel Web site. He does not want the company's Web address formatted as a hyperlink, so you will have to remove the hyperlink after typing the Web address. He has saved the newsletter text in a document named Clothes. You'll begin by opening the document that contains the unformatted text of the newsletter, often called **copy**.

To open the newsletter document and add the Web address:

1. Start Word, and place your Data Disk in the appropriate drive. Make sure your screen matches the figures in this tutorial. In particular, be sure to display non-printing characters and switch to Normal view.

2. Open the file **Clothes** from the Tutorial folder in the Tutorial.04 folder on your Data Disk.

3. To avoid altering the original file, save the document as **Travel Clothes** in the Tutorial folder in the Tutorial.04 folder on your Data Disk.

4. If necessary, change the Zoom setting (in the Standard toolbar) to 100% and switch to Normal view.

5. Click at the end of the second paragraph (after the phone number) press the **spacebar**, and then type the following: **or visit our Web site at www.wideworldtravel.com**

6. Type a period at the end of the Web address, and then press the **Enter** key. The Web address is formatted as a hyperlink, in a blue font with an underline.

7. Move the mouse pointer over the hyperlink. A ScreenTip appears, with the complete URL (including some extra characters that a browser needs to display the Web page). The ScreenTip also displays instructions for displaying the Wide World Travel Web site. See Figure 4-4.

Figure 4-4 **HYPERLINK WITH SCREENTIP**

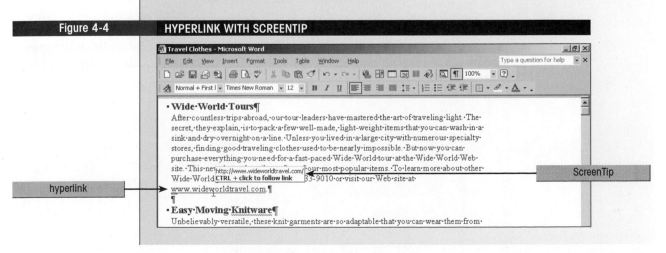

hyperlink

ScreenTip

Max tells you that the Wide World Travel Web site is being updated, so it is not yet available online. So instead of clicking the link to test it, you will remove the hyperlink. This will ensure that the Web address is formatted to match the rest of the paragraph.

To remove the hyperlink:

1. Right-click the text **www.wideworldtravel.com**. A shortcut menu opens, as shown in Figure 4-5.

Figure 4-5   HYPERLINK MENU

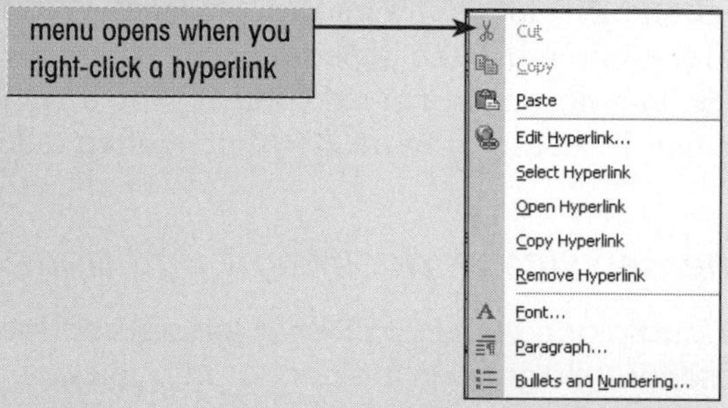

menu opens when you right-click a hyperlink

- Cut
- Copy
- Paste
- Edit Hyperlink...
- Select Hyperlink
- Open Hyperlink
- Copy Hyperlink
- Remove Hyperlink
- Font...
- Paragraph...
- Bullets and Numbering...

2. Click **Remove Hyperlink**. The shortcut menu closes and the text is now formatted in black to match the rest of the paragraph.

You have finished adding the information about the company's Web site to the newsletter. Now that the newsletter contains all the necessary details, you can turn your attention to adding a headline.

Using WordArt to Create a Headline

Max wants the title of the newsletter, "Travel in Style," to be eye-catching and dramatic, as shown earlier in Figure 4-2. WordArt, available in Word and other Microsoft Office programs, provides great flexibility in designing text with special effects that expresses the image or mood you want to convey in your printed documents. With WordArt, you can apply color and shading, as well as alter the shape and size of the text. You can easily "wrap" the document text around WordArt shapes.

Note that you begin creating WordArt by clicking a button on the Drawing toolbar. When you first display the Drawing toolbar, Word switches to Print Layout view. As a rule, Print Layout view is the most appropriate view to use when you are desktop publishing with Word because it shows you exactly how the text and graphics fit on the page. The vertical ruler that appears in Print Layout view helps you position graphical elements more precisely.

REFERENCE WINDOW   **RW**

Creating Special Text Effects Using WordArt

- Click the Drawing button on the Standard toolbar to display the Drawing toolbar.
- Click the Insert WordArt button on the Drawing toolbar.
- Click the style of text you want to insert, and then click the OK button.
- Type the text you want in the Edit WordArt Text dialog box.
- Click the Font and Size list arrows to select the font and font size you want.
- If you want, click the Bold or Italic button, or both.
- Click the OK button.
- With the WordArt selected, drag any handle to reshape and resize it. To keep the text in the same proportions as the original, press and hold down the Shift key while you drag a handle.

You're ready to use WordArt to create the newsletter title. First you will display the Drawing toolbar. Then you will choose a WordArt style and type the headline text.

To create the title of the newsletter using WordArt:

1. Press **Ctrl+Home** to move the insertion point to the beginning of the document.

2. If the Drawing toolbar is not displayed on your screen, click the **Drawing** button on the Standard toolbar. The Drawing toolbar appears at the bottom of the screen. Word switches to Print Layout view.

   TROUBLE? If the Drawing toolbar is not positioned at the bottom of the Document window, drag it there by its title bar. If you do not see the Drawing toolbar anywhere, right-click the Standard toolbar, and then click Drawing on the shortcut menu.

3. If necessary, click **View** on the menu bar and then click **Ruler** to display the vertical and horizontal rulers, and then verify that the Zoom setting is 100%.

4. Click the **Insert WordArt** button on the Drawing toolbar. The WordArt Gallery dialog box opens, displaying 30 different WordArt styles.

5. Click the WordArt style in the second row from the top, second column from the right, as shown in Figure 4-6.

Figure 4-6	WORDART STYLES

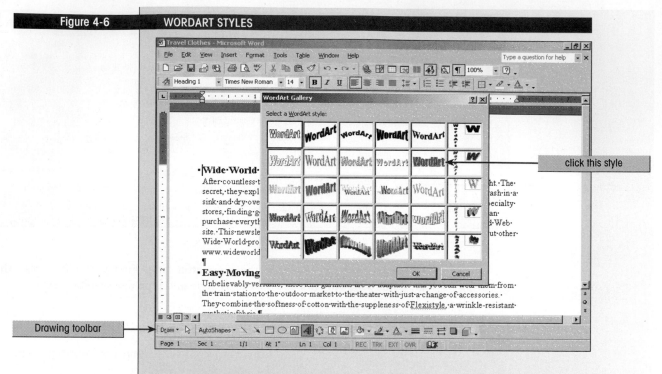

6. Click the **OK** button. The Edit WordArt Text dialog box opens, displaying the default text "Your Text Here," which you will replace with the newsletter title.

7. Type **Travel in Style** to replace the default text with the newsletter title. Notice the toolbar at the top of the Edit WordArt Text dialog box, which you could use to apply boldface and italics, or to change the font or font style. You don't need to use these options now, but you might choose to when creating headlines for other documents.

8. Click the **OK** button. The Edit WordArt Text dialog box closes and the WordArt image is inserted at the beginning of the newsletter. The "Wide World Tours" heading moves to the right to accommodate the new headline. See Figure 4-7.

   TROUBLE? If you see a border around the headline, the WordArt is currently selected. Click anywhere outside of the border to deselect the WordArt.

Figure 4-7	WORDART HEADLINE INSERTED INTO DOCUMENT

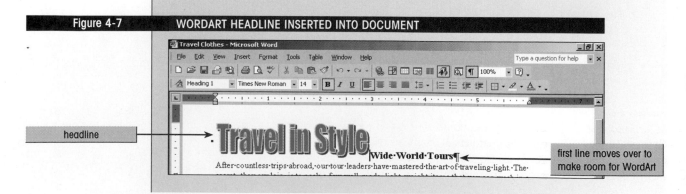

Eventually, you will position the headline so that it appears at the very top of the document, stretching from margin to margin. But for now, you can leave it in its current position.

Selecting a WordArt Object

The WordArt image you have created is not regular text. You cannot edit it as you would other text, by moving the insertion point to it and typing new letters, or by selecting part of it and using the buttons on the Formatting toolbar. Unlike regular text, a WordArt headline is considered an **object**—that is, something that lies on top of the document. To edit a WordArt object in Word, you must first click it to select it. Then you can make changes using special toolbar buttons and dialog boxes, or by dragging it with the mouse.

Max would like you to make several changes to the newsletter headline. Before you can do this, you need to select it.

To select the WordArt headline:

1. Click the WordArt headline. The headline is surrounded by a black border with eight small black squares (called resize handles). The WordArt toolbar also appears. See Figure 4-8.

Figure 4-8	SELECTED HEADLINE

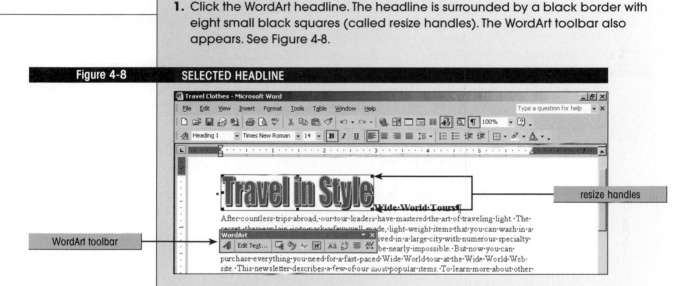

Editing a WordArt Object

Now that the WordArt object is selected, you can modify its appearance (color, shape, size, and so forth) using the buttons on the Drawing toolbar or the WordArt toolbar. First of all, Max would like you to edit the WordArt by adding an exclamation mark at the end of the headline. While you're making that change, he would like you to format the headline in italics.

To change the font and formatting of the WordArt object:

1. Verify that the WordArt object is selected, as indicated by the resize handles.

2. Click the **Edit Text** button on the WordArt toolbar. The Edit WordArt Text dialog box opens. As you recall, you used this dialog box earlier when you first created the WordArt headline.

3. Click at the end of the headline (after the "e" in Style) and type **!** (an exclamation mark).

4. Click the **Italic** button in the Edit WordArt Text dialog box. The headline in the Text box is now formatted in italics, with an exclamation mark at the end.

5. Click the **OK** button. The Edit WordArt Text dialog box closes, allowing you to see the edited headline in the document.

Changing the Shape of a WordArt Object

You can quickly change the shape of a WordArt object using the **WordArt Shape** button on the WordArt toolbar. Right now, the WordArt headline has a straight shape, without any curve to it. Max wants to use an arched shape.

To change the shape of the WordArt object:

1. Verify that the WordArt headline is selected, and then click the **WordArt Shape** button [Abc] on the WordArt toolbar.

2. Move the mouse pointer over the options in the palette to display a ScreenTip with the name of each shape. As you can see, the Plain Text shape (a straight line) is currently selected.

3. Click the **Inflate Top** shape (fourth row down, fifth column from the left), as shown in Figure 4-9.

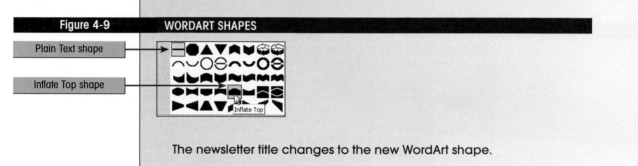

Figure 4-9   WORDART SHAPES

Plain Text shape

Inflate Top shape

The newsletter title changes to the new WordArt shape.

The headline has the shape you want. Now you can take care of positioning the WordArt object above the newsletter text.

Wrapping Text Below the WordArt Object

At this point, the WordArt object is on the same line as the heading "Wide World Tours." Max would like you to set the WordArt on its own line at the top of the document. To do this, you need to change the way the text flows, or **wraps**, around the WordArt object.

You can wrap text around objects many different ways in Word. For example, you can have the text wrap above and below the object, through it, or wrap the text to follow the shape of the object, even if it has an irregular shape. Text wrapping is often used in newsletters to prevent text and graphics from overlapping, to add interest, and to prevent excessive open areas, called white space, from appearing on the page. The Text Wrapping button on the WordArt or Picture toolbar provides some basic choices, whereas the Layout tab of the Format Picture dialog box provides more advanced options. Because you want to use a relatively simple option—wrapping text so that it flows below the WordArt headline—you'll use the Text Wrapping button on the WordArt toolbar. You'll have a chance to use the Format Picture dialog box in the Case Problems at the end of this tutorial.

To wrap the newsletter text below the WordArt headline:

1. With the WordArt object selected, click the **Text Wrapping** button [ ] on the WordArt toolbar. A menu of text wrapping options opens.

2. Click **Top and Bottom**. The text drops below the newsletter title. The WordArt is still selected, but instead of handles in the shape of square boxes, you see small circles. A number of other items appear around the WordArt object, as shown in Figure 4-10. You can use the handles shown in Figure 4-10 to change the size and position of the WordArt object. You'll learn the meaning of the anchor symbol shortly. Don't be concerned if yours is not in the same position as the one in Figure 4-10.

Figure 4-10	WORDART AFTER WRAPPING TEXT

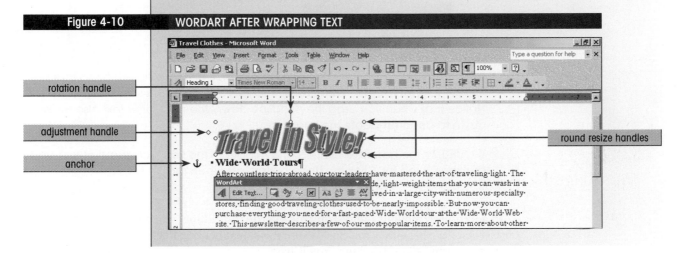

rotation handle

adjustment handle

anchor

round resize handles

Positioning and Sizing the WordArt Object

After you choose a text wrap style for a WordArt object, you can adjust its size and position in the document. To position a WordArt object, click it and drag it with the mouse pointer. To widen any WordArt object, drag one of its resize handles. To keep the object the same proportion as the original, hold down the Shift key as you drag the resize handle. This prevents "stretching" the object more in one direction than the other.

Max asks you to widen the headline so it fits neatly within the newsletter margins. As you enlarge the headline, you can practice dragging the WordArt object to a new position.

To position and enlarge the WordArt object:

1. Move the mouse pointer over the headline.

2. Use the ⊹ pointer to drag the WordArt object to the right, until it is centered over the top of the newsletter.

3. Click the **Undo** button 🔙 on the Standard toolbar to undo the move. The headline returns to its original position, aligned along the left-hand margin. Note that you can use this same technique to drag a WordArt object to any location in a document. (You'll learn more about dragging objects later in this tutorial, when you insert a picture into the newsletter.)

4. With the WordArt object still selected, position the pointer over its lower-right resize handle. The pointer changes to ↘.

5. Press and hold the **Shift** key while you drag the resize handle to the right margin, using the horizontal ruler as a guide. See Figure 4-11. As you drag the handle, the pointer changes to ✛. If necessary, repeat the procedure to make the exclamation mark line up with the right margin.

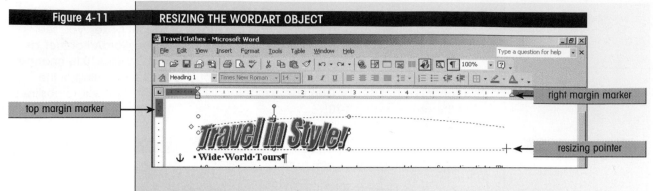

| Figure 4-11 | RESIZING THE WORDART OBJECT |

6. If necessary, use the ⬌⬍ pointer to drag the headline down slightly, so that the top of the headline does not extend into the top margin, as shown in Figure 4-11. Notice that when you drag the headline down, the newsletter text also moves down to accommodate the headline.

TROUBLE? If the headline jumps to the middle of the first paragraph of text, you dragged it too far. Click the Undo button, and then repeat Step 6.

In addition to moving and resizing the WordArt headline, you can drag the rotation handle to rotate the headline. You can also use the adjustment handle to increase or decrease the arch at the top of the headline. You'll have a chance to practice these techniques in the Review Assignments at the end of this tutorial. Right now you need to turn your attention to the anchor symbol on the left side of the WordArt object.

Anchoring the WordArt Object

At some point after you wrap text around a document, you need to make sure the WordArt object is properly positioned within the document as a whole—a process known as **anchoring**. The process draws its name from the anchor symbol in the left margin, which indicates the position of the WordArt relative to the text. (The anchor symbol is only visible after you wrap text around the document.) To ensure that changes to the text (such as section breaks) do not affect the WordArt, you need to anchor the WordArt to a blank paragraph before the text. At this point, the WordArt anchor symbol is probably located to the left of the first paragraph (the heading "Wide World Tours"). However, yours may be in a different position (for instance, it might be positioned above and to the left of the WordArt). In the next set of steps, you will move the anchor to a new, blank paragraph at the beginning of the document.

To anchor the WordArt object to a blank paragraph:

1. Press **Ctrl+Home**. The insertion point moves to the beginning of the newsletter text (that is, to the left of the first "W" in the heading "Wide World Tours"). The WordArt object is no longer selected; you cannot see the anchor at this point.

2. Press the **Enter** key. A new paragraph symbol is inserted at the beginning of the document.

3. Click the WordArt object. The selection handles and the anchor symbol appear.

4. Click the anchor and drag it to the left of the new, blank paragraph, as shown in Figure 4-12.

Figure 4-12	PROPERLY ANCHORED WORDART

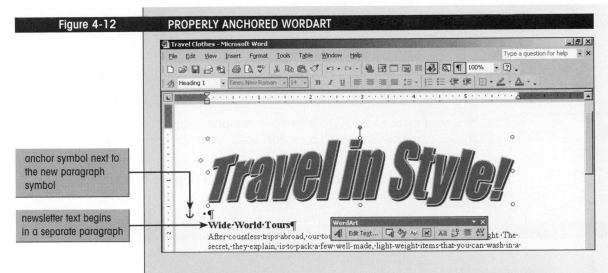

anchor symbol next to the new paragraph symbol

newsletter text begins in a separate paragraph

TROUBLE? If your WordArt headline is positioned below the new paragraph symbol, drag it up slightly to position it above the new paragraph symbol. If you notice any other differences between your headline and the one shown in Figure 4-12, edit the headline to make it match the figure. For example, you may need to drag the WordArt left or right slightly, or you may need to adjust its size by dragging one of its resize handles.

5. Click anywhere in the newsletter to deselect the WordArt, and then save your work.

Your WordArt is now finished. Max congratulates you on your excellent work. The headline will definitely draw attention to the newsletter, encouraging potential customers to read the entire document.

Formatting Text in Newspaper-Style Columns

Because newsletters are meant for quick reading, they are usually laid out in newspaper-style columns. In newspaper-style columns, a page is divided into two or more vertical blocks, or columns. Text flows down one column, continues at the top of the next column, flows down that column, and so forth. The narrow columns and small type size allow the eye to take in a lot of text, thus allowing a reader to scan a newspaper quickly for interesting information.

When formatting a document in columns, you can click where you want the columns to begin and then click the Columns button on the Formatting toolbar. However, the Columns command on the Formatting menu offers more options. Using the Columns command, you can insert a vertical line between columns. The Columns command also gives you more control over exactly what part of the document will be formatted in columns.

Max wants you to divide the text below the title into two columns and add a vertical line between them.

To apply newspaper-style columns to the body of the newsletter:

1. Position the insertion point at the beginning of the second paragraph (to the left of the first "W" in "Wide World Tours").

2. Click **Format** on the menu bar, and then click **Columns**. The Columns dialog box opens.

3. In the Presets section, click the **Two** icon.

4. Click the **Line between** check box to select it. The text in the Preview box changes to a two-column format with a vertical rule between the columns.

You want these changes to affect only the paragraphs after the WordArt headline, so you'll need to insert a section break and apply the column formatting to the text after the insertion point.

5. Click the **Apply to** list arrow, and then click **This point forward** to have Word automatically insert a section break at the insertion point. See Figure 4-13.

Figure 4-13	COMPLETED COLUMNS DIALOG BOX

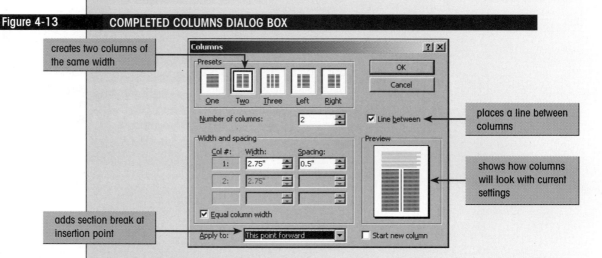

creates two columns of the same width

places a line between columns

shows how columns will look with current settings

adds section break at insertion point

6. Click the **OK** button to return to the Document window. A continuous section break appears below the WordArt title. The word "continuous" indicates that the new section continues on the same page as the preceding page—in other words, the newsletter text and the WordArt title will print on the same page, even though they lie in different sections. The text in Section 2 is formatted in two columns.

To get a good look at the columns, you need to change the zoom setting so you can see the entire page at one time.

To zoom out to display the whole page:

1. Click the **Zoom** list arrow on the Standard toolbar, and then click **Whole Page**. Word displays the entire page of the newsletter so that you can see how the two-column format looks on the page. See Figure 4-14. Note that the Whole Page Zoom setting is only available in Print Layout view. You should use it whenever you want to have the entire page displayed as you edit it.

Figure 4-14   **WHOLE PAGE VIEW SHOWING TWO COLUMNS**

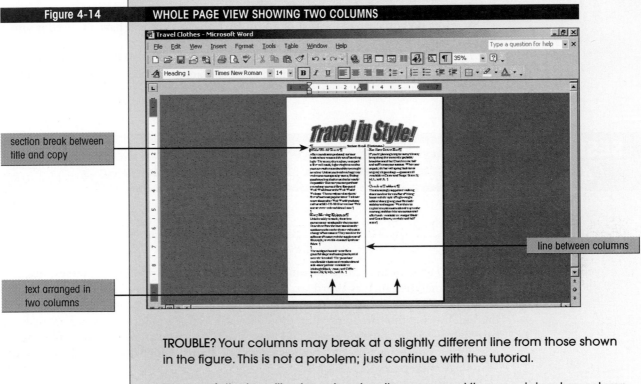

section break between title and copy

line between columns

text arranged in two columns

TROUBLE? Your columns may break at a slightly different line from those shown in the figure. This is not a problem; just continue with the tutorial.

The newsletter headline is centered on the page, and the copy is in a two-column format. The text fills the left column but not the right column. You'll fix this later, after you add a graphic and format some of the text.

2. Click the **Zoom** list arrow again, and then click **Page Width**. The Page Width option reduces the zoom setting enough to make the page span the width of the document window. Now you can read the text again.

3. Save your work.

Keep in mind that you can modify the structure of columns in a document by reformatting the document with three or more columns, or return the document to its original format by formatting it as one column. You can also insert column breaks to force text to move from one column to the next. You'll have a chance to practice modifying the columns in the Case Problems at the end of this tutorial.

Session 4.1 QUICK CHECK

1. Describe four elements commonly associated with desktop publishing.
2. Describe at least two differences between a desktop-published document and a Web page.
3. In your own words, define the following terms:
   a. desktop publishing
   b. Web page
   c. copy
   d. anchor
4. True or False: When using Word's desktop-publishing features, you should display your document in Normal view.

5. True or False: You can edit WordArt just as you would edit any other text in Word.
6. How do you change the text of a WordArt object after you have inserted it into a Word document?
7. What is the purpose of the WordArt Shape button on the WordArt toolbar?
8. True or False: When you first format a document into newspaper-style columns, the columns will not necessarily be of equal length.

SESSION 4.2

In this session you will insert, resize, and crop clip art, and change the way the text wraps around the clip art. Then you'll create drop caps, insert typographic symbols, balance columns, place a border around the newsletter, and print the newsletter.

Inserting Graphics

Graphics, which can include drawings, paintings, photographs, charts, tables, designs, or even designed text such as WordArt, add variety to documents and are especially appropriate for newsletters. Word allows you to draw pictures in your document, using the buttons on the Drawing toolbar. To produce professional-looking graphics, it's easier to create a picture in a special graphics program and then save the picture as an electronic file. (You may already be familiar with one graphics program, **Paint**, which is included as part of the Windows operating system.)

Instead of creating your own art in a graphics program, you can take a piece of art on a piece of paper (such as a photograph) and scan it—that is, run it through a special machine called a scanner. A **scanner** is similar to a copy machine except that it saves a copy of the image as an electronic file, instead of reproducing it on a piece of paper. (As you may know, many modern copy machines also function as scanners.) You can also use a digital camera to take a photograph that is then stored as an electronic file.

Electronic files come in several types, many of which were developed for use in Web pages. In desktop publishing, you will most commonly work with **bitmaps**—a type of file that stores an image as a collection of tiny dots, which, when displayed on a computer monitor or printed on a page, make up a picture. There are several types of bitmap files, the most common of which are:

- **BMP:** Used by Microsoft Paint to store graphics you create. These files, which have the .bmp file extension, tend to be very large.
- **GIF:** Suitable for most types of simple art. A GIF file is compressed, so it doesn't take up much room on your computer. A GIF file has the file extension .gif.
- **JPEG:** Suitable for photographs and drawings. Even more compressed than GIF files. A JPEG file has the file extension .jpg.
- **TIFF:** Commonly used for photographs or scanned images. TIFF files have the file extension .tif and are usually much larger than GIF or JPEG files.

Once you have stored a piece of art as an electronic file, you can insert it into a document using the Picture commands on the Insert menu. You'll have a chance to explore some of these commands in the Review Assignments and Case Problems at the end of this tutorial.

If you don't have time to prepare your own art work, you can take advantage of **clip art**—a collection of pre-made, copyright-free images included along with Word. A number of clip art selections are stored on your computer when you install Microsoft Word. You can also download additional clip art from the Web. (You'll have a chance to look for clip art on the Web in the Case Problems at the end of this tutorial.) You begin inserting clip art by opening the Clip Art Task Pane. From there you can open the Clip Organizer, which gives you access to a series of folders containing various categories of clip art. Then you copy an image to the Office Clipboard, close the Clip Organizer, and paste the image into the document.

To add visual appeal to the Wide World Travel newsletter, you will insert a piece of clip art now. Max wants you to use a graphic that reflects the newsletter content.

To insert the clip art image of an airplane into the newsletter:

1. If you took a break after the previous session, make sure Word is still running, the Travel Clothes newsletter is open, the document is in Print Layout view, and the nonprinting characters are displayed. Also verify that the Drawing toolbar is displayed.

2. Click the **Insert Clip Art** button 🖻 on the Drawing toolbar. The Insert Clip Art Task Pane opens, as shown in Figure 4-15. You can use the top part of this Task Pane to search for graphics related to a specific topic. You can also click the Clip Organizer option (near the bottom) to open a dialog box where you can browse among the various images stored on your computer. You'll use the Clip Organizer in the next step.

| Figure 4-15 | INSERT CLIP ART TASK PANE |

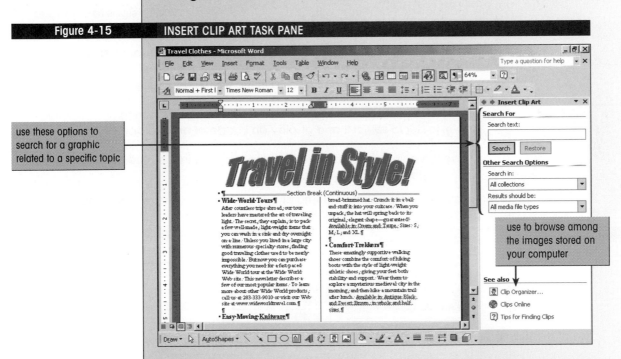

use these options to search for a graphic related to a specific topic

use to browse among the images stored on your computer

TROUBLE? If you see the Add Clips to Organizer dialog box, click Now. This will organize the clip art installed on your computer into folders, so that you can then use the Clip Organizer dialog box to select a piece of clip art. This dialog box will appear the first time you attempt to use clip art on your computer.

3. Click **Clip Organizer** near the bottom of the Task Pane. The Microsoft Clip Organizer opens, with the Favorites folder selected in the Collection List. This dialog box works similar to Windows Explorer. You click the plus signs next to folders to display subfolders. The images stored in subfolders are displayed in the right-hand pane. Clip art in Word is stored in subfolders within the Office Collections folder. See Figure 4-16. (You might see different folders from those shown in Figure 4-16, but you should see the Office Collections folder.)

Figure 4-16   **MICROSOFT CLIP ORGANIZER**

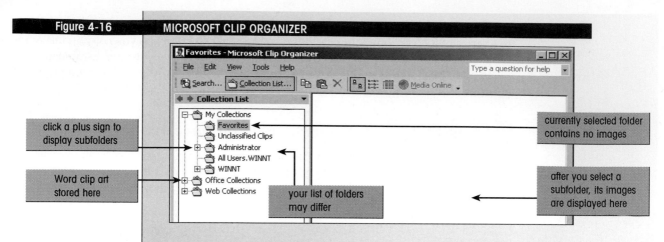

click a plus sign to display subfolders

Word clip art stored here

your list of folders may differ

currently selected folder contains no images

after you select a subfolder, its images are displayed here

4. Click the plus sign next to the **Office Collections** folder. A list of subfolders within the Office Collections folder appears. This list of folders, which is created when you install Word, organizes clip art images into related categories. The folders with plus signs next to them contain subfolders or clip art images.

5. Scroll down and examine the list of folders. Click any plus signs to open subfolders, and then click folders to display clip art images in the right-hand pane.

6. Click the plus sign next to the **Transportation** folder to display its subfolders, and then click the **Transportation** folder to select it. Three images stored in the Transportation folder are displayed in the right-hand pane.

   TROUBLE? If you don't see any images in the Transportation folder, click the Travel folder to select it and display an image of an airplane in a blue circle.

7. Move the pointer over the image of the airplane in the blue circle. An arrow button appears.

8. Click the arrow button. A menu of options opens, as shown in Figure 4-17.

Figure 4-17   **IMAGE IN THE TRANSPORTATION FOLDER SELECTED**

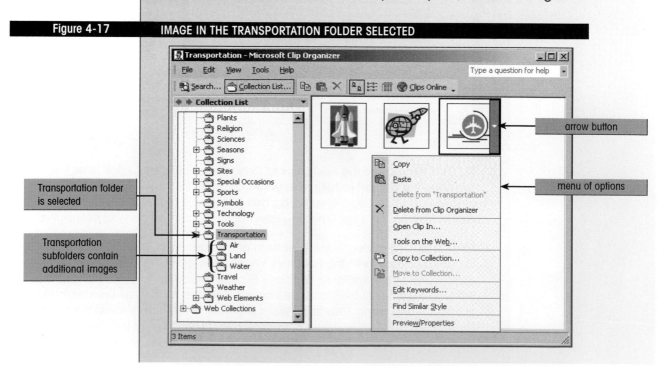

Transportation folder is selected

Transportation subfolders contain additional images

arrow button

menu of options

9. Click **Copy** in the menu. The image is copied to the Office Clipboard.

10. Click the **Close** button ☒ to close the Microsoft Clip Organizer, and then click **Yes** when you see a dialog box asking if you want to save the item on the Clipboard. You return to the Document window.

Now that you have copied the image to the Clipboard, you can paste it into the document at the insertion point. Max asks you to insert the graphic in the paragraph below the heading "Tours." Before you insert the image, you will close the Task Pane.

To paste the clip art into the document:

1. Close the Insert Clip Art Task Pane.

2. Position the insertion point to the left of the word "After" in the beginning of the first paragraph below the heading "Wide World Tours."

3. Click the **Paste** button 📋 on the Standard toolbar. The image is inserted into the document at the insertion point. The image nearly fills the left column.

4. Save the document.

5. Click the airplane image to select it. Like the WordArt object you worked with earlier, the clip art image is an object with resize handles that you can use to change its size. The Picture toolbar appears whenever the clip art object is selected. See Figure 4-18.

| Figure 4-18 | NEWSLETTER WITH THE CLIP ART OBJECT INSERTED |

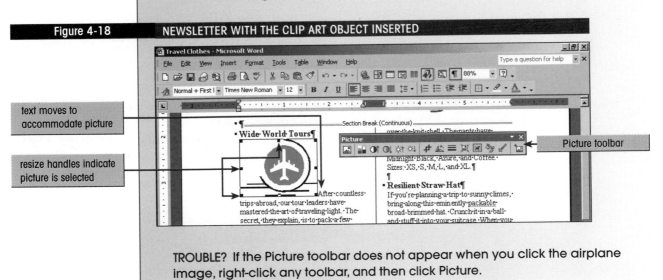

text moves to accommodate picture

resize handles indicate picture is selected

Picture toolbar

TROUBLE? If the Picture toolbar does not appear when you click the airplane image, right-click any toolbar, and then click Picture.

Max would like the image to be smaller so it doesn't distract attention from the text. You'll make that change in the next section.

Resizing a Graphic

You often need to change the size of a graphic so that it fits better into your document. This is called **scaling** the image. You can resize a graphic by either dragging its resize handles or, for more precise control, by using the Format Picture button on the Picture toolbar.

For Max's newsletter, the dragging technique will work fine.

To resize the clip art graphic:

1. Make sure the clip art graphic is selected.

2. Drag the lower-right resize handle up and to the left until the dotted outline forms a rectangle about 1.5 inches wide. Remember to use the horizontal ruler as a guide. See Figure 4-19. *Note:* You don't have to hold down the Shift key, as you do with WordArt, to resize the picture proportionally.

Figure 4-19	RESIZING THE GRAPHIC

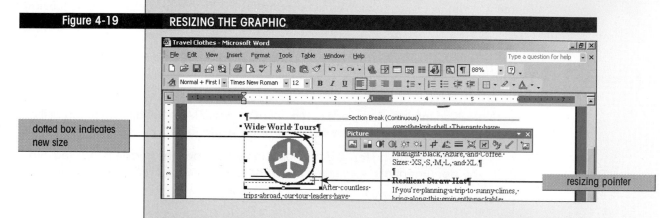

dotted box indicates new size

resizing pointer

3. Release the mouse button. The airplane image is now about half as wide as the left-hand column.

Max wonders if the graphic would look better if you deleted part of the horizontal line on the left side of the image. You'll make that change in the next section.

Cropping a Graphic

You can **crop** the graphic—that is, cut off one or more of its edges—using either the Crop button on the Picture toolbar or the Format Picture dialog box. Once you crop a graphic, the part you cropped is hidden from view. It remains a part of the graphic image, so you can change your mind and restore a cropped graphic to its original form.

To crop the airplane graphic:

1. If necessary, click the clip art to select it. The resize handles appear.

2. Click the **Crop** button on the Picture toolbar. The pointer changes to . To crop the graphic, you must position this pointer over a middle handle on any side of the graphic.

3. Position the pointer directly over the middle resize handle on the left side of the picture.

4. Press and hold down the mouse button. The pointer changes to .

5. Drag the handle to the right. As you drag, a dotted outline appears to indicate the new shape of the graphic. Position the left border of the dotted outline along the left border of the blue circle. See Figure 4-20.

Figure 4-20	CROPPING THE GRAPHIC

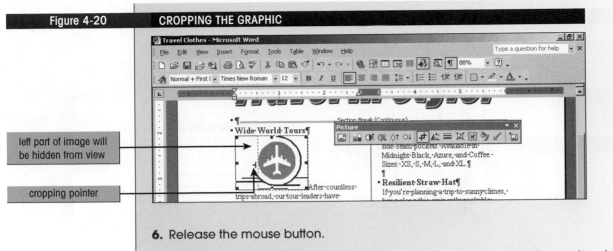

left part of image will be hidden from view

cropping pointer

6. Release the mouse button.

Max decides he prefers to display the whole airplane, so he asks you to return to the original image.

7. Click the **Undo** button on the Standard toolbar. The cropping action is reversed, and the full image reappears.

Rotating a Graphic

Max still isn't happy with the appearance of the graphic, because of the amount of white space on the left side. He suggests rotating the image, so that the airplane is positioned horizontally on the page. Use the Rotate Left button on the Picture toolbar to rotate the image.

To rotate the airplane graphic:

1. If necessary, click the clip art to select it. The resize handles appear.

2. Click the **Rotate Left** button on the Picture toolbar. The graphic rotates 90 degrees to the left. The resize handles change to circles, just as they did when you adjusted the position of the WordArt headline earlier. You can drag the green rotation handle to rotate the graphic, but it's easier to continue using the Rotate Left button.

3. Click again. The graphic rotates another 90 degrees, leaving the airplane upside down.

4. Click again. The graphic rotates another 90 degrees. Now the airplane appears to be flying across the page from left to right. See Figure 4-21.

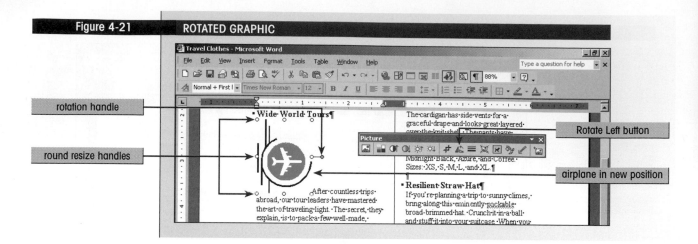

Figure 4-21   ROTATED GRAPHIC

Now Max wants you to make the text wrap to the right of the graphic, making the airplane look as if it's flying into the text.

Wrapping Text Around a Graphic

For the airplane to look as though it flies into the newsletter text, you need to make the text wrap around the image. Earlier, you used the Top and Bottom text wrapping to position the WordArt title above the columns of text. Now you'll try the Tight text wrapping option to make the text follow the shape of the plane.

To wrap text around the airplane graphic:

1. Verify that the airplane graphic is selected.
2. Click the **Text Wrapping** button ![icon] on the Picture toolbar. A menu of text wrapping options appears.
3. Click **Tight**. The text wraps to the right of the airplane, following its shape.
4. Click anywhere in the text to deselect the graphic, and then save the newsletter. Your screen should look similar to Figure 4-22.

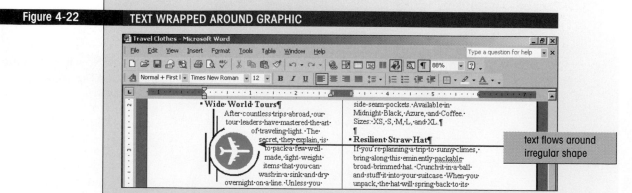

Figure 4-22   TEXT WRAPPED AROUND GRAPHIC

The Text Wrapping button should provide all the options you need for most situations. In some cases, however, you might want to use the more advanced options available in the Format Picture or Format WordArt dialog box. You'll have a chance to explore these options in one of the Case Problems.

Moving a Graphic

Finally, Max asks you to move the graphic down to the middle of the paragraph, so that it is not so close to the heading. You can do this by dragging the graphic to a new position. Like WordArt, a clip art graphic is anchored to a specific paragraph in a document. When you drag a graphic (including WordArt) to a new paragraph, the anchor symbol moves to the top of that paragraph. When you drag a graphic to a new position within the same paragraph, the anchor symbol remains in its original position and only the graphic moves. You'll see how this works when you move the airplane graphic.

To move the graphic:

1. Verify that the graphic is selected. You should see an anchor symbol to the left of the graphic, indicating that the graphic is anchored to the first paragraph below the heading "Wide World Tours." (It may look like the graphic is actually anchored to the heading.)

2. Move the mouse pointer over the graphic.

3. Click and drag the pointer 🔧 down. As you move the pointer, a dotted outline appears indicating the new position of the graphic.

4. Position the dotted outline in the middle of the paragraph, aligned along the left margin, and then release the mouse button. The graphic moves to its new position, but the anchor remains at the top of the paragraph. See Figure 4-23.

Figure 4-23	GRAPHIC IN NEW POSITION

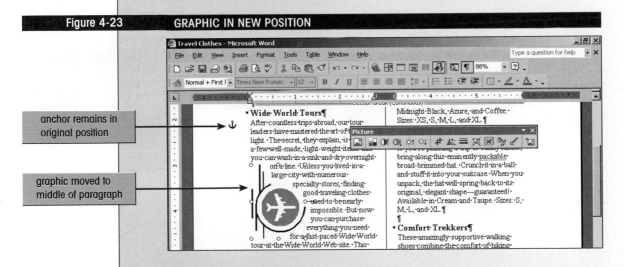

anchor remains in original position

graphic moved to middle of paragraph

5. Click anywhere outside the graphic to deselect it.

TROUBLE? If paragraph text wraps to the left of the graphic, you need to drag the graphic further to the left, so that it aligns along the left-hand margin.

The image of the airplane draws the reader's attention to the beginning of the newsletter, but the rest of the text looks plain. Max suggests adding a drop cap at the beginning of each section.

Inserting Drop Caps

A **drop cap** is a large, capital letter that highlights the beginning of the text of a newsletter, chapter, or some other document section. The drop cap usually extends from the top of the first line of the paragraph down two or three succeeding lines of the paragraph. The text of the paragraph wraps around the drop cap. Word allows you to create a drop cap for the first letter of the first word of a paragraph.

You will create a drop cap for the first paragraph following each heading in the newsletter. The drop cap will extend two lines into the paragraph.

To insert drop caps in the newsletter:

1. Click in the paragraph below the heading "Wide World Tours" (the paragraph where you inserted the graphic).

2. Click **Format** on the menu bar, and then click **Drop Cap**. The Drop Cap dialog box opens.

3. In the Position section, click the **Dropped** icon.

4. Click the **Lines to drop** down arrow once to change the setting from 3 to 2. You don't need to change the default distance from the text. See Figure 4-24.

Figure 4-24	DROP CAP DIALOG BOX

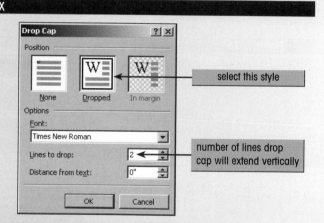

5. Click the **OK** button to close the dialog box, and then click anywhere in the newsletter to deselect the new drop cap. Word formats the first character of the paragraph as a drop cap.

6. Click anywhere in the newsletter text to deselect the drop cap.

   Note: Word re-wraps the text around the graphic to accommodate the drop cap above. If the paragraph text wraps to the left of the graphic, drag it closer to the left margin. See Figure 4-25.

   TROUBLE? Don't be concerned if Word now marks the "fter" of "After" as a grammatical error. Word considers drop caps to be objects, not regular text. By formatting the *A* in "After" as a drop cap, you essentially deleted the regular character *A*. Because the remaining regular characters "fter" do not appear in the dictionary, Word marks it as a potential error.

| Figure 4-25 | DROP CAP BEGINS THE PARAGRAPH |

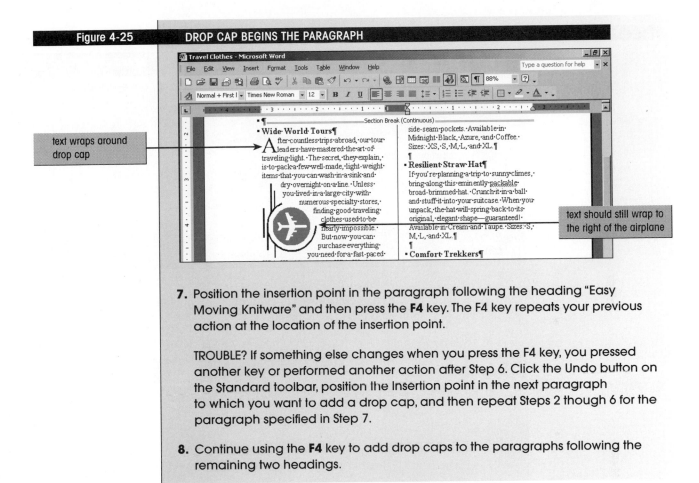

7. Position the insertion point in the paragraph following the heading "Easy Moving Knitware" and then press the **F4** key. The F4 key repeats your previous action at the location of the insertion point.

   TROUBLE? If something else changes when you press the F4 key, you pressed another key or performed another action after Step 6. Click the Undo button on the Standard toolbar, position the insertion point in the next paragraph to which you want to add a drop cap, and then repeat Steps 2 though 6 for the paragraph specified in Step 7.

8. Continue using the **F4** key to add drop caps to the paragraphs following the remaining two headings.

The newsletter looks more lively with the drop caps. Next, you turn your attention to inserting a registered trademark symbol beside a trademark name.

Inserting Symbols and Special Characters

In printed publications, it is customary to change some of the characters available on the standard keyboard into more polished looking characters called **typographic symbols**. For instance, while you might type two hyphens to indicate a dash, in a professionally produced version of that document the two hyphens would be changed to one long dash (called an em dash because it is approximately as wide as the letter "m"). In the past, desktop publishers had to rely on special software to insert and print a document containing typographic symbols, but now you can let Microsoft Word do the work for you.

Word's AutoCorrect feature automatically converts some standard characters into more polished looking typographic symbols as you type. For instance, as Max typed the information on the Resilient Straw Hat, he typed two hyphens after the words "elegant shape." As he began to type the next word "guaranteed," Word automatically converted the two hyphens into an em dash. Figure 4-26 lists some of the other characters that AutoCorrect automatically converts to typographic symbols. In most cases you need to press the spacebar and type more characters before Word will insert the appropriate symbol. You'll have a chance to practice using AutoCorrect to insert typographic symbols in the Review Assignments at the end of this tutorial.

Figure 4-26   COMMON TYPOGRAPHIC SYMBOLS

TO INSERT THIS SYMBOL OR CHARACTER	TYPE	WORD CONVERTS IT TO
em dash	word--word	word—word
smiley	:)	☺
copyright symbol	(c)	©
registered trademark symbol	(r)	®
trademark symbol	(tm)	™
ordinal numbers	1st, 2nd, 3rd, etc.	1st, 2nd, 3rd, etc.
fractions	1/2, 1/4	½, ¼
arrows	--> or <--	→ or ←

To insert typographic characters into a document after you've finished typing it, you can use the Symbol command on the Insert menu.

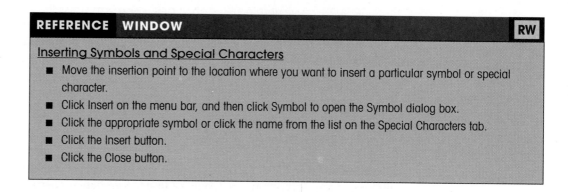

REFERENCE WINDOW   RW

Inserting Symbols and Special Characters

- Move the insertion point to the location where you want to insert a particular symbol or special character.
- Click Insert on the menu bar, and then click Symbol to open the Symbol dialog box.
- Click the appropriate symbol or click the name from the list on the Special Characters tab.
- Click the Insert button.
- Click the Close button.

Max noticed that he forgot to insert a registered trademark symbol (®) after the trademarked name "Flexistyle." He asks you to insert this symbol now, using the Symbol command on the Insert menu.

To insert the registered trademark symbol:

1. Scroll down to display the paragraph below the heading "Easy Moving Knitware," and then click to the right of the word "Flexistyle." (Take care to click between the final "e" and the comma.)

2. Click **Insert** on the menu bar, and then click **Symbol** to open the Symbol dialog box.

3. If necessary, click the **Special Characters** tab. See Figure 4-27.

Figure 4-27 INSERTING A TYPOGRAPHIC SYMBOL

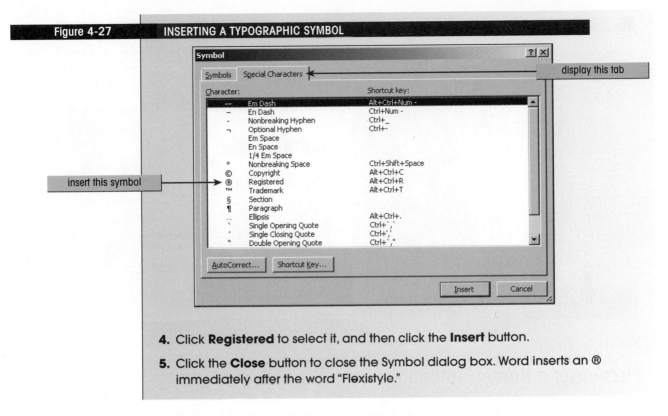

4. Click **Registered** to select it, and then click the **Insert** button.

5. Click the **Close** button to close the Symbol dialog box. Word inserts an ® immediately after the word "Flexistyle."

Next, you decide to adjust the columns of text so they are approximately the same length.

Balancing the Columns

You can shift text from one column to another by adding blank paragraphs to move the text into the next column or by deleting blank paragraphs to shorten the text so it will fit into one column. The problem with this approach is that any edits you make could throw off the balance. Instead, Word can automatically **balance** the columns, or make them of equal length.

To balance the columns:

1. Position the insertion point at the end of the text in the right column, just after the period following the word "sizes."

   Next, you need to change the zoom to Whole Page so you can see the full affect of the change.

2. Click the **Zoom** list arrow on the Standard toolbar, and then click **Whole Page**.

3. Click **Insert** on the menu bar, and then click **Break**. The Break dialog box opens.

4. Below "section break types," click the **Continuous** option button.

5. Click the **OK** button. Word inserts a continuous section break at the end of the text. As shown in Figure 4-28, Word balances the text between the two section breaks.

Figure 4-28   NEWSLETTER WITH BALANCED COLUMNS

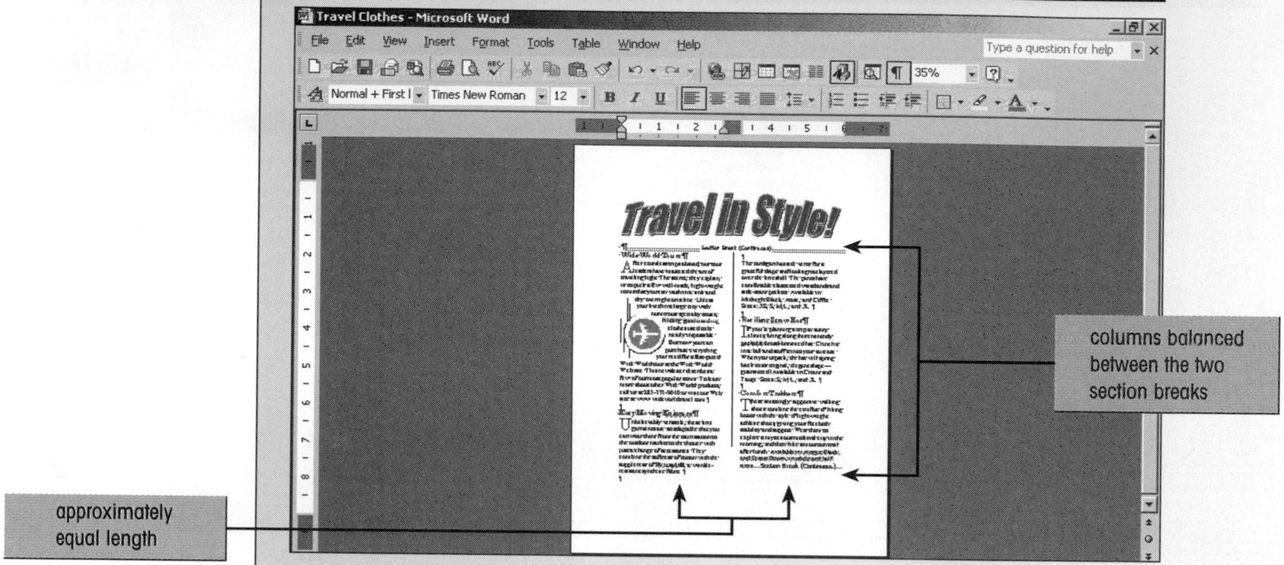

columns balanced between the two section breaks

approximately equal length

Drawing a Border Around the Page

You can add definition to a paragraph or an entire page by adding a border. Right now, Max wants to add a border around the newsletter. (In the Case Problems at the end of this tutorial, you'll learn how to add a border around individual paragraphs.)

To draw a border around the newsletter:

1. Make sure the document is in Print Layout view and that the zoom setting is set to Whole Page so that you can see the entire newsletter.

2. Click **Format** on the menu bar, and then click **Borders and Shading**. The Borders and Shading dialog box opens.

3. Click the **Page Border** tab. You can use the Setting options on the left side to specify the type of border you want. In this case, you want a simple box.

4. In the Setting section, click the **Box** option. Now that you have selected the type of border you want, you can choose the style of line that will be used to create the border.

5. In the Style list box, scroll down and select the ninth style down from the top (the thick line with the thin line underneath), and then verify that the Apply to list option is set to **Whole document**. See Figure 4-29. (While the Borders and Shading dialog box is open, notice the Shading tab, which you can use to add a colored background to a page. You'll have a chance to use this tab in the Case Problems at the end of this tutorial.)

Figure 4-29	ADDING A BORDER TO THE NEWSLETTER

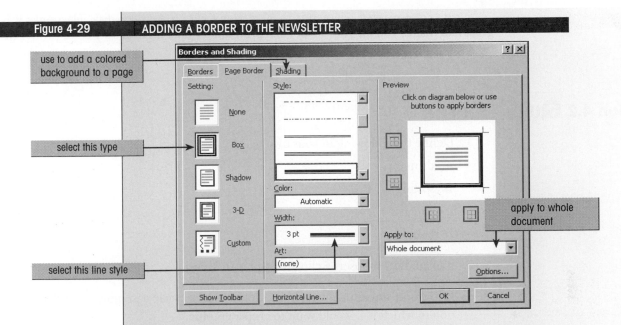

6. Click the **OK** button, and then save your work. The newsletter is now surrounded by an attractive border, as shown in Figure 4-30.

Figure 4-30	NEWSLETTER WITH BORDER

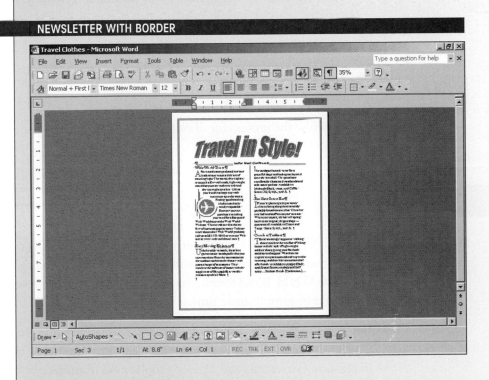

7. Create a footer that centers **Prepared by your name** and the current date at the bottom of the document. Be sure to replace **your name** with your first and last name. Format the footer in a small font to make it as unobtrusive as possible.

8. Preview the newsletter and then print it. Unless you have a color printer, the WordArt headline and the airplane will print in black and white.

9. If necessary, click the **Close** button on the Print Preview toolbar to return to Print Layout view, then close the newsletter and exit Word.

You give the printed newsletter to Max, along with a copy on disk. He thinks it looks great and thanks you for your help. He'll print it later on a high-quality color printer (to get the best resolution for printing multiple copies).

Session 4.2 QUICK CHECK

1. Define the following in your own words:
   a. **drop cap**
   b. scaling
   c. clip art
   d. balance

2. Explain how to insert a clip art graphic in Word.

3. Describe a situation in which you would want to scale a graphic. Describe a situation in which you would want to crop a graphic.

4. True or False: When inserting a drop cap, you can specify the number of lines you want the drop cap to extend into the document vertically.

5. Describe two different methods for inserting the registered trademark symbol in a document.

6. Besides the Symbol command on the Insert menu, what is another way of entering typographic symbols?

7. Describe the process for drawing a border around the page.

REVIEW ASSIGNMENTS

Max's Wide World Travel newsletter was a success; the sales for the advertised items were brisk. Now he has been asked to create a newsletter describing the highlights of some recent Wide World Travel tours. Max has already written the text of the newsletter and asks you to transform it into a professional-looking newsletter. Complete the following:

1. If necessary, start Word and make sure your Data Disk is in the appropriate disk drive. Check your screen to make sure your settings match those in the tutorial and that the nonprinting characters and Drawing toolbar are displayed.

2. Open the file **Travel** from the Review folder for Tutorial 4 on your Data Disk, and then save it as **Travel Highlights** in the same folder.

3. In the first paragraph after the heading "Wide World Tours," replace "YOUR NAME" with your first and last name.

4. In the first paragraph after the heading "Wide World Tours" (after the phone number), insert the following: "or visit our Web site at www.wideworldtravel.com." Then press Enter to insert a blank line. Remove the hyperlink from the Web address.

5. At the top of the document, create the headline "Wide World Highlights" using WordArt. In the WordArt Gallery, choose the third style from the right in the third row down from the top (the rainbow style with the shadow).

6. Change the shape of the WordArt object to Triangle Up, and then edit the WordArt text to add italics.

7. Apply the Top and Bottom wrapping style to the WordArt object.

8. Insert a blank paragraph at the beginning of the document, anchor the WordArt headline to the new paragraph, and then save your work. If the WordArt moves below the new paragraph symbol, drag it up above the new paragraph. When you are finished, the anchor symbol should be positioned to the left of the new paragraph symbol, with the WordArt object positioned above the new paragraph symbol.

9. If necessary, enlarge the WordArt object to span the entire width of the page. Be sure to hold down the Shift key while you drag. When you are finished, the WordArt object should be approximately .5 inches high on the left end, and about 1 inch tall at the center.

Explore ▸ 10. Practice dragging the adjustment handle (the yellow diamond on the left) up and down to change the slope of the WordArt image. Click the Undo button to undo each change. When you are finished, the adjustment handle should be located to the left of the middle resize handle on the left edge of the WordArt object.

Explore ▸ 11. Practice dragging the rotation handle to rotate the WordArt object. When you are finished, return the headline to its original, horizontal position.

12. Position the insertion point to the left of the first word in the first heading, and then format the newsletter text in two columns using the Columns dialog box. Insert a section break so that the columns formatting is applied to the part of the newsletter after the insertion point. Do not insert a line between columns. View the new columns in Print Layout view, using the Whole Page zoom setting.

13. Return to Page Width zoom, and then click to the left of the paragraph that begins "We prefaced our adventure . . . "

14. Insert the clip art graphic of the Eiffel Tower from the Buildings folder.

15. Select and resize the graphic so it is approximately 1.5 inches square.

16. Crop the image vertically on the left and right. When you are finished, the image

should be approximately 1 inch wide.

17. Use the Undo button to undo the cropping.

18. Wrap text around the graphic using the Tight wrapping option.

19. Add a drop cap for the first paragraph following each heading, using the default settings for the Dropped position.

Explore   20. Scroll to display the paragraph below the heading "Wide World Tours." Click after the last "s" in "Wide World Adventures," press the spacebar, and then type "(tm)" (without the quotation marks). Word's AutoCorrect feature converts the letters in parentheses to the trademark symbol. Save your work and then open a new, blank document, and practice using AutoCorrect to insert the typographic symbols shown earlier in Figure 4-26. When you are finished, close the document without saving your changes.

Explore   21. You can change the alignment of text in newspaper-style columns using the alignment buttons on the Formatting toolbar. Select both columns of text by clicking before the first word of the heading "Wide World Tours," pressing and holding down the Shift key, and then clicking after the last word of text in the second column ("square"). Use the Justify button on the Formatting toolbar to justify the text.

22. Balance the columns. If the words in the last line of the newsletter text are spaced too far apart after you insert the section break, click at the end of the line and then press Enter to move the section break to the next line.

23. Add a border around the page using a border style of your choice.

24. Preview, save, and print the newsletter. When you are finished, close the document and exit word.

CASE PROBLEMS

Case 1. City of Santa Fe, New Mexico   Caroline Hestwood is the manager of information systems for the city of Santa Fe. She and her staff, along with the city manager, have just decided to convert all city computers from the Windows 98 operating system to Windows 2000 and to standardize applications software on the latest version of Microsoft Office. Caroline writes a monthly newsletter on computer operations and training, so this month she decides to devote the newsletter to the conversion. Complete the following:

1. If necessary, start Word, make sure your Data Disk is in the appropriate drive, and check your screen to make sure your settings match those in the tutorial.

2. Open the file **Convert** from the Cases folder for Tutorial 4 on your Data Disk, and then save the file as **Software Conversion** in the same folder.

Explore   3. If the text you want to format as WordArt has already been typed, you can begin creating your WordArt by selecting the text in the document. Select the text of the newsletter title, "Software Update." (Do not select the paragraph symbol at the end of the title.) Click the Insert WordArt button on the Drawing toolbar, and then choose the WordArt style in the third row down, first column on the left. Verify that "Software Update" appears in the Edit WordArt Text dialog box, and then click OK.

4. Set the wrapping style to Top and Bottom, insert a new paragraph, and then anchor the WordArt to the new paragraph.

5. Edit the WordArt object to set the font to 32-point Arial bold, and then apply the Arch Up (Curve) shape to the object. Resize the WordArt object so that it spans the width of the page from left margin to right margin and so that its maximum height is about 1 inch. (*Hint*: Use the resize handles while watching the horizontal and vertical rulers in Print Layout view to adjust the object to the appropriate size.)

6. Center and italicize the subtitle of the newsletter, "Newsletter from the Santa Fe Information Management Office."

7. Replace "INSERT YOUR NAME HERE" with your name, then center and italicize the line containing your name.

8. Insert a continuous section break before the subtitle.

Explore   9. You can emphasize paragraphs within a document by putting a border around one or more paragraphs and by adding shading. To learn how, select the subtitle and the line after it (containing your name). Click Format on the menu bar, and then click Borders and Shading. In the Borders and Shading dialog box, select the Box style on the Borders tab, click the Shading tab, select a light, see-through color from the Fill grid, such as Gray-15%, and then click OK.

10. Select everything in the newsletter from the heading "The Big Switch" through the last word in the document. Then use the Columns button in the Standard toolbar to format the body of the newsletter into two newspaper-style columns. Examine the newsletter to find the new section break.

Explore   11. Position the insertion point at the beginning of the first paragraph under the heading "Training on MS Office," and then open the Insert Clip Art Task Pane. In the Search text box, type Computer and then click Search. A group of clip art images appears in the Insert Clip Art Task Pane. Click an image that illustrates the newsletter content. The image is inserted into the newsletter. Close the Insert Clip Art Task Pane.

Explore   12. Resize the picture so that it is 35% of its original size. Instead of dragging the resize handles as you did in the tutorial, select the picture, and then click the Format Picture button on the Picture toolbar to open the Format Picture dialog box. Click the Size tab. Adjust the Height and Width settings to 35% in the Scale section, and make sure the Lock aspect ratio check box is selected. Click OK.

13. Use the appropriate Picture toolbar button to select the Tight wrapping option.

Explore 14. You can use the Replace command to replace standard word processing characters with typographic characters. To replace every occurrence of two dashes (– –) with an em dash (—), position the insertion point at the beginning of the first paragraph of text. Click Edit on the menu bar, and then click Replace. In the Find what text box, type two hyphens (--), and then press the Tab key to move the insertion point to the Replace with text box. Click the More button to display additional options, and then click the Special button at the bottom of the dialog box. Click Em Dash in the list. Word displays the special code for em dashes in the Replace with text box. Click the Replace All button. When the operation is complete, click the OK button, and then click the Close button.

Explore 15. Preview the newsletter. If it does not fit on one page, click the Shrink to Fit button on the Print Preview toolbar.

16. Insert a border around the newsletter. Use a border style of your choice.

17. If necessary, balance the columns.

18. Save and print the newsletter, and then close it and exit Word.

Case 2. *Morning Star Movers* Martin Lott is the executive secretary to Whitney Kremer, director of personnel for Morning Star Movers (MSM), a national moving company with headquarters in Minneapolis, Minnesota. Whitney assigned you the task of preparing the monthly newsletter News and Views, which provides news about MSM employees. You decide to update the layout and to use the desktop-publishing capabilities of Word to design the newsletter. You will use text assembled by other MSM employees for the body of the newsletter. Complete the following:

1. If necessary, start Word, make sure your Data Disk is in the appropriate drive, and check your screen to make sure your settings match those in the tutorial.

2. Open the file **Movers** from the Cases folder for Tutorial 4 on your Data Disk, and then save it as **Movers Newsletter** in the same folder.

3. Use the Find and Replace command to replace all instances of the name "Katrina" with your first name. Then replace all instances of "Pollei" with your last name.

4. Click at the end of the first section (to the right of the space after "contact her at") and then type "thurlow@msm.net" (without the quotes) followed by a period. Press Enter to insert a blank line, and then remove the hyperlink.

5. Create a "News and Views" WordArt title for the newsletter. Use the WordArt style in the third row down, fourth column from the left, and set the font to 24-point Arial bold. Set the wrapping style to Top and Bottom, and then anchor the WordArt to a new, blank paragraph.

6. Resize the WordArt object proportionally so that the title spans the width of the page from left margin to right margin and so that the height of the title is about 1 inch. (*Hint*: Use the resize handles while watching the horizontal and vertical rulers in Print Layout view to adjust the object to the appropriate size.)

7. Make sure the WordArt object is positioned above the new paragraph, and then format the body of the newsletter into two newspaper-style columns. Place a vertical rule between the columns.

Explore   8. You can change the structure of a newsletter by reformatting it with additional columns. Change the number of columns from two to three using the same technique you used in the previous step (that is, the Columns command on the Format menu). Make sure that the Equal column width check box is selected.

Explore   9. You can insert your own graphics, stored as an electronic file, just as quickly as you can insert clip art. Position the insertion point at the beginning of the paragraph below the heading "MSM Chess Team Takes Third." Click Insert on the menu bar, point to Picture, and then click From File. Look in the Cases folder for Tutorial 4 on your Data Disk, select the file named Knight, and then click the Insert button.

Explore   10. You can delete a graphic by selecting it, and then pressing the Delete key. To practice this technique, click the Knight graphic to select it, and then press the Delete key. To reinsert the graphic, click the Undo button.

11. Scale the height and the width of the picture to 60% of its original size. (*Hint*: To scale the size, click the Format Picture button on the Picture toolbar, and then set the Scale values on the Size tab, making sure the Lock aspect ratio check box is selected.) Close the Format Picture dialog box when you are finished.

Explore   12. In addition to cropping a picture with the Crop button, you can use the Format Picture dialog box. Using this dialog box allows you to be more precise because you can specify exact cropping measurements. To try it now, click the Format Picture button on the Picture toolbar, click the Picture tab, and change the values in the Crop from text boxes. Crop 0.3, 0.4, 0.2, and 0.4 inches from the left, right, top, and bottom of the picture, respectively.

Explore   13. You already know how to wrap text around a graphic or WordArt object using the Text Wrapping button. In some situations, however, you might need additional options to gain even more control over how text wraps in a document. To view these options now, click the Format Picture button on the Picture toolbar, click the Layout tab, and then click Advanced. Click the Tight icon, and notice the additional settings at the bottom of the Advanced Layout dialog box. Among other things, you can specify to what side the text should wrap and the distance to preserve between the text and the graphic. Click the Right only option button, click OK, and then click OK again. Keep in mind that you can also access the Advanced Layout dialog box from the Format WordArt dialog box.

Explore

14. Format drop caps in the first paragraph after each heading except the "MSM Chess Team Takes Third" heading. Use the default settings for number of lines, but change the font of the drop cap to Arial.

15. View the entire page. If necessary, decrease the height of the WordArt title or change the page margins until the entire newsletter fits onto one page and until each column starts with a heading.

16. Add a border around the entire page of the newsletter using the Page Border command.

17. Save the newsletter, and then preview and print it. Close the document and exit Word.

Case 3. *Wild Grains Grocery Cooperative* Mary Ann Hansen is the publicity director for Wild Grains Grocery Cooperative in Athens, Georgia. Local residents pay a membership fee to join the co-op, and then receive a 10% discount on all purchases. Many members don't realize that they can take advantage of other benefits—such as free cooking classes and monthly mailings with recipe cards and coupons. To spread the word, Mary Ann would like to create a brochure describing the benefits of joining the co-op. She has already written the text of the brochure. She would like the brochure to consist of one piece of paper folded in three parts, like a standard business letter, with text on both sides of the paper. Complete the following:

1. If necessary, start Word, make sure your Data Disk is in the appropriate drive, and check your screen to make sure your settings match those in the tutorial.

2. Open the file **Grains** from the Cases folder for Tutorial 4 on your Data Disk, and then save it as **Wild Grains Brochure**.

3. Below the cornucopia graphic, click after the Web address, insert a blank line and then type your first and last name. Remove the hyperlink from the Web address.

4. Format the entire document in three columns of equal width. Do not include a vertical line between columns. Don't be concerned that part of the text overflows onto a second page.

5. Click at the end of the list of member benefits (after the word "country") and press Ctrl+Enter to insert a page break. Click the Bullets button to remove the bullet from the new paragraph.

Explore

6. You are already familiar with adding section breaks and page breaks to a document. You can also add a column break, which forces the text after the insertion point to move to the next column. Click at the beginning of the heading "Join Now!" (just to the left of the "J"), click Insert on the menu bar and then click Break. Under Break Types, click Column break, and then click OK. Insert another column break before the heading "Member Benefits." On the second page, click at the top of the left-hand column, press Enter a few times to insert some blank paragraphs, and then insert another column break. (Don't be concerned if the new paragraph marks don't align.) Press Ctrl+End to move the insertion point to the end of the document and insert another column break.

7. Change the zoom setting to Whole Page and review your work. The document should consist of two pages, with three columns each. The graphic and the co-op address should appear in the middle column on the second page.

Explore ▷ 8. Click the cornucopia graphic in the second page, click the Copy button on the Standard toolbar, click to the left of the heading "Join Now!" and then add two blank paragraphs. Click in the first new paragraph (at the top of the column) and then click the Paste button on the Standard toolbar. The middle column of the first page now contains the graphic, with the heading "Join Now!" below, followed by two paragraphs of text.

9. Click in the left-hand column of page 2, and then delete all but one of the paragraph marks. With the insertion point located at the only remaining paragraph mark in the left-hand column, insert the WordArt text "WHY JOIN?" In the WordArt Gallery select the style in the fourth column from the left, third row down (the rainbow style with a shadow). Be sure to type "WHY JOIN?" in all uppercase letters in the Edit WordArt Text dialog box, and format the text in boldface. Save your work.

Explore ▷ 10. Select the WordArt object, and then click the WordArt Vertical Text button on the WordArt toolbar. The heading is positioned vertically in the left-hand column of page 2.

11. Increase the size of the WordArt object (by dragging a resize handle) so that the WordArt spans the height of the column—do *not* press Shift as you drag the handle—and the letters spread out to fill the height of the column. When you are finished, the WordArt object should be approximately 6 inches high. If you increase the size too much, the WordArt will jump to the next column. If that happens, click the Undo button and try again.

Explore ▷ 12. Click the Format WordArt button on the WordArt toolbar. In the Format WordArt dialog box, click the Colors and Lines tab, click the Color list arrow, click the black square in the upper-left hand corner of the palette, and then click OK. The WordArt changes from a rainbow style to all black. Save your work.

Explore ▷ 13. Use the Copy button on the Formatting toolbar to copy the "WHY JOIN?" WordArt object to the Office Clipboard. Paste a copy of the WordArt object in the right-hand column of page 2, and then change the text to "WILD GRAINS". When you are finished, page 2 should consist of the "WHY JOIN?" WordArt in the left-hand column, the graphic and address information in the middle column, and the "WILD GRAINS" WordArt in the right-hand column. Zoom to Whole Page view and examine your work.

14. If necessary, add paragraph breaks to the center column to center the graphic and the text vertically in relation to the WordArt titles. Adjust the size of the WordArt as necessary.

15. Use the Page Setup command on the File menu to center both pages vertically. (*Hint*: Use the Vertical alignment setting in the Layout tab.)

Explore   16. To print the brochure, you need to print the first page and print the second page on the reverse side. Click File on the menu bar, click Print, click the Pages option button, type 1, and then click OK. Retrieve the printed page, and then insert it into your printer's paper tray so that "WHY JOIN?" prints on the reverse side of the list of member benefits; likewise, "WILD GRAINS" should print on the reverse side of the "Welcome to Wild Grains" text. Whether you should place the printed page upside down or right-side up depends on your printer. You may have to print a few test pages until you get it right. When you finish, you should be able to turn page 1 (the page with the heading "Welcome to Wild Grains") face up, and then fold it inward like a business letter, along the two column borders. Fold the brochure so that the "WILD GRAINS" column lies on top.

17. Save and close the document, and then exit Word.

Case 4. New Job Newsletter You've just moved to a new part of the country and decide to send out a newsletter to friends and family describing your new job. In the one-page newsletter, you'll include articles about you and your colleagues, your new job, your new responsibilities, and future plans. You'll desktop publish the copy into a professional-looking newsletter. Complete the following:

1. If necessary, start Word, make sure your Data Disk is in the appropriate drive, and check your screen to make sure your settings match those in the tutorial.

2. Write two articles to include in the newsletter; save each article in a separate file.

3. Plan the general layout of your newsletter.

4. Create a title for your newsletter with WordArt.

5. Save the document as **New Job** in the Cases folder for Tutorial 4.

Explore   6. Insert the current date and your name as author below the title.

7. Insert the articles you wrote into your newsletter. Position the insertion point where you want the first article to appear, click Insert on the menu bar, click File, select the article you want to insert, and then click the Insert button. Repeat to insert the second article.

Explore   8. Format your newsletter with multiple columns.

9. Insert at least one clip art picture into your newsletter. If your computer is connected to the Internet, use the Clips Online option in the Insert Clip Art Task Pane to access Microsoft's online collection of clip art. Follow the directions on the screen to search for an image that illustrates the content of your newsletter. Download the image to your computer, and then insert it into the newsletter.

Explore   10. Wrap text around the graphic, and then add at least two drop caps in the newsletter.

11. Create a border around the page and then add shading to the entire document using the Shading tab in the Borders and Shading dialog box. (*Hint*: Press Ctrl+A to select the entire document, open the Borders and Shading dialog box, select a page border, click the Shading tab, select a light, transparent color from the Fill grid, such as Gray-15%, and then click OK.)

12. Save and print the newsletter, and then close the document and exit Word.

INTERNET ASSIGNMENTS

Student Union

The purpose of the Internet Assignments is to challenge you to find information on the Internet that you can use to create effective documents. The actual assignments are updated and maintained on the Course Technology Web site. Log on to the Internet and use your Web browser to go to the Student Union on the New Perspectives Series site at **www.course.com/NewPerspectives/studentunion**. Click the Online Companions link, and then click the link for this text.

QUICK CHECK ANSWERS

Session 4.1

1. List any four of the following: The printing is of high-quality; the document uses multiple fonts; the document incorporates graphics; the document uses typographic characters; the document uses columns and other special formatting features.

2. List any two of the following: In desktop publishing the reader sees the entire page at one time while in a Web page the reader sees only part of the page at a time; in desktop publishing the use of color increases printing costs, while in Web design, color itself does not affect the cost of producing a Web page; in desktop publishing the quality of the printer greatly affects the appearance of graphics in the printed page, while in Web design the quality of graphics is most affected by the type of electronic file in which the graphic is stored; in desktop publishing the page is static, while in Web design parts of the page can be animated, or include video and audio; the reader cannot interact with a desktop-published document, while it is possible to interact with a Web page by clicking hyperlinks.

3. (a) Using a desktop computer system to produce commercial-quality printed material. With desktop publishing, you can enter and edit text, create graphics, lay out pages, and print documents. (b) A document that can contain specially formatted text, graphics, video, and audio. A Web page is stored on a computer as a collection of electronic files and is designed to be viewed in a special program called a browser. (c) Unformatted text (d) A symbol that appears in the left margin, which shows a WordArt object's position in relation to the text.

4. False

5. False

6. To resize a WordArt object, select the object and drag its resize handles. To resize the WordArt object proportionally, press and hold the Shift key as you drag a resize handle.

   To change the text of a WordArt object, click the object to select it, click the Edit Text button on the WordArt toolbar, edit the text in the Edit WordArt Text dialog box, and then click OK.

7. The WordArt Shape button allows you to change the basic shape of a Word-Art object.

8. True

Session 4.2

1. (a) a large, uppercase letter that highlights the beginning of the text of a newsletter, chapter, or some other document section; (b) resizing an image to better fit a document; (c) existing, copyright-free artwork that you can insert into your document; (d) to make columns of equal length

2. Position the insertion point at the location where you want to insert the image, click the Insert Clip Art button on the Drawing toolbar, click Clip Organizer in the Task Pane, open the folder containing the image you want, click the arrow button on the image, click Copy, and then close the Clip Organizer. Finally, paste the graphic into the document.

3. You might scale a graphic to better fit the width of a column of text. You might crop a graphic to emphasize or draw attention to a particular part of the image or to eliminate unnecessary borders.

4. True

5. Click where you want to insert the symbol in the document, click Insert on the menu bar, click Symbol, click the Special Characters tab in the Symbol dialog box, click Registered Trademark in the list, click the Insert button, and then click the Close button. Type "(tm)".

6. using the AutoCorrect feature, which lets you type certain characters and then changes those characters into the corresponding symbol

7. Click Format on the menu bar, click Borders and Shading, click the Page Border tab in the Borders and Shading dialog box, select the border type you want in the Setting section, choose a line style from the Style list box, make sure Whole document appears in the Apply to list box, and then click OK.

New Perspectives on

MICROSOFT WORD 2002

Read This Before You Begin

To the Student

Data Disks

To complete the Level II tutorials, Review Assignments, and Case Problems, you need three Data Disks. Your instructor will either provide you with the Data Disks or ask you to make your own. You will also need storage space on your computer's hard drive.

If you are making your own Data Disks, you will need **three** blank, formatted high-density disks. You will need to copy a set of files and/or folders from a file server, standalone computer, or the Web onto your disk. Your instructor will tell you which computer, drive letter, and folders contain the files you need. You could also download the files by going to **www.course.com** and following the instructions on the screen.

The information below shows you which folders go on your disks, so that you will have enough disk space to complete all the tutorials, Review Assignments, and Case Problems:

Data Disk 1

Write this on the disk label:
Data Disk 1: Word 2002 Tutorial 5

Put this folder on the disk:
Tutorial.05

Data Disk 2

Write this on the disk label:
Data Disk 2: Word 2002 Tutorial 6 (Tutorial and Review)

Put these folders on the disk:
Tutorial.06\Tutorial and Tutorial.06\Review

Data Disk 3

Write this on the disk label:
Data Disk 3: Word 2002 Tutorial 6 (Cases)

Put this folder on the disk:
Tutorial.06\Cases

Before you begin Tutorial 7, copy the Tutorial.07 folder to your hard drive.

When you begin each tutorial, be sure you are using the correct Data Disk (or that you have copied the necessary files to your hard drive). Refer to the "File Finder" chart at the back of this text for more detailed information on which files are

used in which tutorials. See the inside front or inside back cover of this book for more information on Data Disk files, or ask your instructor or technical support person for assistance.

Course Labs

The Word Level II tutorials feature an interactive Course Lab to help you understand Internet: World Wide Web concepts. The Lab Assignments at the end of Tutorial 7 refer to this Lab.

To start a Lab, click the **Start** button on the Windows taskbar, point to **Programs**, point to **Course Labs**, point to **New Perspectives Course Labs**, and click the name of the Lab you want to use.

Using Your Own Computer

If you are going to work through this book using your own computer, you need:

- **Computer System** Microsoft Windows 98, NT, 2000 Professional, or higher must be installed on your computer. This book assumes you have installed Microsoft Word 2002 on your computer. To complete Tutorial 7, you also need to have Microsoft Excel 2002 installed on your computer. Depending on the options chosen when you installed Word, you may need access to the Microsoft Office XP installation CD in order to install additional features. (The tutorial steps provide information on installing these features as you need them.)

- **Data Disks** You will not be able to complete the tutorials or exercises in this book using your own computer until you have your Data Disks.

- **Course Labs** See your instructor or technical support person to obtain the Course Lab software for use on your own computer.

Visit Our World Wide Web Site

Additional materials designed especially for you are available on the World Wide Web. Go to www.course.com/NewPerspectives.

To the Instructor

The Data Disk Files and Course Labs are available on the Instructor's Resource Kit for this title. Follow the instructions in the Help file on the CD-ROM to install the programs to your network or standalone computer. For information on creating Data Disks or the Course Labs, see the "To the Student" section above. Please note:

students need to install the data files for Tutorial 7 onto their hard drives due to the complexity of the tutorial.

You are granted a license to copy the Data Files and Course Labs to any computer or computer network used by students who have purchased this book.

OBJECTIVES

In this tutorial you will:

- Use the Thesaurus

- Create a new folder

- Use fonts appropriately to add interest to a document

- Use fonts and styles

- Attach a template to a document and create a new template

- Create and modify an outline

- Hyphenate a document

- Add footnotes and endnotes

- Insert text with Click and Type and apply text highlighting

- Adjust character and paragraph spacing

- Create a table of contents

CREATING
STYLES, OUTLINES, TABLES, AND TABLES OF CONTENTS

Writing a Business Plan for Safe Site Inc.

CASE

SafeSite Inc.

Pamela Morris and Maya Siu have been friends since college, where they both majored in computer science. Since graduation a few years ago, they have been working for e-commerce companies—companies that sell their products over the Web. Typically, customers make e-commerce purchases by typing information into a form on a Web page and then clicking a button. The information is then sent to the company via the Internet. One problem with this arrangement is that many customers hesitate to send private information, such as credit card numbers, over the Internet because they fear that a third party might intercept this information and use it for fraudulent purposes. To help protect their customers' privacy, e-commerce companies employ a variety of security measures. Still, many consumers continue to avoid e-commerce sites because they don't understand how effective these security measures are.

With this in mind, Pamela and Maya are developing a new Web site, called SafeSite, that will allow consumers to look up security ratings for e-commerce companies. Pamela and Maya have already established a new business, SafeSite Inc., which will market the Web site. Like many Web businesses, SafeSite Inc. will ultimately generate revenue by selling advertising space. The more popular their site becomes with e-commerce customers, the more Maya and Pamela will be able to charge for advertising on SafeSite.

Maya and Pamela are ready to quit their jobs to work full-time on SafeSite. Before they can do that, they must secure a start-up loan from First Bank of the Pacific. To obtain the loan, they must write a business plan—a report that details all aspects of starting a new business, including the market for the business, operations, financial, and personnel information. They have written part of the plan and have asked you to help them work on it.

SESSION 5.1

In this session, you will see how Maya and Pamela planned their report. Then you'll open the report and use the Microsoft Word Thesaurus to edit the report. You'll learn about using fonts and templates, and then modify, create, and apply template styles to format the report. Finally, you will create a new template for use in future SafeSite documents.

Planning the Document

Before they began working on their business plan, Maya and Pamela consulted a number of resources, including the U.S. government Small Business Administration (SBA). They know that a thorough business plan informs prospective investors about the purpose, organization, goals, and projected profits of the proposed business. It also analyzes the target industry, including available market research. Most importantly, a business plan should convince potential investors that the venture is viable, well-conceived, and worthy of funding.

Maya and Pamela want to organize their business plan in a standard manner. According to information on the SBA's Web site, the body of a business plan can be divided into four parts: the description of the business; the marketing plan; the financial management plan; and the management plan. In addition, a business plan should include an executive summary, supporting documents, and financial projections. Maya and Pamela have completed some of these sections, and have saved them in a Word document named SafeSite.

Maya and Pamela have begun to format the document, but want you to check the fonts, headers, and styles and make sure the formatting is consistent. They also need you to create a table of contents and create a new folder in which to store your version of the document.

Creating a New Folder

You'll begin by opening the current draft of the business plan. Pamela wants you to create a new folder in which to store the business plan and any related files. That way she can easily copy the entire folder to a floppy disk and transfer the files to her home computer. You'll create the folder, and then save the document in the new folder, using a different filename.

To open the document and save it in a new folder:

1. Start Word, if necessary, make sure your Data Disk is in the appropriate drive, and check the screen. Make sure that nonprinting characters are displayed.

2. Open the file **SafeSite** from the Tutorial subfolder in the Tutorial.05 folder on your Data Disk.

3. Switch to Normal view, if necessary.

4. Click **File** on the menu bar, and then click **Save As** to display the Save As dialog box. You'll now create a new folder called Business Plan within the Tutorial folder.

5. Click the **Create New Folder** button 📵 located near the top of the Save As dialog box. The New Folder dialog box opens, as shown in Figure 5-1.

Figure 5-1 NEW FOLDER DIALOG BOX

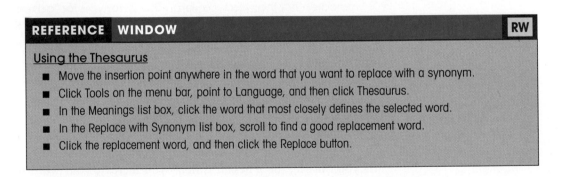

6. Type **Business Plan** in the Name text box, and then click the **OK** button. The new folder appears in the Save in list box at the top of the Save As dialog box.

7. Save the Safe Site document in the new Business Plan folder using the filename **SafeSite Business Plan**.

Before you begin formatting the SafeSite business plan, read through it carefully to check for word usage. You can find synonyms for overused words by using Word's built-in Thesaurus.

Using the Thesaurus

In the paragraph above the last heading in the SafeSite business plan document, the word "market" occurs twice in one sentence. Pamela asks you to replace the second occurrence with another word that has the same meaning. You can do this using the Thesaurus. The **Thesaurus** is a Word feature that contains a list of words and their synonyms. Similar to a thesaurus reference book, the Word Thesaurus lets you look up a specific word to find its synonyms and related words. Then you can immediately insert an appropriate synonym into a document. The Thesaurus is a useful editing tool that helps make your word choices varied and exact.

REFERENCE WINDOW	RW

Using the Thesaurus
- Move the insertion point anywhere in the word that you want to replace with a synonym.
- Click Tools on the menu bar, point to Language, and then click Thesaurus.
- In the Meanings list box, click the word that most closely defines the selected word.
- In the Replace with Synonym list box, scroll to find a good replacement word.
- Click the replacement word, and then click the Replace button.

You'll now use the Thesaurus to find a synonym for the word "market."

To find synonyms using the Thesaurus:

1. Click **Edit** on the menu bar, click **Find**, and then use the Search and Replace dialog box to find the sentence that begins "We are prepared to refine our site."

2. In the sentence that begins "We are prepared to refine our site," click the second occurrence of the word **market**.

3. Click **Tools** on the menu bar, point to **Language**, and then click **Thesaurus**. The Thesaurus: English (U.S.) dialog box opens. The word "market" appears in the Looked Up list box. A list of possible meanings for "market" appears in the Meanings list. "Marketplace" is selected in the Meanings list. A list of synonyms for "marketplace" appears to the right. Your Thesaurus dialog box should look similar to Figure 5-2, although your list of synonyms may differ.

Figure 5-2	FINDING SYNONYMS FOR MARKET

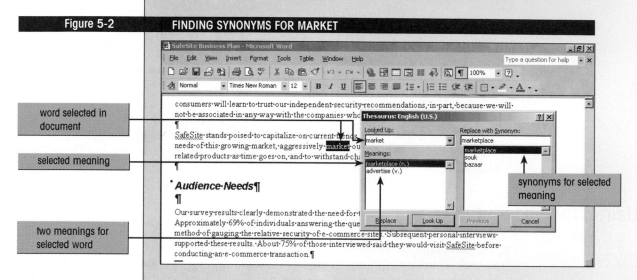

word selected in document

selected meaning

two meanings for selected word

synonyms for selected meaning

Whenever you use the Thesaurus, be sure to select the correct meaning for the word you're looking up. For example, in the business plan, the selected occurrence of "market" means advertise, not marketplace. You need to select this meaning before you can view the correct synonyms.

4. Click **advertise (v.)** in the Meanings list box. (Note that the "v." in parentheses indicates that the word is a verb.) The synonyms for "advertise" appear in the Replace with Synonym list box on the right. Pamela thinks that "promote" is the best synonym.

5. Click **promote** in the Replace with Synonym list box to highlight it, and then click the **Replace** button. The Thesaurus dialog box closes, and the word "promote" replaces the word "market" in the document.

6. Save your work.

As you can see, the Thesaurus helps you increase your word power as you write. Now that the text of the chapter is finished, you can work on its appearance. To create a professional-looking document, you need to understand how to use fonts effectively.

Choosing Fonts

The Word default font, Times New Roman, is useful for many situations. But in some cases, you may want to choose a different font. Times New Roman was specifically designed for narrow-column newspaper text. For reports (such as business plans), Web pages, and other documents that have wider columns, a wider font is sometimes easier to read. Here are some general principles that might help you decide which fonts to use in your documents:

■ It's common practice to use a serif font for the main text. A **serif** is a small embellishment at the tips of the lines of a character, as shown in Figure 5-3. "Sans" is French for "without," thus, a **sans serif font** is a font without embellishments.

Figure 5-3	SERIF AND SANS SERIF FONTS

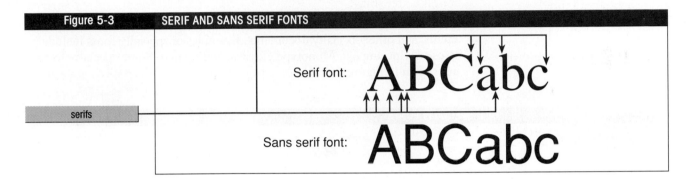

■ Common serif fonts include Book Antiqua, Courier, Garamond, and Times New Roman, some of which are shown in Figure 5-4. Because serif fonts are easy to read, they are appropriate not only for main text, but also for titles and headings.

Figure 5-4	SAMPLE SERIF FONTS

■ Examples of common sans serif fonts include Arial, Arial Narrow, Century Gothic, and Lucida Console, some of which are shown in Figure 5-5. Large blocks of text in sans serif font can be harder to read than serif fonts, so you should use sans serif fonts for titles, headings, headers and footers, captions, and other special parts of a document.

Figure 5-5	SAMPLE SANS SERIF FONTS

Arial
Arial Narrow
Century Gothic

- Avoid all-uppercase sans serif text, which is difficult to read. All-uppercase serif font is easier to read, but mixed uppercase and lowercase text in any font is better still.

- Avoid unusual or fancy fonts except in certificates, invitations, advertisements, and other specialty documents. Examples of specialty fonts include Brush Script, Impact, Monotype Corsiva, and Stencil. Some specialty fonts are shown in Figure 5-6.

Figure 5-6	SAMPLE SPECIALTY FONTS

Brush Script

Monotype Corsiva

STENCIL

- Avoid excessive changes in fonts and font attributes. Typically, the text of a document should include only one or two fonts—one for the main paragraphs and another one for the titles and headings. Excessive use of boldface and italics makes a document appear cluttered and sloppy and detracts attention from the document's content.

- You can add special effects to most fonts by adjusting the formatting settings in the Font dialog box. (To open this dialog box, click Format on the menu bar, and then click Font.) For example, you can format a font as small caps (a reduced version of regular capital letters), superscript (slightly above the main line), subscript (slightly below the main line), outline (only the outline of the letters), or with shadows. Figure 5-7 shows some common font effects. Take care not to overuse special effects, or your document will look messy.

Figure 5-7	COMMON FONT EFFECTS

SMALL CAPS

Super^{script}

Sub_{script}

Outline

Shadow

Pamela wants you to choose some appropriate fonts and apply them to the business plan.

Applying Styles

Now that you understand how to use fonts effectively, you're ready to learn how to apply them quickly to text. It's often helpful to use the Format Painter to copy formatting (including fonts) from one paragraph to another. However, when you're working on a long document, it is easier to use the sets of predefined formats known as **styles**. Every Word document opens with a set of styles that includes Normal (the default style for paragraphs in a Word document), Heading 1, Heading 2, and Heading 3. Word's default Normal style is 12-point Times New Roman, left alignment, with single-line spacing.

All styles used in a document are listed in the Style list on the Formatting toolbar. Figure 5-8 shows the default styles available with a new, blank document. Note that the Style list will rarely be so short, because every time you change the formatting in a document (for example, by adding a bulleted list or underlining a heading), Word adds your formatting choices to the Style list as new styles.

Figure 5-8 **DEFAULT STYLES**

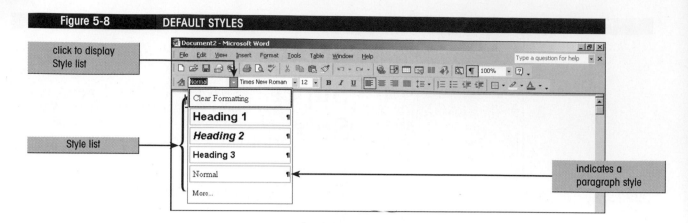

The easiest way to apply a style is to select the text you want to format, and then select a style in the Style list. However, if you plan to work extensively with styles in a document, you may prefer to use the options in the Styles and Formatting Task Pane. You can also use the Reveal Formatting Task Pane, which summarizes all the formatting applied to selected text. (You'll have a chance to use the Styles and Formatting Task Pane later in this tutorial. You'll use the Reveal Formatting Task Pane in the Case Problems at the end of this tutorial.)

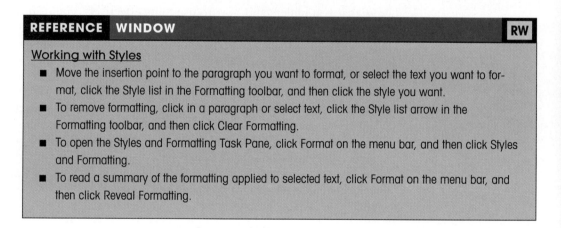

REFERENCE WINDOW **RW**

Working with Styles

- Move the insertion point to the paragraph you want to format, or select the text you want to format, click the Style list in the Formatting toolbar, and then click the style you want.
- To remove formatting, click in a paragraph or select text, click the Style list arrow in the Formatting toolbar, and then click Clear Formatting.
- To open the Styles and Formatting Task Pane, click Format on the menu bar, and then click Styles and Formatting.
- To read a summary of the formatting applied to selected text, click Format on the menu bar, and then click Reveal Formatting.

Pamela and Maya used Word's default styles to format the headings in their business plan. However, after looking over the document, Pamela notices some inconsistencies. For example, she forgot to apply the Heading 1 style to the "Executive Summary" heading at the beginning of the document. You'll use the Style list to apply the Heading 1 style.

To apply a style:

1. Scroll up to the beginning of the document, and then click anywhere in the **Executive Summary** heading.

2. Click the **Style** list arrow in the Formatting toolbar. The Style list opens, as shown in Figure 5-9. The Style list contains the default styles included with all new Word documents (shown earlier in Figure 5-8), and styles for additional formatting (such as the bulleted list format) applied by Maya and Pamela. You want to apply the Heading 1 style.

Figure 5-9	STYLE LIST FOR SAFESITE BUSINESS PLAN DOCUMENT

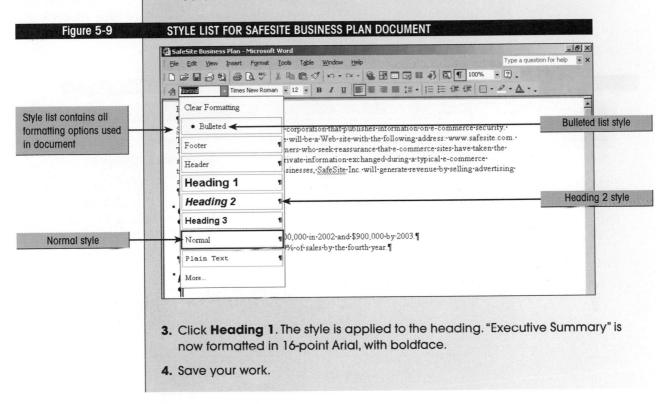

Style list contains all formatting options used in document

Bulleted list style

Heading 2 style

Normal style

3. Click **Heading 1**. The style is applied to the heading. "Executive Summary" is now formatted in 16-point Arial, with boldface.

4. Save your work.

Now that you are familiar with the Word Style list, you are ready to learn how to add other predefined styles to a document. You do this by using a Word template.

Using a Template

A **template** is a set of predefined styles designed for a specific type of document. For example, Word provides templates for formatting reports, brochures, memos, letters, and resumes. The Word default template, the Normal template, contains the Normal paragraph style described earlier. You can change the available styles by attaching a different template to a document. You can also use a Word template as the basis for a completely new document.

Another Word feature related to templates is known as a theme. A **theme** is a unified design for a document and can include background colors, horizontal and vertical lines, and graphics. Themes include colorful backgrounds and borders, and are designed for Web pages and other documents that you plan to present online. Typically, they are not suitable for business-related reports (such as a business plan).

Pamela wants to use the Word Professional Report template to format the business plan. She explains that you can see the styles available in this template by opening it from the New Documents Task Pane.

To review the styles in the Professional Report template:

1. Click **File** on the menu bar, and then click **New**. The New Document Task Pane opens.

2. Under the "New From Template" heading, click **General Templates**. The Templates dialog box opens. The tabs in this dialog box list a variety of templates which you can use as the basis for letters, reports, memos, and many other kinds of documents.

3. Click the **Reports** tab, if necessary. As shown in Figure 5-10, the Reports tab displays the templates that you can use to create reports. (Your Templates dialog box might contain more or fewer templates than the ones shown in Figure 5-10.) You're interested in the Professional Report template.

Figure 5-10	TEMPLATES DIALOG BOX

tabs contain templates for several types of documents

Reports template tab

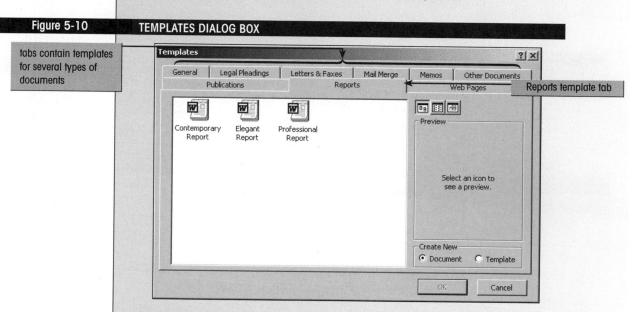

4. Click **Professional Report** and then click **OK**. The template opens in the Document window. It contains placeholder text formatted with the template styles.

   TROUBLE? If you see a message indicating that the Professional Report template is not installed, insert the Microsoft Office XP CD into your CD-ROM drive, and then click the OK button. If the Office XP CD is not available to you, choose another template.

5. Click the **Style** list arrow on the Formatting toolbar, examine the styles included in the template, press **Esc** to close the Style list, scroll through the document to view the formatted text, and then close the template.

You could use this template to create a new document by selecting the placeholder text and typing new text. However, the SafeSite Business Plan document already contains formatted headings. In this case, it makes more sense to attach the template to the existing document (that is, to the SafeSite Business Plan document), and then have Word apply the template styles automatically. (You'll use a template as the basis for a new document in the Review Assignments at the end of this chapter.)

Attaching a Template

You attach a template to a document using the Templates and Add-ins command on the Tools menu. Typically, Word's template files are stored in a subfolder of the Microsoft Office folder, in the Program Files folder. However, they may be stored in a different folder on your computer. Once you select the template file you want to attach, you need to select the "Automatically update document styles" check box in the Templates and Add-ins dialog box. This checkbox ensures that the templates styles are added to the document's Style list.

REFERENCE WINDOW   **RW**

Attaching a Word Template to a Document

- Click Tools on the menu bar, click Templates and Add-ins, and then click the Attach button.
- In the Attach Template dialog box, navigate to the folder containing the Microsoft Office Templates, select the template you want, and then click the Open button. You return to the Templates and Add-ins dialog box.
- Click the "Automatically update document styles" check box to select it. (You must select this check box so the template styles will appear in the document's Style list.)
- Click the OK button.

Pamela asks you to attach the Professional Report template to the SafeSite Business Plan document. The Professional Report template file is included on your Data Disk.

To preview and attach the Professional Report template to the business plan:

1. Click **Tools** on the menu bar, and then click **Templates and Add-ins**. The Templates and Add-ins dialog box opens.

2. Click the **Attach** button. The Attach Template dialog box opens. Use the Look in list arrow to open the Tutorial subfolder within the Tutorial.05 folder on your Data Disk.

3. If necessary, click **Professional Report** in the file list, as shown in Figure 5-11.

| Figure 5-11 | TEMPLATE SELECTED IN ATTACH TEMPLATE DIALOG BOX |

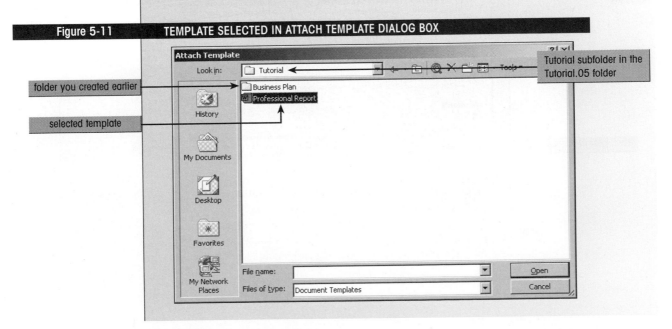

4. Click the **Open** button. The Attach Template dialog box closes, and you return to the Templates and Add-ins dialog box.

5. Click the **Automatically update document styles** check box to select it. Your Templates and Add-ins dialog box should look similar to the one in Figure 5-12.

Figure 5-12   **TEMPLATES AND ADD-INS DIALOG BOX**

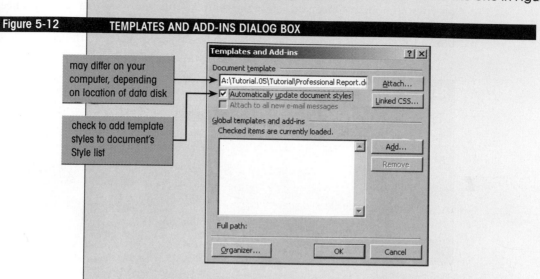

may differ on your computer, depending on location of data disk

check to add template styles to document's Style list

6. Click the **OK** button. The Templates and Add-ins dialog box closes, and you return to the Document window. The document is now formatted using the styles of the Professional Report template, as shown in Figure 5-13.

Figure 5-13   **DOCUMENT FORMATTED WITH TEMPLATE STYLES**

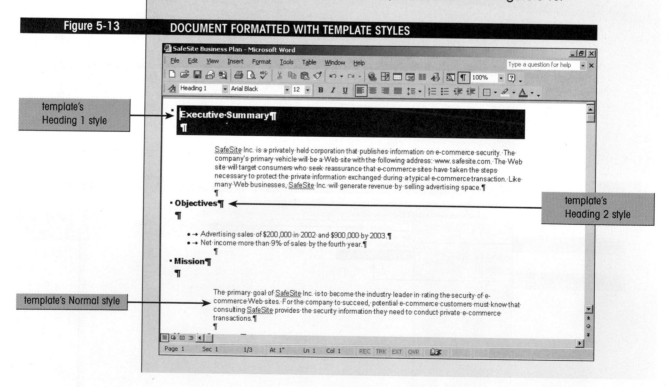

template's Heading 1 style

template's Heading 2 style

template's Normal style

7. Click the **Executive Summary** heading and read the style name in the Style list box. The template's Heading 1 style includes a black background and white text.

8. Click in the paragraph below the "Executive Summary" heading, and read the style name in the Style list box. The template's Normal style includes a paragraph indentation, and a 10-point Arial font.

9. Click the **Style** list arrow on the Formatting toolbar, and scroll through the list of template styles. Note that the styles with paragraph marks next to them are considered paragraph styles. When you click a paragraph style, the paragraph containing the insertion point is formatted (whether or not the entire paragraph is selected). The styles with lowercase a's are character styles. When you select a character style, only the text you have selected is formatted. You'll learn more about character and paragraph formatting later in this tutorial. Figure 5-14 shows examples of character and paragraph styles.

Figure 5-14	TEMPLATE CHARACTER AND PARAGRAPH STYLES

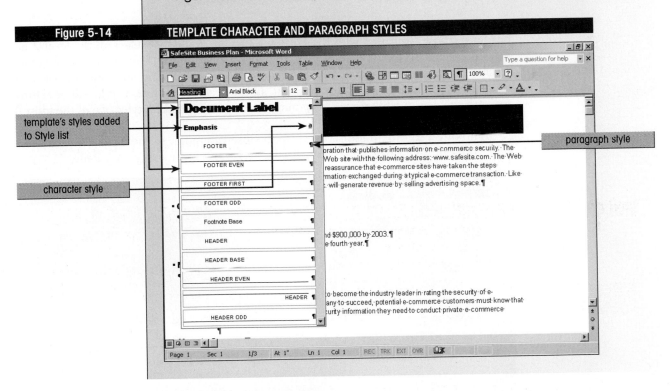

Applying Template Styles

After you attach a template to a document, you often need to correct formatting problems. For instance, the Normal style paragraphs in the report document are indented slightly. However, the bulleted lists in the document are not. Pamela asks you to fix this problem by applying the template's List Bullet 2 style, a bulleted list style that includes paragraph indentation.

To apply template styles to the document:

1. Press the **Esc** key to close the style list.

2. Select the bulleted list of objectives near the beginning of the document. Take care to select both items in the list, as well as the paragraph mark at the end of each item. Do not, however, select the paragraph mark below the bulleted list.

3. Click the **Style** list arrow on the Formatting toolbar, scroll down, and then click **List Bullet 2**. The list of objectives is indented further to the right and formatted with square bullets.

   TROUBLE? If the list is formatted without bullets, you may have clicked "List 2" rather than "List Bullet 2." Click the Undo button on the Standard toolbar and try again.

4. Use the List Bullet 2 style to format the bulleted lists below the headings "Keys to Success" and "Market Analysis Summary."

5. Save your work.

Modifying a Style

After looking over the document, Pamela decides that she wants to italicize the second-level headings (those formatted with the Heading 2 style). You could select all the level-2 headings, and then click the Italic button on the Formatting toolbar. However, it's more efficient to change the style definition, which specifies the particular font, size, and format for that style. Once you change the style definition, all the headings with that style will be reformatted with the new, modified style. This automatic updating makes styles one of the most flexible and helpful Word tools.

To modify a style definition, you move the insertion point to the text formatted with the style you want to change, and then open the Styles and Formatting Task Pane.

REFERENCE WINDOW	RW

Modifying a Style

- Click Format on the menu bar, and then click Styles and Formatting to open the Styles and Formatting Task Pane.
- In the Styles and Formatting Task Pane, right-click the style you want to modify, and then click Modify.
- In the Modify Style dialog box, use the toolbar buttons to select formatting. For other formatting changes, use the Format list button.
- If you want to save your style changes to the original template file, select the Add to template check box. If you don't select this check box, your style changes will be saved only to the template attached to the active document.
- To update all text in the document with the modified style, select the Automatically update check box.

You're ready to add italics to the Heading 2 style. You'll start by moving the insertion point to a heading formatted with the Heading 2 style.

To change the Heading 2 style to italics:

1. Click the **Objectives** heading near the beginning of the document.

2. Click **Format** on the menu bar, and then click **Styles and Formatting**. The Styles and Formatting Task Pane opens. As shown in Figure 5-15, it contains a list that you can use to apply styles. The box at the top of the Task Pane contains the name of the style applied to the paragraph that contains the insertion point—in this case, the Heading 2 style. Note that you could click the Select All button to select all the text in the document that is formatted with the Heading 2 style.

Figure 5-15	STYLES AND FORMATTING TASK PANE

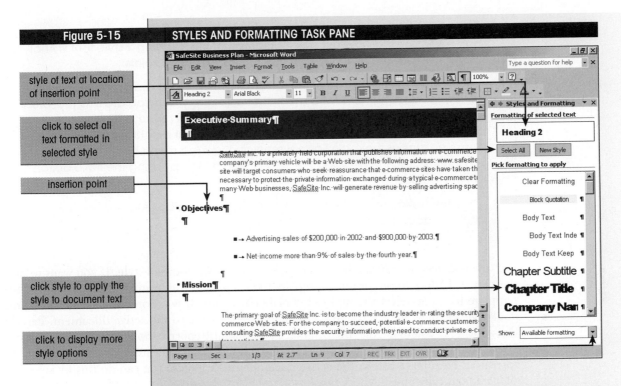

style of text at location of insertion point

click to select all text formatted in selected style

insertion point

click style to apply the style to document text

click to display more style options

3. Scroll the Pick formatting to apply list until you can see "Heading 2" in the list.

4. In the Pick formatting to apply list, right-click **Heading 2**. A shortcut menu opens.

5. Click **Modify** in the shortcut menu. The Modify Style dialog box opens, as shown in Figure 5-16. This dialog box contains a toolbar that you can use to apply common formatting options. For other formatting changes, you can use the Format list button. The dialog box also includes a preview of the selected style and a description of all its formatting attributes.

Figure 5-16	MODIFY STYLE DIALOG BOX

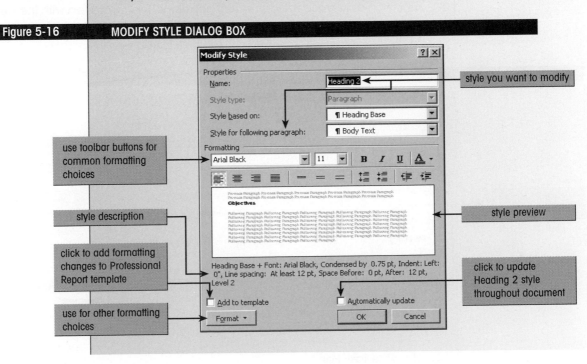

use toolbar buttons for common formatting choices

style description

click to add formatting changes to Professional Report template

use for other formatting choices

style you want to modify

style preview

click to update Heading 2 style throughout document

6. In the Modify Style dialog box, point to the toolbar buttons and read their names. Notice that the Font box indicates that the Heading 2 style font is Arial Black. The Font Size box indicates that the font size is 11 points.

7. Click the **Format** list button in the lower-left corner of the dialog box, and review the commands on the menu that appears. When you are finished, press the **Esc** key to close the menu. (You'll use this Format menu in the Case Problems at the end of this tutorial. Keep in mind that it includes many of the same options as the main Format menu in the Word menu bar.) Now, you want to add italics to the Heading 2 style. You can do this by using the Italic button on the toolbar.

8. Click the **Italic** button I on the Modify Style dialog box toolbar. The word "Italic" is added to the style description.

Now you need to indicate how you want to apply the modified style. If you want to save your style changes to the original template file (that is, to the original Professional Report template file), you select the Add to template check box. If you don't select this check box, your style changes are saved only to the template attached to the active document. Pamela does not want you to change the original Professional Report template file, so you will not select the Add to template check box. However, you need to indicate that you want Word to format all Heading 2 text in the active document with italics. You can do this by selecting the Automatically update check box.

To update the Heading 2 style and return to the document:

1. Click the **Automatically update** check box to insert a check mark, and then click the **OK** button. The Modify Style dialog box closes. You return to the Document window, where the Styles and Formatting Task Pane remains open.

2. Save your work and then scroll through the document to view the new style definition applied to the document headings. Text formatted with the Heading 2 style is now italicized, making the headings more noticeable. Note that the Heading 2 style is also italicized in the Task Pane. See Figure 5-17.

| Figure 5-17 | NEW FONT DEFINITION APPLIED DOCUMENT |

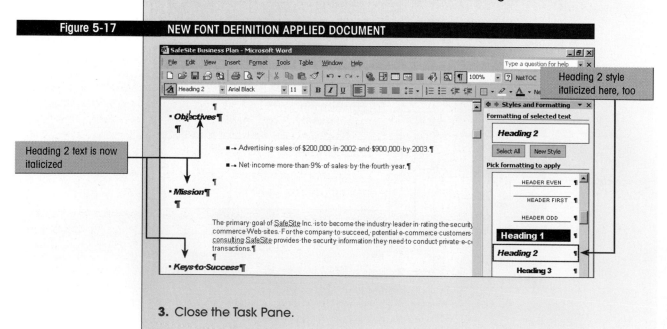

3. Close the Task Pane.

Defining New Styles

To add interest to the business plan, Maya asks you to create, or define, a new style that includes all the characteristics of the Normal style, plus a light gray background. She plans to use this new style to emphasize the paragraph under the "Executive Summary" heading, and for other parts of the business plan that she hasn't written yet.

Defining, or creating, a new style is similar to modifying an existing style. To define a new style, you assign it a name and give it a new style definition. You can define a style two different ways: by example and by using the New Style dialog box.

REFERENCE WINDOW   **RW**

Defining New Styles

- Select text formatted with a style that you want to use as the basis of the new style.
- Apply the formatting you want to include in the style.
- With the newly formatted text selected, type a name for the new style in the Style list box, and then press the Enter key.

or

- Select text formatted with a style that you can use as the basis of the new style.
- Open the Styles and Formatting Task Pane, and then click the New Style button.
- In the New Style dialog box, use the toolbar buttons or the Format button to specify the formatting you want to include in the style.
- Type a name for the style in the Style text box.
- Click the Style Type list arrow, and click Paragraph or Character.
- To add the new style to the template file attached to the document, select the Add to template check box.
- To update the document with the new style, select the Automatically update check box.

Maya wants you to define a new style called Summary that contains all the formatting elements of the Normal style, plus a light gray background. She also wants the style to align the paragraph along the left margin. You'll start by selecting a paragraph that is formatted with the Normal style, and then apply the formatting you want.

To apply the formatting you want to include in the style:

1. Select the paragraph of text under the heading "Executive Summary" (the paragraph that begins "SafeSite Inc. is a privately held corporation"). This paragraph is formatted with the Normal style. You want the new style to include all the characteristics of this paragraph, plus a light gray shading. You can add this shading by using the Borders and Shading command on the Format menu.

2. Click **Format** on the menu bar, and then click **Borders and Shading**. The Borders and Shading dialog box opens.

3. Click the **Shading** tab, and in the palette of shading options, click the fourth square from the left on the top row (gray 12.5%), and then click the **OK** button. The Borders and Shading dialog box closes.

4. Click the **Decrease Indent** button ▤ twice. The paragraph moves left, so that it is aligned on the left margin.

5. Deselect the paragraph and review the formatting change. A light gray background has been added to the paragraph, as shown in Figure 5-18. It is also aligned on the left margin.

Figure 5-18	NEWLY FORMATTED PARAGRAPH

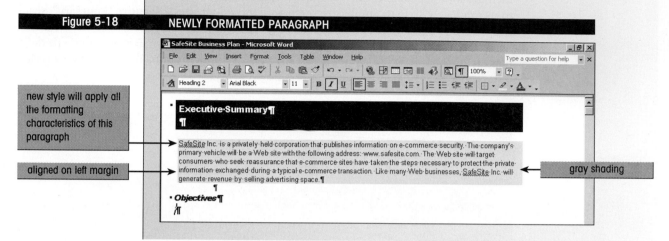

new style will apply all the formatting characteristics of this paragraph

aligned on left margin

gray shading

Now that the paragraph is formatted the way you want, you can use its formatting to define a new style. As you will see in the next set of steps, Word added the new formatting (with the 12.5% gray screen) to the Style list.

To define a new style:

1. Click the **Style** list arrow in the Formatting toolbar, and scroll down until you see Left .08". Word created this new style when you applied the gray shading to the selected paragraph. You could use this new style whenever you want to format a paragraph in Arial 10-point text, with a gray background, and aligned on the left margin. However, the style's name (Left .08") is not very descriptive. Instead of using the styles created automatically by Word, it is usually better to create a new style yourself, with a descriptive name of your choice. Pamela wants to name the new style "Summary," so that she and Maya remember that it is designed for summary paragraphs at the beginning a document.

2. Press the **Esc** key. The Style list closes.

3. Click anywhere within the paragraph with the gray background.

4. Click the **Style** list box, type **Summary**, and then press **Enter**.

5. Open the **Style** list. As shown in Figure 5-19, the style named Left .08" has been replaced with a style named "Summary." (The styles in the list are arranged alphabetically, so you'll find "Summary" near the end of the list.)

Figure 5-19 | **NEWLY DEFINED STYLE**

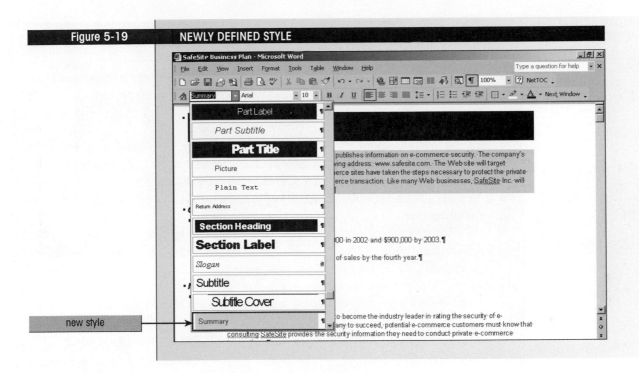

new style

Creating a New Template

The document now contains all the styles that Pamela and Maya will use when creating other important documents for SafeSite Inc. They ask you to save these styles as a new template, which they can use to create SafeSite documents.

By default, Word offers to save your new template in the Template folder. You can access any templates saved to this folder later using the New command on the File menu. For this tutorial, however, you'll save your template in the same folder as the rest of your data files.

REFERENCE WINDOW   **RW**

Creating and Using a New Template

- Create a new document containing all the styles you want to include in your template, save it as a Word document, and then delete all text from the document.
- Click File on the menu bar, click Save As, click the Save as type list arrow, and then click Document Template.
- Verify that the Templates folder is displayed in the Save in list box. If you save your template to this folder, it will appear as one of the options in the Templates dialog box. If you prefer, you can save the template in a different location, such as a folder on your Data Disk.
- Type a descriptive name for the template in the File name text box, click the Save button, and then close the template.
- To begin creating a document based on a template stored in the Template folder, click File on the menu bar, click New, click General Templates in the New Document Task Pane, click the icon for your template in the General tab, and then click the OK button. Create the document, applying styles as necessary. Save the new document as a Word document.
- To begin creating a document based on a template saved in any location, open a blank document, and then attach the template (as described earlier in this tutorial) using the Templates and Add-ins command on the Tools menu. If you prefer, you can open the template and then save it as a Word document.

You're ready to save the styles in the document as a new template. You'll save the template to the Business Plan folder that you created earlier, so that you can easily give it to Pamela and Maya. Your first step is to save the SafeSite Business Plan document, preserving your work so far. Then you will delete the text in the document and save it with a new name as a template.

To save the styles of the current document as a new template:

1. Click the **Save** button 🖫 on the Standard toolbar to preserve your work. Be certain you have saved the document before proceeding to the next step.

2. Press **Ctrl+A** and then press **Delete**. The text of the document is selected and then deleted, but the styles are still available from the Style list box.

3. Click **File** on the menu bar, click **Save As**, click the **Save as type** list arrow, and then click **Document Template**. The Templates folder is displayed in the Save in list box. Because you want your new template handy, you'll save it to a different location.

4. Use the **Save in** list arrow to switch to the Business Plan folder on your Data Disk, where you originally saved the Safe Site Business Plan document. Now you need to enter a descriptive name for the template, which will be used as the basis for all future SafeSite company documents.

5. Change the filename to **SafeSite Company Documents**, and then click the **Save** button.

The new template is now saved and ready for whenever Pamela wants to create a SafeSite document. To begin creating a document based on this template, she must open a blank document, and then attach the template (as described earlier in this tutorial) using the Templates and Add-ins command on the Tools menu. Alternately, she can open the template and then save it as a Word document. Either way, the template styles will be available to her via the Style list.

To verify that the new template contains all the necessary styles:

1. Click the **Style** list arrow and review the Style list. Note that it contains the new Summary style you created earlier.

2. Press the **Esc** key to close the Style list, and then close the template as you would close any Word document.

The template you have just created will make it easy for Pamela and Maya to create new documents. You'll give them a copy on a disk after you have completed your work on the business plan.

Session 5.1 QUICK CHECK

1. Explain how to create a new folder.

2. What is the Thesaurus?

3. Use the Thesaurus to find at least two synonyms for the word "business" when it is used to refer to an individual company.

4. Define serif and sans serif fonts. When would you use each of these types of fonts? Give two examples of each type of font.

5. Explain how to attach a Word template to a document.

6. Explain how to create a new template and attach it to a document.

7. How do you modify a predefined style?

8. Explain how to define a new style by example.

SESSION 5.2

In this session, you will learn how to rearrange parts of a document using Outline view. You'll also learn how to improve the appearance of the right margin by hyphenating the document. Finally, you'll add a footnote to the document that will help readers locate additional information.

Using Outline View

An **outline** is a list of the basic points of a document and the order in which they are presented. Once you have formatted a document with heading styles, you can use Word's Outline view to display an outline that shows as much of the document as you specify. For instance, you can display only text formatted with Heading 1, text formatted with Heading 1 and Heading 2, or all the text in the document, including text formatted with the Normal style. In Outline view, you can see and edit as many as nine levels of headings in a document. As with any outline, the broadest or most general topic is the level-1 heading (that is, text formatted in the Heading 1 style), and the remaining topics become increasingly narrow or more specific with second-level headings (text formatted in the Heading 2 style) and subsequent headings (Heading 3 style, and so on).

Outline view simplifies the process of reorganizing a document. To select an entire section, you click the white plus sign next to that section's heading. To move a section after you select it, you click the Move Up or Move Down button on the Outlining toolbar. You can also use the Outlining toolbar to change the precedence of headings. For instance, you might want to demote a level-1 heading to a level-2 heading, or to promote a level-3 heading to a level-1 heading. Note that some kinds of formatting (such as the Heading 1 formatting with the black background) are not visible in Outline view. To ensure that you can see all the text, including text with special formatting, you need to deselect the Show Formatting button in the Outlining toolbar.

REFERENCE WINDOW   RW

Creating and Editing Outlines

- Format a document with heading styles.
- Click the Outline View button.
- To ensure that you can see all the text, including text with special formatting, click the Show Formatting button to deselect it.
- Use the Show Level list arrow to display the desired number of headings.
- To move a section, click the white plus sign next to the section's heading, and then click the Move Up button or the Move Down button until the section has moved to the desired location.
- Use the Promote button or the Demote button to increase or decrease the levels of headings.
- Click the Show Level list arrow, and then click to display the entire document again.
- Click the Normal View button.

After reviewing the organization of the business plan, Maya decides that the topic "Current Competition" should appear before the topic "Market Definition." You start by switching to Outline view.

To use Outline view:

1. Open the **SafeSite Business Plan** document. Display nonprinting characters in Normal view.

2. Make sure the insertion point is at the beginning of the document, and then click the **Outline View button** in the lower-left corner of the Document window. The Outlining toolbar appears. This toolbar contains two list boxes. You can use the Outline Level list box to apply a heading level to text. You can use the Show Level list box to display the desired number of levels in an outline. In this case, you need to use the Show Level list box to display the first- and second-level headings in the document.

3. Locate the Show Level list arrow by using the mouse pointer to display its name in a ScreenTip. (The Show Level box currently displays the text "Show All Levels".)

4. Click the **Show Level** list arrow, and then click **Show Level 2**. You see only the level-1 and level-2 headings in the document.

5. If you see the level-2 headings (beginning with "Objectives") but not the level-1 headings (beginning with "Executive Summary"), you need to click the **Show Formatting** button ![icon] in the Outlining toolbar to deselect it. At this point, your outline should look similar to Figure 5-20. Notice that the headings are displayed in the outline without the rest of the document text. The plus sign next to each line of text indicates that the text is a heading, rather than part of the main text of the document. The underlines indicate text that is not visible.

Figure 5-20	DOCUMENT IN OUTLINE VIEW

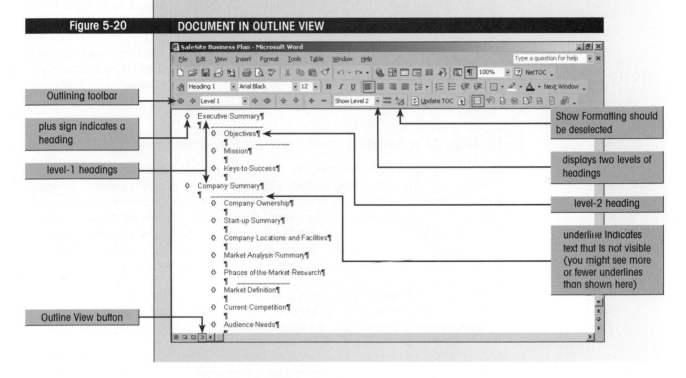

Now that you see only the headings of the business plan, you can change the organization by reordering some headings and changing the level of others.

Moving Headings in an Outline

You can rearrange the order of topics in an outline by moving the headings up and down. When you move a heading in Outline view, any text below that heading (indicated by the underline) moves with it. First, you'll move the section "Current Competition" so that it appears before the topic "Market Definition." As you work in Outline view, keep in mind that the Undo button reverses any mistakes, just as in Normal view.

To move headings in Outline view:

1. Click the **white plus sign** next to the heading "Current Competition." The heading and the paragraph mark following it are selected.

2. Click the **Move Up** button ![icon] on the Outlining toolbar. The heading and the text below it move above the heading "Market Definition." Note that each time you click the Move Up button, the selected section moves above the preceding section. To move a section down, you would use the Move Down button. You can also use the mouse to drag sections up and down.

Now that the topics of the outline are in logical order, you realize that one level-2 heading (formatted in the Heading 2 style) should actually be a level-3 heading (formatted in the Heading 3 style).

Promoting and Demoting Headings in an Outline

You can easily change the levels of headings in Outline view. To **promote** a heading means to increase the level of a heading—for example, to change a level-3 heading to a level-2 heading. To **demote** a heading means to decrease the level—for example, to change a level-1 heading to a level-2 heading.

While reviewing the business plan, Maya notices that the heading "Audience Needs" should be a level-3 heading, below the level-2 heading "Market Definition." She also wants to add other level-3 headings below the "Market Definition" heading. You'll demote the "Audience Needs" heading, and then add two new level-3 headings.

To demote a heading and then add new headings:

1. Click anywhere in the heading "Audience Needs," and then click the **Demote** button ⇨ on the Outlining toolbar. (Take care not to click the Demote to Body Text button by mistake, which would make the heading part of the main text of the document, rather than a heading.) The heading moves right and becomes a level-3 heading, formatted with the Heading 3 style. Note that promoting a heading in Outline view is similar to demoting a heading. You place the insertion point in the desired heading and click the Promote button.

   TROUBLE? If the heading now has a square next to it rather than a plus sign, you clicked the Demote to Body Text button by mistake. Click the Undo button on the Formatting toolbar, and then repeat Step 1.

2. Click at the beginning of the heading "Audience Needs," and then press the **Enter** key. A new heading is inserted in the outline.

3. Click in the new heading and type **Audience Demographics**. The new level-3 heading is now formatted in the Heading 3 style. You can't see the formatting, however, because the Show Formatting button in the Outlining toolbar is deselected.

4. Press the **Enter** key, verify that Level 3 is still selected in the Outline Level list box, and then type **Potential for Audience Growth**. Your outline, with the new level-3 headings, should now look like the one in Figure 5-21. You will probably see rectangles next to the first two level-3 headings and a plus sign next to the last level-3 heading. All that matters is that the last three headings are level-3 headings.

Figure 5-21	REVISED OUTLINE

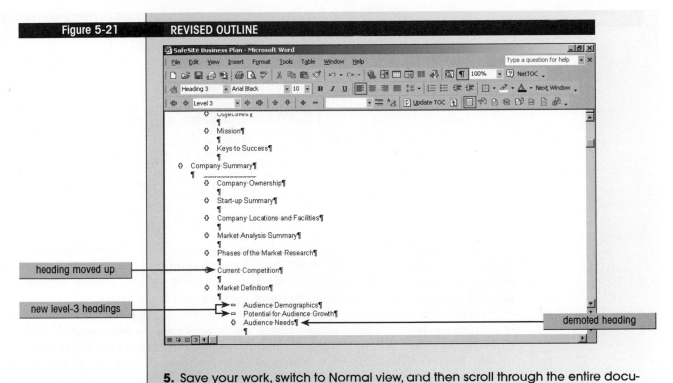

5. Save your work, switch to Normal view, and then scroll through the entire document. The heading you demoted ("Audience Needs") is now formatted in Heading 3 style, as are the two new headings you added. Note that when you moved the Current Competition heading, the entire section moved with it.

Pamela explains that she will print the outline later. To do so, she will display the document in Outline view, display the number of headings she wants to include in the outline, and then click the Print button on the Standard toolbar.

Now you're ready to address some other concerns. First, Pamela has noticed that the right edges of most of the paragraphs in the document are uneven. You'll correct this problem in the next section.

Hyphenating a Document

One potential problem with left-aligned text is excessive raggedness along the right margin. You can reduce raggedness by justifying the text, but that introduces another problem: Word inserts extra white space between words to stretch the lines of text to align along the right margin. Sometimes, this causes unsightly **rivers**, that is, blank areas running through the text of a page, as shown in Figure 5-22.

Figure 5-22 **RIVERS WITHIN JUSTIFIED TEXT**

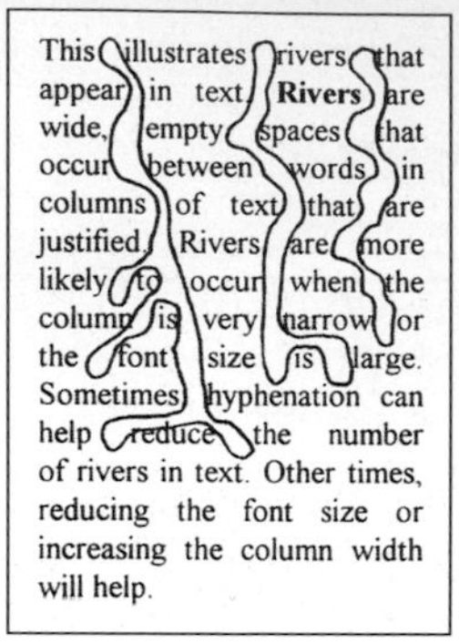

This illustrates rivers that appear in text. **Rivers** are wide, empty spaces that occur between words in columns of text that are justified. Rivers are more likely to occur when the column is very narrow or the font size is large. Sometimes hyphenation can help reduce the number of rivers in text. Other times, reducing the font size or increasing the column width will help.

Hyphenating the text can sometimes reduce the raggedness in left-aligned text or reduce the rivers in justified text. Use the Word Hyphenation feature to hyphenate a document one or two ways: automatically, in which case Word decides where to divide a word; or manually, in which case you can accept, reject, or change the suggested hyphenation.

To hyphenate a document, you need to specify a width for the **hyphenation zone**, which is the distance from the right margin within which words will be hyphenated. A smaller hyphenation zone results in more words being hyphenated, but creates a less-ragged right margin. A larger hyphenation zone results in fewer hyphenated words but a more-ragged right margin. In justified text, increasing the number of hyphenated words reduces the amount of white space inserted between words. You also can specify the number of successive lines that can end with hyphenated words. Too many lines in a row ending in a hyphen can be distracting and difficult to read.

Pamela asks you to hyphenate the business plan to eliminate as much raggedness as possible. This means you need to decrease the hyphenation zone.

To set the hyphenation zone and hyphenate the newsletter:

1. Verify that the document is displayed in Normal view.

2. With the insertion point anywhere in the document, click **Tools** on the menu bar, point to **Language**, and then click **Hyphenation**. The Hyphenation dialog box opens.

3. Decrease the Hyphenation zone to **0.1"**.

4. Change the Limit consecutive hyphens setting to **3**. This prevents Word from hyphenating words at the end of more than three lines in a row.

5. Click the **Automatically hyphenate document** check box to insert a check. See Figure 5-23.

Figure 5-23 **HYPHENATING A DOCUMENT**

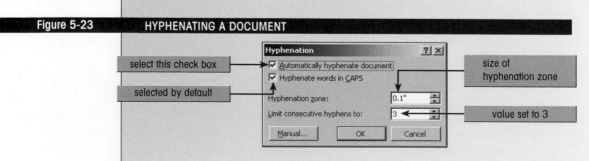

6. Click the **OK** button. Word hyphenates the document as needed. Scroll the document so that the paragraph under the heading "Phases of Market Research" is at the top of the Document window. You can now see several hyphenated words, as shown in Figure 5-24.

TROUBLE? If your document is not hyphenated as shown in Figure 5-24, repeat Steps 1-6, making sure to click the Automatically hyphenate check box to insert a check.

Figure 5-24   **DOCUMENT WITH AUTOMATIC HYPHENATION**

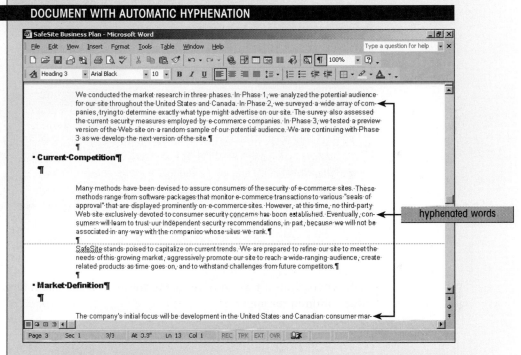

TROUBLE? If you see a dialog box indicating that the Hyphenation feature is not currently installed, click Yes, and, if necessary, insert the Office XP CD into the CD-ROM drive. If you don't have access to the Office XP CD, click No, and then simply read the rest of this section. Your document will not be hyphenated as described here.

7. Save your work.

Look through your document to make sure you like how Word has hyphenated it. If you don't like the hyphenation, you can click the Undo button, repeat the preceding steps, and then click the Manual button instead. Word now will stop at each word before it is hyphenated to let you accept or reject the suggested hyphenation. In this case, Pamela is satisfied with the automatic hyphenation.

Adding Footnotes and Endnotes

The sentence under the heading "Audience Needs" refers to the results of a survey. Pamela wants to include the survey results in an appendix at the end of the business plan and reference these results in a footnote.

A **footnote** is a line of text that appears at the bottom of the printed page and often includes an explanation, the name of a source, or a cross-reference to another place in the document. When all notes for a document are gathered together and printed at the end of the document, instead of at the bottom of each page, they are called **endnotes**. Usually, a document will contain footnotes or endnotes, but not both. You can insert footnotes and endnotes into a Word document with the Footnote command on the Insert menu. When you insert footnotes and endnotes in Normal view, Word opens a special window where you can type the footnote (or endnote text) and see the footnote (or endnote) number at the same time.

REFERENCE WINDOW   **RW**

Inserting Footnotes or Endnotes
- Switch to Normal view, and position the insertion point where you want the footnote or endnote number to appear.
- Click Insert on the menu bar, point to Reference, and then click Footnote to open the Footnote and Endnote dialog box.
- Click the Footnote button if you want the note to appear at the bottom of the page, or click the Endnote button if you want the note to appear at the end of the document, and then click Insert.
- Type the text of the footnote or endnote in the Footnotes window.
- Close the Footnotes window.
- To delete a footnote or endnote, highlight the footnote or endnote number in the document and press the Delete key.

Now you'll insert a footnote in the business plan that refers the reader to the survey information in the appendix.

To insert a footnote:

1. Make sure the document is in Normal view, click **Edit** on the menu bar, click **Find**, and then use the Find and Replace dialog box to find the phrase **for the service SafeSite will provide**. Close the Find and Replace dialog box.

2. Click at the end of the sentence (to the right of the period after "provide"). This is where you will add the footnote number.

3. Click **Insert** on the menu bar, point to **Reference**, and then click **Footnote**. The Footnote and Endnote dialog box opens.

4. Make sure the **Footnotes** option button is selected, the Number format is set to "1, 2, 3...," and the Start at setting is set to 1.

5. Click the **Insert** button. A footnote number is inserted into the text, and the insertion point moves to the Footnotes window. See Figure 5-25.

Figure 5-25   **CREATING A FOOTNOTE**

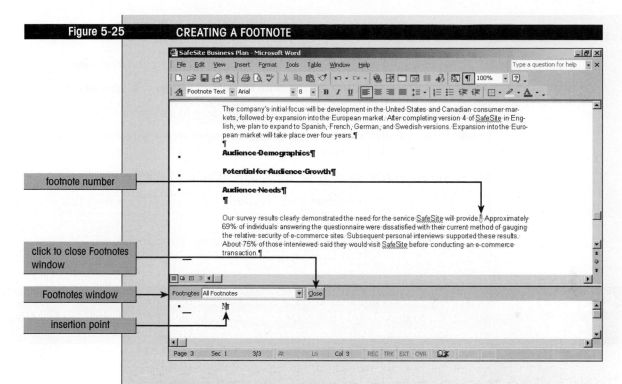

6. Type the following text: **See Appendix A.** (Be sure to include the period, and do not press the Enter key.)

   TROUBLE? If you make a typing mistake, use any Word editing feature to edit the footnote.

7. Click the **Close** button in the Footnotes window to return to the main document window, and then move the pointer over the footnote number in the text. The footnote is displayed in a box over the number. Next, to see the footnote as it will print at the bottom of the page, you need to switch to Print Layout view.

8. Switch to Print Layout view, and scroll to the bottom of page 3 to view the footnote.

9. Save your work.

To delete a footnote or endnote, highlight the footnote or endnote number in the document and press the Delete key. When you delete the number, Word automatically deletes the text of the footnote or endnote and renumbers the remaining notes consecutively.

You can move a footnote or endnote using the cut-and-paste method. Select and cut the note number from the document, and then paste it anywhere in your document. Again, Word renumbers the notes consecutively and places the footnote on the same page as its reference number. You can edit the text of an endnote or footnote by clicking in the footnote or endnote while in Print Layout view, or by double-clicking the footnote number in the main text.

Session 5.2 QUICK CHECK

1. Why would you want to move headings up and down in an outline?

2. What happens when you promote a heading? When you demote a heading?

3. Explain how to promote or demote a heading in a Word outline.

4. True or False: To take full advantage of Outline view, you should apply the Word predefined heading styles first.

5. What does the term "river" mean in relation to justified text?

6. What is the hyphenation zone? If you increase its size, how does that affect the number of hyphenated words?

7. What is the difference between a footnote and an endnote?

SESSION 5.3

In this session, you will learn how to position the insertion point with Click and Type and how to insert the current date. You'll also learn how to highlight text with colors and adjust character and paragraph spacing. Finally, you'll create a table of contents.

Positioning the Insertion Point with Click and Type

Maya and Pamela plan to revise the business plan several times. To help them keep track of who worked on each draft and the date each draft was created, they ask you to create a temporary cover page containing the necessary information. To draw attention to the text of the new cover page, you want it to appear in the middle of a separate page. You could position the insertion point at the beginning of a blank page and press the Enter key until you have inserted the appropriate number of paragraph marks. But it is much easier to use the Word **Click and Type** feature, which allows you to double-click a blank area of a page and immediately begin typing. Word inserts the necessary paragraph marks and applies the proper formatting to position the text in that particular area of the page. Keep in mind that Click and Type only works in Print Layout view.

To create the new cover page for the document, you'll first verify that the Click and Type feature is turned on. Then you'll insert a new page, double-click the center of the blank page, and begin typing the centered text.

To create a title page using Click and Type:

1. Verify that the **SafeSite Business Plan** document is open, that nonprinting characters are displayed, and that the document is displayed in Print Layout view.

2. Display the horizontal and vertical rulers.

3. Click **Tools** on the menu bar, and then click **Options**. The Options dialog box opens.

4. Click the **Edit** tab, verify that the **Enable click and type** check box (in the lower-left corner of the Edit tab) contains a check mark, and then click the **OK** button.

5. Press **Ctrl+Home** to move the insertion point to the beginning of the document. Before inserting the new page, you need to insert a blank paragraph, and then clear formatting from it. Otherwise, the Heading 1 style would apply to the cover page.

6. Press **Enter** to insert a new paragraph, press ↑ to move the insertion point up to the new paragraph, click the **Style** list arrow on the Formatting toolbar, scroll to the top of the Style list, and then click **Clear Formatting**.

7. Press **Ctrl+Enter** to insert a page break, and then press ↑ to move the insertion point up to the new page. As you will see, when you move the pointer over a blank area of a page, the pointer changes shape to reflect the alignment that will be applied to text in that area.

You've inserted a new page that is formatted in the Normal style. Now you're ready to use Click and Type. As you will see, when you move the pointer over a blank area of a page, the pointer changes shape to reflect the alignment that will be applied to text in that area.

To use Click and Type to insert new text in a blank page:

1. Move the pointer over a blank area of the page, near the left margin. The pointer changes to $\underset{\equiv}{\text{I}}$, indicating that if you click in that spot, the text will be left-aligned.

2. Move the pointer over a blank area of the page, near the right margin. The pointer changes to $\overset{\equiv}{\text{I}}$, indicating that if you click in that spot, the text will be right-aligned.

3. Move the pointer over the center of the page, about 4 inches down from the top margin. (Use the vertical ruler on the left side of the screen as a guide.) The pointer changes to $\underset{\equiv}{\text{I}}$, indicating that if you click in that spot the text will be center-aligned.

4. Double-click. Word inserts the appropriate number of paragraph marks and positions the insertion point where you double-clicked. See Figure 5-26.

   TROUBLE? If the paragraph marks appear and then disappear, you may have triple-clicked. Repeat Steps 3 and 4.

Figure 5-26   **INSERTION POINT POSITIONED WITH CLICK AND TYPE**

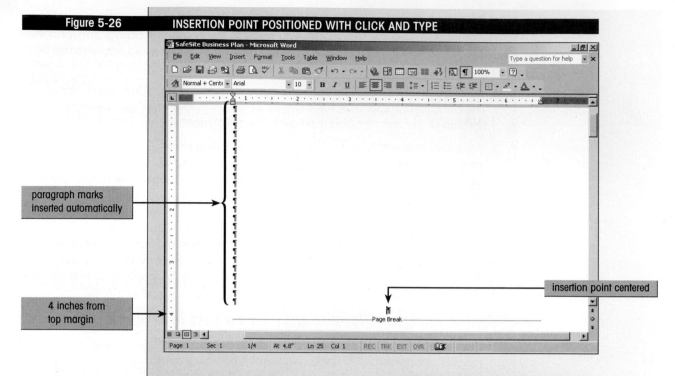

paragraph marks inserted automatically

4 inches from top margin

insertion point centered

5. Type the title page text shown below, making sure to replace "Evan Brillstein" with your name.

   TROUBLE? If Word breaks "SafeSite" into two words, move the pointer over the word **Safe**, click the **AutoCorrect Options** button ⚡, and then click **Change back to "SafeSite"**.

   SafeSite Business Plan

   Partial Draft

   Prepared by Evan Brillstein

6. Format the cover page text in **18-point Times New Roman, bold**, and then save your work. (Because the cover page will not be included in the final document, its font doesn't have to match the rest of the document.)

Inserting the Current Date

Next, Pamela asks you to add the current date to the cover page. You could begin typing the date and have Word finish it for you using AutoComplete. But by using the Insert Date and Time command on the Insert menu, you can take advantage of its formatting options. You can use this command to insert both the current date and the time into a document.

To insert the date into the title page:

1. Click at the end of your name, and then press the **Enter** key to move the insertion point to a new line.

2. Click **Insert** on the menu bar, and then click **Date and Time**. The Date and

Time dialog box opens, as shown in Figure 5-27. The Available formats list box contains the current date and time in a variety of formats. Notice the Update automatically check box, which you could click if you wanted Word to update the date and time each time you open the document. In this case, you want to insert today's date, without Word updating it when you reopen the document.

Figure 5-27	DATE AND TIME DIALOG BOX

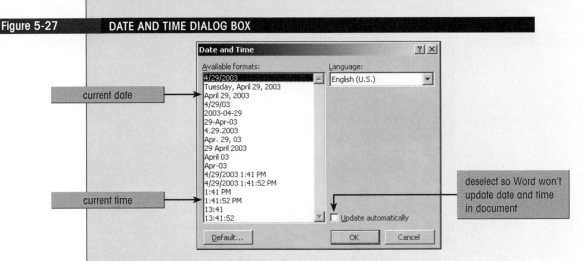

3. In the Available formats list box, click the format that provides the day of the week and the date –for example, Monday, April 29, 2003.

4. Click the **OK** button. Word inserts the date into the title page.

5. Verify that the date is formatted in 18-point Times New Roman, bold, to match the rest of the title page text.

Next, Pamela explains that she plans to ask several colleagues to review the business plan, and she wants to makes sure they know that the document is not yet completed. She asks you to draw attention to the words "Partial Draft" in the cover page.

Highlighting Text with Color

The **Highlight** button on the Formatting toolbar works like an electronic highlighting pen; you use it to shade parts of a document with color. It is useful when you need to draw attention to specific text. If you want, you can click the Highlight list arrow to select a highlighting color from the palette of options. But most people prefer yellow (which is selected by default) because its light shade makes it easy to read the text.

Pamela asks you to use the yellow highlighting to draw attention to the words "Partial Draft" on the cover page.

To highlight the title page text:

1. Select the words **Partial Draft**.

2. Click the **Highlight** list arrow ✎ in the Formatting toolbar. A color palette appears. Yellow background is applied to the selected text. The highlighting will alert anyone who reviews the plan that it is not yet final. See Figure 5-28.

3. Click the yellow square (in the upper-left corner).

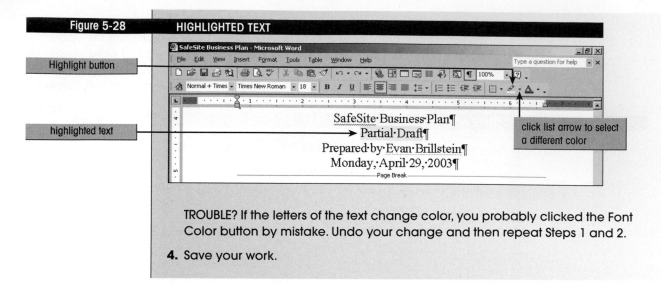

Figure 5-28 HIGHLIGHTED TEXT

TROUBLE? If the letters of the text change color, you probably clicked the Font Color button by mistake. Undo your change and then repeat Steps 1 and 2.

4. Save your work.

Finally, you decide the cover page text would be easier to read if you added space between the characters. While you're at it, you'll also adjust some paragraph spacing within the business plan.

Changing Character and Paragraph Spacing

As you know, you can quickly change the spacing between lines of a document to make it single-spaced, 1.5-spaced, or double-spaced. (If you prefer, you can choose even more precise line-spacing options by using the Paragraph command on the Format menu.)

To add polish to a document, you can also adjust the spacing between characters or between individual paragraphs. Adjusting **character spacing** is useful when you want to emphasize titles, whereas adjusting **paragraph spacing** allows you to fine-tune the appearance of specially formatted elements, such as a bulleted list.

Adjusting Spacing Between Characters

Word offers a number of ways to adjust the spacing between characters. In some situations, you might want to use kerning, the process of adjusting the spacing between combinations of characters to improve their appearance. In most documents, however, it's easiest to select a group of characters and then uniformly expand or condense the spacing between them. Notice that space between characters is measured in points, with one point equal to $\frac{1}{72}$ of an inch.

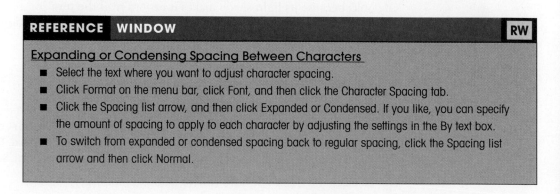

REFERENCE WINDOW **RW**

Expanding or Condensing Spacing Between Characters
- Select the text where you want to adjust character spacing.
- Click Format on the menu bar, click Font, and then click the Character Spacing tab.
- Click the Spacing list arrow, and then click Expanded or Condensed. If you like, you can specify the amount of spacing to apply to each character by adjusting the settings in the By text box.
- To switch from expanded or condensed spacing back to regular spacing, click the Spacing list arrow and then click Normal.

You want to expand the spacing between the characters in the cover page. You'll do that now.

To adjust character spacing in the cover page:

1. Select the cover page text.

2. Click **Format** on the menu bar, and then click **Font**. The Font dialog box opens.

3. Click the **Character Spacing** tab, if necessary. This tab, shown in Figure 5-29, offers a number of ways to adjust the spacing between characters.

Figure 5-29   **ADJUSTING CHARACTER SPACING**

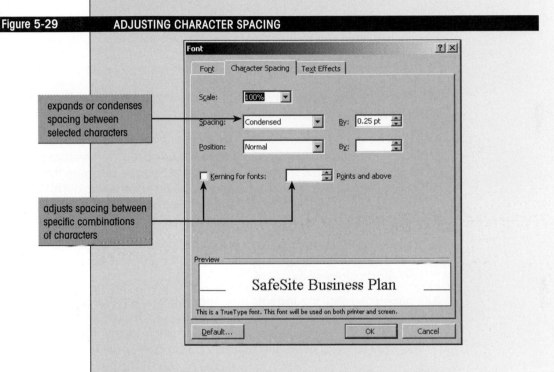

expands or condenses spacing between selected characters

adjusts spacing between specific combinations of characters

4. Click the **Spacing** list arrow, and then click **Expanded**.

5. Change the number of points between characters (in the top By text box) to **1.5**.

6. Observe the expanded spacing (applied to the first line of the selected text) in the Preview box.

7. Click the **OK** button, and then click anywhere in the cover page to deselect the text. Notice the increased space between characters in the title page text.

Now that the cover page is finished, you turn your attention to adjusting the spacing before and after the bulleted list on page 3.

Adjusting Spacing Between Paragraphs

In a single-spaced document, such as the SafeSite business plan, you might need to insert extra space before specially formatted items, such as bulleted lists. As with character spacing, paragraph spacing is measured in points.

Adjusting Spacing Between Paragraphs:
- Move the insertion point to the paragraph in which you want to adjust spacing.
- Click Format on the menu bar, click Paragraph, and then click the Indents and Spacing tab.
- Use the Before box to specify, in points, the amount of space you want to insert above the selected paragraph. Use the After box to specify the amount of space you want to insert below the selected paragraph.

Pamela has asked you to insert extra space before the bulleted list on page 3, under the heading "Market Analysis Summary."

To change the paragraph spacing before and after the bulleted list:

1. Click **Edit** on the menu bar, click **Find**, use the Find and Replace dialog box to find the paragraph that begins **Before we began**, and then close the Find and Replace dialog box. You need to insert some space between this paragraph (which begins "Before we began") and the bulleted list below it. To accomplish this, you could insert space after the paragraph, or insert space before the first bullet. You'll insert space after the paragraph.

2. With the insertion point located in the paragraph that begins "Before we began," click **Format** on the menu bar, and then click **Paragraph**. The Paragraph dialog box opens.

3. If necessary, click the **Indents and Spacing** tab. See Figure 5-30. As mentioned earlier, you can use the Line spacing settings to choose precise line-spacing options. You'll use the After box now to specify, in points, the amount of space you want to insert below the selected paragraph.

Figure 5-30 CHANGING PARAGRAPH SPACING

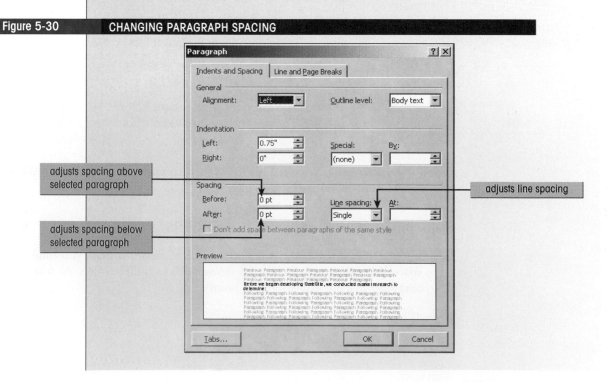

adjusts spacing above selected paragraph

adjusts line spacing

adjusts spacing below selected paragraph

4. Click the up arrow in the After text box twice to change the setting to **12 pt**.

5. Observe the effects of this new setting in the Preview box.

6. Click the **OK** button. Space is added between the paragraph that begins "Before we began" and the first bullet. The first bullet is now positioned 12 points (about ⅙ of an inch) below the preceding paragraph.

Your work on this draft of the business plan is almost completed. Before you finish, Pamela asks you to create a table of contents, which usually is one of the last tasks you perform when creating a document.

Creating a Table of Contents

Word can create a table of contents with page numbers for any document to which you have applied heading styles in the form of Heading 1, Heading 2, and so forth. Note that if you add or delete text later and one or more headings moves to a new page, the table of contents will not be updated automatically to reflect the change. However, you can easily update the table of contents by right-clicking anywhere in the table of contents, and then clicking Update Field. The page numbers in a Word table of contents are actually hyperlinks that you can use to jump to a particular part of the document.

REFERENCE WINDOW   **RW**

Creating a Table of Contents
- Make sure you have applied heading styles such as Heading 1, Heading 2, and Heading 3. (Note that it is possible to create a table of contents from other heading styles, but Word uses the Heading 1, Heading 2, etc., styles by default.)
- Click Insert on the menu bar, point to Reference, and then click Index and Tables.
- Click the Table of Contents tab in the Index and Tables dialog box.
- Click the Formats list arrow and select a style, set Show levels to the number of heading levels you want to show, verify that the Show page numbers check box is selected, and then click the OK button.
- To delete a table of contents, select it and press the Delete key.
- To update a table of contents, right-click it, click Update Field, and then click Update entire table.

The current draft of the SafeSite business plan is fairly short, but the final document will be much longer. Pamela asks you to create a table of contents for the business plan now, and insert it on a new page, just after the title page. Then, as Pamela adds sections to the business plan, she can update your original table of contents.

To insert the table of contents:

1. Move the insertion point to the end of the date on the cover page, and press **Ctrl+Enter** to insert a new page. Before inserting the table of contents, you need to clear formatting from this new page.

2. Click the **Style** list arrow, and then click **Clear Formatting**. The new paragraph is formatted in the Normal style. Next, you need to add a heading for the table of contents.

3. Click the **Bold** button [B] on the Formatting toolbar, type **Contents**, click [B] again to turn off bold formatting, and then press **Enter** three times. The insertion point is now located where you want to insert the table of contents.

4. Click **Insert** on the menu bar, point to **Reference**, and click **Index and Tables**. The Index and Tables dialog box opens.

5. Click the **Table of Contents** tab, if necessary. Word provides a variety of formats for a table of contents. In this case, you'll use the Classic format.

6. Click the **Formats** list arrow and then click **Classic**. The Print Preview box shows a sample of a table of contents formatted with the Classic format. (The Web Preview box shows you what the table of contents would look like if you saved your Word document as a Web page and viewed it in a Web browser such as Microsoft Explorer.)

Note that the Show page numbers check box is selected by default, so the table of contents will include a page number for each heading. By default, the Use hyperlinks instead of page numbers check box is selected. This setting means that Word will make each entry in the table of contents (each heading and page number) a hyperlink that links to the relevant section in the document. You can accept this default setting. Even if you deselected this check box, Word would still format the page numbers as hyperlinks. Finally, because the document contains three levels of headings, you can leave the Show levels setting at 3. See Figure 5-31.

Figure 5-31   **INSERTING A TABLE OF CONTENTS**

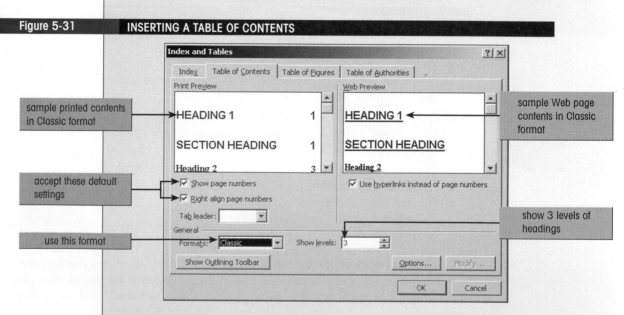

7. Click the **OK** button. Word searches for any text formatted with styles Heading 1, Heading 2, and Heading 3, and then assembles that text and its corresponding page number in a table of contents. The table of contents appears below the "Contents" heading.

8. The text is gray to indicate that Word considers the table of contents a single object. Note that this gray highlighting does not indicate that the table of contents is selected. To select the entire table of contents, you would have to click and drag to its left, in the selection bar.

9. Press **Ctrl** and click a heading in the Table of Contents. That section of the document is displayed in the Document window. Continue experimenting using the hyperlinks in the table of contents.

You'll have a chance to experiment with Word's table of contents feature more extensively in the Review Assignments and Case Problems at the end of this tutorial. Among other things, you will update a table of contents and delete one. You'll also learn another way to move quickly among the headings in a document—browsing by heading with the Select Browse object button in the vertical scroll bar.

With the table of contents inserted in the business plan, you're ready to print the document.

To print the document:

1. Save your work.

2. Preview, and then print the business plan. If you see a dialog box asking about updating the table of contents, go ahead and update the entire table. Your completed document should look like Figure 5-32. Notice that the yellow highlighting on the cover page appears as a gray background on a black and white printout.

Figure 5-32   COMPLETED DOCUMENT (PAGES 1 AND 2)

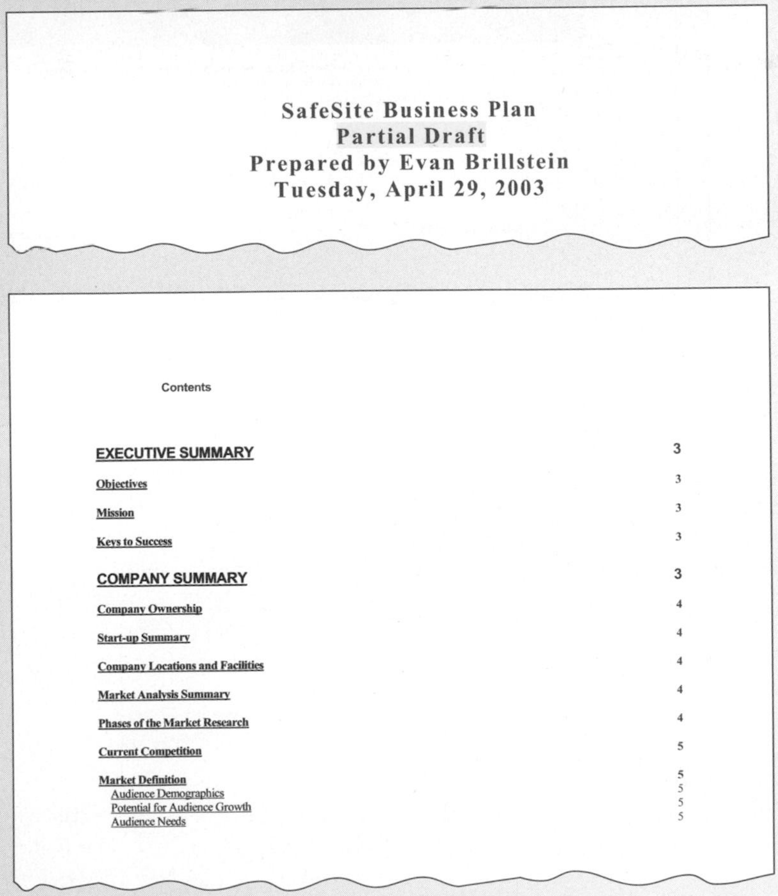

SafeSite Business Plan
Partial Draft
Prepared by Evan Brillstein
Tuesday, April 29, 2003

Contents

EXECUTIVE SUMMARY	3
Objectives	3
Mission	3
Keys to Success	3
COMPANY SUMMARY	3
Company Ownership	4
Start-up Summary	4
Company Locations and Facilities	4
Market Analysis Summary	4
Phases of the Market Research	4
Current Competition	5
Market Definition	5
Audience Demographics	5
Potential for Audience Growth	5
Audience Needs	5

Figure 5-32   **COMPLETED DOCUMENT (PAGE 3)**

Executive Summary

SafeSite Inc. is a privately held corporation that publishes information on e-commerce security. The company's primary vehicle will be a Web site with the following address: www.safesite.com. The Web site will target consumers who seek reassurance that e-commerce sites have taken the steps necessary to protect the private information exchanged during a typical e-commerce transaction. Like many Web businesses, SafeSite Inc. will generate revenue by selling advertising space.

Objectives

- Advertising sales of $200,000 in 2002 and $900,000 by 2003.
- Net income more than 9% of sales by the fourth year.

Mission

The primary goal of SafeSite Inc. is to become the industry leader in rating the security of e-commerce Web sites. For the company to succeed, potential e-commerce customers must know that consulting SafeSite provides the security information they need to conduct private e-commerce transactions.

Keys to Success

- The ability to supply unfailingly accurate information on industry-wide e-commerce security.
- Reputation for respectability and reliability in the e-commerce community, as evidenced by favorable reviews in trade magazines.
- Up-to-date assessments of consumer needs.

Company Summary

SafeSite Inc. is a new company that seeks to publish the most accurate information on e-commerce security in the industry. The company's Web site will serve consumers who seek reassurance before making online purchases.

Figure 5-32   **COMPLETED DOCUMENT (PAGE 4)**

Company Ownership

SafeSite Inc. has been established as a Limited Liability corporation based in Santa Clara County. As of this writing, the corporation is entirely owned by its principal operators.

Start-up Summary

Total start-up expenses (including legal costs, initial Web site design and testing, and computer equipment) are $26,175. We require start-up assets of $75,000 in initial cash to cover additional site development and office expenses.

Company Locations and Facilities

The company will soon move to new office space in the Silicon Valley area of California, the heart of the U.S. high-tech industry. Initially, SafeSite Inc. requires a four-room suite of offices, with fiber-optic network cabling and a full T1 connection.

Market Analysis Summary

Before we began developing SafeSite, we conducted market research to determine:

- Profile of target audience

- Size of target audience

- Profile of potential advertisers

- Number of potential advertisers

The answers to these questions are crucial to the continued development and the future marketing of SafeSite. We must understand the nature of our audience (the people who will access SafeSite to look up security information). In addition, we must accurately identify our potential advertisers.

Phases of the Market Research

We conducted the market research in three phases. In Phase 1, we analyzed the potential audience for our site throughout the United States and Canada. In Phase 2, we surveyed a wide array of companies, trying to determine exactly what type might advertise on our site. The survey also assessed the current security measures employed by e-commerce companies. In Phase 3, we tested a preview version of the Web site on a random sample of our potential audience. We are continuing with Phase 3 as we develop the next version of the site.

Figure 5-32   **COMPLETED DOCUMENT (PAGE 5)**

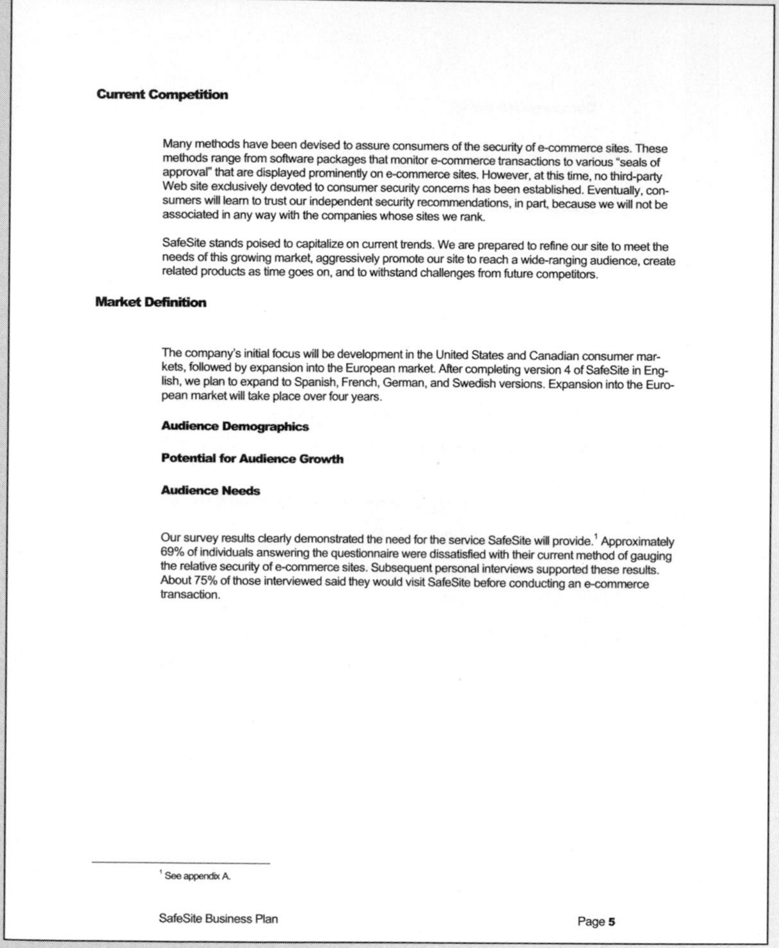

Current Competition

Many methods have been devised to assure consumers of the security of e-commerce sites. These methods range from software packages that monitor e-commerce transactions to various "seals of approval" that are displayed prominently on e-commerce sites. However, at this time, no third-party Web site exclusively devoted to consumer security concerns has been established. Eventually, consumers will learn to trust our independent security recommendations, in part, because we will not be associated in any way with the companies whose sites we rank.

SafeSite stands poised to capitalize on current trends. We are prepared to refine our site to meet the needs of this growing market, aggressively promote our site to reach a wide-ranging audience, create related products as time goes on, and to withstand challenges from future competitors.

Market Definition

The company's initial focus will be development in the United States and Canadian consumer markets, followed by expansion into the European market. After completing version 4 of SafeSite in English, we plan to expand to Spanish, French, German, and Swedish versions. Expansion into the European market will take place over four years.

Audience Demographics

Potential for Audience Growth

Audience Needs

Our survey results clearly demonstrated the need for the service SafeSite will provide.[1] Approximately 69% of individuals answering the questionnaire were dissatisfied with their current method of gauging the relative security of e-commerce sites. Subsequent personal interviews supported these results. About 75% of those interviewed said they would visit SafeSite before conducting an e-commerce transaction.

---

[1] See appendix A.

SafeSite Business Plan   Page **5**

Page breaks in your document occur at different locations, depending on the fonts you used. Don't be concerned about this. Scroll through your document and add return characters as necessary so that the lines of text are well-grouped.

3. Close the document, and then exit Word.

You now have a printed copy of the business plan, which you take to Pamela and Maya.

Session 5.3 QUICK | CHECK

1. Explain how to position the insertion point in the middle of a blank page without pressing Enter to insert paragraph marks.

2. True or False: If you use the Date and Time dialog box to insert the current date in your document, Word will automatically revise the date each time you open the document.

3. Describe a situation in which you would highlight text in a document, and then explain how to do so.

4. What is the difference between character spacing and paragraph spacing?

5. True or False: It is only possible to adjust the spacing before a paragraph.

6. Explain the steps required to create a table of contents in Word.

REVIEW ASSIGNMENTS

Maya and Pamela received the start-up funding they wanted and successfully launched SafeSite, which has proven popular with e-commerce consumers. Now that they have the Web site up and running, they would like to expand SafeSite Inc. by selling a software package called SafeDesign. Web designers can use SafeDesign to build security into their e-commerce sites from the bottom up. Before Pamela and Maya can begin marketing SafeDesign, they need to develop a technical support strategy. They have written a summary of their customer training and support policies, and have asked you to help edit and format the document.

1. Start Word, if necessary, and open the file SafeDesign from the Review folder for Tutorial 5 on your Data Disk.

2. Make sure that nonprinting characters and the ruler are displayed. If necessary, switch to Normal view.

3. Create a new folder called **SafeDesign Technical Support** (within the Review folder for Tutorial 5).

4. Save the file in the new folder as **SafeDesign Policies**.

5. Use the Thesaurus to replace "personnel" (in the second paragraph after the heading "Introducing SafeDesign") with a different word.

6. Attach the Professional Report template to the document. (This template is in the Review folder for Tutorial 5.) Remember to select the Automatically update document styles check box.

7. Apply the Heading 1 style to the first line of the document, "SafeDesign Support Policies." Apply the Heading 2 style to all of the headings in the body of the document: "Introducing SafeDesign," "Classes," "Technical Support," "Using Technical Support," "Average Wait Times," and "Frequently Asked Questions." Do not apply a style to the company address and phone number at the top of the document.

8. Create a new style by example for the company address, phone numbers, and Web address at the top of the document. The style should format text in 12-point Arial bold, centered on the page, with character spacing expanded (insert 1.5 points between each character). Name the style "Company Address." Click anywhere in the document outside the first six lines, and verify that the new style is available in the Style list box on the Formatting toolbar.

Explore 9. Create a new character style (a style that formats only selected characters) for the word "SafeDesign." To create the style: open the Styles and Formatting Task Pane, click the New Style button, type Software Name in the Name text box, click the Style type list arrow, click Character, click the Bold button, click the Italic button, click the Format list arrow, click Font, click the Character Spacing tab, change the spacing to expanded with 1.5 points between characters, and then click the OK button twice. Select the second instance of "SafeDesign" in the document (in the sentence that begins "Our new software, SafeDesign"). Click Software Name in the Task Pane. Apply the Software Name style to the third instance of "SafeDesign" (in the next paragraph, in the sentence that begins "That's why we are committed").

Explore ➤ 10. Modify the Heading 1 style so that it formats text with center alignment, using the small caps font effect, in 16-point Arial Black. (*Hint*: To make the font changes, click the Font list button in the Modify Style dialog box, click Font, and then use the tabs of the Font dialog box to make your selections.) Close the Styles and Formatting Task Pane when you are finished.

11. Under the heading "Using Technical Support," select the list of three technical support options (beginning with "Call our telephone support" and ending with "and your technical support plan"), and then apply the List Bullet style. Under the heading "Average Wait Times," apply the List Bullet style to the list of waiting times for the four technical support plans (Levels I through IV). Add 12 points of space before the first bullet in each list.

12. Using Outline view, reorganize the document so the "Classes" section comes after the "Average Wait Times" section.

13. Demote the headings "Using Technical Support" and "Average Wait Times" to make them level-3 headings, and then switch to Normal view to review your changes.

14. Below the heading "Technical Support," after the period at the end of the second sentence, insert the following footnote: "As the needs and resources of your company change, you can modify your technical support plan. Changes can be made only at the expiration of the current contract period."

15. Hyphenate the document with a hyphenation zone of 0.1", using automatic hyphenation. Limit consecutive hyphens to 2.

16. Create a cover page for the document. To prevent the formatting of the document title from affecting the new page, insert a new paragraph at the beginning of the document, clear formatting from it, and then insert a new page. Switch to Print Layout view. Use Click and Type to insert your name on one line, and the word "Draft" on another line in the center of the page. Highlight the word "Draft" to call attention to it.

Explore ➤ 17. Start a new line and insert the current date and time, using a format that includes seconds. Click the Update automatically check box. (If the date is highlighted in yellow, select the date, click the Highlight list arrow, and then click None.) Note the time inserted into the document, save your work, and close the document. Reopen the document and notice that the time has been updated. Wait a few seconds, click the date and time, and then press F9. Note that the time is updated again.

18. Insert a table of contents on a new page immediately after the cover page as follows: insert a new page after the cover page, clear formatting, and insert the boldface heading "Contents". Insert a table of contents formatted with the Fancy format for your table of contents. (If the Fancy format is not available, choose another.) Be sure to include the necessary number of heading levels. Test one of the headings to make sure it links to that section in the document.

Explore ➤ 19. In addition to using the table of contents to move around in a document, you can use the Select Browse Object button on the vertical scroll bar. Press Ctrl+Home to move the insertion point to the beginning of the document, click the Select Browse Object button (the circle near the bottom of the vertical scroll bar). A palette of options opens. Move the pointer over the buttons in the palette and review the name of each option. Click the Go To button in the palette, and then use the Go To tab of the Find and Replace dialog box to move the insertion point to the top of page 3. Close the Find and Replace dialog box. Click the Select Browse Object button again, click the Browse by Heading button, and then click the double blue down arrow button (at the bottom of the vertical scroll bar) to move from one heading to the next. Use the double blue up arrow button to browse up through the document by heading.

20. Save the document and then print it. If you are asked if you want to update the table of contents, go ahead and update the entire table.

21. Use the SafeDesign Policies document to create a new blank template called **SafeDesign Template**. Save the new template in the SafeDesign Technical Support folder on your Data Disk.

Explore ▸ 22. To keep a Style list from getting overcrowded, you can delete unnecessary styles. (Note that you can't delete default styles, such as Heading 1 and Heading 2.) Delete the block quotation style from the template as follows: open the Styles and Formatting Task Pane, right-click the block quotation style in the Task Pane Style list, click Delete, and then click Yes. Save your changes to the template and then close it.

23. Open a blank document and attach the SafeDesign Template to it. Be sure to select the Automatically update document styles check box. Verify that the template headings are available in the Styles and Formatting Task Pane, save the new document as **Additional Policies** in the SafeDesign Technical Support folder on your Data Disk, and then close the document.

Explore ▸ 24. To experiment with using a Word template as the basis for a new document, click File on the menu bar, and then click New. Click General Templates in the New Document Task Pane. Click the tabs in the New dialog box to review the various templates provided with Word. Some tabs include icons for Wizards, which guide you through the steps involved in creating complicated documents such as Web pages. Click the General tab. Note that if you create a new template and save it in the Templates folder, it will appear as an option on this tab. Click the Letters and Faxes tab, click the Elegant Fax icon, and then click the OK button. A document opens with placeholder text for all the elements of a fax cover sheet. Following instructions in the template, create a fax sheet that you could use to fax the SafeDesign document from SafeSite Inc. to Peter Bennigan at First Bank of the Pacific. Use information that you make up, and type a brief message in the Notes/Comments area. To select a check box, double-click it. Save the document as **Fax Cover Sheet** in the SafeDesign Technical Support folder on your Data Disk, preview it, print it, and then close it.

25. Close any open documents and exit Word.

CASE PROBLEMS

Case 1. Rosewood Interiors Geoffrey Browne is the sales manager for Rosewood Interiors, a furniture store in Boulder, Colorado, that until recently specialized in contemporary furnishings. In response to customer requests, the store has begun stocking more traditional style furniture. Now Geoffrey needs to provide his sales associates with some tips on selling this new stock. He has created a draft of a document and has asked for your help.

1. Start Word, if necessary, open the file **Furniture** from the Cases folder for Tutorial 5 on your Data Disk, and save it as **Rosewood Traditional Furniture**.

2. Switch to Outline view, display two levels of headings, and then promote the section "Guidelines for Helping Customers" to a level-1 heading. Reorder the document so the introduction section is the first section of the document.

Explore ▸ 3. Print the outline without showing the formatting of the headings.

4. Switch to Normal view, and change the font of the Title style and the Heading 1 style to a sans serif font. (*Hint*: Use the Font list box in the Modify Style dialog box.)

5. Change the font of the Normal style to a serif font other than Times New Roman.

6. Click at the end of the telephone number at the top of the document, press the Enter key twice, type "Draft Prepared by", and then type your name. Highlight the new line, using the color of your choice.

7. Format the four lines containing the store's name, address, and phone number using one of the font effects (such as small caps) available in the Font dialog box. Adjust the character spacing as necessary to make the text easy to read.

8. In the last paragraph of the document, change "consult" to one of its synonyms in the Thesaurus.

9. At the end of the first bullet (following the word "brochure"), insert the following footnote: "The Traditional Interiors brochure is available at the Customer Service desk."

10. Hyphenate the document using automatic hyphenation with a hyphenation zone of .25. Limit consecutive hyphens to 3.

11. Click in the paragraph above the table (which begins "Here is a list"), and change the paragraph spacing after the paragraph to 12 points.

12. Insert a table of contents for the document above the introduction, using the Formal style. Because the document is so short, you do not need page numbers, so you can deselect the Show page numbers check box. Keep the Use hyperlinks instead of page numbers check box selected. Check the headings in the table of contents to make sure they work as hyperlinks.

Explore 13. In the body of the document, change the heading "Guidelines for Helping Customers" to "Guidelines for Assisting Customers". Now that you've changed the heading, you need to update the table of contents as follows: right-click the table of contents, and then click Update Field in the shortcut menu.

14. Save your changes. Preview the document for problems, fix any formatting problems, and then print the document.

Explore 15. Word's AutoCorrect feature allows you to preserve formatted text and then insert it into documents later simply by typing a few characters. To see how this works, select the store's name, address, and phone number at the top of the document, as well as the blank paragraph below the phone number. Click Tools on the menu bar, click AutoCorrect Options, click the AutoCorrect tab, type "Rosewood Address" (without the quotation marks) in the Replace text box, verify that the Formatted text option button is selected, click the Add button, and then click the OK button. To try out the new AutoCorrect entry, close the Rosewood Traditional Furniture document, open a blank document, type Rosewood Address, and then press the spacebar. Verify that the formatted text is inserted into the document, and save the document as **Store Address** in the Cases folder for Tutorial 5. Now you can delete your AutoCorrect entry as follows: click Tools, click AutoCorrect Options, scroll down and select the Rosewood Address entry in the list box, click the Delete button, and then click the OK button. Close the Store Address document and exit Word.

Case 2. Brochure for Meals & Menus Clarissa Ruffolo and Tom Jenkins own Meals & Menus, an upscale catering service that specializes in home entertaining for people who like to socialize but don't have time to cook. Tom has prepared a brochure with the company's latest menu choices, which he formatted using the Word default heading styles. However, he is not happy with the brochure's appearance and has asked for your help.

1. Start Word, if necessary, and check your screen, making sure that nonprinting characters are displayed.

2. Open the file **Meals** from the Cases folder for Tutorial 5 on your Data Disk, and save it as **Meals & Menus**. Notice that the headings in the document are formatted using the Word default Heading1 and Heading 2 styles.

3. Attach the template named **Menu Template**, which is stored in the Cases folder for Tutorial 5, to the current document. Remember to select the Automatically update document styles check box. Verify that the document's styles are updated to reflect the template's styles.

4. Apply the Bulleted List style (with the diamond-shaped bullet) to all the bulleted lists in the document. (If you find that Word automatically transformed the bullets in the document to diamonds, go ahead and apply the style anyway so that all the bullets have the same line spacing.)

Explore ▶ 5. You can use the Reveal Formatting Task Pane to check the formatting in a document. To try it now, click Format on the menu bar, click Reveal Formatting, select the heading "Our Famous Desserts," and then, in the Reveal Formatting Task Pane, review the description of formatting applied to this text. Note that the Task Pane even lists the outline level for the selected text, which in this case is Level 2. Select the heading "A Final Word" and review the heading applied to it. Note that this is a Level 1 heading.

Explore ▶ 6. Click the list arrow in the Task Pane title bar, and then click Styles and Formatting to open the Styles and Formatting Task Pane. Select the heading "Our Famous Desserts" (which is formatted in the Heading 2 style), and then click Select All in the Styles and Formatting Task Pane. All the text in the document formatted with the Heading 2 style is selected. Scroll through the document to review these headings. Close the Task Pane.

7. In Outline view, display two levels of headings, and then promote the headings "Lunch," "Dinner," and "Our Famous Desserts," to level-1 headings.

Explore ▶ 8. Move the "Our Famous Desserts" heading up, to make it the first heading in the document, above "Bagel Brunch." This time, instead of clicking the Move Up button, select the heading, and then drag it up to the beginning of the document.

9. Print the outline with only the headings displayed, and then switch back to Normal view.

10. In the first sentence under the heading "Our Famous Desserts," use the Thesaurus to find a synonym for "delectable."

Explore ▶ 11. Switch to Print Layout view, press Ctrl+Home, press Ctrl+Enter, and then clear formatting from the new page. Scroll down to display the heading "Our Famous Desserts," and notice that you inadvertently cleared formatting from this heading. Click the Undo button until "Our Famous Desserts" is again formatted in the Heading 1 style, and the new page is removed. Now insert a new paragraph at the beginning of the page. Clear formatting from the new paragraph, insert a new first page, move the insertion point up to the new page, select the Company Name style, and then use Click and Type to insert "Meals & Menus" (without the quotation marks) about 3 inches down, in the center of the page. Notice how the Click and Type Feature automatically applies the selected style.

12. Press Enter, select the Company Address style, and then type the following:

2567 Rowley

Madison, Wisconsin 53708

Prepared by Your Name

Be sure to replace "Your Name" with your first and last name.

Explore

13. Insert the current date below your name, in the format of your choice. Click the Update automatically check box so that Word shows the current date each time you open the document. Right-click the date to open a shortcut menu. Notice the command "Update Field," which you can use to update the date the next time you open the document.

14. Modify the Company Address style so that it applies a sans serif font with expanded character spacing. (*Hint*: To select expanded character spacing, click the Format button in the Modify Style dialog box, and then click Font.)

Explore

15. You can use the Styles and Formatting Task Pane to display a list of all the styles currently in use in a document. To display this list now, open the Styles and Formatting Task pane, click the Show list arrow (at the bottom of the Task Pane), and then click Formatting in Use. A list of the styles used in the document appears. Review the list and then close the Task Pane.

16. Save, preview, and print the document, and then exit Word.

Case 3. The Business of Basketball As part of the requirements for your advanced writing class, your writing group has written a term paper on "The Business of Basketball." Your assignment is to edit the preliminary outline.

1. Start Word, if necessary, and check your screen, making sure that nonprinting characters are displayed. Open the file **Business** from the Cases folder for Tutorial 5 on your Data Disk.

2. In the Cases folder for Tutorial 5, create a new folder called **Writing Project**, and then save the document in the new folder as **Business of Basketball**.

3. Using Outline view, reorder the headings so that "Team Philosophy" follows "Management Style."

4. Demote the section "Marketing" to make it a second-level heading.

5. Print the completed outline of the document, with the Show Formatting feature turned off.

6. Use the Thesaurus to find a synonym to replace "lucrative" in the first sentence under the heading "Introduction."

Explore

7. Scroll to the table in the document, and add the following endnote to the table heading: "Data taken from www.basketballnews.com, May 25, 2002." Take care to select the Endnotes option button rather than the Footnotes option button in the Footnote and Endnote dialog box. In the Endnotes list box, make sure that End of document is selected, so that the note will be placed at the end of the report. When you are finished typing the note, scroll up to the end note number in the document, and place the pointer over the number to display the end note text.

8. Change the Heading 1 style to a sans serif font.

Explore

9. Create a new character style (a style that formats only selected characters) for the author names. To create the style: open the Styles and Formatting Task Pane, click New Style, type Author Name in the Name text box, click the Style type list arrow, click Character, click the Bold button, if necessary, click the Italic button, select 12-point Arial, and then click OK. Apply the new style to the author names (on the first page).

10. Add your name to the list of authors on the first page, format it with the Author Name style, and then add highlighting to your name.

11. Create a table of contents on a separate page, following the heading "Table of Contents." Use the Formal style.

Explore

12. Drag in the Selection bar to select the table of contents, and then press Delete. Insert a new table of contents using the Classic style.

13. Save your work, preview the document, print it, and then close it. When you are finished, exit Word.

Case 4. Washington State Budget Mona Parks is an economic analyst for the governor's office in the state of Washington. She is responsible for compiling a preliminary draft of the governor's annual budget proposal, a document that will ultimately incorporate information from over 100 state agencies. Each year she begins her work on the budget draft by creating an outline using Word's outline numbered list feature. She has asked you to help.

1. Start Word, if necessary, making sure that nonprinting characters are displayed.

2. Open a new Word document, and save it as **Preliminary Budget Draft** in the Cases folder for Tutorial 5 on your Data Disk.

Explore

3. In addition to creating an outline using document headings, you can create a numbered list in outline format using the Numbering button on the Formatting toolbar. To begin creating the budget outline: display the document in Normal or Print Layout view, insert a new line, click the Numbering button on the Formatting toolbar, and type "Governor's Message". Press Enter and type "Budget Highlights". Press Enter and type "Summaries by Agencies".

Explore

4. To demote a level-1 heading to a level-2 heading, you can click the Increase Indent button on the Formatting toolbar. To demote a level-2 heading to a level-3 heading, you click the Increase Indent button again. You'll use these options now as you type the list of agencies under the heading "Summaries by Agencies." To type this list: press Enter, click the Increase Indent button, type "Department of Agriculture", press the Enter key, click the Increase Indent button, type "Research", press Enter, type "County Outreach", press Enter, click the Decrease Indent button once, and then type "Department of Commerce".

5. Continue using the techniques described in Step 4 to add the following text to the outline:
   c. Department of Justice
      i. Juvenile Justice Program
      ii. Appeals Court
      iii. Public Defenders
   d. Department of Parks and Recreation
   e. Department of Education

Explore

6. Now that you have created your outline, you can format it using the Word default heading styles. Select your outline numbered list, click Format on the menu bar, click Bullets and Numbering, and then click Outline Numbered tab. Click the second style from the right, in the bottom row (which uses the form I. Heading 1, A. Heading 2), and then click OK.

7. Switch to Outline view, and reorganize the list of departments in alphabetical order. Print the outline and then switch to Normal view.

8. Click at the beginning of the document, click the Numbering button to deselect it, and then add the following title and subtitle to the beginning of the document: Preliminary Budget for the State of Washington, Draft Prepared by Your Name. (Replace "Your Name" with your first and last name.) On a line after your name, insert the current date in a format that includes the day of the week.

9. Format the title, subtitle, and date appropriately, and then save this formatting as a new style named "Budget Title".

10. Save your work, preview the document, and print it.

11. Create a new template named **Budget Template**, based on the Preliminary Budget Draft document. Save the template in the Cases folder for Tutorial 5, close it, and then exit Word.

QUICK CHECK ANSWERS

Session 5.1

1. In the Save As dialog box, click the New Folder button, type the name of the folder, and then click the OK button.

2. The Thesaurus is a feature you can use to find synonyms for words in a document.

3. The following are synonyms for "business" when it is used to refer to an individual company: company, corporation, conglomerate, establishment, partnership, firm, multinational, transnational, small business, enterprise, venture, concern, and organization.

4. A serif font is a font in which each character has a small embellishment (called a serif) at its tips. A sans serif font is a font in which the characters do not have serifs. Serif fonts are useful for the main text of a document because they are easy to read. Sans serif fonts are best for headings and titles. Two examples of serif fonts are Times New Roman and Garamond. Two examples of sans serif fonts include Arial and Century Gothic.

5. Click Tools on the menu bar, and then click Templates and Add-ins. Click the Attach button. In the Attach Template dialog box, navigate to the folder containing the template, select the template you want, and then click the Open button. Click the Automatically update document styles check box to select it. Click the OK button to attach the template to your document.

6. First, create a new document containing all the styles you want to include in the new template, save it as a Word document, and delete all text from the document. Then save the file as a Document Template. Verify that the Templates folder is displayed in the Save in list box. If you save your template to this folder, it will appear as one of the options in the New dialog box. If you prefer, you can save the template in a different location.

7. Move the insertion point to text formatted with the style you want to modify. Click Format on the menu bar, and then click Styles and Formatting. In the Styles and Formatting Task Pane, click the Show list arrow and then click Custom. In the Format Settings dialog box, click the Styles button (in the lower-left corner). In the Style dialog box, verify that the style you want to modify is selected in the Styles text box and then click Modify. In the Modify Style dialog box, use the toolbar buttons for common formatting options. For other formatting changes, use the Format button. If you want your style changes saved in the original template file, select the Add to template check box. If you don't select this check box, your style changes will only be saved to the template attached to the active document. To update all text in the document with the modified style, select the Automatically update check box. Click the OK button. In the Style dialog box, click the Close button.

8. Format a paragraph with the font, margins, alignment, spacing, and other elements that you want for the style, and then select the paragraph. Click the Style text box on the Formatting toolbar. Type the name of the new style (replacing the current style name), and then press the Enter key.

Session 5.2

1. By moving the headings in an outline, you can reorganize the document text.

2. When you promote a heading, it becomes a higher-level heading in the outline. For example, you could promote a level-2 heading to a level-1 heading. When you demote a heading, it becomes a lower-level heading. For example, you could demote a level-1 heading to a level-2 or level-3 heading.

3. To promote a heading, click that heading in Outline view, and then click the Promote button on the Outlining toolbar. To demote a heading, click that heading, and then click the Demote button.

4. True

5. A river is a blank area running through the text of a page.

6. The hyphenation zone is the distance from the right margin within which words will be hyphenated. Increasing its size reduces the number of hyphenated words.

7. A footnote appears at the bottom of a page, whereas an endnote appears at the end of a document.

Session 5.3

1. Double-click a blank area of a page using the Click and Type pointer.

2. False

3. It is sometimes helpful to highlight text that you want to delete from a document later, or to draw a colleague's attention to an important section. To highlight text, first select it, and then click the Highlight button on the Formatting toolbar.

4. Character spacing affects the positioning of individual characters, whereas paragraph spacing affects the spacing between paragraphs.

5. False

6. Make sure you have applied heading styles such as Heading 1, Heading 2, and Heading 3. Click Insert on the menu bar, point to Reference, and then click Index and Tables. Click the Table of Contents tab in the Index and Tables dialog box. Select a predefined style in the Formats list box, set the show-levels number to the number of heading levels you want to show, verify that the Show page numbers check box is selected, and then click the OK button.

CREATING
FORM LETTERS AND MAILING LABELS

Writing a Form Letter for Palm Tree Athletic Club

CASE

Palm Tree Athletic Club

Maria Fuentes is the facilities manager for Palm Tree Athletic Club, a chain of health and fitness clubs with branches located throughout the state of Florida. The chain has just completed major renovations at several branches, which forced club members to endure a lot of dust, noise, and inconvenience. Maria wants to show the club's gratitude by inviting each member to sign up for three free hours with a certified personal trainer. She plans to send a letter to each member announcing the free offer.

Maria doesn't have time to type personal letters to each of the club's many members. Instead, she plans to create a **form letter** that contains the information she wants to send all members. The form letter will also contain specific details for individual members, such as name, address, and favorite type of exercise equipment. Maria will create the form letter using Word's Mail Merge features. She has already written the letter, but she needs to add the personal information for each member. She asks you to create the form letter, as well as the mailing labels for the envelopes.

In this tutorial, you'll use Word's Mail Merge Wizard to help Maria create a form letter, mailing labels, and a telephone directory. First you'll open the letter that will serve as the main document. Next you'll create a data source that contains the name and address of each member who will receive the customized letter. Then you'll have Word merge the main document with the data source. Finally, you'll use the data source document to create mailing labels for the envelopes. You'll also create a telephone list containing the number of each branch of the Palm Tree Athletic Club.

SESSION 6.1

In this session, you will see how Maria planned her letter. You'll open the form letter, start the Mail Merge Wizard, create a data source with specific member information that will be inserted into the form letter, and then merge the form letter with the data source.

Planning the Form Letter

Maria hopes to generate good will for the Palm Tree Athletic Club by offering each member three free hours with a personal trainer. Maria's letter is designed to inform members about the offer and mention improvements to the club that might appeal to each member. Her letter is organized to capture the reader's attention. First she thanks club members for their patience during the renovations, and then she briefly describes the free offer. Finally, she encourages members to review the new schedules for their favorite type of exercise class.

Maria writes in a friendly, informal style. She uses a standard business-letter format and plans to print the letters on stationery preprinted with the company letterhead.

Understanding the Merge Process

Maria asks you to use Word's Mail Merge features to create the form letters. The term **merge** refers to the process of combining information from two separate documents to create many final documents, each containing customized information. In Word, the two separate documents are called a main document and a data source.

A **main document** is a document (such as a letter) that contains standard text and placeholders (called **merge fields**) that mark where variable information (such as a name or an address) will be inserted. Maria's main document is a letter that looks like Figure 6-1, except that merge fields will replace the red text.

Figure 6-1   MARIA'S MAIN DOCUMENT

[Date]

[First Name] [Last Name]
[Address Line 1]
[City], FL [ZIP Code]

Dear [First Name]:

As you've probably noticed, your branch of the Palm Tree Athletic Club has been
undergoing major renovations. You'll be happy to know that we have finally cleared
away the rubble. We've installed the new equipment, including a new suite of [Favorite
Equipment] machines, and are laying the new carpet next week. We want to thank you
for your patience while we knocked down walls and expanded our facilities. We realize
you put up with a lot of inconvenience (not to mention noise and dust).

As a sign of our gratitude, we invite you to sign up for three free hours with one of our
certified personal trainers. Just bring this letter to your branch of the Palm Tree Athletic
Club and sign up for six half-hour sessions at times that are convenient for you. Our
trainers are available Monday through Saturday.

While you're at the club, take a look at our new schedule for [Favorite Class] classes. We
hope you'll like the additional weekend options. (We've had many requests for these over
the past few months.)

We look forward to seeing you at Palm City Athletic Club.

Sincerely yours,

Maria Fuentes
Facilities Manager

A **data source** is a document that contains information, such as members' names and addresses, that will be inserted into the main document. Maria's data source will include the name and address of each club member, as well as information about each member's preferred exercise machine and favorite class.

Inserting information from a data source into a main document produces a final document called a **merged document**. Figure 6-2 illustrates how the data source and main document combine to form a merged document.

Figure 6-2 **MERGING A MAIN DOCUMENT WITH A DATA SOURCE TO CREATE A MERGED DOCUMENT**

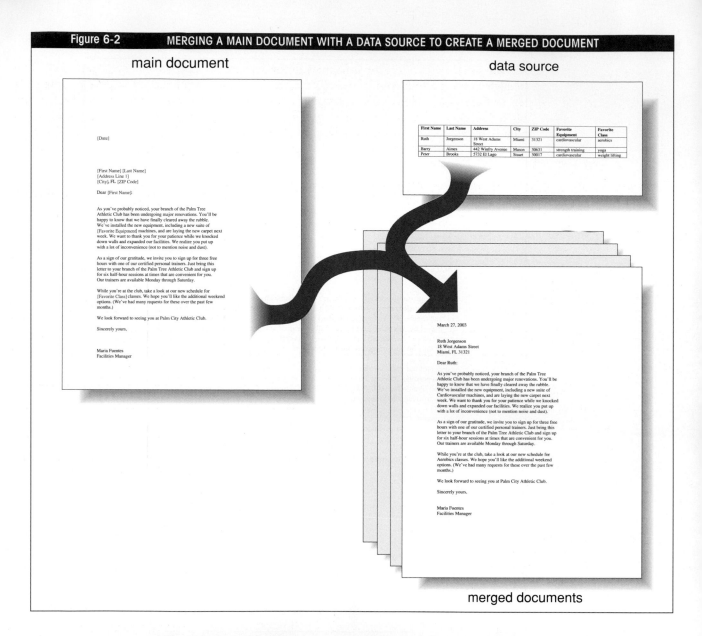

Mail Merge Fields

During a merge, the merge fields (the placeholders for text that changes in the main document) instruct Word to retrieve information from the data source. For example, one merge field in the main document might retrieve a name from the data source; another merge field might retrieve an address. For each club member listed in the data source, Word will create a new, separate letter in the final merged document. Thus, if the data source contains five sets of member names and addresses, the merged document will contain five separate letters, each one containing a different member name and address in the appropriate places.

You insert merge fields in a main document using the Insert Merge Fields dialog box. You can distinguish merge fields from the other text of the main document because each merge field name is enclosed by pairs of angled brackets—like this: << >>.

Data Fields and Records

A data source is a table of information similar to the one shown in Figure 6-3. The **header row**, the first row of the table, contains the name of each merge field. The cells below the header row contain the specific information that replaces the merge field in the main document. This information is called **data**. Each row of data in the table makes up a complete **record**, or all the information about one individual or object. For a mail merge to work smoothly, every record in the data source must have the same set of merge fields.

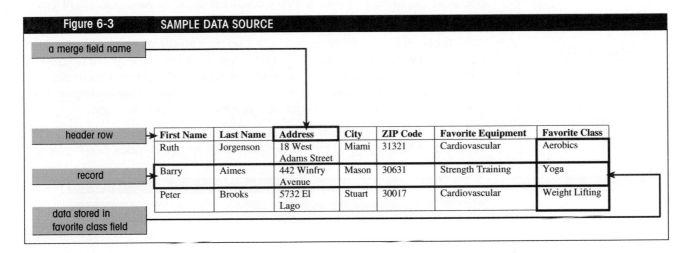

Figure 6-3	SAMPLE DATA SOURCE

a merge field name

header row

First Name	Last Name	Address	City	ZIP Code	Favorite Equipment	Favorite Class
Ruth	Jorgenson	18 West Adams Street	Miami	31321	Cardiovascular	Aerobics
Barry	Aimes	442 Winfry Avenue	Mason	30631	Strength Training	Yoga
Peter	Brooks	5732 El Lago	Stuart	30017	Cardiovascular	Weight Lifting

record

data stored in favorite class field

Data sources are commonly used to store names and addresses. However, you can also create data sources with inventory records, records of suppliers, or records of equipment. After you understand how to manage and manipulate the records in a data source, you'll be able to use them for many different types of information.

Using the Mail Merge Wizard

Word's **Mail Merge Wizard** is a special feature that walks you through the six steps involved in merging documents. These steps are:

- Select the type of document you want to use as the main document. Possible types of main documents include letters, envelopes, and e-mails.
- Select the document you want to use as the main document. You can type a new document or edit an existing one.
- Select the list of recipients (that is, the data source) you want to use for the merge. You can use an existing data source or create a new one.
- Complete the main document by adding merge fields.
- Preview the merged document.
- Complete the mail merge.

You can access the Mail Merge Wizard via the Mail Merge Task Pane. Once you are familiar with merging documents, you can also use the buttons on the Mail Merge toolbar to perform the same tasks described by the Mail Merge Wizard. Maria asks you to start the Mail Merge Wizard now.

> *To start Word and open the Mail Merge Wizard:*
>
> **1.** Start Word, insert your Data Disk in the appropriate drive, verify that a new, blank document is displayed in Normal view, and then close the New Document Task Pane, if necessary.
>
> **2.** Click **Tools** on the menu bar, point to **Letters and Mailings**, and then click **Mail Merge Wizard**. The Mail Merge Task Pane opens and the Document window switches to Print Layout view. The Mail Merge Task Pane displays information and options related to the first step in merging documents. Depending on how your computer is set up, you might also see the Mail Merge toolbar.
>
> **3.** If you do not see the Mail Merge toolbar, click **Tools** on the menu bar, point to **Letters and Mailings**, and then click **Show Mail Merge Toolbar**. See Figure 6-4.

Figure 6-4	WORD'S MAIL MERGE FEATURES

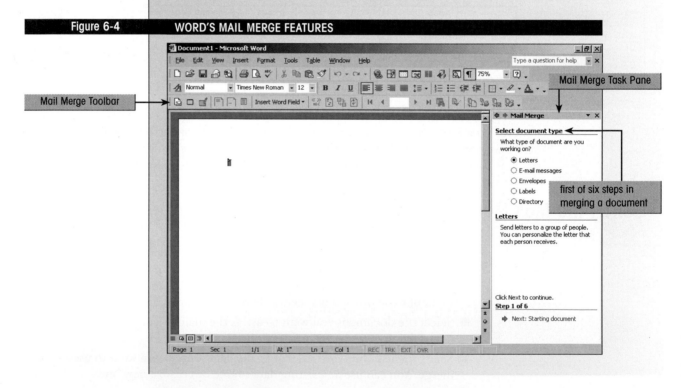

With the Mail Merge Task Pane open, you are ready to perform the first two steps in merging a document.

Selecting a Main Document

According to the Mail Merge Wizard, your first task is to specify the type of main document you want to use for the merge. The Mail Merge Wizard provides a number of options, including e-mail messages and labels. In this case, you want to create a letter.

To specify the type of merged document to create:

1. Verify that the **Letters** option button is selected in the Mail Merge Task Pane.

2. At the bottom of the Task Pane, click **Next: Starting document**. The Mail Merge Task Pane displays information and options that you can use to select a starting document—that is, to select a main document.

When selecting a main document, you have three choices: use the document currently displayed in the Document window; start a new document from a template; or open an existing document. Maria has already written the letter she wants to send to all Palm Tree Athletic Club members, so you don't need to create a new document. Instead, you'll use an existing document.

To select a starting, or main, document:

1. In the Mail Merge Task Pane, click the **Start from existing document** option button (just below the "Select starting document" heading). A list box appears, with an Open button below it.

2. Click **Open**. The Open dialog box appears. You'll use this dialog box to open Maria's document.

3. Use the Look in list arrow to select the **Tutorial** folder in the Tutorial.06 folder on your Data Disk.

4. Click **Club** and then click **Open**. The document named Club opens.

5. Switch to **Normal** view, zoomed to **100%**. Note that the "Use the current document" option button is now selected in the Task Pane, indicating that you will use the current document. Also, note that the title bar indicates that the newly opened document (which was originally named "Club") is now named "Document1." At the bottom of the Task Pane, you can see the next step in the mail merge process. See Figure 6-5.

Figure 6-5	MAIN DOCUMENT OPEN IN DOCUMENT WINDOW

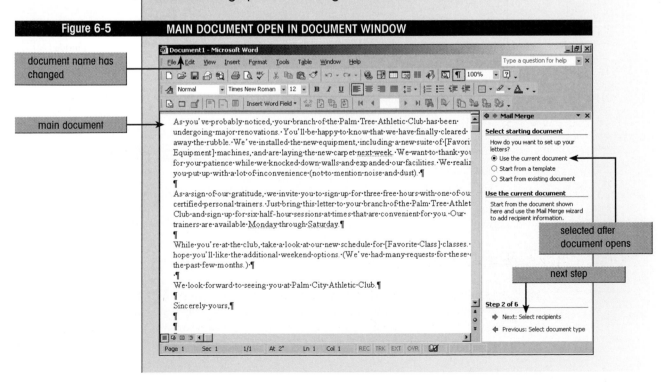

Next you need to tell Word where to find the list of recipients for Maria's letter.

Selecting a Data Source

As you learned earlier, a data source is a table of information. In a typical mail merge, the data source contains a list of names and addresses, but it can also contain additional, customized fields. You can use many kinds of files as data sources for a mail merge including simple Word tables, Excel worksheets, Access databases, or a special file designed to store addresses for Microsoft Office applications.

When performing a mail merge, you can select a data source file that already contains names and addresses, or you can create a new data source, enter names and addresses into it, and then merge it with the main document. In this section, you will create a data source using the tools provided by the Mail Merge Wizard. This involves two steps: deciding which fields to include in the data source, and entering address information.

Selecting Fields to Include in the Data Source

You need to create a data source that contains club member information, including address, favorite exercise equipment, and preferred type of class. Maria compiled all the necessary information by asking each member to fill out a form when they first joined the club. Figure 6-6 shows one of these forms.

Figure 6-6	MEMBER INFORMATION FORM

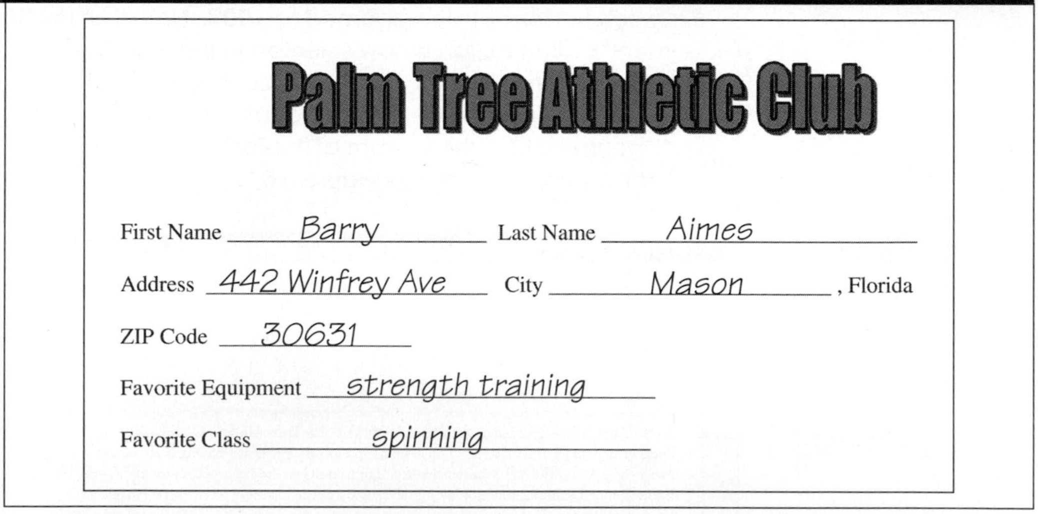

Palm Tree Athletic Club

First Name _____Barry_____ Last Name _____Aimes_____

Address _442 Winfrey Ave_ City _____Mason_____ , Florida

ZIP Code _30631_

Favorite Equipment _strength training_

Favorite Class _spinning_

Your job is to create a data source to store all the data found in the member information forms. When you create your data source, therefore, you must include the field names shown in Figure 6-7.

Figure 6-7	FIELD NAMES TO INCLUDE IN DATA SOURCE

Field Names	Description
First Name	Member's first name
Last Name	Member's last name
Address	Member's street address
City	Member's city (in Florida)
ZIP Code	Member's ZIP code
Favorite Equipment	Member's favorite type of exercise equipment
Favorite Class	Member's favorite type of exercise class

When you create a new data source from within the Mail Merge Wizard, Word provides a number of default fields such as First Name, Last Name, and Company. You can customize the data source by adding new fields and removing the default fields that you don't plan to use. As you create a data source, keep in mind that each field name must be unique; you can't have two fields with the same name. Although the order of field names in the data source doesn't affect their placement in the main document, arrange them logically so you can enter information quickly and efficiently. For example, you'll probably want the First Name field next to the Last Name field. Finally, note that if you include spaces in your field names, Word will replace the spaces with underscores. For example, Word transforms the field name First Name into First_Name.

REFERENCE WINDOW   **RW**

Creating a Data Source

- In Step 3 of the Mail Merge Wizard, select the Type a new list option button, and then click Create.
- In the New Address List dialog box, click the Customize button.
- In the Customize Address List dialog box, click a field you want to delete, click the Delete button, and then click the Yes button. Continue to delete any unnecessary fields.
- To add a new field, click the Add button, type the name of the field in the Add Field dialog box, and then click the OK button.
- To rearrange the order of the field names, click a field name, and then click the Move Up or Move Down button.
- Click the OK button to close the Customize Address List dialog box.
- In the New Address List dialog box, enter information for the first record, click the New Entry button, and type another record. Continue until you are finished entering information into the data source, and then click the Close button.

You're ready to begin creating the data source for Maria's form letter.

To begin creating the data source:

1. In the bottom of the Task Pane, click **Next: Select recipients**, and then click the **Type a new list** option button in the Task Pane.

2. Below the heading "Type a new list" click **Create**. The New Address List dialog box opens, as shown in Figure 6-8. You will use this dialog box to enter a complete set of information for one person—that is, enter one record into the data source. Before you begin entering information, you need to customize the list of fields to match the list shown earlier in Figure 6-7.

Figure 6-8	CREATING A DATA SOURCE

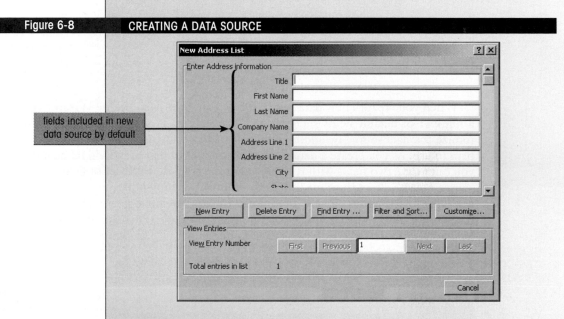

fields included in new data source by default

3. Click the **Customize** button. The Customize Address List dialog box opens. Here you can delete the fields you don't need, and add new ones. You'll start by deleting fields.

4. In the Field Names list box, click **Title** (if necessary), and then click the **Delete** button. A message appears asking you to confirm the deletion.

5. Click the **Yes** button. The Title field is deleted from the list of field names.

6. Continue using the Delete button to delete the following fields: Company Name, Address Line 2, State, Country, Home Phone, Work Phone, and E-mail Address. Next you need to add some new fields. When you add a new field, it is inserted below the selected field, so you will start by selecting the last field in the list.

7. Verify that **ZIP Code** is selected, and then click the **Add** button. The Add Field dialog box opens, instructing you to type a name for your field.

8. Type **Favorite Equipment**, click the **OK** button, and then use the Add button to add a **Favorite Class** field. When you are finished, your Customize Address List dialog box should look like the one shown in Figure 6-9. You could use the Move Up and Move Down buttons to rearrange the field names (for instance, to move the Favorite Class field above the Favorite Equipment field), but in this case the order is fine. You are finished customizing the list of field names.

Figure 6-9   CUSTOMIZED LIST OF FIELD NAMES

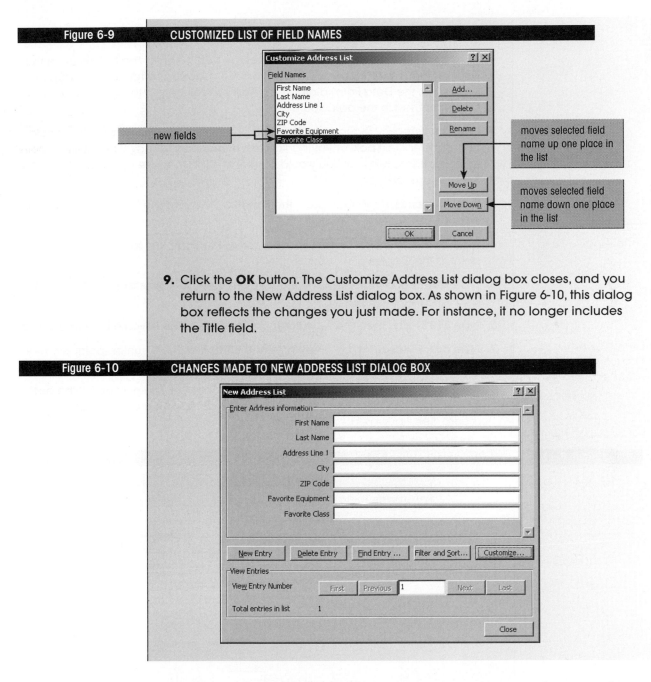

new fields

moves selected field
name up one place in
the list

moves selected field
name down one place
in the list

9. Click the **OK** button. The Customize Address List dialog box closes, and you
return to the New Address List dialog box. As shown in Figure 6-10, this dialog
box reflects the changes you just made. For instance, it no longer includes
the Title field.

Figure 6-10   CHANGES MADE TO NEW ADDRESS LIST DIALOG BOX

Now that you have specified the fields you want to use, you are ready to enter the member information into the data source.

Entering Data into a Data Source

You are now ready to begin entering information about each club member into the data
source. Maria gives you three completed Member Information Forms (shown earlier in
Figure 6-6). She asks you to transfer the information from the paper forms into the data
source. Each paper form will equal one new record in the data source. You'll use the New
Address List dialog box to begin entering information.

To enter data into a record using the data form:

1. Click the **First Name** text box, and then type **Ruth** to enter the first name of the first member. Make sure you do not press the spacebar after you finish typing an entry in the Data Form dialog box. Add spaces only in the text of the main document, not in the data source.

2. Press the **Enter** key to move the insertion point to the Last Name field. You could also click that text box, or you could press the Tab key to move the insertion point to the next field text box. You would press Shift + Tab to move the insertion point to the previous text box.

3. Type **Jorgenson** and then press the **Enter** key to move the insertion point to the Address Line 1 field.

4. Type **18 West Adams Street**, and then press the **Enter** key to move the insertion point to the City field.

5. Type **Miami** and then press the **Enter** key to move the insertion point to the ZIP Code field.

6. Type **31321** and then press the **Enter** key to move to the Favorite Equipment field.

7. Type **cardiovascular**, and then press the **Enter** key. The insertion point is now in the Favorite Class field.

8. Type **step aerobics** but do *not* press the Enter key yet. The number at the bottom of the dialog box tells you that so far, the data source contains only one record. See Figure 6-11.

Figure 6-11	COMPLETED RECORD 1

insertion point in last field

indicates number of records currently in data source

You have completed the information for the first record of the data source document. Now you're ready to enter the information for the next two records. You can create a new record by clicking the New Entry button, or by pressing the Enter key twice. In the steps below, you use the New Entry button.

To add additional records to the data source:

1. Click the **New Entry** button. This creates a new, blank record. The Total entries in list number, at the bottom of the dialog box, tells you that you're editing the second record.

2. Enter the information shown in Figure 6-12 into the new record.

Figure 6-12	COMPLETED RECORD 2

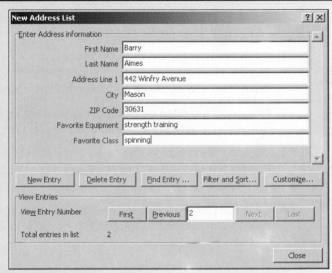

3. After entering data into the last field, press **Enter** twice. Note that you can use the Enter key or the New Entry button to create a blank record.

4. Enter the information for the third record, as shown in Figure 6-13.

Figure 6-13	COMPLETED RECORD 3

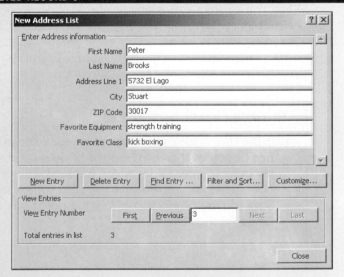

TROUBLE? If a new, blank record opens, you pressed the Enter key twice at the end of the third record or you clicked the New Entry button in the New Address List dialog box. Click the Delete Entry button to remove the unneeded fourth record.

You have entered the records for three members. Next you need to proofread each record to make sure you typed the information correctly. Any misspelled names or other typos in the final letters will reflect poorly on Palm Tree Athletic Club.

Displaying Records in a Data Source

You can display specific records in the data source by using the First, Previous, Next, and Last buttons. You'll use these buttons now to proofread each record in the data source.

To display the first record:

1. Click the **First** button at the bottom of the New Address List dialog box. The current record number (to the right of the Previous button) changes to 1, and the first record appears, with information about Ruth Jorgenson.

2. Proofread the data by comparing your information with Figure 6-11. Make any necessary corrections by selecting the text and retyping it.

3. Click the **Next** button. The "View Entry Number" changes to 2, and the information for the second record (for Barry Aimes) appears. Compare your record with Figure 6-12.

4. Click the **Last** button to review the last record (for Peter Brooks) in the data source. Compare your record with Figure 6-13. Make any necessary corrections.

Maria's data source eventually will contain hundreds of records for Palm Tree Athletic Club members. The current data source, however, contains only the records Maria wants to work with now.

You are finished entering records into the data source. Next you need to save the data source.

Saving a Data Source

When you create a data source in the Mail Merge Wizard, Word saves it as a Microsoft Office Address List, which is a special file designed to store address information for any Microsoft Office program.

Maria asks you to close the New Address List dialog box. In the process, you will save the data source as a Microsoft Office Address List.

To save the data source:

1. In the New Address List dialog box, click **Close**. The Save Address List dialog box opens, as shown in Figure 6-14. By default, Word offers to save the file to the My Data Sources folder, which is a subfolder of the My Documents folder. In this case, however, you will save the data source to your Data Disk. Notice that the Save as type box indicates that the data source will be saved as a Microsoft Office Address Lists file.

Figure 6-14	SAVING THE DATA SOURCE

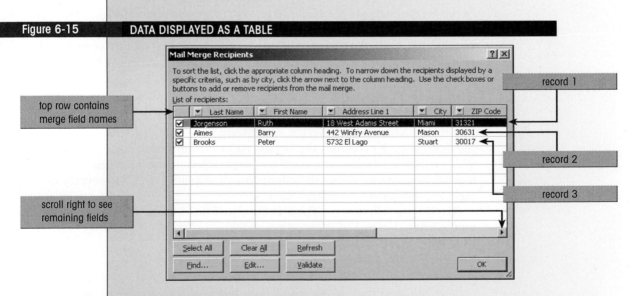

default folder is subfolder of My Documents folder

default file type

2. Use the Save in list arrow to select the **Tutorial** folder within the Tutorial.06 folder on your Data Disk.

3. Click the **File name** text box, type **Club Data**, and then click the **Save** button. The Mail Merge Recipients dialog box opens, as shown in Figure 6-15. Here you can see the data source displayed as a table. The header row, at the top, contains the names of each field in the table. Each row below the header row consists of one complete record. (You need to scroll right to see all the fields.) You can use this dialog box to rearrange the records in the list and to choose which members you want to include in the mail merge. You'll use this dialog box later in this tutorial. For now, you'll close it.

Figure 6-15	DATA DISPLAYED AS A TABLE

top row contains merge field names

scroll right to see remaining fields

record 1

record 2

record 3

Mail Merge Recipients

To sort the list, click the appropriate column heading. To narrow down the recipients displayed by a specific criteria, such as by city, click the arrow next to the column heading. Use the check boxes or buttons to add or remove recipients from the mail merge.

List of recipients:

	Last Name	First Name	Address Line 1	City	ZIP Code
☑	Jorgenson	Ruth	18 West Adams Street	Miami	31321
☑	Aimes	Barry	442 Winfry Avenue	Mason	30631
☑	Brooks	Peter	5732 El Lago	Stuart	30017

Select All   Clear All   Refresh

Find...   Edit...   Validate   OK

4. Click the **OK** button. The Mail Merge Recipients dialog box closes. You return to the Document window. The Mail Merge Task Pane indicates that you have selected an Office Address List file named Club Data.mdb as your data source.

The Task Pane also indicates that the next step in the mail merge process is writing (in this case, editing) the main document. Finally, note that you could click Edit recipient list to reopen the Mail Merge Recipients dialog box. See Figure 6-16.

Figure 6-16   SELECTED DATA SOURCE

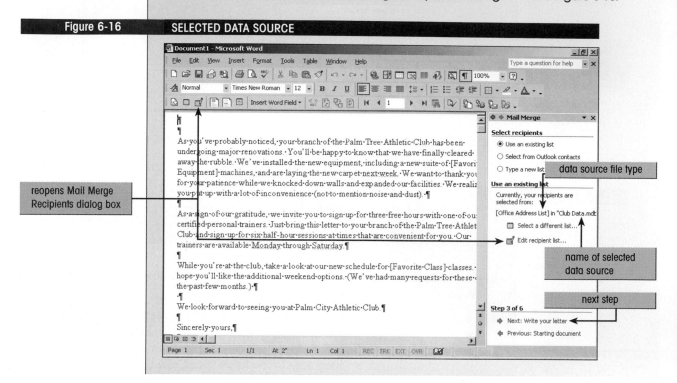

Editing a Main Document

In the first two steps of the Mail Merge Wizard, you selected Maria's letter as your main document. This letter is open on your screen, next to the Mail Merge Task Pane. In the third step, you selected, created, and saved the data source. Now you will turn your attention back to the main document. You'll edit Maria's letter to add the current date and the merge fields.

Adding a Date Field

You already know how to use the Insert Date and Time dialog box to add the current date to a document. If you select the Update automatically check box, Word inserts a **date field**, which tells Word to provide the current date each time the document is opened. A date field is similar to a merge field—the information it displays varies. However, you do not have to include a date field in the data source.

Maria wants the date to appear at the top of the document, just below the company logo on the printed stationery.

To insert the date field:

1. In the Mail Merge Task Pane, click **Next: Write your letter**. The Mail Merge Task Pane displays information and options related to working with the main document. If you had originally selected a new, blank document as your main document, you would need to write the text of the form letter now. In this case, you will edit the existing letter.

2. Make sure the insertion point is at the beginning of the form letter, on the first blank line. Maria already adjusted the page's top margin to leave room for the letterhead on the company stationery. You will insert the date on the first line of the document.

3. Click **Insert** on the menu bar, and then click **Date and Time**. The Date and Time dialog box opens. You will use the Update automatically check box to have Word revise the date every time you open the document.

4. Click the third month-day-year format in the Available formats list, and then click the **Update automatically** check box to select it. See Figure 6-17.

Figure 6-17	INSERTING A DATE FIELD

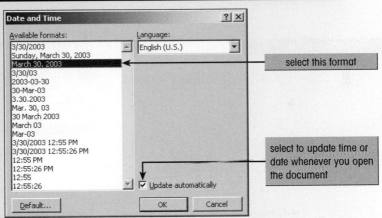

TROUBLE? The date in your Date and Time dialog box will differ from the one shown in Figure 6-17. Just click the format that includes the month, the day, and the year, as in March 3, 2003.

5. Click the **OK** button. The current date appears in the document. Now, whenever you or Maria print the merged document letter for Palm Tree Athletic Club's members, the current date will appear.

TROUBLE? If you see {TIME \@ "MMMM d, yyyy"} instead of the date, your system is set to display field codes. To view the date, click Tools on the menu bar, click Options, click the View tab, click the Field codes check box to remove the check mark and then click the OK button.

You're now ready to insert the merge fields for the letter's inside address.

Inserting Merge Fields

Maria's letter is a standard business letter, so you'll place the member's name and address below the date. You'll use merge fields for the member's first name, last name, address, city, and zip code. You must enter proper spacing and punctuation around the fields so that the information in the merged document will be formatted correctly. The Mail Merge Task Pane includes links, such as the Address block link, that you can use to insert a standard set of fields. The More items link offers more flexibility because it allows you to insert fields one at a time, rather than in predefined groups.

To insert a merge field:

1. Press the **Enter** key six times to leave space between the date and the first line of the inside address.

2. Click **More items** in the Mail Merge Task Pane. The Insert Merge Fields dialog box opens. (You could also use the Insert Merge Field button on the Mail Merge toolbar to open this dialog box.) As shown in Figure 6-18, the Database Fields option button is selected, indicating that the dialog box displays all the fields in the data source.

   TROUBLE? If you see a different list, the Address Fields option button may be selected rather than the Database Fields option button. Click the Database Fields option button to select it.

Figure 6-18	INSERTING MERGE FIELDS INTO THE MAIN DOCUMENT

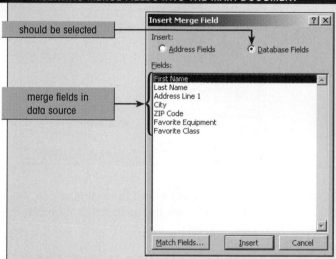

3. In the Fields list, click **First Name** if necessary, click the **Insert** button, and then click the **Close** button. The Insert Merge Fields dialog box closes, and a special instruction called a merge code is inserted into the document. The merge field consists of the field name surrounded by angled brackets << >> (also called chevrons).

   TROUBLE? If you make a mistake and insert the wrong merge field, select the entire merge field, including the chevrons, press the Delete key, and then insert the correct merge field.

4. Depending on how your computer is set up, you might see a gray background behind the merge field. If you do *not* see the gray background, click **Tools** on the menu bar, click **Options**, and then click the **View** tab in the Options dialog box. If necessary, change the **Field Shading** setting to **Always**, and then click the **OK** button.

Later, when you merge the main document with the data source, Word will replace the field code with information from the First Name field in the data source. Now, you're ready to insert the merge fields for the rest of the inside address. You'll add the necessary spacing and punctuation to the main document as well.

To insert the remaining merge fields for the inside address:

1. Press the **spacebar** to insert a space after the First Name field, click the **Insert Merge Fields** button [icon] on the Mail Merge toolbar, click **Last Name** in the Insert Merge Field dialog box, click the **Insert** button, and then click the **Close** button. Word inserts the Last Name merge field into the form letter.

2. Press the **Enter** key to move the insertion point to the next line, click [icon], click **Address Line 1** in the Insert Merge Field dialog box, click the **Insert** button, and then click the **Close** button. Word inserts the Address Line 1 merge field into the form letter.

3. Press the **Enter** key to move the insertion point to the next line, click [icon], click **City** in the Insert Merge Field dialog box, click the **Insert** button, and then click the **Close** button. Word inserts the City merge field into the form letter.

4. Type **,** (a comma), press the **spacebar** to insert a space after the comma, and then type **FL** to insert the abbreviation for the state of Florida. If Palm Tree Athletic Club had members outside Florida, you would need to use the State field name in the data source and also in the main document form letter. Because all of the members live in Florida, you can make the state name part of the main document, where it will be the same for every letter.

5. Press the **spacebar** to insert a space after FL, and then insert the ZIP Code merge field. Word inserts the ZIP Code merge field into the form letter. See Figure 6-19.

Figure 6-19	FORM LETTER WITH MERGE FIELDS

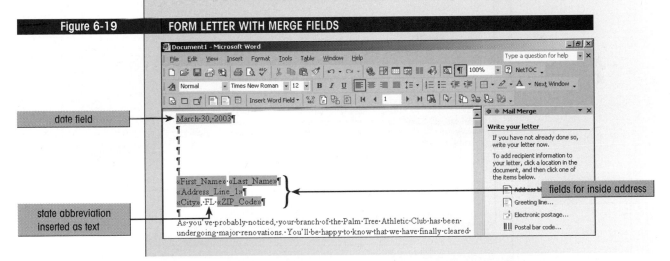

The inside address is set up to match the form for a standard business letter. You can now add the salutation of the letter, which will contain each member's first name.

To insert the merge field for the salutation:

1. Press the **Enter** key twice to leave a line between the inside address and the salutation, type **Dear**, and then press the **spacebar**.

2. Insert the **First Name** field into the document.

3. Type **:** (a colon). This completes the salutation.

   TROUBLE? If the Office Assistant asks if you want help writing the letter, click "Just type the letter without help."

You'll personalize the letter even more by including references to each member's favorite class and exercise equipment.

To finish personalizing the letter:

1. Select the placeholder **(Favorite Equipment)** (including the brackets) in the first paragraph of the form letter. You'll replace this phrase with a merge field.

2. Use the Insert Merge Field dialog box to insert the **Favorite Equipment** merge field. Word replaces your placeholder with the Favorite Equipment merge field.

3. If necessary, press the **spacebar** to insert a space between the field and the next word, "machines."

4. Replace **(Favorite Class)** in the first sentence of the third main paragraph of the form letter with the **Favorite Class** field, and make sure there is a space between the merge field and the next word, "classes." Your document should look like Figure 6-20.

Figure 6-20	FORM LETTER AFTER INSERTING MERGE FIELDS

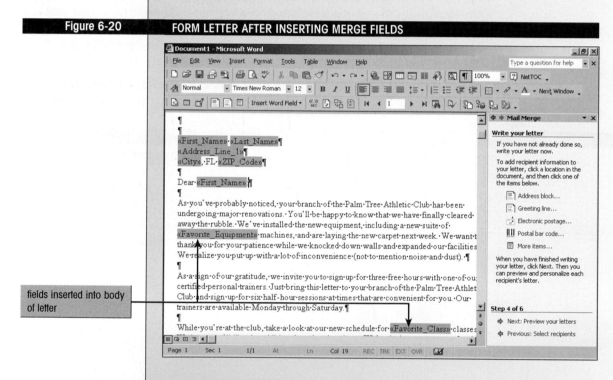

fields inserted into body of letter

5. Carefully check your document to make sure all the field names and spacing are correct. Now that you have inserted all the merge fields, you need to save the main document with a new name.

   TROUBLE? If you see an error, edit the document as you would any other Word document. If you inserted an incorrect merge field, delete the entire merge field, and then insert the correct one.

6. Save the letter as **Club Letter with Field Codes** in the Tutorial subfolder within the Tutorial.06 folder on your Data Disk.

The main document now contains all the necessary merge fields, but not the data. To include data, you merge the main document and the data source. First, however, you should preview the merged document.

Previewing the Merged Document

According to the Mail Merge Wizard, your next step is to preview the merged document to see how the letter will look after Word inserts the information for each member. When you preview the merged document, you can check one last time for any missing spaces between the merge codes and the surrounding text. You can also look for any other formatting problems, and, if necessary, make final changes to the data source.

To preview the merged document:

1. In the Mail Merge Task Pane, click **Next: Preview your letters**. The Task Pane displays information and options related to previewing the merged document. The data for the first record replaces the merge fields in the form letter. See Figure 6-21. Scroll to the top of the document so you can see the inside address and salutation. Carefully check the letter to make sure the text and formatting are correct. In particular, check to make sure that the spaces before and after the merged data are correct because it is easy to omit spaces or add extra spaces around merge fields. Finally, notice that both the Task Pane and the Go to Record box in the Mail Merge toolbar indicate which record is currently displayed in the document.

Figure 6-21	FIRST LETTER WITH MERGED DATA

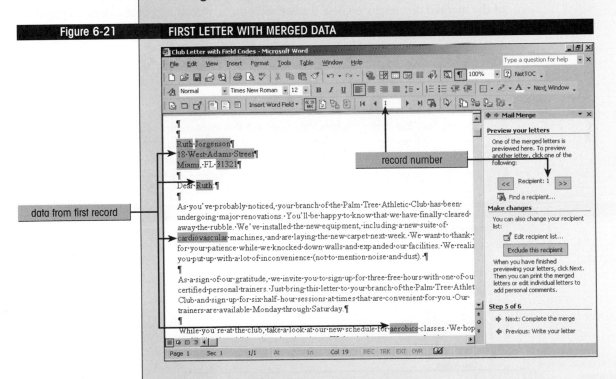

2. If you need to make any changes to the form letter, click **Previous: Write your letter** in the Task Pane, edit the document, save your changes, and then click **Next: Preview your letters** in the Task Pane. When you are finished, your screen should look like Figure 6-21. Before you finish previewing your merged document, you should review the data for the other two records.

3. Click the **Next Record** button ▶ in the Mail Merge toolbar to display the data for Barry Aimes in the letter. (*Note:* You can also use the right-facing double-arrow button in the Task Pane to display the next record.)

> **4.** Click ▶ in the Mail Merge toolbar to display the data for Peter Brooks in the letter.
>
> **5.** Click the **First Record** button ◀ in the Mail Merge toolbar to redisplay the first record in the letter (with data for Ruth Jorgenson).

The form letter (main document) of the mail merge is completed. At this stage you could also use the Mail Merge Task Pane to make changes to the data source, but Maria says the data source is fine for now. You are ready for the final step, completing the merge.

Merging the Main Document and Data Source

Now that you've created the form letter (main document) and the list of member information (data source), you're ready to merge the two files and create personalized letters to send to Palm Tree Athletic Club members. Because the data source consists of three records, you'll create a merged document with three pages, one letter per page.

You could merge the data source and main document directly to the printer using the Merge to Printer button on the Mail Merge toolbar. Then Word immediately prints the merged document without saving it as a separate file. However, Maria wants to keep a copy of the merged document on disk for her records. So you'll merge the data source and main document to a new document.

> *To complete the mail merge:*
>
> **1.** In the Mail Merge Task Pane, click **Next: Complete the merge**. As shown in Figure 6-22, the Task Pane displays options related to merging the main document and the data source. You can use the Print option (or the Merge to Printer button 🔳 on the Mail Merge toolbar) to merge directly to the printer. Or, you can use the Edit individual letters option (or the Merge to New Document button 🔳 on the Mail Merge toolbar) to merge to a new document.

| Figure 6-22 | LAST STEP OF MAIL MERGE WIZARD |

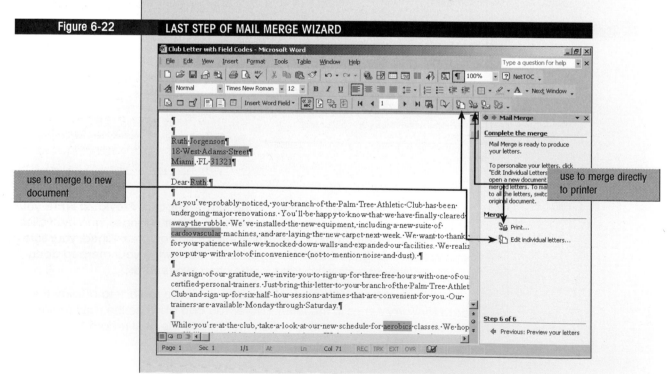

use to merge to new document

use to merge directly to printer

2. Click **Edit individual letters** in the Mail Merge Task Pane. The Merge to New Document dialog box opens. Here, you need to specify which records you want to include in the merge. You want to include all the records in the data source.

3. Verify that the All option button is selected, and then click the **OK** button. Word creates a new document called Letters1, which contains three pages, one for each record in the data source. The form letter with the merge field codes (Club Letter with Field Codes) remains open, as indicated by its button in the taskbar. See Figure 6-23.

| Figure 6-23 | MERGED DOCUMENT |

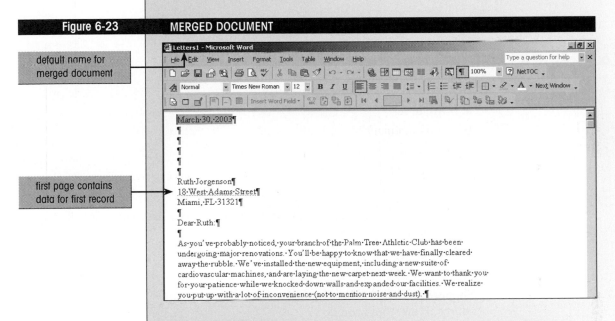

default name for merged document

first page contains data for first record

4. Save the merged document in the Tutorial subfolder in the Tutorial.06 folder, using the filename **Club Merged Letters1**.

5. Click the **Print Preview** button on the Standard toolbar to switch to Print Preview.

6. Click the **Zoom Control** list arrow on the Print Preview toolbar, and then click **Page Width** so the text is large enough to read. Next you will use the Select Browse Object button (at the bottom of the vertical scroll bar) to move from one page to the next.

7. Click the **Select Browse Object** button, click the **Browse by Page** button in the palette, and then click the **Previous Page** button or **Next Page** button below the vertical scroll bar to move to the beginning of each letter. Note that each letter is addressed to a different member and that the favorite equipment and class vary from one letter to the next.

8. Click the **Close** button on the Print Preview toolbar to return to Normal view, and then save and close the Club Merged Letters1 document. The document named Club Letter with Field Codes reappears, along with the last step of the Mail Merge Wizard.

> **9.** Close the Mail Merge Task Pane but leave the Mail Merge toolbar displayed. If you are not taking a break before the next session, you can leave the Club letter with Field Codes document open. If you are taking a break, close all open documents (saving any changes) and exit Word.

You have completed the six steps of the Mail Merge Wizard and generated a merged document. In the next session you will learn how to use additional features of the Mail Merge Wizard.

Session 6.1 QUICK CHECK

1. Define the following in your own words:
   a. form letter
   b. main document
   c. data source
   d. merge field
   e. record

2. All the information about one individual or object in a data source is called a _____.

3. True or False: For a mail merge to work properly, every record in the data source must have the same set of fields.

4. Suppose you want to insert information for a field named "Gender" into the data source. How would you do it?

5. What type of file do you create when you create a data source from within the Mail Merge Wizard?

6. Explain how to insert a field code into a main document.

7. Explain how to merge to a new document.

SESSION 6.2

In this session you will edit a data source, sort records in a data source, filter a data source to display only certain records, create mailing labels, and create a telephone directory.

Editing a Data Source

After you complete a mail merge, you may find that you need to make some changes to the data source and redo the merge. For instance, now Maria wants to add some records to the data source.

You can edit a data source in two ways—from within the program used to create the data source in the first place, or from within the Mail Merge Wizard. If you are familiar with the program used to create the data source, it's often simplest to edit the file from within that program. For example, if you were using an Excel worksheet as your data source, you could open the file in Excel, edit it (perhaps by adding new records), save it, and then reselect the file as your data source. You can use Microsoft Access to edit a data source created in Word, but it's easier to edit it from within Word, using the buttons on the Mail Merge toolbar.

REFERENCE **WINDOW**   RW

Editing a Data Source

- If you did not use the Mail Merge Wizard to create your data source, open the program you used to create the data source, edit the file, save it and close it.
- Click the Open Data Source button on the Mail Merge toolbar, navigate to the folder containing the data source, select the data source, and then click the Open button.

or

- Click the Mail Merge Recipients button on the Mail Merge toolbar and then click the Edit button.
- To add a record, click the New Field button and then type a new record.
- To delete a record, display it and then click the Delete button.
- To add or remove fields from the data source, click the Customize button, make any changes, and then click the OK button. Remember that if you remove a field, you will delete any data already entered into that field.
- Click the Close button.

You'll try the second method now as you add some new records to Maria's data source. After you complete a merge using the Mail Merge Wizard, it's usually easiest to change the merge documents by using the Mail Merge toolbar, rather than the Task Pane. (Note that you only have to perform Step 1 if you took a break from the last session.)

To add records to Maria's data source:

1. If you took a break after the last session, start Word, open the document named **Club Letter with Field Codes**, display the Mail Merge toolbar (if necessary), click the **Open Data Source** button 🔲 on the Mail Merge toolbar, and then use the Select Data Source dialog box to open the data source file named **Club Data** (from the Tutorial subfolder in the Tutorial.06 folder on your Data Disk). Next, click the **View Merged Data** button 🔲 on the Mail Merge Toolbar to display the data for Ruth Jorgenson (just as you saw it earlier in Figure 6-21).

2. If the Mail Merge Task Pane is open, close it and verify that the Mail Merge toolbar is still visible. The main document still displays the data for Ruth Jorgenson, which first appeared when you previewed the merged document. You can redisplay the merge fields using a button on the toolbar.

3. Click 🔲 on the Mail Merge Task Pane. The merge field codes are displayed in the main document.

4. Click the **Mail Merge Recipients** button 🔲 on the Mail Merge toolbar. The Mail Merge Recipients dialog box opens. You saw this dialog box earlier, when you first selected the data source to use for the mail merge.

5. Click the **Edit** button. The Club Data.mdb dialog box opens. Note that this dialog box looks similar to the New Address List dialog box, which you used earlier when you first entered information into the data source.

6. Use the New Entry button to enter the information shown in Figure 6-24 into the data source. When you are finished, you should have added three new records, for a total of six.

Figure 6-24   NEW DATA

First Name	Last Name	Address Line 1	City	ZIP Code	Favorite Equipment	Favorite Class
Violette	Wolfgramm	3004 Falcon Parkway	Tampa	30902	cardiovascular	low-impact aerobics
Kathy	Armstrong	19284 White Sands	Tampa	30902	strength training	Pilates
Pablo	Orozco	248 North River Road	Aurora	30010	strength training	yoga

7. After you finish entering the data for Pablo Orozco, use the buttons in the View Entries section of the dialog box to review your work and make any necessary corrections.

8. Click the **Close** button. The Club Data.mdb dialog box closes, and you return to the Mail Merge Recipients dialog box, as shown in Figure 6-25. If your records look different from those in Figure 6-25, click the Edit button, edit the data source, and then click the Close button.

Figure 6-25   NEW RECORDS ADDED TO DATA SOURCE

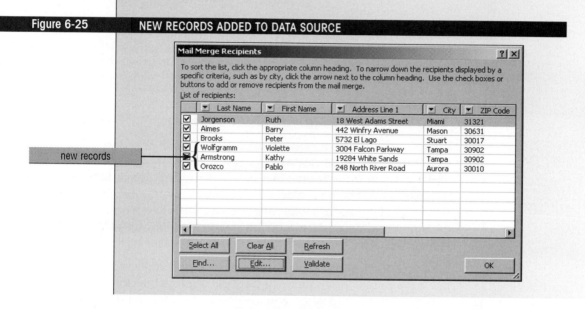

new records

You'll leave the Mail Merge Recipients dialog box open so you can use it to make other changes to the data source.

Sorting Records

As Maria looks through the letters to Palm Tree Athletic Club members in the merged document, she notices one problem—the letters are not grouped by ZIP codes. Currently, the letters are in the order in which members were added to the data source file. She plans to use bulk mailing rates to send her letters, and the U.S. Postal Service requires bulk mailings to be separated into groups according to ZIP code. She asks you to sort the data file by ZIP code and perform another merge, this time merging the main document with the sorted data source.

You can sort information in a data source table just as you sort information in any other table. Recall that to **sort** means to rearrange a list or a document in alphabetical, numerical, or chronological order. You can sort information in ascending order (A to Z, lowest to highest, or earliest to latest) or in descending order (Z to A, highest to lowest, or latest to earliest) by clicking a column heading in the Mail Merge Recipients dialog box. The first time you click the heading, the records are sorted in ascending order. If you click it twice, the records are sorted in descending order.

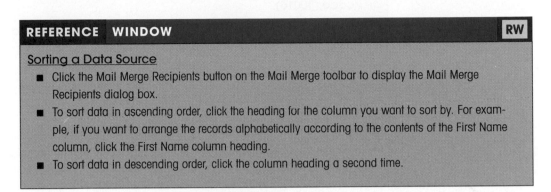

REFERENCE WINDOW **RW**

Sorting a Data Source
- Click the Mail Merge Recipients button on the Mail Merge toolbar to display the Mail Merge Recipients dialog box.
- To sort data in ascending order, click the heading for the column you want to sort by. For example, if you want to arrange the records alphabetically according to the contents of the First Name column, click the First Name column heading.
- To sort data in descending order, click the column heading a second time.

Currently, the records in the data source appear in the order you entered them, with the information for Ruth Jorgenson first. You'll sort the records in an ascending order, based on the contents of the ZIP Code column.

To sort the data source by zip code:

1. Verify that the Mail Merge Recipients dialog box is still open. If it is not, click the **Mail Merge Recipients** button on the Mail Merge toolbar.

2. Click the **ZIP Code** column heading. Word sorts the rows of the data table from lowest zip code number to highest. The information for Pablo Orozco is now at the top of the list. See Figure 6-26.

Figure 6-26 **RECORDS SORTED IN ASCENDING ORDER BY ZIP CODE**

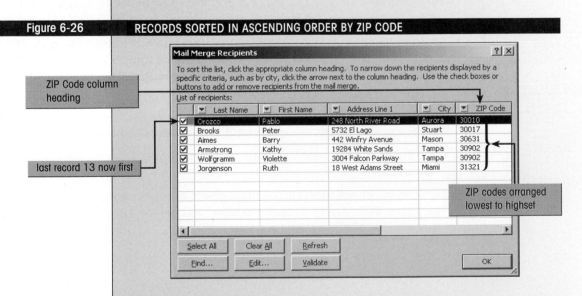

When you merge the data source with the form letter, the letters will appear in the merged document in the same order.

3. Click the **OK** button. The Mail Merge Recipients dialog box closes.

4. Click the **Merge to New Document** button 🔲 on the Mail Merge toolbar, and then click the **OK** button in the Merge to New Document dialog box. Word generates the new merged document with six letters, one letter per page as before, but this time the first letter is to Pablo Orozco, who has the lowest ZIP code (30010).

5. Scroll through the letters in the newly merged document to see that they are arranged in ascending order by ZIP code.

6. Save the new merged document in the Tutorial subfolder in the Tutorial.06 folder, using the filename **Club Merged Letters2**, and then close it. You return to the main document.

As Maria requested, you've created a merged document with the letters to Palm Tree Athletic Club members sorted by zip code. She then tells you that the letters to members who frequent the Tampa club need additional information.

Selecting Records to Merge

Maria plans to offer an extra hour of personal trainer time to members of the Tampa club, because renovations at that branch caused the most inconvenience. Maria wants to modify the form letter slightly, and then merge it with only those records of Palm Tree Athletic Club members who live in Tampa. To select specific records in a data source, you need to use the Mail Merge Recipients dialog box.

To select specific records for a merge:

1. Make sure the document named Club Letter with Field Codes is displayed in the Document window. Use the Find command on the Edit menu to find the sentence that begins "As a sign of our gratitude."

2. Change "three" to **four** in the part of the sentence that reads "...sign up for three free hours," and then save the document as **Tampa Club Letter with Field Codes** in the Tutorial subfolder in the Tutorial.06 folder on your Data Disk.

3. Click the **Mail Merge Recipients** button 🔲 on the Mail Merge toolbar. The Mail Merge Recipients dialog box opens. To remove an individual record from the merge, you can deselect its check box in the leftmost column.

4. Click the check box next to the first record (for Pablo Orozco). The check mark is removed.

5. Remove the check marks for all the records *except* those for Tampa residents. See Figure 6-27. Now that you have selected only the Tampa records, you can complete the Merge.

Figure 6-27   **FILTERING RECORDS**

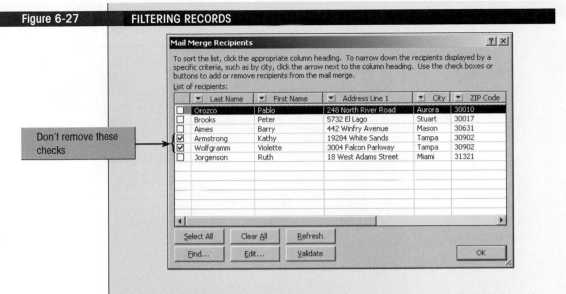

Don't remove these checks

6. Click the **OK** button. The Mail Merge Recipients dialog box closes.

7. Click the **Merge to New Document** button 🖺 on the Mail Merge toolbar, and then click the **OK** button in the Merge to New Document dialog box. Word generates the new merged document with two letters, one letter per page. This time the first letter is to Kathy Armstrong.

8. Scroll through the letters in the new merged document to see that they are both addressed to members who live in Tampa.

9. Save the new merged document in the Tutorial subfolder in the Tutorial.06 folder, using the filename **Club Merged Letters3**, close it, save your changes to the document named Tampa Club Letter with Field Codes, and then close it.

You give the completed file to Maria, who will print the letters on the company stationery. Next you'll create and print mailing labels for the form letter envelopes and also create a telephone list—both using the Mail Merge Wizard.

Creating Mailing Labels

Now that you've created and printed the personalized sales letters, Maria is ready to prepare envelopes in which to mail the letters. She could print the names and addresses directly onto envelopes, or she could create mailing labels to stick on the envelopes. The latter method is easier because she can print 14 labels at one time; by comparison, printing envelopes is far too time-consuming. Maria asks you to create the mailing labels.

She has purchased AveryLaser Printer labels, product number 5162 Address. These labels, which are available in most office-supply stores, come in 8½ × 11-inch sheets designed to feed through a laser printer. Each label measures 4 × 1.33 inches; each sheet has seven rows of labels with two labels in each row, for a total of 14 labels per sheet, as shown in Figure 6-28. Word supports most of the Avery label formats.

Figure 6-28	LAYOUT OF A SHEET OF AVERY 5162 LABELS

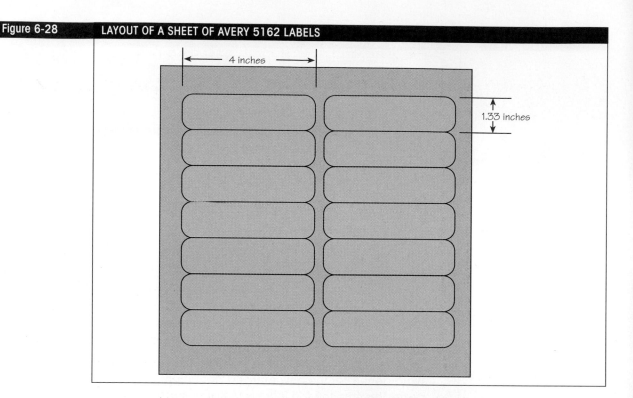

Creating mailing labels is similar to creating form letters, and the Mail Merge Wizard walks you through all six steps. You'll begin creating the mailing labels by starting the Mail Merge Wizard. You can use the same data source file (Club Data) as you used earlier.

To specify the main document and data source for creating mailing labels:

1. Open a new, blank document.

2. Click **Tools** on the menu bar, point to **Letters and Mailings**, and then, click **Mail Merge Wizard.** Next you will change the document view so you can see the entire document.

3. If necessary, switch to **Print Layout** view and change the zoom setting to **Whole Page.**

4. Under "Select Document Type" click the **Labels** option button, and then click **Next: Starting document.** The Task Pane displays information and options relating to setting up the document layout for labels. (Note: If Maria wanted you to print envelopes instead of mailing labels, you would have selected Envelopes as the type of main document.)

5. Under "Select starting document" click the **Change document layout** option button to select it (if necessary), and then, under "Change document layout," click **Label options.** The Label Options dialog box opens.

6. If necessary, click the **Label products list arrow** and select **Avery standard.**

7. Scroll the Product number list box, and then click **5162 - Address.** Your Label Options dialog box should look like Figure 6-29.

TROUBLE? If your printer is a dot matrix printer, select the Dot matrix option button rather than the Laser and ink jet option button.

Figure 6-29 | LABEL OPTIONS DIALOG BOX

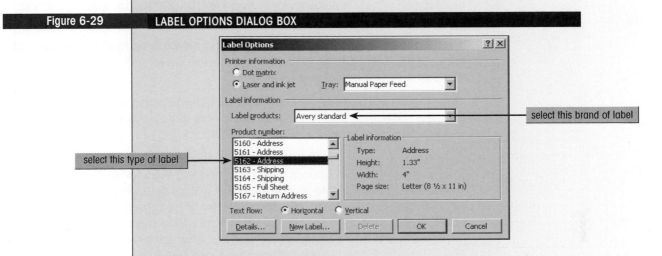

8. Click the **OK** button. The Label Options dialog box closes.

9. Click **Tools** on the menu bar, click **Options**, click the **View** tab, click the **Text boundaries** check box (in the lower-left corner) to select it, and then click the **OK** button. The document is now subdivided into label-sized rectangles, as shown in Figure 6-30.

Figure 6-30 | DOCUMENT SETUP FOR LABELS

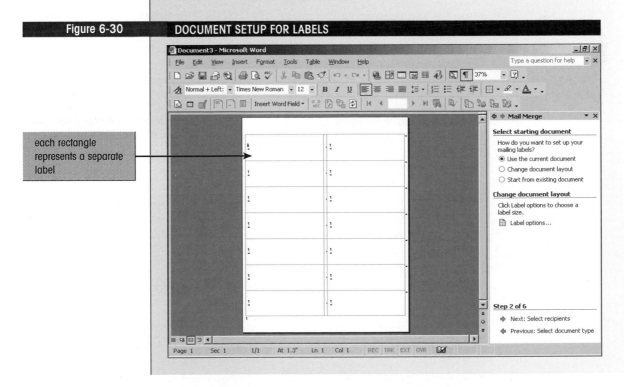

You are finished setting up the document. Next you need to select the data source you created earlier.

To continue the mail merge:

1. Click **Next: Select recipients**. Under "Select recipients," click the **Use an existing list** option button (if necessary), and then, under "Use an existing list," click **Browse**. The Select Data Source dialog box opens.

2. Use the Look in list arrow to select the file named **Club Data** in the Tutorial subfolder in the Tutorial.06 folder, and then click the **Open** button. The Mail Merge Recipients dialog box opens.

3. Verify that all the records are displayed with check boxes selected and then click the **OK** button. The Mail Merge Recipients dialog box closes. Now you are ready to insert field codes into the document.

4. Click **Next: Arrange your labels**, and then change the Zoom setting to **100%**. The Task Pane displays options related to inserting field codes into the document. Note that if the data source included a State field, you could use the Address block option to insert a complete set of fields for a single address. However, because the data source does not include a State field, you need to insert the field codes individually, as you did when creating the form letter. (You'll have a chance to use the Address block option in the Review Assignments and Case Problems at the end of this tutorial.)

5. Verify that the insertion point is located in the upper-left label in the document, click **More Items** in the Task Pane, and then use the Insert Merge Field dialog box to insert the First Name field into the document. Click the **Close** button. The First Name field code is inserted into the document.

6. Press the **spacebar** to add a space after the First Name field code, insert the **Last Name** field code, press **Enter**, insert the **Address Line 1** field code, press **Enter**, insert the **City** field code, type **,** (a comma), press the **spacebar** to insert a space, type **FL**, press the **spacebar**, and then insert the **ZIP Code** field code. You are finished inserting the field codes for the first label. Now you can copy your work to the remaining labels.

7. Click the **Update all labels** button, near the bottom of the Task Pane. (You may have to scroll down to see it, using the scroll button at the bottom of the Task Pane.) The address field codes are inserted into all the labels in the document, as shown in Figure 6-31. Note that the Next Record code is a special code that tells Word how to insert the data into the document. You can ignore it. You are now ready to preview the labels and complete the merge.

Figure 6-31 | FIELD CODES INSERTED INTO DOCUMENT

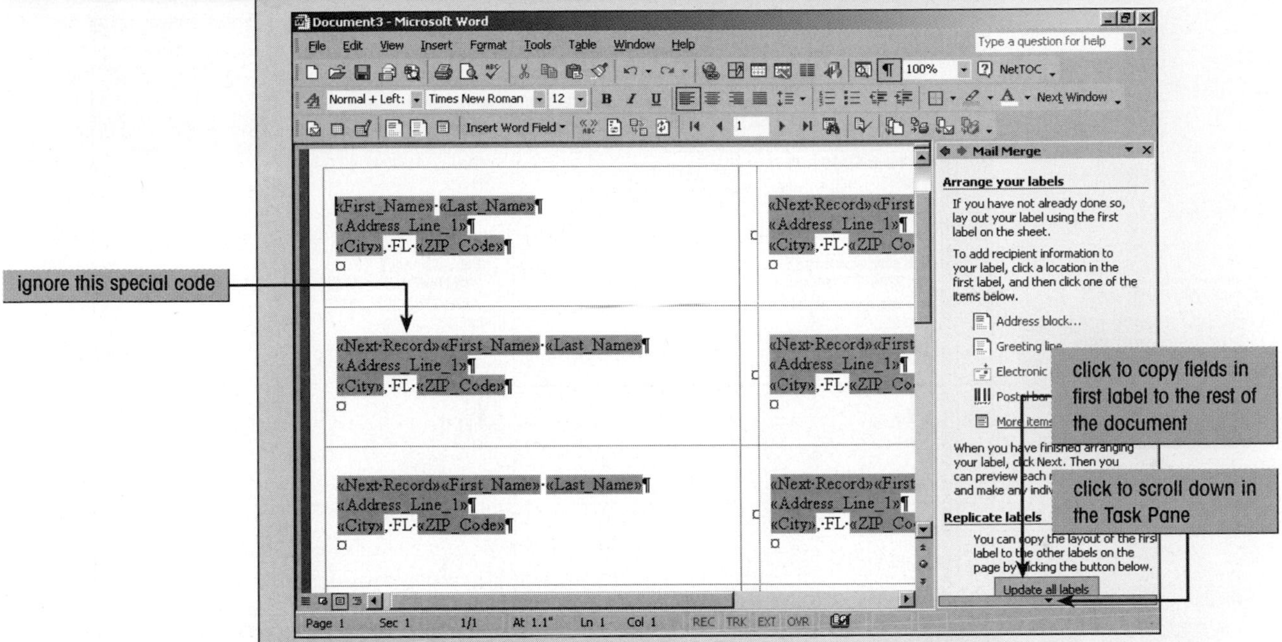

ignore this special code

click to copy fields in first label to the rest of the document

click to scroll down in the Task Pane

8. Click **Next: Preview your labels** in the Task Pane. (You may have to scroll down to display this option, again using the scroll button at the bottom of the Task Pane.) The data for the club members is displayed in the labels. (If you see some extra text in labels that would otherwise be blank, ignore it for now.) You are ready to merge to a new document.

9. Click **Next: Complete the merge** in the Task Pane, click **Edit individual labels** in the Task Pane, and then click the **OK** button in the Merge to New Document dialog box. The finished labels are displayed in a new document.

The labels are almost finished. All you need to do is edit the document to remove any extra text, save the document, and print the labels. For now, you'll just print the labels on an 8½ X 11-inch sheet of paper so you can see what they look like. Later, Maria will print them on the sheet of labels.

To save and print the labels:

1. Scroll through the document. Note that the document contains space for 14 labels, but that the data source only contained six records. However, when you clicked the Update Labels button in the Task Pane earlier, the comma and the state abbreviation (FL) were copied to all the labels, including those that don't contain any address information. See Figure 6-32. You can solve this problem by deleting the extra text in the bottom four rows of labels. (As you'll see in the Review Assignments at the end of this tutorial, you can avoid this issue entirely by using the Address block option for inserting field codes. However, as mentioned earlier, the Address block option is only useful when your data source contains all the necessary address fields.)

| Figure 6-32 | EXTRA TEXT IN LABELS DOCUMENT |

comma and state
abbreviation in labels
that would otherwise
be blank

2. Change the Zoom setting to **Whole Page**, drag the mouse pointer to select the bottom four rows of labels, and then press the **Delete** key. The extra text is deleted.

3. Save the merged document in the Tutorial subfolder in the Tutorial.06 folder using the filename **Club Labels**.

4. Print the labels on a sheet of paper, just as you would print any other document.

   TROUBLE? If you want to print on a sheet of labels, ask your instructor or technical support person how to feed the sheet into the printer. If you're using a shared printer, you may need to make special arrangements so other users' documents aren't accidentally printed on your label sheet.

5. Close the merged document.

6. Save the main document to the Tutorial subfolder in the Tutorial.06 folder using the filename **Club Labels with Field Codes**, and then close the document.

Creating a Telephone Directory

As your final task, Maria wants you to create a list of telephone numbers for all the branches of Palm Tree Athletic Club. Maria has already created a Word document containing the phone numbers for each branch. She asks you to use that document as the data source for the merge. You'll set up a mail merge as before, except this time you'll select Directory as the main document type. You'll start by examining the Word document that Maria wants you to use as the data source.

To prepare for creating the telephone list:

1. Open the document named **Phone** from the Tutorial subfolder in the Tutorial.06 folder on your Data Disk, and review the document. Note that the information is arranged in a table, with two column headings, "Branch" and "Number." Maria wants the telephone directory in alphabetical order by branch. She asks you to sort the table before using it as the data source in the Mail Merge Wizard.

2. Display the Tables and Borders toolbar, use the Sort Ascending button ⬇ on the Tables and Borders toolbar to sort the table alphabetically by branch, close the Tables and Borders toolbar, and then save the document as **Sorted Phone List** in the Tutorial subfolder in the Tutorial.06 folder on your Data Disk.

3. Close the Sorted Phone List document, open a new, blank document, start the Mail Merge Wizard, and then display the blank document in Print Layout view.

4. If you see a gray border on the page margins, click **Tools** on the menu bar, click **Options**, click the **View** tab, click the **Text boundaries** check box to deselect it, and then click the **OK** button.

5. Display the rulers, and change the zoom setting to **85%** (or a setting that will let you see the 6-inch mark on the horizontal ruler).

6. In the Mail Merge Task Pane, under "Select document type" click the **Directory** option button, click **Next: Starting document**, verify that the **Use the current document** option button is selected, click **Next: Select recipients**, verify that the **Use an existing list** option button is selected, and then click **Browse**. The Select Data Source dialog box opens.

7. Select the file named **Sorted Phone List** (in the Tutorial subfolder in the Tutorial.06 folder on your Data Disk) as the data source, click the **Open** button, review the records in the Mail Merge Recipients dialog box, and then click the **OK** button.

8. In the Task Pane, click **Next: Arrange your directory**.

You're ready to insert the field codes in the main document and merge the main document with the data source. Maria wants the telephone list to include the name of the club branch at the left margin of the page and the phone number at the right margin. You'll set up the main document so that the phone number is preceded by a dot leader. A **dot leader** is a dotted line that extends from the last letter of text on the left margin to the beginning of text aligned at a tab stop.

To create the main document:

1. With the insertion point at the top of the blank document, insert the **Branch** merge field. Now you'll set a tab stop at the right margin (at the 6-inch mark on the ruler) with a dot leader.

2. Click **Format** on the menu bar, and then click **Tabs**. The Tabs dialog box opens.

3. Type **6** in the Tab stop position text box, click the **Right** option button in the Alignment section, and then click the **2 ....** option button in the Leader section to create a dot leader. See Figure 6-33.

Figure 6-33   CREATING A TAB WITH A DOT LEADER

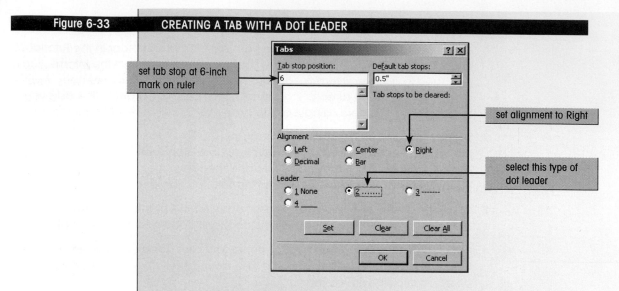

set tab stop at 6-inch mark on ruler

set alignment to Right

select this type of dot leader

4. Click the **OK** button. Word clears the current tab stops and inserts a right-aligned tab stop at the 6-inch mark on the horizontal ruler.

5. Press the **Tab** key to move the insertion point to the new tab stop. A dotted line stretches across the page, from the Branch field code to the right margin.

6. Insert the **Number** merge field at the location of the insertion point, and then press the **Enter** key. You must insert a hard return here so that each name and telephone number will appear on a separate line. Notice that the dot leader shortened to accommodate the inserted field code. The completed main document should look like Figure 6-34.

Figure 6-34   COMPLETED MAIN DOCUMENT FOR TELEPHONE DIRECTORY

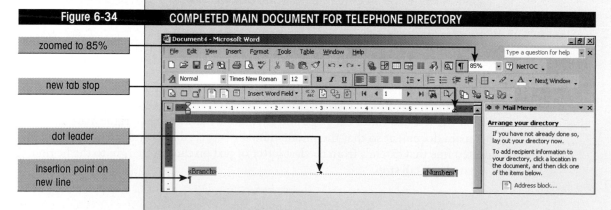

zoomed to 85%

new tab stop

dot leader

insertion point on new line

7. Save the main document in the Tutorial subfolder in the Tutorial.06 folder using the filename **Club Phone Directory with Field Codes**.

You are now ready to merge this file with the data source.

To merge the files:

1. In the Task Pane, click **Next: Preview your directory**, review the data in the document, click **Next: Complete the Merge** in the Task Pane, click **To New Document** in the Task Pane, verify that the All option button is selected in the Merge to New Document dialog box, and then click the **OK** button. Word creates a new document that contains the completed telephone list. See Figure 6-35.

Figure 6-35   **COMPLETED TELEPHONE DIRECTORY**

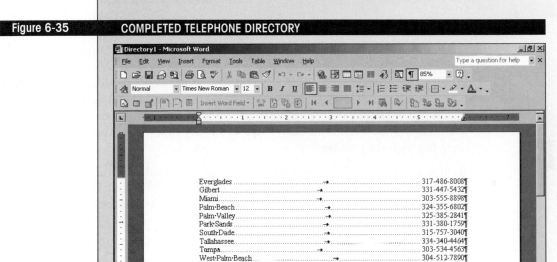

2. Save the document as **Club Phone Directory** in the Tutorial subfolder in the Tutorial.06 folder on your Data Disk and then close it.

3. Save and then close the document named Club Phone Directory with Field Codes.

   TROUBLE? If you see a dialog box asking if you want to save changes to the data source, click the Yes button.

4. Exit Word.

You have created the telephone list. Maria will have it printed and distributed to each branch of the club. Now that you are familiar with the many types of documents you can create using Word's Mail Merge Features, you can use them whenever you need to distribute customized information to a group of people. As you will learn in the Case Problems at the end of this tutorial, you can even use the Mail Merge Wizard to send out mass e-mail messages.

Session 6.2 QUICK CHECK

1. True or False: To create mailing labels, you can use the same data source file you used for a form letter.

2. Explain how to create mailing labels.

3. What is a dot leader? (The telephone directory you created in this tutorial used a dot leader.)

4. Explain how to filter a data source to display only the records with Iowa entered in the State field.

5. Explain how to alphabetize a data source by last name.

REVIEW ASSIGNMENTS

The club's free personal training offer was a great success, and Maria was pleased with how convenient it was to send out form letters with the Word Mail Merge feature. Now Radine Robbins, the club's special events coordinator, wants to use the Mail Merge Wizard to send out a letter inviting members to sign up for their annual health assessments. Members will be invited for either a cardiovascular screening or a strength training screening, depending on what type of assessment they chose when they first joined the club. Radine asks you to help her with the mailing.

1. If necessary, start Word and make sure your Data Disk is in the appropriate drive. Open the file **Assess** from the Review folder for Tutorial 6 on your Data Disk, and then save it with the filename **Health Assessment** in the Review folder for Tutorial 6 on your Data Disk.

2. With the Health Assessment document open, start the Mail Merge Wizard, select Letters as the type of main document, and then select the current document as the main document.

3. In Step 3 of the Mail Merge Wizard, create a new data source with the following fields: First Name, Last Name, Address Line 1, City, ZIP Code, and Type. Remove any extra fields so that the data source contains only six fields.

4. Create records using the following information:
   - Sandy Martinez, 2483 Anderson Ferry Drive, Tampa, 30307, cardiovascular
   - April Matthews, 471 S. Valley View, Flambeau, 31321, strength
   - Thomas Peacemaker, 372 Wildwood Avenue, Greeley, 30631, strength
   - David Menaker, 988 Heather Circle #32, Tampa, 30204, cardiovascular

5. Save the data source as **Assessment Data** in the Review folder for Tutorial 6 on your Data Disk.

6. Sort the data source by zip code from the lowest to the highest zip code.

7. In Step 4 of the Mail Merge Wizard, replace the field names in brackets with actual merge fields. Remember to replace [Date] with a Word date field.

8. Save your changes to the main document, and then preview the merged document. Correct any formatting problems or extra spaces.

9. In Step 6 of the Mail Merge Wizard, click Edit individual letters to merge to a new document. Save the merged document as **Merged Health Assessment Letters**, and then close it.

10. Return to Step 5 in the Mail Merge Wizard, edit the data source to select only records for members interested in cardiovascular assessments, and then complete a second merge. Save the new merged document as **Cardio Health Assessment Letters**, and then print the first letter. Close all documents, saving changes as needed.

Next Radine wants you to create envelopes to use for mailing the form letters. She wants you to use the Address block option in the Mail Merge Wizard to insert the address fields, so you will have to edit the data source to insert a State field. To learn how, complete these steps:

11. Open a new, blank document, start the Mail Merge Wizard, and select Envelopes as the type of main document.

Explore 12. In Step 2 of the Mail Merge Wizard, verify that the Change document layout button is selected, and then click Envelope Options. In the Envelope Options dialog box, verify that Size 10 (4⅛ × 9 inches) is selected in the Size box, and then click the OK button.

Explore 13. In Step 3 of the Mail Merge Wizard, select the **Assessment Data** file you created earlier as the data source. Edit the data source to add a State field after the City field, and then add "FL" to the state field in each record.

Explore 14. In Step 4 of the Mail Merge Wizard, click the recipient address area of the envelope, and click Address block in the Task Pane to open the Insert Address Block dialog box. Select the "Joshua Randall Jr." name format, and deselect the Insert company name check box. Verify that the Insert postal address check box is selected and then click the OK button. The Address Block merge field codes are inserted into the main document. Save the main document as **Envelopes with Field Codes** in the Review folder for Tutorial 6.

15. Preview the merged envelopes, merge to a new document, save the document as **Merged Envelopes**, print the first envelope, and then close all open documents, saving changes as necessary.

As you learned in the tutorial, you can use many types of files as your data source. For example, right now Sam Lee, the club's human resources manager, needs to send a memo to all club employees regarding their health insurance plans. The data you'll need for this mail merge is stored in a Microsoft Excel worksheet named Insurance Data. This file contains the following field names: First Name, Last Name, Address Line 1, Work Phone, and Number. To merge this alternate data source with a Word document, complete the following:

16. Open the document named **Memo** from the Review folder in the Tutorial.06 folder on your Data Disk, and then save it as **Insurance Memo** in the same folder.

17. With the Insurance Memo document open, start the Mail Merge Wizard, and complete the first two steps. Select Letters as the document type, and use the current document (the Insurance Memo document) as the main document.

Explore 18. In Step 3 of the Mail Merge Wizard, select the Use an existing list option button, click Browse, navigate to the Review folder for Tutorial 6, click the file named **Insurance Data** and then click Open. In the Select Table dialog box, click the OK button, and then review the records in the Mail Merge Recipients dialog box. Click the OK button.

19. In Step 4 of the Mail Merge Wizard, insert the merge field codes into the main document. Move the insertion point after the colon(:) in TO:, press the Tab key, insert the First Name field (for the employee's first name), press the spacebar, and then insert the Last Name field (for the employee's last name).

20. To the right of DATE: in the memo, press the Tab key, and insert the Word date field in a format that matches "April 26, 2003."

Explore 21. Select the Word date field and the name fields, and then toggle off the Bold button. Notice that character formatting can be applied to fields just as to regular text.

22. In the body of the memo, immediately before the word individual(s), insert the Number field followed by a space.

WORD WD 6.40 TUTORIAL 6 CREATING FORM LETTERS AND MAILING LABELS

23. Save the main document with the changes. Then preview the merged document and check each record for any mistakes.

24. Merge to a new document. Scroll through the new document to verify that the information has been correctly inserted into the memos, and then save the new merged document as **Merged Insurance Memos**.

25. Print the memo for Minh Lien, and then close all documents, saving any changes.

26. Create an e-mail directory using the same format as the telephone directory you created in the tutorial. Use the Insurance Data file as the data source. The directory should include the first name, last name, and e-mail address for each employee in the Insurance Data Excel file. Set a right tab at six inches, and use a dot leader to separate the names from the e-mail addresses. Be sure to press Enter after you insert the merge field for the e-mail addresses. Save the main document as **Directory with Field Codes** and the merged document as **Merged Directory**. When you are finished, close all documents and exit Word.

CASE PROBLEMS

Case 1. Friends of Sugar Creek Justin Chambers is chair of The Friends of Sugar Creek, an organization working to prevent a convenience store from being built on a wetlands area in northern Wisconsin. He is sending a letter to community leaders, asking for their support. He asks you to help with the mail merge.

1. If you are working from a floppy disk, verify that you have copied the Cases folder for Tutorial 6 to a new, blank floppy disk. (This will ensure that you can fit all the solution files for all the case problems on one disk.) If necessary, start Word and make sure your Data Disk is in the appropriate drive. Open the file **Creek** from the Cases folder for Tutorial 6 on your Data Disk, and then save it as **Sugar Creek Letter**.

2. Start the Mail Merge Wizard and create a form letter main document using the **Sugar Creek Letter** file.

3. Create a data source with the following field names: Last Name, First Name, Nickname, Title, Company, Address Line1, and E-mail Address. Arrange the field names in the order given in this step.

4. Enter the following four records into the data source. (Don't include the commas in the records.)
   - Joliet, Pierre, Pierre, Chief Medical Officer, Peshtigo Medical Center, 1577 Cooperville Drive, joliet@pmc.org
   - Regenbogen, David, Dave, President, Regenbogen and Associates, 633 Wentworth, d_regenbogen@world.net
   - Suyemoto, Mae, Mae, Chief Engineer, Taylor and Culkins Engineering Services, 4424 Bedford, m_suyemoto@TaylorCulkins.com
   - James, Theodore, Tad, Principal, Peshtigo High School, 844 Tiger Way, tad_james@peshtigo-high-school.peshtigo.edu

5. Save the data source as **Sugar Creek Data** in the Cases folder for Tutorial 6, and then sort the records alphabetically by last name.

6. Change the Zoom setting to 100%. In Step 4 of the Mail Merge Wizard, insert the merge field codes into the document. Replace the field names in brackets with the actual merge field codes. Remember to insert the merge field code for Nickname in the body of the letter.

7. Save your changes to the main document.

8. Preview the merged document, and then complete the merge.

9. Save the merged letters document as **Merged Sugar Creek Letters** in the Cases folder for Tutorial 6.

10. Print the first letter and then close all open documents, saving any changes.

11. Open a new blank document, save it as **Sugar Creek Envelopes** in the Cases folder for Tutorial 6, and then start the Mail Merge Wizard.

Explore ▶ 12. In Step 1 of the Mail Merge Wizard, select Envelopes as the type of main document. In Step 2 of the Mail Merge Wizard, verify that the Change document layout button is selected, and then click Envelope Options. In the Envelope Options dialog box, verify that Size 10 (4⅛ × 9 inches) is selected in the Size box, and then click the OK button. In Step 3 of the Mail Merge Wizard, select the **Sugar Creek Data** file you created earlier as the data source. In Step 4 of the Mail Merge Wizard, click the recipient address area of the envelope, and then insert the necessary merge field codes to print a first name, last name, company name, and street address on each envelope. For the last line of the address, type "Peshtigo, WI 53734".

13. Preview the merged envelopes, merge to a new document, and then save the document as **Merged Sugar Creek Envelopes**.

14. Print the first envelope and then close all open documents, saving changes as necessary.

15. Create an e-mail directory of prospective contributors. Use the file named **Sugar Creek Data** (which you created earlier) as the data source. Use a dot leader to separate the name on the left from the e-mail address on the right.

16. Save the main document for the e-mail directory as **Sugar Creek E-mail Directory** in the Cases folder for Tutorial 6.

17. Save the merged document as **Merged Sugar Creek E-mail Directory**.

18. Print the e-mail directory and then save and close all open documents. Exit Word.

Case 2. Joseph's Gems   Joseph Brennan owns a small jewelry store in Dubuque, Iowa. Frequently, he notifies regular customers (who live in nearby communities in Iowa, Wisconsin, and Illinois) of upcoming sales. He decides to prepare personalized form letters to mail to all his regular customers one month before their birthdays. He'll mail the letters along with a two-page color catalog and a gift certificate. He asks you to help perform a mail merge using Word.

1. If you are working from a floppy disk, verify that you have copied the Cases folder for Tutorial 6 to a new, blank floppy disk. (This will ensure that you can fit all the solution files for all the case problems on one disk.) If necessary, start Word and make sure your Data Disk is in the appropriate drive. Open the file **Gems** from the Cases folder for Tutorial 6, and then save it as **Gems Letters** in the Cases folder for Tutorial 6.

2. Start the Mail Merge Wizard and create a form letter main document using the Gems Letter document.

3. Create a data source with the following field names: First Name, Last Name, Address Line 1, City, State, ZIP Code, Birthday, Birth Month, Birthstone.

4. Enter the following five records into the data source. (Don't include the commas in the records.) Enter months by numbers (1, 2, 3), not names (January, February, March), so you can sort in chronological order.

   ■ Kayleen, Mitchell, 882 River Way, Dubuque, IA, 52001, 23, 1, garnet
   ■ Tammy, Minervini, 8244 Westbrook Way, Platteville, WI, 52143, 31, 9, sapphire
   ■ Susan, Gardner, 804 Derby Road, Dubuque, IA, 52001, 14, 6, pearl

■ Garth, Poduska, 77 Catskill Circle, Rockford, IL, 51345, 7, 1, garnet

■ Oscar, Pike, 402 Waverly Avenue, Waterloo, IA, 53400, 22, 9, sapphire

5. Save the data source as **Gems Data** in the Cases folder for Tutorial 6.

6. At the beginning of the main document, insert a date field and merge fields for the inside address and salutation, in a proper business-letter format. Remember to include the state field in the inside address. Use the member's first name in the salutation.

7. In the body of the letter, insert the Birth Month, Birthday, and Birthstone fields at the locations indicated by the bracketed words. Put a slash (/) between the Birthday and Birth Month fields. Save your changes to the main document.

8. Use the Mail Merge Recipients button on the Mail Merge toolbar to display the data source and sort records alphabetically by last name. Then select only the records for customers with January birthdays.

9. Preview the merged document, and then merge to a new document. Save the merged document as **Merged Gems Letters** in the Cases folder for Tutorial 6.

10. Print the letters that result from the merge.

11. Create a main document for generating mailing labels on sheets of Avery 5162 Address labels, using the **Gems Data** file as your data source. Save the main document as **Gems Labels** in the Cases folder for Tutorial 6. (*Note:* In the tutorial, you used the Options command on the Tools menu to display the rectangular outlines of the labels, but that is not strictly necessary. If you do not see the label outlines now, do *not* display them.).

Explore   12. In Step 4 of the Mail Merge Wizard, click the label in the upper-left corner of the main document, and then click Address block in the Task Pane to open the Address Block dialog box. Select the "Joshua Randall Jr." name format, and deselect the Insert company name check box. Verify that the Insert postal address check box is selected and then click the OK button. The Address block merge field code is inserted into the main document. Click Update all labels to insert the Address block field in all the labels. Save your changes to the main document.

13. Preview the merged document and then merge to a new document.

14. Print the labels on an 8½ × 11-inch sheet of paper, and save the merged document as **Merged Gems Labels** in the Cases folder for Tutorial 6. Close all open documents, saving any changes.

15. Open a new, blank document, save it as **Gems Customer Directory** in the Cases folder for Tutorial 6, start the Mail Merge Wizard, select Directory as the main document type, and then select the **Gems Data** file as your data source. Close the Mail Merge Recipients dialog box.

Explore   16. In Step 4 of the Mail Merge Wizard, insert merge fields into the main document to create a directory entry that looks like the example below. Use the Address block option (as described above in Step 12) to insert the complete address, and the More items option to insert the birthday, birth month, and birthstone.

Garth Poduska
77 Catskill Circle
Rockford IL 51345
1/7
garnet

17. Insert two blank lines after the last line of merge field codes, and then save your work.

Explore

18. In the tutorial you learned how to select specific records in a data source by using the checkboxes to the left of each record. You can also filter a data source to display only records that meet certain conditions, Filtering is a good option for a data source containing numerous records; however, you may find that this feature doesn't work as reliably as the checkbox method. To filter the Gems Data data source: Open the data source, click the list arrow at the top of the City column, and then click Dubuque. The data source displays only the records for Dubuque residents. (Note that to redisplay all the records in the data source, you can click the list arrow at the top of the City column and then click All.)

19. Preview the merged document, and then complete the merge to a new document. Save the merged document as **Merged Gems Dubuque Directory** in the Cases folder for Tutorial 6, and then print the directory.

20. Close all open documents, saving any changes, and then exit Word.

Case 3. Liberty Auto Sales   Tom Reynolds is the customer relations manager for Liberty Auto Sales in Cadillac, Michigan. After a customer purchases a new car, Tom sends out a Sales Satisfaction Survey accompanied by a personalized letter. He wants you to help him use the Word Mail Merge feature to perform this task.

1. If you are working from a floppy disk, verify that you have copied the Cases folder for Tutorial 6 to a new, blank floppy disk. (This will ensure that you can fit all the solution files for all the case problems on one disk.) If necessary, start Word and make sure your Data Disk is in the appropriate drive.

2. In a new, blank document, create a Word table with six rows and eight columns. Insert the following labels in the heading row: First Name, Last Name, Address Line 1, City, ZIP Code, Car Make, Car Model, Sales Rep.

3. Enter the following five records into the Word table. Don't include the commas in the records.
   - Donald, Meyers, 344 Spartan Avenue, Detroit, 48235, Honda, Civic, Bruce
   - Arlene, Snow, 46 North Alberta Road, Ecorse, 48229, Toyota, Camry, Lillie
   - Lance, Nakagawa, 4211 Livonia Drive, Kentwood, 49508, Honda, Accord, Martin
   - Peter, Siskel, 92 Waterford Place, Walker, 49504, Toyota, Corolla, Bruce
   - Marilee, Peterson, 8211 University Drive, Detroit, 48238, Honda, Civic, Lillie

4. Save the file as **Auto Sales Data** in the Cases folder for Tutorial 6 and then close it.

5. Open the file **Auto** from the Cases folder for Tutorial 6, and then save it as **Auto Sales Letters**.

6. Create a letter main document using the current document.

7. Select the **Auto Sales Data** document that you created earlier as the data source.

8. Edit the main document to include the following in the letter, using a proper letter format: date, inside address, and salutation. You'll need to add the state (MI) as text.

9. Edit the body of the form letter to replace words in brackets with their corresponding merge field names.

10. Save your changes to the main document.

11. Preview the merged document and merge to a new document. Save the merged document as **Merged Auto Sales Letters** in the Cases folder for Tutorial 6.

12. Print the first letter in the merged document.

13. Create a directory that lists the make of car purchased by each customer. Use a dot leader to separate the name from the make of car. Save the main document as **Auto Sales Directory** in the Cases folder for Tutorial 6. Use the **Auto Sales Data** file as the data source.

14. Preview the merged document, merge to a new document, and then save the merged document as **Merged Auto Sales Directory** in the Cases folder for Tutorial 6.

15. Print the directory, and then close all open documents, saving any changes as needed.

Explore ▷ 16. Open a new blank document, start the Mail Merge Wizard, select Letters as the document type, use the current document as the main document, select the **Auto Sales Data** document that you created earlier as the data source, close the Mail Merge Recipients dialog box, and then, in Step 4 of the Mail Merge Wizard, experiment with the Greeting line, which you can use to insert a salutation in a letter. Use the Greeting line link to insert a salutation that includes the customer's first name, followed by a colon. Keep in mind that you can use the Greeting line link to personalize form letters. Close all documents without saving any changes. Exit Word.

Case 4. E-Mail Merge for DataTech Software You are an associate product manager for DataTech, a software firm that sells a popular line of database products. Your manager asked you to learn how to use the Mail Merge Wizard to send out mass e-mails to the company's sales representatives. To learn how to use the Mail Merge Wizard, follow these steps:

1. If you are working from a floppy disk, verify that you have copied the Cases folder for Tutorial 6 to a new, blank floppy disk. (This will ensure that you can fit all the solution files for all the case problems on one disk.) If necessary, start Word and make sure your Data Disk is in the appropriate drive.

2. Open a new, blank document, and save it as **E-mail Message**.

3. Start the Mail Merge Wizard, and, in Step 1, select E-mail messages as the main document type. In Step 2, select the current document as the main document.

4. In Step 3, create a new data source that contains three fields: First Name, Last Name, and E-mail Address. Add four records to the data source, using the names and e-mail addresses of your friends, fellow students, or colleagues. One of the records should include your name and e-mail address, so you can verify that the e-mail message is sent as planned.

5. Save the data source as **E-mail Data** in the Cases folder for Tutorial 6.

6. Type a message in the main document indicating that you are sending an e-mail in order to test Word's E-mail Merge option. Ask the recipient to reply to your message, so you can confirm that the messages were sent to the correct address. The message should begin with a brief salutation that includes the First Name field.

7. Save your changes to the main document.

8. Preview the merged document.

Explore ▷ 9. In Step 6 of the Mail Merge Wizard, click Electronic mail. In the Merge to E-mail dialog box, verify that the E-mail Address field is selected in the To text box. Type "Testing Word E-mail Merge" in the Subject text box and verify that the All option button is selected.

10. If you have Outlook Express or Outlook selected as your default e-mail program, and your computer is already connected to the Internet, Word will send your e-mail messages when you click the OK button. If you do not have Outlook or Outlook Express installed on your computer, or if your computer is not connected to the Internet, the Merge to E-mail dialog box will close without any visible change to the E-mail Message main document. Click the OK button.

11. If you see a new, merged document, save the merged document as **Merged E-mail Message** in the Cases folder for Tutorial 6.

12. If your computer was set up to send the e-mail messages, check your e-mail account to see if you received the message. Watch for replies from the other recipients.

13. Create an e-mail directory using the **E-mail Data** file as the data source. Save the main document as **My E-mail Directory** in the Cases folder for Tutorial 6, and save the merged document as **My Merged E-mail Directory** in the Cases folder for Tutorial 6.

14. Print the merged directory, and then close all open documents, saving any changes.

Explore   15. If you have Outlook installed on your computer and have selected Outlook as your default e-mail client, you can use your Outlook address book as the data source for a mail merge. To learn how: Open a new blank document, and start the Mail Merge wizard. In Step 1 of the Mail Merge wizard, select e-mail message. In Step 2 use the current document. In Step 3, click the Select from outlook contacts option button and then click Choose contacts folder. (If you see the Choose Profile dialog box, select your user profile. If you don't have the option of selecting a specific user profile, accept the default setting. Click the OK button.) In the Select Contact List folder dialog box, double-click your address book. Your Outlook contacts are displayed in the Mail Merge Recipients dialog box. Use the checkboxes to deselect all of the records except the records for three friends, fellow students, or colleagues to whom who can send a test e-mail message.

16. In Step 4 of the Mail Merge Wizard, type an e-mail message indicating that you are testing Word's e-mail merge feature. Use the Insert Merge Fields button on the Mail Merge toolbar to insert a first name field in the document, just as you would for an ordinary mail merge. Complete the e-mail merge as described in Steps 7 through 10 of this case problem. If you see a new, merged document, save it as **Merged Outlook E-mail** document in the Cases folder for Tutorial 6.

17. Close all open documents, saving any changes, and exit Word.

QUICK | CHECK ANSWERS

Session 6.1

1. **a.** A form letter is a document containing general information to be sent to many recipients, and to which you can add personalized data, such as name, and address.

   b. A main document is a document (such as a letter or a contract) that, in addition to text, contains placeholder text to mark where variable information from the data source (such as a name or an address) will be inserted.

   c. A data source is a document (often in the form of a table) that contains information, such as members' names and addresses, which can be merged with the main document.

   d. A merge field is placeholder text in a main document. When the main document and the data source are merged, merge fields are replaced by specific information from each record in the data source.

   e. A record is a collection of information about one individual or object in a data source. For example, a record might include the first name, last name, address and phone number for a member.

2. record

3. True

4. From within the New Address List dialog box, click Customize, click Add, type the Gender, click OK, and then click OK again.

5. Microsoft Office Address Lists

6. Click More Items in the Mail Merge Task Pane, or click the Insert Merge Fields button on the Mail Merge toolbar. In the Insert Merge Field dialog box, click the field you want to insert, click Insert, and then click Close. Adjust the spacing or formatting around the merge field code as necessary.

7. Click Edit individual letters in the Mail Merge Task Pane (or click the Merge to New Document button on the Mail Merge toolbar) and then click OK. Save the merged document.

Session 6.2

1. True.

2. In Step 1 of the Mail Merge Wizard, select the Labels as the main document type; in Step 2 click Label options to select a label type, in Step 3 select a data source, in Step 4 insert merge field codes in the main document, click Update Labels, and then preview the merged document and the merge to a new document. Delete unnecessary text from labels that would otherwise be blank.

3. A dot leader is a dotted line extending from text on the left margin to text at the tab stop.

4. Open the Mail Merge Recipients dialog box, click the list arrow in the State column, and then click Iowa..

5. Open the Mail Merge Recipients dialog box, and then click the Last Name column heading.

OBJECTIVES

In this tutorial you will:

- Compare and merge documents

- Embed and modify an Excel workbook

- Link an Excel chart

- Modify and update a linked chart

- Modify a document for online distribution

- Use Web Layout view

- Insert and edit hyper-links

- Save a Word document as a Web page

- Format a Web document

- View a Web document in a Web browser

LABS

The Internet: World Wide Web

COLLABORATING WITH OTHERS AND CREATING WEB PAGES

Writing a Grant Proposal for Space Station Education

CASE

Space Station Education

Nalani Tui is assistant principal of Thoreau Elementary and Middle School. For the past six months she has been developing a new science program inspired by the International Space Station (ISS), a permanent laboratory orbiting the earth. Requiring the collaboration of 16 nations and costing over $60 million, the ISS will take at least eight years and 46 separate space flights to complete. Scientists aboard the space station will perform experiments that could lead to important breakthroughs in technology.

Nalani's program, called Space Station Education, will allow students to communicate directly with the astronauts at the space station via the Internet. At the same time, students will use data generated by the space station scientists in their own research projects. Nalani hopes that a combination of speakers, field trips, and hands-on activities will encourage students to learn about the link between space travel and technology. In the process, she hopes her students will become more confident computer users.

Nalani has finished planning the Space Station Education curriculum. Now she needs to apply for a grant from the U.S. Department of Education to fund the program. Nalani has completed part of a grant proposal—a document that outlines the scope of the program and provides details on its implementation. Because Nalani has applied for other grants in the past, she knows that writing a grant proposal is a group process. In particular, she understands the value of having a grant proposal reviewed by colleagues, professional editors, and other qualified readers. As a first step, she asked Tom Jenkins and Karen Goldberg, principals at neighboring schools, to review a draft of her proposal. Both Tom and Karen edited the proposal document in Word, made some grammatical corrections, and inserted comments. Now Nalani has to merge the two edited versions of the proposal into one document.

After Nalani creates a new version of the document, she wants to add budget figures compiled by her assistant, Jeremy Woods. She also has to add a pie chart created by Margarita Lopez, an administrator for the county school district. Finally, she wants several teachers at Thoreau School and other colleagues scattered throughout the state's school districts to review her proposal. Nalani can simply hand deliver printed copies of her proposal to the teachers at Thoreau School. However, to make the proposal available to teachers throughout the state, she plans to publish it on her school's Web site.

SESSION 7.1

In this session, you will merge two edited copies of the proposal with Nalani's original document. Then you'll see how Nalani planned the proposal. Next, you'll embed an Excel workbook in the proposal, modify the workbook within Word, and insert a link to an Excel chart. You'll use Excel to modify the chart, and then update it in Word.

Comparing and Merging Documents

Nalani asks you to help her combine, or **merge**, three copies of the grant proposal. The first document, named Grant, contains Nalani's original draft of the proposal. The second document, named Tom, contains Tom Jenkins' edited copy of the proposal. The third document, named Karen, contains Karen Goldberg's edited copy. Nalani asks you to use the Compare and Merge Documents command on the Tools menu to merge these three documents into a new document. In the new document, Tom and Karen's changes will be underlined and highlighted in color. In addition, a vertical line will appear in the left margin next to every edited line of text. In Word, these special underlines, font colors, and vertical lines are known as **revision marks**.

Once you have merged two documents into one new document, you can merge that new document with a third document. When you have merged all the documents you want to compare, you can use the buttons on the Reviewing toolbar to accept or reject individual editing changes.

REFERENCE WINDOW   RW

Comparing and Merging Documents
- Open the original document.
- Click Tools on the menu bar, and then click Compare and Merge Documents.
- Select an edited version of the original document.
- Click the Merge list arrow, and then click Merge into new document.
- To merge an additional document, click Tools on the menu bar, click Compare and Merge Documents, select a document, click the Merge list arrow, and then click Merge into current document.
- Use the Next button on the Reviewing toolbar to move the insertion point from one edit to the next.
- Click the Accept Change or Reject Change buttons on the Reviewing toolbar to accept or reject changes.

In the following sections you will practice comparing documents that contain some simple edits. The steps in this tutorial are designed to give you a general idea of how to compare and merge documents. Keep in mind, however, that Word's Compare document feature can sometimes produce unexpected results, especially with heavily edited documents.

Merging Changes in a New Document

You'll start by opening Nalani's original draft of the grant proposal. Then you will merge it with Tom's edited copy of the proposal. Before you begin, you will verify that you have copied the Tutorial.07 folder to your computer's hard drive. The files you'll create in this tutorial are fairly large. Storing them on the hard drive allows Word to save and update files more quickly than if they were stored on a floppy disk.

To merge Nalani's proposal with Tom's edited copy:

1. Verify that you have copied the Tutorial.07 folder to your computer's hard drive, and then start Word.

2. Open the document named **Grant** from the Tutorial subfolder in the Tutorial.07 folder on your hard drive.

3. Switch to Print Layout view (if necessary), and quickly read through the proposal. Notice the photograph in the last section, which like any graphic, is not visible in Normal view.

4. Click **Tools** on the menu bar, and then click **Compare and Merge Documents**. The Compare and Merge Documents dialog box opens. First you must select the document you want to compare to the Grant document.

5. If necessary, use the **Look in** list arrow to select the Tutorial subfolder in the Tutorial.07 folder on your hard drive.

6. In the file list, click **Tom**. Next, you need to indicate where you want the revision marks to appear.

7. Click the **Merge** list arrow, as shown in Figure 7-1. A menu with three options appears. If you click Merge, Word will open the document selected in the file list (in this case, Tom), and highlight with revision marks any differences between the Tom document and the Grant document. Clicking Merge into current document will insert revision marks into the current document (Grant), leaving the document selected in the file list (Tom) unopened. However, to avoid confusion between the original document and edited copies, use the Merge into new document option.

Figure 7-1	SELECTING A LOCATION FOR REVISION MARKS

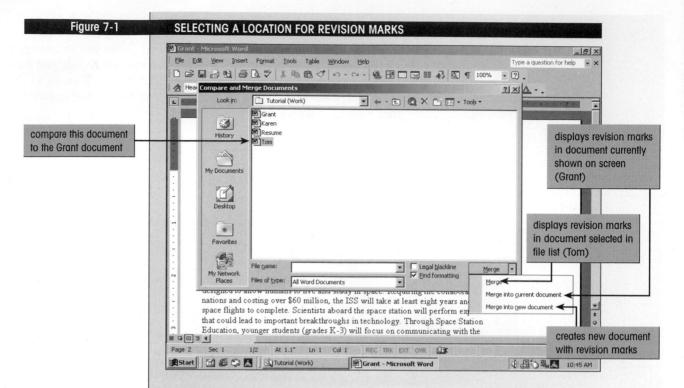

TROUBLE? If the document named Tom opens, you accidentally clicked the Merge button, rather than the Merge button list arrow. Close the Tom document without saving any changes, and begin again with Step 4.

8. Click **Merge into new document**. A new document opens and the Reviewing toolbar appears.

    TROUBLE? If a new document does not open, or if the document named Tom opens, close all open Word documents without saving changes, and start again with Step 2.

9. Scroll down to review the revision marks shown in Figure 7-2. (The revision marks on your computer might be a different color from the ones in Figure 7-2.) A note in the right margin indicates that Tom deleted the text "fully functional." Notice that Tom added a comment to the words "National Radio Astronomy Observatory." (You might have to scroll right to read the text of this comment.)

Figure 7-2	REVISION MARKS IN NEW DOCUMENT

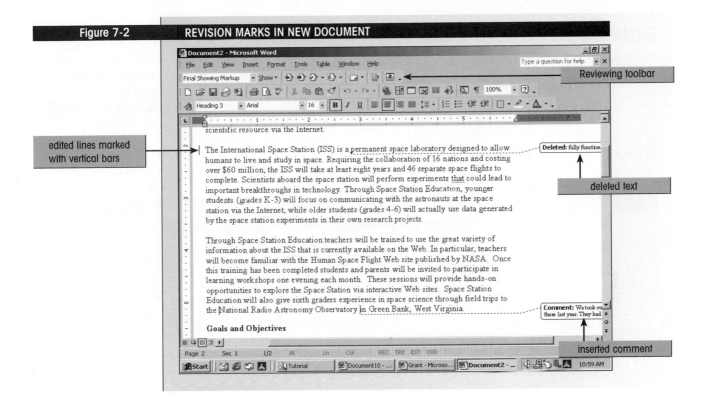

edited lines marked with vertical bars

Reviewing toolbar

Deleted: fully function

deleted text

Comment: We took ou there last year. They had

inserted comment

Merging Changes in the Current Document

The revision marks in Document2 show you Tom's edits to the original grant proposal. Next, you need to merge Karen's edits with Tom's. To do this, you can merge the document named Karen with the Tom's current document. When you merge, Karen's edits will be added to Document2. However, the original document named Karen will remain unchanged.

To merge Karen's edits with the current document:

1. Click **Tools** on the menu bar, and then click **Compare and Merge Documents**. The Compare and Merge Documents dialog box opens.

2. If necessary, use the **Look in** list arrow to select the Tutorial subfolder in the Tutorial07 folder on your hard drive, and then click **Karen** in the file list.

3. Click the **Merge** list arrow, and then click **Merge into current document**. Additional revision marks are added to Document2, reflecting Karen's changes to the original grant proposal.

4. Scroll through the Document2 text and review the edits. Notice that, at the beginning of the document, Karen added a comment to the title. She also replaced the passive verb "be trained" with the active verb "learn" in the beginning of the third paragraph of the Project Abstract section. Also notice that Tom and Karen's changes appear in different colors. (Exactly what colors you see depends on how your computer is set up.)

5. Place the mouse pointer over the box containing the text "Deleted: be trained" in the right margin. A ScreenTip appears with the name of the person who made the change (in this case, Karen Goldberg), and the date and time the change was made. See Figure 7-3. (Note that the name in this ScreenTip is the name specified in the User Information tab of the Options dialog box on Karen's computer. You'll see the Options dialog box in the Review Assignments at the end of this tutorial.)

TROUBLE? If you see a name other than Karen Goldberg in the ScreenTip (for instance, your own name), ignore it and continue with the steps.

| Figure 7-3 | SCREENTIP WITH NAME OF EDITOR |

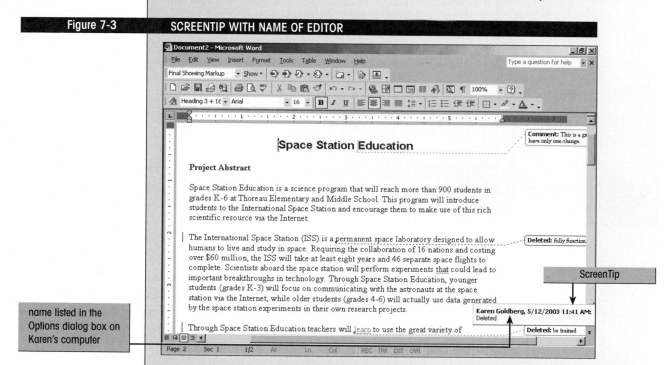

6. Place the mouse pointer over the box containing the text "Deleted: fully functional," in the right margin. A box appears indicating that Tom Jenkins made this change.

TROUBLE? If you see a name other than Tom Jenkins in the ScreenTip (for instance, your own name), ignore it and continue with the steps.

7. Place the mouse pointer over Tom's comment (just before the Goals heading). Again, a box appears indicating the author of the comment (in this case, Tom Jenkins).

8. Switch to Normal view and notice that the boxes are no longer visible in the right margin. Now, instead of a note indicating that "fully functional" was deleted, the words are crossed out in the paragraph.

9. Switch back to Print Layout view.

Accepting and Rejecting Changes

After you merge documents, you must decide which changes you want to accept. To do this, you can use the buttons on the Reviewing toolbar. To simply accept an individual change (including the addition of a comment), you click the Accept Change button. To reject a change (or to delete a comment), you click the Reject Change/Delete Comment button. You can also use the list arrows on these buttons to make decisions about all the changes in a document. For example, you can accept all the edits in a document by clicking the Accept Change list arrow, and then clicking Accept All Changes in Document. Likewise, you can reject all the edits in a document by clicking the Reject Change/Delete Comment buttons, and then clicking Reject All Changes in Document.

To accept and reject changes in Document2:

1. Press **Ctrl+Home** to move the insertion point to the beginning of the document.

2. Click the **Next** button on the Reviewing toolbar. The insertion point moves to the first change—Karen's comment at the beginning of the document. You've read this comment, so there's no reason to keep it.

3. Click the **Reject Change/Delete Comment** button in the Reviewing toolbar. The comment is deleted.

4. Click. The deleted text "fully functional," is highlighted in the right margin. You will accept this change.

5. Click the **Accept Change** button in the Reviewing toolbar. You could continue to accept and reject individual changes, but Nalani wants to accept all the remaining changes. The only exception is Tom's comment (just before the Goals heading), which she has already read, and wants to delete.

6. Click the **Reject Change/Delete Comment** list arrow on the Reviewing toolbar. A menu of options appears, as shown in Figure 7-4.

| Figure 7-4 | REJECTING CHANGES IN A DOCUMENT |

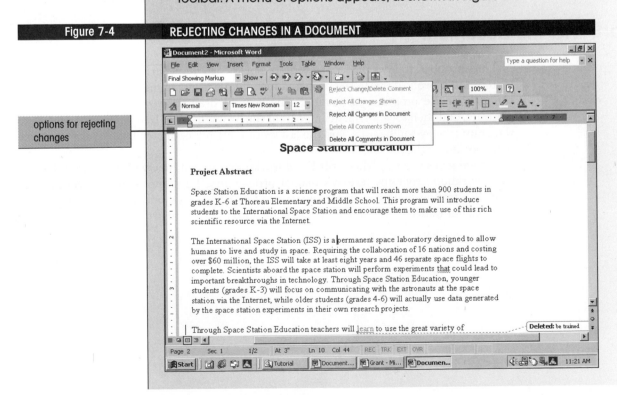

options for rejecting changes

7. Click **Delete All Comments in Document**, and then scroll down to verify that Tom's comment has been deleted. Now you will accept the remaining changes.

8. Click the **Accept Change** list arrow ▨▾ on the Reviewing toolbar, and then click **Accept All Changes in Document**. The remaining revision has been incorporated into the document, and the revision marks disappear. Now you will save this new copy of the grant proposal.

9. Save the document as **Grant Proposal** in the Tutorial subfolder in the Tutorial.07 folder on your hard drive.

You are finished reviewing Tom and Karen's edits to the original grant proposal. Finally, you need to close Nalani's original draft of the document.

To close the Grant document:

1. Click the taskbar button for the document named **Grant**.

2. Close the document named **Grant** without saving any changes.

3. If necessary, redisplay the document named **Grant Proposal**.

4. Close the Reviewing toolbar.

Revision marks allow you to see any changes in a document, and they simplify the process of combining multiple copies of a document. As you become an experienced Word user, you will learn how to use revision marks even more extensively.

Now that you have incorporated Karen and Tom's suggestions, you are ready to add Jeremy's budget and Margarita's pie chart. This is a good time to plan your work on the grant proposal.

Planning the Document

Nalani's proposal follows the format required by the agency offering the grant. She will ultimately add more sections to the proposal, including a project timeline and detailed explanations about the program curriculum. The current draft, however, begins with a Project Abstract, and then reviews the main goals of the program. The Budget section explains how the grant money will be used, and the last section introduces Peter Brooks, the teacher who will coordinate the program.

Nalani gives you two Microsoft Excel workbooks to combine with the Word document. One workbook contains Jeremy's budget projections. The other contains Margarita's pie chart illustrating computer ownership data in the Thoreau school district. Figure 7-5 shows how Nalani wants to combine these elements into a complete proposal.

Figure 7-5   **PROPOSAL PLAN**

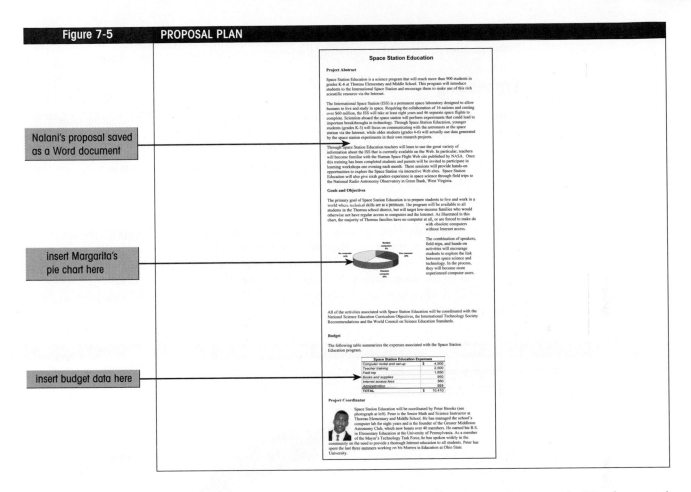

Your immediate task is to place the Excel data and the pie chart into the Word proposal document.

Integrating Objects from Other Programs

Every software program is designed to accomplish a set of specific tasks. As you've seen with Microsoft Word, you can use a word-processing program to create, edit, and format documents such as letters, reports, newsletters, and proposals. A **spreadsheet program**, on the other hand, allows you to organize, calculate, and analyze numerical data. A spreadsheet created in Microsoft Excel is known as a **worksheet**. An Excel file typically consists of multiple worksheets, and is called a **workbook**. Jeremy Woods created the budget for Space Station Education in an Excel worksheet. Margarita also used Excel to create her chart.

Both the worksheet and the chart are Excel objects. An **object** is an item such as a graphic image, clip art, WordArt image, chart, or section of text that you can modify and move from one document to another. Nalani asks you to place the worksheet and chart objects into her proposal, but she also wants to be able to modify the Excel objects after they are inserted into the document. A technology called **object linking and embedding**, or **OLE** (pronounced "oh-lay"), allows you to integrate information created in one program (such as Excel), into a document created in another program (such as Word), and then to modify that information using the tools originally used to create it, such as the Excel menus and toolbars for information created in Excel.

The program used to create the original version of the object is called the **source program** (in this case, Excel). The program into which the object is integrated is called the **destination program** (in this case, Word). Similarly, the original file is called the **source file**, and the file into which you insert the object is called the **destination file**.

The next two sections describe embedding and linking: two options for transferring data between source files and destination files.

Embedding

Embedding is a technique that allows you to insert a copy of an existing object into a destination document. In the destination document, you can double-click an embedded object to access the toolbar buttons and menus of the source program. This allows you to edit the object within the destination document. Because the embedded object is a copy, any changes you make to it are not reflected in the original source file, and vice versa. For instance, you could embed a workbook named "Itemized Expenses" in a Word document named "Travel Report." Later, if you change the Itemized Expenses workbook, those revisions will not appear in the embedded version of the workbook in the Travel Report document. The opposite is also true. If you edit the embedded version of the workbook, those changes will not show up in the original Itemized Expenses workbook. The embedded workbook retains a connection to the source program, Excel, but not to the source workbook.

Figure 7-6 illustrates the process of embedding Jeremy's Excel worksheet in Nalani's Word proposal.

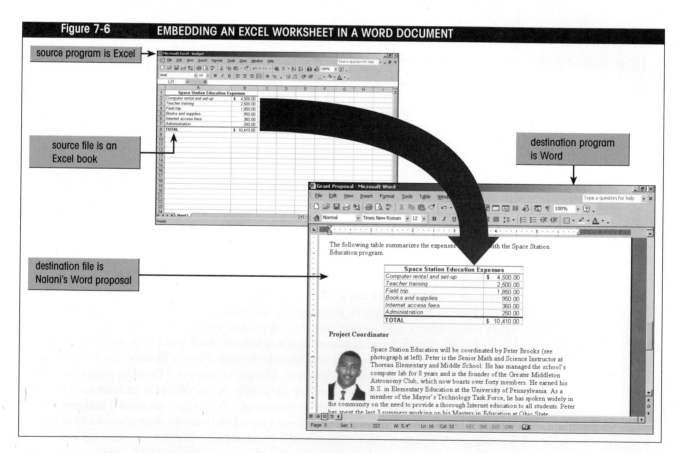

Figure 7-6   **EMBEDDING AN EXCEL WORKSHEET IN A WORD DOCUMENT**

Linking

Linking is similar to embedding, except that the object inserted into the destination file maintains a two-way connection between the source file and the destination file. Just as with an embedded object, you can double-click a linked object to access the toolbar buttons and menus of the source program. However, any changes you make to a linked object within the destination program also appear in the original source file. Likewise, if you edit the original file in the source program, those changes appear in the linked object. The linked object in the destination document is not a copy; it is a representation of the original object in the source file. As a result, a document that contains a linked object usually takes up less space on a disk than does a document containing an embedded version of the same object. Figure 7-7 illustrates how you can use linking to place Margarita's Excel chart into Nalani's Word document proposal.

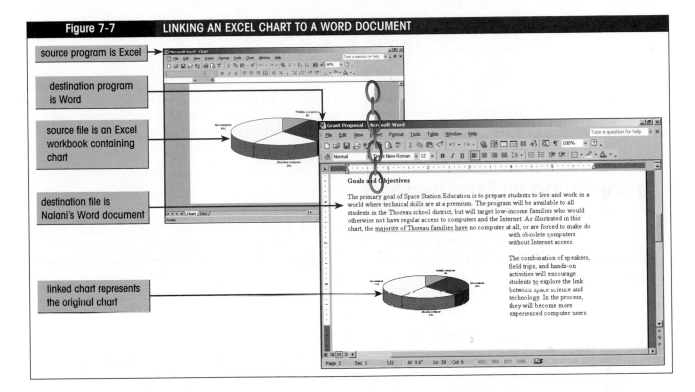

Figure 7-7   LINKING AN EXCEL CHART TO A WORD DOCUMENT

- source program is Excel
- destination program is Word
- source file is an Excel workbook containing chart
- destination file is Nalani's Word document
- linked chart represents the original chart

One drawback to linking is that by moving files or folders, you can accidentally disrupt the connection between the source file and the document containing the linked object. For example, suppose you insert a linked workbook in a document, and then close the document and go home. Later that evening, a colleague moves the source file (the workbook) to a different folder, or deletes the workbook. As a result, the next time you open the document containing the linked object, you might get an error message, or find that you can't update the linked object.

Choosing Between Embedding and Linking

Embedding and linking are useful when you know you must edit an object after inserting it into Word. (If you don't need to edit the object, you can consider a simpler option: pasting a copy of the object into a Word document, similar to the way you paste a selection of copied text. You'll practice this technique in the Case Problems at the end of this tutorial.) Before you can use either embedding or linking, you must verify that you have the source program installed on your computer. Then you can decide if you want to embed or link the object.

Embedding is best if you won't have access to the original source file in the future, or if you don't need to maintain the connection between the source file and the document containing the linked object. In general, embedding is simpler than linking because you can change the embedded object without changing any other file. The source file is unaffected by any editing in the destination document. You could even delete the source file from your disk without affecting the copy embedded in your Word document.

Link a file whenever you have data that is likely to change over time, or if someone else updates your data regularly. For example, suppose you created a Word document called "Refinancing Options" into which you want to insert an Excel workbook containing the latest interest rates for home mortgages. Suppose also that your assistant updates the Excel workbook daily to make sure it reflects current rates. By linking the workbook to the Refinancing Options document, you can be certain that the mortgage rates are updated every time your assistant updates the Excel workbook. The advantage to linking is that the data in both the Excel workbook and the Word document can reflect recent revisions. A disadvantage to linking is that you must have access both to Excel and to the linked file on your computer.

Keep in mind that files containing embedded and linked objects can be very large. For that reason, you'll usually want to store such files on your computer's hard drive or network drive rather than on a floppy disk. Also note that you must have Excel installed on your computer to perform the steps in the rest of this session. If Excel is not installed on your computer, read the remainder of this session, but do not attempt to perform the steps.

Embedding an Excel Workbook

Nalani asks you to insert Jeremy's worksheet in the document. You will embed the entire Excel workbook into the Budget section of the proposal, replacing the "[Insert Excel worksheet]" placeholder. You'll use the Object command on the Insert menu to embed the existing Excel workbook in the proposal. Then you can use Excel commands to modify the expense workbook within Word.

To embed the Excel workbook:

1. Click **Edit** on the menu bar, click **Find**, find the placeholder **(Insert Excel worksheet)**, click **Cancel** to close the Find and Replace dialog box, and then press **Delete**. The placeholder (Insert Excel worksheet) is deleted. The insertion point should be located on a blank line, two lines above the heading "Project Coordinator." This is where you will embed the Excel workbook.

2. Click **Insert** on the menu bar, and then click **Object** to open the Object dialog box, which has two tabs—Create New and Create from File.

3. Click the **Create from File** tab. You'll use the Browse feature to find the Excel worksheet file in the Tutorial folder for Tutorial 7 on your hard drive.

4. Click the **Browse** button. The Browse dialog box opens.

5. If necessary, use the **Look in** list arrow to select the Tutorial folder for Tutorial 7, click **Budget** in the file list, and then click the **Insert** button. The Browse dialog box closes, and you return to the Object dialog box. The name of the selected file (Budget.xls), and the names of the folders in which it is stored, appear in the File name text box. See Figure 7-8. Make sure the Link to file check box is not selected. You don't want to link the worksheet—only embed it.

Figure 7-8	EMBEDDING A FILE

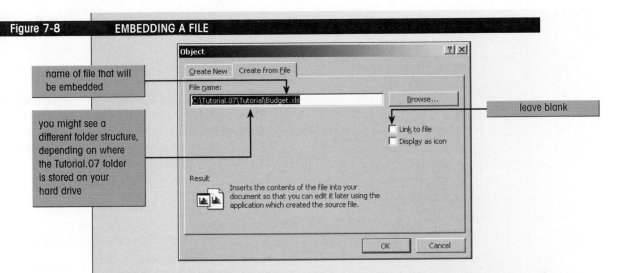

name of file that will be embedded

you might see a different folder structure, depending on where the Tutorial.07 folder is stored on your hard drive

leave blank

6. Click the **OK** button. The Excel worksheet appears in the document. It would look better, however, if it were centered between the left and right margins.

7. Click the **worksheet** to select it. Black selection handles appear around the outside of the worksheet.

8. Click the **Center** button ▤ on the Formatting toolbar. The Excel worksheet is centered horizontally in Nalani's proposal document. See Figure 7-9.

Figure 7-9	EMBEDDED WORKSHEET CENTERED HORIZONTALLY

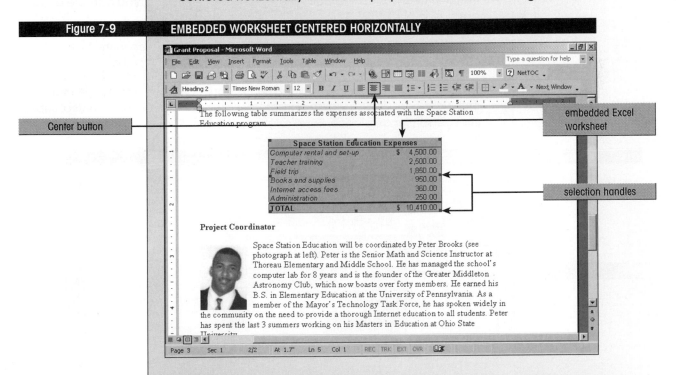

Center button

embedded Excel worksheet

selection handles

TROUBLE? Depending on how your computer is set up, you may see the embedded worksheet on a white background, rather than on a gray background (as in Figure 7-9). To display the worksheet on a gray background, click Tools on the menu bar, click Options, click the View tab, click the Field Shading list box, and then click Always. Note, however, that displaying the gray background is optional, and that the background will not be visible in the printed document.

9. Click anywhere in the document outside the worksheet to deselect the embedded object.

Because the workbook object is embedded, you can make changes to the object within Word, which you'll do in the next section.

Modifying the Embedded Workbook

If Excel is installed on your computer, you can edit the embedded workbook by double-clicking it and using Excel commands and tools. After you modify the workbook, you can click anywhere else in the Word document to deselect the workbook and redisplay the usual Word editing commands and tools. Any changes that you make in the embedded workbook affect only the copy in Word and not the original Budget file.

Because all the cost figures are large and rounded to the nearest $100 increment, Nalani wants you to remove the decimal points and trailing zeroes.

To eliminate the decimal places in the embedded workbook:

1. Double-click the workbook. After a moment, the workbook opens in an Excel window. See Figure 7-10. Depending on how your computer is set up, the Excel toolbars may appear one on top of the other, as in Figure 7-10, or side by side on one row.

   Notice that an Excel worksheet is arranged in rows and columns, just like a Word table. The intersection between a row and column is called a **cell** and takes its name from its column letter and the row number. For example, the intersection of column B and row 2 is "cell B2." To remove the decimal places from the cells containing dollar signs (cell B2 and cell B8), you can use a toolbar button. First, you must select these two cells.

   TROUBLE? If you see the Excel menus and toolbars displayed in the Word window (rather than in a separate window), just continue with these steps.

   TROUBLE? If you don't see the Excel menus and toolbar, or a message indicates that Word can't find the source program, ask your instructor or technical support person for assistance. Excel might not be installed on your computer.

Figure 7-10   EDITING THE EMBEDDED WORKSHEET

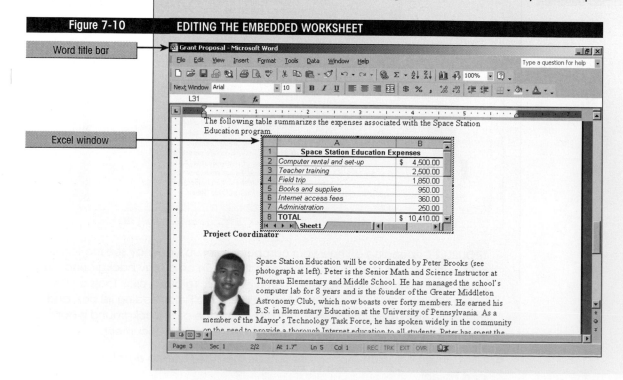

2. Click cell **B2**, which contains the figure $4,500.00, press and hold the Ctrl button, click cell **B8** (which contains the figure $10,410.00), and then release Ctrl. Cell B2 is highlighted, and cell B8 is outlined by a thin black line, indicating that the two cells are highlighted.

3. Click the **Decrease Decimal** button on the Excel Formatting toolbar twice. The numbers in the selected cells change to whole dollar amounts. Next, you'll use the Format Cells dialog box to remove the decimal places from cells B3 through B7.

   TROUBLE? If you don't see the Decrease Decimal button on your screen, click Format on the menu bar, and then click Cells. The Format Cells dialog box opens. Click the Number tab, if necessary, click Currency in the Category list box, change the setting in the Decimal places box to 0, click the Symbol list box, click $, and then click the OK button.

4. Click cell **B3** (which contains the number 2,500.00), and then drag the mouse down to cell **B7** (which contains the number 250.00). Cells B3 through B7 are selected. See Figure 7-11.

Figure 7-11	SELECTING CELLS IN A WORKSHEET

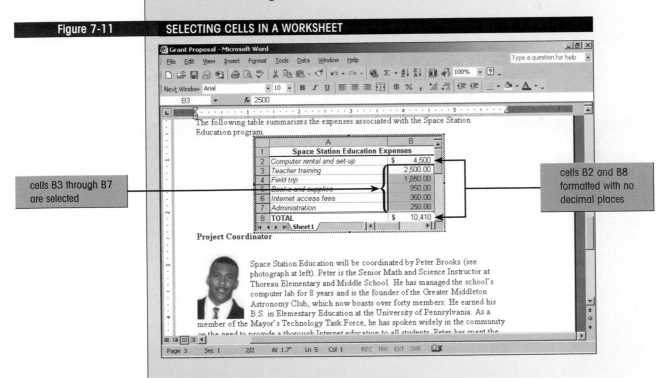

cells B3 through B7 are selected

cells B2 and B8 formatted with no decimal places

5. Click **Format** on the Excel menu bar, and then click **Cells**. The Format Cells dialog box opens.

6. Click the **Number** tab, if necessary, click **Currency** in the Category list box, change the setting in the Decimal places box to **0**, and verify that the entry in the Symbol box is **None**. Your Format Cells dialog box should look like Figure 7-12.

Figure 7-12   SELECTING A CURRENCY FORMAT

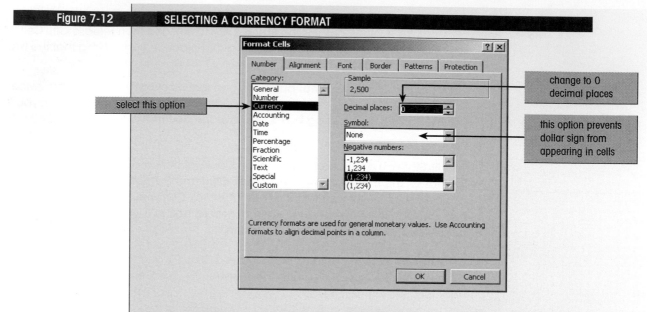

7. Click **OK** to close the Format Cells dialog box, and then click outside the worksheet. You return to the Grant Proposal document, where the embedded worksheet displays the newly formatted budget figures.

8. Click anywhere outside the Excel worksheet in the proposal to deselect it, if necessary. See Figure 7-13.

Figure 7-13   EDITED WORKSHEET EMBEDDED IN PROPOSAL

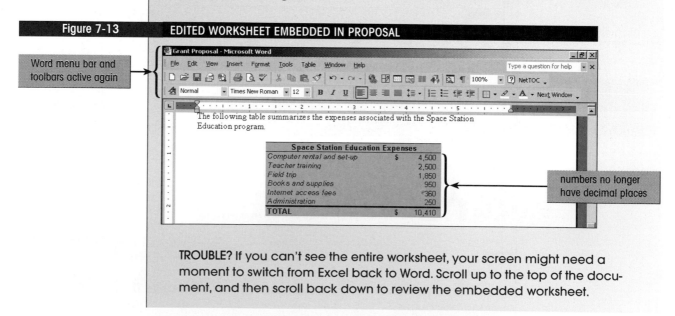

TROUBLE? If you can't see the entire worksheet, your screen might need a moment to switch from Excel back to Word. Scroll up to the top of the document, and then scroll back down to review the embedded worksheet.

The Excel workbook, Budget, remains in its original form on your disk, with the two decimal places. You have modified only the embedded copy in Nalani's proposal.

Linking an Excel Chart

Next, Nalani wants you to incorporate the chart that illustrates data on computer ownership in the Thoreau school district. Because Margarita plans to revise her data soon, Nalani decides to insert a linked version of the chart rather than embedding it. That way, once Margarita updates the chart, the latest version will appear in Nalani's proposal.

You'll link to the Chart file in the Tutorial folder the proposal document. Because you'll make changes to the chart after you link it, you'll make a copy of the chart as you link it. This leaves the original file in the Tutorial folder unchanged in case you want to repeat the tutorial steps later. Note that you don't always have to copy a file before you link it to a Word document.

To link an Excel chart to the proposal document:

1. Click **Edit** on the menu bar, click **Find**, find the placeholder **(Insert Excel chart)**, click **Cancel** to close the Find and Replace dialog box, and then press **Delete** to delete the placeholder (Insert Excel chart). Make sure the insertion point is positioned on a blank line between two paragraphs of text.

2. Click **Insert** on the menu bar, and then click **Object** to open the Object dialog box. You used this dialog box earlier to embed the Excel workbook in the proposal. This time, you'll use it to insert a linked object.

3. Click the **Create from File** tab.

4. Click the **Browse** button to open the Browse dialog box, and then, if necessary, use the **Look in** list arrow to open the Tutorial subfolder in the Tutorial.07 folder. The Browse dialog box lists the files in the Tutorial folder for Tutorial 7. Because you want to leave the original file unchanged in your Tutorial folder, you'll make a copy of it now.

5. Right-click the filename **Chart**. A shortcut menu opens.

6. Click **Copy** and then press **Ctrl+V**. A new file, Copy of Chart, appears in the file list.

7. Click **Copy of Chart** and then click the **Insert** button. The name of the selected file appears in the File name text box. Now you must specify that you want the chart file linked to, not embedded in, the proposal document.

8. Click the **Link to file** check box to select it. See Figure 7-14.

Figure 7-14   **INSERTING A LINKED OBJECT**

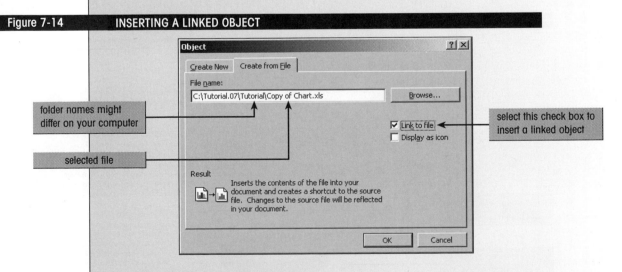

9. Click the **OK** button. After a moment, the chart image appears in the proposal.

The chart is far too large for the document. You can change its size easily, just as you would change the size of any graphic in a Word document. You can either drag its resize handles, or use a command on the Format menu.

To resize the chart and wrap text around it:

1. Click the chart. Black resize handles appear around its border.

2. Click **Format** on the menu bar, and then click **Object**.

3. Click the **Size** tab, and in the Scale section, use the **Height** down arrow to decrease the Height and Width settings to **40%**. Both the height and width of the selected object will be reduced to 40% because the Lock aspect ratio check box is selected. (If it is not selected, select it now.)

4. Click the **OK** button.

5. Scroll up, if necessary, to display the chart. After a pause, the chart appears in the Word document in a smaller size. Next, you'll wrap text around the chart.

   TROUBLE? If the chart is no longer located below the first paragraph after the heading "Goals," just continue with the steps. You will have a chance to adjust its position later.

   TROUBLE? Don't be concerned if it takes a few moments for the chart to appear. Some computers need extra time to display graphics. You might notice similar delays throughout this tutorial. You also might observe that the colors of your graphics change slightly.

6. If necessary, click the **chart** to select it, click **Format** on the menu bar, click **Object**, and then click the **Layout** tab in the Format Object dialog box.

7. Click the **Square** icon, click the **Left** option button to align the chart on the left margin, and then click the **OK** button. After a pause, the document text wraps to the right of the chart.

8. If necessary, drag the chart to position it on the second page, as shown in Figure 7-15.

Figure 7-15   **LINKED EXCEL CHART IN WORD PROPOSAL**

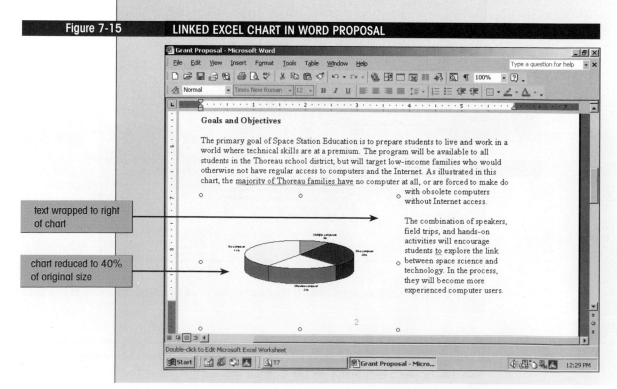

text wrapped to right of chart

chart reduced to 40% of original size

> **9.** Click anywhere in the **document** to deselect the chart, and then save the document. Review the percentages in the chart. (You might need to temporarily increase Word's Zoom setting to read the percentages easily. When you are finished, remember to return the zoom setting to 100%.)

Because you linked the file, you did not insert a copy of the file in the proposal, but merely a visual reference to the original. The size of the proposal file on disk has not increased significantly as a result of the link. If you double-click the chart, Excel will start and display the original source file. Instead of seeing the Word title bar at the top of the screen, you would see the Excel title bar, along with the Excel menus and toolbars, just as you did earlier when you edited the embedded workbook.

Modifying the Linked Chart

The advantage of linking a file over embedding it is that the destination file is updated whenever you modify the source file. Furthermore, you can update the source file either within the source program or within the destination program. In the following steps, you'll simulate what would happen if Margarita modified the source file in Excel. You'll open the file named Copy of Chart in Excel, change some values, and then view the updated information in the Word proposal.

> ### To modify the chart in the source program:
>
> **1.** Click the **Start** button 🏁Start on the taskbar, point to **Programs**, and then click **Microsoft Excel**. The Excel program window opens.
>
>   TROUBLE? You must have Microsoft Excel version 2002 installed on your computer to complete this section. If you do not see Microsoft Excel on your Programs menu, ask your instructor or technical support person for help.
>
>   TROUBLE? If the Office Assistant opens asking if you want help, click the Start Using Excel button.
>
> **2.** Click the **Open** button 📂 on the Excel Standard toolbar to display the Open dialog box.
>
> **3.** Use the **Look in** list arrow to open the Tutorial folder for Tutorial 7.
>
> **4.** Double-click **Copy of Chart**. The Excel workbook with the computer ownership chart opens. If necessary, maximize the Excel window. Notice that 41% of students in the Thoreau school district have no computer at home, and 21% have only an obsolete computer at home. See Figure 7-16.

Figure 7-16 | **CHART DISPLAYED IN THE SOURCE PROGRAM—EXCEL**

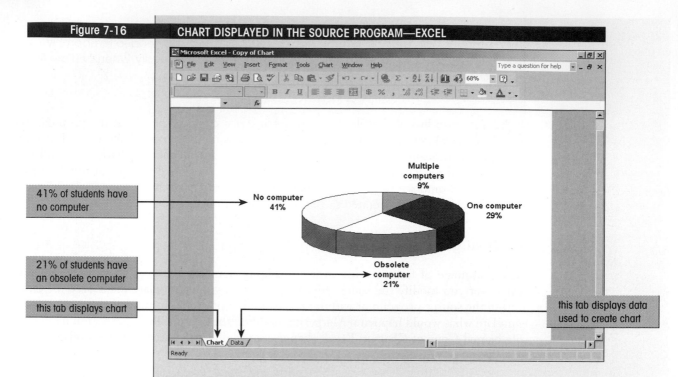

41% of students have no computer

21% of students have an obsolete computer

this tab displays chart

this tab displays data used to create chart

At the bottom of the window are two tabs. The Chart tab contains the chart, and the Data tab contains the data Margarita used to create the chart. Any changes made to the data on the Data tab will automatically be reflected in the chart. Assume Margarita has audited her data and found that the number of students with no computer at home is actually higher than she had originally thought. You'll enter that revised data next.

5. Click the **Data** tab. The worksheet containing the computer ownership data appears.

6. Click cell **B7**, which currently contains the value "350."

7. Type **400**, and press the **Enter** key. Now you'll look at the chart in Excel and see the effect of this change.

8. Click the **Chart** tab, and note that the "No computer" percentage changed from 41% to 44%, reflecting the new value you entered. See Figure 7-17.

Figure 7-17   **EXCEL CHART REFLECTING INCREASE IN STUDENTS WITH NO COMPUTERS**

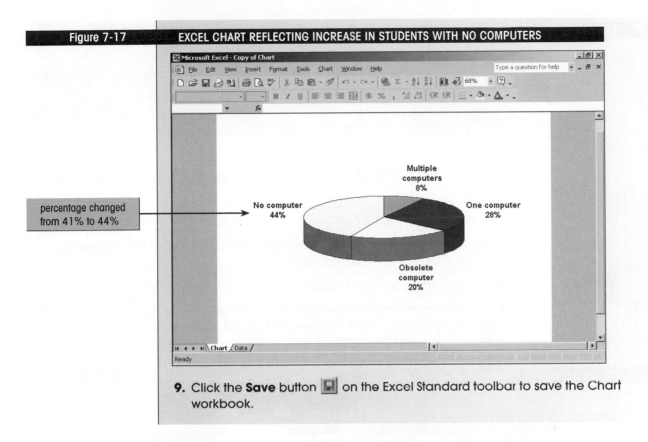

percentage changed
from 41% to 44%

9. Click the **Save** button on the Excel Standard toolbar to save the Chart workbook.

Now you'll return to the proposal and view the linked version.

To view the linked chart in the proposal:

1. Close Excel. The Word program window reappears, with the linked version of the chart displayed in the Grant Proposal document.

Notice that in the linked version of the chart, the "No computer" value is still 41%. Why doesn't it reflect the change you made in the source program? To make sure the changes are carried over to the linked version, you must perform one more step: updating the link.

Updating the Link

When you **update** a link, you ensure that the linked object in the destination file reflects the latest version of the source file. If you modify a linked object in the source program while the Word document to which it's linked is closed, Word will automatically update the link the next time you open the document. (In some cases, Word might ask if you want to update the link before you open the document.) But if you modify a linked object in the source program while the Word document is open, you have to tell Word to update the link.

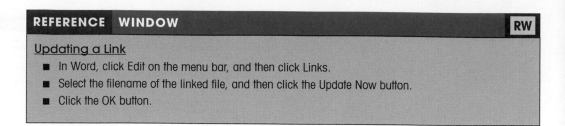

REFERENCE WINDOW · RW

Updating a Link
- In Word, click Edit on the menu bar, and then click Links.
- Select the filename of the linked file, and then click the Update Now button.
- Click the OK button.

Once the linked chart in Word is updated, it will reflect the change you made in Excel.

To update a linked file:

1. Make sure Microsoft Word appears in the title bar, and that you still see the linked chart in the Document window.

2. Click anywhere in the Microsoft Word window to activate it if necessary.

3. Click **Edit** on the menu bar, and then click **Links**. The Links dialog box opens. See Figure 7-18. A list of linked objects appears; in this case it consists of only one file named Copy of Chart. (You probably can't see the entire filename, however.)

Figure 7-18   **UPDATING LINKS IN A DOCUMENT**

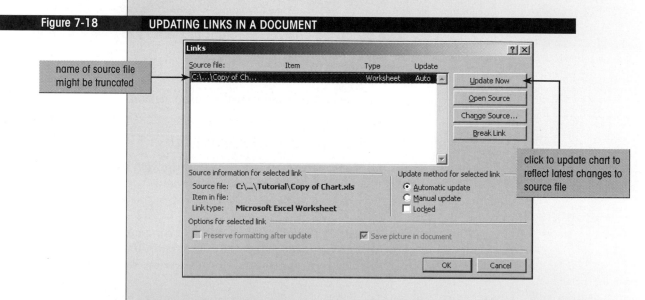

name of source file might be truncated

click to update chart to reflect latest changes to source file

4. Click **Copy of Ch...**, if necessary to select it, and then click the **Update Now** button. Word updates the linked object to reflect the latest changes to the source file.

5. Click the **OK** button in the Links dialog box. The Links dialog box closes.

6. If necessary, deselect the chart. The updated version of the chart appears in Word.

7. Change Word's Zoom setting to 175%, scroll to display the chart in the Word window, and review the percentages. The "No computer" percentage is now 44%. See Figure 7-19.

   TROUBLE? If the percentage has not changed in your chart, save the Grant Proposal document and close Word. Then start Word again and re-open the Grant Proposal document.

Figure 7-19	UPDATED CHART IN PROPOSAL DOCUMENT

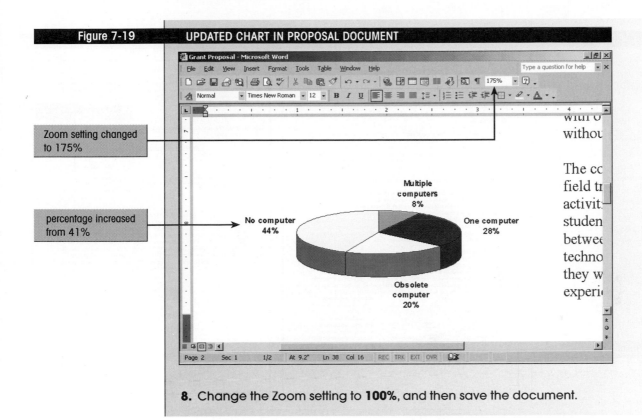

Zoom setting changed to 175%

percentage increased from 41%

8. Change the Zoom setting to **100%**, and then save the document.

Now you can be assured that any updates Margarita makes to the chart will be reflected whenever the proposal is opened.

Keep in mind that although you just edited the source file by opening it in the source program (Excel), you can just as easily edit the source file in the destination program. You would double-click the linked object in the destination document window. The source program would start, and the source file would open. After editing the source file, you would simply close the source program. The linked object in the destination file would update automatically.

Your grant proposal document is finished. You are ready to print it for distribution to the teachers at Thoreau School.

To print and then close the document:

1. Switch to Header and Footer view, and then click the **Format Page Number** button.

3. Preview the document. Don't be concerned if one line of the Goals section appears by itself at the top of the second page. Nalani will add additional text to the proposal after her colleagues review it, so at this point she isn't concerned about adjusting page breaks in the document.

3. Print the document. Your two-page document should look similar to Figure 7-20, although the exact layout of the text and graphics might differ.

Figure 7-20 **PRINTED DOCUMENT READY FOR DISTRIBUTION**

Space Station Education

Project Abstract

Space Station Education is a science program that will reach more than 900 students in grades K-6 at Thoreau Elementary and Middle School. This program will introduce students to the International Space Station and encourage them to make use of this rich scientific resource via the Internet.

The International Space Station (ISS) is a permanent space laboratory designed to allow humans to live and study in space. Requiring the collaboration of 16 nations and costing over $60 million, the ISS will take at least eight years and 46 separate space flights to complete. Scientists aboard the space station will perform experiments that could lead to important breakthroughs in technology. Through Space Station Education, younger students (grades K-3) will focus on communicating with the astronauts at the space station via the Internet, while older students (grades 4-6) will actually use data generated by the space station experiments in their own research projects.

Through Space Station Education teachers will learn to use the great variety of information about the ISS that is currently available on the Web. In particular, teachers will become familiar with the Human Space Flight Web site published by NASA. Once this training has been completed students and parents will be invited to participate in learning workshops one evening each month. These sessions will provide hands-on opportunities to explore the Space Station via interactive Web sites. Space Station Education will also give sixth graders experience in space science through field trips to the National Radio Astronomy Observatory in Green Bank, West Virginia.

Goals and Objectives

The primary goal of Space Station Education is to prepare students to live and work in a world where technical skills are at a premium. The program will be available to all students in the Thoreau school district, but will target low-income families who would otherwise not have regular access to computers and the Internet. As illustrated in this chart, the majority of Thoreau families have no computer at all, or are forced to make do with obsolete computers without Internet access.

linked chart

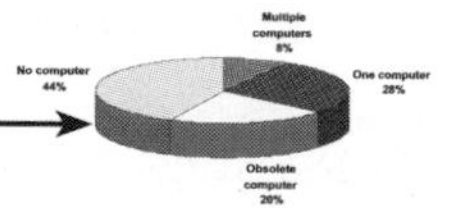

The combination of speakers, field trips, and hands-on activities will encourage students to explore the link between space science and technology. In the process, they will become more experienced computer users.

1

All of the activities associated with Space Station Education will be coordinated with the National Science Education Curriculum Objectives, the International Technology Society Recommendations and the World Council on Science Education Standards.

Budget

embedded worksheet

The following table summarizes the expenses associated with the Space Station Education program.

Space Station Education Expenses		
Computer rental and set-up	$	4,500
Teacher training		2,500
Field trip		1,850
Books and supplies		950
Internet access fees		360
Administration		250
TOTAL	$	10,410

Project Coordinator

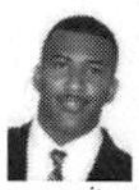

Space Station Education will be coordinated by Peter Brooks (see photograph at left). Peter is the Senior Math and Science Instructor at Thoreau Elementary and Middle School. He has managed the school's computer lab for eight years and is the founder of the Greater Middleton Astronomy Club, which now boasts over 40 members. He earned his B.S. in Elementary Education at the University of Pennsylvania. As a member of the Mayor's Technology Task Force, he has spoken widely in the community on the need to provide a thorough Internet education to all students. Peter has spent the last three summers working on his Masters in Education at Ohio State University.

2

3. Close the Grant Proposal document, saving any changes.

You give the completed proposal to Nalani, who then distributes it to the teachers at Thoreau School. She asks them to mark their suggestions directly on the printed document with a brightly colored pen. Now she wants you to focus on the task of distributing the document electronically, which you'll do in the next session.

Session 7.1 QUICK CHECK

1. Explain how to merge two edited copies of a document with the original document.
2. Define the following in your own words:
   a. source file
   b. object
   c. source program
   d. destination file
3. What is the difference between embedding and linking?

4. In what situations would you choose linking over embedding?

5. How do you embed an Excel workbook into a Word document? How do you link an Excel chart to a Word document?

6. Explain how to create a copy of a file within the Browse dialog box.

7. How do you modify an embedded object from the destination program?

8. True or False: When you modify an embedded object, your changes are also made to the source file.

SESSION 7.2

In this session, you will modify the proposal so that it is easier for Nalani's statewide colleagues to read online. You'll begin by creating hyperlinks that allow users to navigate through the document more easily and to access additional information. Then you'll see how the document looks in Web Layout view. Finally, you'll modify the document's appearance to make it more interesting.

Distributing Word Documents Online

In addition to printing the proposal for teachers at Thoreau, Nalani wants to make the proposal available to other colleagues **online**, which means they will read it on the computer screen rather than on a printed page. You can make a document available online in one of two ways—you can either e-mail the document to specific people, or you can make it available as a Web page.

Whichever online option you choose (Web page or e-mail), keep in mind that reading a document online is different from reading it in printed form. If you are certain a document will only be read online (and therefore don't have to worry about how the document will look when printed on a black and white printer), you can sometimes use more interesting formatting options, such as a fancy background or colored fonts. Because it is difficult to "flip through pages" online, you might also need to organize online information for easy access, or provide a quick method (such as a hyperlink) for opening related files. (You'll learn more about hyperlinks later in this tutorial.) Finally, remember that when distributing documents online, large document files can be problematic.

The following section provides information on e-mailing Word documents. After that, you'll learn more about working with Web pages.

E-Mailing Word Documents

Nalani plans to e-mail copies of the proposal to Tom Jenkins and Karen Goldberg so they can review the revised proposal. To e-mail a Word document, you need to use an e-mail program such as Microsoft Outlook. First you create an e-mail message, type the recipient's e-mail address, and then type the text of the e-mail. Finally, you need to attach the Word document to the e-mail message. The exact steps to attach a document to an e-mail message vary from one e-mail program to another, but they are similar to opening a document in Word: you need to find and then select the file you want to attach.

When you e-mail documents you should know a few basic rules:

■ Many e-mail programs have difficulty handling large attachments. Consider using a compression program (such as WinZip) to reduce a large file to a more manageable size before e-mailing it. Alternately, you could convert the Word document to a Web page (as described later in this tutorial).

A Web page is usually much smaller than a Word document containing the same amount of text.

■ You might find that early versions of Word cannot open files created in the most recent versions of Word. Before e-mailing a file, ask the recipient which version of Word he or she is using. To avoid problems with conflicting versions, save the Word document as a rich text file (using the Rich Text File document type in the Save As dialog box) before e-mailing it.

■ If you plan to e-mail a document that contains links to other files, remember to e-mail all the linked documents.

■ E-mail attachments, including Word documents, are sometimes used maliciously to spread computer viruses. Remember to include an explanatory note with any e-mail attachment so that the recipient can be certain the attachment is legitimate. If you plan to send and receive e-mail attachments, install a reliable virus checker program on your computer.

E-mailing Word documents is especially useful when you are collaborating with a group. You can exchange documents with colleagues in the office or around the world with just a click of the mouse. In Nalani's case, e-mailing documents enabled her to get Tom and Karen's comments on her proposal in the space of a few hours.

To make a document available to a wider audience, however, it's easier to publish it as a Web page, because then you don't have to take time to read and manage several e-mail messages. You'll learn more about working with Web pages in the next section.

Publishing Word Documents as Web Pages

Web pages are special documents designed to be viewed in a program called a **browser**. The two most popular browsers are **Microsoft Internet Explorer** and **Netscape Navigator**. You can create a Web page on just about any kind of computer, but if you want other people to open your Web page in a browser, you must store it on a special network computer called a **Web server**. Browsers send messages through a computer network to a Web server. The Web server responds by sending a file containing the Web page back to the browser, which then displays the Web page in the browser window. When you make a Web page available to others via a Web server, you are **publishing** the Web page.

Web servers are found on two different types of networks—intranets and the Internet. An **intranet** is a self-contained network, belonging to a single organization, which relies on Web servers and related technology. For example, the science and math teachers at Thoreau School recently created an intranet to connect all the computers in the school. Because Nalani's computer is connected to the Thoreau School intranet, she can use her browser to retrieve school-related Web pages from a Web server that is down the hall from her office.

At the same time, Nalani's computer is also connected to the largest, most widely used computer network in the world, the **Internet**. The part of the Internet that transfers and displays Web pages is called the **World Wide Web**, or simply, the **Web**. Each Web page has its own specific **address** (or **URL**), such as *www.microsoft.com* or *www.cnn.com*. A group of related Web pages is called a **Web site**. The main Web page within a Web site (the one that is usually displayed first) is called a **home page**. When her computer is connected to the Internet, Nalani can use her browser to access well-known Web sites such as *www.microsoft.com* or *www.cnn.com*.

You probably have experience using a browser to view Web pages. If so, you know that Web pages usually contain text and graphics, and also can contain audio and video. Web pages include **hyperlinks** (or **links**) which you can click to open, or "jump to," additional information. A hyperlink can be a word, a phrase, or a graphic. Text hyperlinks are usually underlined and appear in a different color from the rest of the document.

While hyperlinks are widely used in Web pages, you can also use them in ordinary Word documents that are intended for online reading. (You already have some experience using hyperlinks in Word documents.) In the next section, you will learn more about using hyperlinks in online Word documents and Web pages.

Using **Hyperlinks in Word**

As you know, you can include a hyperlink to a Web page in a Word document. You can also include e-mail links that you can click to type an e-mail message. In addition, you can include a link that opens another Word document, or that jumps to another part of the same document. If you have many Office XP documents that are related to each other, you can create a useful hyperlink system that allows users to retrieve and view related material. For example, a business proposal might include links to a budget stored in an Excel workbook and to product photographs stored in a PowerPoint presentation. In fact, instead of using Margarita's chart as a linked object, you could have inserted a hyperlink that users click to open the chart in Excel. (You used a linked object because you wanted the chart to appear in the printed version of the proposal.)

Nalani wants you to add two hyperlinks to the proposal document—one hyperlink that targets a location within the proposal, and one that targets a different document.

Inserting a Hyperlink to a Bookmark in the Same Document

According to Nalani, one of the strengths of her proposed Education Space Station program is the project's coordinator, Peter Brooks. A teacher at Thoreau School, Peter is well known in the community for helping introduce students to new technology. Nalani decides to add to the Project Abstract a sentence that introduces Peter. She also wants to include a hyperlink that jumps to the "Project Coordinator" section at the end of the proposal.

Creating a hyperlink that jumps from one location to another in the same document requires two steps. First, you insert an electronic marker called a **bookmark** at the location you want the link to jump to. Second, you enter the text that you want users to click, and format it as a hyperlink. Figure 7-21 illustrates this process.

| Figure 7-21 | HYPERLINK THAT TARGETS A BOOKMARK |

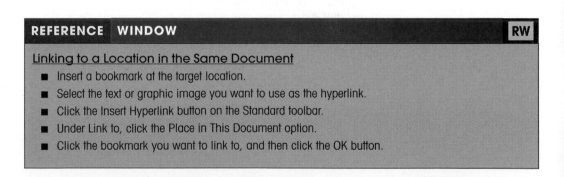

enter text here and format it as a hyperlink

when user clicks hyperlink, Word jumps to target bookmark

place bookmark here

First you'll open the document you saved at the end of the previous session, and then insert a bookmark in the Project Coordinator section. Next, you'll insert the hyperlink in the Project Abstract section.

To insert a hyperlink to a location within the same document:

1. If you took a break after the last session, make sure Word is running, and then open the **Grant Proposal** document.

2. Use the **Find** command on the Edit menu to find the **Project Coordinator** heading, close the Find and Replace dialog box, and verify that the heading "Project Coordinator" is selected. This is where you'll insert a bookmark required for the hypertext link.

3. Click **Insert** on the menu bar, and then click **Bookmark**. The Bookmark dialog box opens. You can now type the bookmark name, which must be one word, without spaces.

4. Type **Coordinator**, and click the **Add** button. The Bookmark dialog box closes. Although you can't see it, a bookmark has been inserted before the heading. This bookmark will be the target of the hyperlink. When you click the hyperlink (which you will create next), the insertion point will jump to this bookmark.

5. Press **Ctrl+Home** to move the insertion point to the beginning of the document, and then click at the end of the first paragraph under the heading "Project Abstract." The insertion point should be positioned immediately following the phrase "...via the Internet."

6. Insert a space, if necessary, and then type: **The project coordinator is Peter Brooks, a Thoreau teacher who is well known in the community for introducing students to new technology.** (Include the period.) Next, you'll format part of this sentence as a hyperlink.

7. Select the name **Peter Brooks** in the sentence you just typed, and then click the **Insert Hyperlink** button 🔗 on the Standard toolbar. The Insert Hyperlink dialog box opens.

8. Under Link to, click **Place in This Document**. See Figure 7-22. The right side of the dialog box now lists the headings and bookmarks in the document. Here you can click the item you want the hyperlink to jump to. You can create a hyperlink that jumps to a specific document heading, rather than to a bookmark. However, notice that in this document Word considers the sentence that begins "Through Space Station Education..." to be a heading, even though it's really part of a paragraph. Because you can't always predict what text will appear in the heading list, it's usually easier to link to bookmarks rather than headings. (In the Review Assignments at the end of this tutorial you'll learn how to create hyperlinks that jump to document headings.)

Figure 7-22   **INSERTING A HYPERLINK**

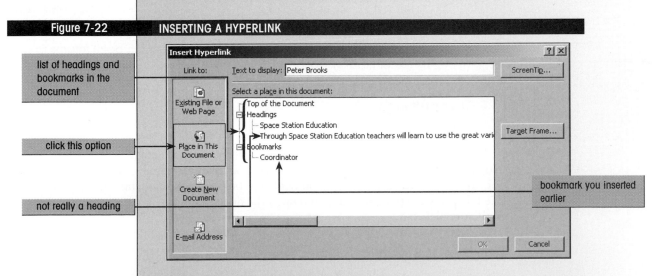

TROUBLE? If you see only three items in the right side of the dialog box, click the plus signs next to "Headings" and "Bookmarks."

9. Click **Coordinator**, and then click the **OK** button. The name "Peter Brooks" appears in underlined blue text. The hyperlink now targets the Coordinator bookmark.

> TROUBLE? If you formatted the wrong text as a hyperlink, click the Undo button and begin again with Step 7.

Now that you have inserted a hyperlink into the document, you should test it. When working with hyperlinks in a document, it's helpful to display the **Web toolbar**, which contains buttons that simplify the process of working with hyperlinks and Web pages. So before testing the hyperlink, you'll display the Web toolbar.

To test the hyperlink in your document:

1. Right-click the **Formatting toolbar**, and then click **Web** on the shortcut menu. The Web toolbar appears.

2. Move the mouse pointer over the blue underlined text (the hyperlink). After a moment, a ScreenTip (yellow rectangle) appears with the name of the bookmark (Coordinator) and instructions for following the link. See Figure 7-23.

| Figure 7-23 | DISPLAYING THE HYPERLINK SCREENTIP |

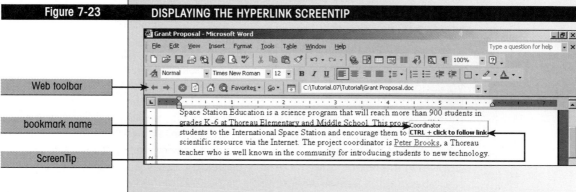

3. Press and hold **Ctrl** and then click the **hyperlink**. The insertion point jumps to the Coordinator bookmark, and the Project Coordinator section appears. You'll use one of the Web toolbar buttons to return to the beginning of the document.

4. Click the **Back** button on the Web toolbar. The insertion point returns to the hyperlink (Peter Brooks). Notice that the hyperlink is now purple. The color change indicates that you have already used, or followed, the hyperlink.

5. Save your work.

In this document it's not important that the hyperlink changes color after you use it. However, hyperlinks can also jump to other documents, including Web documents on the World Wide Web. In that environment, it's helpful to know which links you've already tried. If you were to close and then reopen the document, the hyperlink would again be blue until you clicked it.

Creating Hyperlinks to Other Documents

The greatest power of hyperlinks lies not in jumping to another location within the same document, but in jumping to other documents. These documents can be located on the World Wide Web, on your computer's hard drive, or on your company's network server. When you add a hyperlink to another document, you don't necessarily target a bookmark as you do for hyperlinks pointing to a location within the same document.

Instead, you target either the URL of a Web page, or the path and filename of a file on your computer or network.

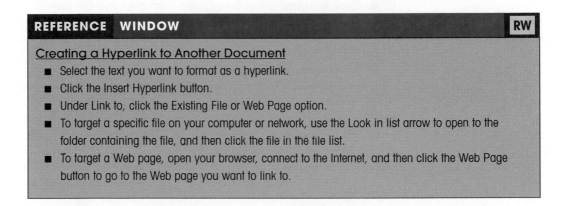

REFERENCE WINDOW RW

Creating a Hyperlink to Another Document
- Select the text you want to format as a hyperlink.
- Click the Insert Hyperlink button.
- Under Link to, click the Existing File or Web Page option.
- To target a specific file on your computer or network, use the Look in list arrow to open to the folder containing the file, and then click the file in the file list.
- To target a Web page, open your browser, connect to the Internet, and then click the Web Page button to go to the Web page you want to link to.

Nalani wants to insert a hyperlink that will open a Word document containing Peter's resume. Because this hyperlink will take users to a different document, you don't need to insert a bookmark. Instead, you use the name of the target document.

To create a hyperlink to another document:

1. Use the hyperlink again to jump to the Project Coordinator section.

2. Click at the end of the Project Coordinator section. The insertion point should be located immediately to the right of the phrase "at Ohio State University." This is where you'll insert text, some of which will become the hyperlink.

3. Press the **spacebar**, and type **(See his resume.)** making sure to include the parentheses.

4. Select the word **resume** in the text you just typed. See Figure 7-24.

Figure 7-24 **SELECTING TEXT TO FORMAT AS A HYPERLINK**

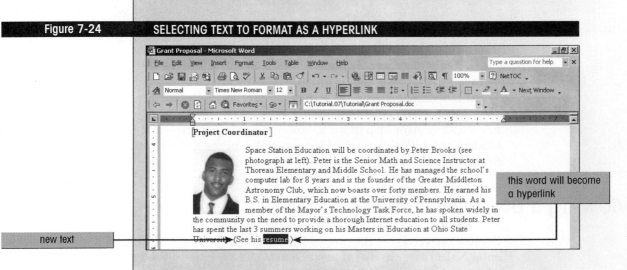

5. Click the **Insert Hyperlink** button 🔗 on the Standard toolbar. The Insert Hyperlink dialog box opens.

6. Under Link to, click the **Existing File or Web Page** option. The right side of the dialog box displays options related to selecting a file or a Web page.

7. If necessary, use the **Look in** list arrow to open the Tutorial subfolder in the Tutorial.07 folder on your hard drive.

8. Click **Resume** in the file list, and then click the **OK** button. The word "resume" is now formatted in blue with an underline, as a hyperlink.

When your documents include hyperlinks to other documents, you must keep track of where you store those target documents. If you move a target document to a different location, any hyperlinks to it contained in other documents might not function properly. In this case, you created a hyperlink in the Grant Proposal document that links to the Resume document. Both documents are stored in the Tutorial subfolder in the Tutorial.07 folder, which is most likely located on a hard disk. To ensure that the hyperlink in the Proposal document will continue to function, you must keep the two documents in the same folder.

Now you're ready to test the hyperlink you just created.

To use a hyperlink to jump to another file:

1. Move the pointer to the hyperlink **resume**.

2. Press and hold **Ctrl** and then click **resume**. Word opens the document named Resume.

3. Read through the resume, and then click the **Back** button ⇦ on the Web toolbar to return to the Proposal document. Notice that the hyperlink color has changed, indicating that you have used the hyperlink.

4. Use the hyperlink again to return to the Resume document, and then close the Resume document without saving any changes.

5. Save your changes to the Grant Proposal document.

As you can see, hyperlinks allow you to display information instantaneously. When used thoughtfully, hyperlinks make it possible to navigate a complicated document quickly and easily. If you don't want to include hyperlinks in your document, but still require an easy method for moving among sections while you are editing the document, you can use the **Word Document Map**. This feature displays a list of all the headings in the document. To move the insertion point to a specific section, you click that heading in the Document Map. For the Document Map to work, however, headings must be formatted with Word's default heading styles. (You'll use the Document Map in the Review Assignments at the end of this tutorial.)

Viewing a Document in Web Layout View

Because the version of the proposal you are now working on is intended for an online audience, Nalani suggests that you switch to Web Layout view. **Web Layout view** offers several advantages for online viewers:

- Text appears larger in Web Layout view.
- Text wraps to the window, not to the printed page. Each line of text spans the width of the document window.

■ Documents can be displayed with different background effects.

■ Page setup elements, such as footers, headers, and breaks, are not displayed. (Because users don't view the document as printed pages, these elements aren't necessary.)

Web Layout view is useful when you need to format a document for online viewing. Text wrapping doesn't always survive the conversion from a Word document to a Web page, and graphics often shift position when you save a document as a Web page. Web Layout view prepares you for this by showing you what the graphics look like in their new positions.

Keep in mind that, despite its name, Web Layout view does not show you exactly how a document will look when saved as a Web page. Some features you see in Web Layout view (such as the animation you will add in the next section) do not appear when you save the document as a Web page. (You will learn more about saving a document as a Web page later in this tutorial.)

If you switch to Web Layout view and then save the document in that view, it will open automatically in Web Layout view. Nalani asks you to display the Grant Proposal document in Web Layout view and then save it. Then when she e-mails the file to Karen and Tom, it will open for them in Web Layout view.

To display a document in Web Layout view:

1. Click the **Web Layout View** button (next to the Normal View button, just above the status bar). Notice that paragraphs now span the width of the document window. The line widths are no longer constrained by the margin settings for the printed page. This makes the document easier to read online. See Figure 7-25.

Figure 7-25	DOCUMENT DISPLAYED IN WEB LAYOUT VIEW

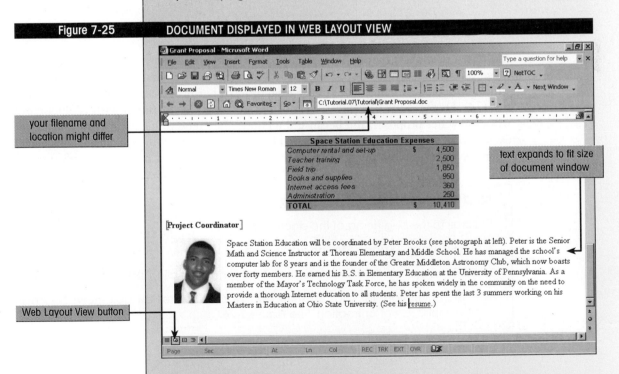

your filename and location might differ

text expands to fit size of document window

Web Layout View button

TROUBLE? Depending on the size of your monitor, the line breaks in your document may differ from those in Figure 7-25. This has to do with the fact the Web Layout View wraps text to fit the size of the screen, and is not a problem.

2. Scroll through the document to review its appearance in Web Layout View. Depending on the size of your computer screen, you might find that all the text in the first paragraph of the Goals and Objectives section has wrapped to the

right of the chart, leaving the heading "Goals and Objectives" floating over the chart. You could correct this problem now by dragging the chart down, until part of the first paragraph wraps over the top of the chart. However, if you move the chart, the text wrapping will not look right when you switch back to Print Layout view. Because Nalani wants Tom and Karen to be able to switch between Web Layout view and Print Layout view, she decides to leave the chart where it is for now. You'll have a chance to adjust its position later when you create a Web page version of the Grant Proposal.

3. Save your changes to the Grant Proposal document.

Next, you'll make some changes to the Grant Proposal document that will improve its online appearance.

Improving **the Appearance of an Online Document**

To make the online version of the proposal more visually interesting for online viewers, Nalani suggests you use two features—animated text and a colored background. You'll add these features now to improve the appearance of the document Nalani will e-mail to Karen and Tom. However, keep in mind that some features that appear in Web Layout view do not appear when you convert the document to a Web page. (You will learn more about converting a document to a Web page in the next session.)

Animating Text

Animated text is text that blinks, sparkles, shimmers, or displays a moving border. Most of these animations are not appropriate for official, professional documents, and Nalani would not consider using them in the final draft of her proposal, which she will submit to the U.S. Department of Education. But because she is acquainted with the people who will review her proposal, and because she knows they tend to be informal when reviewing each other's work, she thinks it's acceptable to use some animated text in this draft. Nalani suggests you try animating the proposal title, "Space Station Education," with sparkles.

To animate the title of the proposal:

1. Scroll to the beginning of the document.

2. Select the title **Space Station Education**.

3. Click **Format** on the menu bar, click **Font**, and then click the **Text Effects** tab.

4. In the Animations list, click **Sparkle Text**. Notice the Preview box shows a sample of this type of animation. See Figure 7-26.

Figure 7-26	PREVIEWING ANIMATED TEXT

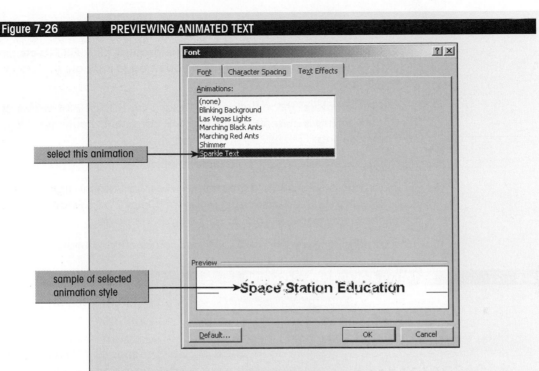

5. Click the **OK** button, and then click anywhere outside the title to deselect it. Rainbow colored sparkles have been added to the title.

Animation draws an online viewer's eyes immediately to the animated text, so use this feature only for your most important words or phrases. Overusing animated text makes your document difficult to view. Also keep in mind that animation effects don't appear in printed documents, nor will they survive the conversion to a Web page.

Applying a Background Effect

You also can make an online document more visually appealing by applying background effects. As with animated text, backgrounds do not appear in printed documents. You can apply one of the following background effects:

- Solid color
- Gradient—a single color or combination of colors that varies in intensity
- Texture—choose from a collection of textures
- Pattern—choose from a collection of interesting patterns; you designate the colors in the pattern
- Picture—a graphic image

When choosing a background color or texture, make sure your text is still readable. In poorly designed online documents, the background might be so dark or the pattern so obtrusive that the text is illegible. In addition, a background that contains a complicated pattern will increase the file size and take longer to appear on a user's screen. Nalani suggests you use a gradient background that ranges from white to pale blue.

To apply a background effect to a document:

1. Click **Format** on the menu bar, point to **Background**, click **Fill Effects**, and then click the **Gradient** tab, if necessary. First you need to indicate that you want to use two colors for the background.

2. Click the **Two colors** option button. The Color 1 and Color 2 list arrows appear. The Color 1 setting is currently white, which is correct. You only need to change the Color 2 setting.

3. Click the **Color 2** list arrow. A color palette appears.

4. Click the **pale blue square** in the bottom row, third from the right. The palette closes and the selected color appears in the Color 2 box. Finally, you need to specify how you want the color to vary across the page.

5. In the Shading styles section, click the **From corner** option button. See Figure 7-27.

| Figure 7-27 | SELECTING A GRADIENT BACKGROUND |

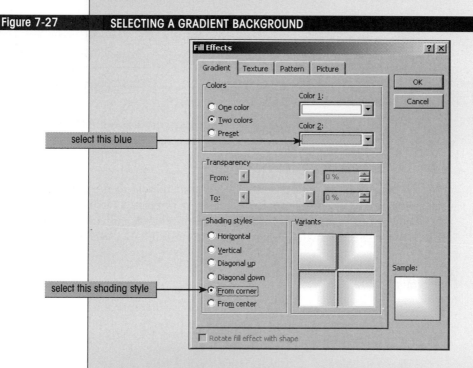

6. Click the **OK** button. The blue and white gradient fills the background of the Grant Proposal document.

7. Save the Grant Proposal document in Web Layout view, and then close it.

The gradient background is attractive and light enough to make the document text easy to read. The proposal is ready to be e-mailed to Karen and Tom. However, before Nalani e-mails the proposal, she will add a similar background to the Resume document. Then both of the linked documents will have a consistent look.

Session 7.2 QUICK CHECK

1. What is a hyperlink?

2. What is a browser?

3. What's the difference between an intranet and the Internet?

4. Explain how to insert a hyperlink to a location in the same document containing the hyperlink.

5. Which name is an invalid bookmark name? a) Recommendations, b) Executive Summary, c) README

6. What does a change in the color of a hyperlink indicate?

7. True or False: Web Layout view shows you exactly what your document will look like when saved as a Web page.

SESSION 7.3

In this session, you will convert Nalani's proposal into a Web page for publication on the World Wide Web, and then format the Web page to make it easier to read in a Web browser. Finally, you'll insert and edit hyperlinks that link the Proposal and Resume documents, and then preview your Web page in a browser.

Saving a Word Document as a Web Page

So far, Nalani has created printed copies of her proposal to hand out to teachers at Thoreau School and an online version to e-mail to Karen and Tom. Next, she wants to convert the Grant Proposal document to a Web page so she can make it available on the World Wide Web. Another term for a Web page is **HTML document**. The letters HTML are short for **Hypertext Markup Language**, a special programming language that tells a Web browser how a Web page should look on the screen. When you save a Word document as a Web page, you are really inserting HTML codes that tell the browser exactly how to format the text and graphics. Fortunately, you don't have to learn the Hypertext Markup Language to create Web pages. When you save the document as a Web page, Word creates all the necessary HTML codes (called markings, or tags). This process is transparent to you, so you won't actually see the HTML codes in your Web pages.

The relatively small size of Web pages makes them easy to share on the Internet. For example, a Word document containing a moderate amount of formatting and a few graphics might be 500 KB in size. The same document saved as a Web page might be only 20 KB in size, along with about 50 KB of graphics files. To help keep your Web page file small, Word puts any graphics into a separate folder. This folder also contains other small files that your Web browser needs to display the Web page correctly. By default, this folder has the same name as your Web page, plus an underscore and the word "files." For instance, a Web page saved as "Finance Summary" would be accompanied by a folder named "Finance Summary_files."

Although saving a Word document as a Web page is easy, it's not foolproof, particularly when it comes to formatting. Some Word formatting features (such as paragraph borders or certain font effects) will not translate into HTML. When you save your document as a Web page, document formatting might be lost, or the formatting will look different. In some cases, the original document might contain special features, such as animation, that don't survive the translation to HTML. Sometimes you might need to reapply formatting after a document has been saved as a Web page. As a general rule, once you save a document as a Web page, you'll want to modify it to make it more attractive for users of the World Wide Web. At the very least, you will probably need to reposition graphics.

To create sophisticated Web pages (or entire Web sites), you'll probably want to use a dedicated HTML editor, such as Microsoft FrontPage. But to create a simple Web page from an existing document, you can save the document as a Web page.

REFERENCE WINDOW   **RW**

<u>Saving a Word Document as a Web Page</u>
- Click File on the menu bar, and then click Save as Web Page.
- If desired, give the file a new filename. Word will add the file extension .htm at the end of the document, although this extension probably won't be visible in the Save As dialog box.
- Click the Save button.
- If Word warns you that the document has formatting not supported by Web browsers, click the Continue button.

You are ready to save the Grant Proposal document as a Web page.

To save the document as a Web page:

1. If you took a break after the last session, make sure Word is running. Close any Internet-related programs, such as e-mail editors or browsers, and then open the **Grant Proposal** document.

2. Click **File** on the menu bar, and then click **Save as Web Page**. The Save As dialog box, which you have used many times, opens. The only difference between this dialog box and the one you previously used is that the Save as type text box indicates that the document will be saved as a Web page.

3. Change the filename so it reads **Grant Proposal Web Page**.

4. Click the **Save** button. Word displays a warning message indicating that some elements of the document cannot be displayed in commonly used browsers (Microsoft Internet Explorer 4.0 and Netscape Navigator 4.0). The dialog box explains that animated text (the document heading, which is currently formatted with sparkles) will become italicized instead. Also, any pictures or objects with text wrapping will become left- or right-aligned. See Figure 7-28. You'll see exactly what this means after you finish saving the document as a Web page.

| Figure 7-28 | WARNING MESSAGE |

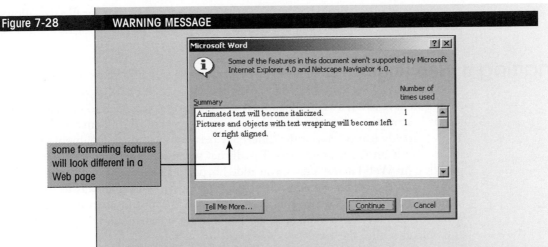

some formatting features will look different in a Web page

5. Click **Continue**. After a pause, the document is converted into a Web page.

   TROUBLE? If you think that Word is taking a long time to convert and save the file in HTML format, don't worry. Depending on the speed of your system, it could take several minutes.

6. If necessary, display the Web toolbar. Your document should now look similar to Figure 7-29.

| Figure 7-29 | GRANT PROPOSAL WEB PAGE |

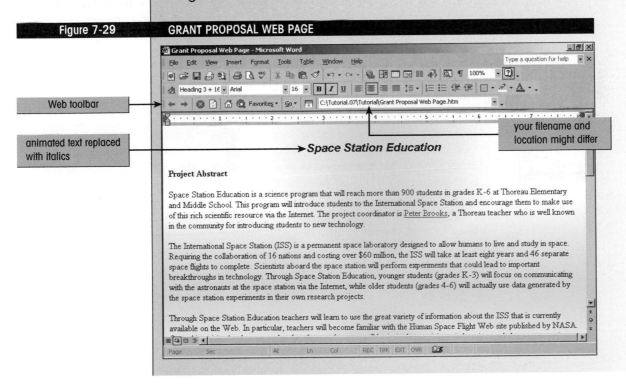

Web toolbar

animated text replaced with italics

your filename and location might differ

At first glance, the new Grant Proposal Web page might look identical to the Grant Proposal Word document when you displayed it in Web Layout View. But as you review the Web page, you'll notice at least one difference: the animated title is now formatted in italics. Another major difference is not actually apparent on the screen: The file size has decreased from about 66 KB to only about 17 KB (plus about 33 KB of related files). This reduced size is a tremendous advantage for Web pages that must be transferred electronically over long distances and often through slow network connections. The smaller file size allows the Web pages to appear as quickly as possible in a browser window.

Formatting a Web Page

After you have saved a Word document as a Web page, you need to format the Web page so that it is attractive when displayed in a browser—you need to format it for online viewing. You've already learned about the difference between reading a document online as opposed to reading it on the printed page. Recall that when you prepared an online version of the proposal (in Web Layout View), you added hyperlinks and a colored background. But when you created the earlier version of the grant proposal, your goal was to create a document suitable for e-mailing. Now you need to format the proposal to improve its appearance when it is displayed in a Web browser. You'll begin by correcting the placement of graphics and objects within the text.

Moving and Editing Text and Graphics

You can edit and format text and graphics in a Web page the same way you edit and format a normal Word document. First, Nalani asks you adjust the placement of the Excel chart. Depending on the size of your computer screen, this object (which had text wrapped around it) might have shifted to an awkward position when you first viewed the grant proposal in Web Layout view. Nalani didn't want you to adjust its position in Web Layout view, because then the text would have wrapped incorrectly in Print Layout view. However, now that you have converted the grant proposal to a Web document that is only meant to be viewed in a browser, you don't have to worry about how graphics will look in Print Layout view. You can position the chart for viewing in a browser.

To change the text wrapping around graphics:

1. Scroll down to display the Excel chart in the section below the "Goals and Objectives" heading, as shown in Figure 7-30. (Depending on the size of your computer monitor, the text on your screen might have wrapped around the chart differently). In Figure 7-30, the entire heading "Budget" (which used to be left-aligned) has wrapped to the right of the chart. You could adjust the position of the chart by adjusting settings in the Format Object dialog box, but it's easier to drag the chart up a few lines.

Figure 7-30	CHART WITH BUDGET HEADING WRAPPED TO THE RIGHT

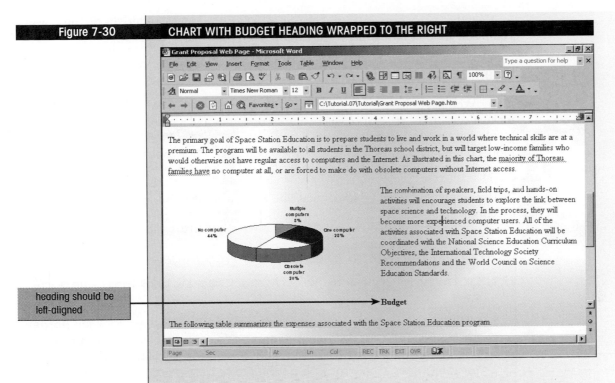

heading should be left-aligned

2. If necessary, click the **chart** to select it, and then drag it up so that it is positioned similarly to the one in Figure 7-31, with the heading "Budget" left-aligned below the chart. Deselect the chart.

Figure 7-31	CHART WITH BUDGET HEADING IN PROPER POSITION

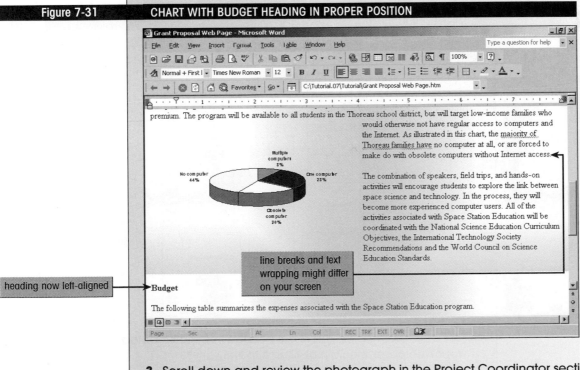

heading now left-aligned

line breaks and text wrapping might differ on your screen

3. Scroll down and review the photograph in the Project Coordinator section. Adjust its position, if necessary, so that the entire paragraph wraps to the right of the photograph. It's okay if the top of the photograph doesn't align perfectly with the top of the paragraph of text.

Now that you've corrected the placement of the text and graphics in Nalani's proposal, you'll add another formatting feature to the Web page.

Inserting Horizontal Lines

Many Web pages have horizontal lines that separate sections of a document. These lines make it easy to see at a glance where one section ends and another begins. You can also add horizontal lines to Word documents that you plan to read in Web Layout view, but they are more commonly used in Web pages. If you don't like a horizontal line after you insert one into a document, you can delete it by clicking the line and then pressing Delete.

Nalani wants you to add a horizontal line below the title and at the end of each section except the last one.

To insert horizontal lines into the Web page:

1. Click to the left of the "P" in "Project Abstract" near the beginning of the document.

2. Click **Format** on the menu bar, click **Borders and Shading**, click the **Borders** tab in the Borders and Shading dialog box, and then click the **Horizontal Line** button. The Horizontal Line dialog box opens, and lists many styles of horizontal lines. (There may be a short pause before you see the borders displayed within the dialog box.)

3. Scroll down until you see a red line in the left column.

4. Click the **red line**, as shown in Figure 7-32.

Figure 7-32   SELECTING A HORIZONTAL LINE STYLE

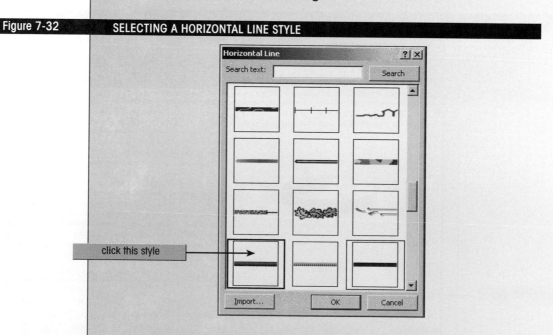

5. Click the **OK** button. A red line is inserted into the Web page below the title. Your Web page should look similar to Figure 7-33.

Figure 7-33	NEWLY INSERTED HORIZONTAL LINE

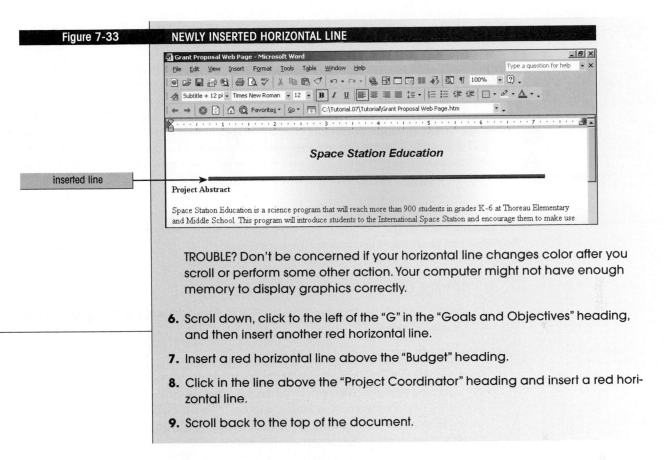

TROUBLE? Don't be concerned if your horizontal line changes color after you scroll or perform some other action. Your computer might not have enough memory to display graphics correctly.

6. Scroll down, click to the left of the "G" in the "Goals and Objectives" heading, and then insert another red horizontal line.

7. Insert a red horizontal line above the "Budget" heading.

8. Click in the line above the "Project Coordinator" heading and insert a red horizontal line.

9. Scroll back to the top of the document.

Now that you've used horizontal lines to give shape to the document, you decide to improve the appearance of the document's text.

Modifying Text Size and Color

Web pages use colored text to enhance the appearance of the page and to call attention to important information. You also can adjust text size on a Web page just as you would on a printed document. To improve the proposal's readability and appearance, Nalani wants you to increase the font size of the title text and change its color to red, to match the horizontal lines.

To change the size and color of text:

1. Select the title **Space Station Education** at the beginning of the Web page.

2. Use the **Font Size** list arrow on the Formatting toolbar to change the font size from 16-point to **24-point**.

3. Click the **Font Color** list arrow on the Formatting toolbar, click the **red square** (third row from the top, first column on the left), and then deselect the text. The title "Space Station Education" is formatted in red, to match the horizontal lines.

4. Save your work.

You've formatted Nalani's proposal document so that it will be visually appealing when displayed in a browser. Next, you'll create additional hypertext links and edit an existing link.

Creating and Editing Hyperlinks in a Web Page

As you looked through the HTML version of the proposal, you probably noticed that it still contains two hyperlinks. The Peter Brooks link jumps to the Project Coordinator section at the end of the Web page. The resume link jumps to a Word document containing Peter's resume. Nalani wants to save the Resume document as a Web page, and then format it to match the Grant Proposal document. She also wants you to add a hyperlink to the resume that will jump back to the Grant Proposal Web page. Finally, because you'll save the Resume document with a new name, you have to edit the resume hyperlink (in the Grant Proposal Web page) to make sure it opens the right file.

In the following steps, you will convert the resume to a Web page, create a new link from the resume back to the proposal, and then modify the hyperlink in the proposal so that browsers can easily jump between the two documents.

To convert the resume to a Web page:

1. Open the file named **Resume** from the Tutorial subfolder in the Tutorial.07 folder on your hard drive.

2. If necessary, switch to Print Layout View.

3. Save the document (in the Tutorial folder for Tutorial 7) as a Web page using the filename **Resume Web Page**. While the Save As dialog box is open, notice that Word has created a new folder, named "Grant Proposal Web Page_files," in which to store the files related to the proposal Web page. Note that you should never save any other documents in this folder.

4. Click the **Save** button to close the Save As dialog box. Word automatically switches to Web Layout view.

Next, you'll make some formatting changes to give the Resume Web page the same look as the proposal Web page. You'll use the procedures you learned earlier in this tutorial.

To format the Resume Web Page:

1. Click **Format** on the menu bar, point to **Background**, click **Fill Effects**, click the **Gradient** tab, and then apply a white and pale blue background to the Web page, using the From corner shading style.

2. Select the text **Peter Brooks** at the top of the page, and format it in red.

3. Save your work.

The resume and the proposal now have a similar appearance.

Inserting a Hyperlink to a Web Page

After users read Peter's resume they most likely will want to return to the proposal, so Nalani asks you to insert a hyperlink that jumps to the proposal. You insert hyperlinks into Web pages the same way as in Word documents.

To insert a hyperlink:

1. Press **Ctrl+End** to move the insertion point to the end of the Web page, and then type **Return to Grant Proposal**.

2. Select the text **Grant Proposal** in the phrase you just typed, click the **Insert Hyperlink** button on the Standard toolbar and then, under Link to, click **Existing File or Web Page**.

3. If necessary, use the **Look in** list arrow to open the Tutorial subfolder in the Tutorial folder on your hard drive, click **Grant Proposal Web Page**, and then click the **OK** button. Word inserts the hyperlink to the proposal.

4. Save and close the Resume Web page. You return to the proposal.

The resume now contains a hyperlink that takes users back to the proposal.

Editing a Hyperlink

Recall that the proposal itself contains the hyperlink that targets a Word document containing the resume. You need to edit the hyperlink so that it targets the resume with its new Web page name. Rather than deleting the hyperlink and reinserting a new one, you can edit the existing hyperlink to target the Resume Web Page.

To edit a hyperlink:

1. Scroll to the end of the proposal, and position the pointer over the hyperlink. A ScreenTip appears indicating that the link will jump to a document named Resume.doc.

2. Right-click the **resume** hyperlink. A shortcut menu opens.

3. Click **Edit Hyperlink** in the shortcut menu. The Edit Hyperlink dialog box opens.

4. Verify that the Existing File or Web Page option is selected under "Link to."

5. If necessary, use the **Look in** list arrow to open the Tutorial folder for Tutorial 7.

6. Click **Resume Web Page** in the file list, and then click the **OK** button. You return to the proposal Web page.

7. Place the mouse pointer over the resume hyperlink. A ScreenTip appears, indicating that the link will now jump to a Web page named "Resume Web Page.htm."

8. Save your work.

The edited hyperlink in the proposal Web page correctly targets the Resume Web page. You're now ready to view the finished Web pages in a Web browser and to test the hyperlinks.

Viewing the Web Page in a Web Browser

While you're editing a Web page in Word, the document window shows how the document will look when viewed from a Web browser. However, it's always a good idea to view your Web pages with a Web browser to see exactly how they will look. This can help you discover unexpected formatting problems that you might not notice otherwise.

To view the Web page in a Web browser and test the links:

1. Click **File** on the menu bar, and then click **Web Page Preview**. Word opens your default Web browser and displays the Grant Proposal in its document window. See Figure 7-34. Regardless of your type of browser, your view of the Grant Proposal Web page should be similar to Figure 7-34. Maximize the browser window, if necessary.

Figure 7-34	PROPOSAL DISPLAYED IN BROWSER WINDOW

Internet Explorer title bar

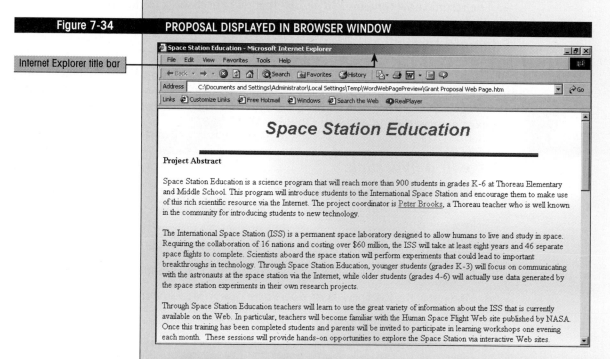

TROUBLE? If a message informs you that Internet Explorer is not your default browser and asks you if you want to make it your browser, click the No button.

2. Scroll through the document so you can see how it looks in the browser. (If you notice any formatting problems at this point, you will have to close the browser window, edit the document in Word, save your changes, and then preview it in the browser again). Next, you should check the hyperlinks to make sure they work properly. In a browser, you don't have to press the Ctrl key to use a hyperlink. Instead, you simply click the link.

3. Move the insertion point to the beginning of the document, and click the **Peter Brooks** hyperlink. The heading "Project Coordinator" is displayed in the browser window.

4. Click the **resume** hyperlink in the last paragraph of the document. The browser opens the Resume Web page.

5. Scroll through the document to view it. Notice that when you view the resume in the browser, the table format disappears and Peter's address information is

left-aligned. In this case, the format is still acceptable, so you don't have to make any additional changes in Word.

6. Click the **Grant Proposal** hyperlink. The browser now returns to the proposal Web page.

TROUBLE? If any of the hyperlinks don't work properly, edit them so they link to the proper document.

7. Close the browser window. You return to the grant proposal in the Word window.

8. If necessary, press **Ctrl+End** to move the insertion point to the bottom of the Web page, press **Enter** twice, and insert the text **Prepared by** followed by your first and last name.

9. Print the document, save, and close the proposal. The printed Web page looks similar, but not identical, to the printed Word document.

You have now finished preparing two Web pages, the proposal and the resume, for online viewing. The Grant Proposal Web page contains an embedded Excel worksheet, as well as a linked Excel chart. As long as you keep the Excel file "Copy of Chart" and the Web page file "Grant Proposal Web Page" in the same folder (the Tutorial subfolder in the Tutorial.07 folder) the links between the two should be maintained.

In this tutorial you have integrated Word with two other programs—Excel and a browser. In doing so, you were able to progress far beyond simple word-processed text. In the Review Assignments and Case problems at the end of this tutorial, you will use other programs and features of Word to produce even more advanced documents. Among other things, you will create your own diagrams, charts, and graphics.

Session 7.3 QUICK CHECK

1. True or False: A Web page is the same thing as an HTML document.

2. Name two types of document formatting that will not survive the conversion to a Web page.

3. True or False: After you convert a Word document to a Web page, you need to re-create all hypertext links.

4. Explain how to insert a horizontal line into a Web page. What is the purpose of such a line?

5. List the various tasks you should perform after converting a Word document into a Web page.

6. Describe the steps necessary to preview a Web page in your default Web browser.

REVIEW ASSIGNMENTS

Nalani's grant proposal for the Space Station Education program was accepted. The school received the grant and the program was extremely successful. Now Nalani needs to submit a program evaluation report to the U.S. Department of Education, the agency that provided the funding. Nalani wrote the body of the report in Word, and then e-mailed it to Tom Jenkins and Karen Goldberg for their comments. Both Tom and Karen returned edited copies of the report document, and now Nalani wants you to merge their files with her original report document. She also wants you to embed a worksheet of actual budget figures and then link a graph illustrating ratings from student evaluation forms. Next, she wants you to create an online version of the report that she can e-mail back to Tom and Karen. This online version will include some hyperlinks. Finally, she asks you to save the report as a Web page for publication on the World Wide Web, and add a hyperlink to NASA's Human Space Flight Web site.

1. Verify that you have copied the Tutorial.07 folder to your hard drive.

2. Make sure that Word is running, and open the file named **Report** from the Review folder for Tutorial7.

3. Merge the Report document with Karen's edited copy (named **KGReport**). Merge these two documents to a new document. Then merge the new document with Tom's edited copy (named **TJReport**). Save the new document as **Evaluation Report** in the Review folder for Tutorial 7, and then close the original Report document without saving any changes.

4. Review all the edits in the Evaluation Report document, and read all the comments. If necessary, display the Reviewing toolbar.

5. Delete all the comments in the document, accept Karen's three edits (the insertion of "while", the insertion of "orbit around the earth", and the deletion of "space), and then reject Tom's three changes in the sentence that begins "Program volunteers participated in…" The end of the sentence should read "the Human Space Flight Web site published by NASA." Accept all remaining changes in the document, and then save your work.

Explore ▶ 6. Click Tools on the menu bar and then click Options. Click the User Information tab. Note the name in the Name box is the name that would appear in the revision mark ScreenTips if you used this computer to edit a document. Click Cancel to close the Options dialog box. Switch to Header and Footer view, click along the left margin of the Footer section, click Insert on the menu bar, click Field, in the Field Name list box scroll down and click User Name. The name you saw in the Options dialog box is inserted in the footer as field. If this is not your name, type a forward slash (/) to the right of the field and then type your own name. Use the Format Page Number button on the Header and Footer toolbar to make the page number field begin at 1 rather than 2, and then close Header and Footer view.

7. Delete the placeholder [Insert Excel chart], verify that the insertion point is positioned on a blank line between two paragraphs of text, and embed the Excel file named **EvalCht**. Use the Object command on the Format menu to reduce the chart's height and width to 30%, and then wrap text to the right of the chart, using the Square wrapping option (with the Left horizontal alignment option). Click at the beginning of the paragraph that begins "Space Station Education also gave sixth graders…" and insert a page break to move the chart and the related text to page 3. Nalani will eventually add more text to the first page, so you don't have to be concerned about the blank space at the bottom of page 1. Save your work.

8. Delete the placeholder [Insert Excel worksheet], verify that the insertion point is positioned on a blank line between two blank lines, and insert a linked copy of the workbook named **FinlBgt**. Remember to make a copy of the Excel file, so that the Excel file you actually link to the Word document is named **Copy of FinlBgt**. Also remember to click the Link to file check box to select it. Review the worksheet in the Word document, and notice that the figure for Computer rental and setup is 4.00. Center the worksheet in the page, save your work, and then close the Evaluation Report document.

9. Start Excel, open the workbook named **Copy of FinlBgt** from the Review subfolder in the Tutorial.07 folder, click cell B2 (the cell containing the number "4.00"), type 4000, press Enter, click the Save button on the Standard toolbar, and then close Excel. Open the Evaluation Report document in Word, and verify that the Computer rental and setup figure has been updated to $4,000. If it has not been updated automatically, right-click the worksheet, and then click Update Link in the shortcut menu. Save your work.

10. Print the proposal document.

11. Switch to Web Layout view, display the Web toolbar, if necessary, and then review the proposal and note any problems with text wrapping around the chart. You'll fix any text-wrapping problems later, when you save the proposal as a Web page.

12. Near the end of the document, select the phrase "Peter was assisted" and insert a bookmark named "Volunteers." In the paragraph following the "Introduction" heading, format the phrase "Five teachers" as a hyperlink that targets the Volunteers bookmark. Test the hyperlink to make sure it works.

Explore ▶ 13. In documents that have been formatted using Word's default heading styles (Heading 1, Heading 2, and Heading 3), you can create hyperlinks that target specific headings. To try this now, select the phrase "International Space Station" in the paragraph under the "Introduction" heading, click the Insert Hyperlink button, click Place in This Document, and then review the list of headings in the Insert Hyperlink dialog box. (If you can't see the document headings, click the plus sign next to Headings.) Click "What is the International Space Station?" and then click OK. In the document window, test the International Space Station hyperlink to make sure it jumps to the heading "What is the International Space Station?"

Explore ▶ 14. In addition to using hyperlinks to move from one part of a document to another, you can use Word's Document Map feature. This feature is available in Normal, Page Layout, and Web Layout view. To learn how use the Document Map, click the Document Map button on the Standard toolbar. A Document Map window opens on the left side of the document window. Click Budget in the Document Map window to move the insertion point to the Budget section. Practice using the Document Map to move the insertion point to other sections of the document. Click the Document Map button again to close the Document Map window.

15. Format the report with a two-color gradient background, with pink as Color 1, and lavender as Color 2. Use the Horizontal shading style. Format the title and subtitle with animated text, using the Marching Black Ants animation style.

16. Switch to Print Layout view. Notice that the colored background is no longer visible. Switch back to Web Layout view and save your work.

17. Save the report as a Web page in the Review folder for Tutorial 7, using the name **Evaluation Report Web Page**.

18. Adjust the position of the Excel chart to make the text wrap around it properly. Make

sure the "Curriculum Objectives" heading is aligned on the left margin, below the chart.

19. Insert a horizontal line of your choice before each section heading (including the "Introduction" heading). Format the title, subtitle, and section headings using a font color of your choice. Save your work.

Explore
20. In the tutorial you inserted a hyperlink to another document stored on your computer. You can also insert hyperlinks to Internet Web sites. To learn how, use the Find command on the Edit menu to select the word "NASA," and then click the Insert Hyperlink button on the Standard toolbar. Click Existing File or Web Page, click in the Address text box, type "www.nasa.gov", and then click OK. Next, test the link. If your computer is already connected to the Internet, the NASA Web page will open in your browser. If your computer is not connected, your computer may attempt to connect and display the NASA Web page. (If necessary, click Connect in the Dial-up Connection dialog box.) If your computer cannot establish a connection, the browser might open and display a message indicating that the specified Web page could not be found. Close your browser and any dialog boxes. Save your changes to the report Web page.

21. Use the Web Page Preview command to view the report in your Web browser. Fix any formatting problems and test all the hyperlinks. (Don't test the NASA link if it didn't work for you earlier.)

22. Right-click the Start button, click Explore, and then use Windows Explorer to display the contents of the Evaluation Report Web Page_files folder (which you'll find in the Review folder for Tutorial 7). How many files does this folder contain? What is their total size? What size is the Evaluation Report Web Page file, in the Review folder?

23. Close your browser, save any changes to the report Web page, and then close Word.

24. Use your e-mail program to send the Evaluation Report Word document to a fellow student. In most e-mail programs, you need to create a new message, and then attach the file to the message. Ask the recipient of the file to open it, display it in Web Layout view, and test the various links. Can he or she access the source file for the Excel workbook? Why or why not? Do the other links in the document work? Why or why not?

Explore
25. Close all open files and programs.

CASE PROBLEMS

Case 1. Office Location for Vista Insurance Company Steven Woodhouse works for the Vista Insurance Company, a new, rapidly growing company. Emma Knightly, vice president of operations for the company, has proposed that Vista open a new downtown office, and has assigned Steven the responsibility of finding a good location. Steven has contacted local real estate agencies through the World Wide Web, and he has located an available office building that seems satisfactory. He has downloaded an image of the office building and asks you to prepare a memo to Emma describing the office site. He'd like you to include the image in the memo. When you've finished, he requests that you e-mail the memo to Emma for online viewing. Emma won't be viewing the memo in her browser; she'll just open it directly in Word.

1. If necessary, start Word. Open the file **Office** from the Cases folder for Tutorial 7 and then save it to the same folder as **Office Rental Memo**.

2. In the From: section of the memo, replace "Steve Woodhouse" with your name.

3. After the third paragraph, delete the bracketed phrase "[insert chart]," and embed the workbook called **Rates** from the Cases folder for Tutorial 7.

4. Reduce the size of the chart to 40% of its original size, and center it between the left and right margins.

5. Double-click the chart to display the Excel tools. Click the chart title, click before the "R" in "Rental," type "Monthly", and then press the spacebar so that the title reads "Monthly Rental Rates ($)." Click outside the chart to return to the Word menu and toolbars.

6. Click in the blank line above the heading "Interoffice Memo" and then insert "Vista Insurance" as a piece of WordArt, using the WordArt style with green letters and a shadow. Center the WordArt Logo.

7. Format the document with a solid, light green background. (*Hint:* Click Format on the menu bar, point to Background, then click the light green tile on the color palette.) Notice how Word switched automatically to Web Layout view, when you added the green background. Preview the Office Rental Memo document in Web Layout view, and note any problems with the formatting. Save your work.

8. Open the document named **Downtn** from the Cases folder for Tutorial 7, save it as **Downtown Development** in the Cases folder for Tutorial 7, switch to Web Layout view, and then format the document using the same background you used for the memo. Remove any SmartTags in the document, save your work, and close the document. (*Note:* that SmartTags can adversely affect the formatting when a Web page is viewed in a browser. For example, text with a SmartTag attached might appear on a white background, even though the rest of the document has a green background.)

9. In the Office Rental memo, in the paragraph above the photograph, just after the sentence that ends with "…in the heart of the downtown business district," insert the following text: See New Development Projects in the Downtown Area for a list of new renovations. Make "New Development Projects in the Downtown Area" a hyperlink, targeting the **Downtown Development** file in the Cases folder for Tutorial 7.

10. Test the hyperlink in the memo. When the Downtown Development document opens, insert a hyperlink at the end that takes users back to the memo. Test this new hyperlink.

11. Test all the links in the two documents one last time, and then close the Downtown Development document, saving your work, if necessary.

12. Print the Office Rental Memo document while it is displayed in Web Layout view. Save your work and close the document.

13. Use your e-mail program to send the Office Rental Memo document to a fellow student. (If you prefer, send the file to yourself.) In most e-mail programs, you need to create a new message, and then attach the file to the message. Ask the recipient of the file to open it, display it in Web Layout view, and test the various links. Do all the links in the document work? Why or why not?

Case 2. Mountain Time Web Page Sophie Kurtz is a marketing manager for Mountain Time Inc., a company that offers guided tours to many popular tourist sites in the western United States. She recently prepared a flyer describing upcoming tours to selected western national parks. She asks you to help finish the project, and then convert it to a Web page so she can post it on the company's Web site and make it available to prospective tourists.

1. If necessary, start Word. Open the file **Parks** from the Cases folder for Tutorial 7, and then save it as **Mountain Time Parks Tour** in the same folder.

2. Position the photograph of the arch against the left margin, wrap text around it, and enlarge it so that the entire second paragraph wraps to the right of the photo.

Explore
3. In this tutorial you learned how to link and embed objects using the Object command on the Insert menu. If you prefer, you can also link or embed an object by copying it to the Clipboard, and then pasting it into the destination file using the Paste Special command on the Edit menu. To experiment using Paste Special now, press Ctrl+End to move the insertion point to the last line of the document, start Excel, and open the workbook named **TourInf** from the Cases folder for Tutorial 7. Click cell A1, and then drag down and to the right to cell E7. The worksheet data should now be selected. Click the Copy button on the Excel toolbar, click the Microsoft Word button on the taskbar, click Edit on the menu bar, and then click Paste Special. The Paste Special dialog box allows you to paste objects from the Clipboard in a variety of formats, including HTML, unformatted text, and formatted text. To embed the entire workbook, you could select the Microsoft Excel Worksheet Object option. To link the worksheet to the Word document, you could select the Paste link option button. In this case, you will experiment with pasting the worksheet data as formatted text. Click the Formatted Text (RTF) option in the As list box, verify that the Paste option button is selected, and then click OK. The worksheet is inserted into the document as a Word table.

4. If the Cost/person column is truncated by the right margin, move the mouse pointer over the table to display the Table move handle in the upper-left of the table, click the Table move handle, and then drag the entire table slightly left until you can see the entire Cost/person column. Add the heading "Accommodations" to the second-to-last column on the right. Delete the first row containing the text "Western Tours." Adjust column widths as necessary to make the table span the width of the current margins. Format the new table as necessary to make it attractive and easy to read.

Explore

5. When creating Web pages and online documents, you sometimes might need to create simple graphics. To learn how, open the Paint program from the Accessories submenu on the Start menu. Click Image on the menu bar, click Attributes, and then change the Width settings to 200 and the height setting to 50. Click View on the menu bar, point to Zoom, click Custom, click the 200% option button, and then click OK. Use the Brush button on the toolbar to draw some mountain peaks with a sun overhead. (If you don't like your first attempt, use the Erase button to erase your work.) Don't expect to produce a perfect work of art; your goal is just to get familiar with using Paint. Use the Rectangle tool to draw a rectangle the same size as the image, and then use the Fill tool to fill the rectangle with a lavender color. You also might need to click inside some of the shapes you drew to fill them with color. (*Hint:* Use the Undo command on the Edit menu to reverse any mistakes. Use the Magnifier tool to zoom in on the image, if necessary, to make it easier to edit.) Save the logo as a 24-bit bitmap file named **Logo** in the Cases folder for Tutorial 7, and then close Paint.

6. Insert a linked copy of the logo at the top of the Mountain Time Tours document, and then save your work. Open Paint, open the Logo file, change the background color to yellow, save your work, and then close Paint. Right-click the logo in the Word document, and then click Update Link to change the logo background to yellow.

7. At the bottom of the document type "Prepared by:" followed by your first and last name.

8. Save and print the document.

9. Switch to Web Layout view, and note any formatting problems.

10. Save the document as a Web page with the name **Mountain Time Parks Tour Web Page**. Adjust the placement of text and graphics as necessary. You might want to reduce the size of the photograph so that it doesn't extend below the two paragraphs of text. Add an appropriate background color, and one or two horizontal lines.

11. Open the file named **Comment** from the Cases folder for Tutorial 7, save it as a Web page named **Comment Web Page** in the Cases folder for Tutorial 7, format it to match the tour Web page, and then save and close the Comment Web Page. At the bottom of the tour Web page, insert the following text: "Click here to read comments about last year's tour!" Format this new text as a hyperlink that targets the file named **Comment Web Page**.

12. Place a hyperlink at the bottom of the Comment Web Page that takes the user back to the tour Web page. Test both links, save both files, and then close the Comment Web Page file.

13. Preview the Mountain Time Parks Tour Web Page in your browser. Fix any formatting problems in Word and test all links. (If your Web pages contain any SmartTags, you might want to delete them in Word, save your changes, and then preview the Web page in your browser again.) If you see the File Download dialog box when you click a link, click Open this file from its current location, and then click OK.

14. Print both Web pages from your browser, close your browser, and then close any open documents in Word and Excel, saving changes as necessary. Close Excel if it is still open.

Case 3. Bayside Health Web Page Susan Dague, publications director at Bayside Health Inc., is often asked to develop newsletters on a variety of topics related to health and fitness. To broaden the audience for these newsletters, she wants to transform them into Web pages and allow clients to read them over the World Wide Web. Susan asks you to open a blank Web page in Word, and then use it to create a Health News home page.

Explore

1. Click File on the menu bar, click New, and then click Blank Web Page in the New Document Task Pane. A blank document opens, similar to a regular Word document.

2. Save the Web page in the Cases folder for Tutorial 7 as **Health News Home Page**.

3. Type "Bayside Health Inc." and press Enter twice. Type "Welcome to Our Health News Home Page" and press Enter twice. Type "Our Health News reports give you quick updates on these important topics:" and press Enter twice. Click the Bullets button ▤ in the Formatting toolbar, and then type the following list:
   - Exercise
   - Pain management
   - Low-fat cooking

4. Select the heading "Bayside Health Inc." and the subheading "Welcome to our Health News Home Page," and then format them in 26-point Arial with a red font color. Finally, center the heading and subheading.

Explore

5. Now that you have formatted the text, you can transform the look of the Web page itself by selecting a collection of formatting options known as a theme. Click Format on the menu bar, and then click Theme to open the Theme dialog box. In the Choose a Theme list box, click Blends. If you see a message indicating that the Blends theme is not installed on your computer, select another theme. Otherwise, click OK. Save your work.

6. Open the document named **Exercise** in the Cases folder for Tutorial 7, and then display the document in Print Layout view, zoomed to Whole Page. Review the document's format, and then switch to Web Layout view. The two-column portion of the document changes to a single column and the border is hidden. The graphic (which was originally near the end of the document, in the bottom of the right column) moves to the top of the second section, under the heading "Excessive Hype over Exercise Type."

7. Save the document as a Web page named **Exercise Web Page**.

8. Drag the graphic down to position it in the paragraph below the heading "Stress on Stress Management." Format the Exercise Web Page using the Blends theme you used earlier for the home page. (You might have to re-format the list of exercise guidelines with bullets after you apply the Blends theme.) Also, delete the WordArt headline, and then format the "Excessive Hype over Exercise" heading and the "Stress on Stress Management" heading to match the main heading in the Health News home page.

9. Insert a hyperlink at the bottom of the page that returns the user to the Health News home page. Save and close the Exercise Web Page, and display the Health News home page.

10. Select the text "Exercise" in the first bullet, and format it as a hyperlink that targets the file named **Exercise Web Page**. Test the hyperlinks in both pages, and then close the Exercise Web Page file.

11. Preview the Health News Home page in your browser, review the formatting, and check all links.

12. Correct any problems in Word, save your work, and then close your browser and any open documents.

Case 4. *Financial Aid FAQ Page* Your local high school recently sponsored a workshop for parents of prospective college students. The goal of the workshop was to teach parents how to apply for financial aid. Now the program coordinator wants to provide some follow-up information on the Web. She asks you to create a FAQ (Frequently Asked Questions) page that answers questions raised at the seminar. In addition to the FAQ page, she asks you to create a Web page summarizing the cost of going to college. You will use a Word template to begin creating the FAQ page. Finally, she wants you to create a diagram illustrating the process of applying for financial aid, and which she can use as a handout in future workshops.

1. Click File on the menu bar, click New, and then click General Templates in the New Document Task Pane. In the Templates dialog box, click the Web Pages tab, click Frequently Asked Questions, and then click OK. A FAQ template opens, with placeholder text for questions and answers and a table of contents at the top. The document headings are already formatted as hyperlinks, as is the text "Back to top" which appears after each answer placeholder.

2. Save the template as a Word document named **Financial Aid FAQ** in the Cases folder for Tutorial 7.

3. Delete the ellipses in the heading "How do I...?", press the spacebar, and then type "apply for financial aid". When you are finished, the heading should read "How do I apply for financial aid?" Edit the hyperlink "How do I...?" in the table of contents (at the top of the page) so that it also reads "How do I apply for financial aid?"

4. After the "How do I apply for financial aid?" heading, replace the placeholder "This is the answer to the question" with a few sentences explaining how to apply for financial aid. For example, you might say: "You need to fill out a financial aid form for each college to which you apply. Typically these forms request detailed income and tax information."

5. Edit the heading "Where can I find...?" so that it reads, "Where can I find the necessary forms?" Edit the hyperlink in the table of contents to match, and then insert an answer to this question.

6. Delete the placeholder questions and answers for the "Why doesn't...?" heading, the "Who is..." heading, and the "When is...?" heading. Delete the corresponding links in the table of contents, as well as the extra "Back to top" links.

7. Edit the heading "What is...?" so that it reads "What are the costs associated with a college education?" Edit the hyperlink in the table of contents to match, and then insert an answer to this question. The last sentence in the answer should read: "For more information, click here."

8. At the bottom of the page, replace the word "Date" with the current date, followed by your first and last name. Edit the title on the FAQ page so that it describes the page's content. Save your work.

Explore ▷ 9. If you need to create a chart quickly, and you don't have access to Microsoft Excel, you can use Word's chart feature. To learn how, click the New Web Page button on the Standard toolbar (this button appears in place of the New Document button when you are working on a Web page), click Insert on the menu bar, point to Picture, and then click Chart. In the Datasheet window, replace the row labels "East," "West," and "North" with three major college expenses. Replace the column labels (1st Qtr, and so on) with the labels 1st Yr, 2nd Yr, 3rd Yr, and 4th Yr. Replace the existing numbers with expense data for four years of college, and then click outside the chart window to embed the completed chart in the Web page.

10. Save the Web page as **College Expense Chart** in the Cases folder for Tutorial 7.

11. On the FAQ page, format the text "For more information, click here" as a hyperlink that targets the College Expense Chart page. Insert the text "Back to FAQ" at the bottom of the chart page, and format it as a link that targets the FAQ page.

Explore ▷ 12. Format the FAQ and the chart Web pages with a textured background, using an option on the Texture tab on the Fill Effects dialog box. Be sure to pick a texture that is light enough to make the text easy to read.

13. Finish formatting the Web pages using the techniques you learned in this tutorial. Remember to make the pages look similar. Increase the size of the chart to make it easy to read. Save your work.

14. Close the Chart page.

15. Preview the FAQ document in your browser, and test all the links, including the link to the chart. Test the link in the chart that jumps back to the FAQ. Adjust any formatting problems in Word, and then save your work.

16. Print both pages from the browser window.

17. Close your browser, and then close any open documents.

Explore ▷ 18. You can create a variety of diagrams in Word using the tools on the Drawing toolbar. To learn how, open a new, blank document, and save it as **Application Process** in the Cases folder for Tutorial7. Switch to Print Layout view and display the rulers. In the Help box on the right side of the menu bar, type diagram, press Enter, and then click About diagrams. Read all the information Help provides about creating diagrams (including flowcharts) in Word, and then close the Help window. Click the Drawing button on the Standard toolbar to display the Drawing toolbar. In the Drawing toolbar, click the Insert Diagram or Organization Chart button to open the Diagram Gallery dialog box. Click the middle option in the top row (Cycle Diagram), and then click OK. A diagram opens with placeholder text. Click the leftmost instance of "Click to add text," press Enter twice, and then type: "Estimate costs for upcoming school year." Replace the placeholder text on the rightmost side with "Apply for financial aid". (Use extra paragraph marks to center the text vertically.) Replace the bottom placeholder text with "Compare aid received with actual costs". In the Diagram toolbar, click the AutoFormat button, and then select a format that appeals to you. Preview your diagram, make any changes using Word's editing tools, then save and print your diagram.

LAB ASSIGNMENTS

**The Internet:
World Wide
Web**

This Lab Assignment is designed to accompany the interactive Course Lab called Internet World Wide Web. To start the Lab, click the Start button on the taskbar, point to Programs, point to Course Labs, point to New Perspectives Applications, and click Internet World Wide Web. If you do not see Course Labs on your Programs menu, ask your instructor or technical support person for help.

The Internet: World Wide Web

One of the most popular services on the Internet is the World Wide Web. This lab is a Web simulator that teaches you how to use Web browser software to find information. You can use this lab whether or not your school provides you with Internet access.

1. Click the Steps button to learn how to use Web browser software. As you proceed through the steps, answer all of the Quick Check questions that appear. After you complete the steps, you'll see a Quick Check summary report. Follow the instructions on the screen to print this report.

2. Click the Explore button. Use the Web browser to locate a weather map of the Caribbean Virgin Islands. What is its URL?

3. Enter the URL **http://www.atour.com**. A SCUBA diver named Wadson Lachouffe has been searching for the fabled treasure of Greybeard the pirate. A link from the Adventure Travel Web site leads to Wadson's Web page called "Hidden Treasure." Locate the Hidden Treasure page, and answer the following questions:
   a. What was the name of Greybeard's ship?
   b. What was Greybeard's favorite food?
   c. What does Wadson think happened to Greybeard's ship?

4. In the steps, you found a graphic of Jupiter from the photo archives of the Jet Propulsion Laboratory. In the Explore section of the lab, you can also find a graphic of Saturn. Suppose one of your friends wants a picture of Saturn for an astronomy report. Make a list of the blue underlined links your friend must click to find the Saturn graphic. Assume that your friend begins at the Web Trainer home page.

5. Jump back to the Adventure Travel Web site. Write a one-page description of the information at the site. Include the number of pages the site contains, and diagram the links it contains.

6. Chris Thomson, a student at UVI, has his own Web page. In Explore, look at the information Chris included on his page. Suppose you could create your own Web page. What would you include? Use word-processing software to design your own Web page. Make sure to indicate the graphics and links you would use.

QUICK | CHECK ANSWERS

Session 7.1

1. Open the original version of the document, click Tools on the menu bar, click Compare and Merge Documents, select the first edited copy of the document, click the Merge list arrow, and then click Merge into new document. Open the Compare and Merge dialog box again, select the second edited copy of the document, and this time select Merge into current document.

2. a. A source file is the file containing the original object.

   b. An object is an item such as a graphic image, clip art, a WordArt image, a chart, or a section of text that you can modify and move from one document to another.

   c. The source program is the program in which an object was originally created.

   d. A destination file is the file into which you want to insert an object.

3. With embedding, you place an object into a document and retain the ability to use the tools of the source program. With linking, you place a representation of an object into a document. With embedding, there is no connection maintained between the source file and the destination file; with linking there is.

4. Link a file whenever you have data that is likely to change over time, or if you are using data that is updated regularly by someone else.

5. To embed an existing workbook, click Insert on the menu bar, click Object, click the Create from File tab, select the file, click Insert, and then click OK without selecting the Link to file check box. To link an Excel chart, follow the same procedure, but select the Link to file check box.

6. To copy a file, right-click it, click Copy, and then press Ctrl+V.

7. To modify an embedded object from within the destination program, double-click the object, and then use the tools and menus of the source program.

8. false

Session 7.2

1. A hyperlink is a word, phrase, or graphic image that you can click to jump to another document or Web page.

2. A browser is a program designed to retrieve files from a Web server and display Web pages.

3. An intranet is a self-contained web-based network that is owned by a single organization. The Internet is a worldwide network incorporating many organizations. Part of the Internet, the World Wide Web is used to transfer Web pages between Web servers and browsers.

4. Insert a bookmark at the location you want the hyperlink to jump to. Select the text you want to format as a hyperlink, click the Insert Hyperlink button on the Standard toolbar, click Place in this Document, click the bookmark you want to link to, and then click the OK button.

5. "Executive Summary" (b) is an invalid bookmark name because it has a space.

6. A change in the color of hyperlink text indicates that the link has been used, or followed.

7. false

Session 7.3

1. true

2. text wrapping around graphics and animated text

3. false

4. Click Format on the menu bar, click Borders and Shading, click the Borders tab, click the Horizontal Line button, select a line style, and then click the OK button. A horizontal line separates sections of a document to make it easier to read and navigate.

5. After converting a Word document to a Web page, you should adjust the formatting to make it more suitable for online viewing and possibly add some special formatting features such as a background color, that are not always available in printed documents. In some cases, the original document might already contain special features, such as text wrapping, that don't translate to HTML. In that case, you might need to reapply the feature once the document has been saved as a Web page. At the very least, you will probably need to reposition graphics.

6. To preview a Web page in the default Web browser, click File on the menu bar, and then click Web Page Preview.

New Perspectives on

MICROSOFT®
WORD 2002

Read This Before You Begin

To the Student

Data Disks

To complete the Level III tutorials, Review Assignments, and Case Problems, you need five Data Disks. Your instructor will either provide you with the Data Disks or ask you to make your own. You will also need storage space on your computer's hard drive.

If you are making your own Data Disks, you will need **five** blank, formatted high-density disks. You will need to copy a set of files and/or folders from a file server, standalone computer, or the Web onto your disk. Your instructor will tell you which computer, drive letter, and folders contain the files you need. You could also download the files by going to www.course.com and following the instructions on the screen.

The information below shows you which folders go on your disks, so that you will have enough disk space to complete all the tutorials, Review Assignments, and Case Problems:

Data Disk 1

Write this on the disk label:
Data Disk 1: Word 2002 Tutorial 8

Put this folder on the disk:
Tutorial.08

Data Disk 2

Write this on the disk label:
Data Disk 2: Word 2002 Tutorial 9

Put this folder on the disk:
Tutorial.09

Data Disk 3

Write this on the disk label:
Data Disk 3: Word 2002 Tutorial 10 (Tutorial and Review)

Put these folders on the disk:
Tutorial.10\Tutorial and Tutorial.10\Review

Data Disk 4

Write this on the disk label:
Data Disk 4: Word 2002 Tutorial 10 (Cases)

Put this folder on the disk:
Tutorial.10\Cases

Data Disk 5

Write this on the disk label:
Data Disk 5: Word 2002 Additional Cases

Put this folder on the disk:
AddCases

When you begin each tutorial, be sure you are using the correct Data Disk (or that you have copied the necessary files to your hard drive). Refer to the "File Finder" chart at the back of this text for more detailed information on which files are used in which tutorials. See the inside front or inside back cover of this book for more information on Data Disk files, or ask your instructor or technical support person for assistance.

Using Your Own Computer

If you are going to work through this book using your own computer, you need:

- **Computer System** Microsoft Windows 98, NT, 2000 Professional, or higher must be installed on your computer. This book assumes you have installed Microsoft Word 2002 on your computer.

- **Data Disks** You will not be able to complete the tutorials or exercises in this book using your own computer until you have your Data Disks.

Visit Our World Wide Web Site

Additional materials designed especially for you are available on the World Wide Web.
Go to www.course.com/NewPerspectives.

To the Instructor

The Data Disk Files are available on the Instructor's Resource Kit for this title. Follow the instructions in the Help file on the CD-ROM to install the programs to your network or standalone computer. For information on creating Data Disks, see the "To the Student" section above.

You are granted a license to copy the Data Files to any computer or computer network used by students who have purchased this book.

OBJECTIVES

In this tutorial you will:

- Apply advanced features to a document template

- Define and modify styles within the document template

- Apply borders and shading to a paragraph

- Create, insert, and print AutoText entries

- Use Smart Tags

- Create a watermark

- Customize the toolbars

- Automate parts of a document using field codes

- Record, edit, and run macros

- Create and modify a chart using data from an Excel worksheet

CUSTOMIZING WORD AND AUTOMATING YOUR WORK

Automating a Magazine Article Query Letter

CASE

Home Business: Freelance Writing

In 1995, Armand Collier graduated from San Jose State University with a major in English and a minor in journalism. He then accepted a job as a technical writer at a San Jose software company. His dream, however, was to become a full-time freelance writer, combining his training as a writer with his hobbies of digital photography and travel. He began writing articles in the evenings and on weekends, first for newspapers and then for travel and photography magazines. By 2001, his freelance writing business had grown sufficiently for him to quit his day job and freelance full-time from his home office.

Armand's success as freelance writer depends on his receiving a steady flow of assignments from magazines, so he spends much of his time writing **queries**, which are article ideas he proposes to magazine editors. He asks you to help him create a document template he can use to prepare his queries. As you know, a **document template** is a blueprint for the text, graphics, and format of a document. First, you'll format the template and insert a graphic (Armand's business logo) into the template. You'll also add AutoText entries to the document template and learn about Smart Tags. Next, you'll modify the toolbars and add field codes to the template to automate much of the work of creating queries. Then you'll record macros, including an AutoNew macro, and attach them to the template. Finally, you'll use the document template to create a query to propose an article, "Photographing Peoples of Peru," for the magazine *Travel Photography*.

SESSION 8.1

In this session, you'll set up a document template, add graphics to it, and create and change styles within the template. You'll also apply a border and shading to a paragraph, and you'll create AutoText entries so you can quickly insert common phrases into a document. Finally, you'll learn how to use Smart Tags to manage your contact information.

Planning the Query Letter

The magazine query and its document template will follow the standard content, organization, style, and presentation that many freelance authors use.

Each query contains the following five sections:

- **Logo and contact information.** This appears at the top of the first page and includes Armand's full name, mailing address, phone number, e-mail address, and Web page URL.
- **Date, magazine name, and proposed article title.** This information appears just below Armand's logo and contact information.
- **Overview.** This section includes one attention-grabbing paragraph (the hook), which usually becomes the first paragraph in the printed magazine article. The second paragraph provides a rationale for the article.
- **Main points.** This section includes the information necessary to convince the magazine editor that the article will be interesting and well written.
- **Credentials.** This section contains a brief biography of Armand to let the magazine editor know that he's qualified to complete the proposed article.

Armand wants every query to be clear, direct, and succinct so magazine editors can read it quickly. Each query also must have an appealing layout to promote a positive image of Armand's experience and professionalism as a freelance writer.

Understanding Document Templates

The template you'll create for Armand will ensure that all queries include the same type of information in the same order with the same format. You already know how to use a template to apply styles to text.

In addition to styles, a document template can contain a variety of helpful features designed to streamline the process of creating a document. The following list describes some common template elements:

- Boilerplate text and graphics that you want to appear in every document created using the template
- AutoText that helps users quickly and accurately insert common words and phrases
- Custom toolbars, menus, and shortcut keys that contain the most frequently used commands
- Fields, which are special codes that insert information automatically
- Macros, which automate a series of keystrokes or mouse operations

You'll include most of these features in the document template you prepare for Armand. Figure 8-1 shows some of the template features that will appear in the printed document.

Figure 8-1	FEATURES OF QUERY DOCUMENT TEMPLATE

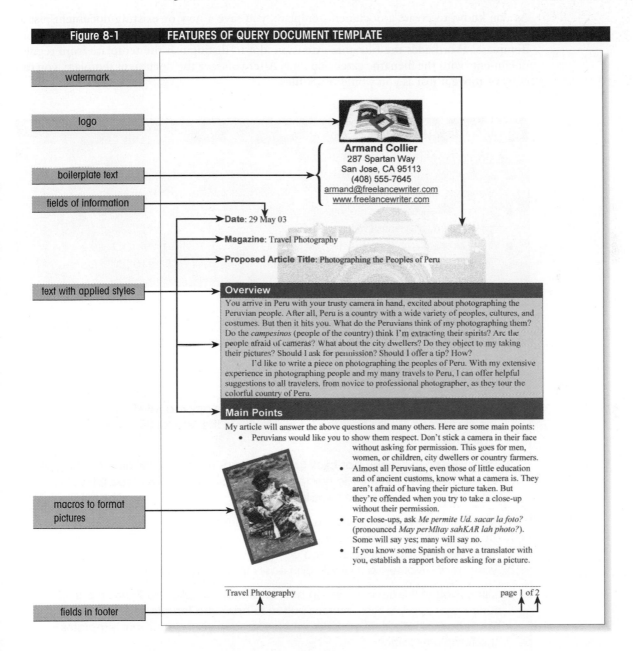

You can define document templates for many kinds of frequently used documents: proposals, invoices, fax cover sheets, reports, contracts, or any document for which you want to automate your work and maintain a consistent look and feel. Using a template to create a document has the following advantages:

- **Consistency.** All documents based on the template will have the same format.
- **Accuracy.** Including boilerplate text or graphics in a template helps prevent a user from introducing typos and other errors into the document.
- **Efficiency.** Customized toolbars, menus, shortcut keys, AutoText, and macros help simplify and automate the process of creating a document.

You'll begin creating Armand's template by adding graphics and boilerplate text.

Creating the Query Template

As you know, to create a document template, you save a new or existing document just as you would any other Word document, except that you change the file type to Document Template. Word adds the filename extension .dot to distinguish the template from regular documents with the filename extension .doc. After you save the document template, you can copy or move it just as you would other files.

REFERENCE   WINDOW   **RW**

<u>Creating a Document Template</u>
- Insert graphics and boilerplate text, format the document, create and modify styles, or make other changes to the document.
- Customize the toolbars, menus, and shortcut keys, record macros, create AutoText entries, and make other modifications to Word.
- Click File on the menu bar, click Save As, type the filename in the File name text box, click the Save as type list arrow, click Document Template, and then click the Save button.

Armand already typed some boilerplate text and applied some formatting changes he wants to include in the template. You'll save his document as a template file now.

To create the document template:

1. Start Word as usual, insert your Data Disk into the appropriate drive, and open the file named **Query** from the Tutorial folder in the Tutorial.08 folder on your Data Disk.

2. Click **File** on the menu bar, click **Save As** to open the Save As dialog box, type **Magazine Query** in the File name text box, click the **Save as type** list arrow, and then click **Document Template**.

   The default Templates folder on your computer's hard disk automatically opens in the Save in list box. You need to switch to the Tutorial.08 folder on your Data Disk instead. But before you do that, you'll add the Templates folder to your list of Favorites so that you can easily find it when you need it later.

3. Click **Tools** in the Save As dialog box, and then click **Add to Favorites**. In the future, you can use the Favorites button to open the Templates folder quickly. You'll do that later in this tutorial, when you save your document templates in the Templates folder.

   TROUBLE? If you see a dialog box indicating that you can't add the Templates folder to your favorites list, the Templates folder has already been added to your Favorites list. Click OK and continue with the next step.

4. Change the **Save in** list box to the Tutorial subfolder within the Tutorial.08 folder on your Data Disk, and then click the **Save** button in the Save As dialog box. The Magazine Query file is saved as a document template.

With a few exceptions, the Magazine Query template looks similar to the **Normal** template (also called the global template), which is the template you usually use when you start a new document. First, note that the Magazine Query template contains boilerplate text and graphics, whereas the Normal template is blank. Also, Armand made sure the Normal style is 12-point Times New Roman, and then modified the Heading 1 style to 14-point, bold Arial. He also set up the Heading 1 style to add 12 points before each paragraph formatted with this style and 3 points after each paragraph formatted with this style. Finally, he changed the text flow setting to "Keep with next" to prevent a heading from appearing alone at the bottom of the page; this setting ensures that a heading always appears with at least two lines of the paragraph that follows it. (To access the text flow settings and the Space Before and Space After settings, point to a style in the Styles and Formatting Task Pane, click the style's list arrow, click Modify in the drop-down list, click the Format button, and then click Paragraph.) Now you'll continue to add features to the template that will help automate the creation of query letters.

Inserting Graphics into a Document Template

Next you'll insert two graphics into the document template—Armand's logo at the beginning of the query template and a photograph of Armand near the end of the document. The logo and the photo are JPEG files (with the filename extension .jpg), which you can import into the template just as you would into a normal document.

To insert the graphics into the document template:

1. If necessary, switch to Print Layout View, make sure the nonprinting characters are displayed, and verify that the insertion point is centered in the blank line above Armand's name at the beginning of the document.

2. Click **Insert** on the menu bar, point to **Picture**, and then click **From File**. The Insert Picture dialog box opens.

3. Use the **Look in** list arrow to open the Tutorial subfolder for Tutorial 8 on your Data Disk, and then double-click **ACLogo**. Armand's logo appears at the top of the document template. Notice that because the insertion point was centered when you inserted the picture, the picture is automatically centered between the left and right margins.

   You'll resize the logo, maintaining the **aspect ratio**, which is the relative height and width of the picture. If the aspect ratio changes, the picture becomes too wide for its height or too tall for its width.

4. Click the logo to select it. The Picture toolbar appears.

   TROUBLE? If the Picture toolbar does not appear, right-click any toolbar and then click Picture.

5. Click the **Format Picture** button 🖼 on the Picture toolbar to open the Format Picture dialog box, click the **Size** tab, make sure the **Lock aspect ratio** and **Relative to original picture size** check boxes are selected, change the Height (in the Scale section) to **40%**. See Figure 8-2.

Figure 8-2   **FORMAT PICTURE DIALOG BOX AFTER SETTING SCALE TO 40%**

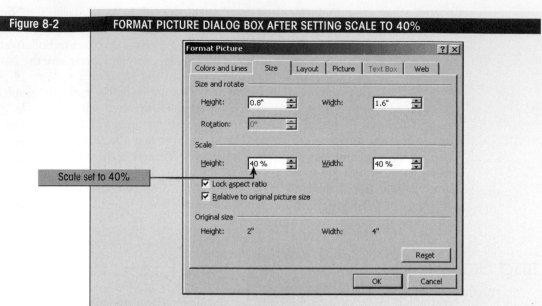

Scale set to 40%

6. Click the **OK** button to close the Format Picture dialog box. Deselect the picture by clicking anywhere else in the document window. See Figure 8–3.

Figure 8-3   **INSERTED AND RESIZED LOGO**

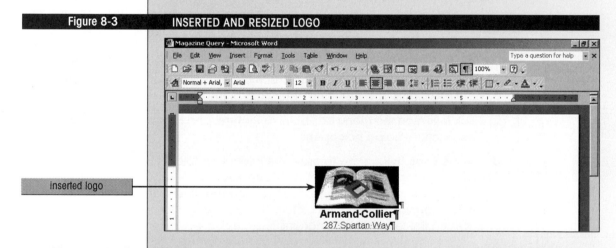

inserted logo

7. Move the insertion point to the beginning of the last paragraph in the query template, just below the Credentials heading, and insert the graphic file **Armand**. Now you'll resize the picture and wrap the text around it.

8. Select the picture of Armand, click [icon], click the **Size** tab, change the size of the picture so its height is **1.25** inches, click the **Layout** tab in the Format Picture dialog box, click the **Advanced** button in the lower-right corner of the dialog box, click the **Square** icon, click the **Right only** option button, and then click the **OK** button to close the Advanced Layout dialog box. Selecting the Right only option forces text to wrap around the graphic on its right side only.

9. Click the **OK** button to close the Format Picture dialog box, and then deselect the picture. See Figure 8–4.

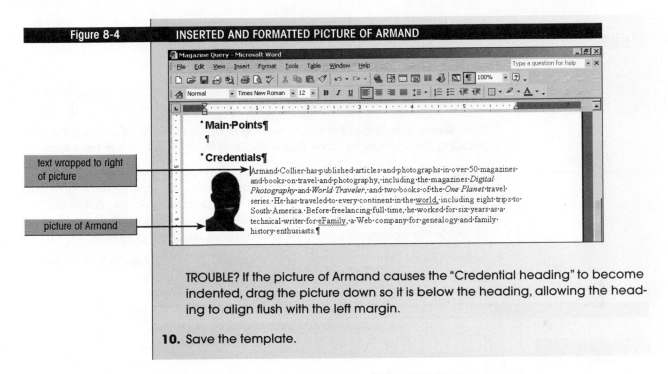

Figure 8-4 — INSERTED AND FORMATTED PICTURE OF ARMAND

text wrapped to right of picture

picture of Armand

TROUBLE? If the picture of Armand causes the "Credential heading" to become indented, drag the picture down so it is below the heading, allowing the heading to align flush with the left margin.

10. Save the template.

Now any document based on this template will contain Armand's logo and picture.

Creating and Modifying Styles in a Document Template

Armand wants you to create a new style and further modify the Heading 1 style in the query template. Both styles will be available in any document created from the template.

Defining and Applying a New Style

Currently, the query headings Date, Magazine, and Proposed Article Title are 12-point Times New Roman—the Normal style. You'll define and then use a new character style called Query Heading. Recall that a character style includes only character-level formats, such as font type and size, italic, or small caps. In this case, the character-level formats will be 12-point, blue, bold Arial.

To define the new style for query headings:

1. Click the **Styles and Formatting** button 🄰 on the Formatting toolbar to open the Styles and Formatting Task Pane.

2. Click the **New Style** button in the Task Pane to open the New Style dialog box.

3. Type **Query Heading** in the Name text box, click the **Style type** list arrow, and then click **Character**. The Style based on list box changes to Default Paragraph Font, and the Style for following paragraph list box becomes blank.

4. In the Formatting section of the dialog box, change the Font to **Arial**, the Font size to **12**, the Font style to **Bold**, and the Font color (using the **Font color** list arrow 🄰 ▾) to **Blue**. Notice that if you rest the mouse pointer on a color tile, a ScreenTip appears with the name of the color.

5. Click the **OK** button in the New Style dialog box.

Now you'll use the Query Heading style to format some text.

To apply the new style:

1. Select the heading **Date** (but not the colon that follows it), located just below Armand's contact information.

2. Click **Query Heading** in the Pick formatting to apply section of the Task Pane. The heading "Date" changes to the Query Heading style: 12-point, blue, bold Arial.

3. Select the heading **Magazine** (but not the colon), and then repeat Step 2 (or press the **F4** key to repeat the previous action). The Query Heading style is applied. Note that if Query Heading was a paragraph style, the colon also would change to 12-point, blue, bold Arial because paragraph styles affect all text in the paragraph, whereas character styles affect only selected text.

4. Apply the Query Heading style to the heading **Proposed Article Title** (but not the colon), and then deselect any selected text. See Figure 8–5.

Figure 8-5	APPLIED CHARACTER STYLE

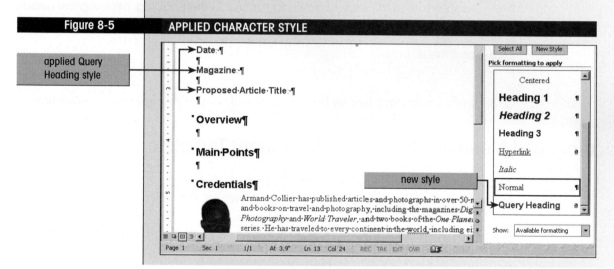

The newly formatted text is now part of the template, and will be included in any document based on this template. The Query Heading style is also part of the template, and can be used to format other text.

Applying Borders and Shading with a Style

You'll now create another style, called Key Paragraph. This will be a paragraph style that emphasizes a particular paragraph, such as the Overview paragraph near the beginning of the query. This time you'll create the style by example.

To create a new style by example:

1. Position the ⌔ pointer to the left of the blank line located below the "Overview" heading and click. This selects the entire paragraph, which currently contains no text. Now you will apply borders and shading, which will appear around any text you type in the paragraph.

2. Click **Format** on the menu bar, click **Borders and Shading** to open the Borders and Shading dialog box, and, if necessary, click the **Borders** tab.

3. Click the **Box** icon in the Setting section of the dialog box. This places a box (or a border) around the paragraph.

4. Click the **Shading** tab, and then click the **Yellow** tile located in the seventh row down, third column from the left, in the grid of color tiles. This creates a yellow shaded background for the paragraph.

5. Click the **OK** button in the Borders and Shading dialog box to return to the document, and then deselect the paragraph. See Figure 8–6.

| Figure 8-6 | CREATING A NEW PARAGRAPH STYLE |

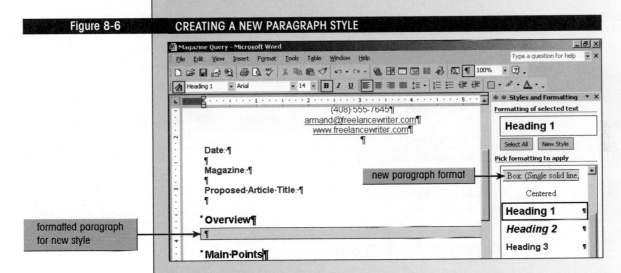

Now you're ready to create a style based on the formatting of this paragraph.

6. Select the **paragraph** below the Overview heading again, and click the **New Style** button in the Task Pane. The New Style dialog box opens.

   TROUBLE? If the Styles and Formatting Task Pane isn't open, click the Styles and Formatting button 🅰 on the Formatting toolbar.

7. Name the style **Key Paragraph**. Leave the Style type set to Paragraph. You don't need to change any formatting because all the new formatting features appear in the Description section of the New Style dialog box. Within the New Style dialog box, make sure the **Add to template** check box is unchecked, and check the **Automatically update** check box to select it. This tells Word that if you change the format of any paragraph in the Key Paragraph style, the change will appear in all paragraphs with that style applied.

8. Click the **OK** button in the New Style dialog box. The New Style dialog box closes, and you return to the document window. The new style appears in the Style and Formatting Task Pane, as shown in Figure 8–7.

Figure 8-7   KEY PARAGRAPH STYLE

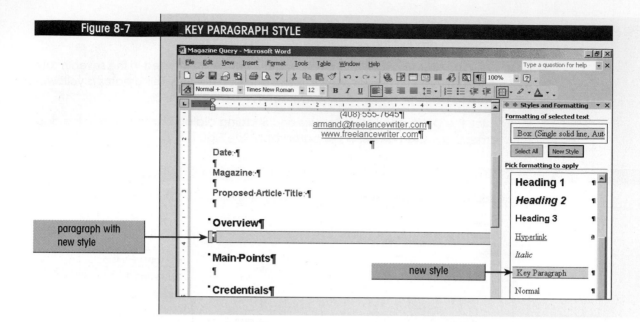

paragraph with new style

new style

You can use the new style you just created to highlight any key paragraph in the query document.

Modifying an Existing Style

Next Armand wants you to add borders and shading to the Heading 1 style. You decide to place a box border around the heading, fill the box with blue, and make the text white so it stands out.

To modify the Heading 1 style:

1. Point to the **Heading 1** style in the Task Pane to display the Heading 1 list arrow, click the **Heading 1** list arrow, and then click **Modify**. The Modify Style dialog box opens.

   TROUBLE? If you clicked the Heading 1 style rather than its list arrow, click the Undo button 🔄 on the Standard toolbar to remove the Heading 1 style, and then carefully repeat Step 1.

2. Click the **Format** button, and then click **Border**. The Borders and Shading dialog box opens.

3. Using the procedure you learned earlier, change the border setting to **Box** and the shading to **Blue** (fifth row down, sixth column from the left).

4. Click the **OK** button to close the Borders and Shading dialog box. You return to the Modify Style dialog box. Next you'll change the font color to white so that the heading appears as white text on a blue background.

5. Click the **Font Color** list arrow ⚏▾, and then click the **White** color tile.

6. Click the **OK** button in the Modify Style dialog box. Word applies the new formatting to any existing Heading 1 text, and all the headings change to white text on a blue background, as shown in Figure 8–8.

Figure 8-8   **HEADING 1 STYLE AFTER MODIFICATIONS**

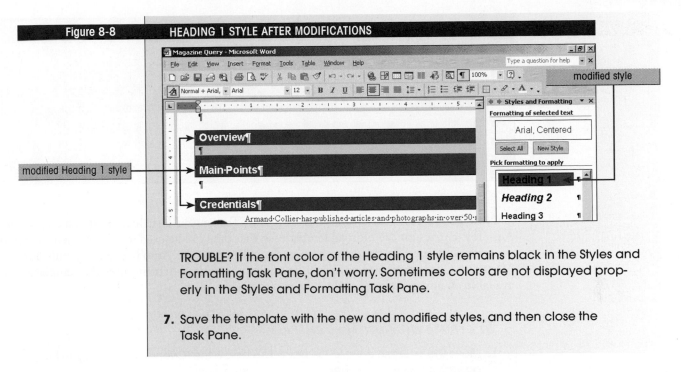

> **TROUBLE?** If the font color of the Heading 1 style remains black in the Styles and Formatting Task Pane, don't worry. Sometimes colors are not displayed properly in the Styles and Formatting Task Pane.

7. Save the template with the new and modified styles, and then close the Task Pane.

You're now ready to begin automating the template by creating AutoText entries.

Automating Word with AutoText

AutoText enables you to insert frequently used text (such as a phrase or blocks of text) or graphics (such as a drawing or scanned photograph) into your documents quickly and efficiently, with just a few keystrokes or mouse clicks. For example, you might make your signature block for a letter (Sincerely, four blank lines, your name, and title) an AutoText entry so you can instantly insert that text; or, you might create an AutoText entry that is a company name and a sized logo.

Two advantages of AutoText are its speed and accuracy. After you create an error-free AutoText entry, you can easily insert it into documents. This is especially valuable for difficult-to-type text such as phone numbers, serial numbers, e-mail addresses, or other words and numbers not in the Word dictionary. Furthermore, Word provides a useful set of default AutoText entries for inserting common phrases, such as "Sincerely Yours," "CONFIDENTIAL," and "Dear Sir or Madam."

Creating AutoText Entries

In the query template, you'll create AutoText entries for phrases that Armand uses frequently: digital photography, digital darkroom, and image editing software.

REFERENCE WINDOW **RW**

<u>Creating an AutoText Entry</u>
- Select the text or graphics you want to be an AutoText entry.
- Click Insert on the menu bar, point to AutoText, and then click AutoText. (Clicking New adds the entry to the default template, usually Normal.dot, and not necessarily to the template you're creating.)
- Click the Look in list arrow, and select the template to which you want the AutoText attached.
- Type a new name (an abbreviation) for the AutoText entry.
- Click the Add button.

Now you're ready to create your own AutoText entry. Usually, you'll want to create AutoText entries for the Normal template, so that they can be used in all documents created on your computer. In this case, however, you'll create the AutoText entries only for the Magazine Query template, so they'll be available any time Armand uses the template, and available on any computer to which he copies the template.

To create an AutoText entry:

1. Move the insertion point to the blank line below the "Overview" heading, in the paragraph with the border and yellow background.

2. Type **With digital photography** (no ending punctuation). Correct any misspelled words.

3. Select the phrase **digital photography**, but don't select the end-of-paragraph symbol. Remember that any text you select, including typos, spaces, and symbols, will be included in the AutoText entry.

4. Click **Insert** on the menu bar, point to **AutoText**, and then click **AutoText** to open the AutoCorrect dialog box with the AutoText tab selected. Click the **Look in** list arrow, and then click **Magazine Query (template)**. This ensures that the AutoText is attached to the current template and not to the Normal template.

   Next you'll type a new name for the AutoText entry. Select a short abbreviation so you can insert the AutoText entry into your document by typing only a few letters.

5. If necessary, click the **Enter AutoText entries here** text box, and then type **dp** as the abbreviation for "digital photography." See Figure 8-9.

Figure 8-9	CREATING A NEW AUTOTEXT ENTRY

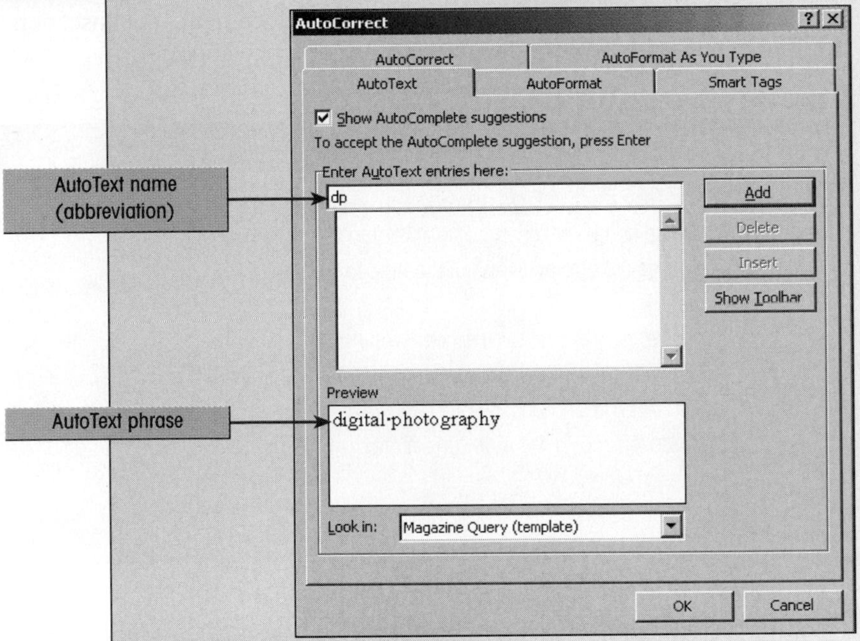

6. Click the **Add** button in the AutoCorrect dialog box. The AutoCorrect dialog box closes and your new entry is added to Word's list of AutoCorrect entries.

Now Armand can use AutoText to insert the phrase "digital photography" into any query document. After you create two more AutoText entries, you'll test them to see how easy they are to use.

To create additional AutoText entries:

1. With "digital photography" still selected, type **digital darkroom** to replace the selected text.

2. Select **digital darkroom**, but not the end-of-paragraph symbol.

3. Click **Insert** on the menu bar, point to **AutoText**, click **AutoText**, type the abbreviation **dd**, and then click the **Add** button. You didn't have to change the Look in list box because you already set the default template to Magazine Query.

4. Repeat Steps 1 through 3, only this time type **image editing software**, and use the abbreviation **ies** in the AutoCorrect dialog box.

5. Use the Backspace key to delete all the text in the current paragraph, but leave a blank line so you can see the end-of-paragraph symbol and the yellow background. (You must delete the text so it doesn't become boilerplate in the template.)

6. Save the template.

You can add as many AutoText entries to a template as you like, but for now you'll work with these three entries.

Inserting an AutoText Entry into a Document

When you use AutoText to insert text into a document, the insertion point should be located exactly where you want the AutoText entry to appear.

REFERENCE   WINDOW   **RW**

<u>Inserting AutoText into a Document</u>
- Move the insertion point to where you want to insert the entry.
- Type the name (or abbreviation) of the AutoText entry.
- Press the F3 key.

Or, if you don't remember the AutoText entry abbreviation
- Move the insertion point to where you want to insert the entry.
- Click Insert on the menu bar, point to AutoText, and then click AutoText.
- Click the AutoText tab in the AutoCorrect dialog box, and then click a name (or abbreviation) in the list of AutoText entries.
- Click the Insert button.

You'll test the three AutoText entries you created for this template. Because this is only a test, the insertion location isn't important.

To insert an AutoText entry:

1. Leave the insertion point in the blank line below the "Overview" heading.

2. Type **dp**, and then press the **F3** key. The phrase "digital photography" appears.

   This is the simplest way to insert an AutoText entry.

3. Delete **digital photography** from the current line.

4. Click **Insert** on the menu bar, point to **AutoText**, and then click **AutoText** to open the AutoCorrect dialog box. Next, you'll use the Insert menu to insert an AutoText entry.

5. Double-click **dd** in the list of AutoText entries. The phrase "digital darkroom" appears in the text. Both methods of inserting AutoText are simpler than typing the full entry each time.

6. Test the "ies" AutoText entry using either method.

7. Delete any text you inserted with AutoText so it doesn't become boilerplate in the template. Do not delete the blank line below the "Overview" heading.

Later, you'll use these AutoText entries to help Armand create a magazine query.

Printing a List of the AutoText Items

If you create many AutoText entries, you might find it difficult to remember them all. Also, if you plan to share your template, you might want to let others know what AutoText entries are available in the template. In either case, it would be helpful for you to have a printed list of all the AutoText entries.

REFERENCE WINDOW **RW**

Printing a List of the AutoText Entries
- Click File on the menu bar, and then click Print.
- Click the Print what list arrow, and then click AutoText entries.
- Click the OK button.

So Armand will know what AutoText entries and abbreviations you've created, you'll print a list for him.

To print AutoText entries:

1. Click **File** on the menu bar, and then click **Print** to open the Print dialog box.

2. Click the **Print what** list arrow, and then click **AutoText entries**.

3. Click the **OK** button. Word prints a list of AutoText entries for the Magazine Query template. The printed list also includes the default entries in the Normal template.

4. Save the template.

Now that you've learned how to use AutoText, you'll learn how to customize a closely related feature, AutoCorrect.

Customizing AutoCorrect

Recall that **AutoCorrect** checks your document for errors as you type and automatically corrects common typing errors, such as letter transposition (adn to and), a sentence that begins with a lowercase letter, and two initial capital letters (PHotography to Photography).

Sometimes, however, AutoCorrect makes unwanted corrections. For example, Armand wants to be able to type "IF" for "image file" and "IFs" for "image files". But every time he types "IFs" in a document, AutoCorrect automatically changes it to "if". So he can type "IFs" in a document, Armand wants you to make "IFs" an AutoCorrect exception. An **exception** is a word or phrase that AutoCorrect doesn't automatically modify.

To create an exception in AutoCorrect:

1. Click **Tools** on the menu bar, click **AutoCorrect Options**, and then, if necessary, click the **AutoCorrect** tab.

2. Make sure the seven check boxes are all checked. Now you're ready to create an exception.

3. Click the **Exceptions** button in the AutoCorrect dialog box to open the AutoCorrect Exceptions dialog box, and then click the **INitial CAps** tab. Here you'll type the text you want as an exception to the AutoCorrect initial capitalization rule.

4. Type **IFs** in the Don't correct text box, and then click the **Add** button.

   TROUBLE? If you find that "IFs" already appears in the list of exceptions in the AutoCorrect Exceptions dialog box, skip Step 4.

   You can use the First Letter tab to add abbreviations (with their ending periods) that you don't want followed by a capitalized word.

5. Click the **OK** button in the AutoCorrect Exceptions dialog box, and then click the **OK** button in the AutoCorrect dialog box.

Now when Armand types "IFs", AutoCorrect won't change the word to "Ifs." Note that this AutoCorrect exception applies to all documents created or edited only with your installation of Word; it doesn't become part of the Magazine Query template or the Normal template. Therefore, Armand has to make the same AutoCorrect exception on any other computer he uses.

Using Smart Tags

So far you have learned about several features that you can use to automate your work. Another useful automated option in Word is the Smart Tag feature. As you have seen in earlier tutorials, Word automatically marks certain words or phrases (names, dates, addresses and so forth) as smart tags. A **smart tag** appears as a dotted purple underline in a document. When you place the mouse pointer over the smart tag (or when the insertion point is located within the smart-tagged text) a Smart Tags Actions button appears. This button displays a menu of commands that you can use to perform certain actions involving the smart-tagged word or phrase. The commands available on this menu depend on the type of information that has been marked with a smart tag. For example, you can use a smart-tagged name to send that person an e-mail message, or add that person to the Microsoft Outlook address book (or another electronic address book). You can use a smart-tagged address to open your browser and display a map (from the Internet) showing you how to get to that address; you can also choose to add that address to Outlook (or to another electronic address book).

REFERENCE WINDOW **RW**

Using Smart Tag Actions
- Move the pointer over text marked with a smart tag, or click anywhere within the tagged text to display the Smart Tag Actions button
- Click the Smart Tag Actions button to open the shortcut menu.
- Click the desired action item in the shortcut menu, and then complete the actions as directed.

Recall that you can delete smart tags from documents by clicking Remove this Smart Tag in the Smart Tag Actions menu. Note that you can only see smart tags in a document if the Smart Tag feature is turned on.

REFERENCE	WINDOW	RW

Turning On Smart Tags
- Click Tools on the menu bar, click AutoCorrect Options to open the AutoCorrect dialog box, and then click the Smart Tags tab.
- Select the Label text with smart tags check box.
- Click the OK button.

You'll have a chance to use smart tags in the first case problem at the end of this tutorial. In the next session, you'll turn your attention back to the template. At this point, the template contains boilerplate text and graphics, modified styles, and AutoText entries. In the next session you'll add a watermark, customize the toolbars, and insert fields.

Session 8.1 QUICK CHECK

1. What is a template? List three types of documents for which you might create a template.

2. What is boilerplate? How are templates and boilerplates related?

3. List five features a template might contain.

4. List three advantages of using templates.

5. Briefly describe how to create and save a template.

6. How would you define the Heading 1 style as white characters on a blue background?

7. What are the advantages of AutoText?

8. What is an AutoCorrect exception?

SESSION 8.2

In this session, you'll add a special kind of graphic called a watermark to the template, and you'll customize the toolbars in the template. Also, you'll automate the template by inserting fields.

Creating a Watermark

A **watermark** is a graphic that appears behind or in front of existing text on the pages of a document. Usually, the watermark appears in a light shade in the background of each printed page. You add a watermark to a header or footer so that it appears on every page in the document (or on every page on which the header or footer appears).

REFERENCE WINDOW   **RW**

Creating a Watermark

- Click View on the menu bar, and then click Header and Footer.
- Insert a graphic (for example, clip art, drawing, WordArt, or picture) into the header.
- Select the graphic, click the Text Wrapping button on the Picture toolbar, and then click Behind Text.
- Click the Color button on the Picture toolbar, and then click Washout.
- Move the watermark graphic to any location in the page.
- Click the Close button in the Header and Footer toolbar.

Armand wants you to add a picture of a camera as a watermark to the query template.

To add a watermark to the template:

1. If you took a break after the last session, make sure Word is running, the Magazine Query template is open, Word is in Print Layout View, and nonprinting characters are displayed.

2. Click **View** on the menu bar, and then click **Header and Footer**. The Header and Footer toolbar appears in the window, a Header text box opens at the top of the page, and the main text of the document becomes dimmed. Next you'll insert a JPEG image of a camera.

3. Click **Insert** on the menu bar, point to **Picture**, click **From File** to open the Insert Picture dialog box, and then insert the picture **Camera** located in the Tutorial folder for Tutorial.8 on your Data Disk. See Figure 8-10.

Figure 8-10   **HEADER WITH INSERTED PICTURE**

picture in header
to create watermark

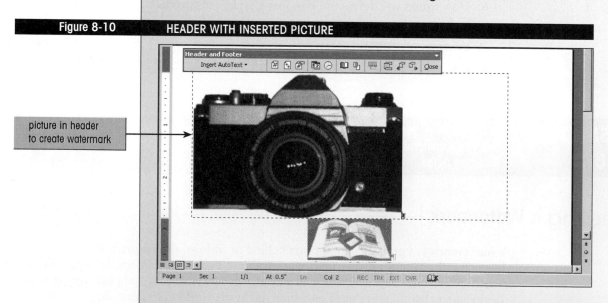

4. Click the camera picture to select it and to display the Picture toolbar.

5. Click the **Text Wrapping** button ⊞ on the Picture toolbar, and then click **Behind Text**. The camera image moves behind the text in the document template.

6. Click the **Color** button on the Picture toolbar, and then click **Washout**. This changes the camera image to a light, low-contrast (washed out) color. Even if you don't convert the color to Washout, Word automatically lightens a watermark. However, you'll usually want to make the image even lighter by converting it to Washout.

7. With the camera image still selected, drag it so its top is centered just below the URL, as shown in Figure 8–11.

Figure 8-11	WATERMARK IN DOCUMENT TEMPLATE

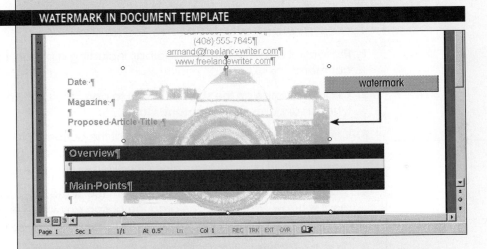

8. Click the **Close** button in the Header and Footer toolbar, and then save the template.

Every page of a query created from the Magazine Query document template will contain the camera background watermark. To edit the watermark, click View on the menu bar, click Header and Footer to open the Header and Footer toolbar, scroll to the watermark, and click the watermark. Then you can modify the size, color, contrast, and position of the watermark.

Customizing the Toolbars

You can customize every part of a template, including the toolbars, menus, and shortcut keys to suit your specific needs.

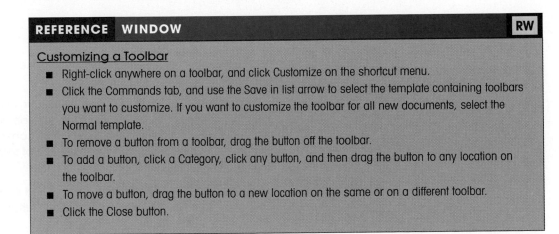

REFERENCE WINDOW   **RW**

Customizing a Toolbar
- Right-click anywhere on a toolbar, and click Customize on the shortcut menu.
- Click the Commands tab, and use the Save in list arrow to select the template containing toolbars you want to customize. If you want to customize the toolbar for all new documents, select the Normal template.
- To remove a button from a toolbar, drag the button off the toolbar.
- To add a button, click a Category, click any button, and then drag the button to any location on the toolbar.
- To move a button, drag the button to a new location on the same or on a different toolbar.
- Click the Close button.

Armand wants you to customize the Standard and the Formatting toolbars in the template to meet his special needs for preparing magazine queries.

Removing Buttons from the Toolbars

Armand asked you to remove the Insert Hyperlink button from the Standard toolbar and the Highlight buttons from the Formatting toolbar because he doesn't use these features in magazine query documents.

To remove buttons from the toolbars:

1. Right-click anywhere on any toolbar, including a button, to open the shortcut menu.

2. Click **Customize** on the shortcut menu to open the Customize dialog box. If necessary, click the **Commands** tab.

3. If necessary, click the **Save in** list arrow at the bottom of the dialog box, and then click **Magazine Query**. This ensures that the changes you make to the toolbars affect only the Magazine Query template, not the Normal template.

4. Drag the **Insert Hyperlink** button from the Standard toolbar into the document window. (*Note*: You can drag the button anywhere except to another location on a toolbar.) This removes the button from the toolbar.

5. Drag the **Highlight** button off the Formatting toolbar.

The buttons you removed are no longer visible in the Word window. Remember that if you change the Magazine Query document template by removing or adding buttons (which you'll do next), these changes apply only to that document template, not to the Normal template. Therefore, during your work with other documents, the toolbars will not be modified.

Adding Buttons to the Toolbars

With the Customize dialog box still open, you're ready to add new buttons to the toolbars. As you can see, the dialog box displays a list of categories and the buttons available for the current category. Armand wants you to add the View Field Codes button to the Standard toolbar, which will be useful later when you add field codes to the template. Then he wants you to create an AutoText button that he can use to insert the phrase "digital photography." He wants this button added to the Formatting toolbar.

To add buttons to the toolbars:

1. Verify that the Customize dialog box is still open, and make sure the Save in list box is still set to the Magazine Query template.

2. Click **View** in the Categories list box. The Commands list box displays the buttons associated with the various View commands. The list includes the View Field Codes button, which you'll add to the toolbar in a moment. Note that you can click the Description button to display a description of the button that is currently selected in the Commands list box.

3. Scroll down in the Commands list box, click the **View Field Codes** button in the Commands list box, and then click the **Description** button. See Figure 8–12.

Figure 8-12   **CUSTOMIZING THE TOOLBARS**

former locations of removed buttons

description of button

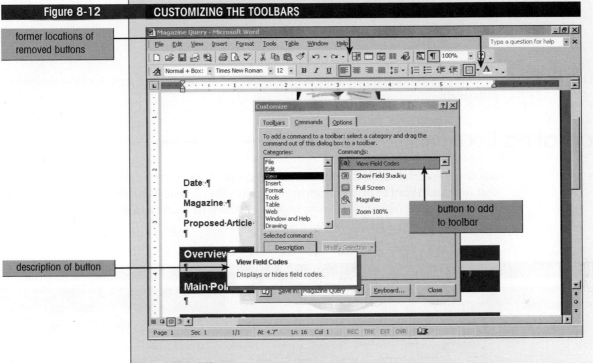

4. Drag {a} from the Customize dialog box to the spot between the Show/Hide ¶ button ¶ and the Zoom list box on the Standard toolbar. As you drag {a} to the toolbar, an I-beam pointer ⌶ marks the location in which the new button will appear when you release the mouse button.

Next you'll add an AutoText button to the Formatting toolbar.

To add an AutoText button to the toolbar:

1. Verify that the Commands tab of the Customize dialog box is still open, and then click **AutoText** near the end of the Categories list. The AutoText entries you created earlier appear in the Commands list box. You want to create a toolbar button for the "dp" (digital photography) entry.

2. Drag **dp** to the immediate right of the **Borders** button ▦ on the Formatting toolbar, right-click the **dp** AutoText button to display a shortcut menu, point to **Change Button Image**, and then click the button that has an image of a video camera, located on the third row down, first column on the left of the button palette. The AutoText button contains an image and text. Now you'll delete the text.

TROUBLE? If you release the mouse button and the dp AutoText button doesn't appear on the toolbar, you might have positioned the button too far to the right of the Borders button. Make sure the I-beam pointer appears on the toolbar before you release the mouse button.

3. Right-click the **dp** AutoText button again, and then click **Default Style**. The default style for a button is only the button image, no text. Now the button just contains the camera image.

4. Click the **Close** button in the Customize dialog box.

5. Save the template.

Using these customized toolbars, Armand will be able to create query documents more efficiently.

Automating Documents Using Fields

Another powerful method for automating a document is using fields. A **field** is a special code that instructs Word to insert information, such as the current date, filename, or author's name, into a document. You already know how to use fields to create a mail merge. Figure 8–13 lists the fields that you'll include in the query template.

Figure 8-13	FIELD EXAMPLES	
FIELD	**CODE (EXAMPLE)**	**ACTION**
Date	{DATE \@ "MMMM d, yyyy"}	Inserts current date/time according to date-time picture
Fill-in	{FILLIN "Your name?" * MERGEFORMAT }	Inserts information filled in by user
NumPages	{NUMPAGES}	Inserts total number of pages in document
Page	{PAGE}	Inserts current page number
Ref	{REF BookmarkName}	Inserts contents of specified bookmark

When you insert a field into a document, the corresponding code includes the name of the field and optional instructions and switches enclosed in braces { }, also called French brackets or curly brackets, that mark the beginning and end of the code. An **instruction** is a word or phrase that specifies what the field should do, such as display a prompt (a phrase that tells the user how to proceed). A **switch** is a command following *, \#, \@, or \! that turns on or off certain features of the field. For example, a switch can specify how the result of the field is formatted. Figure 8–14 shows a field code that contains a field name, instructions, and a switch. The field name, FILLIN, specifies that this field asks the user to supply (fill-in) some information. The instruction is a prompt (Product name:) that tells the user what to type. The switch (\@ MERGEFORMAT) specifies that the field's result (the user fill-in information) should retain any formatting applied to the field even if the user fills in new information.

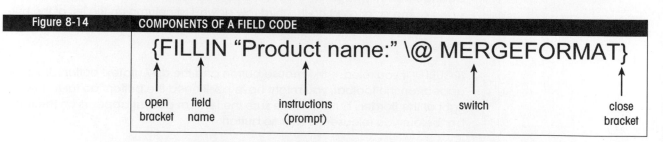

Figure 8-14	COMPONENTS OF A FIELD CODE

{FILLIN "Product name:" \@ MERGEFORMAT}

open bracket | field name | instructions (prompt) | switch | close bracket

All field codes must include braces and a field name, but not all field codes include instructions and switches. The Field dialog box, which you'll access later, shows which elements each field code must contain.

Inserting and Editing the Date Field

You're already familiar with the Date field, which inserts the current date and time or specified parts of the date and time in the format you select, such as the full name for the current month (for example, February) without the day, year, or any part of the time.

You can designate the exact format of the date and time by changing the date-time picture field switch. The **date-time picture** is a pattern of abbreviations and punctuation that follows the switch code \@ and specifies the content and format of the date and time. Figure 8–15 shows the date-time picture options.

Figure 8-15	DATE-TIME PICTURE OPTIONS	
CHARACTER	**PURPOSE**	**EXAMPLE**
M	Month in numeric format	2 (for Feb)
MM	Month in numeric format with leading zero	02
MMM	Month as three-letter abbreviation	Feb
MMMM	Month as full name	February
d	Day in numeric format	5 (for 5th day of month)
dd	Day in numeric format with leading zero	05
ddd	Day of week as three-letter abbreviation	Mon
dddd	Day of week as full name	Monday
yy	Year in two-digit format	01
yyyy	Year in four-digit format	2001

You can use the characters in Figure 8-15 to create a date-time picture in any date and time format. For example, the full Date code for the date format "Monday, June 7, 2004" is: {DATE \@ "dddd, MMMM d, yyyy"}. For query documents, Armand uses the "07 June 04" date format.

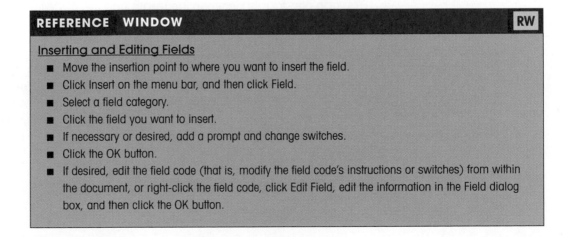

REFERENCE WINDOW   **RW**

Inserting and Editing Fields
- Move the insertion point to where you want to insert the field.
- Click Insert on the menu bar, and then click Field.
- Select a field category.
- Click the field you want to insert.
- If necessary or desired, add a prompt and change switches.
- Click the OK button.
- If desired, edit the field code (that is, modify the field code's instructions or switches) from within the document, or right-click the field code, click Edit Field, edit the information in the Field dialog box, and then click the OK button.

You'll insert the Date field into the template with the Field command (not with the Date command) so you can modify the date-time picture.

To insert the Date field using the Insert Field command:

1. Move the insertion point to the right of the space after "Date" near the beginning of the document.

2. Click **Insert** on the menu bar, and then click **Field**. The Field dialog box opens.

3. Click the **Categories** list arrow, click **Date and Time**, and then click **Date** in the Field names list. See Figure 8–16.

| Figure 8-16 | FIELD DIALOG BOX |

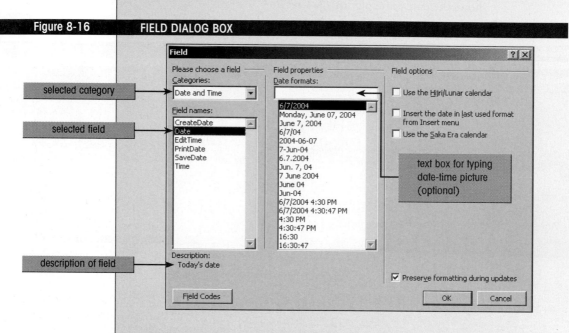

4. Click the **OK** button in the Field dialog box to insert the Date code in the document. Don't worry about the date-time picture at this point; you'll edit it later.

5. If you see today's date (that is, the result of the field code) but not the date code itself, click the **View Field Codes** button {a} on the customized Standard toolbar. Notice that the View Field Codes button is a toggle switch; click it to alternate between showing the results of the fields and showing the field codes. You can also toggle between the results and the codes by pressing the Alt+F9 key combination.

Currently, the format switch in the Date field code is * MERGEFORMAT, which tells Word to retain the current formatting even if the result changes. For example, if you change the current field result to bold, Word retains the bold characters even if the date changes. Because Armand always uses the regular font for the date, you'll edit the field code to remove the MERGEFORMAT switch and insert the date-time picture switch using the usual Word editing commands. You need to change the format so that it displays dates similar to 07 June 04—the date format that Armand prefers.

To edit the Date field code:

1. Click the **View Field Codes** button [a] on the customized Standard toolbar so you can see the field results—today's date in the format "6/7/2004."

2. Click [a] again to view the field code. Notice that you can see the field code for the date field and also for the Hyperlink fields that mark Armand's e-mail address and Web site URL.

3. Select **\ * MERGEFORMAT** (and the space after it) in the Date field code. The background for the unselected part of the code is gray, and the selected part of the code is white on a darker gray background. See Figure 8-17.

| Figure 8-17 | DATE FIELD CODE IN DOCUMENT TEMPLATE |

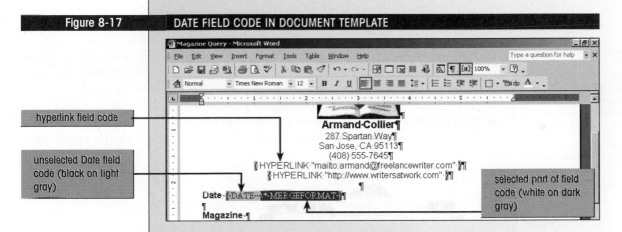

hyperlink field code

unselected Date field code (black on light gray)

selected part of field code (white on dark gray)

TROUBLE? If the field code does not have a gray backround, click Tools on the menu bar, click Options, click the View tab, click the Field shading list arrow in the Show section, click When selected, and then click the OK button.

4. Type **\@ "dd MMMM yy"** (including the quotation marks). Be sure to type the letter "M" in uppercase. The complete field code is: { DATE \@ "dd MMMM yy"}.

TROUBLE? If the quotation marks on your screen are curly rather than straight, don't worry. Word accepts either the typographic (curly) or the straight quotation marks in field codes. Normally, however, Word automatically uses straight quotation marks in a field.

5. Click [a] on the customized Standard toolbar.

The date still appears in the format "6/7/2004" or a format other than "07 June 2004." Before the date will appear in the new format, you need to update the field.

Updating a Field

The date format hasn't changed even though you changed the format switch. This is because you simply changed the text of the field code in the document, not the underlying field itself. For the change to take effect in the field, you must update the field.

To update the Date field:

1. Click anywhere in the date (the result of the field code).

2. Press the **F9** key. The date changes from the "6/7/04" format to the "07 June 04" format (but with today's date).

3. Click the **View Field Codes** button {a} on the customized Standard toolbar to view the field code.

Now every magazine query document will contain the current date in the desired format.

Inserting and Editing the Fill-In Field

When Armand begins a new document using the query template, he wants Word to prompt him to fill in the Magazine information (the name of the magazine to which the query is addressed) and the Proposed Article Title information (the name of the article that Armand wants to write). The purpose of a **Fill-in field** is to provide such prompts. When this field is updated, Word prompts you to fill in specific information.

First you'll insert the Fill-in field, and then you'll edit it to provide an appropriate prompt.

To insert a Fill-in field:

1. Move the insertion point to the right of the space after "Magazine."

2. Click **Insert** on the menu bar, and then click **Field**. The Field dialog box opens.

3. Select the **Mail Merge** category, and then click **Fill-in** in the Field names list box.

4. Click in the **Prompt** text box in the Field Properties section of the dialog box, and type **Type the magazine name** (with no punctuation at the end). Leave the Field options check boxes unchecked.

5. Uncheck the **Preserve formatting during updates** check box. When you clear this check box, you tell Word to update formatting whenever you update the field. Now, if someone using the document changes the formatting of the text in the field, Word will change it back to the original formatting whenever the field is updated. If you want Word to retain any changes to text formatting in the field, you would leave this check box checked.

6. Click the **OK** button. A blank Microsoft Word dialog box appears with the prompt you typed, "Type the magazine name".

7. Click the **OK** button without entering any text. Armand will fill in the requested information in the text box when he creates his queries.

8. If necessary, click the **View Field Codes** button {a} in the customized Standard toolbar to view the field code.

The Fill-in field code appears in your template. This field code has no switch—because you chose not to preserve formatting during updates—but it does include the text you specified for the prompt. You can click anywhere in the field code to modify the prompt or to add a switch.

When Armand uses this template to create new queries, the template will prompt him to insert the name of the magazine for which he wants to write an article. Now you'll use the Fill-in field to create a prompt for the proposed magazine article name.

To insert and edit another Fill-in field:

1. Move the insertion point to the right of the space after "Proposed Article Title."

2. Insert a Fill-in field as you did before, except this time type the prompt **Type the proposed magazine article title** (with no punctuation at the end).

3. Uncheck the **Preserve formatting during updates** check box as you did earlier, click the **OK** button in the Field dialog box, and then click the **OK** button in the Microsoft Word dialog box.

4. Save the template with the three field codes that you just inserted.

Having added a date field and two Fill-in fields, now you're ready to insert another type of field.

Inserting a Reference Field

Armand wants the template to include a footer with specific information about the document. In particular, he wants to print the name of the magazine and the page number at the bottom of every page. You'll use fields to insert both items in the footer. When Armand prepares a query, he'll never need to edit the footer; all the information will appear automatically.

How can you ensure that the magazine name appears automatically in the footer? Recall that the template prompts Armand to type the magazine name in a Fill-in field. You can mark that Fill-in field as a **bookmark**, which is text, graphics, tables, or a location that you select and assign a name, and then use a **Ref field** to cross-reference (or insert into another part of the document) the information contained in that bookmark. In the query template, the Ref field will duplicate the text of the Fill-in field in the footer.

REFERENCE WINDOW   **RW**

Creating a Reference Using the Ref Field
■ Select the information you want to reference, such as a Fill-in field.
■ Click Insert on the menu bar, click Bookmark, type a name for the bookmark, and then click the Add button to create a bookmark.
■ Move the insertion point to where you want to reference the contents of the bookmark (in other words, where you want it repeated).
■ Click Insert on the menu bar, click Field, select the Links and References category, click Ref in the Field names list, click the Bookmark name list box, select any field options as desired, and then click the OK button.

You'll mark the magazine name Fill-in field as a bookmark, create a footer, and then insert the Ref field to insert the magazine name. As you create the new bookmark, keep in mind that a bookmark name must be a single word that begins with a letter and can be as many as 40 letters or numbers; it can't contain any spaces or symbols, such as a hyphen, slash, or asterisk.

To mark the Fill-in field as a bookmark:

1. Make sure the document field codes are visible.

2. Select the entire field **{FILLIN "Type the magazine name" }** (but not the end-of-paragraph symbol). Make sure the field is selected (dark gray or black), and not just shaded (light gray); the text should be white.

3. Click **Insert** on the menu bar, and then click **Bookmark**. The Bookmark dialog box opens.

4. Type **Magazine** as the name of the bookmark, and then click the **Add** button. The bookmark "Magazine," is added to the list of bookmarks.

With the magazine name Fill-in field bookmarked, you're ready to create a footer and insert the Ref field.

To create a footer and insert the Ref field:

1. Click **View** on the menu bar, and then click **Header and Footer**. The Header and Footer toolbar opens with a blank Header text box.

2. Click the **Switch Between Header and Footer** button 🔳 in the Header and Footer toolbar to display the blank Footer text box. Armand asks you to draw a horizontal line above the footer to separate it from the body text.

3. Click the **Borders** list arrow 🔳 on the Formatting toolbar to open the Borders toolbar, and then click the **Top Border** button 🔳 to insert a horizontal line across the top of the Footer text box. Now you can type the text of the footer and insert the Ref field.

4. Type **Magazine:** (including the colon), and press the **spacebar**.

5. Click **Insert** on the menu bar, click **Field**, select **Links and References** in the Categories list box, and then click **Ref**.

6. Click **Magazine** in the Bookmark name list box. See Figure 8–18.

Figure 8-18   FIELD DIALOG BOX WITH REF FIELD CODE

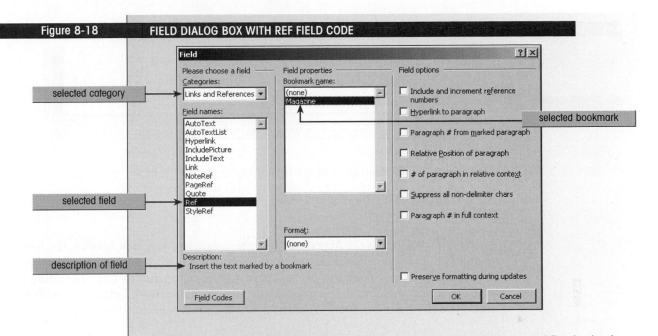

7. Click the **OK** button in the Field dialog box. Leave the Header and Footer toolbar open in the window.

In the future, when Armand uses the Magazine Query template, the text he enters in the Magazine Fill-in field (at the top of the Magazine Query document) will be displayed in the document's footer.

Inserting the Page Number and Number of Pages Fields

Armand also wants the footer to show the current page number and the total number of pages in the magazine query document in the double-number format, page *x* of *y*, where *x* is the current page and *y* is the total number of pages. You can use the Page field and the NumPages field to insert the page number and the total number of pages, respectively.

To insert the fields for the page number and the number of pages:

1. Press the **Tab** key twice to move the insertion point from the end of the Ref field to the right margin of the footer.

2. Type **page**, press the **spacebar**, and then click the **Insert Page Number** button 🔢 on the Header and Footer toolbar. This button is a quick way to insert the Page field into a document. The { PAGE } field appears in the footer.

3. Press the **spacebar**, type **of**, and then press the **spacebar** again. Next you'll insert the NumPages field, which inserts the total number of pages in the document.

4. Click the **Insert Number of Pages** button 🔢 on the Header and Footer toolbar. (Alternately, you can open the Field dialog box, select Document Information in the Categories list, click NumPages in the Field names list, and then click the OK button. Using the Insert Number of Pages button, however, is a quicker method.) The completed footer now contains the page x of y information, as shown in Figure 8-19.

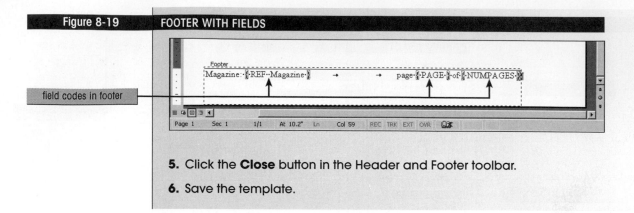

Figure 8-19   FOOTER WITH FIELDS

field codes in footer

Footer
Magazine··{·REF··Magazine·}   →   →   page·{·PAGE·}·of·{·NUMPAGES·}

Page 1   Sec 1   1/1   At 10.2"   Ln   Col 59   REC TRK EXT OVR

5. Click the **Close** button in the Header and Footer toolbar.

6. Save the template.

When Armand uses the Magazine Query template to create new queries, the footers will contain the magazine name, the page number, and the total number of pages in the query.

You have inserted fields into the template to help automate the task of creating a magazine query document. In the next session you'll record macros to further automate the template, and then you'll create a magazine query document based on the template.

Session 8.2 QUICK CHECK

1. What is a watermark?

2. How do you add and remove buttons from a toolbar?

3. What is a field? Name and describe three fields.

4. What would the Date field look like if today is June 7, 2004, and you want the date to appear in the format 07 June 2004?

5. How do you update a field?

6. What is a Ref field?

7. To set up page numbering in the form page 2 of 5, what two fields do you use?

SESSION 8.3

In this session, you will import two macros, record a macro for the Magazine Query template, and edit a macro using Visual Basic for Applications. You'll also start a new document based on the template you created, and then write a specific magazine article query using all the features of the template.

Automating Word with Macros

Armand knows that every time he writes a new query, he has to perform several routine tasks: resize digital photographs, position photographs at the right (or left) margin with text wrapping around to the left (or right), and add a border to photographs. Such tasks are prime candidates for macros. A macro, in its simplest form, is a recording of keystrokes and mouse operations that you can play back at any time by pressing a key combination or by using the mouse. In its fullest form, a macro is a computer program that can perform complex functions based on document conditions or user input.

Recording or programming a macro to run frequently executed commands has several advantages. Combining a number of keystrokes and mouse operations into a macro saves time and helps you complete your work faster. If you record a macro accurately—without typos or other mistakes—the keystrokes and mouse operations will always play back error-free. A macro that inserts text or performs formatting operations will consistently insert the same text and perform the same formatting operations.

Before you record the steps (keystrokes and mouse clicks) of a macro, you should usually do the following:

- **Name the macro.** A macro name must begin with a letter and can contain a maximum of 80 letters and numbers; the name can't contain spaces, periods, or other punctuation. The macro name should summarize its function. For example, if you record a macro to resize a picture, you could name the macro "PictureBorder".

- **Describe the macro (optional).** You should provide a detailed description of a macro to help you recall its exact function. This is especially important if a macro performs a complex series of operations that can't be summarized in the macro name. For example, a simple macro name, such as PositionPicLeft, doesn't describe the picture features, such as borders and text wrapping. You could include that type of information in the description.

- **Attach the macro to a template.** Unless you specify otherwise, every macro you create is attached to the global template, Normal.dot, and is available in every Word document, regardless of what template you used to create the macro. If you attach a macro to only the template you're editing, the macro is available only in documents created from that template. For example, in this tutorial you'll record three macros and attach them to the Magazine Query template so they'll be available only in magazine query documents.

- **Assign the macro to a toolbar button, menu, or keyboard shortcut (optional).** A macro is easier to run if you assign it to a toolbar button, menu, or keyboard shortcut. For example, you can run a macro with one mouse click or a combination of keystrokes if you assign it to a toolbar button or to a shortcut key; if you assign it to a menu you can run a macro with two mouse clicks. Otherwise, it requires four mouse clicks to run.

You'll first import two macros into the query template, and then you'll record and edit a third macro to help Armand automate writing magazine query documents.

Armand has already written two macro programs, **ResizePictureLeft** and **ResizePictureRight**. The two are similar: each opens a simple dialog box, asks the user to type a percentage, expands or reduces the picture size by the given percentage, and then positions the picture at the left or right margin. To create these macros, Armand did more than record keystrokes. Because the macro uses programming commands not available by recording keystrokes, Armand also used the Visual Basic for Applications (VBA) editor. **VBA editor** is a feature built into Word and other Office applications and provides a complete environment for writing new VBA code and editing existing VBA code and procedures. The Visual Basic Editor contains a complete debugging tool set for finding syntax, run-time, and logic problems in a VBA program. Writing complete VBA programs and using most of the VBA editor features are beyond the scope of this tutorial, but you'll learn how to record macros and use the VBA editor for simple editing.

Importing and Running a VBA Macro

Armand wrote the two VBA macros in a Word document, and then he exported them from Word into the file PicMacro.bas. The **.bas** filename extension indicates that the file contains one or more Visual Basic macros. Your next task is to import PicMacro.bas into the Magazine Query template and then to test Armand's two macros.

To import a VBA macro:

1. If you took a break after the last session, make sure Word is running, the Magazine Query template is open, Word is in Print Layout view, and nonprinting characters are displayed.

2. Click **Tools** on the menu bar, point to **Macro**, and then click **Visual Basic Editor**. The Microsoft Visual Basic window opens. This window contains the VBA Editor, with various smaller windows (called panes) for creating and editing macros.

3. Click **File** in the VBA Editor menu bar, click **Import File** to open the Import File dialog box, change the Look in folder to the Tutorial folder in the Tutorial.08 folder of your Data Disk, click **PicMacs.bas** (or simply **PicMacs**), and then click **Open**. If necessary, drag the scroll bar in the Projects - TemplateProjects pane until you can see Modules below TemplateProject (Magazine Query).

   TROUBLE? If the Projects - Template Projects pane isn't open, click View, and then click Project Explorer.

4. Double-click the **Modules** folder in the Projects - Template Projects pane to open it. You can now see PicMacs, which is the name of the set of macros that you imported.

5. Double-click **PicMacs** to open the macro window with the picture macros. See Figure 8–20. As you can see, the first macro is ResizePictureLeft, which resizes a digital photograph and positions it at the left margin of your Word document. If you scroll down the macro window, you can see the second macro, ResizePictureRight, which has the same function as ResizePictureLeft, except that it positions the picture at the right margin.

Figure 8-20   **VBA EDITOR WITH PICMACS MACROS**

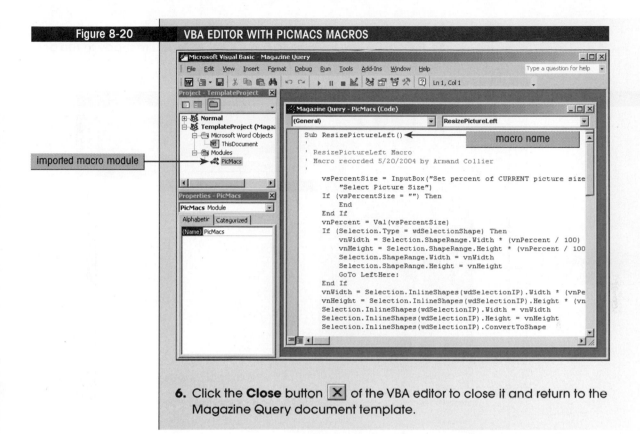

6. Click the **Close** button ☒ of the VBA editor to close it and return to the Magazine Query document template.

The two picture macros are imported, and you're now ready to run them.

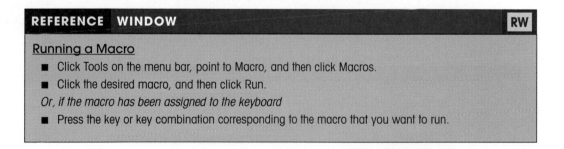

REFERENCE WINDOW   **RW**

Running a Macro

■ Click Tools on the menu bar, point to Macro, and then click Macros.

■ Click the desired macro, and then click Run.

Or, if the macro has been assigned to the keyboard

■ Press the key or key combination corresponding to the macro that you want to run.

Running a Macro

To run the macros (which are designed to format pictures), you must have a picture inserted into your document, and the picture must be selected.

To insert and select a picture, and then run a macro:

1. Move the insertion point to the blank line below the Main Points heading.

2. Using the method given earlier in this tutorial, insert the picture file **PeruBoys** into the document.

3. Click the picture to select it. See Figure 8–21. The resize handles appear around the picture, indicating that the picture is selected. Now you're ready to run one of the macros.

Figure 8-21   **DOCUMENT WITH INSERTED PICTURE**

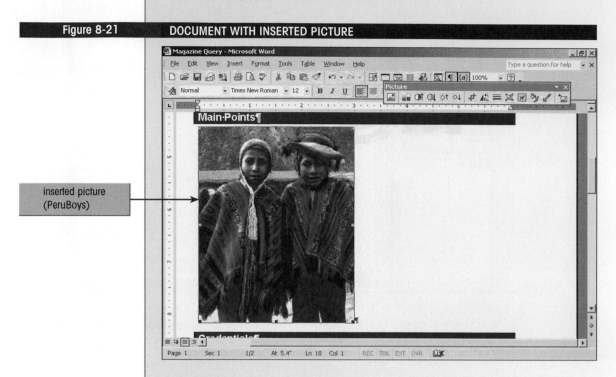

inserted picture
(PeruBoys)

TROUBLE? If your Word window has any toolbars open other than the Picture toolbar, close them.

4. Click **Tools** on the menu bar, point to **Macro**, and then click **Macros**. The Macros dialog box opens, as shown in Figure 8–22.

Figure 8-22   **THE MACROS DIALOG BOX**

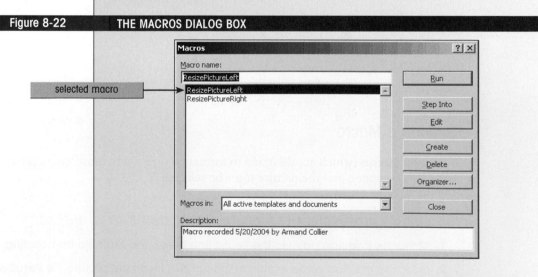

selected macro

TROUBLE? If you see other macros listed in the Macros dialog box, they are probably from your Normal template. Just continue with the next step.

5. If necessary, click **ResizePictureLeft** (the first of the two macros), and then click the **Run** button. The macro displays a dialog box and waits for you to type a percentage of the current picture size. (For example, if you wanted the height and width of the picture to be half their current values, you would type 50; if you wanted the height and width to be double their current values, you would type 200.)

   TROUBLE? If a dialog box appears with a message indicating that macros are disabled, you should change your security settings. Save the current document, click Tools on the menu bar, click Options to open the Options dialog box, click the Security tab, click the Macro Security button, and then click the Low option button. (If you're concerned about macro security, you might want to change this option to Medium or High after you have finished this tutorial). Repeat Step 5. If the macro still won't run, close the Word window, reopen it, open this document, and try the step again.

6. Type **50** and click the **OK** button. The macro frames the picture as a shape (as indicated by the round resize handles and the round, green rotation handle), sets the picture so that the document text wraps around it on the right side, and positions the picture at the left margin. See Figure 8-23.

   TROUBLE? If you can't see the entire picture of the two Peruvian boys as shown in Figure 8-23, scroll the document window until you can.

| Figure 8-23 | PICTURE AFTER PLAYING RESIZEPICTURELEFT MACRO |

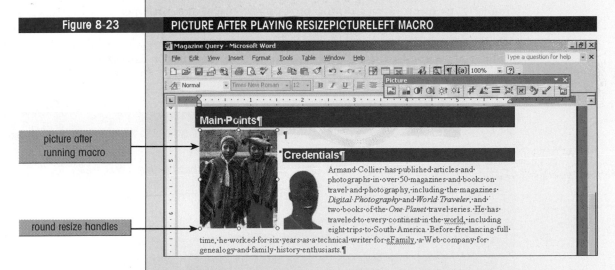

picture after running macro

round resize handles

Next you'll test the other macro, ResizePictureRight.

7. With the picture of the two Peruvian boys still selected, follow the procedure given earlier, except this time run **ResizePictureRight** and type **75** as the percentage, so that the macro reduces the picture width and height to 75% of the current values. See Figure 8-24. Notice that the picture dimensions are 75% of the current picture size, not 75% of the original size. Also note that the picture is positioned at the right margin.

Explore

6. Create a new toolbar called "OfficePlus Memo Template." Make it available only to the OfficePlus Memo document template. To the new toolbar, add the View Field Codes button, the Field... button, the Bookmark... button, and the AutoText button. Keep the Field and Bookmark buttons in text format, so that "Field..." and "Bookmark..." appear on the toolbar. (*Hint*: To create a new toolbar, open the Customize dialog box, and then click the New button in the Toolbars tab.)

7. After the colon in the memo heading "Date:", insert a tab, and then insert the Date field code. Use the Field button on the Formatting toolbar to insert this field. Format the date-time field so that the date appears in the style 08 Sep 2004.

8. After the colon in the memo heading "To:", insert a tab, and then use your custom OfficePlus Memo toolbar to insert a Fill-in field with the prompt "Type recipient of the memo".

Explore

9. With View Field Codes and nonprinting characters turned on, select the Fill-in field and the tab to the right of "To:", and copy them to the position immediately to the right of the colons after "Company:" and "Project Name." Change the Fill-in field codes to "Type recipient's company" and "Type name of project", respectively. Sometimes copying fields is faster than individually inserting them.

10. Select the Fill-in field code for the company name, and use the custom toolbar to bookmark it with the bookmark name "CompanyName." Repeat this for the next Fill-in field code and bookmark it with the bookmark name "ProjectName." As you create the bookmarks, make sure you don't include the end-of-paragraph symbol.

11. Select [Company] in the first paragraph of the memo body, delete it, and insert in its place a Ref field to insert the company name. Repeat this for [Project Name] to automatically insert the name of the project.

12. Insert a Fill-in field to the right of the dot-leader after "Game Room(s)", with the prompt "Number of game rooms". Set the default response to "1".

Explore

13. Copy the Fill-in field code that you just inserted to the right of the other dot-leaders below "Game room(s)", and then change the prompts to "Number of ", followed by the name of the room.

14. In the paragraph below the heading "OfficePlus Personnel," select each of the six names one by one, click the AutoText button on the custom OfficePlus Memo toolbar, and create an AutoText entry for each name. Use the person's initials as the AutoText abbreviation. Delete both lists of names and the brackets around them. Leave two spaces where a name should be located.

15. Create an AutoNew Macro that moves the insertion point to the paragraph below "OfficePlus Personnel" and also to where the first name goes. You might want to use a bookmark when creating the macro.

16. Save the completed document template using the default filename and location, and then save the document template to the Templates folder. Close the template and open a new document using the OfficePlus Memo document template.

17. When prompted by the Fill-in fields, use "John Tulley" as the memo recipient, "First Security Bank," as the recipient's company, "Park Plaza Building" as the project name, "0" as the number of game rooms, "2" as the number of weight training rooms, "1" as the number of basketball courts, "0" as the number of racquetball courts, and "0" as the number of sauna rooms.

18. When the insertion point automatically moves to the location to insert the name of the chief architect, use the "jdp" AutoText entry to insert "J. David Pilati", move the insertion point to the location for inserting the name of the construction foreman, and use the "rs" AutoText entry to insert Ravae Soddano.

19. Save the new letter using the filename **OfficePlus Project Memo**, and then print it.

20. Delete the OfficePlus Memo document template from the Templates folder. Exit Word.

Case 4. Job Application Cover Letter You have recently been hired by your college or university placement center, which not only has the responsibility of helping college graduates find job openings, but also of training students in the art of applying for jobs. Your supervisor asks you to prepare a Word document template that students can use to help them write complete, well-organized cover letters, which the students will then include with their resumes when applying for jobs. Do the following:

1. Start Word (if necessary), open the file **CovrLetr** from the Cases subfolder for Tutorial 8 on your Data Disk, and then save it as a document template (in the same folder on your Data Disk) with the filename **Cover Letter**.

2. Read through the cover letter, making note of the text in brackets. The text in brackets represents possible boilerplate or Fill-in field text.

3. Replace some (or all) of the bracketed text with appropriate Date, Fill-in, or Ref field codes. Keep in mind that the letter should have enough boilerplate text and enough prompts that any student can use your document template to create a standard four-paragraph cover letter. Also keep in mind that students should be able to select and replace bracketed text without using a field.

4. Insert a date field at the appropriate location in the letter.

5. As part of the document template, create at least one macro. For example, create an AutoNew macro to move the insertion point to a certain location within the document.

6. Create or modify at least two styles. For example, you might want the personal information at the beginning of the letter to be in one or two styles, and you might want to change the Normal style from Times New Roman font to a book font, such as Garamond or Century.

7. Create at least two AutoText entries. For example, one might be the name of your college or university; the other might be the name of your major.

8. Save the template in the Cases for Tutorial 8 folder, and save a copy to the Templates folder.

9. Start a new document based on the Cover Letter document template. Use real or fictitious fill-in information for the letter recipient, company name, address, job number, job title, and job description. If you use fictitious information, make it realistic (don't try to be clever or humorous). Use your real name as the applicant (person writing the letter), and use real information regarding your personal qualifications for the job.

10. Save the completed cover letter as **My Cover Letter** and print it.

11. Delete the document template from the Templates folder. Exit Word.

Quick | Check answers

Session 8.1

1. Blueprint for the text, graphics, and formatting that ensures all documents follow a specified pattern; memos, invoices, contracts.
2. Text and graphics that are used repeatedly. Templates can contain boilerplate text or graphics that automatically appear in every document based on the template.
3. Styles; AutoText; custom toolbars, menus, and shortcut keys; fields; macros
4. consistency, accuracy, efficiency
5. Create a normal Word document, customize or modify toolbars, menus, and shortcut keys, add fields, create macros, and save as a document template.
6. Open the Style dialog box, select the style to change, click Modify, click Format, click Border, change the shading to blue, and then change the font color.
7. AutoText allows you to insert frequently used text or graphics into a document with speed and accuracy.
8. A word or phrase that AutoCorrect doesn't automatically modify.

Session 8.2

1. Text or graphics, usually in a lighter shade, that usually appear behind existing text on each page of a document.
2. Right-click anywhere on a toolbar, click Customize, click the Command tab, click a category, drag a button from the dialog box to a toolbar, or drag buttons off the toolbar.
3. Special code used to insert information into a document. Date: inserts current date and/or time; Ref: inserts text marked with a specified bookmark. Fill in: prompts user to fill-in specified information; Page: inserts current page number; NumPages: inserts number of pages in document.
4. dd MMMM yyyy
5. Select the field and press the F9 key.
6. A field that refers to or references some other object in the document (often a bookmark) and repeats that text at the location of the REF field.
7. Page and NumPages

Session 8.3

1. A recording of keystroke or mouse operations that you can perform by pressing fewer key combinations or mouse operations.
2. speed, accuracy, consistency
3. Double-click the REC button on the status bar, give the macro a name and a description, optionally assign it to a keyboard or toolbar, record the keystrokes and mouse operations, and then click the Stop Record button.
4. If you've typed the wrong text or performed the wrong keyboard or mouse operations. Click the name of the macro in the Macro dialog box, click Edit, change the macro, and then return to the document.
5. Macros that run automatically with certain Word events. AutoExec runs when you open Word; AutoNew runs when you open a blank document; AutoOpen runs when you open an existing document.

6. An Auto New macro might be used to automatically perform some operation when a new document is opened based on that template.

7. Click File, click New, and then click the desired template name in the "New from template" section of the Task Pane.

8. Click Tools, point to Macros, click Macros, click MyMacro, and click Run.

9. Insert the chart as an object newly created by the program Microsoft Graph, click the upper-left corner of the datasheet, click Edit, click Import File, and import the Excel worksheet.

OBJECTIVES

In this tutorial you will:

- Learn how to design an effective on-screen form

- Draw and erase rules and gridlines, rotate text, shade cells, and insert graphics in a form table

- Split cells, merge cells, use reverse type, and move gridlines in a form table

- Create text form fields to store numbers, dates, and regular text

- Create drop-down list form fields, and check box form fields

- Set up a form to perform automatic calculations

- Record macros to perform special functions in an on-screen form

- Protect, save, fill in, route, and fax an on-screen form

CREATING
ON-SCREEN FORMS USING ADVANCED TABLE TECHNIQUES

Developing an Order Form for GPS Sales and Service

CASE

Global Positioning Systems Sales and Service

Marissa Wurzburg is owner and manager of GPS Sales and Service, a small company located In Idaho Falls, Idaho. GPS Sales and Service sells, installs, services, and provides training on global positioning system receivers and related supplies and equipment (print and electronic topological maps, computer-interface cables and adaptors, compasses, altimeters, and pedometers). A GPS receiver is an instrument used by hikers, sailors, surveyors, and other wide-ranging travelers for determining exact locations (to within about 20 feet) on the surface of the earth. The GPS instrument receives radio signals from at least four of the 24 GPS satellites that circle the globe and send signals back to earth, day and night, every day of the year. With its built-in computer, the GPS instrument then calculates important information including longitude, latitude, and distances from a specified point.

Because GPS Sales and Service (which is also known as GP3S) is a small company, with fewer than 10 employees, Marissa and her employees currently use paper-only order forms to take orders from walk-in and telephone customers. She asks you to create an on-screen (also called online or computerized) order form based on her design, that all sales personnel can use when taking orders. Sales representatives will fill in an order form for each GPS order, print a copy of the order form for the customer, and save the form data for the store records.

In this tutorial, you'll create and then test an on-screen order form template. First, you'll open a partially completed order form table and then modify it by drawing and erasing parts of borders, making font-related changes, rotating text, shading cells, splitting and merging cells, creating reverse type and other font effects, and moving gridlines. Next, you'll create form fields to accept certain types of information and add help messages and status bar prompts. Finally, you'll automate the form field with macros and text form fields that perform calculations; you'll test the template by filling in an order form; and then you'll print, fax, and save only the data for the order form. You'll also learn how to route a document.

SESSION 9.1

In this session, you will create a table for an on-screen order form. You'll modify the form table by drawing and erasing parts of borders, making font-related changes, rotating text, shading cells, splitting and merging cells, creating reverse type and other font effects, and moving gridlines.

Planning the Document

The GP3S on-screen form will consist of text and a Word table formatted to be attractive and easy to read, both when displayed on-screen and when printed. The order-form table will contain the GP3S store address, phone number, fax number, and e-mail address, as well as information (such as taxes and handling fees) required to process the order. The form will allow sales representatives to enter the following information:

- **Item:** usually a GPS receiver
- **GPS receiver information:** brand and model
- **GP3S sales:** name of sales representative
- **Customer information:** name, address, and phone number
- **Order information:** date and time of order, item purchased, price per item, sales tax, shipping and handling fee, and total cost
- **Credit card information:** account type, card number, expiration date, and name on card (if different from customer name)

As you work on the form, keep in mind that your goal is to make the form useful for Marissa's sales force. These people, who will use the final form in their daily work, are referred to as the **users**.

Creating and Using On-Screen Forms

You already have some experience working with Word templates, which are blueprints for the text, graphics, and format of a document. An **on-screen form** is a Word template that contains spaces for entering information. In addition to the usual template elements (text, graphics, styles, AutoText, customized toolbars, menus, shortcut keys, fields, and macros), an on-screen form template can contain form fields. A **form field** (sometimes also called a form control) is a space that stores a certain type of information, such as a name or a price. You can assign a specific format to the information stored in a field, and specify rules that govern what kind of information the field will accept. For example, Figure 9-1 shows a form with a number of form fields, including one that accepts only integers (not letters, decimals, or other characters). This integer form field wouldn't accept "two" or "2.5," but only "2." Figure 9-1 also shows a form field set up to accept only currency values. In this instance, Word wouldn't accept "four hundred nineteen ninety-nine," so you'd have to type "419.99" into the field; Word would then automatically add the dollar sign to make the complete entry read "$419.99." If you entered a number such as "419.9934" into the field, Word would automatically round the number to "$419.99."

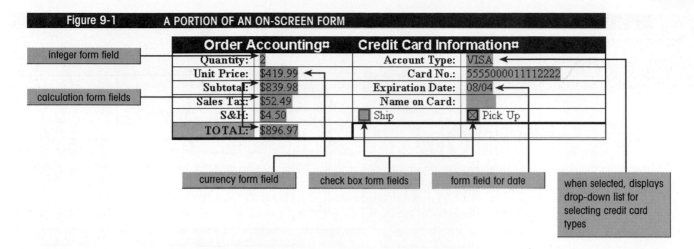

Figure 9-1   **A PORTION OF AN ON-SCREEN FORM**

A form's ability to format information and to allow only certain types of data helps prevent users from entering incorrect information. To help the users even more, you can insert form fields that provide drop-down lists, check boxes, and numeric calculations. You can see some of these elements in Figure 9-1. Also, for each field you can specify a prompt (a brief message) that appears in the status bar and tells the user what information is required for that particular field. Finally, you can allow the user to access additional information about the field by pressing the F1 (Help) key.

Designing an On-Screen Form

Figure 9-2 shows Marissa's design for the on-screen order form.

Figure 9-2   **TABLE STRUCTURE OF ORDER FORM**

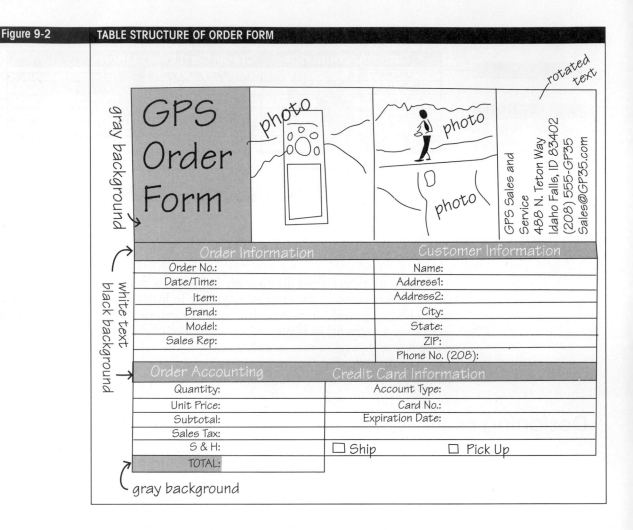

Marissa designed the order-form template as a table with the following features:

- The table includes two fonts (Times New Roman and Arial), two font styles (normal and bold), two font colors (black and white), and rotated text.
- The table design includes border lines of different weights (½-point and 2½-points), cells of different shading (none or white, 20%, and 100% or black), and cells with different types of contents (text, graphics, and form fields, or a combination of these).
- The table structure has cells of different heights and widths.

When designing an on-screen form, you don't need all of the features shown in Figure 9-2. In fact, you don't even need to use a table. If you prefer, you can insert form fields into regular text or frames instead. This flexibility makes it possible to design nearly any type of on-screen form. For example, you might create a business contract with fields for entries such as payment terms and contract length.

Modifying **the Form Table**

Marissa already began creating the table for the on-screen form. You'll open her document, save it as a template, and then modify the table to include the features shown in Figure 9-2.

To open the document and save it as a template:

1. Start Word as usual, insert your Data Disk in the appropriate drive, and then open the **OrdrForm** file from the Tutorial subfolder in the Tutorial.09 folder on your Data Disk.

2. Save the file as a document template in the Tutorial subfolder in the Tutorial.09 folder on your Data Disk, using the filename **GP3S Order Form**.

3. Make sure that the document is displayed in print layout view, that the default Normal style is defined as 12-point Times New Roman, that the Task Pane is closed, and that the Ruler and nonprinting characters are visible. You want to work in Print Layout view so you can see exactly how the form will look when you print the document.

   Next you'll turn off the feature that automatically defines new styles based on your formatting, because it sometimes causes problems in formatting a complex table.

4. Click **Tools** on the menu bar, click **AutoCorrect Options**, click the **AutoFormat As You Type** tab (if necessary), click the **Define styles based on your formatting** check box (if necessary) to deselect it, and then click the **OK** button.

Marissa's table already has the proper dimensions and most of the necessary text. Your first formatting job is to change the lines around some cells.

Drawing and Erasing Rules

A table **border** is a box that frames tables and table cells; it consists of four rules. A **rule** is a horizontal or vertical line drawn along one or more edges of a cell or group of cells. By contrast, a **gridline** is a horizontal or vertical line that defines the location and size of the rows, columns, and cells of a table. The gridlines, which define the structure of a table and are usually visible on your screen, don't show up in the printed table. You can use commands on the Table menu to display or hide gridlines; but even when hidden, the gridlines still define the table's structure. When you create a table, ½-point borders usually appear along all the gridlines.

You'll modify the table by drawing borders of different weights (thicknesses) and by removing some borders. This will help to distinguish sections of the order form.

You'll begin by removing the right border of cells A3 to A9 and of cells C3 to C9.

To remove borders from a group of cells:

1. Click the **Tables and Borders** button ⊞ on the Standard toolbar to open the Tables and Borders toolbar.

2. Click the **Line Style** list arrow on the Tables and Borders toolbar, and then click **No Border**. With No Border selected, you can use the Draw Table pointer ∥ to remove borders without erasing gridlines. When you remove a border, the rule along the gridline becomes invisible, but the gridline separating cells remains intact. (You might wonder why you can't use the Eraser button on the Tables and Borders toolbar to remove borders in the table. When you erase a border, the underlying gridline is also erased, causing two or more cells to merge into one cell. For that reason, you should never use the Eraser ⌫ button to remove borders in tables.)

3. If necessary, click the **Draw Table** button 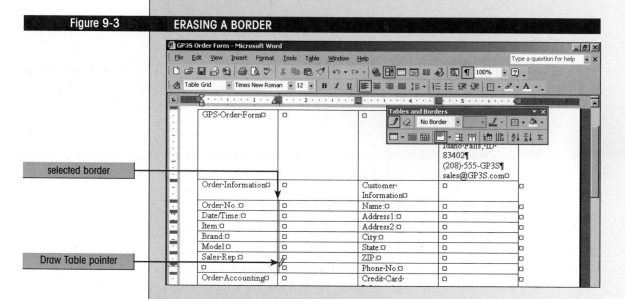 on the Tables and Borders toolbar so that the pointer changes to 🖉.

   TROUBLE? If the pointer does not look like the Draw Table pointer, click the Draw Table button again.

4. Drag 🖉 along the right border of cells A3 through A9 (to the right of the cells below the label "Order information"), as shown in Figure 9-3, and then release the mouse button. The dark black border is removed, revealing the light gray gridline that actually defines the structure of the cells.

   TROUBLE? If you can't see the gridlines after removing borders, click Table on the menu bar, and then click Show Gridlines.

| Figure 9-3 | ERASING A BORDER |

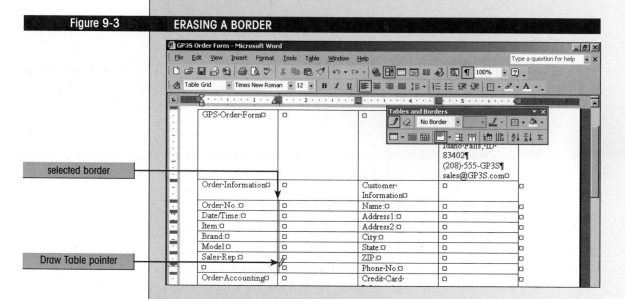

5. Drag 🖉 along the right border of cells C3 through C9 (to the right of the Name, Address1, Address2, City, State, ZIP, and Phone No); drag it again along the right border of cells A11 through A16 (to the right of all the labels below "Order Accounting"); and drag it again along the right border of cells C11 through C16 (to the right of all the cells below "Credit Card Information").

You've used the Draw Table pointer to remove rules without actually erasing gridlines. Now you'll use the same tool to draw rules.

To draw rules:

1. Change the Line Style back to a solid single line.

2. Click the **Line Weight** list arrow ⎯ on the Tables and Borders toolbar, and then click **2 ¼ pt**. Now any borders you insert will be 2¼ points thick rather than the default ½ point.

3. If necessary, scroll up so you can see the top of the table, and then drag 🖉 along the top rule of the table, above the entire row 1.

TROUBLE? If you didn't draw the top rule properly, click the Undo button, and try again. This time, start dragging the pointer in the middle of the top border of cell A1, and finish dragging in the middle of the top border of cell D1.

4. In three separate operations, drag ⌀ along the bottom of cells A16 and B16 (at the very bottom of the table), then along the right border of cell B16 (just click the middle of that border), then along the bottom of cells C15 and D15 (the next-to-the-bottom cells on the right half of the table). The bottom of your table should look like Figure 9-4.

Figure 9-4	TABLE AFTER DRAWING THICK LINES

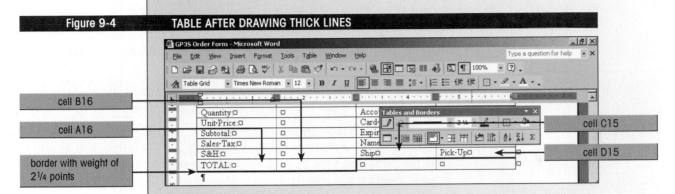

TROUBLE? If you make a mistake, click the Undo button on the Standard toolbar until the new border disappears, and then repeat the necessary steps to draw the borders correctly.

TROUBLE? If you find that the mouser pointer keeps jumping to the top row of the table each time you draw a new border (making it impossible to see the new borders), consider using the Zoom list arrow in the Standard toolbar to decrease the zoom setting to 75% (or even smaller) so that you can see the entire table on the screen at one time. You may then need to return your zoom setting to 100% late, to make it easier for you to read the table as you edit it.

5. Click the **Line Style** list arrow on the Tables and Borders toolbar, click **No Border**, drag ⌀ along the bottom border of cells C16 and D16, and then along the vertical rule to the right of cell D16. Those rules disappear from the table, leaving only the gridlines. See Figure 9-5.

Figure 9-5	TABLE AFTER ERASING BORDERS

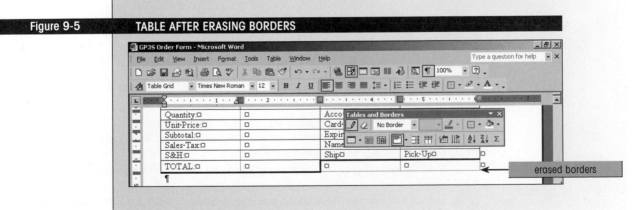

6. Save the template.

As you continue to modify the table, you'll draw or erase other rules.

Changing Fonts, Font Sizes, and Font Effects

Next Marissa wants to make the text in the top row of the table more professional looking. You'll improve its appearance by changing the text's orientation, font, font size, and styles.

To change the font of the existing text within the table:

1. Click ⬚ on the Standard toolbar to close the Tables and Borders toolbar so you can see more of the table.

2. Select row 1 in the table. Recall that you can select a row by clicking ⬀ in the %margin to the left of the row.

3. Click the Font list arrow on the Formatting toolbar, click Arial to change the font of the selected text to Arial, and then deselect the row.

4. Select the phrase **GPS Order Form** in cell A1, click **Format** on the menu bar, and then click **Font** to open the Font dialog box. See Figure 9-6.

   You'll use this dialog box to change the font size to 36 points, the font style to Bold, and the font effects to Engrave. You can also use this dialog box to %change the underline style by clicking the Underline list arrow and selecting from among the 17 underline styles.

Figure 9-6	FONT DIALOG BOX

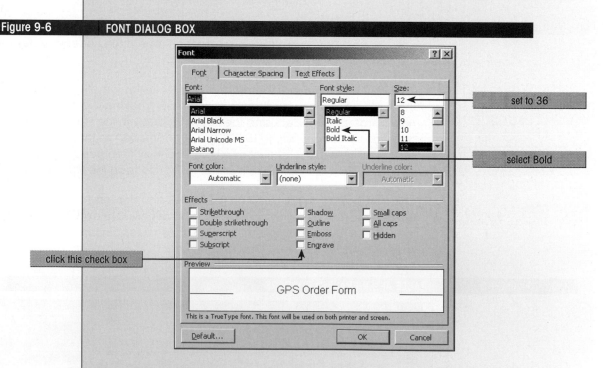

5. Click **36** in the Size list, click **Bold** in the Font style list, click the **Engrave** check box in the Effects section, click the **OK** button, and then deselect the text. The Engrave effect sets the letters in white with a gray-shaded edge. Later you'll fill the cell with a gray background to make these letters stand out.

6. Select the phrase **GPS Sales and Service** in cell D1, and then change the font to 16-point Arial bold.

7. Select the address information in cell D1 (beginning with "488 North Teton Way" and ending with the e-mail address), change the font size to **10** points, and then deselect the text. See Figure 9-7.

Figure 9-7	FORM AFTER MODIFYING TEXT

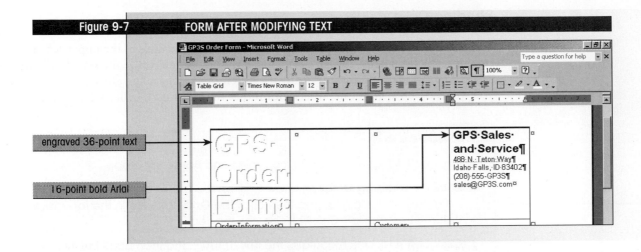

engraved 36-point text

16-point bold Arial

Later you'll make additional font and font style changes. Next you'll rotate the text in cell D1.

Rotating Text in a Table

The text in cell D1 looks crowded in such a narrow cell. Marissa asks you to rotate the text so that it fits more naturally into cell D1. In general, rotating text in tables allows you to fit long phrases or numbers into narrow columns. For example, if a table has many columns of three- and four-digit numbers, you could rotate the numbers in each cell to keep the columns narrow.

To rotate text in the table:

1. Click anywhere in **cell D1**, click **Format** on the menu bar, and then click **Text Direction**. The Text Direction - Table Cell dialog box opens. In the next step, you will select the orientation that formats text from bottom to top. See Figure 9-8.

Figure 9-8	TEXT DIRECTION – TABLE CELL DIALOG BOX

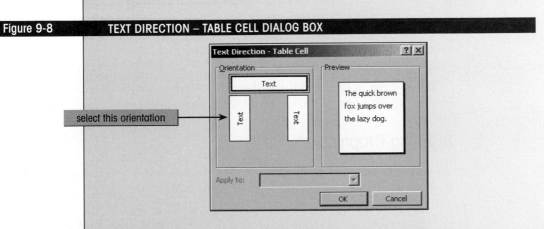

select this orientation

2. In the Orientation section of the dialog box, click the lower-left icon with "Text" written from bottom to top. The Preview box shows you an example of the selected text orientation.

3. Click the **OK** button. The dialog box closes, and the text in the table rotates. Now it stretches from the bottom of cell D1 to the top. The text looks rotated in Print Layout view but not in normal view, so make sure Word is still in print layout view.

4. Save the template.

Shading Cells

To add emphasis to the table, Marissa wants you to add shading to the upper-left cell, which contains the text "GPS Order Form," and the lower-left cell, which contains the word "TOTAL." Shades of gray are usually measured by the amount of black mixed with white. You will use a 20% grayscale, which means that the color is 20% black (and 80% white).

To shade cells:

1. Click **cell A1**, and then open the Tables and Borders toolbar.

2. Click the **Shading Color** list arrow 🖌️ ▾ on the Tables and Borders toolbar to open the color palette, and then click the **Gray-20%** tile in the top row, sixth column from the left. Cell A1 becomes shaded.

3. Click **cell A16**, which contains the text "TOTAL," and then press the **F4** key to repeat your previous action. See Figure 9-9.

Figure 9-9	FORM AFTER SHADING CELLS

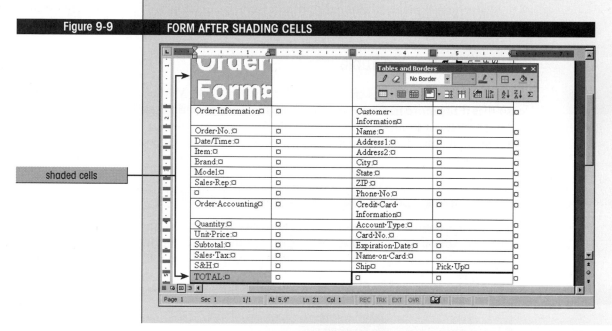

shaded cells

If you refer to Figure 9-1, you'll see that Marissa wants some cells to have a black background (instead of a gray one). You'll shade those cells later.

Inserting Graphics into Cells

To make the order form more attractive, Marissa wants you to insert digital photographs into the two empty cells in the top row of the table.

To insert graphics into cells:

1. Move the insertion point into cell B1, click **Insert** on the menu bar, point to **Picture**, and then click **From File**.

2. Change the Look in folder to the Tutorial folder for Tutorial 9, and then double-click the picture filename **GPSRecvr**. The picture appears in cell B1.

3. Using the same method, insert the picture file **GPSScene** into cell C1. GPSScene shows a scenic picture of a man using a GPS receiver to determine his longitude and latitude. See Figure 9-10.

| Figure 9-10 | FORM AFTER INSERTING PICTURES |

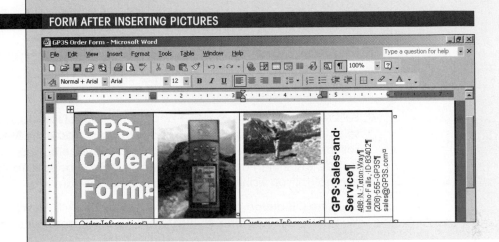

In addition to the two photos you've already added, Marissa would like to add a picture of a topographic map to the form. Marissa wants the map to appear below the GPSScene picture, in a separate cell. To transform cell C1 (which currently contains the GPSScene picture) into two cells, you need to split it.

Splitting Cells

When you **split** cells you divide one cell into two or more cells. You can split cells vertically (to increase the number of columns in a row), or horizontally (to increase the number of rows in a column).

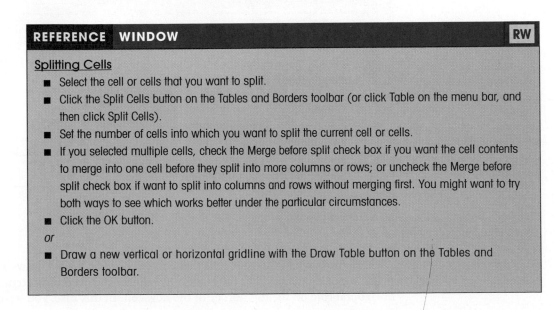

REFERENCE   WINDOW   **RW**

Splitting Cells
- Select the cell or cells that you want to split.
- Click the Split Cells button on the Tables and Borders toolbar (or click Table on the menu bar, and then click Split Cells).
- Set the number of cells into which you want to split the current cell or cells.
- If you selected multiple cells, check the Merge before split check box if you want the cell contents to merge into one cell before they split into more columns or rows; or uncheck the Merge before split check box if want to split into columns and rows without merging first. You might want to try both ways to see which works better under the particular circumstances.
- Click the OK button.

or
- Draw a new vertical or horizontal gridline with the Draw Table button on the Tables and Borders toolbar.

Marissa wants you to convert the current cell C1 into two rows (two stacked cells) so you can insert a picture of a map below the GPSScene picture.

To split a cell into multiple rows:

1. Make sure the Tables and Borders toolbar is visible.

2. Make sure the insertion point is in cell C1 or that cell C1 is selected.

3. Click the **Split Cells** button ▦ on the Tables and Borders toolbar to display the Split Cells dialog box.

4. Set the number of columns to **1** and the number of rows to **2**. Because you've selected only one cell, you don't have to worry about the Merge cells before split check box. If you had selected two or more cells, then you'd have to decide whether or not to merge the cells before the split. You'd merge them, for example, if you wanted to make three columns from two.

5. Click the **OK** button. Now that you have split the cells, Word renumbers all the rows below the new one, so that what was row 2, now becomes row 3; what was row 3, now becomes row 4; and so forth.

6. Insert **GPSMap** into the new cell C2 below GPSScene.

7. Select the **GPSMap** picture and drag its lower-right resize handles up and to the left until the width of the GPSMap is the same width as the GPSScene picture, and then deselect the picture. You might have to hold down the Alt key as you drag the resize handle to get the desired size; don't worry if you can't get the size exactly right. See Figure 9-11.

Figure 9-11	FORM AFTER SPLITTING CELLS AND INSERTING NEW PICTURE

8. Save the template.

Sometimes when you split cells that contain borders, Word draws a rule along an edge of the new cell that you might or might not want. In the preceding steps, Word inserted a 2¼" horizontal rule on the top border of the new cell. In this case, you want to keep that rule. In other cases, you might want to alter or remove the rule.

Merging Cells

Just as you can split cells, you can also merge cells. To **merge** cells means to join two or more adjacent cells into one cell. You can merge adjacent cells in the same row, the same column, or the same rectangular block of rows and columns.

REFERENCE   WINDOW   **RW**

Merging Cells

- Select two or more adjacent cells in a rectangular block.
- Click the Merge Cells button on the Tables and Borders toolbar (or click Table on the menu bar, and then click Merge Cells).

or

- Click the Erase button on the Tables and Borders toolbar, and drag the Eraser pointer across existing borders or gridlines.

Marissa wants you to merge cells to keep each heading on a single line, and to label sections of the table.

To merge cells in a table:

1. Select cells **A3** and **B3**—that is, the cell containing "Order Information" and the blank cell to its right. Remember that because you added an extra row when you split cell C1, all the row numbers below it increased by one, so the cell with "Order Information" is now cell A3.

2. Click the **Merge Cells** button 🔲 on the Tables and Borders toolbar. The two cells combine into one.

3. With the two cells still selected, click the **Center** button 📃 on the Formatting toolbar, and change the font to **14-point, bold Arial**.

4. Select the cell containing "Customer Information" and the blank cell to its right, merge the cells, center the text in the merged cells, and then change the font to **14-point, bold Arial**.

5. Repeat Step 4 for the cell "Order Accounting" and the blank cell to its right, and again for the cell "Credit Card Information," and the blank cell to its right. See Figure 9-12.

Figure 9-12   **MERGED CELLS WITH MODIFIED TEXT**

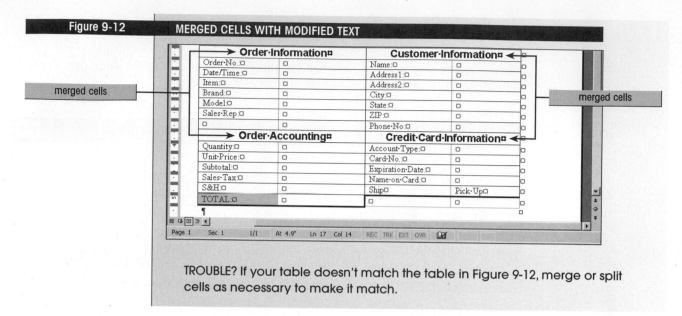

merged cells

merged cells

TROUBLE? If your table doesn't match the table in Figure 9-12, merge or split cells as necessary to make it match.

As you can see, by merging cells you can create cells that span more than one column, and use them to enter major headings. Merging cells is especially useful when you need to enter large amounts of information into a single cell.

Formatting Text as Reverse Type

Besides merging cells, another way to make some of the section headings stand out from the rest of the order form is to set them in reverse type. **Reverse type** (also called **dropout** or **surprinted** type) is white text on a black background, the opposite of the usual black text on a white background. Reverse type is effective for making a line of text or a title attract the reader's eye; however, large amounts of reverse type can be difficult to read.

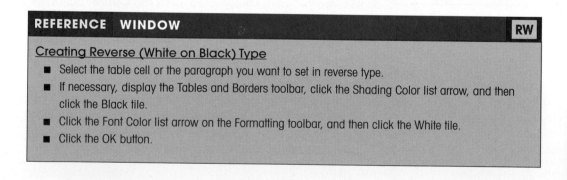

REFERENCE WINDOW   **RW**

Creating Reverse (White on Black) Type
- Select the table cell or the paragraph you want to set in reverse type.
- If necessary, display the Tables and Borders toolbar, click the Shading Color list arrow, and then click the Black tile.
- Click the Font Color list arrow on the Formatting toolbar, and then click the White tile.
- Click the OK button.

You'll change the section headings to reverse type now.

To create reverse type:

1. Select the entire **row 3**, which contains the headings "Order Information" and "Customer Information."

2. Click the **Shading Color** list arrow on the Tables and Borders toolbar, and then click the **Black** tile (fourth row down, first column on the left). The cells become black—which you can't see because the cells are selected. When you select text on a white background, the background changes to black. On the other hand, selected text on a black background changes the background to white.

3. With row 3 still selected, click the **Font Color** list arrow ![A] on the Formatting toolbar, and then click the **White** tile (bottom row, rightmost column) to change the text color to white.

4. Select **row 11** ("Order Accounting" and "Credit Card Information"), click the **Shading Color** button ![icon] (which is already set to black), click the **Font Color** Button (which is already set to white), close the Tables and Borders toolbar, and then deselect the row. See Figure 9-13.

| Figure 9-13 | FORM AFTER CREATING REVERSE TYPE |

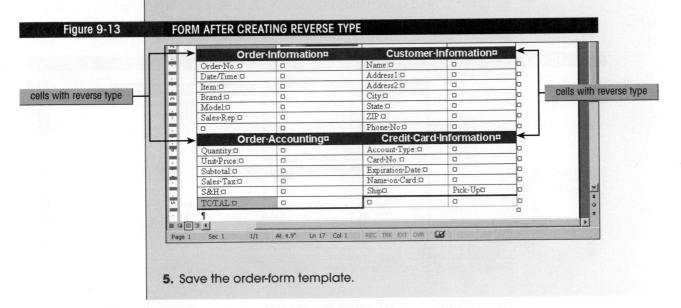

cells with reverse type

cells with reverse type

5. Save the order-form template.

The table structure for the order form is essentially completed. You just have to align some of the text within cells and move some of the gridlines.

Aligning Text in Cells

You've already center-aligned the section headings. Next, to make the order-form more attractive and easier to read, you'll right-align the text in some of the cells. Recall that to change the alignment of text in table cells, you select the cells, and then click the Align Left, Center, Align Right, or Justify button on the Formatting toolbar.

To right-align text in cells:

1. Select cells **A4** through **A9**—the cells below the heading "Order Information" (from "Order No." to "Sales Rep"). Don't select the blank cells to the right of these cells.

TROUBLE? If the cell numbering confuses you, remember that because you split a cell in row 1, all the rows below row 1 increased by one, so now "Order No." is in row 4.

2. Click the **Align Right** button ▤ on the Formatting toolbar. The text and the end-of-cell markers move to the right edge of the cells.

3. With cells A4 to A9 still selected, click the **Bold** button **B** on the Formatting toolbar. The text is formatted in boldface.

4. Select the seven cells in column C below the heading "Customer Information" (from "Name" through "Phone No."), click ▤, and then click **B**. The text is right-aligned and formatted in boldface.

5. Similarly, right-align the six cells in column A below "Order Accounting" (from "Quantity" through "TOTAL"), and format the text in bold.

6. Likewise, right-align the first four cells in column C below "Credit Card Information" (from "Account Type" through "Name on Card"), and format the text in bold. Do not make any changes to the cell containing the text "Ship." See Figure 9-14.

Figure 9-14	FORM AFTER CHANGING TEXT ALIGNMENT

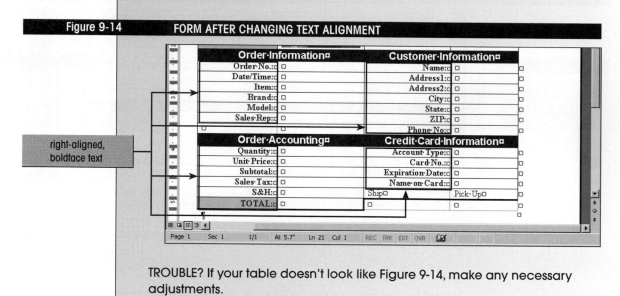

right-aligned, boldface text

TROUBLE? If your table doesn't look like Figure 9-14, make any necessary adjustments.

Now you'll make some cells wider and others narrower.

Moving Gridlines

You can change the width of an individual cell or a group of cells without changing the entire column width. To do this, select the cell or cells, and drag the gridlines (the cell boundaries) to a new location.

The cells with the right-aligned text now contain extra white space to the left of the text. Also, the blank cells to the right of each of these cells could be wider to accommodate the information users will enter into the table. You'll decrease the width of the right-aligned cells, which automatically increases the width of the blank cells.

To change the width of cells by moving gridlines:

1. Select cells **A4** through **A10** (the text and blank cell below the "Order Information" heading), the cells whose widths you want to decrease. The changes in width that you'll make are shown in Figure 9-15.

Figure 9-15	CELLS TO BE REFORMATTED

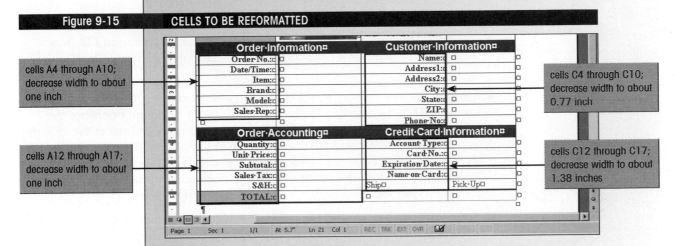

cells A4 through A10; decrease width to about one inch

cells A12 through A17; decrease width to about one inch

cells C4 through C10; decrease width to about 0.77 inch

cells C12 through C17; decrease width to about 1.38 inches

2. Press and hold the Alt key. Recall that if you keep this key pressed while dragging the gridlines, you can see the precise width of the selected column on the Ruler.

3. Move the pointer to the gridline between columns A and B (the right side of the selected rectangle) until it becomes ◄‖►, and then drag the gridline left until the column A width is about 1.0 inch. See Figure 9-16.

Figure 9-16	MOVING A GRIDLINE

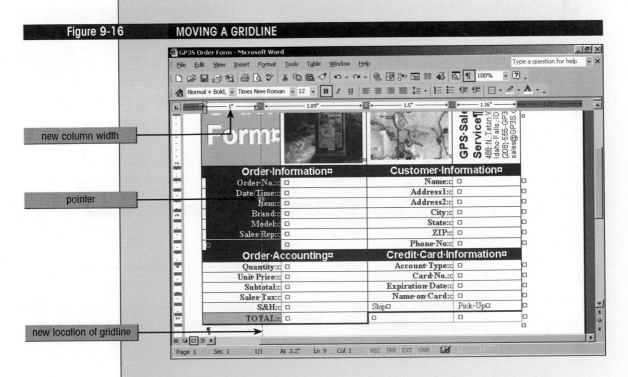

new column width

pointer

new location of gridline

4. Release the **Alt** key and the mouse button.

5. Select the seven cells **C4** through **C10** (see Figure 9-15) below "Customer Information" ("Name" through "Phone No."), move the pointer ←‖→ to the gridline between columns C and D (that is, the rightmost edge of the selected cells), and then hold down the **Alt** key while you drag the gridline left until the width of column C is about **0.77** inch.

6. Release the **Alt** key and the mouse button.

7. Using this same method, decrease the width of cells A12 through A17 (see Figure 9-15) below "Order Accounting" (from "Quantity" through "TOTAL") to **1** inch.

8. Using the same method, select cells **A11** (which contains "Order Accounting") through **B17** (the blank cell to the right of "TOTAL"), and then decrease the width of column B to about **1.25** inches. Note that here you select two columns (cells in columns A and B) to decrease the column width of only column B. You can't just select columns B11 through B17. Because A11 and B11 are merged into one cell (the "Order Information" cell), both columns of cells automatically become selected.

9. Select cells **C12** through **C17** (see Figure 9-15) below the heading "Credit Card Information" (from "Account Type" through the blank cell at the bottom), and then decrease the width of column C to about **1.38** inches (so that the border-line between the selected column C and column D is aligned with the C-D bor-derline in the Customer Information section. Deselect any selected cells. See Figure 9-17.

   TROUBLE? If the border on the far right of the table also moves to the left, undo the operation and repeat the steps, being careful to select only the desired cells.

| Figure 9-17 | TABLE WITH COMPLETED TEXT AND BORDERS |

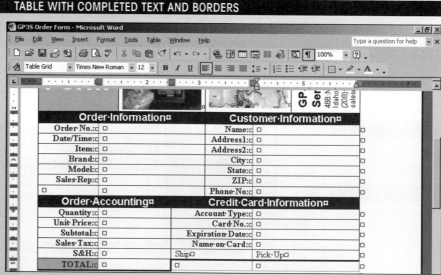

TROUBLE? If the text alignment, text style, column widths, and other features are not the same as those in Figure 9-17, make any necessary adjustments.

10. Save the template.

You have completed the table structure and inserted all the boilerplate text—that is, the text that won't vary—in the order-form template. In the next session, you'll add form fields to the order-form table.

Session 9.1 QUICK CHECK

1. What is an on-screen form?

2. What is a form field?

3. In a table, what is a border? How does it differ from a gridline?

4. How do you rotate text in a table cell?

5. What does it mean to merge cells in a table?

6. What does it mean to split cells in a table?

7. How do you shade a cell with 20% gray?

8. What is reverse type?

SESSION 9.2

In this session, you will create and format text form fields that will be used to store numbers, dates, and regular text. You'll also create prompts and help messages designed to help the user enter the correct information in each field. In addition to the text form fields, you'll create and format drop-down form fields and check box form fields.

Using Form Fields

You have formatted the order form table to make it attractive and easy-to-read, but you still need to insert the most important elements of an on-screen form—form fields. The form fields will help Marissa and the GP3S employees enter information into the order form quickly and efficiently. Recall that a form field stores a certain type of information, such as a name or a price, to which you can assign a specific format.

Word allows you to use three types of form fields:

- **Text form fields**, into which you can enter text, numbers, or other characters for the form, or in which you can perform calculations
- **Drop-down form fields**, list boxes from which you can select an item
- **Check box form fields**, which you can check or uncheck

The text form field is the most versatile of the three. It allows you to:

- Specify the type of information the field will accept (that is, the input type). When specifying an input type, you can choose regular text (any string of alphanumeric characters), numbers only, or dates only.
- Set the maximum number of input characters. For example, if you want the field to accept only three digits for the telephone area code, you would specify 3 as the maximum number of characters. Or, if you want the field to accept a name, but want the number of letters limited to 20, you would set the maximum number of characters to 20.

- Create a message (called a prompt) that appears in the status bar when the insertion point moves into that text field.
- Compose a help message about that text field that appears in a dialog box when the user presses the F1 (Help) key.
- Perform calculations based on values in other cells in the table.

Inserting Text Form Fields

As you have learned, text form fields allow the user to input regular text, numbers, dates, and calculations. In general, you should use text form fields for any type of input. It's not surprising then, that most of the fields you'll add to the GP3S form will be text form fields. You can insert text form fields using buttons on the Forms toolbar.

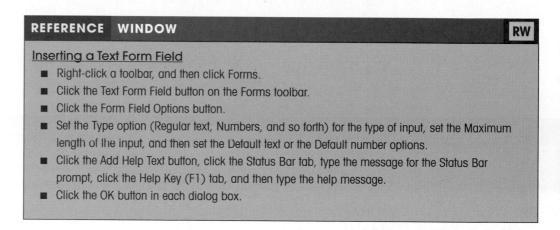

REFERENCE WINDOW   **RW**

Inserting a Text Form Field
- Right-click a toolbar, and then click Forms.
- Click the Text Form Field button on the Forms toolbar.
- Click the Form Field Options button.
- Set the Type option (Regular text, Numbers, and so forth) for the type of input, set the Maximum length of the input, and then set the Default text or the Default number options.
- Click the Add Help Text button, click the Status Bar tab, type the message for the Status Bar prompt, click the Help Key (F1) tab, and then type the help message.
- Click the OK button in each dialog box.

Inserting Text Form Fields for Numbers

When you insert a text form field that will be used to enter numbers, you can specify the kind of number the field will accept, as well as how that number will be formatted on the screen. The key to controlling the content and format of a number is selecting an appropriate numeric picture. A **numeric picture** is a pattern of digits and symbols (such as $#,###,### or 00.00). While numeric pictures might seem a little mysterious at first, once you learn the meaning of the various symbols used in a numeric picture, you can use them to format numbers in a field any way you want.

When you assign a numeric picture to a field, Word takes the number entered by the user, and formats it in a certain way. In some cases, Word also prevents the user from entering improper characters. For example, you could use a numeric picture that would take a single digit entered by the user and display it with a decimal point and a trailing zero. (That is, if the user entered "5" Word would display "5.0" in the field.) The numeric picture doesn't change the number itself (provided you enter an appropriate number), but only how it is displayed within the field. To understand numeric pictures, you first need to understand the symbols used in them. Figure 9-18 shows the most commonly used numeric picture symbols.

Figure 9-18	NUMERIC PICTURE SYMBOLS	
SYMBOL	**PURPOSE**	**EXAMPLE**
0 (zero)	Displays a digit in place of the zero in the field result. If the result doesn't include a digit in that place, the field displays a zero.	Numeric picture "00.0" displays "05.0" Numeric picture "0" diplays an integer of any number of digits
#	Displays a digit in place of the # only if the result requires it. If the result doesn't include a digit in that place, the field displays a space.	Numeric picture "$##.00" displays "$ 5.00"
. (decimal point)	Determines the decimal point position	See examples above
, (comma)	Separates a series of three digits	Numeric picture "$#,###,###" displays "$3,450,000"
- (hyphen)	Includes a minus sign if the number is negative or a space if the number is positive	Numeric picture "-0" displays an integer as " 5" or "-5"
; (semicolon)	Separates the positive and negative numeric picture	Numeric picture "$##0.00;-$##0.00" displays "$ 55.50" if positive, "-$ 55.50" if negative
(parentheses around negative number)	Puts parentheses around a negative result	Numeric picture ""$##0.00;($##0.00)" displays "$ 55.50" if positive, "($ 55.50)" if negative
$, %, etc.	Displays a special character in the results	Numeric picture "0.0%" displays "5.0%"

You'll insert several text form fields that accept only numbers into the order-form template. The first number form field you'll add is one that will be used to enter the order number. When you insert this form field, you'll specify several options. First, you'll specify that the field can only accept a number. Second, you'll indicate a maximum of eight characters of numeric text, because order numbers have no letters and have exactly eight characters. Third, you'll specify a message that will appear in the status bar when the insertion point is positioned in the field. Fourth, you'll specify the text that should appear in the Help dialog box. (The user can open the Help dialog box by pressing the F1 key when the insertion point is located in this field of the form.)

To insert a text form field and set the number options:

1. If you took a break after the last session, make sure that Word is running, that the GP3S Order Form template is open in print layout view, that nonprinting characters are displayed, and that Word displays table gridlines.

2. Move the insertion point to **cell B4**, to the right of the "Order No." cell and just below the "Order Information" heading.

   You could insert the text form field using the Form Field command on the Insert menu, but it's easier to use the Forms toolbar.

3. Right-click any toolbar to display the shortcut menu, and then click **Forms**. The Forms toolbar opens.

4. If necessary, double-click the title bar of the floating Forms toolbar so it becomes a row of buttons below the Formatting toolbar. Now you're ready to insert the text form field.

5. Make sure the insertion point is still in cell B4, and then click the **Text Form Field** button [abl] on the Forms toolbar. Word inserts a text form field with the default options. See Figure 9-19.

Figure 9-19   TABLE WITH NUMBER FORM FIELD

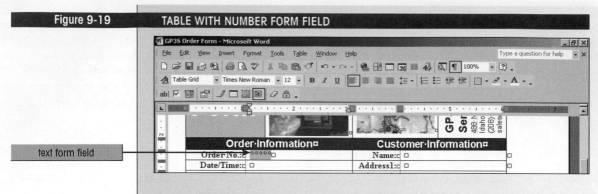

text form field

TROUBLE? If the form field doesn't appear in a gray box, click the Form Field Shading button 📰 on the Forms toolbar.

TROUBLE? If you see { FORMTEXT }, which is the name of the field code, press Alt+F9 to switch from field code view to results view.

Next you'll change the options for the text form field.

6. With the insertion point still immediately to the right of the form field, click the **Form Field Options** button 📑 on the Forms toolbar. The Text Form Field Options dialog box opens. First you'll tell Word that this field should accept only numbers, not text.

7. Click the **Type** list box, click **Number**, press the **Tab** key to select the contents of the **Maximum length** text box, and then type **8**. Next you need to specify the number format.

8. Click in the **Number format** text box, and then type **00000000** (eight zeros), the desired numeric picture. This numeric picture of eight zeros tells Word that the field code accepts only integer values, not decimal numbers, and that regardless of the number of nonzero digits the user types, the field will display eight digits. For example, if the user types 385, the field results would display 00000385. See Figure 9-20. Leave the dialog box open.

Figure 9-20   TEXT FORM FIELD OPTIONS DIALOG BOX

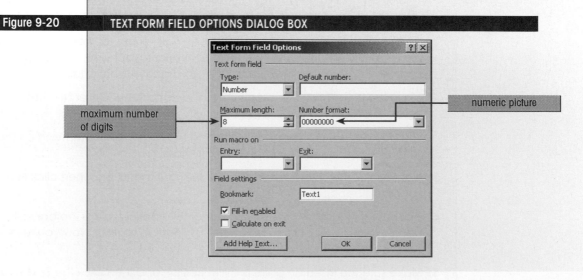

maximum number of digits

numeric picture

You have completed all the options for the text form field except for specifying the help information.

Creating Prompts and Help Messages

Usually, the user knows what information to enter into a field. However, someone using the form for the first time might need some instructions for every field, and both new and experienced people sometimes need clarification regarding what to enter into fields requiring specialized information (such as an order number). To assist in answering user questions, you can create prompts that appear in the status bar, as well as Help dialog boxes that contain even more information.

When the GP3S sales representatives open a new on-screen order form, the insertion point will appear in the text form field you're currently creating (that is, the "Order No." field), because that's the first field in the form. Although the "Order No." label should be enough to inform the sales representatives to type the order number, new users might not know the correct number of digits, or the fact that the number can contain only digits and no decimal or other character. Therefore, Marissa suggests you create a prompt and a help message for this form field.

To add a prompt and a help message to the text form field:

1. Click the **Add Help Text** button in the Text Form Field Options dialog box. The Form Field Help Text dialog box opens.

2. If necessary, click the **Status Bar** tab, and then click the **Type your own** option button. The insertion point moves to the text box.

3. Type **Enter the eight-digit order number** (don't type a period). This text will appear in the status bar whenever the insertion point is in the "Order No." field.

   You'll also create a Help dialog box with more information about what to type into the field.

4. Click the **Help Key (F1)** tab on the dialog box, click the **Type your own** option button, and then type the following text (including the two periods): **The order number is an eight-digit integer. To determine the number, add one to the previous order as listed in the Order Log Book.**

5. Click the **OK** button in the Form Field Help Text dialog box, and then click the **OK** button in the Text Form Field Options dialog box. You return to the GP3S Order Form.

Selecting a Default Value

You have inserted the first number form field. Now you'll insert other number fields, beginning with a number form field to the right of the prompt "ZIP." When you insert this field, you will specify a default value that will automatically appear in the field unless the user enters a different number. In this case, the default will be the major Zip code for the city of Idaho Falls, the source of most of the GP3S orders.

To insert number form fields:

1. Move the insertion point to **cell D9**, below the "Customer Information" heading and to the right of "ZIP."

2. Click the **Text Form Field** button [ab|] on the Forms toolbar to insert the form field, and then double-click the gray-shaded field. Notice that when you double-click a form field, the Text Form Field Options dialog box opens, as it does if you click the Form Field Options button [⊞] on the Forms toolbar.

3. Change the Type to **Number**, the Maximum length to **5**, and the Number format to **00000** (the numeric picture for an integer with five digits). Now you're ready to specify the Idaho Falls ZIP code as the default value.

4. Click the **Default number** text box, and type **83402**.

5. Click the **Add Help Text** button, click the **Status Bar** tab, click the **Type your own** option button, and then type **Enter ZIP code of customer who will receive the order** into the text box.

6. Click the **Help Key (F1)** tab, click the **Type your own** option button, and then type **Enter a five-digit ZIP code.** (Remember to include the period at the end of the sentence.)

7. If necessary, correct any typing errors in the text you just typed, click the **OK** button to close the Form Field Help Text dialog box, and then click the **OK** button to close the Text Form Field Options dialog box. Notice that this text field shows a number because you typed a default value.

8. Repeat Steps 2 through 7 to insert a number text form field in cell B12, to the right of the cell labeled "Quantity." Set the Type to **Number**, the Maximum length to **4**, the Default number to **1**, and the Number format to **0**. Use the text **Enter the number of items** as the Status Bar prompt, but don't create a Help dialog box for this field.

9. Click the **OK** button twice, and then save the template.

Now you're ready to add the remaining number text fields to the on-screen order form.

To add more number text fields:

1. Move the insertion point to **cell D10**, located to the right of the "Phone No." label.

   Here you'll insert one form field for the area code and another for the rest of the telephone number. This demonstrates that you can create more than one form field in a cell.

2. Type **(** (an open parenthesis), insert a text form field, and then open the Text Form Field Options dialog box. Click **Number** in the Type list box, type **208** (the Idaho area code) in the Default number text box, type **3** (the number of digits in an area code) in the Maximum length text box, type **0** (a zero) in the Number format list box to ensure the number is an integer, and then type **Enter three-digit area code** for the Status Bar prompt. Don't type a help message.

3. Click the **OK** button in each dialog box to return to the order form, press the **Right Arrow** key to deselect the field and position the insertion point to its right, type **)** (a close parenthesis), and then press the **spacebar**. You're ready to insert the text form field for the rest of the telephone number.

4. Insert a text form field, and open the Text Form Field Options dialog box. Leave the Type list box set to Regular text so the sales representatives can type a phone number that includes a hyphen (for example, "555-1234"), which is not considered a numeric character.

5. Type **8** in the Maximum length text box to leave enough space for sales representatives to enter the seven-digit phone number and the hyphen, leave the Default text box and the Text format list box blank, and then type **Enter daytime telephone number with a hyphen** for the Status Bar prompt.

6. Click the **OK** button in each dialog box to return to the order form, click **cell D13**, which is to the right of the cell labeled "Card No.," insert a text form field, and then open the Text Form Field Options dialog box.

7. Click **Number** in the Type list box, leave the Default number box blank, type **20** in the Maximum length text box because no credit card has more than 20 digits, type **0** in the Number format list box to ensure the number is an integer, and then type **Enter credit card number without any spaces or hyphens** for the status bar prompt. Disallowing spaces and hyphens in the credit card number prevents a sales representative from entering a nonnumeric character.

8. Click the **OK** button in each dialog box to return to your order-form template, and then save the template. See Figure 9-21.

Figure 9-21   **TABLE WITH VARIOUS NUMBER FORM FIELDS**

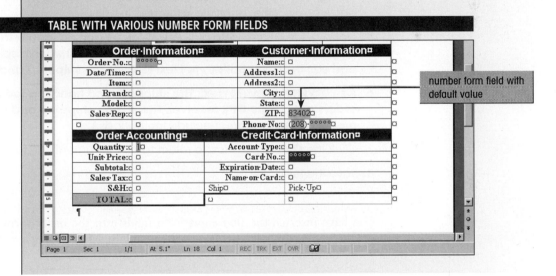

You've inserted all the text form fields that accept only integers as numeric input in your order form template. Next you'll insert text form fields that format input as currency. Later you'll insert other form fields that perform calculations.

Selecting Currency Format

The cells to the right of "Unit Price" and "S&H" (shipping and handling) require fields that format input as currency. When you format input as currency, Word displays it with a dollar sign and usually with a decimal and two digits to the right of the decimal. (Other cells will also store currency values, but it's not necessary to format all money values with the currency format.)

To insert number form fields in the currency format:

1. Move the insertion point to **cell B13**, located to the right of "Unit Price."

2. Insert a text form field, open the Text Form Field dialog box, change the Type to **Number**, leave the maximum length as **Unlimited**, don't include a default number, click the **Number format** list arrow, and then click **$#,##0.00;($#,##0.00)**. This number picture converts any number entered in this form field to a currency format; it displays negative numbers in parentheses.

3. For the Status Bar prompt, type **Enter the unit price**, and then click the **OK** button in each dialog box to return to the order form. Because the S&H form field will be identical (except for the Status Bar prompt), you can copy the form field you just inserted.

4. Make sure the "Unit Price" form field is selected (the form field will display white characters on black, rather than black characters on gray), click the **Copy** button 📑 on the Formatting toolbar, move the insertion point to **cell B16** (to the right of "S&H"), and then click the **Paste** button 📋 on the Formatting toolbar. A copy of the form field is inserted in cell B16.

5. Open the Text Form Field dialog box for the copied form field, change the default number to **4.5** (which will appear as $4.50 when displayed in the form), and edit the Status Bar prompt text to **Enter the shipping and handling fee**.

6. Also add Help Key (F1) text: **The shipping and handling fee is $4.50 for all orders of a single GPS receiver. There is no shipping and handling cost for orders of two or more.** (Include the periods.)

7. Click the **OK** button twice to return to the document window.

8. Save the template.

You have inserted the first eight form fields into the order form template. Before you insert the rest of the form fields into the template, Marissa suggests you test the first eight to verify that they work.

Protecting and Testing a Form

To test an on-screen form, you must first **protect** the form—you must prohibit any changes to the text or structure of the on-screen form. In a protected on-screen form, the insertion point will move only from form field to form field, and not to any other locations; therefore, the user is only allowed to enter information in the form fields, and nowhere else in the form.

The GP3S order form contains eight form fields. After you protect the form, the insertion point will move only from one field to the next, and not to any other location in the form.

To protect the form and test the form fields:

1. Click the **Protect Form** button 🔒 on the Forms toolbar. Because you can't edit the form now, the entire Formatting toolbar and many buttons on the Standard and Forms toolbars become inactive (dimmed). Word doesn't check spelling in protected forms, so there are no red wavy lines beneath any words that might be misspelled. Furthermore, if you click anywhere in the document window, except within a form field, the insertion point automatically moves to the first form field after the location where you clicked.

2. Press the **Tab** key until the order number field in cell B4 (to the right of "Order No." is selected. The field becomes selected, and the prompt "Enter the eight-digit order number" appears in the status bar below the horizontal scroll bar.

3. Press the **F1** key. The Help dialog box opens. See Figure 9-22.

Figure 9-22	TESTING THE FORM FIELD

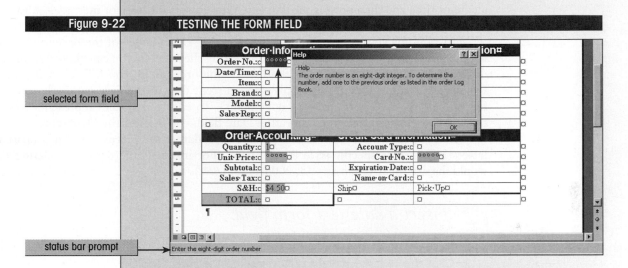

selected form field

status bar prompt

4. Read the message in the Help dialog box, and then click the OK button. You'll now enter an order number.

5. Type **87654**, press the **Tab** key several times to move the selection to the ZIP form field, and then read the Status Bar prompt. Notice that the "Order No." value appears as "00087654," with three leading zeros. When you created the form field, you specified that the field should display 8 digits, so even though you entered only 5 digits, Word added three more for a total of 8.

6. Press the **F1** key to open the Help dialog box, read the Help text for the ZIP code box, and then click the **OK** button. If you were actually taking a customer order, you would have to choose between typing the customer's ZIP code or accepting the default value, 83402. In this case, you'll accept the default.

7. Press the **Tab** key to move the selection to the phone number form field, read the prompt, and then press the **F1** key. This form field has no Help dialog box, so nothing happens.

8. Continue pressing the **Tab** key to move from one field to the next, reading the Status Bar prompts, pressing F1 to read the help messages, and typing any input you desire. Try typing alphabetic characters into the Unit Price field (or one of the other fields that are set up to accept only numbers). As you can see, Word tries to convert your input into an integer, but since you didn't type a valid number, Word simply displays $0.00.

9. When you finish testing all the fields, click 🔒 again to turn off protection so you can continue to edit the form. Notice that the toolbars become active again.

You're finished testing the text fields you've inserted so far.

Inserting Text Form Fields for Dates

As you have seen, you can use the Type option to customize text form fields so they accept only numbers. You can also use the Type option to make the text form field accept only a date or time. If a user enters information in a date text field that Word doesn't recognize as a date or time and then presses the Tab key, Word displays the error message, "A valid date or time is required," and returns the insertion point to the field.

Marissa wants you to insert a form field for the "Date/Time" of the order and also one for the credit card expiration date. When inserting these fields, you can choose from several different date and time types. For the Date/Time order field, you will select the Current Date type, which automatically displays the current date in the field (similarly to the date fields you have used in other word documents). To ensure that sales representatives enter the correct information in the Expiration Date field, you'll select the Date type.

When you specify a date or time type, you use a **date-time picture**, which is a pattern of letters indicating a specific style for the date. (For instance, the date-time picture d/m/y would display the date January 13, 2004 as 13/1/04.)

To insert a date text form field:

1. Move the insertion point to **cell B5**, to the right of the "Date/Time" label.

2. Click the **Text Form Field** button [ab|] on the Forms toolbar to insert a new form field, and then open the Text Form Field Options dialog box.

3. Click the **Type** list arrow, and then click **Current date**. This tells Word to insert the current date in the field. Depending on the date-time picture you select, you can also use the Current Date type to display a time in the form field. You'll do that in the next step.

4. Click the **Date format** list box, and then type **d MMM yy h:mm am/pm** (which is the date-time picture for a date in the format "20 Jun 04 4:15 PM").

5. Click the **OK** button. You don't need a prompt or help text for this form field because it automatically displays the necessary information. See Figure 9-23.

| Figure 9-23 | TABLE WITH DATE FORM FIELD |

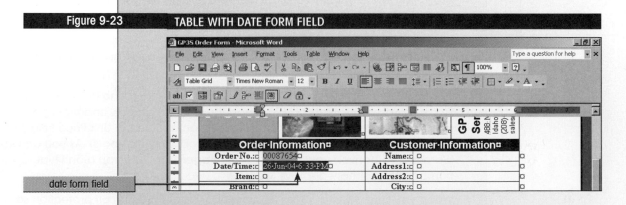

6. Move the insertion point to cell D14, located to the right of "Expiration Date."

7. Insert a text form field into the cell, set the Type to **Date**, click the **Date format** text box, type **MM/yy** (which displays a date in the format "06/04"). Note that you can also select preset date-time pictures in the Date format list box. For additional information about date-time pictures, refer to Tutorial 8 or see Microsoft Word Help.

8. Add the Status Bar prompt **Enter the expiration date in the style 06/04 (month/year)** but do not type a Help message.

9. Click the **OK** button in each dialog box to return to the document window, and then save the template.

You have specified all form fields that will be used to store a date or time.

Inserting Regular Text Form Fields

The remaining text form fields in the order form template should accept any type of character. That means you need to select the Regular Text type when inserting the fields. Note that with Regular Text fields, you can specify default text that will automatically appear in the field. You can also specify a format for the text, for example, Uppercase (all letters will appear capitalized), Lowercase (all letters will appear uncapitalized), First capital (the first letter in the field will appear capitalized), and Title case (the first letter of each word will appear capitalized). You'll start by inserting a field for the "Item" being ordered. For the default text, you'll use the name of the company's most popular product.

To enter a regular text form field:

1. Move the insertion point to **cell B6**, to the right of the label "Item."

2. Insert a text form field, and then open the Text Form Field Options dialog box.

3. Leave the Type set to **Regular text**, leave the Maximum length set to **Unlimited**, click the **Default text** box, type **GPS Receiver**, and leave the Text format box blank.

4. Click **Add Help Text** and type **Enter the type of item ordered** as the Status Bar prompt. Type **Enter the type of item, such as GPS Receiver or Topological Map CDs, and not the brand or model.** (including the period) as the Help Key (F1) text.

5. Click the **OK** button twice to return to the document window.

6. Now, using Figure 9-24 as your guide, insert regular text form fields at the locations specified, using the options specified in Figure 9-24. Don't enter any Help text in these form fields.

Figure 9-24		INFORMATION FOR CREATING TEXT FORM FIELDS				
LABEL	**CELL**	**TYPE**	**MAX. LENGTH**	**DEFAULT TEXT**	**TEXT FORMAT**	**STATUS BAR TEXT**
Brand	B7	Regular text	20	Garmin	(none)	Enter the product brand
Model	B8	Regular text	Unlimited	(none)	(none)	Enter the product model
Name	D4	Regular text	Unlimited	(none)	(none)	Enter the customer's name
Address1	D5	Regular text	Unlimited	(none)	(none)	Enter the customer's street address, including apartment number
Address2	D6	Regular text	Unlimited	(none)	(none)	Enter the second line of the address, if needed
City	D7	Regular text	Unlimited	Idaho Falls	Title case	Enter the customer's city
State	D8	Regular text	2	ID	Uppercase	Enter the customer's state
Name on Card	D15	Regular text	Unlimited	(none)	Uppercase	Enter the name on the card if different from customer name

7. Save the template. Your document should now look like Figure 9-25.

Figure 9-25	TABLE WITH REGULAR TEXT FORM FIELDS

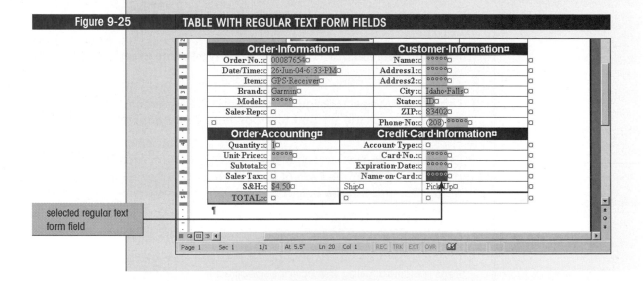

selected regular text form field

Inserting Drop-Down Form Fields

So far you've entered only one of the three major types of form fields—text fields. Now you're ready to use the two other main types of form fields—drop-down fields and check box fields.

When the required information is limited to a short list of entries, you can use a **drop-down form field**, which displays a list of possible entries. The user can then click the correct entry in the list. Using drop-down form fields makes it possible to complete a form faster and without making any spelling errors.

The only individuals who sell GPS receivers and related products are Marissa and her three sales representatives, Dan Redd, Christie Williams, and Paul Crockett. Rather than requiring that they type their own names repeatedly, Marissa suggests you create a drop-down form field so each user can select his or her name.

To insert a drop-down form field:

1. Move the insertion point to the end of the text in cell B9, to the right of the "Sales Rep" label.

2. Click the **Drop-Down Form Field** button 🖳 on the Forms toolbar, and then click the **Form Field Options** button 🖫 on the Forms toolbar. The Drop-Down Form Field Options dialog box opens.

3. In the Drop-down item text box, type **Marissa Wurzburg**, and then press the **Enter** key (or click the **Add** button). The name "Marissa Wurzburg" appears in the "Items in the drop-down list" list box.

4. Repeat Step 3 for each of the other three sales representatives: **Dan Redd**, **Christie Williams**, and **Paul Crockett**. See Figure 9-26.

Figure 9-26   **DROP-DOWN FORM FIELD OPTIONS DIALOG BOX**

TROUBLE? If your dialog box doesn't match Figure 9-26, correct any typing errors by clicking the incorrect name, clicking the Remove button, making the correction, and then clicking the Add button.

You can change the order of the items in the list by clicking the entry you want to move and then clicking the appropriate Move arrow. You decide to leave the list as is because the sales representatives are listed from the most senior to the least senior employee.

Next you'll specify a Status Bar prompt, using the same method you used for text form fields.

5. Click the **Add Help Text** button, click the **Type your own** option button, and then type **Select the sales representative** for the Status Bar prompt.

6. Click the **OK** button in each dialog box to return to the order form. The name "Marissa Wurzburg" appears in cell B9.

You have inserted a drop-down form field that lists the sales representatives. Next Marissa asks you to insert another one for the credit card account type. The GP3S Store accepts VISA, MasterCard, American Express, and Discover.

To insert another drop-down form field:

1. Move the insertion point to **cell D12**, to the right of the label "Account Type" in the Credit Card Information section.

2. Insert a drop-down form field, and then open the Drop-Down Form Field Options dialog box.

3. Type **VISA** in the Drop-down item text box, and then press **Enter** to enter the first item in the "Items in drop-down list" list box.

4. Repeat Step 3 to add **MasterCard**, **American Express**, and **Discover** to the list.

5. Enter **Select the credit card account type** for the Status Bar prompt.

6. Click the **OK** button in each dialog box to return to the document window. See Figure 9-27.

Figure 9-27   **TABLE WITH DROP-DOWN FORM FIELDS**

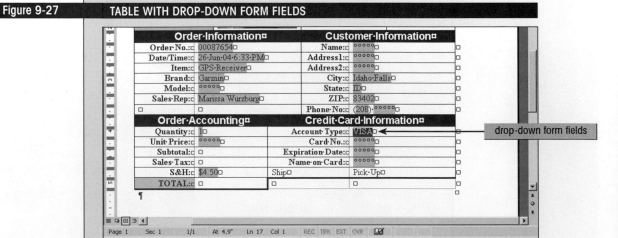

7. Save the template.

If you ever want to modify a form field, click the form field to select it, and then click the Form Fields Options button on the Form toolbar. Then make any change you desire to the field options, such as adding another item to a drop-down list or modifying the text format. Next you need to insert some check box form fields.

Inserting Check Box Form Fields

As you probably know, Microsoft Word dialog boxes often include check boxes that you can click to display or remove a checkmark. Similarly, a **check box form field** is a box-shaped field that that users can click to insert or remove an X. Inserting check box form fields is similar to inserting other form fields. If you want to allow users to select any number of options in a list, you can include each option as text in the template, and then place a check box form field before each item in the list. Unlike a drop-down form field, you can select more than one entry in a list of check box form fields. You might include check box form fields in an on-screen survey form for questions such as, "Which of the following items do you plan to purchase in the next six months?"

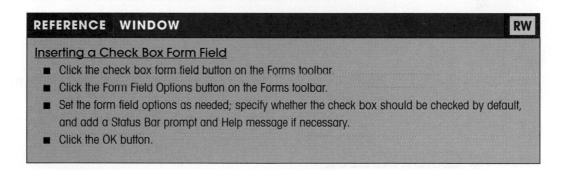

REFERENCE   WINDOW   **RW**

Inserting a Check Box Form Field
- Click the check box form field button on the Forms toolbar.
- Click the Form Field Options button on the Forms toolbar.
- Set the form field options as needed; specify whether the check box should be checked by default, and add a Status Bar prompt and Help message if necessary.
- Click the OK button.

According to Marissa's design, the GP3S order form will indicate whether the orders are to be shipped or picked up. For this reason, you'll add two check box form fields to the order form.

To insert two check box form fields:

1. Click **cell C16**, immediately to the left of the label "Ship."

2. Click the **Check Box Form Field** button ☑ on the Forms toolbar to insert a check box.

3. Click the **Form Field Options** button 📑 on the Forms toolbar to open the Check Box Form Field Options dialog box.

4. Click the **Checked** option button in the Default value section of the dialog box so this box will be checked when a sales representative starts a new form.

5. Enter **Press the spacebar or click with the mouse to insert or remove a check** as the Status Bar prompt.

6. Click the **OK** button in each dialog box to return to the order form.

7. Press the **Right Arrow** key to deselect the form field, verify that the insertion point is positioned between the form field and the word "Ship," and then press the **spacebar**. A space is inserted to the right of the check box form field.

8. Select and then copy the check box form field and the space after it to the position immediately to the left of the phrase "Pick Up" in cell D16, but set the Default value to **Not checked**. See Figure 9-28.

TROUBLE? If your order form doesn't match Figure 9-28, make any necessary changes.

Figure 9-28	TABLE WITH CHECK BOX FORM FIELDS

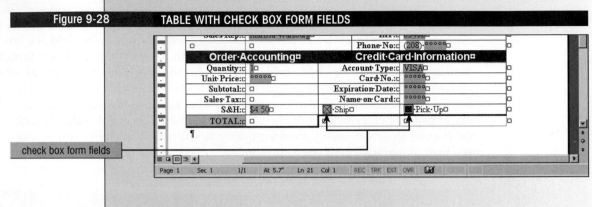

check box form fields

9. Save the template.

You've completed all the form fields the sales representatives will need to enter or select information.

Session 9.2 QUICK CHECK

1. Describe each of the following types of text form fields:
   a. text form fields used to store regular text
   b. text form fields used to store numbers
   c. text form fields used to store dates

2. What is the difference between a Status Bar prompt and a Help message in a form field?

3. True or False. The date-time picture MMM dd, YYYY in a text form field displays the date in the form 03 February 2004.

4. What is a numeric picture? What numeric picture would you use if you want a numeric form field to display a number in the style 3.50%?

5. Why would you use a drop-down form field?

6. How do you create a list of items for a drop-down form field?

7. Why would you use a check box form field?

8. How do you set the default value of a check box form field to checked?

SESSION 9.3

In this session, you will automate the on-screen form by inserting text form fields that perform calculations. You will attach macros that help users enter information in the most logical order. You'll also protect and save the on-screen form, use the template to prepare a sample order, fax a filled-in form, and save only the data for an order. You'll also learn how to route a document.

Using Fields to Perform Calculations

The Order Accounting section of the form already contains the fields for entering the quantity, unit price, and the shipping and handling fee. When filling out the form, a sales representative could multiply the quantity by the unit price to get a subtotal, multiply the subtotal by the tax rate (6.25%, or 0.0625) to determine the sales tax, add the shipping and handling fee, and then sum all these numbers to determine a total amount for the order.

But why have the sales representative perform these routine calculations? Not only is it time-consuming, but it also increases the chance for mathematical errors. Instead, you can set up a text form field to perform the calculations automatically. To do this, you specify that the text form field is of type Calculation, and then you add an **expression**, which is a mathematical formula that gets data from other cells and computes a result. Using the above example, an expression could get the subtotal from another cell, multiply that result by 0.0625, and then display the results.

REFERENCE WINDOW   **RW**

Performing Calculations with Form Fields
- Move the insertion point to the cell where you want to display the calculation results.
- Insert a text form field, and then open the Text Form Field Options dialog box.
- Click the Type list arrow, and then click Calculation.
- Type an expression (or formula) in the Expression text box. For example, the expression "=B14+B15+B16" yields the sum of the values in cells B14, B15, and B16.
- Set the number format and other options as needed.
- Click the OK button.

To insert the form field that calculates the cost of the subtotal:

1. If you took a break after the last session, make sure that Word is running, that the GP3S Order Form template is open in Print Layout view, that the Forms toolbar and nonprinting characters are displayed, and that the table gridlines are displayed.

2. Move the insertion point to **cell B14**, to the right of the label "Subtotal," click the **Text Form Field** button [abl] on the Forms toolbar to insert a text form field, and then open the Text Form Field Options dialog box.

3. Click the **Type** list arrow, and then click **Calculation**. The Text Form Field Options dialog box displays the Expression text box in which you can type a formula for the calculation you want to perform. Here, you want the contents of cell B12 (quantity of the item ordered) to be multiplied by the contents of cell B13 (the unit price).

4. Click to the right of the equal sign in the **Expression** text box, and then type **b12*b13**. Notice that in most computer programs, an asterisk (*) is used as a multiplication sign.

5. Click the **Number format** list arrow, and then click **$#,##0.00;($#,##0.00)** to set the number format as a dollar amount. See Figure 9-29.

Figure 9-29   **TEXT FORM FIELD OPTIONS DIALOG BOX**

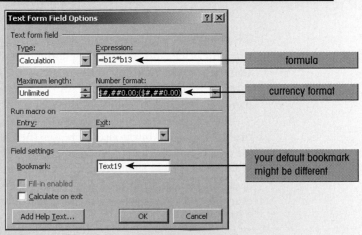

6. Click the **Calculate on exit** check box to insert a checkmark. The Calculate on exit check box ensures that Word performs the calculation when the insertion point moves to the next form field. If the check box isn't selected, Word won't perform the calculation until the field is updated. (To update a field, you select the field, and then press the F9 key.)

7. Click the **OK** button. You return to the document window.

8. Select the text form field that you just inserted and press **F9**. The field is updated and Word displays the results of the calculation—"$0.00."

The number "$0.00," appears in the field because the unit price is blank. You didn't type a Status Bar prompt or a help message because the calculation information is inserted automatically.

You're now ready to insert the form fields that calculate the sales tax, handling fee, and total costs.

To insert the rest of the form fields that will perform calculations:

1. Move the insertion point to **cell B15**, to the right of the cell labeled "Sales Tax," and then repeat Steps 2 through 8 in the previous set of steps, except in Step 4 type **b14*0.0625** after the equal sign in the Expression text box. This formula calculates the sales tax, which is the subtotal multiplied by 6.25%. Remember to check the **Calculate on exit** check box and to choose the **$#,##0.00;($#,##0.00)** number format.

TROUBLE? If you exit the Text Form Field Options dialog box before specifying all the information, just reopen the dialog box and make the necessary changes and selections.

Now you'll insert the form field that calculates the total amount of the order.

2. Move the insertion point to **cell B17**, to the right of the cell labeled "TOTAL." Repeat the procedure to insert a calculation field, except type **b14+b15+b16** after the equal sign in the Expression text box. This will calculate the total order amount, which is the sum of the subtotal (cell B14), the sales tax (cell B15), and the shipping and handling fee (cell B16). Be sure to check the **Calculate on exit** check box and to choose the **$#,##0.00;($#,##0.00)** number format.

3. Save the template. Your order-form template should look like Figure 9-30. Notice that cell B14 (to the right of the "TOTAL" label) displays the current result of the calculation, $4.50.

   TROUBLE? If the results of your calculation fields wrap to more than one line, adjust column widths as necessary.

   TROUBLE? If your form is different—for example, a label is misspelled, text is not aligned properly, or a border is out of place or missing—make the corrections now. You can change the form field options for a field by double-clicking the field to open the Form Field Options dialog box.

| Figure 9-30 | TABLE WITH CALCULATION FORM FIELDS |

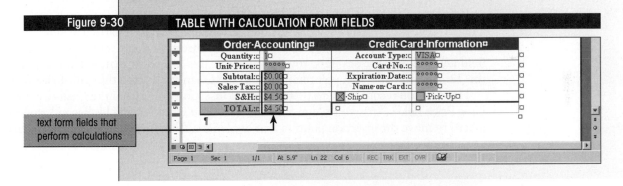

text form fields that perform calculations

The order form now contains all the form fields that perform calculations. When a sales representative enters the Quantity and Unit Price, the calculation text form fields will compute the subtotal, sales tax, shipping and handling fee, and total amount. Keep in mind that a text form field that is set up to perform calculations, displays the result of the calculation, and not the formula used in the calculation. You should also be aware that, when the user fills in a protected form, the insertion point doesn't stop at calculation fields, but skips past them to the next form field that requires input.

Recording a Macro to Change Field Order

After you finish inserting fields in a form, you need to decide the order in which the user will fill in the fields. As you know, the user must press the Tab key to move the insertion point from one field to the next. But where is the "next" field? Microsoft Word selects the next field the same way your eyes find the next word to read in a paragraph of text. When you read, your eyes scan from left to right until they reach the end of a line, and then they move down to the left edge of the next line. Similarly, when you press the Tab key, the insertion point moves to the next field in the same cell if there is another field in that same cell, to the next field on that same row, or to the first (leftmost) field on the next row.

Sometimes, however, the order in which Word selects fields may not be suitable for your form. After all, when filling in fields, it's usually easiest to enter similar information as a group. For example, in the GP3S form it makes sense to enter all the order information before entering any of the customer information, and all the order information before entering any of the credit card information.

When sales representatives fill out the GP3S order form, they'll want to enter, for example, the quantity followed by the unit price and then enter the shipping and handling fee. But right now, when a sales representative enters the quantity and presses the Tab key, the insertion point moves to the Account Type field in the Credit Card Information section. The sales representative must press the Tab key again to move the insertion point to the Unit Price field. Figure 9-31 shows how the insertion point moves among the fields of the Order Information and Customer Information sections of the form.

| Figure 9-31 | NORMAL MOVEMENT OF INSERTION POINT WHEN TAB IS PRESSED |

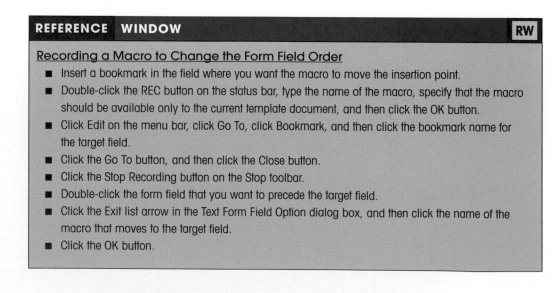

If you want to control the movement of the insertion point in a form, you need to create a macro that runs whenever the insertion point enters or exits a particular field. For example, you might record a macro that runs when the insertion point is located in the Quantity field and the user presses Tab. You could design this macro so that, when the user presses the Tab key, the insertion point moves from the Quantity field to the Unit Price field.

How do you record a macro that moves the insertion point from the Quantity field to the Unit Price field? First, you assign a bookmark to the Unit Price field. Second, you record a macro to move the insertion point to that bookmark. And third, you assign the macro to the Quantity field.

REFERENCE WINDOW   **RW**

Recording a Macro to Change the Form Field Order
- Insert a bookmark in the field where you want the macro to move the insertion point.
- Double-click the REC button on the status bar, type the name of the macro, specify that the macro should be available only to the current template document, and then click the OK button.
- Click Edit on the menu bar, click Go To, click Bookmark, and then click the bookmark name for the target field.
- Click the Go To button, and then click the Close button.
- Click the Stop Recording button on the Stop toolbar.
- Double-click the form field that you want to precede the target field.
- Click the Exit list arrow in the Text Form Field Option dialog box, and then click the name of the macro that moves to the target field.
- Click the OK button.

Marissa's first concern is to ensure that the insertion point moves from one field to the next within the Order Information section of the form. Right now, when the insertion point is in the "Order No." field and the user presses the Tab key, the insertion point moves to the "Name" field. In the following steps, you'll record a macro that moves the insertion point to the "Item" form field instead. This macro will run only when the insertion point is located in the "Order No." field and the user presses the Tab key.

To record a macro that will change the field order:

1. To make sure that your installation of Word will allow macros to run, click **Tools** on the menu bar, click **Options**, click the **Security** tab, click the **Macro Security** button, click the **Medium** or **Low** option buttons, and then click the **OK** button twice. Now after you create macros in any document and open the document in Word, you can run the macros. If you left the Security set to High, you wouldn't be able to run your macros after you closed and then reopened the document.

2. Double-click the **Item** form field in cell B6. The Text Form Field Options dialog box opens; here you can assign a bookmark to this form field.

3. In the Field settings section of the dialog box, double-click the **Bookmark** text box to highlight its contents (if the text box is blank, click in it), type **ItemField** (all one word, without spaces), and then click the **OK** button. You've now assigned a bookmark to the field. Next you'll record the macro that moves the insertion point to the ItemField bookmark.

4. Double-click the **REC** button on the status bar to open the Record Macro dialog box, type **MoveToItemField** in the Macro name text box, click the **Store macro in** list arrow, click **Documents Based On GP3S Order Form**, select the text in the **Description** text box, type **Go to Item field**, and then click the **OK** button. You return to the document window, where each of your actions will be recorded.

5. Click **Edit** on the menu bar, click **Go To**, click **Bookmark** in the Go to what list, click the **Enter bookmark name** list arrow, click **ItemField** in the list of bookmarks, click the **Go To** button, and then click the **Close** button.

   (You used the Go To command to move the insertion point to the bookmark, rather than using the Bookmark command on the Edit menu, because the Bookmark command allows you to edit the document. You must avoid any command related to editing the document, because later in this tutorial you'll protect the form to prevent users from changing it inadvertently. Once you protect the form, all editing commands become unavailable. If you use the Bookmark command now, the macro will not work later after you protect the document.)

6. Click the **Stop Recording** button ■ on the Stop toolbar. You have recorded the entire macro. Now you need to tell Word to execute this macro whenever the Tab key is pressed in the "Order No." field.

7. Open the Text Form Field Options dialog box for the "Order No." text form field in cell B4.

8. Click the **Exit** list arrow in the Run macro on section of the dialog box, and then click **MoveToItemField**. See Figure 9-32.

Figure 9-32   TEXT FORM FIELD OPTIONS DIALOG BOX WITH EXIT MACRO

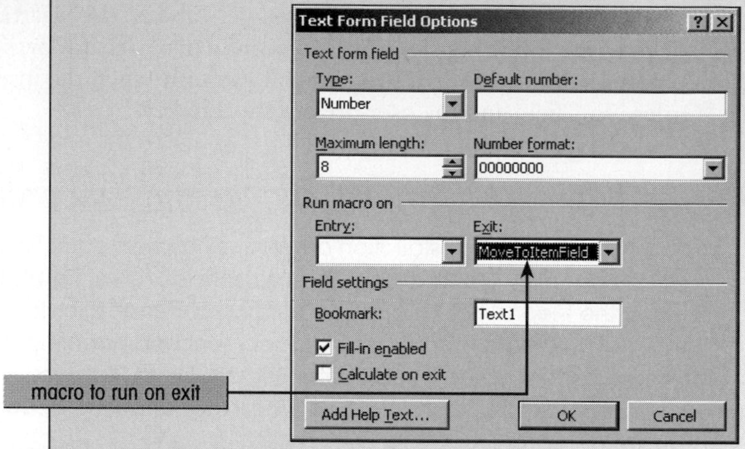

9. Click the **OK** button to return to the document window, and then save the order-form template.

Now whenever a GP3S sales representative presses the Tab key after entering the order number, the insertion point will move to the Item field, not to the Name field. You'll have a chance to test this macro later, to make sure it works as planned. But first, you need to create several more macros. Each macro will move the insertion point from one form field to another form field. Once all the macros are all completed, they will ensure that the insertion point moves among the fields in a logical sequence. Rather than record each macro, you'll use the Visual Basics for Applications (VBA) Editor to copy and modify the macro you already created.

To create the other macros using the VBA Editor:

1. Using the procedure given in the preceding set of steps, assign the bookmark names shown in Figure 9-33.

Figure 9-33	BOOKMARK AND MACRO NAMES TO ASSIGN IN FORM FIELDS		
LABEL NEXT TO FIELD	CELL NUMBER OF FIELD	BOOKMARK NAME	MACRO NAME (TO RUN WHEN INSERTION POINT LEAVES FIELD)
Brand	B7	BrandField	MoveToModelField
Model	B8	ModelField	MoveToSalesRepField
Sales Rep	B9	SalesRepField	MoveToNameField
Name	D4	NameField	MoveToAddress1Field
Address1	D5	Address1Field	MoveToAddress2Field
Address2	D6	Address2Field	MoveToCityField
City	D7	CityField	MoveToStateField
State	D8	StateField	MoveToZIPField
ZIP	D9	ZIPField	(none)
Quantity	D12	(none)	MoveToUnitPriceField
Unit Price	B13	UnitPriceField	MoveToSHField
S&H	B16	SHField	MoveToAccountTypeField
Account Type	B12	AccountTypeField	MoveToCardNoField
Card No.	B13	CardNoField	(none)
Ship	C16	ShipField	(none)
Name on Card	D15	(none)	MoveToShipField

You don't need to assign bookmark names to the Order No., Phone No., Quantity, Subtotal, Expiration Date, Sales Tax, Name on Card, or Pick Up fields. This is because some of the fields automatically appear in the correct order and because the insertion point doesn't stop at form fields with calculations. You should also note that "S&HField" isn't a valid bookmark name, so you used "SHField" instead.

2. Click **Tools** on the menu bar, point to **Macro**, click **Macros**, click MoveToItemField, and then click the **Edit** button. The VBA Editor window appears on-screen.

3. Make sure the insertion point is in the window containing the Sub MoveToItemField macro, press the **Ctrl+A** key combination to select all the macro code, press the **Ctrl+C** key combination to copy the code to the Clipboard, and then press the **Down Arrow** key to deselect the code and move the insertion point to the end of the macro.

4. Press the **Ctrl+V** key combination to make another copy of the macro code.

5. Scroll up so you can see the beginning of the second copy of the macro code (just below the horizontal line), change both occurrences of the macro name from "MoveToItemField" to **MoveToBrandField**. (Do not delete the parentheses to the right of the macro name.)

6. Find the following line of code: Selection.GoTo What:=wdGoToBookmark, Name:="ItemField". This is the line of the macro that specifies which bookmark the insertion point should move to. By changing the name of the bookmark in this line, you can change which field the insertion point will move to.

7. Change "Name:=ItemField" to **Name:=BrandField** (with no punctuation at the end of the line).

8. Press **Ctrl+End** to move the insertion point to the end of the macro code, and then repeat Steps 4 through 7, but this time change the macro name to **MoveToModelField**, and the bookmark name to **ModelField**.

9. Repeat Steps 4 through 7 again, once for each of the remaining bookmarks listed in Figure 9-33. (*Hint*: Each time you repeat this process, change the word "Item" to the desired field name.) When you are finished, close the VBA Editor window. You return to the document window.

You have now created all the macros. Next you need to open the Form Field Options dialog box for each field mentioned in the preceding steps, and indicate that you want a macro to run when the insertion point exits that field.

To set macros to run on exit from fields:

1. Open the Text Form Field Options dialog box for the "Item" text form field.

2. Click the **Exit** list arrow in the Run macro of section of the dialog box, and then click **MoveToBrandField**.

3. Click the **OK** button to return to the document window.

4. Continue specifying the macro that should run upon exit for the remaining fields listed in Figure 9-33.

TROUBLE? If you try to specify a macro but can't find the proper macro name, you probably have made a mistake renaming copied macro code, or you have forgotten to create the macro. To correct any mistakes or create macros, return to the VBA Editor, edit the macros, and save your changes.

You have finished creating the macros and specifying which macro should run when the insertion point leaves each form field.

Protecting and Saving the On-Screen Form

Your next task is to test your macros. Before you can test them, however, you need to protect the document template. As you saw earlier, after you protect the form, the insertion point can only move from one field to another. It can't move to any other location in the document.

To protect the form and test the macros:

1. Click the **Order No.** form field to move the insertion point there, and then click the **Protect Form** button 🔒 on the Forms toolbar. Now when you press the Tab key, the insertion point will move from one field to the next.

2. Press **Tab** (you might have to press it twice) to move the insertion point to the Item form field, press the **Tab** key again (once or twice) to move the insertion point to the Brand form field, and press the **Tab** key again (once or twice) to move the insertion point to the Model form field.

> TROUBLE? If in either the preceding or the following steps, the insertion point doesn't move to the correct form field, unprotect the form and edit the macros and the form field options (including bookmark names, if necessary) so that the macros work properly.
>
> **3.** Continue pressing the **Tab** key to move the insertion point from one field to the next, testing to make sure that the insertion point moves to each field in the proper order.
>
> **4.** Unprotect the document, if necessary, and make any necessary changes to the form field options or to the macros to make sure the form works properly.

The order form template is now completed. With the table formatted, all the form fields in place, and the macros recorded, you're ready to protect the order form template one last time. You'll also need to save the file to the Templates folder so it's readily available when the GP3S sales representatives use the New command on the File menu.

To protect and save the on-screen form:

1. Click the **Protect Form** button 🔒 on the Forms toolbar to protect the document. Most of the toolbar buttons become unavailable, indicating that the form is now protected.

2. Save the template.

With the template protected and saved, you'll copy it to the Templates folder on your computer. Once the template is stored in this folder, you will use it as the basis of a new document. In the next step, you will find the location of the Templates folder on your computer, and then add the folder to your Favorites list.

3. Click **Tools** on the menu bar, click **Options**, click the **File Locations** tab, click **User templates**, click the **Modify** button, click **Tools**, and then click **Add to Favorites**.

TROUBLE? If you see an error message, you probably already added the Templates folder to your Favorites list. Click the Cancel button on the error message dialog box, and continue with the next step.

4. Click the **Cancel** button on the Modify Location dialog box, and then click the **Close** button on the Options dialog box. Next you will save the order form template in the Templates folder.

5. Click **File** on the menu bar, click **Save As**, click the **Favorites** button on the Save As dialog box, double-click the **Templates** folder, and then click the **Save** button.

Before you continue, you'll close the Forms toolbar to regain the space in the document window.

6. Right-click any toolbar and then click **Forms** on the shortcut menu. The Forms toolbar closes.

7. Close the GP3S Order Form template but leave Word open.

In addition to (or instead of) saving template files in this default Template folder, you can, if you desire, save your template files in other folders, and then tell Word that templates are stored in this other folder. Alternately, you could save templates in a folder that you specify as your template folder for workgroup templates (template files available to your entire workgroup). To change an existing file location or to set a new file location, go to the File Locations tab of the Options dialog box, as described in Step 3 above, click the file type whose location you want to change, and then click the Modify button. You then can change or set the path to the desired folder.

You have finished protecting the form and saving it in the Templates folder. Now you are ready to use the GP3S order-form template to fill out an order form.

Filling in the On-Screen Form

So far you have been acting as a form designer and creator. Now it's time to try out the form from the user's point of view. You can do this by filling in the form just as a sales representative would.

> **REFERENCE WINDOW**   **RW**
>
> Filling in On-Screen Forms
> - Click File on the menu bar, and then click New. (Don't click the New button on the Standard toolbar.)
> - Click General Templates in the New from template section of the New Document Task Pane.
> - Double-click the icon of the document template you want.
> - Read the Status Bar prompt for directions, and then type the requested information in the first field. If you need additional help, press the F1 key.
> - Press the Tab key to move to the next field, or press Shift+Tab to move to the previous field. If you don't want to change the information in a field, press the Tab key to go to the next field. (*Note*: The Shift+Tab key combination will not move the insertion point to the previous field if a macro has been assigned to run when the insertion point leaves the field.)
> - Save and print, fax, or route the completed form.

You'll open a new order form and fill in information for a customer's order.

To open a new order form and fill in some information:

1. Click **File** on the menu bar, and then click **New**. The New Document Task Pane opens. (Recall that you only use the New button on the Standard toolbar to start a document based on the Normal template.)

2. Scroll down in the New Document Task Pane to display the New from template section, and then click **General Templates**. The Templates dialog box opens.

3. Double-click the **GP3S Order Form** icon. A new document window opens with a blank order form. The "Order No." form field is selected, ready for you to type the order number.

4. Press the **F1** key, read the Help dialog box, click the **OK** button to close it, and then type **35891**. (Because you specified that the field should store 8 digits, Word will add the leading-zero digits to the order number after you press the Tab key.)

TROUBLE? If you type the wrong number, edit it. If you type the wrong number and press the Tab key, double-click the Order No. field and retype the correct number. (Normally, you'd be able to single-click the field that you want to edit, no matter where it is, but because the macros run when you leave the current field, the insertion point jumps to the field specified by the macro, not to where you clicked.)

5. Press the **Tab** key. The Item field becomes highlighted, and a Status Bar prompt appears. The default item, "GPS Receiver," appears in the form field.

6. Press the **Tab** key without typing anything to accept the default entry (GPS Receiver). The insertion point moves to the Brand field.

7. Press the **Tab** key again to accept the default entry (Garmin) in the Brand field. The insertion point moves to the Model field.

8. Type **G-12 MAP** in the Model field, press the **Tab** key to move the insertion point to the Sales Rep field, click the list arrow in that field, and then click **Christie Williams**. See Figure 9-34.

| Figure 9-34 | FILLING IN THE FORM |

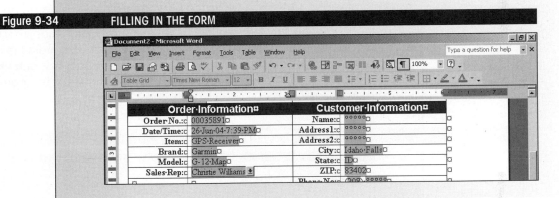

You have completed the first section of the GP3S order form. Now you'll test the customer information sections.

To complete the order form:

1. Press the **Tab** key to move the insertion point to the Name field, type **Kyle Galetka**, press the **Tab** key to move the insertion point to the Address1 field, type **1388 Yellowstone Road**, and then press the **Tab** key twice to move the insertion point past the Address2 field to the City field.

2. With the insertion point in the City field, press the **Tab** key (to accept the default city, Idaho Falls). The insertion point moves to the State field.

3. Press the **Tab** key (to accept the default state, ID), and then press the **Tab** key again (to accept the default ZIP code). The insertion point moves to the area code field.

4. Press the **Tab** key (to accept the default area code, 208), and then type **555-8831** in the phone number field. You've completed the Customer Information section of the form.

TROUBLE? If, in this and subsequent steps, you press Tab and the next field doesn't become highlighted, press Tab a second time.

TROUBLE? If you press Tab too many times and move the insertion point past the Item field, double-click the Item field.

5. Press the **Tab** key to move the insertion point to the Quantity field, type **2**, and then press the **Tab** key. The insertion point moves to the Unit Price field.

6. Type **419.99** and press the **Tab** key to move the insertion point to the S&H field (you'll accept the default value of $4.50). Press the **Tab** key again to leave the Order Accounting section and move the insertion point to the Account Type field in the Credit Card Information section.

7. Press **Tab** to accept the default account type (VISA). The insertion point moves to the "Card No." field.

8. Type **5555000011112222** (a hypothetical credit card number), press the **Tab** key to move the insertion point to the Expiration Date field, type **8/2004**, and then press the **Tab** key to move the insertion point to the Name on Card field.

9. Without entering any information in the Name on Card field, press the **Tab** key again to move the insertion point to the Ship check box, press the **spacebar** to remove the checkmark in the check box, press the **Tab** key, and then press the **spacebar** to add a checkmark to the Pick Up check box. This completes the form. See Figure 9-35.

Figure 9-35	COMPLETED ON-SCREEN FILL-IN FORM

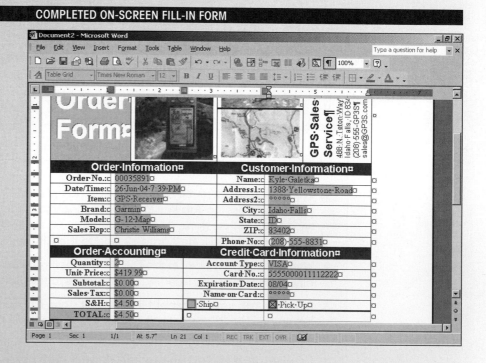

TROUBLE? If the information in your form is not the same as in Figure 9-35, fix it now.

Even though you have filled out the form completely, the calculation fields don't reflect the information you entered in the Order Accounting section; the calculation fields haven't been updated. The only way to update fields in a protected form is to specify that you want the fields updated when you print the form.

To update fields when you print a form:

1. Click **Tools** on the menu bar, click **Options** to open the Options dialog box, and if necessary, click the **Print** tab.

2. In the Printing options section, if necessary, click the **Update fields** check box to make sure that option is selected.

3. Click the **OK** button. Now whenever you print a completed order form, Word will update the fields. You only have to set this option once, not each time you want to print an order form.

4. Click the **Print** button 🖨 on the Standard toolbar to print the order form. Your printed order form should look like Figure 9-36. Notice also that after you printed the form, the calculation fields in the on-screen version display the correct information. For instance, the TOTAL field displays the value $896.97.

Figure 9-36	COMPLETED AND PRINTED ON-SCREEN FORM

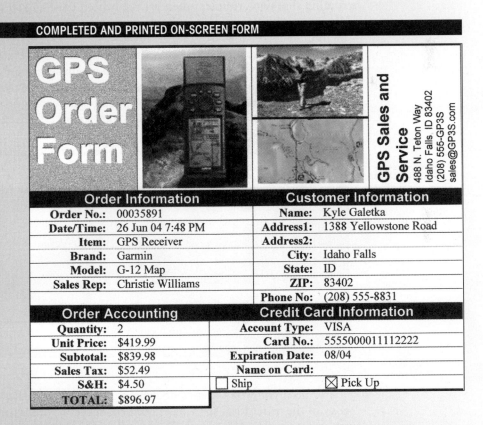

Finally, you'll save the filled-in order form as a Word document because you need to fax it to the customer. Later, you'll save only the filled-in data, which uses less disk space.

5. Save the document as **GP3S Customer Order** in the Tutorial subfolder in the Tutorial .09 folder on your Data Disk.

Now that you've finished filling in the form, you can be satisfied that it works as Marissa planned.

Faxing or Routing an Order Form

After completing an order, the sales representative is supposed to mail or fax a printed form to the customer. With Word's **Fax Wizard**, you can quickly prepare an electronic facsimile (fax) of a document. If you have a fax program, such as Microsoft Fax, installed on your computer and a modem, you can send a fax directly from your computer. Or you can print a cover sheet and the document, and then fax it from a separate fax machine.

If you want to share a document with a group of people who have access to e-mail that supports attachments, and if you want to accumulate comments and corrections from members of the workgroup, then you might want to route the document instead of faxing it. When you **route** a document, you send it as an attachment to an e-mail message; the message (with the document attached) then travels to a group of people, one person at a time. The recipients of the e-mail are specified in a **routing slip**. After each person reads the document and makes comments and corrections, he or she sends it to the next recipient on the routing slip. Each recipient then has the benefit of seeing all the comments and corrections of previous reviewers. When the document returns to you, it will have accumulated comments and corrections from all the reviewers.

To understand another use of routing, suppose that GPS is preparing to host a series of classes on using GPS products. Each time a group signs up for a course, a sales representative prepares an order form. The sales representative then routes the order form to Marissa for approval, then to the course coordinator who arranges accommodations for the class participants, then to the class teacher, and so on. If any person in the routing doesn't approve the form, it doesn't go on to the subsequent members of the workgroup. Whether the form is approved or not, it returns to Marissa, the originator of the routed document.

REFERENCE WINDOW   **RW**

Routing a Document
- Log on to the Internet, and then return to your Word document.
- Click File on the menu bar, point to Send To, and then click Routing Recipient.
- Click the Address button, and then select or enter the names and e-mail addresses for all recipients.
- Click the Route button, or click the OK button, and then click File on the menu bar, point to Send To, and then click Next Routing Recipient.

For now, you won't route a document. Instead, Kyle Galetka requests that you fax him a copy of the order form so he has a permanent record of his order. You'll create and send the fax using the Fax Wizard. (Even if you're not actually faxing the document, you should complete these steps.)

To create and send a fax:

1. Click **File** on the menu bar, point to **Send To**, and then click **Fax Recipient**. The Fax Wizard dialog box opens. Read the information in the dialog box.

    TROUBLE? If you don't see the Fax Recipient in the Send To submenu, ask your instructor or technical support person for help.

2. Click the **Next** button. The next Fax Wizard dialog box opens, where you can select the document you want to fax. The default document name is GP3S Customer Order.doc, which is the document you want to fax.

3. Make sure the **With a cover sheet** option button is selected so that the Wizard will create a cover sheet for your fax, and then click the **Next** button. The next Fax Wizard dialog box opens, where you can select the fax program you want to use. In this case, you'll print the document on the default Windows printer rather than actually fax it.

   TROUBLE? If the With a cover sheet option button is dimmed, just continue the following steps as best you can without creating a cover letter.

   TROUBLE? If you actually want to send a fax, you must have a fax program and know a fax number to which you can send the form. For more information, ask your instructor or technical support person for help.

4. At this point (assuming you have Microsoft Fax installed on your computer), you can select the Microsoft Fax option button; or you can select a different fax program. In this case, you should click the **I want to print my document so I can send it from a separate fax machine** option button, and then click the **Next** button. The next Fax Wizard dialog box appears, where you can type the name and fax numbers of the recipients.

5. With the Insertion point in the First Name text box, type **Kyle Galetka**, press the **Tab** key, type **1-208-555-8835**, and then click the **Next** button. The next Fax Wizard dialog box appears, where you can select a style for the cover sheet.

6. Make sure the Professional option button is selected, click the **Next** button, and fill in the information as shown, except type your name instead of Marissa Wurzburg, as shown in Figure 9-37.

Figure 9-37	FAX WIZARD WITH INFORMATION FOR FAX FORM

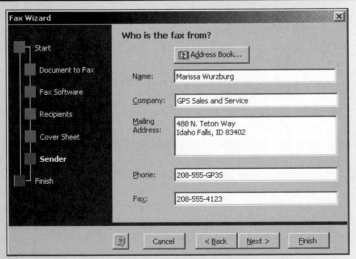

7. Click the **Next** button, read the information in the final Fax Wizard dialog box, and then click the **Finish** button. Word creates a document for the Fax cover sheet. The Fax Wizard closes.

8. Click in each of the five "(Click here . . .)" regions of the document, and type the information as shown in Figure 9-38. This is optional information, and is different from the information you filled in with the Fax Wizard. Even though optional, it is sometimes helpful to the recipient.

9. Save the cover letter as **Galetka Fax** to the Tutorial subfolder in the Tutorial .09 folder. Print the cover letter, and then close it.

| Figure 9-38 | DOCUMENT WINDOW WITH FAX COVER SHEET |

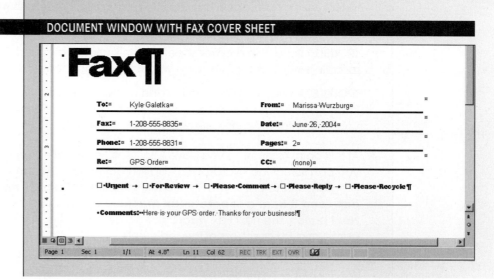

You're almost finished working on the order form. Your last task is to save the order information in case Marissa needs to refer to it later.

Saving Only the Data from a Form

After you fill in a form, it's important to keep a copy for your records. You could print a copy and store it in a filing cabinet. Or you could save the entire on-screen form as a Word document, as you did earlier. To save space in a filing cabinet or on your computer's hard drive, however, you can choose to save only the information entered into the form. When you choose this option, Word saves the information as a text file.

When you save on-screen form information as a text file, you save only the data entered into or calculated by the fields, not the table, graphics, fields, or anything else in the document. Word saves the data in a text file, with the filename extension ".txt." The advantage of this method is that you save disk space. A file with only data uses about ¼ kilobyte of disk space.

By contrast, when you save an on-screen form as a Word document, you save the complete document, including the table, graphics, fields, and information. A complete GP3S order document saved as a normal Word document uses about 80 kilobytes of disk space. The advantage of this method is that any time you want to view or print the completed form, you can open the document just as you would any other Word document.

Be aware that after you save a form as a text file with only the data, you can't retrieve the data and display it in the form again. You can, however, import the data into a spreadsheet or database program, and then analyze the data you have collected. By using a feature in the Options dialog box, you can set up Word so that every time you save a form document, Word saves only the data (as a text file).

REFERENCE   WINDOW   **RW**

Setting up Word to Save Only Form Data
- Click Tools on the menu bar, click Options, and then click the Save tab.
- Click the Save data only for forms check box in the Save options section to select it.
- Click the OK button.

In the future, Marissa wants Word to save only the data in the form, and not the complete, filled-in form documents. You'll use the Options dialog box to select the appropriate setting now.

To set the Save data only for forms option:

1. Make sure the GP3S Customer Order is still visible in the document window, click **Tools** on the menu bar, click **Options**, and then click the **Save** tab in the Options dialog box. Notice the "Save data only for forms" check box in the Save options section. When this check box is selected, Word saves only the data entered into form documents. It does not save the entire form document. (*Note*: Choosing this setting has no effect on the original form template.)

2. If necessary, click the **Save data only for forms** check box to select it.

3. Click the **OK** button. The Options dialog box closes.

With the Save data only for forms option set, you can save the form that you just completed for Kyle Galetka.

To save the completed form:

1. Click the **Save** button 🖫 on the Standard toolbar. Because you haven't yet saved this document as data only, the Save As dialog box opens.

2. Make sure the Save in list box is set to the Tutorial subfolder in the Tutorial .09 folder on your Data Disk. Leave the default filename **GP3S Customer Order** in the File name text box, leave **Plain Text** as the default file type, and then click the **Save** button. Word now displays a dialog box indicating that you are about to save the file as text only. The dialog box also shows you the text file that will be created after you finish saving the data. See Figure 9-39

Figure 9-39   **SAVING THE FORM AS DATA-ONLY PLAIN TEXT**

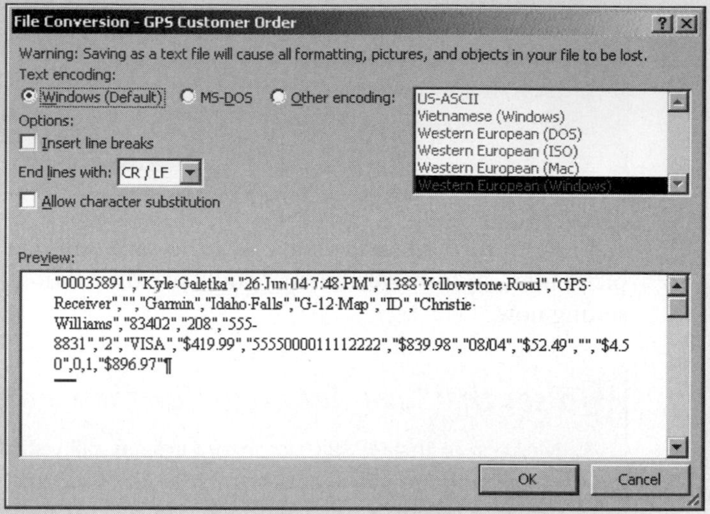

3. Click the **OK** button. Word saves the data with the filename extension ".txt" because it is a text file.

   Now that you're finished working with the GP3S form, you need to deselect the "Save data only for forms check box" on the Save tab in the Options dialog box. You'll do that now.

4. Click **Tools** on the menu bar, click **Options**, click the **Save** tab, click the **Save data only for forms** check box to deselect it, and then click the **OK** button.

5. Close any open documents. Click the **No** button if you're prompted to save changes to any open document.

6. Delete the **GP3S Order Form** template from the Templates folder on your computer.

7. Exit Word.

   In this tutorial you formatted a table using advanced table features and added form fields to make the document an on-screen form template. Then you used the template to create a Word document with all the information filled in for a GPS order. Finally, you printed the document, prepared it for faxing, and saved just the document data.

   Marissa is pleased with the appearance of the form you created and with how well it works. She's sure it will speed up the order-taking process as well as improve the accuracy of the records kept at the GP3S Store.

Session 9.3 QUICK CHECK

1. In a text form field that performs calculations, what is an expression?

2. Briefly describe how you would tell Word to calculate the sum of the values in two cells of a table in an on-screen form.

3. When you're filling out an on-screen form, what key or keys do you press to move from one field to the next? To move from one field to a previous field?

4. Briefly describe how you would change the order in which the insertion point moves from one field to another in a form.

5. Why do you protect a form template before you save it?

6. What are the two ways that you can save a completed form? Name one advantage and one disadvantage of each.

7. How do you save only the data in a form, rather than the entire form, as a normal Word document?

REVIEW ASSIGNMENTS

Martsen Vohwinkle is course director and teacher for Global Positioning Systems Sales and Service. His responsibilities include developing course materials for classes that explain how to use GPS equipment, recruiting students for these classes, and, finally, teaching the classes. He asks you to help him develop an on-screen form that he can use when registering students for his classes.

1. If necessary, start Word and make sure your Data Disk is in the appropriate drive. Open the file **GPCourse** from the Review subfolder in the Tutorial.09 folder on your Data Disk, and then save it in the same folder as a document template with the filename **GP3S Course Sign-Up Form**.

2. At the bottom of the document, insert "Prepared by [Your Name]". (Remember to replace "[Your Name]" with your first and last name.)

3. Insert the picture file **GPSRocks** (from the Review folder for Tutorial 9) into cell B1.

4. Change the font of the text in cell A1 to 12-point Arial, and then change the font of the company name "GPS Sales and Service" to 26-point, bold, engrave Arial.

5. Rotate the text in cell A1 so that it reads bottom to top. Set the shading color of cell A1 to Gray-30%. Set the weight (thickness) of the lines on all four sides of the table to 3 points. Similarly, set the center vertical border (the line separating the left and right halves of the table) to the same weight.

6. Change the text in row 2 (cells A2 and B2, "Course Information" and "Customer Information") to reverse type, and then change the font in those cells to 16-point bold Arial.

Explore ▶ 7. Split column A from cells A3 to A9 into two columns. (*Hint*: Select the specified cells and then click the Split Cells button on the Tables and Borders toolbar. Do not merge the cells before splitting.)

8. Remove the border line (but not the gridline) to the right of cells A3 to A9.

9. Set the text alignment of cells A3 to A9 to Align Right. Set the width of cells A3 to A9 to 1 inch. Finally, set the width of the new cells B3 to B9 to 1.4 inches.

10. Merge cells C3 to C6 (the four cells below "Customer Information") to make one large cell. In this new, large cell (below "Customer Information"), insert a text form field that accepts regular text. Type "Enter the customer name and address" as the Status Bar prompt, and, for the help text, use: "Type the name and address in standard format on three or four lines." Don't set any default text; keep the maximum length set to Unlimited, and don't specify a Text format. With the Text and Field Options dialog box still open, assign the bookmark "NameAddress."

11. In the same cell as the label "Phone" and between the two parentheses, insert a text form field that accepts only numbers. Set the maximum length to 3, the default text to "208," the number format to "000," and enter "AreaCode" as the bookmark. Set the Status Bar prompt to "Enter the customer's area code." Don't enter any Help text.

12. In the Phone cell, click to the right of the space after the close parenthesis, insert a text form field that accepts regular text. Set the maximum length to 8, don't include default text, and leave the text format blank. Leave the bookmark with its default name; you won't be referring to this field in any macros.

13. To the right of the space after "E-mail," insert a text form field that accepts regular text. Set the length to unlimited. Change the bookmark to "Email." Set the Status Bar prompt to "Enter the customer's e-mail address, if available." Don't enter any Help text.

14. In cell B3, to the right of "Course Title," insert a drop-down form field. Enter the following names of GPS courses into the drop-down list: "Introduction to GPS," "GPS in the Field," and "GPS and Maps." Type "Select the course title" for the Status Bar prompt. Don't enter any Help text.

15. In cells B4 and B5, to the right of "Start Date" and "End Date," enter text form fields that accept only dates. Use a date-time picture that formats the date in the form 07 Jun 04. For the Status Bar prompts, type "Enter the date of the first day of class" and "Enter the date of the last day of class," for the two respective cells. Don't enter any Help text. Set the respective bookmarks to "StartDate" and "EndDate."

16. In cell B6, to the right of "Day of Week," enter a drop-down form field. Because all classes are taught on Tuesday, Wednesday, or Thursday, include the name of those three days as the items in the drop-down items. Set the bookmark to "DayofWeek." Type "Select the day of the week for the classes" as the Status Bar prompt.

17. In cells B7 and B8, to the right of "Course Fee" and "Materials," insert two text form fields that accept only numbers, and format them in currency format. Set the bookmarks to "CourseFee" and "Materials," respectively. Set the default values to "75" and "35," respectively. For the Status Bar prompts, type "Enter the course tuition fee" and "Enter the total cost of course books, handouts, reference materials, and so forth." Do not enter any Help text.

18. In cell B9, to the right of "TOTAL," enter a text form field that sums the course fee and the cost of materials and formats the total as currency.

19. Create as many macros as needed, all of which should be stored in the GP3S Course Sign-Up Form template, so that as a GP3S employee uses the template, the insertion point moves from one field to the next in the Course Information column (column B), and then from one field to the next in the Customer Information column (column C). Choose descriptive names for the macros, but use the bookmark names assigned in previous steps. Select the Run macro on Exit setting as needed for each form field.

20. Test the macros. Make any changes or additions as needed so that all the macros work properly.

Explore ▶ 21. Record a macro (for this template only) named "PrintForm" that prints two copies of the form.

Explore ▶ 22. To the right of the space after "Check Here to Print," insert a check box form field, and set the Run macro on Entry to "PrintForm." This sets up the form so that whenever a GP3S employee presses Tab to move to the check box, two copies of the form are printed.

23. Protect and save the completed document template form. Don't copy it to the Template folder. Close the document template window.

Explore 24. Start a new document based on this form. (*Hint*: Use the New command on the File menu to open the New Document Task Pane, and then click Choose document in the "New from existing document" section.)

25. Fill in the form using real or fictitious (but reasonable) information. For the customer information, use your own name, address, phone number, and e-mail address. Make sure that after you press the Tab key to move the insertion point to the check box at the bottom of the form, Word prints two copies of the form.

26. Save the completed form (not just the date) to the Tutorial.09 Review folder using the filename **GP3S Course Sheet**. (Word will automatically append .doc as the filename extension.)

27. Save the data from the form in plain text format, using the filename **GP3S Course Sheet**. (Word will automatically append .txt as the filename extension.) Close the document window and exit Word.

CASE PROBLEMS

Case 1. San Antonio Disaster Kleenup Jose Herrera is owner and operator of a small business called San Antonio Disaster Kleenup (SADK) in San Antonio, Texas. The company specializes in the clean-up of homes, apartments, and businesses that have been affected by fires, floods, and storms. SADK removes smoke and soot; extracts water and repairs water-damaged structures; cleans, restores, and deodorizes carpets; repairs, cleans, and deconta-minates electronic equipment; recovers print and electronic data; and serves as a general contractor for services such as drywall and flooring construction, electrical and plumbing work, and roofing and structural restoration. Jose wants to automate his preinspection forms, which SADK agents use to get initial information from potential clients and to set up an appointment to inspect the disaster site. Jose asks you to help him by preparing a Word on-screen form.

1. If necessary, start Word and make sure your Data Disk is in the appropriate drive. Open the file **SADKForm** from the Cases subfolder in the Tutorial.09 folder on your Data Disk, and then save it in the same folder as a document template with the filename **SADK Pre-Inspection Form**.

2. At the bottom of the document, insert "Prepared by [Your Name]". (Remember to replace "[Your Name]" with your first and last name.)

3. Format the text in cell A1 in 12-point Arial, and then change the font of the company name, "San Antonio Disaster Kleenup," to 22-point, bold, Arial.

4. Rotate the text in cell A1, using the Tables and Border toolbar, so that the text reads bottom to top. (*Hint*: Use the Change Text Direction button on the toolbar.) Increase the height of the row so that the street address of SADK all fits on one vertical line. (*Hint*: Drag the gridline below row 1 or use the Table Properties dialog box to set the row height to about 2.4 inches.)

Explore 5. Set the width of column A automatically so that the widest row of text barely fits on one line. (*Hint*: Click Table on the menu bar, click Table Properties, click the Column tab in the Table Properties dialog box, and deselect the Preferred width check box. Now Word will automatically select an appropriate width.)

6. Change the width of column B to 4 inches.

7. Change the font in cell B1 to white, 36-point, bold Arial, and change the background of the cell to Gray-60%.

Explore   8. Change the alignment in cell B1 so that text is centered both horizontally and vertically. (*Hint*: Use the Align Center button on the Tables and Borders toolbar. Make sure this change affects only cell B1.)

9. Merge cells A2 and B2 so that the heading "Customer Information" is in one cell that spans the table. Make sure this text is centered in the merged cell (this should happen automatically when you merge the cells), and change its font to 18-point, bold, Arial.

10. Set the weight (thickness) of the horizontal lines above and below row 2 (the newly merged cell) to 3 points.

11. Repeat the two previous steps for cells A9 and B9 ("Damage Information") and then again for cells A12 and B12 ("Inspection Charges").

12. Draw a 3-point horizontal line between rows 19 and 20, just above the cell with the text "Inspection Appointment Date."

13. Remove any remaining border line (but not the gridline) between columns A and B.

14. Apply the Align Right text alignment to cells A3 through A8, cells A10 through A11, and cells A13 through A19.

15. In cells B3 through B8, insert appropriate form fields, each of which requests information about the customer. Create an appropriate Status Bar prompt for each form field, but don't include Help text. Insert two form fields for the Phone Number: one field for the area code (put parentheses around the area code), and one for the 7-digit number (including a hyphen). Use the following default values, where appropriate: San Antonio, TX, 78265, and area code 210. In the State form field, set the maximum length to 2, and the text format to Uppercase.

16. To the left of each of the five labels in cell B10 (to the right of "Type of Structure(s)"), insert a check box form field. Keep all the defaults (for instance, keep the check boxes unchecked, and do not enter Status Bar prompts). Similarly, to the left of each of the five labels in cell B11 (to the right of "Type of Damage"), insert a check box form field, keeping all the defaults.

17. In cells B13 to B19, insert an appropriate form field. Specify the form field type based on the type of information that will be stored in the cell. Set the default number of rooms to 1, the default inspection fee per room to $50, the base fee to $100, and the travel fee to $0. (No travel fee is assessed unless the location is outside the greater San Antonio area.) In cell B17, insert a text form of type Calculation with an expression that multiplies cell B13 (number of rooms) times cell B14 (inspection fee per room), and adds cells B15 (base fee) and B16 (travel fee). The result should be the total Estimated Inspection Cost.

18. Set the format for the Inspection Appointment Date field to "MMMM d, yyyy" and the Inspection Appointment Time to "HH:mm" (military clock time). Don't enter any Status Bar prompts or help text for these fields.

Explore   19. Record a macro (for this template only) named "PrintForm" that prints the form (one copy).

Explore   20. To the right of the space after "Print Form:," insert a check box form field, and set the Run macro on Entry to "PrintForm." This sets up the form so that whenever the user presses Tab to select the check box, a copy of the form is printed.

21. Protect and save the completed document template form. Don't copy it to the Template folder. Close the document template window.

Explore   22. Start a new document based on this form. (*Hint*: Use the New command on the File menu to open the New Document Task Pane, and then click Choose document in the "New from existing document section.")

23. Fill in the form using real or fictitious (but reasonable) information. For the customer information, use your own name, address, and phone number. Make sure that when a user presses the Tab key to select the check box at the bottom of the form, Word prints a copy of the form.

24. Save the completed form (not just the data) to the Cases folder for Tutorial 9 using the filename **SADK Pre-Inspection Sheet**. (Word automatically adds the filename extension .doc.)

25. Save the data from the form in plain text format. Use the same filename, **SADK Pre-Inspection Sheet**. (Word automatically appends .txt as the filename extension.) Close the document window and exit Word.

Case 2. Living Sea Aquarium Living Sea Aquarium in Calgary, Alberta, Canada, is a world-class exhibition hall that features fish, coral, reptiles, birds, plants, and insects from around the world. The 100,000-square-foot, state-of-the-art facility has four major exhibition halls, each representing a different major waterway ecosystem. The Living Sea Aquarium emphasizes research and education for students of all ages.

Carol Tanaka, the director of Living Sea Aquarium, wants you to help her create a form that Living Sea Aquarium employees can fill out when school groups order tickets and register for educational classes.

1. If necessary, start Word and make sure your Data Disk is in the appropriate drive. Open the file **LSAForm** from the Cases subfolder in the Tutorial.09 folder on your Data Disk, and then save it in the same folder as a document template with the filename **Living Sea Aquarium Form**.

2. At the bottom of the document, insert "Prepared by [Your Name]". (Remember to replace "[Your Name]" with your first and last name.)

3. Insert into cell A1 the file **LSALogo**, the Living Sea Aquarium logo.

4. Remove the borders (but not the gridlines) along the top and the left edge of cell A1.

5. Draw a 3-point border along the bottom edge of cell A1, along the left edge of B1, and along the top of B1. Also draw a border of the same weight along the bottom border (that is, along the bottom of cells A12 and B12).

6. Format the organization name "Living Sea Aquarium" in cell B1 in 36-point, bold, Book Antiqua. (If you don't see Book Antiqua in your Font list, use another serif font of your choice.)

Explore   7. Set the text alignment in cell B1 so the text is centered both horizontally and vertically. (*Hint*: Use the Align Center button on the Tables and Borders toolbar. Make sure this change affects only cell B1.)

8. Apply a Gray-20% background to cell B1.

9. Set the width of column A to 2 inches, allowing the width of column B to increase accordingly to about 3.85 inches.

10. Remove the border line (but not the gridline) that separates columns A and B from the second row to the bottom row.

11. In each of the following steps in which you're asked to insert a form field, follow the directions as indicated, but also create an appropriate Status Bar prompt. Do not, however, include Help Key (F1) text. If any of the other options are not specified, you may keep the default options or choose appropriate options on your own.

12. Insert three text form fields in cell B4 (to the right of "City, Province, Postal Code"). Use the following settings for each field:

    a. A text form field (for the city) with the default of "Calgary." After the field, insert a comma and a space.

    b. A text form field (for the Province) with the default of "AB" (abbreviation for the Province Alberta), with a maximum length of 2, and the text format set to Uppercase. After the field, insert a space.

    c. A text form field (for the Postal Code) of type Regular text to accommodate the mixed alphanumeric characters in Canadian postal codes, with the default of "T1Y3C2," a maximum length of 6, and the text format set to Uppercase.

13. Insert two form fields in cell B6 (to the right of "Phone Number"):

    a. A text form field in number format (for the area code) enclosed in parentheses, with the default "403," the maximum length of 3, and the number format set for integers). After the field, insert a space.

    b. A text form field in regular text format for the seven-digit (and one hyphen) telephone number, of maximum length 8.

14. In Cell B8 (to the right of "Number of Students), insert a text form field that accepts only numbers, with the default set to "50," the maximum length set to 3 (because the aquarium can accommodate a maximum of 250 students at a time), and the number format set for integers. For the Status Bar prompt, type "Enter the number of students (don't enter the number of teachers or parents, who get in free)."

15. In cell B9 (to the right of "Cost per Student"), insert a text form field that accepts only numbers with the default set to "$2.50," and the number format set to currency.

16. In cell B10 (to the right of "Discount [percent]"), insert a text form field that accepts only numbers, with the default value set to "0.1" and the number format set to "0%." Note that the default value of 0.1 will appear as "10%." For the Status Bar prompt, type "Enter the discount (0% for fewer than 25 students, 10% for 25-50 student, and 20% for more than 50 students)."

17. In cell B11 (to the right of "Total cost"), insert a text form field of type Calculation, with the numeric form set to currency, and with an expression that multiplies the number of students times the cost per student times the quantity (1 minus the discount percentage). If you have entered the proper formula, the default result should be $112.50. Don't include a Status Bar prompt.

18. In cell B12 (to the right of "Program"), insert a drop-down form field with the following three drop-down items: "Tour Only", "Lecture Only", and "Tour and Lecture".

Explore   19. After you type the items into the drop-down form field, change the order of the items so that "Tour and Lecture" is the first item—that is, the default value in the drop-down list. (*Hint*: Use the Move arrows in the Drop-Down Form Field Options dialog box.)

20. In cells B2 to B12 that don't already contain form fields, insert an appropriate form field, each of which accepts the information referred to in the corresponding labels in column A.

21. Protect and save the completed document template form. Don't copy it to the Template folder. Close the document template window.

Explore   22. Start a new document based on this form. (*Hint*: Use the New command on the File menu to open the New Document Task Pane, and then click Choose document in the "New from existing document" section.)

23. Fill in the form using "Stampede Middle School" as the organization; "4872 Jasper

Drive" as the street address; the default values for the city, province, and postal code; your own name and phone number for the contact person and phone number; today's date as the date of visit; "60" as the number of students; the default of "$2.50" as the cost per student; "0.2 (20%)" as the discount; and "lecture only" as the program.

24. Print a copy of your completed form. Save the completed form (not just the data) in the Cases folder for Tutorial 9 using the filename **Living Sea Aquarium Sheet**. (Word automatically adds the filename extension .doc.)

25. Save the form data in plain text format. Use the same filename, **Living Sea Aquarium Sheet**. (Word automatically appends .txt as the filename extension.) Close the document window and exit Word.

Case 3. New N' Old CD Exchange Aaron Goetzinger owns and operates a small store, called New N' Old CD Exchange, that buys, sells, and exchanges new and used music CDs. He and his four employees would like to use a simple computerized system to create and print sales slips for the company and its customers. Aaron asks you to create the fill-in forms.

1. Read through each step of this entire case problem. Then, using paper and pencil, design an on-screen fill-in form with the features mentioned in the following steps. As you plan, make function and appearance your main concerns.

2. Create the fill-in form table with two columns and as many rows as needed.

3. Design the form so that it includes the purchase (by either the customer or the company) or exchange of only one CD. That is, if a customer purchases, sells, or exchanges more than one CD, more than one of your fill-in forms is required.

4. In row 1 include the following company information: New N' Old CD Exchange, 9814 Forsyth Avenue, Greensboro, NC 27420, (336) 555-4336. In the other cell, include one or more digital pictures (use a photo file of your own or use the company logo, named **CDXchng.jpg**, which is located in the Cases folder for Tutorial 9).

5. Merge row 2 into one cell, and add a heading in reverse type. Select an appropriate heading text, such as "Trade-In CD Information," "New CD Information," or "Customer Information."

6. Include at least one other heading row with the same format as the one in row 2.

7. Include at least one cell with rotated text.

Explore   8. Include labels and form fields for the following types of information: Customer name, address, phone number, and e-mail; customer's trade-in CD title (if any), main artist, label (brand), music classification (soft rock, classic rock, hard rock, R&B, alternative, country, jazz, Latin, inspirational, classical, other), and dollar value; customer's new CD title (if any), main artist, label (brand), music classification, and dollar value; the net dollar amount owed by the customer or by the company, including handling fee (determined by a calculation form field). (*Hint*: After creating labels and form fields for the trade-in CD, copy those labels and fields to use for the new CD information, and make any necessary modifications.)

9. Include at least one drop-down form field (for example, to select the type of music), at least two number form fields, at least one calculation form field (as indicated in the previous step), and at least one check box form field.

10. Set default values for at least four of the form fields.

Explore   11. Set at least two form fields that specify a type of text format: Uppercase (for example, to use with a postal two-letter state abbreviation), Title case (for example, to use with CD Titles), or First capital (for example, to use with a city name or a person's name).

12. Specify appropriate maximum lengths and text, number, or date formats for applicable form fields.

13. Change one or more of the column widths, and split one or more of the cells.

14. Draw some of the borders with a line weight of one point or more, and erase the borders (but not the gridlines) at other locations in the table.

15. Change the font attributes of some of the text in the table.

16. Make any other modifications or additions to the form so it is more attractive and easier to use.

17. Write at least one macro (attached to the form document template) that automatically runs in the form document template. For example, create a macro to change the order in which the user fills in the fields, a macro to automatically print the completed form, or a macro to automatically save the form both in full, and in data-only form.

18. At the bottom of the document, insert "Prepared by [Your Name]". (Remember to replace "[Your Name]" with your first and last name.)

19. Save your fill-in form as a document template using the filename **CD Exchange Form** in the Cases folder for Tutorial 9.

Explore ▷ 20. Start a new document based on this form. (*Hint*: Use the New command on the File menu to open the New Document Task Pane, and then click Choose document in the New from existing document section.)

21. Fill in the information for the form using real or fictitious (but reasonable) information. For the customer name and address, use your name and address.

22. Make sure your computer is set up to update the fields upon printing.

23. Protect and save the completed form using the filename **CD Exchange Sheet** as a Word document (a .doc file). Using the same filename, save the form as a plain text document (a .txt file). Save these files in the Cases folder for Tutorial 9.

Case 4. Campus Activity Application Form You have recently been asked to be the director of a campus activity. You decide to prepare an on-screen fill-in form to process participant applications for the event. You may select the event. Examples include a fun run, chess tournament, bowling night, dating service, mountain hike, volunteer clean-up day, text-book exchange, and fund-raiser.

1. Read through each step for this entire case problem. Then, using paper and pencil, design an onscreen fill-in form with the features mentioned in the following steps. As you plan, make function and appearance your main concerns.

2. Include a table of at least two columns and ten rows.

3. Design the form with titles, labels, and form fields.

4. Include form fields for all the information you might need from the applicants.

5. Include all the information the applicant might need: location, date, and time. Also add disclaimers and other information (these might or might not appear in form fields).

6. In the design of the table, merge at least one set of two cells, and split at least one cell.

7. Include at least two merged heading rows with the same format. Include at least one cell with rotated text.

8. Include at least one drop-down form field, at least two number form fields, and at least one check box form field.

9. Set default values for at least four of the form fields.

Explore 10. Include at least two form fields that specify a type of text format: Uppercase (for example, to use with a postal two-letter state abbreviation), Title case (for example, to use with the activity name), or First capital (for example, to use with a city name or a person's name).

Explore 11. Include at least two adjacent rows for expense items, such as entrance fee and supplies fee. Include a text form field for currency for each of the items of expense. Create a separate Total row (where you'll include the total expense) just below the adjacent expense rows. Move the insertion point to the cell where you want to calculate the sum of the cells just above it, and then click the AutoSum button. This automatically sums the numbers in the cells directly above the current one. If the cells above it are numeric fields, the AutoSum button inserts a calculation form field that sums the cells above it.

12. Specify appropriate maximum lengths and text, number, or date formats for applicable form fields.

13. Change one or more of the column widths.

14. Draw some of the borders with a line weight of one point or more, and erase the borders (but not the gridlines) at other locations in the table.

15. Change the font attributes of some of the text in the table.

16. Make any other modifications or additions to the form so it is more attractive and easier to use.

17. Write at least one macro (attached to the form document template) that automatically runs in the form document template. For example, create a macro to change the order in which users fill in the fields, a macro to automatically print the completed form, or a macro to automatically save the form both in full, and in data-only form.

18. At the bottom of the document, insert "Prepared by [Your Name]". (Remember to replace "[Your Name]" with your first and last name.)

19. Protect and save your fill-in form as a document template using the filename **Campus Activity Application Form** in the Cases folder for Tutorial 9.

Explore 20. Start a new document based on the newly created form. (*Hint*: Use the New command on the File menu to open the New Document Task Pane, and then click Choose document in the New from existing document section.)

21. Fill in the information for the form using real or fictitious (but reasonable) information. For the customer name and address, use your own real name and address.

22. Set your computer to update the fields upon printing.

23. Protect and save the completed form using the filename **Campus Activity Sheet** as a Word document (a .doc file), and then using the same filename as a plain text document (a .txt file), save both files in the Cases folder Tutorial 9.

QUICK | CHECK ANSWERS

Session 9.1

1. Word template used for entering information at the computer
2. a space in a document that stores a certain type of information, such as a name or a price, to which you can assign a specific format

3. Outside lines (rules) of a cell or group of cells. Borders appear when you print the table, whereas gridlines appear only on the screen.

4. Click Format on the menu bar, click Text Direction, click an orientation icon, and then click the OK button.

5. Join two or more adjacent cells into one cell.

6. Divide one cell into two adjacent cells, or divide one column or row of cells into two or more columns or rows of cells.

7. Click the Shading Color list arrow on the Tables and Borders toolbar, and then click Gray-20%.

8. white text on a black background

Session 9.2

1. a. accepts both letters and numbers

   b. accepts only numbers

   c. accepts information only in a valid date/time format

2. A status bar prompt appears on the status bar when the insertion point enters the form field; a help message appears when you press F1 with the insertion point in the form field.

3. false

4. digits and symbols that specify the content and format of numbers in form field; 0.00%

5. to enable users to select only from certain options

6. Click the Drop-Down Form Field option on the Forms toolbar, and then enter a list of items in the Drop-Down Item text box.

7. allows user to check a box by clicking the mouse or pressing the spacebar

8. Set the default value to "Not Checked" in the check box form field Options dialog box

Session 9.3

1. a formula that Word uses to perform mathematical calculations

2. Insert a text form field in the cell where you want the results, set the type to Calculations, enter an expression such as = A1 + A2 in the Expressions text box.

3. Tab, Shift+Tab

4. Assign a bookmark to the second (target) field, create a macro to move the insertion point to that bookmark, and then attach the macro to the first field.

5. to prevent the form from being changed by anyone else, and so that the insertion point moves from one field to the next when a new document is created using that template

6. You can save a form as a normal Word document, or you can save only the data as a text file. The advantage of saving as a normal Word document is that you can open and view the form like any other document; the disadvantage is that you must save the complete document, which uses a lot of disk space. The advantage of saving data only as a text file is that the data uses less disk space than a normal Word document; the disadvantage is that you can't reinsert the data back into the form.

7. Click Tools on the menu bar, click Options, click the Save tab, and then click the Save data only in forms check. Then save the document using the Save button on the Standard toolbar.

In this tutorial you will:

- Create a master document, and create, split, merge, and remove subdocuments

- Control text flow and page breaks

- Use automatic heading numbers, numbered captions, and cross-references

- Create a graph with Microsoft Graph

- Track revisions, merge revisions, insert comments, and create versions

- Protect a document with digital signatures

- Use advanced page numbering techniques and style references

- Create an index, table of contents, and table of figures

MANAGING LONG DOCUMENTS

Creating a Survey Report

CASE

Decision Data, Inc.

Decision Data, Inc. (DDI) is a market research company headquartered in Lowell, Massachusetts. The company's clients rely on DDI for help with marketing decisions such as choosing packaging designs and advertising campaigns. Each client is assigned a DDI research team, which consists of three or four marketing experts. The research team is responsible for researching the client's particular market and writing a report summarizing the most important information.

To obtain information for DDI clients, the research teams rely on Internet survey forms (sometimes called cybersurveys) and focus groups. The DDI research teams ask customers, clients, employees, contractors, and others to fill out and submit cybersurveys via the Internet. Focus groups consist of 8 to 12 people who assemble in a room for about two hours and discuss a product or issue in depth.

Recently, the American Association of Recreation Homebuilders (AARH) hired DDI to provide marketing information about its magazine, *Cabin and Condo Living.* Three of DDI's market researchers, Albert Kjar, Bonnie Langarica, and Cindy Myrup, have been assigned to the research team for this project; Albert will oversee the entire project. In networking terminology, the team is considered a **workgroup**, a group of colleagues who have access to the same network server and work together on a common project. The group has just finished conducting surveys over the Internet and holding focus group meetings, all designed to elicit opinions from the subscribers of *Cabin and Condo Living,* as well as from the magazine's pool of freelance writers. The research team is now working on a six-section report summarizing its findings. Each member of the workgroup has written two of the six sections. It's your job to help the workgroup combine the multiple sections of the report into one master document. Then you'll help the team edit the report to make it more attractive and easier to read.

In this session, you will see how Albert planned the report. You'll then create a master document by inserting existing document files into the master document. You'll split, merge, and remove subdocuments. Finally, you'll use some pagination settings to control text flow and page breaks in the document.

Planning a Document

The report will follow DDI's specifications for content, organization, style, and presentation. The complete report will contain six sections explaining the opinions of both the writers and the subscribers of *Condo and Cabin Living*.

The market research team will use a consistent organization and format. Each section of the report will contain a main heading (the section title) and subheadings that label the various topics included in the section. The report will include front matter (title page, table of contents, and list of figures), several sections in the body of the report, and an index.

The team members will write in a user-friendly style—that is, personal and informal, yet straightforward. They will avoid jargon and clearly define any technical terms. The sections will have a uniform, attractive appearance and follow standard desktop-publishing principles. The team will set up the report to print on both sides of the paper, so the report will require different formats and footers for even and odd pages.

Working with Master Documents

Manipulating many pages in a long document can be cumbersome and time-consuming. On the other hand, splitting a long document into several shorter documents makes it hard to keep formatting consistent and to ensure that section and page numbering are always correct. To avoid these problems, you can use Word's Master Document feature, which combines the benefits of splitting documents into separate small, manageable files with the advantages of working with a single, long document. A **master document** is a long document divided into several smaller, individual files, called **subdocuments**. Figure 10-1 illustrates the relationship between master documents and subdocuments.

Figure 10-1	MASTER DOCUMENT AND SUBDOCUMENTS

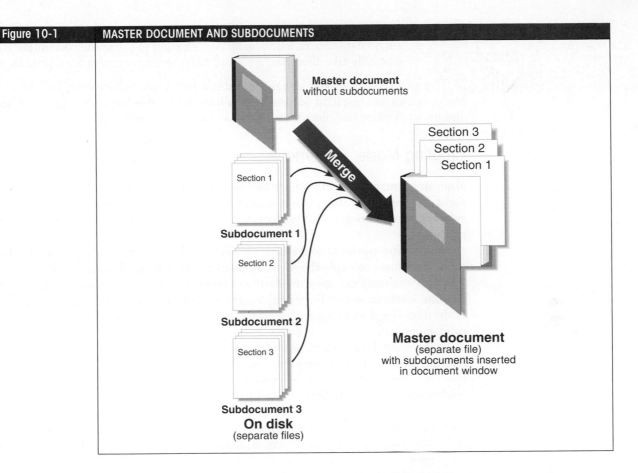

Using a master document is helpful when you are working with a document that consists of multiple sections. By working on each section individually, you avoid the extra time required to open, save, and edit a very large file. The Master Document feature is also helpful when several people are simultaneously working on different parts of the same document. Each member of the team can submit a separate document; you can then quickly organize these individual documents into a single, complete document by creating a master document. Finally, you might also want to use the Master Document feature when working with a document that contains many graphics, which require a large amount of computer memory and disk space. You can divide the graphics among the various subdocuments to reduce the amount of time you spend opening, saving, and editing documents.

Although you could work with and print smaller documents individually, combining them into a master document has several advantages:

- **Consistent formatting elements**. You set up styles, headers, footers, and other formatting elements in only the master document; all the subdocuments use those same formatting elements.

- **Accurate numbering**. You can number the entire master document, including all subdocuments, with consecutive page numbers, section numbers, and figure numbers. If you rearrange, delete, or add material, Word automatically updates all the numbers to reflect your changes.

- **Accurate cross-referencing**. You can refer to figures or tables in other sub-documents and have Word update the cross-reference fields in the master document if you alter the document.

- **Complete table of contents and index**. You can easily compile a table of contents and create an index for a master document.

■ **Faster editing**. You can edit the master document all at once, or you can edit each subdocument individually. Any changes in the master document automatically take effect and are saved into the subdocument files, and vice versa.

The various workgroups at DDI often use the Master Document feature to combine multiple files into one long document. You'll learn how this feature works as you help Albert and his workgroup complete their report on *Cabin and Condo Living*.

Creating Master Documents

You can create a master document by converting an existing document into a master document and converting its parts into subdocuments. Alternately, you can insert existing files as subdocuments into an existing document. You also can use a combination of these two methods.

In the first method, converting an existing document into a master document and subdocuments, you apply the Word built-in heading styles (Heading 1, Heading 2, and so forth) to the text, and then divide the document into subdocuments at the location of a heading level you select. For example, if you divide a master document into subdocuments at the Heading 1 style, each Heading 1 and its accompanying text are saved as a separate subdocument.

In the second method, creating a master document from existing documents, you insert existing files as subdocuments into an open Word document. Word converts the inserted files into subdocuments and the open document file into the master document. Unlike the first method, the subdocuments don't have to begin with a built-in heading style.

In practice, you probably will use both methods to create and manage a master document. For example, you might divide your original document into a master document and subdocuments, and then insert separate files as subdocuments into the master document.

You can convert any document into a master document. After you do create a master document, you can open, edit, and print its subdocuments individually; or you can open, edit, and print the entire master document as a single unit. When you save a master document, Word saves the file for each subdocument. The master document file contains only the filenames of its subdocuments, but not their text and objects (such as graphics).

Inserting subdocuments into a master document is different from importing files into a document. Imported files become part of the document in which they're inserted, whereas the files of subdocuments remain separate from the master document in which they're inserted.

Preparing to Use Master Documents

Before you begin working with master documents, you must first switch to master document view. In **master document view** you can insert, create, or remove subdocuments. You can also reorganize the document just as you can in outline view.

If you plan to take a document created by someone else and convert it into a master document, you also need to adjust some settings in the document's Properties dialog box (sometimes called the Properties sheet). The Properties dialog box, shown in Figure 10-2, lists several settings for the document file, including the name of the person who created the document (the Author). But how does Word know the Author name? It automatically makes the Author name identical to the name entered in the User Information tab of the Options dialog box.

Figure 10-2   **DOCUMENT PROPERTIES**

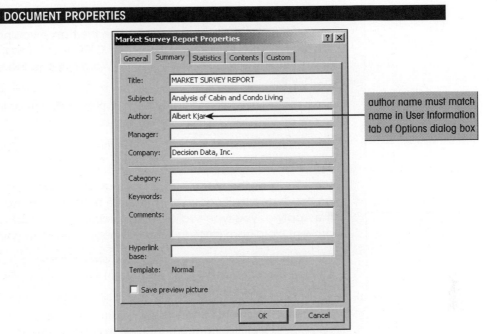

For the Master Document feature to work correctly, the Author name (in the Properties dialog box) and the user name in the Options dialog box must be identical. So if you take a document created by someone else and convert it into a master document, you first must change the Author name to match the user name on your computer's Options dialog box. If you don't match the Author and user name, Word will think you're trying to modify a document that you don't "own"—that you are trying to edit a document for which you don't have editing rights. Word will then lock the subdocument files, making them unavailable for editing. You'll learn how to match these two names in the next section, when you begin working with Albert's document.

Converting a Document into a Master Document

Albert has already written the title page and Background section of the report using the company's standard styles. Because he created the document, his name appears in the document's Properties dialog box. Before you convert his document to a master document, you should open it and change the Author name to match the user name in your Options dialog box. You'll do that now. You'll also make sure Word is set up so that it doesn't apply built-in styles as you type. Finally, you'll convert the document into a master document.

To convert an existing file into a master document:

1. Start Word as usual, insert your Data Disk in the appropriate drive, and then open the **MrktRep** file from the Tutorial subfolder in the Tutorial.10 folder on your Data Disk.

2. Click **Tools** on the menu bar, click **Options**, and then click the **User Information** tab. On a piece of paper, write down the name exactly as shown in the Name text box, and then click the **Cancel** button.

3. Click **File** on the menu bar, click **Properties**, click the **Summary** tab, replace "Albert Kjar" (in the Author text box) with the name you noted earlier from the Options dialog box, and then click the **OK** button. Now the same person "owns" the master document and the Word file, and therefore has full rights to modify it.

4. Save the file as **Market Survey Report** in the Tutorial subfolder in the Tutorial.10 folder on your Data Disk.

5. Click the **Show/Hide ¶** button ¶ on the Standard toolbar, if necessary, to display nonprinting characters.

6. Click **Tools** on the menu bar, click **AutoCorrect Options**, click the **AutoFormat As You Type** tab, if necessary, clear the **Built-in Heading styles** check box (in the Apply as you type section of the dialog box). By turning off this feature, you prevent Word from applying styles to headings when you don't want it to.

7. Click the **OK** button to close the AutoCorrect dialog box, and then click the **Outline View** button 🔲. The document switches to outline view, and the Outlining toolbar opens.

8. If necessary, click the **Show Level** list arrow, and then click **Show All Levels** so you can see all your document's text in outline view.

9. If necessary, click the **Master Document View** button 🔲 on the Outlining toolbar to make sure it's selected (framed with a blue border). When the Master Document View button is selected, the Outlining toolbar displays a set of buttons for managing master documents. See Figure 10-3.

Figure 10-3	MASTER DOCUMENT VIEW

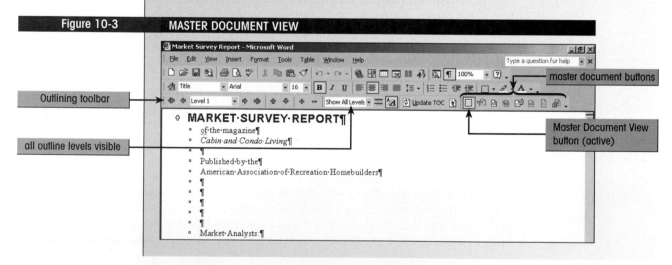

Even though the Master Document View button is selected, the Market Survey Report won't be a true master document until you insert a subdocument. Before you do this, however, Albert asks you to make backup copies of the files you'll use as subdocuments. Then, if a problem arises as you compile your master document and its subdocuments, you can start again with the original files. It's always important to make backup copies when working with any document, but backups are especially important when you are working with master documents and subdocuments. You'll first make a copy of the document written by Bonnie (the analysis of *Cabin and Condo Living's* subscribers) and then the one by Cindy (the analysis of *Cabin and Condo Living's* freelance writers).

To make a backup copy of the subdocuments:

1. Click the **Open** button 🗁 on the Standard toolbar, and then make sure the Tutorial subfolder for Tutorial 10 is displayed in the Look in list box.

2. Right-click the filename **Subscbrs**, and then click **Copy** on the shortcut menu.

3. Press **Ctrl+V** to paste a copy of the Subscbrs file into the Tutorial subfolder in the Tutorial.10 folder. The Copy of Subscbrs file appears in the Open dialog box.

4. Right-click the filename **Copy of Subscbrs**, click **Rename** on the shortcut menu, type **Magazine Subscribers**, and then press the **Enter** key to change the name of the file.

   TROUBLE? If an error message appears indicating that you're trying to change the filename extension, click the No button, and use the filename "Magazine Subscribers.doc" (with the .doc filename extension). If you can't successfully rename files in the Open dialog box, open Windows Explorer, display the files in the Tutorial folder for Tutorial 10, and repeat Step 4.

5. Repeat Steps 2 through 4 to create a copy of the **Authors** file with the filename **Freelance Authors**.

   TROUBLE? Again, if an error message appears indicating that you're trying to change the filename extension, click the No button, and use the filename "Freelance Authors.doc" (with the .doc filename extension).

6. Click the **Cancel** button in the Open dialog box to return to the report.

Now you can insert two subdocuments into the master document.

Inserting Subdocuments

When you insert a subdocument into a master document, the subdocument opens within the master document, at the location of the insertion point. The subdocument appears in a box, marked with a Subdocument icon 📑. Word inserts End of Section breaks at the beginning and end of the subdocument. Sometimes a Lock icon 🔒 appears near the Subdocument icon to indicate that the subdocument is locked. You can't edit locked subdocuments, and all menu commands are unavailable when the insertion point is positioned in a locked subdocument. (The Lock feature is important when more than one person is working on a master document, because it allows only one person at a time to edit a subdocument. Because you matched the Author name and the user name, the subdocuments won't normally be locked.)

REFERENCE   WINDOW   **RW**

Inserting a Subdocument

- Move the insertion point to where you want to insert the subdocument.
- Click the Insert Subdocument button on the Outlining toolbar.
- Select the document you want to insert as the subdocument.
- Click the OK button.

Albert asks you to insert the document named Magazine Subscribers (written by Bonnie) into the master document, and then insert the document named Freelance Authors (written by Cindy).

To insert subdocuments into the master document:

1. Click to the left of "Advertisers," the level-1 heading at the middle of page 3 (section 2). This is where you will insert the first subdocument.

2. Click the **Insert Subdocument** button 🖹 on the Outlining toolbar. You see the Insert Subdocument dialog box, which is similar to the Open dialog box.

3. If necessary, use the Look in list arrow to open the Tutorial folder for Tutorial 10, and then double-click the filename **Magazine Subscribers**. The file is inserted as a subdocument at the location of the insertion point (just above the heading "Advertisers"). Scroll so you can see the beginning of the subdocument. See Figure 10-4. Note that Word creates a section break and displays the Subdocument icon 🗐 and the Expand icon ✛. Don't worry if the box around the subdocument appears larger or smaller in your document window. Word usually marks only the beginning of the subdocument with the box, and then shows broken lines to indicate that the subdocument extends beyond the box.

Figure 10-4	SUBDOCUMENT INSERTED INTO MASTER DOCUMENT

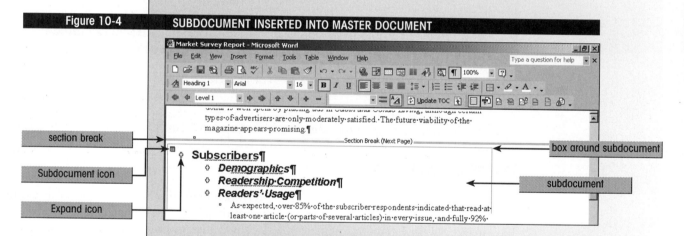

TROUBLE? If a dialog box opens with the message "Style 'Heading 1' exists in both the subdocument you're adding (Magazine Subscribers) and the master document. Would you like to rename the style in the subdocument?," click the No to All button. This tells Word to use the Heading 1 style defined in the master document.

To ensure that you can edit this subdocument, you need to be certain it isn't locked.

4. Look for a **Lock** icon 🔒 near the Subdocument icon at the beginning of the subdocument. If you see 🔒, move the insertion point into the subdocument, and then click the **Lock Document** button 🔒 on the Outlining toolbar to unlock the subdocument.

TROUBLE? If your document is formatted differently than the one in Figure 10-4, click the Show Formatting button 🗛 on the Outlining toolbar to display the document's formatting.

Now you'll insert the document written by Cindy.

5. If necessary, click to the left of the level-1 heading "Advertisers" (now on page 4, section 4), and then repeat Steps 2 through 4 to insert the second subdocument, **Freelance Authors.** See Figure 10-5.

| Figure 10-5 | SECOND SUBDOCUMENT INSERTED AND EXPANDED |

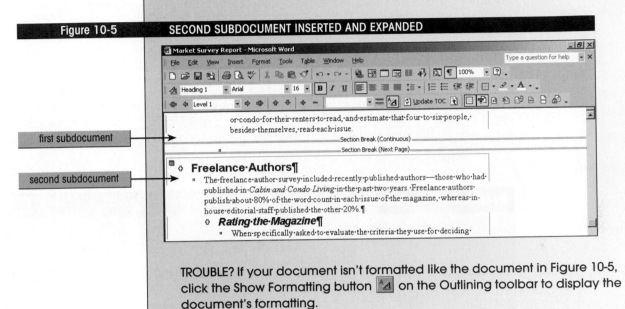

TROUBLE? If your document isn't formatted like the document in Figure 10-5, click the Show Formatting button 🔠 on the Outlining toolbar to display the document's formatting.

The master document Market Survey Report now contains two subdocuments. Even though you can manipulate the subdocuments in the master document, the text of these subdocuments continues to be stored in the files Magazine Subscribers and Freelance Authors, and not in the Market Survey Report file. This is still the case even after you save the master document, which you'll do in the next section.

Saving the Master Document

After you insert subdocuments, you should save the master document. You save the master document the same way you save any other file.

To save the master document:

1. Click the **Save** button 🔲 on the Standard toolbar. Market Survey Report is now saved as a master document with two subdocuments.

The names and locations of the two subdocument files, Magazine Subscribers and Freelance Authors, are recorded in the master document. The subdocuments will continue to appear in the master document as long as the files aren't renamed or moved.

Working with Subdocuments

One benefit of working with master documents is the ability to reorganize subdocuments and their associated files. Another benefit is that you can create additional subdocuments from parts of the master document if the master document itself becomes too long and unwieldy.

Creating a Subdocument

When you **create a subdocument**, you take a part of the master document and make it a subdocument. When you save the master document with the new subdocument, Word creates a new file using the name of the subdocument's first heading. The new subdocument file is saved in the same folder as the master document, and the text of the new subdocument is no longer saved in the master document file.

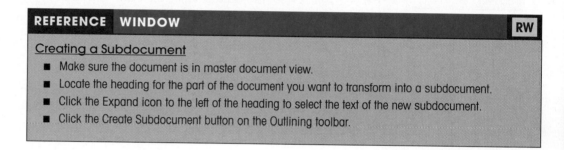

REFERENCE	WINDOW	RW

Creating a Subdocument
- Make sure the document is in master document view.
- Locate the heading for the part of the document you want to transform into a subdocument.
- Click the Expand icon to the left of the heading to select the text of the new subdocument.
- Click the Create Subdocument button on the Outlining toolbar.

Now Albert wants you to transform the "Advertisers" section into a subdocument.

To create a subdocument:

1. Scroll down so you can see the heading "Advertisers" (now on page 5), and then click the **Expand** icon ✛ to the left of "Advertisers." The "Advertisers" heading and all the text and subheadings below it are selected. Now you're ready to create the subdocument.

2. Click the **Create Subdocument** button 🖹 on the Outlining toolbar. Again, Word puts a box around the Advertisers section, inserts section breaks before and after the Advertisers section, and displays the Subdocument icon 📰 and the ✛ at the beginning of the new subdocument.

3. Save the report with the new subdocument. Word creates a new file named "Advertisers," using the subdocument's first heading for the filename. The subdocument is saved in the same folder as the master document.

You have successfully transformed a part of the master document into a subdocument. As you'll see in the next section, you can also split an existing subdocument into two separate subdocuments.

Splitting Subdocuments

If one subdocument becomes too long and unwieldy, or if you want two people to work on what is currently one subdocument, you can **split the subdocument**—you can divide one subdocument into two subdocument files. The next time you save the master document, Word creates a new file using the new subdocument's heading as the filename. Word saves the new file in the same folder as the master document.

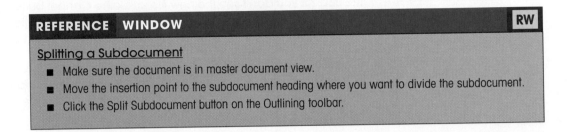

REFERENCE WINDOW   **RW**

Splitting a Subdocument
- Make sure the document is in master document view.
- Move the insertion point to the subdocument heading where you want to divide the subdocument.
- Click the Split Subdocument button on the Outlining toolbar.

Next, Albert wants to split the "Subscribers" subdocument. After the split, the original "Subscribers" subdocument will consist of the level-1 heading "Subscribers" and the level 2-heading "Demographics." The new, second subdocument will have the filename Readership Competition, and will consist of the level-2 heading "Readership Competition" and another level-2 heading, "Readers' Usage." This split will result in one more subdocument. (The subdocument that begins with the heading "Subscribers" will retain it's original filename, "Magazine Subscribers.")

To split the subdocument:

1. Click to the left of the "Readership Competition" heading in the middle of the first subdocument.

   As you can see in the Style list box on the Formatting toolbar, this heading is tagged with the Heading 2 style. In outline view, it's considered a level-2 heading.

2. Click the **Split Subdocument** button 🗒 on the Outlining toolbar. Word draws a box around the new subdocument and inserts section breaks.

3. If you can see text below the headings, click anywhere in the headings, and click the **Collapse** button 🗕 on the Outlining toolbar to display only the headings within this subdocument. See Figure 10-6.

Figure 10-6   **ONE SUBDOCUMENT SPLIT INTO TWO**

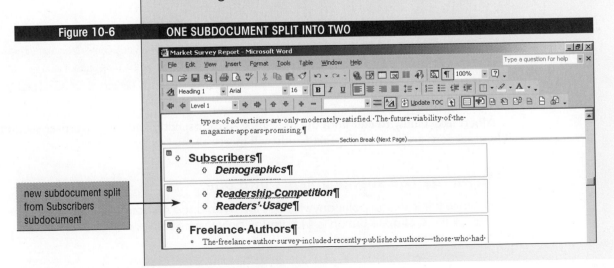

new subdocument split from Subscribers subdocument

4. Save the report with the new subdocument. Word creates a new file named "Readership Competition." Note that this filename matches the new subdocument's first heading. The subdocument is saved in the same folder as the master document.

5. Click the **Open** button 📂 on the Standard toolbar. Verify that the Tutorial folder for Tutorial 10 contains a new file named Readership Competition.

   TROUBLE? If you don't see the new file, click the Cancel button in the Open dialog box, make sure the heading "Readership Competition" appears at the top of the subdocument box, and then repeat Steps 1 and 2.

6. Click the **Cancel** button in the Open dialog box to return to the master document. Note that the master document now contains four subdocuments: Magazine Subscribers, Readership Competition, Freelance Authors, and Advertisers.

So far, you've learned how to insert a subdocument into a master document, to create a subdocument from master document text, and to split an existing subdocument into two subdocuments. Next you'll learn how to combine, or merge, two subdocuments.

Merging Subdocuments

If your master document contains two adjacent subdocuments that happen to be fairly short and simple with few graphics or tables, it's sometimes helpful to merge the subdocuments. When you **merge subdocuments** you combine the files and text of two adjacent subdocuments. Word inserts the text of the second subdocument into the first one, so that when you save the master document, the first subdocument file contains the text of both subdocuments. The second subdocument file remains on your disk but is no longer used by the master document. You could delete this file without affecting your master document. You should merge only subdocuments that will be edited by the same person. If two subdocuments will be edited by different people, it makes more sense to keep them separate, no matter how short they are.

REFERENCE WINDOW   **RW**

Merging Subdocuments
- Make sure the document is in master document view.
- Click the Subdocument icon of the first subdocument.
- Press and hold the Shift key while you click the Subdocument icon of an adjacent subdocument.
- Release the Shift key, and then click the Merge Subdocument button on the Outlining toolbar.

Albert asks Cindy to edit both the Freelance Author section and the Advertiser section. These sections are adjacent, so first Cindy will merge them.

To merge two subdocuments into one:

1. Move the insertion point anywhere in the "Freelance Authors" heading, and click the **Collapse** button − to display only the headings and not the text under them.

2. Click the **Subdocument** icon of the Freelance Authors subdocument. The entire Freelance Authors subdocument is selected.

   TROUBLE? If you click the Subdocument icon but the entire subdocument isn't selected, move the pointer to the center of the icon and try again. Keep trying until the entire subdocument, and not just the heading, is selected.

3. Press and hold the **Shift** key while you click in the "Advertisers" subdocument heading (you might need to scroll to see this subdocument heading), and then release the **Shift** key. With both subdocuments selected, you can merge them.

4. Click the **Merge Subdocument** button on the Outlining toolbar. The two subdocuments become one.

5. Click , if necessary, to collapse the text of the new subdocument, and then deselect the text. See Figure 10-7. Although you can't see it in Figure 10-7, Word maintains the section breaks before the Advertisers heading. However, you can see that the no longer appears next to the Advertisers heading. (You can't see the section breaks because Word doesn't display them in outline view when only the headings are visible.)

| Figure 10-7 | TWO SUBDOCUMENTS MERGED INTO ONE |

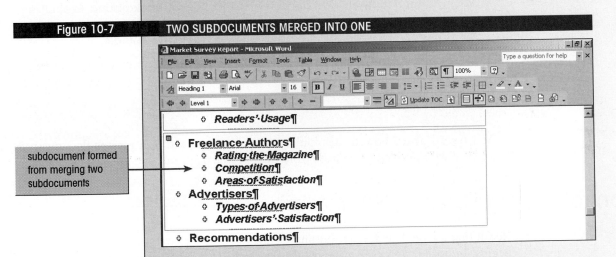

subdocument formed from merging two subdocuments

6. Save the master document. The text from the Advertisers file merges with the document named Freelance Authors; the master document can no longer access the Advertisers file, although it remains on your Data Disk.

The master document now has a title page and three subdocuments: Freelance Authors, Magazine Subscribers, and Readership Competition.

Removing a Subdocument

So far you've learned several techniques for manipulating subdocuments. You've learned how to create subdocuments, split one subdocument into two, and merge two subdocuments into one. It's also possible to **remove a subdocument**—to incorporate the text of a subdocument into the master document. This decreases the number of subdocuments but increases the size of the master document. The removed subdocument file stays on your disk, but the master document file no longer needs access to it. You can delete this unused subdocument file without affecting the master document.

REFERENCE WINDOW   **RW**

Removing a Subdocument

- Click the Subdocument icon for the subdocument you want to move into the master document.
- Click the Remove Subdocument button on the Outlining toolbar.

After reading the short subdocument entitled "Subscribers" (which includes only two headings and two paragraphs), Albert decides that it doesn't need any changes. He asks you to remove this subdocument and return it to the master document.

To remove the Subscribers subdocument:

1. Click the **Subdocument** icon 📇 for the Subscribers subdocument (on page 4) to select all the text in it.

2. Click the **Remove Subdocument** button 📄 on the Outlining toolbar. The "Subscribers" heading and its accompanying text become part of the master document.

 Your master document now consists of the title page, Background, Executive Summary, Subscribers, and Recommendations sections. It also includes the subdocuments Readership Competition and Freelance Authors.

3. Deselect the Subscribers section and save the master document. Your Data Disk has two extra files, Advertisers and magazine subscribers, which are no longer part of the master document.

You have learned how to manipulate subdocuments within a master document. Next you'll deal with problems that arise from undesirable page and line breaks.

Controlling Text Flow and Page Breaks

Recall that a **page break** is a location in a document where one page ends and another one begins. In page layout view, page breaks are marked by a dark gray space between the bottom of one page and the top of the next page. If the page break is part of a section break, the double-line section break appears at the bottom of the page with the text "Section Break (Next Page)." You'll now look at the location of page breaks and the text above and below those breaks.

To view the page breaks in the report:

1. Switch to print layout view and scroll through the document, noting the location of section breaks, the paragraph text that is now visible below the headings, and the page breaks.

2. Look specifically at the text just below the page break at the top of page 3 and just above the page break at the bottom of page 5.

As you scroll through the document, you might notice some problems with the location of page breaks. You might observe the following:

- A page break appears just above the phrase "report are pleased with the response," at the top of page 3. See Figure 10-8. Your document might be different; subtle variations in printer drivers can cause page breaks to appear at different locations.)

Figure 10-8   DOCUMENT WITH WIDOW

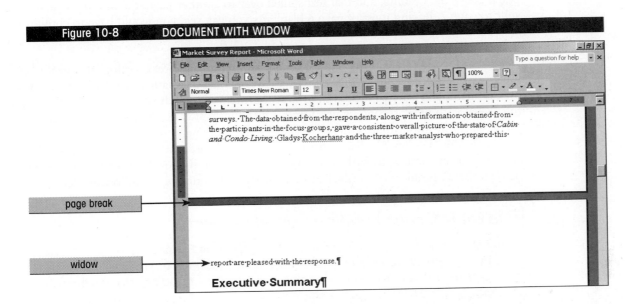

The phrase "report are pleased with the response" is an example of a **widow**, which is the last line of a paragraph appearing alone at the top of a page. A widow looks out of place and can be hard to read when isolated on a page.

■ A page break appears after the first line of the paragraph that begins "Of the three types of respondents . . .," just below the heading "Advertisers' Satisfaction" (at the bottom of page 5). See Figure 10-9. (Again, your document might be different.)

Figure 10-9   DOCUMENT WITH ORPHAN

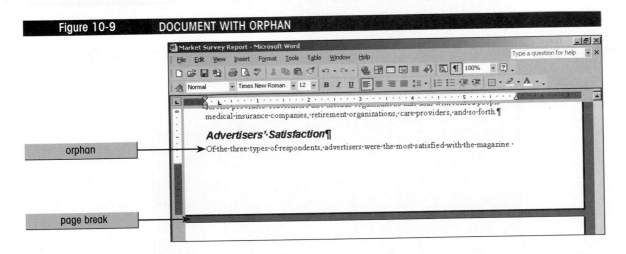

This page break creates an **orphan**, which is the first line of a paragraph isolated at the bottom of a page. If you omit this orphan, however, you then will have a heading isolated at the bottom of the page.

You could insert hard page breaks to solve these specific problems. To create a **hard page break**, you move the insertion point to where you want the page to end, and then press Ctrl+Enter. In most cases, however, hard page breaks create more problems than they solve.

For example, if you insert a hard page break just above the heading near the bottom of page 5, the heading would appear at the top of page 6. But if you then added more text to the paragraph above the heading, and that text spilled over to another page, the heading would then shift to page 7, leaving most of page 6 blank. As you can see, you would have to continually insert and delete hard page breaks to fix widows, orphans, and isolated headings as you edit a document.

In Word, you can avoid these problems by assigning page break settings to specific document styles. Once you do that, Word automatically fixes pagination problems (such as widows, orphans, and isolated headings) in all text formatted with those styles. You'll now apply the "Keep with next" setting, which forces a heading to stay on the same page as the paragraph below it, thus avoiding an isolated heading appearing at the bottom of a page. You'll also apply the "Widow/Orphan control" setting which prevents the occurrence of widows and orphans in paragraphs with two or more lines. (Even if your document doesn't contain the page break problems described earlier, you should complete the following steps.)

To control page breaks in your document:

1. Click the **Styles and Formatting** button ![A] on the Formatting toolbar to open the Styles and Formatting Task Pane, point to **Heading 1** in the Task Pane, and click its list arrow. You'll edit Heading 1 so all level-1 headings stay on the same page as the first paragraph below them.

   TROUBLE? If you accidentally clicked the Heading 1 style, the paragraph in your document that contains the insertion point will automatically convert to that style. Click the Undo button ![undo], point to (but do not click) the Heading 1 style, and then click its list arrow.

2. Click **Modify** to open the Modify Style dialog box, click the **Format** button, and then click **Paragraph**. The Paragraph dialog box opens.

3. If necessary, click the **Line and Page Breaks** tab, which contains various options you can use to control breaks in your document. See Figure 10-10.

| Figure 10-10 | PARAGRAPH DIALOG BOX |

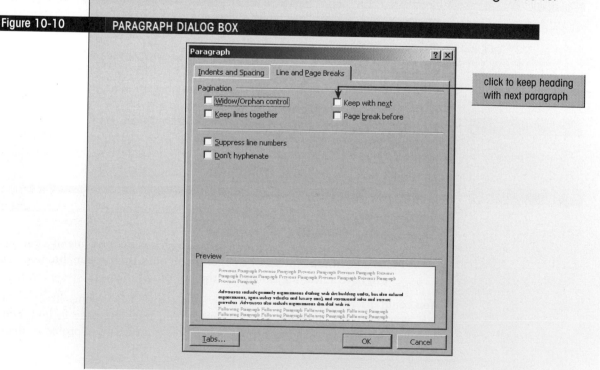

4. Click the **Keep with next** check box in the Pagination section of the dialog box. This instructs Word to force all text in the Heading 1 style onto the same page as the paragraph that follows it. If you want each heading formatted with the Heading 1 style to begin a new page, you click the "Page break before" check box.

5. Click the **OK** button in both dialog boxes to return to the document.

6. Using the same procedure, select the **Keep with next** option for the Heading 2 style. You don't have to modify the other headings because DDI market research reports rarely have more than two levels of headings. But if you were writing a document that included lower-level headings, you would have to select the "Keep with next" option for all the heading styles.

7. Using the same procedure, select **Widow/Orphan control** (also located in the Paragraph dialog box) for the Normal style. This tells Word to prevent the first and last lines of a paragraph from appearing alone on a page.

8. Close the Styles and Formatting Task Pane, save the document, and then scroll through the document to view the page breaks.

From now on, regardless of what changes you make to the document text, a heading will never appear alone at the bottom of a page, and the text formatted in the Normal style will never include widows or orphans.

As you look through your document, notice places where words break at the end of a line. For example, in the last paragraph of the document (on page 6), "e-business" is split between two lines. Although this isn't a serious problem, readers might be confused to see "e-" at the end of a line. To prevent Word from breaking a hyphenated word, you need to use a hard or nonbreaking hyphen. A **nonbreaking hyphen** is a hyphen that won't allow the word or phrase containing it to break between two lines. A **soft hyphen** is a hyphen that allows the words containing it to appear on different lines. To insert a soft hyphen, you simply press the hyphen key on your keyboard.

You'll replace the soft hyphen in both occurrences of the word "e-business" (both singular and plural) with a nonbreaking hyphen.

To insert a nonbreaking hyphen:

1. Move the insertion point immediately to the left of the hyphen in "e-businesses" (plural), located in the last paragraph of the document, on page 6.

2. Press the **Delete** key to delete the soft hyphen. The "e" becomes joined to "businesses," and, as a result, "ebusinesses" appears on the next line. Now you'll insert the nonbreaking hyphen.

   Click **Insert** on the menu bar, click **Symbol** to open the Symbol dialog box, and then click the **Special Characters** tab. As you can see, Word offers a wide variety of special symbols, including the nonbreaking hyphen.

3. Click **Nonbreaking Hyphen** and click the **Insert** button to insert the hyphen into the document at the location of the insertion point. While the Symbol dialog box is still open, notice the shortcut keys for the nonbreaking hyphen: Ctrl+_ (underscore). You'll insert nonbreaking hyphens in other locations by pressing Ctrl+Shift+hyphen. (Note that Shift + hyphen inserts an underscore.)

4. Click the **Close** button in the Symbol dialog box. The Symbol dialog box closes, and you can see that the word "e-businesses" (which now contains a nonbreaking hyphen) has moved to the next line. See Figure 10-11.

Figure 10-11 | **NONBREAKING HYPHEN INSERTED**

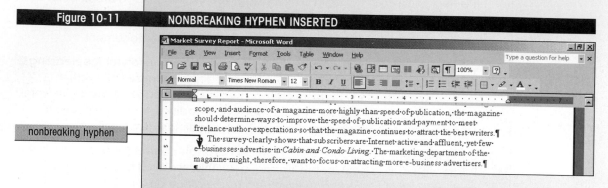

nonbreaking hyphen

Next you'll use a nonbreaking hyphen in "e-business" (singular) in the next line.

5. Move the insertion point between the "e" and the hyphen in the next occurrence of "e-business" in the same paragraph, delete the **hyphen**, and then press **Ctrl+Shift+hyphen**. Now "e-business" will always appear on one line.

6. Save the master document, and then close all open documents, even if you plan to continue to the next session.

Another important special character is the nonbreaking space. A **nonbreaking space** is a space that won't allow the words on either side to break between two lines. For example, the phrase "35 mm" (referring to 35-mm film or a 35-mm camera) might be hard to read or distracting if the "35" appears at the end of one line and "mm" appears at the beginning of the next line. To avoid this problem, you can insert a nonbreaking space between the "35" and the "mm." You can insert the nonbreaking space by using the Special Symbols tab in the Symbols dialog box, or by pressing Ctrl+Shift+spacebar. The Market Survey Report doesn't contain any words that require a nonbreaking space.

You have completed setting up DDI's Market Survey Report using Word's master document feature. In the next session, you'll use Word features to number sections and figures, and then you'll edit the report.

Session 10.1 QUICK CHECK

1. Define the following terms:
   a. master document
   b. subdocument
   c. split subdocuments
   d. merge subdocuments
   e. remove subdocument
   f. widow
   g. orphan

2. What are three advantages of using a master document to manage long documents, rather than working with separate, smaller documents?

3. After you create a subdocument from text in a master document and save the master document, the master document file on the disk becomes bigger. True or false?

4. What are the two methods for creating a master document?

5. When would you split a subdocument?

6. When would you merge two subdocuments?

7. What is a nonbreaking hyphen? A nonbreaking space? Why would you use them?

SESSION 10.2

In this session, you will reopen a master document, automatically number sections of a master document, insert a graph, captions, and figures, number the figures, and then create an automatically numbered cross-reference to the figures. You'll also use revision marks, insert comments, and attach a digital signature.

Reopening a Master Document

When you open a master document that has one or more subdocuments, Word doesn't open the subdocuments, but rather displays their filenames as hyperlinks, as shown in Figure 10-12.

Figure 10-12	SUBDOCUMENT NAME IN UNEXPANDED MASTER DOCUMENT

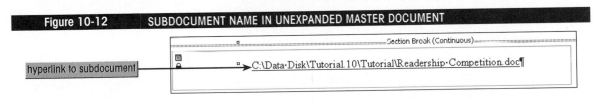

hyperlink to subdocument

As you can see in Figure 10-12, The hyperlink appears in underlined blue text and enclosed in a dotted outline. The subdocument icon 📄 and the lock icon 🔒 are also enclosed in the outline. The lock indicates that you can't edit the hypertext. When you click a subdocument hyperlink, Word opens the subdocument into another document window, not into the master document.

However, in this case, you don't want to open the subdocuments into other document windows. You want to open them into the master document, a process known as expanding the subdocuments. To **expand subdocuments** means to open the subdocuments, currently displayed only as hyperlinks, into the master document so that you can read and edit the text of the subdocuments. When you expand the subdocuments, the lock icon 🔒 disappears, indicating that the text is now available to be modified. Conversely, to **collapse subdocuments** means to close the subdocuments so that the subdocuments appear only as hyperlinks in the master document. You'll open the master document and expand subdocuments now.

To expand subdocuments:

1. Open the master document **Market Survey Report**, switch to outline view, and, if necessary, click the **Master Document View** button 🔲 to select it.

   TROUBLE? If you didn't close the master document at the end of the previous session, close it now and then reopen it so you can follow the subsequent explanation and steps.

2. Display nonprinting characters, scroll so you can see pages 4 and 5, and make sure you can see the subdocument hyperlinks. See Figure 10-13.

Figure 10-13 | MASTER DOCUMENT BEFORE EXPANDING SUBDOCUMENTS

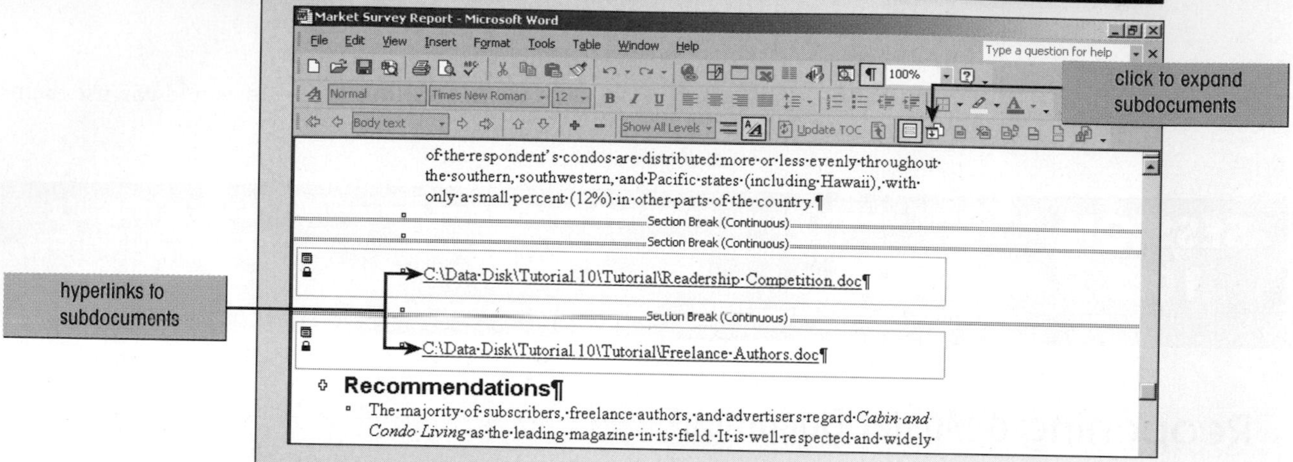

click to expand subdocuments

hyperlinks to subdocuments

of the respondent's condos are distributed more or less evenly throughout the southern, southwestern, and Pacific states (including Hawaii), with only a small percent (12%) in other parts of the country.¶

——————Section Break (Continuous)——————

——————Section Break (Continuous)——————

C:\Data Disk\Tutorial 10\Tutorial\Readership Competition.doc¶

——————Section Break (Continuous)——————

C:\Data Disk\Tutorial 10\Tutorial\Freelance Authors.doc¶

Recommendations¶
  □ The majority of subscribers, freelance authors, and advertisers regard *Cabin and Condo Living* as the leading magazine in its field. It is well respected and widely·

TROUBLE? If, instead of blue underlined hyperlinks, you see code that begins with "{HYPERLINK . . .," press Alt+F9 to display the actual hyperlinks.

3. Click the **Expand Subdocuments** button 🖽 on the Outlining toolbar. Word replaces the hyperlinks with the text of the subdocuments.

You've successfully expanded the subdocuments into the master document. You can now read and modify the subdocument text.

Adding Section Numbers to Headings

Because Albert wants to help readers find the information they need, he asks you to give each major heading a section number—for example, "Section 1. Background," and "Section 2. Executive Summary." You could manually insert text such as "Section 1" before each heading, but what would happen if you had to add, reorder, or delete a section? You would need to review every heading and change the numbers—a time-consuming process, especially in a long document. Instead, you can number sections of a master document by using the Heading Numbering feature. This feature has several advantages:

■ **Automatic sequential numbering.** Word keeps the heading numbers consecutive even if you add, delete, or move a section.

■ **Numbering across subdocuments.** Word formats the same-level headings of all the subdocuments in the master document with consecutive numbering. Then the members of a writing team don't need to know the number of each heading as they write their own subdocument.

■ **Consistent style.** The subdocuments all have the number style specified in the master document.

You'll modify the Heading 1 style in the master document to include automatic numbering. Then each subdocument will be formatted with consecutive section numbers in the same style.

<u>Numbering Headings</u>
- Click Format on the menu bar, and then click Bullets and Numbering.
- Click the Outline Numbered tab, and then select the heading numbering style you want to use.
- If necessary, click the Customize button, select the appropriate formatting options, and then create the heading numbering text.
- Click the OK button in each dialog box.

You're ready to add numbering to the Heading 1 style.

To number headings automatically with the Heading Numbering feature:

1. Click anywhere in the level-1 heading "Background" at the beginning of page 2, click the **Show Level** list arrow on the Outlining toolbar, and then click **Show Level 2** to view only the title and the level-1 and level-2 headings.

2. Click **Format** on the menu bar, click **Bullets and Numbering** to open the Bullets and Numbering dialog box, and then click the **Outline Numbered** tab. Now you'll select the numbering format shown in Figure 10-14.

Figure 10-14	BULLETS AND NUMBERING DIALOG BOX

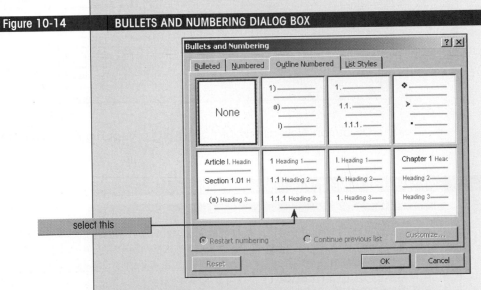

select this

3. Click the numbering format located in the bottom row, second column from the left, as shown in Figure 10-14. This format is sometimes called the legal paragraph numbering format. Next you want to customize the numbering format so that each number is followed by a period. For example, the first level number would be "1." (a period follows the 1), and the second level is "1.1." (a period also follows the second 1).

TROUBLE? If your Outline Numbered tab shows an icon with periods after the first two legal-numbered levels, someone has already customized the styles. Continue with the subsequent steps, but you might not have to type the periods.

4. Click the **Customize** button to open the Customize Outline Numbered List dialog box. You want to change the default setting "1" for Heading 1 styles to "1." (a period follows the number) and Heading 2 styles to "1.1." (with a period following the second number).

5. Make sure **1** is selected in the Level list, click to the right of the number in the Number format text box, type **.** (a period), click **2** in the Level list, click to the right of the number in the Number format text box, and then type **.** (a period). Word automatically inserts another space, so each heading includes two spaces after the period. Make sure your settings match those in Figure 10-15.

Figure 10-15   CUSTOMIZE OUTLINE NUMBERED LIST DIALOG BOX

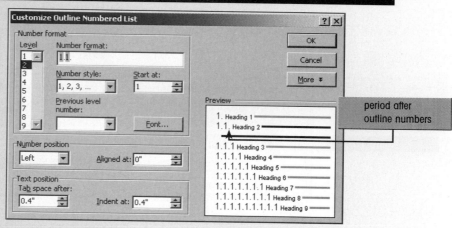

6. Click the **OK** button. Now all text formatted with a heading style has automatic section numbering. See Figure 10-16.

Figure 10-16   COLLAPSED DOCUMENT WITH NUMBERED HEADINGS

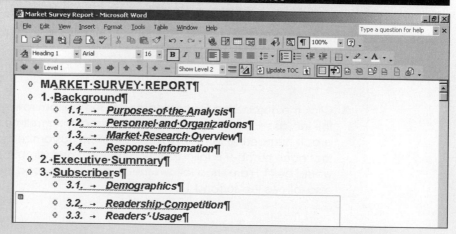

As you scroll through the report, you see that all the headings have section numbers, making it easy to refer to a specific section heading or subheading by its number. Furthermore, from now on, if Albert adds, removes, or rearranges the headings, Word will renumber the section numbers consecutively.

Inserting Numbered Captions

Albert suggests that you include figures to illustrate key points in the report. Specifically, in section "1.2. Personnel and Organizations," he wants you to add a picture of Gladys Kocherhans, the liaison between Decision Data, Inc. and the American Association of Recreation Homebuilders. Also, in section "1.4. Response Information," you need to add a pie chart showing the fraction of each type of respondent. Finally, in section "3.1. Demographics," you need to add a picture of a typical cabin in the Mountain West. Because graphics are not visible in outline view, you'll switch to print layout view.

To insert figures into the report:

1. Switch to print layout view, and then move the insertion point immediately to the left of "Gladys Kocherhans" below "1.2. Personnel and Organizations," on page 2.

2. Click **Insert** on the menu bar, point to **Picture**, click **From File**, use the Look in list arrow to select the Tutorial subfolder in the Tutorial.10 folder on your Data Disk, and then double-click the image file **Gladys** (or **Gladys.jpg**). Word inserts the picture of Gladys into the document. You'll now change the text wrapping resize the picture.

3. Click the picture to select it, click the **Text Wrapping** button on the Picture toolbar, and then click **Square**. The text wraps to the right of the picture.

4. Click the **Format Picture** button on the Picture toolbar, click the **Size** tab, change the Height to **1.5** inches, make sure the **Lock aspect ratio** check box is selected, and then click the **OK** button. If necessary, drag the picture down a little so that it is below (and not to the left of) the heading "1.2. Personnel and Organizations," which should be against the left margin. See Figure 10-17.

Figure 10-17 | DOCUMENT WITH INSERTED PICTURE

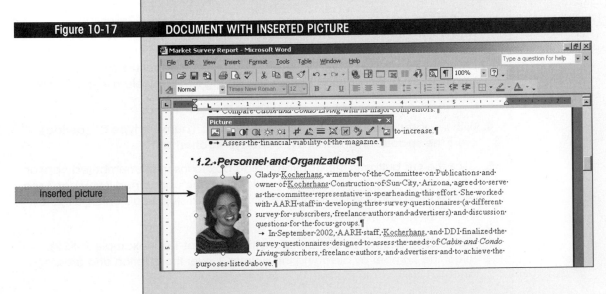

inserted picture

5. Save the master document.

Albert wants to include captions for each figure so the text can refer to them. He asks you to insert captions with automatic figure numbering. Numbering figures manually is time-consuming and error-prone, especially if you rearrange text, reorder sections, and add and delete figures. To make the job easier, you can use the Caption command with automatic figure numbering, in much the same way as you numbered the sections. Word will update the figure numbers if you insert another figure in a section, move a figure to another section, or reorder the sections.

REFERENCE WINDOW   **RW**

Creating Captions

- Select the table or figure to which you want to apply a caption.
- Click Insert on the menu bar, point to Reference, and then click Caption.
- Click the Label list arrow, and then click the type of object to which you're applying the caption (for example, figure or table).
- Set other options as needed.
- If you prefer double-numbering (in the form "Figure 3-1"), click the Numbering button, select the Include chapter number check box, and then set other options as needed. Click the OK button.
- Click the OK button in the Caption dialog box.

You'll create numbered captions for the figure you just inserted.

To create a numbered caption:

1. With the picture of Gladys still selected, click **Insert** on the menu bar, point to **Reference**, and then click **Caption** to open the Caption dialog box.

2. Make sure that in the Options section, **Figure** is selected in the Label list box, and that **Below selected item** is selected in the Position list box.

3. Verify that the Caption text box displays "Figure 1."

   TROUBLE? If the Caption text box does not display "Figure 1," click the Numbering button to open the Caption Numbering dialog box, and uncheck the Include chapter number check box. Now the caption label will take the form "Figure 1" rather than "Figure 1-1" or another numbering style. Click the OK button to close the Caption Numbering dialog box and return to the Caption dialog box.

4. With the insertion point to the right of the caption number, type a . (period), press the **spacebar**, and then type **Gladys Kocherhans**.

5. Click the **OK** button in the Caption dialog box to insert the numbered caption, which is a floating text box with a border. Don't be concerned if you can't see Gladys's last name in the caption box. In the next step, you'll enlarge the text box so you can read the entire name.

   TROUBLE? If the caption number is anything except 1 (for example, if it's 2), select the number by dragging the pointer I over the caption and pressing the F9 key to update the field codes.

6. Drag the right-center resize handle on the caption to the right until "Figure 1. Gladys Kocherhans" is displayed on one line, and then drag the bottom-center resize handle up to reduce the height of the text box, so that the heading "1.3. Market Research Overview" stays at the left margin.

   TROUBLE? If, after performing the above step, the heading still doesn't move to the left margin, drag the entire caption box up closer to the picture to make room for the heading.

7. Right-click the edge of the caption text box, and then click **Format Text Box** in the shortcut menu. The Format Text Box dialog box opens.

8. Click the **Colors and Lines** tab, and then set the line color to **No Line**. This removes the borderlines from around the caption.

9. Click the **Layout** tab in the Format Text Box dialog box, click the **Square** icon, click the **Left** option button in the Horizontal alignment section, and click the **OK** button. The settings you selected in the Layout tab should make the caption stay at the left margin and wrap the text around it to the right. Notice that the lines around the caption box have disappeared. See Figure 10-18.

Figure 10-18	FIGURE WITH CAPTION

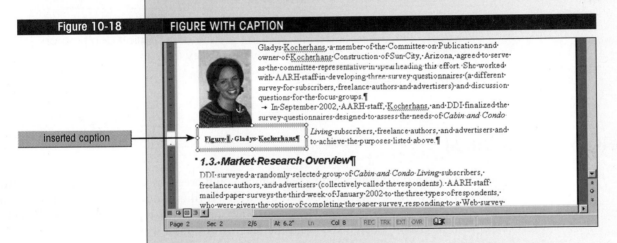

inserted caption

TROUBLE? If the caption isn't positioned and formatted as shown in Figure 10-18, drag it to the correct location and then make any other necessary adjustments. If the caption number is "2" rather than "1", select it and press the F9 key to update it.

Now, using the same procedure, you'll insert another picture with a numbered caption.

To insert a picture with a numbered caption:

1. Click at the beginning of the paragraph below the heading "3.1 Demographics" on page 4 (to the left of the sentence that begins "The subscriber respondents…".

2. Insert the picture **cabin** (or **cabin.jpg**) from the tutorial subfolder in the Tutorial.10 folder, set the Text Wrapping to **Square**, adjust its height to **1.5** inches (keep the original aspect ratio), and then move the picture down, if necessary,

so the "3.1 Demographics" heading stays at the left margin. Now add the numbered caption **Figure 2. Cabin in the Rockies**, adjust the caption box size, if necessary, to fit the text on two lines, and then remove the borderlines around the captions, as shown in Figure 10-19.

Figure 10-19 | **SECOND FIGURE WITH CAPTION**

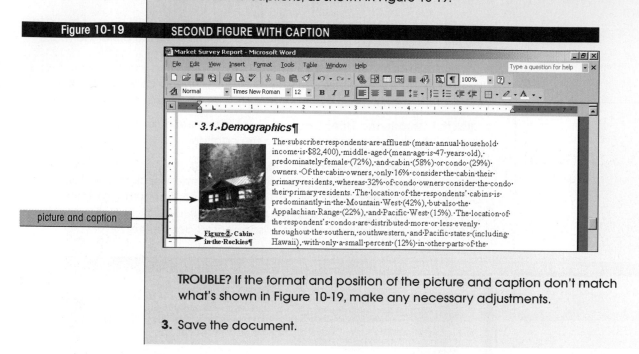

picture and caption

TROUBLE? If the format and position of the picture and caption don't match what's shown in Figure 10-19, make any necessary adjustments.

3. Save the document.

Using Microsoft Graph

Now you'll add a third figure, a pie chart which you'll create as a Microsoft Graph Chart. **Microsoft Graph** is a program you can use with Word and other Office applications to create line charts, bar charts, area charts, pie charts, and other types of charts. To prepare charts with Microsoft Graph, you open the Microsoft Graph window (or make Microsoft Graph available in the Word window), select the type of chart you want, and then modify the information in the datasheet. The **datasheet** is a grid of cells, similar to a Word table (but more like an Excel worksheet), to which you can add data and labels. As you add the data and labels, Microsoft Graph automatically creates the chart. Now you'll use Microsoft Graph to create a pie chart.

To create a pie chart:

1. Move the insertion point to the beginning of the paragraph just below the heading "1.4 Response Information" on page 2 (just to the left of the sentence that begins "Response rates were...").

2. Click **Insert** on the menu bar, click **Object**, click the **Create New** tab, click **Microsoft Graph Chart**, and then click the **OK** button.

   If Microsoft Graph appears in a separate window, maximize the Microsoft Graph window. Note that Microsoft Graph displays two major items, a sample chart (probably a bar chart) and a datasheet (the grid of labels and numbers).

3. Drag the sample chart so that it doesn't cover the datasheet (or drag the datasheet so that it doesn't cover the sample chart), display the Formatting

and Standard toolbars on separate lines, click the **Chart Type** list arrow,
and then click the **Pie Chart** button.

4. Click anywhere in the datasheet, click the blank gray button in the far upper-
left corner of the chart (two rows above row 1, and two columns to the left of
column A) to select the entire datasheet, and then press the **Delete** key to
erase all the current data. Because the datasheet is now blank, the chart
window is also blank.

5. Fill in the datasheet as shown in Figure 10-20. For column labels, use the following: **Subscribers**, **Authors**, and **Advertisers**. For the data, use the following:
1305, **240**, and **38**. Don't be concerned if you can't see the last few letters of
the words "Subscribers" and "Authors" after you enter them.

Figure 10-20	CREATING A PIE CHART WITH MICROSOFT GRAPH

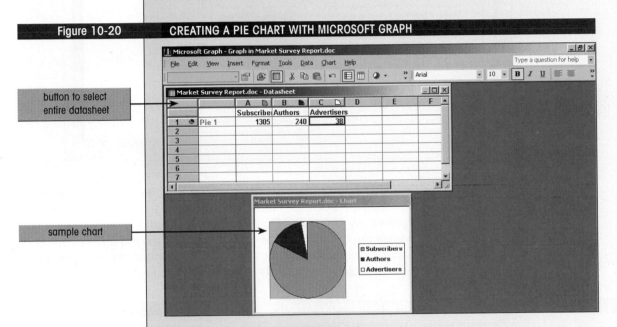

button to select
entire datasheet

sample chart

TROUBLE? If your datasheet and pie chart don't look like those in Figure 10-20,
make any necessary changes. If necessary, ask your instructor or technical
support person for help.

6. If Microsoft Chart is in a separate window, click **File**, and then click **Exit &
Return to . . .** (which is followed by the folder in which your Word document is
located). If the Microsoft Chart elements are in the Word document window,
click anywhere outside the chart or datasheet to deselect Microsoft Chart. You
return to the document window, where the chart has been inserted into the
document.

Next you'll position the chart on the right side of the page, and then wrap the text around
the left side of the chart. You'll also create a caption for the pie chart figure.

To position the chart, wrap the text, and create a caption:

1. Right-click the chart, click **Format Object**, click the **Layout** tab, click the **Square** icon in the Wrapping style section, click the **Right** option button in the Horizontal alignment section, and then click the **OK** button.

2. Drag the chart down until it appears on the next page (rather than in the current page's bottom margin), and align the top of the chart with the top of the text. See Figure 10-21.

Figure 10-21	PIE CHART INSERTED AND POSITIONED

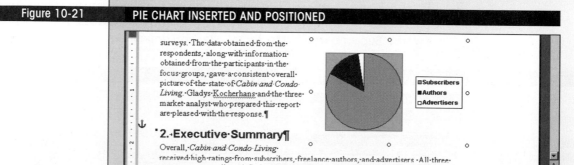

3. Insert a numbered figure caption with the text **Figure 2. Relative number of respondents**. (Word automatically numbers this Figure 2 because you inserted it before the previously numbered Figure 2. The old Figure 2 is renumbered Figure 3.) Remove the border from the caption and adjust the text wrapping so the text flows to the left of the caption. Make any other necessary adjustments so your document looks like Figure 10-22. Save the document.

Figure 10-22	PIE CHART FIGURE WITH CAPTION

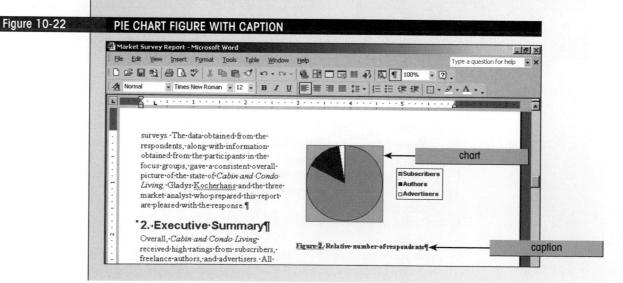

Scroll down and note that the photo of the cabin has been renumbered as Figure 3.

Now that you have inserted three figures with captions, you need to refer to each of them in the text. For that, you'll use cross-references.

Creating Cross-References

A **cross-reference** is a notation within a document that points the reader to another figure, table, or section. If you refer to figures within the text—for example, "See Figure 2"—you need to make sure the reference numbers change if the figure numbers change, which might happen if you add or delete figures or reorganize a document. The Cross-reference feature in Word updates these references just as it updates the heading numbering and figure captions.

REFERENCE WINDOW   **RW**

Creating Cross-References
- Move the insertion point to the location you want to insert the cross-reference.
- Type the text preceding the cross-reference, such as "See" and a space.
- Click Insert on the menu bar, point to Reference, and then click Cross-reference.
- Select the reference type—for example, figure, table, equation, or heading.
- In the "Insert reference to" list box, select the information you want to appear in the cross-reference—for example, entire caption, only label and number, or page number.
- Indicate whether you want the cross-reference formatted as a hyperlink. (When the user clicks a hyperlink cross-reference, the insertion point moves to the item being cross-referenced.)
- Click the Insert button, and then click the Close button.

Albert wants every figure in the report referenced within the text, so you'll insert a cross-reference to the three figures.

To insert a cross-reference to a figure:

1. In the first paragraph under the heading "1.2 Personnel and Organizations," click to the right of "Gladys Kocherhans." (Be sure to click to the right of the name in the paragraph of text, and not in the figure caption.)

2. Press the **spacebar**, type **(see**—that is, an open parenthesis followed by the word "see"—press the **spacebar** again, click **Insert** on the menu bar, point to **Reference**, and then click **Cross-reference**. The Cross-reference dialog box opens.

3. Click the **Reference type** list arrow, click **Figure**, click the **Insert reference to** list arrow, click **Only label and number**, and then make sure **Figure 1. Gladys Kocherhans** is selected in the For which caption list box. See Figure 10-23.

Figure 10-23　CROSS-REFERENCE DIALOG BOX

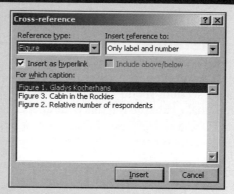

4. Click the **Insert** button to insert this cross-reference, click the **Close** button to close the dialog box, and then type **)** (a close parenthesis) after the cross-reference. The phrase "(see Figure 1)" appears in the report.

TROUBLE? If the figure number changes to 2 (or another number) as you edit the document, select the figure caption, press the F9 key to update the caption field codes, return the insertion point to the body text, press Ctrl+A to select all the body text, and press the F9 key again to update the cross-reference.

Notice that the cross-reference you created is automatically numbered to match the figure caption number. The power of all numbering features in Word—heading numbering, caption numbering, and cross-references—becomes evident when you edit a long document with many figures. Now you'll add cross-reference to the other two figures.

To insert additional cross-references:

1. Move the insertion point to the end of the first sentence below the heading "1.4. Response Information," and insert the sentence (with proper spaces before and after) **See Figure 2.** (with a period but with no parentheses). Don't actually type "Figure 2" but rather insert it as a cross-reference to Figure 2 using the procedure you learned earlier.

2. Move the insertion point to the right of the phrase "Mountain West (42%)" in the paragraph below "3.1. Demographics," and insert the phrase **(see Figure 3)**. Take care to include the parentheses. Don't type "Figure 3" but rather insert it as a cross-reference. See Figure 10-24.

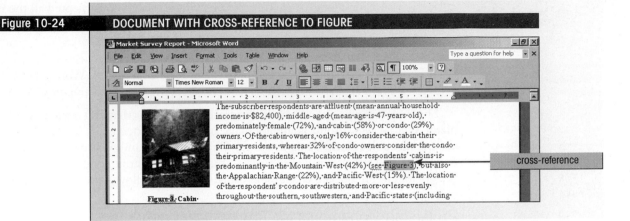

Figure 10-24   **DOCUMENT WITH CROSS-REFERENCE TO FIGURE**

You've finished working on the master document for now, so you'll save and close it.

To save and close the document:

1. Save the master document and close it. Do not exit Word.

Next you'll work with the individual subdocuments of the Market Survey Report.

Tracking **Changes**

The files you received from Albert's workgroup were only drafts. The writers still need to make final edits to their sections. Because Albert wants to know exactly what additions and deletions the other writers make to the text, he asks them to track their changes to the document. They can do this by turning on revision tracking, a feature that marks any revision to the document. (It only marks changes that are made while revision tracking is turned on. It does not mark changes that were made earlier.) Word draws attention to revisions using **revision marks**, a combination of colored text, underlines, vertical bars in the margins, and other features. Revision marks look different depending on whether the document is displayed in print layout view or normal view. When you turn on revision tracking:

- Word marks additions and deletions to text. For deletions, Word inserts (in print layout view) a **callout**, which is a message balloon (like those you see in newspaper comics) and an arrow indicating the location of the deletion. In normal view, deletions appear as colored strikeout characters. For additions, Word underlines and colors the added text.

- You can also choose to mark formatting changes, such as adding or removing boldface, altering margins, and inserting page breaks.

- In a workgroup, each person's edits appear in a unique color.

- Word can show or hide revision marks in the document or printout. You can choose to display all the revision marks in a document, or you can hide the revision marks to see how the text would look if you accepted all the revisions. In addition, you can print the document with or without the revision marks.

■ Word keeps track of the name of the person, date, and time of each revision. (For the name of the person associated with each edit, Word takes the user name from the User Information tab of the Option dialog box.)

These features give you flexibility in tracking revisions that you make in your own documents or that workgroup members make in a shared document. You can choose to track changes for a document using the Track Changes command on the tools menu. If you want to require that other people use revision marks when editing a document, you can protect the document for tracked changes, as explained in the following section.

Protecting Documents for Tracked Changes

Sometimes, you'll want to ensure that you see every change made to a document (or subdocuments), such as when several people revise a report. To do this, you **protect** the document for tracked changes; then anyone who edits the document must use revision marks. After you protect a document this way, Word marks every addition or deletion in the document with revision marks.

REFERENCE WINDOW	RW
Protecting a Document for Tracked Changes	
■ Open the document you want to protect.	
■ Click Tools on the menu bar, and then click Protect Document.	
■ Click the Tracked changes option button.	
■ If necessary, add a password to turn on or off tracked changes.	
■ Click the OK button.	

Once you protect a document for tracked changes, you should keep in mind the following:

■ Revision marks don't necessarily show up even when tracking is on. You can choose to display or hide the tracking marks. Even if you can't see them, they are stored in your document for you or others to view when necessary.

■ You can use the revision-tracking feature without protecting the document. The difference between tracking changes with protection on or off is this: If the document is unprotected, you can turn on and off revision tracking at will. If the document is protected, you can't turn off revision tracking. If you want to ensure that nobody can modify your document without tracking the changes, you must protect the document.

■ When you protect a master document for revision tracking, Word creates revision marks for any change made in the master document text or in the subdocuments that are expanded in the master document. However, even if the master document is protected, you can still open the subdocuments in separate document windows and edit them, without tracking the revisions. In other words, protecting a master document doesn't protect the separate subdocument files.

■ To turn on revision tracking (for an unprotected document), you double-click the TRK button on the status bar at the bottom of the Word window. To turn off revision tracking, double-click the TRK button again.

Albert wants to ensure that any revisions made in the section on Magazine Subscribers are carefully tracked and reviewed.

To protect a subdocument for tracked changes:

1. Open the file **Market Survey Report** from the Tutorial subfolder in the Tutorial.10 folder, but don't expand the subdocuments.

2. Click **Tools** on the menu bar, and then click **Protect Document** to open the Protect Document dialog box.

3. If necessary, click the **Tracked changes** option button to select it, and then click the **OK** button. You could add a password so that only you could unprotect the document, but in this case it isn't necessary. To remind you that all revisions will be tracked, Word darkens the **TRK** button in the status bar.

4. Save the document.

Now that the document is protected for revisions, neither you nor anyone else can make revisions without recording them in the document file.

Editing with Revision Marks

Once a document is protected for tracking changes, Word marks every word or phrase that you or anyone else adds to the document using different font attributes (for example, under-lined red font) and adds a balloon callout to mark deleted text.

Both Cindy and Albert want to make revisions to the Subscribers section (written by Bonnie Langarica) with tracked changes turned on. You'll make the changes as if you were Cindy or Albert. To do this, you start by changing the user name in the Options dialog box.

To edit a document with revision marks:

1. Click **Tools** on the menu bar, click **Options**, click the **User Information** tab, click the **Name** text box, type **Cindy Myrup,** click the **Initials** text box, type **CM**, and then click the **OK** button.

2. Make sure the master document window is in print layout view, and scroll down until you see the heading "3. Subscribers" and the picture of the cabin in the Rockies. Now you're ready to make the first change, which is to delete a word. Cindy realizes that the phrase "online Web" is redundant (a Web survey and an online survey in this context are the same thing), so she wants to delete "online."

3. Double-click the word **online** located in the first sentence below the heading "Subscribers," and press the **Delete** key. Normally, "online" would simply disap-pear, but because you are tracking changes, Word inserts the callout "Deleted: online" in the right margin, with an arrow pointing to the location from which the word was deleted. Now you'll insert a word.

4. Click between the words "The" and "number" in the second sentence of the same paragraph, and insert the word **high**; add a space before or after the word to maintain proper word separation. See Figure 10-25.

Figure 10-25   **REVISION MARKS IN DOCUMENT**

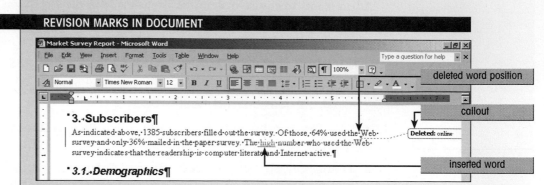

TROUBLE? If your revision marks have a different color from the ones in Figure 10-25, don't worry. Someone might have selected different revision mark colors for your computer.

Cindy's revisions are completed. Now you'll turn off tracked changes by unprotecting the document.

To unprotect the document and turn off revision marks:

1. Click **Tools** on the menu bar, and then click **Unprotect Document**. Now whenever you make changes to the document, Word won't make any revision marks.

You'll see what the document will look like if you accepted all the revisions—that is, if no revision marks appeared in the document.

2. Double-click **TRK** on the status bar at the bottom of the Word window. TRK is highlighted. The Reviewing toolbar appears below the Formatting toolbar. With tracking turned on, any changes you make will insert tracking marks, even though the document is unprotected.

3. Click the **Display for Review** list arrow (located on the left edge of the Reviewing toolbar), and then click **Final**. The document now appears as it would if you accepted all the revisions. Using the Display for Review list arrow, you can also show how the document looked before the revisions and show the original version with changes. In the latter case, a balloon message shows the location of words added (rather than words deleted), and the text includes the words deleted (red strikethrough font). Thus, Word allows you to see the document in all four different views.

4. Change the Display for Review setting back to **Final Showing Markup**.

5. Double-click **TRK** to turn off revision tracking. TRK is a toggle switch; if you double-click it while tracking is off, you turn tracking on; if you double-click it while tracking is on, you turn tracking off. Notice that even though revision tracking is off, the Reviewing toolbar is still on-screen. This shows that tracking can be on or off whether the Reviewing toolbar is present or absent.

6. Right-click anywhere on the Reviewing toolbar, and then click **Reviewing** to close the toolbar.

7. Save the document.

After you make Cindy's suggested changes to the Market Survey Report, Albert reads the document. He decides to make some additional changes.

Using Different Revision Colors

When two or more people edit a document using different computers, Word can mark each person's edits in a unique color. Word knows that a different person is working on a document because of the User Information tab in the Options dialog box. Word checks the name listed in the Options dialog box; if it doesn't match the name of someone who has already worked on the document, then the revisions appear in a different color. When you review revisions, Word shows the person responsible for each revision.

Albert wants his revision marks to look different from Cindy's. To distinguish his edits from Cindy's, you'll again change the User Information name.

To edit the document for Albert:

1. Click **Tools** on the menu bar, click **Options**, and then click the **User Information** tab in the Options dialog box. Type **Albert Kjar** in the Name text box and **AK** in the Initials text box, and then click the **OK** button.

2. Double-click **TRK** on the status bar to turn on tracking and to display the Reviewing toolbar again. Notice that, even though you are tracking changes, the document isn't protected.

   Now when Albert makes any revisions, his markups will be in a different color than Cindy's—provided that Word is set up to mark revisions in a different color for each author. You'll make sure that it is.

3. Click **Show** on the Reviewing toolbar, and then click **Options**. In the "Track Changes options" section, click the **Color** list arrow, click **By author**, and then click the **OK** button. The Track Changes dialog box closes.

   Now you're ready to make Albert's revisions. He sees two errors in the sentence below the "Demographics" heading: two occurrences of "residents" should be "residence."

4. Move the insertion point to the end of the first occurrence of the word "residents," press the **Backspace** key twice to delete the "ts", and then type **ce** to spell the word "residence." Repeat this for the second occurrence of "residents" in the sentence. See Figure 10-26.

Figure 10-26	SECOND SET OF REVISION MARKS

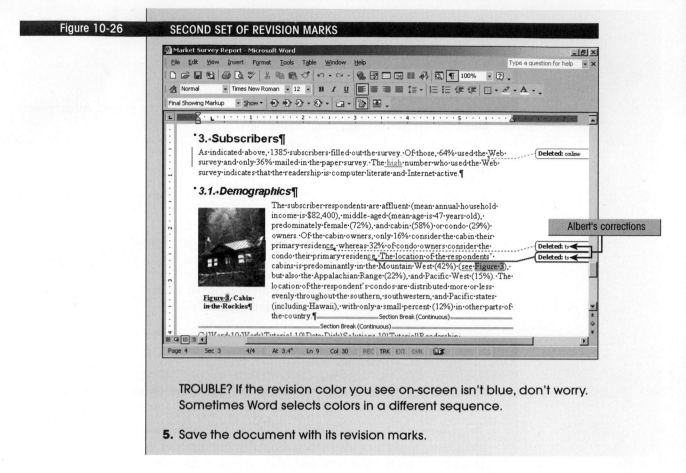

TROUBLE? If the revision color you see on-screen isn't blue, don't worry. Sometimes Word selects colors in a different sequence.

5. Save the document with its revision marks.

Usually a document undergoes more extensive editing than the changes you made for Cindy and Albert. The edits shown in this example, however, are sufficient to show how the revision tracking feature works in Word.

Accepting or Rejecting Revisions

Albert wants to distribute the contents of these early sections of the report to DDI management. But, before he does that, he wants you to review the Magazine Subscribers section and accept or reject the edits as appropriate.

You can accept or reject all the edits at one time, but usually you'll want to look at each revision separately and decide whether to accept or reject it, especially in long documents. Also, keep in mind that before you can accept or reject the revisions in a document, you (or someone else) must make sure the document is unprotected.

REFERENCE WINDOW   **RW**

Reviewing Highlighted Changes
- Make sure the document isn't protected, and move the insertion point to the beginning of the document (or above the revisions that you want to review).
- If necessary, double-click the TRK button on the status bar.
- Click the Next button on the Reviewing toolbar. Word highlights the first revision following the insertion point.
- Click the Accept or the Reject button.
- Continue using the Next button, and then accept or reject revisions until you've reviewed all the revisions in the document.

You can also display and review revisions by each reviewer one at a time. For example, suppose you want to review only Cindy's revisions. To do this, you would click Show on the Reviewing toolbar, point to Reviewers, and then click Cindy Myrup. The Word window would then show only Cindy's revision marks, which you could then accept or reject. Later, if you wanted to review the remaining revision marks, regardless of who made them, you could again click Show on the Reviewing toolbar, point to Reviewers, and then click All Reviewers. Similarly, you can use the Show menu to display and review each kind of revision mark (comments, insertions and deletions, or formatting) one a time or all together.

Now you're ready to review the document revisions. You'll review all types of revision marks for all the reviewers (Cindy and Albert).

To review highlighted changes:

1. Make sure the Reviewing toolbar is displayed. If necessary, click **Tools** on the menu bar, and then click **Unprotect Document** to unprotect the document. If necessary, click **View**, point to **Toolbars**, and then click **Reviewing** to open the Reviewing toolbar.

2. Double-click **TRK** on the status bar to turn off revision tracking. Even though you want the Reviewing toolbar open, you don't want revision tracking turned on. Next you need to position the insertion point before the first revision mark.

3. Click at the beginning of the paragraph below the "3. Subscribers" heading. Now you can use the Reviewing toolbar to select the first revision.

4. Click the **Next** button 🔁 on the Reviewing toolbar. Word highlights the deleted word "online" in the revision mark and increases the thickness of the colored border around the revision balloon. See Figure 10-27.

Figure 10-27   **REVIEWING REVISION MARKS**

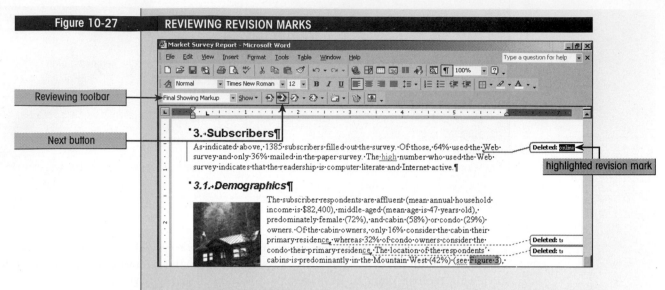

You want to accept this change to avoid the redundancy of "online Web."

5. Click the **Accept Change** button. Word removes the revision mark and "online" is omitted from the document.

6. Click again. Word highlights the inserted word "high." Albert decides that the new word doesn't add anything to the meaning of the sentence, so you'll reject this revision.

7. Click the **Reject Change/Delete Comment** button. Word removes the underlined word "high."

The document now has only two revision marks, both of which Albert wants to accept. Therefore, you decide to accept all revisions (that is, the remaining revisions) in the document.

8. Click the **Accept Change** list arrow, and then click **Accept All Changes in Document**. Word displays a message warning you that at least one of the subdocuments is locked. The subdocuments are locked because you didn't expand them into the master document. This isn't a problem because you haven't made revisions to the subdocuments.

9. Click the **OK** button. Word removes all revision marks in the master document, accepting all the revisions.

10. Close the Reviewing toolbar, save the document, and then close it.

You have rejected one edit and accepted all the others. Word removes the revision marks but keeps the accepted revisions. In this case, you reviewed the subdocument alone, but you could just as easily have reviewed it from within the master document.

In the earlier example, two different authors worked on the *same* document file, that is, both sets of revisions were located in one document. But what if Cindy had one copy of the document file, Albert had another copy of the document file, and they each edited their own file? You would use a similar method of reviewing revisions, except that you would compare and merge the files first, as explained in the Reference Window below. The procedure would occur as follows: You would send each reviewer (in this case each coauthor) a copy of a file; let them each edit the file with change tracking turned on; and have them each send you a copy of their edited files. At this stage, you would have two or more different copies of the same file. You would then compare and merge them all.

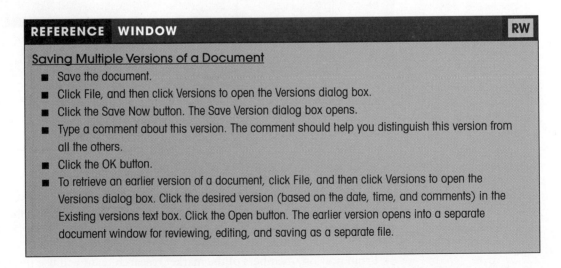

> ### REFERENCE WINDOW   RW
>
> **Comparing and Merging Documents from Different Reviewers**
> - Open one of the edited documents.
> - Click Tools on the menu bar, click Compare and Merge Documents, select another one of the edited files, and then click the Merge button. Word merges the first file with the second in such a way that unmodified text is retained, but both sets of revision marks—each with its own color—appear in the document window.
> - Repeat this procedure for all edited copies of the file.
> - Review the changes and accept or reject each of them.

Saving Multiple Versions of a Document

Normally when you save an existing document, Word overwrites the previous version of the file with a new file. Sometimes, however, it's helpful to be able to recover previous versions of a document—for instance, if a later version gets excessive, unwanted changes. To anticipate that potential problem, you can use the Versions command on the File menu. This command allows you to save an earlier version of the document as part of the main document file; that is, the previous versions as well as the most recent version are all saved in one file. If you want to edit an earlier version, you open that version into a separate document window, and then save it as a separate file. (Note that you can't use the Versions command to save master documents).

> ### REFERENCE WINDOW   RW
>
> **Saving Multiple Versions of a Document**
> - Save the document.
> - Click File, and then click Versions to open the Versions dialog box.
> - Click the Save Now button. The Save Version dialog box opens.
> - Type a comment about this version. The comment should help you distinguish this version from all the others.
> - Click the OK button.
> - To retrieve an earlier version of a document, click File, and then click Versions to open the Versions dialog box. Click the desired version (based on the date, time, and comments) in the Existing versions text box. Click the Open button. The earlier version opens into a separate document window for reviewing, editing, and saving as a separate file.

Now you'll open the subdocument Freelance Authors, make a change, and then save a new version of the subdocument, while keeping the old version.

> ### To save multiple versions of a document:
>
> **1.** Open the document named **Freelance Authors** (from the Tutorial subfolder in the Tutorial.10 folder), double-click **TRK** in the status bar, and then, on the line below the heading "Rating the Magazine," delete the word **specifically**, which Albert thinks is unnecessary. Now you'll save the document as a new version.

2. Click **File** on the menu bar, and then click **Versions**. The Versions in Freelance Authors dialog box opens.

3. Click the **Save Now** button. The Save Version dialog box opens. In the Comments on version text box, you can type a descriptive note to distinguish this version from the others. For example, your note might remind you of the stage of the document's development when you saved this version.

4. Type **Albert's revision**, and then click the **OK** button. Both dialog boxes close, and you return to the document window.

   Now the file contains the saved version and the current version of Freelance Authors. In the next two steps you'll save another version of the document.

5. Use the techniques you learned earlier in this tutorial to accept the revision.

6. Save the file as a new version with the comment **Revision accepted**. Now you can review the list of versions you have created so far.

7. Click **File** on the menu bar, and then click **Versions** to open the Versions in Freelance Authors dialog box again. See Figure 10-28.

Figure 10-28	VERSIONS DIALOG BOX

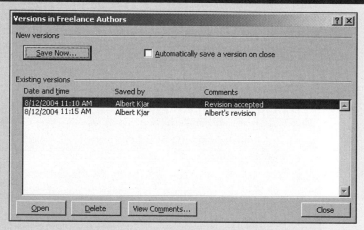

To open any version, you click the version in the Existing versions list box, and then click the Open button.

8. Click the **Close** button on the dialog box, and then close the document.

From now on, members of the market research team will use the Versions feature as they revise and comment on subdocuments. You also can set up Word to save versions automatically each time you close a document. If you want to do this, consult Help for instructions. Keep in mind that if you want to edit a previous version, you first have to open it from within the Versions dialog box, and then save the version as a separate document.

Working with Comments

Recall that Word allows you to insert **comments**, which are the electronic equivalent of sticky notes that you can "attach" to the text. You can use comments, for example, to remind yourself to verify certain information in a report. Comments are most useful when multiple people (such as a workgroup) are editing a single document. For example, one workgroup member might receive copy of a document via e-mail, delete a section, and then insert a comment to explain her revision to the rest of the workgroup.

Comments look different in print layout view than they do in normal view. When the document is in normal view, you need to open a special window (called the Comment pane) to view comments. In print layout view, they appear in callouts in the right margin.

When you insert a comment into a document, Word records your name (taken from the User Information tab of the Options dialog box) and the date the comment was added to the document. To see the author and date information for a comment in print layout view, place the pointer over the comment callout to display a ScreenTip.

You can use the Protect Document command on the Tools menu to protect a document for comments only; then workgroup members can add comments to the document but can't make revisions. Because Albert wants the market research team to make changes as well as comments, you won't protect the subdocuments for comments.

REFERENCE WINDOW   **RW**

Working with Comments

- Move the insertion point to where you want to insert the comment.
- Click Insert on the menu bar, and then click Comment (or click the New Comment button on the Reviewing toolbar). In normal view, Word opens the Reviewing Pane. In print layout view, Word opens a comment callout.
- Type the comment in the Reviewing Pane (in normal view) or in the comment callout (in page layout view).
- Click in the document window (in any view) or press the Esc key (in page layout view) to return the insertion point to the document.
- To protect a document for comments, click Tools on the menu bar, click Protect Document, click the Comments option button, and then click the OK button.
- To make sure your name appears as the author of the comment, click Tools on the menu bar, click Options, and then verify that your name and initials appear in the User Information tab.

Inserting Comments

After reading through the master document Market Survey Report, Albert decides to insert a comment. You'll insert Albert's comment now.

To insert a comment:

1. Open the document named **Market Survey Report** (from the Tutorial subfolder in the Tutorial.10 folder), expand the document (if necessary), and make sure your document is in print layout view and that "Albert Kjar" is the name entered in the User Information tab of the Options dialog box.

2. Move the insertion point to the right of "Mountain West" in the middle of the paragraph, below the heading "3.1. Demographics" on page 4. This is where Albert wants to insert his comment.

3. Click **Insert** on the menu bar, and then click **Comment**. Word adds a colored callout balloon, which now contains the insertion point.

4. Type **Which states constitute the Mountain West?**

5. Press the **Esc** key to return the insertion point to the document. See Figure 10-29.

| Figure 10-29 | DOCUMENT WITH COMMENT |

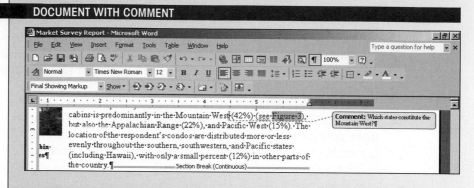

6. Move the pointer ⌶ over the comment balloon in the right margin. Word displays a colored ScreenTip with the name of the person who inserted the comment—in this case, Albert Kjar—and the date and time of the comment.

7. Save the document with Albert's comment.

Inserting comments is an excellent way to communicate with members of a workgroup, allowing you to ask questions, make suggestions, and explain revisions efficiently.

Finding, Viewing, and Deleting Comments

You can see the text of the comments in the Reviewing Pane or (when in print layout view) in the comment callouts. But in a long document, you might not want to scroll through all the pages to find and read the comments. In that case, you can find and view comments in the same way that you find and view revisions—using the Next button on the Reviewing toolbar. When you find a comment, you can then keep it, modify it, or delete it.

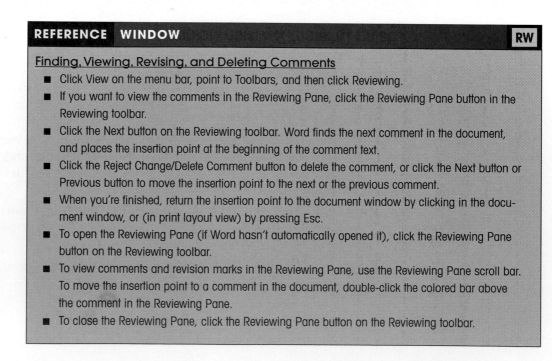

REFERENCE WINDOW   **RW**

<u>Finding, Viewing, Revising, and Deleting Comments</u>
- Click View on the menu bar, point to Toolbars, and then click Reviewing.
- If you want to view the comments in the Reviewing Pane, click the Reviewing Pane button in the Reviewing toolbar.
- Click the Next button on the Reviewing toolbar. Word finds the next comment in the document, and places the insertion point at the beginning of the comment text.
- Click the Reject Change/Delete Comment button to delete the comment, or click the Next button or Previous button to move the insertion point to the next or the previous comment.
- When you're finished, return the insertion point to the document window by clicking in the document window, or (in print layout view) by pressing Esc.
- To open the Reviewing Pane (if Word hasn't automatically opened it), click the Reviewing Pane button on the Reviewing toolbar.
- To view comments and revision marks in the Reviewing Pane, use the Reviewing Pane scroll bar. To move the insertion point to a comment in the document, double-click the colored bar above the comment in the Reviewing Pane.
- To close the Reviewing Pane, click the Reviewing Pane button on the Reviewing toolbar.

Now you're ready to find, view, and delete Albert's comment.

To find, view, and delete a comment using the Reviewing toolbar:

1. Make sure the Market Survey Report document is still open in print layout view.

2. If necessary, display the Reviewing toolbar without turning on revision tracking.

3. Move the insertion point to the beginning of the document. When reviewing a long document, moving the insertion point to the beginning ensures that you find all comments.

4. Click the **Next** button 🔁 on the Reviewing toolbar. Word finds the first comment (in this case, the only comment), highlights the comment balloon (the callout line becomes thick and solid, and the lines around the balloon become thicker), and places the insertion point at the beginning of the comment text. See Figure 10-30. If the document had revision marks, the Next command would have found either the next revision mark or comment.

Figure 10-30	REVIEWING COMMENTS

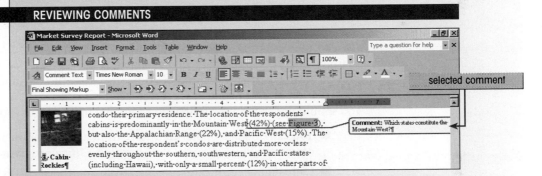

5. Read the comment, and then click the **Reject Change/Delete Comment** button 🗭 to delete the comment. If the document contained other comments or tracked changes, you would repeat Step 4, and continue through the document, reading and handling all the comments.

6. Save the document and then close it.

At this stage, you know how to use revision marks and comments to keep track of changes in a document and to make notes on important parts of the document. These features are designed to simplify the process of editing a document online, especially in a workgroup. But sometimes you'll need to review a printed document, and then the revision marks and comments must appear in printed form. In the next section, you'll learn how to create a printed list of this information.

Printing a List of Revision Marks and Comments

Microsoft Word uses the term **markup** to refer to revision marks and comments collectively. You can print a list of all markups in a document, which is helpful if you want to send a printed copy of the revisions and comments to someone; if you want to read all the markups at once; or if you want to keep a hard copy of the markups on file. Currently, the document doesn't contain any markups, but for future reference you should know how to print them.

(You'll have a chance to print a list of markups in the Case Problems at the end of this tutorial.)

The market analysis workgroup has completed all the subdocuments. The team members have added all their edits and comments for this draft of the report, and you have reviewed all of the edit marks and comments. Next you'll save the Market Survey Report with your digital signature.

Using Digital Signatures

A **digital signature** is an attachment to a file that vouches for its authenticity. A digital signature works much like a handwritten signature: When you sign a letter, you confirm that you wrote the letter and that its contents are accurate, to the best of your knowledge. Similarly, when you attach your digital signature to a Word document, you confirm that you're the author, owner, or reviewer, and certify that the document is unaltered and that the information in the document is correct.

You should understand the following additional information about digital signatures:

- You can obtain a digital certificate from a certification authority or you can create one yourself using the Microsoft Office program SelfCert.
- Only digital certificates obtained from an official certification authority are valid and reliable. Only a certification authority can provide legitimate, certifiable digital signatures.
- When you open a digitally signed document, Word includes the designation "(Signed)" on the title bar of the document window. This notifies you that the file you opened in Word carries a digital signature, but it alone doesn't authenticate the signature.
- To authenticate a digital signature (that is, to verify that the signature is official and authentic), follow the procedure given in the Reference Window, "Authenticating a Digital Certificate." If the digital signature is self-made, Word will warn you that you can't trust the signature.
- If you modify a digitally signed document in any way and then save the modified version, Word will strip the digital signature from the document. (You'll be warned of this when you try to save the document.) Thus, if a document has a certified digital signature, you can be fairly certain that no one has modified the document.
- If you review a document digitally signed by someone else, you can add your own digital signature verifying that you have opened and read the document. If you don't make any modifications, Word will let you save the document with the original and your digital signatures.
- You can't add a digital signature to a master document, but you can add one to each of the subdocuments.

■ You can maintain the security of a document in other ways than using digital signatures—for example, by protecting the document with a password, encrypting the file with a password, and sending the file only through secure networks.

REFERENCE · WINDOW `RW`

Authenticating a Digital Certificate

■ Open the digitally signed Word document in the Word document window. Make sure "(Signed)" appears on the title bar.

■ Click Tools on the menu bar, click Options, click the Security tab, and then click the Digital Signatures button.

■ Select a name from the list of people who have digitally signed the document. Often, the document contains the name of only one signer, the original author.

■ Click the View Certificate button. If the digital signature is certified by a legitimate CA (certification authority), you'll see a trusted certificate. If the digital signature isn't properly registered with a trusted certification authority, you'll be so notified.

■ Click OK in each of the dialog boxes until you return to the Word document.

Creating a Digital Signature Using SelfCert

Albert Kjar asks you to create a digital signature so you can add it to one or more of the files in the market survey report.

You can use the Microsoft Office program SelfCert to create your own digital signature for personal use. Then when you create a document, you can attach your digital signature to the document. This method works if you're sharing your documents only with trusted family, friends, and colleagues. Be aware, however, that anyone could create a digital signature using your name, so self-made digital signatures provide only modest security. To demonstrate how digital signatures work, you'll create your own digital signature using SelfCert.

To create your own digital signature:

1. Click the **Start** button on the task bar, and then click **Run** to open the Run dialog box.

2. Click the **Browse** button to open the Browse dialog box, and then locate the Microsoft Office\Office folder. Typically, the folder path is C:\Program Files\Microsoft Office\Office. In the Office folder, you should see the file "SELFCERT".

   TROUBLE? If SELFCERT isn't in your Office folder, read the remaining steps in this section and the next section, but do not attempt to complete them.

3. Double-click **SELFCERT**. The Browse dialog box closes, and you return to the Run dialog box, where you can see the filename and folder path in the Open text box.

4. Click the **OK** button.

5. Type your name in the Your name text box, and then click the **OK** button.

6. When you see a message indicating that your digital signature was created successfully, click the **OK** button.

You now own a digital signature, even though it not official. In the next section you'll attach it to the Market Survey Report.

Digitally Signing a Document

Albert wants you to add your digital signature to the document Freelance Authors.

To attach a digital signature:

1. Open the document named **Freelance Authors** from the Tutorial subfolder in the Tutorial.10 folder.

2. Click **Tools** on the menu bar, click **Options**, click the **User Information** tab, and then change the name and initials of the user back to their original settings, which would be your name and initials if you are the computer owner.

3. Click the **Security** tab, and then click the **Digital Signatures** button. The Digital Signature dialog box opens.

4. Click the **Add** button. Word warns you that, in the current view, you might not be able to see all the text and pictures. Unless you know what's in a document, you shouldn't add your digital signature. In this case, you have seen everything in the document.

5. Click the **Yes** button.

   TROUBLE? Another warning appears, indicating that this document has tracked changes. Click the **Yes** button, which causes the Word to remove all the tracked changes, and the document reverts back to the state it was in before the tracked changes were made. The Select Certificate dialog box opens.

6. Click your name in the list of issued certificates.

7. Click the **OK** button three times to close the three dialog boxes. Now "(Signed)" appears in the title bar. See Figure 10-31.

Figure 10-31   EDITED SUBDOCUMENT

indicates a digitally signed document

8. Make sure revision tracking is turned off, save the document, and then close it.

   TROUBLE? If Word displays a warning that all digital signatures will be deleted, click Yes. Even though the document won't have a digital signature, the subsequent steps will work properly.

You have attached your digital signature to the document. When you or anyone else opens the document, you can go to the Digital Signature dialog box and see the signature. You'll also always see "(Signed)" on the title bar, as long as the document stays unmodified. If you modify it and save it, Word will strip away all digital signatures.

In the next session, you'll format the document for printing and add a table of contents, list of figures, index, and footers.

Session 10.2 QUICK CHECK

1. Briefly describe how you add automatic numbering to section titles in a master document.

2. What are three advantages of using the Heading Numbering feature?

3. What are two features of using revision marks?

4. Why do you protect a document for revisions?

5. What are comments, and what is their purpose?

6. How can you tell who made a certain revision? How can you tell who made a certain comment?

7. How do you print all the revision marks and comments in a document?

8. What is a digital signature?

SESSION 10.3

In this session, you will set page numbering for all sections of the document, and create odd and even footers. You'll then insert a style reference, compile an index, compile a list of figures, and create a table of contents for the master document.

Numbering Pages with Number Formats

Albert wants to add footers to the Market Survey Report that include the name of the section and page numbers. Like most books, reports, and other long documents, the report will use a different page-numbering scheme for the **front matter**—the material preceding the first page of the first section, and which includes material such as the title page and table of contents. The front matter is usually numbered with lowercase Roman numerals (i, ii, iii, iv), whereas the main sections of the document are numbered with Arabic numerals (1, 2, 3, and so on). The first page of the first section typically begins with page number 1.

You'll begin by formatting the title page and creating several other front matter pages, and then you'll set up the page numbers for the front matter.

To insert new front matter pages and format the title page:

1. Make sure Word is running, open the master document named **Market Survey Report** from the Tutorial subfolder in the Tutorial.10 folder, expand the subdocuments, and then switch to normal view with nonprinting characters displayed. It's easier to insert page breaks in normal view than in print layout view. You'll switch back to print layout view later.

2. Move the insertion point to the end of page 1, immediately to the right of the date "August 4, 2003." Next you need to insert a new section below the title page so that you can format the title page with a format different from the other pages in the front matter.

3. Click **Insert** on the menu bar, click **Break** to open the Break dialog box, click the **Next page** option button, and then click the **OK** button. Word inserts a new page following a section break. The insertion point moves to the new page.

   TROUBLE? If the items on the Insert menu are dimmed and the title bar includes the message "(Read Only)," the User Information name doesn't match the original author of the master document. Click File on the menu bar, click Properties, click the Summary tab, write the name of the author on a piece of paper, and then click the Cancel button. Change the name in the User Information tab of the Options dialog box to match the Properties Summary name, close the current read-only document, and then repeat Steps 1 through 3.

4. Click the **Align Left** button. The insertion point moves to the left margin.

5. Type **Contents**, press the **Enter** key twice to add some space below the heading, press **Ctrl+Enter** to insert another page break, but without a section break, type **List of Figures**, and then press the **Enter** key twice. You've created two new pages, each with a heading.

6. Format each of the two new headings ("Contents" and "List of Figures") in **16-point, bold Arial**. This gives these two headings the same attributes as the Heading 1 style. (You didn't apply the heading style from the Style list because if you had, Word would have automatically numbered the new headings. Currently, the first numbered heading is "1. Background," and you don't want that to change.) See Figure 10-32.

| Figure 10-32 | DOCUMENT WITH NEW PAGES AND HEADINGS |

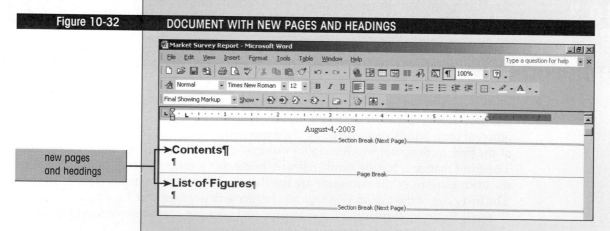

Next you'll center the title page vertically, so that the text is centered between the top and bottom margins.

7. Move the insertion point anywhere on page 1 (the title page), click **File** on the menu bar, click **Page Setup** to open the Page Setup dialog box, and then click the **Layout** tab (if necessary). Make sure **This section** appears in the Apply to list box (in the Preview section of the dialog box), and then, in the Page section, click the **Vertical alignment** list arrow, and click **Center**. Also click the **Different first page** check box to select it; this ensures that page numbering changes you make in the document won't affect the first page—the first page will

remain unnumbered. Your dialog box should now look like Figure 10-33. This tells Word that you want the text on this page to be centered between the top and bottom margins.

Figure 10-33   **PAGE SETUP DIALOG BOX**

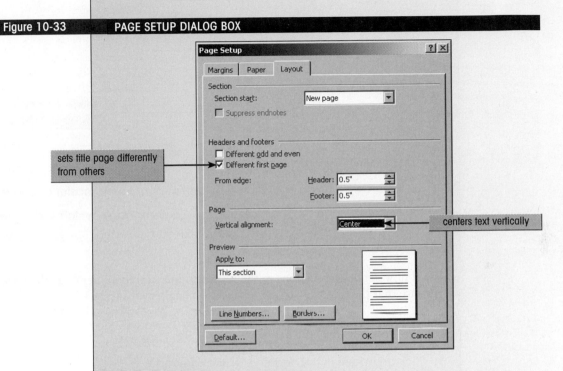

sets title page differently from others

centers text vertically

8. Click the **OK** button and switch to print layout view. Scroll throughout page 1, look over the text, and verify that it is centered vertically as well as horizontally on the page.

Now you're ready to set up the page numbering for the front matter (that is, the title page, table of contents, and list of figures).

To set up page numbers for the front matter:

1. Move the insertion point to the left of the "Contents" heading, on page 2 of the master document. This is where you want to insert Roman numeral i as the page number.

2. Click **Insert** on the menu bar, click **Page Numbers** to open the Page Numbers dialog box, and then click the **Format** button to open the Page Number Format dialog box.

3. Click the **Number format** list arrow, and then click **i, ii, iii, ...** so the page numbers will be lowercase Roman numerals. Make sure that the Include chapter number check box is unchecked.

4. Click the **Start at** option button in the Page numbering section, and then make sure **i** (Roman numeral one) is in the Start at text box. See Figure 10-34. (In your dialog box, the "i" will be selected and possibly hard to read.)

Figure 10-34   **PAGE NUMBER FORMAT DIALOG BOX**

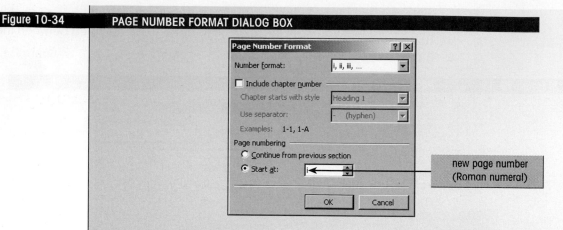

new page number
(Roman numeral)

5. Click the **OK** button in both dialog boxes to return to the master document.

6. Scroll until you can see the footer on the Contents page, which shows the page number "i."

You'll now set up the sections in the report to use Arabic numerals as the page numbers and ensure that the first page of the first section begins with page 1.

To set the first page of Section 1 to page 1:

1. Click anywhere in the heading "1. Background."

2. Click **Insert** on the menu bar, click **Page Numbers** to open the Page Numbers dialog box, and then click the **Format** button to open the Page Number Format dialog box.

TROUBLE? If the Page Number command is dimmed in the Insert menu, your subdocument is locked. To unlock it, switch to master document view, click the Lock Document button on the Outlining toolbar, return to print layout view, and then repeat Step 2.

3. Make sure **1, 2, 3, ...** appears in the Number format list box so the page numbers will be Arabic numerals. Make sure the Include chapter number check box isn't selected. Next you need to indicate that you want the first section to begin with page number 1.

4. Click the **Start at** option button in the Page numbering section, and then make sure **1** (Arabic numeral one) appears in the Start at text box.

5. Click the **OK** button in each dialog box to return to the master document in print layout view.

6. Scroll down through the document so you can see the page numbers in the lower-right corner of each page. As you can see, the numbering starts with page 1 on the "1. Background" page and proceeds through page 5 on the last page.

TROUBLE? If your title page has a page number (Arabic number 1 in the lower-right corner), don't worry about it right now. You'll have a chance to fix it later.

You have set up the page numbering for the master document. All the sections will be numbered with consecutive Arabic numerals, and the front matter with consecutive lower-case Roman numerals. When you create the table of contents and the list of figures later, they'll appear on pages i and ii of the front matter. (The title page is unnumbered.)

Changing the Footer and Page Layout for Odd and Even Pages

Most professionally produced books and reports are printed on both sides of the paper and then bound. When you open a book or report to any page, an odd-numbered page appears on the right, an even-numbered page appears on the left, and sometimes the odd headers or footers have text that differs from the even headers or footers. In this design, the **gutter** is an extra blank space on the side of each page where the pages are bound together.

Albert wants to follow these standards in the Market Survey Report. Specifically, he wants you to use the page layouts shown in Figure 10-35:

Figure 10-35	PAGE LAYOUT FOR ODD AND EVEN PAGES

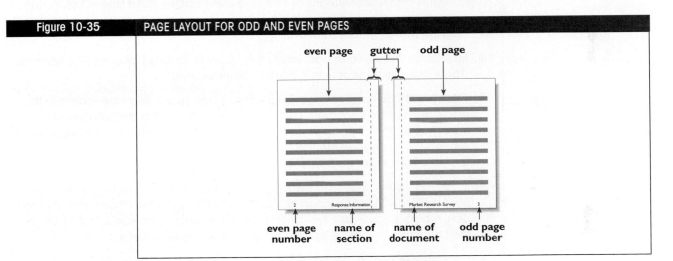

- Set the gutter to one-half inch. Word shifts the text on odd pages to the right (½ inch in this case), leaving a wider margin on the left. Word shifts the text on even pages to the left (again, ½ inch), leaving a wider margin on the right. When the even and odd pages are printed back-to-back (in a printing format called **two-sided printing**), the gutters line up on the same edge of the paper, thus leaving room for the binding.

- Change the location for page numbers so it's different on odd and even pages. In a page layout that distinguishes between odd and even pages, the page numbers usually are printed near the outside edge of the page rather than near the gutter, to make them easier to see in a bound copy. On odd pages, the page numbers appear on the right; on even pages, page numbers appear on the left.

- Type different text for the footers on odd and even pages. In many books, the section title is included in the header or footer of odd pages; at the same time, the book title is included in the header or footer of even pages. Sometimes this text is shifted toward the gutter (just as page numbers are shifted toward the outer edge). DDI's standard style is for the odd-page footers to include the document name (for example, "Market Survey Report"), and the even-page footers to include the section name, (for example, "Magazine Subscribers)" closer to the gutter.

First you'll change the page setup in the master document to distinguish between odd and even page footers, and then you'll increase the size of the gutter to allow enough room to bind the report without obscuring any text.

To change the page setup for printing odd and even pages:

1. Move the insertion point to the second page of the document (numbered page i, with the heading "Contents"), click **File** on the menu bar, and then click **Page Setup** to open the Page Setup dialog box.

2. Click the **Margins** tab, if necessary, and then change the setting in the Gutter text box to **0.5"**

3. Click the **Layout** tab, and then, if necessary, click the **Different odd and even** check box in the Headers and footers section. (The Different first page check box should not be checked). Be aware that this step allows you to enter page numbers and text differently in odd and even pages, but it doesn't automatically change the location of the page numbers currently in your footers. You'll change that manually later on.

4. Make sure **This section** appears in the Apply to list box because you want to apply these settings only to the front matter section.

5. Click the **OK** button. The Page Setup dialog box closes. Now the footers in the odd pages of the front matter will differ from those on the even pages of the front matter. (This change doesn't affect the title page, which is its own, separate section.) You'll change the text and page number position in the front matter footers after you set up odd and even pages for the rest of the document.

6. Move the insertion point to the beginning of page 1 (the first page after the front matter, with the heading "1. Background"). Open the Page Setup dialog box, repeat Steps 2 and 3, click **This point forward** in the Apply to list box (in the Layout tab) so these options apply to the remainder of the report.

7. Click the **OK** button. The Page Setup dialog box closes. Because you set the gutter to ½ inch with odd and even pages different, the body text on each page has shifted. Scroll through the document to see that the body text on odd pages is shifted to the right—the left margin has increased in width, and the right margin has decreased. Conversely, on the even pages the body is shifted to the left—the left margin has decreased in width, and the right margin has increased. You don't see changes in the footers yet (except for the changes in margin size); that will be your next task.

You have specified that odd and even pages should be set up differently. Now you'll type the footer text and format page numbering differently in the odd and even footers.

To format different footers for odd and even pages:

1. Press **Ctrl+Home** to move the insertion point to the beginning of the master document, click **View** on the menu bar, and then click **Header and Footer**. The Header and Footer toolbar opens, and the insertion point appears in the header box at the top of the page.

2. Click the **Switch Between Header and Footer** button ⌸ on the Header and Footer toolbar. The insertion point moves to the footer text box, which should be blank (except for the nonprinting characters).

3. Click the **Show Next** button ⬜ on the Header and Footer toolbar until the insertion point moves to the footer text box labeled "Odd Page Footer - Section 3." The insertion point should be positioned at the left margin of this text box. In the right margin, the footer contains the page number "1". Because this is an odd page, you'll leave the page number at the right and insert the document name at the left.

4. With the insertion point at the left edge of the footer text box, type **Market Survey Report**.

5. Click ⬜ again to move the insertion point to the footer text box labeled "Even Page Footer - Section 3." Now you'll delete the page number from this footer and reinsert it in the left margin.

   TROUBLE? If the page number is already on the left, read through the steps below, but don't delete and then reinsert the page number.

6. Click the page number field (the black "2" with the gray background), and then click the hashed border around it. This selects the page number field on the right edge of the footer.

7. Press the **Delete** key. The page number field is removed from the footer. The insertion point moves back to the left margin of the footer text box.

Next you'll set up the even page footers, with the page number at the left edge and the section title at the right edge. Rather than manually entering the section title in each section, you will tell Word to insert the proper text automatically.

Inserting a Style Reference into a Footer

A **style reference** is a field code that inserts text formatted with a particular style at the location of the field code. Like many of the Word features you've used in this tutorial, style references are useful because they allow Word to update information automatically in one part of a document to reflect changes made in another part of a document. For example, in the footer, Albert wants you to insert a style reference to the Heading 1 style. As a result of this style reference, the footer will include the section name (the only text in the document formatted with the Heading 1 style). As the section heading text changes throughout the document, the section name in the footer automatically changes. Furthermore, if Albert changes a section title, the text in the footer will change accordingly.

To insert a style reference to the section title into the footer:

1. Verify that the insertion point is positioned in the left margin of the Footer text box, and then click the **Insert Page Number** button ⬜ on the Header and Footer toolbar. The page number 2 appears at the left margin.

2. Press the **Tab** key twice to move the insertion point to the right margin.

   TROUBLE? If the insertion point appears outside and to the right of the footer box, drag the right-aligned tab stop marker (in the horizontal ruler) left until it's aligned with the right edge of the footer box.

3. Click **Insert** on the menu bar, and then click **Field** to open the Field dialog box, click the **Categories** list arrow, and then click **Links and References**.

4. In the Field names list box, click **StyleRef** (an abbreviation of "style reference"). Next you'll indicate which style you want the StyleRef field code to refer to.

5. Click **Heading 1** (the style for the section titles) in the Style name list, and then click the **OK** button. The Field dialog box closes. The section title "Executive Summary" appears in the footer, because the Heading 1 style text is "Executive Summary."

6. Click the **Close** button on the Header and Footer toolbar to return to the document window.

7. Scroll through the document to review the footers on other pages. Note that the section name differs from one even page to the next.

TROUBLE? If a footer with a page number (and possibly text) appears on the title page, which is the very first page of the document, move the insertion point to the title page, open the Page Setup dialog box, make sure that Different first page is checked, close the dialog box, click View on the menu bar, click Header and Footer, switch to the First Page Footer - Section 1, delete the page number and any text, and then click Close on the Header and Footer toolbar.

You'll use Print Preview to see how the footers look in the master document, and make sure they're set up according to DDI's style guidelines.

To view the odd and even footers:

1. Verify that the insertion point is positioned at the beginning of the document, and then click the **Print Preview** button [⯐] on the Standard toolbar. If Word displays a message asking if you want to expand the subdocuments into the master document, click the **Yes** button. You'll see a blank page after the title page. This is because you set up the document for different odd and even pages, and then you set two consecutive pages (the title page and the contents page) to be numbered as page 1. You can't have two odd-numbered pages in a row (the margins, gutter spacing, and footer text would be off), so Word inserted a blank, even-numbered page.

2. Click the **Multiple Pages** button [⊞] on the Print Preview toolbar, and then set the number of pages to **1 x 2** so you can see odd and even pages side by side. (At first, you'll only see one page—the title page, which, because it is an odd-numbered page, appears on the right side.)

3. Scroll down until you see pages 2 and 3 (of Section 3). See Figure 10-36.

Figure 10-36 | **PRINT PREVIEW SHOWS EVEN AND ODD PAGES**

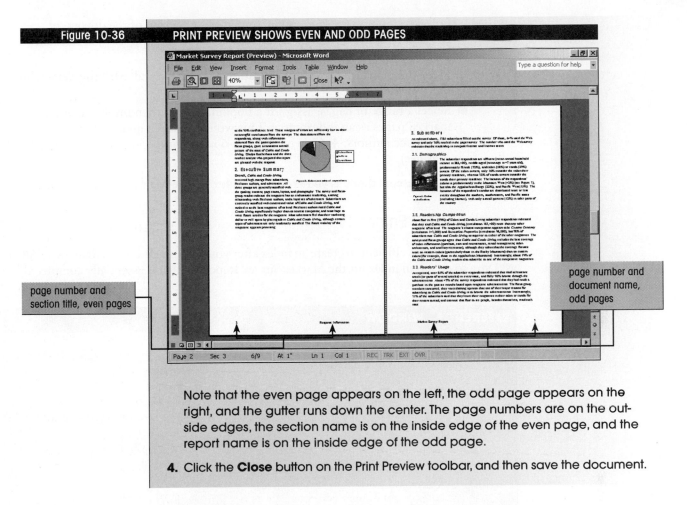

page number and
section title, even pages

page number and
document name,
odd pages

Note that the even page appears on the left, the odd page appears on the
right, and the gutter runs down the center. The page numbers are on the outside edges, the section name is on the inside edge of the even page, and the
report name is on the inside edge of the odd page.

4. Click the **Close** button on the Print Preview toolbar, and then save the document.

The report is set up so Albert can print the document on both sides of the page.

Creating an Index

Albert wants you to create an index to help readers locate specific information in the report.
As you probably know, an **index** is a list of words and phrases (called **entries**) accompanied
by the page numbers on which they appear in a printed document. For example, if
customers want information on "competition," they should be able to look in the index and
find a list of all the pages on which the entry "competition" appears in the report.

Compiling an index by hand is tedious, time-consuming, and error-prone. It's also
inefficient because if you insert, delete, or move text from one part of the document after
you create the index, the page numbers might change. You would then have to go through
the entire index again, making any necessary page number changes. On the other hand,
once you set up an index using the Word Index feature, the page numbering is automatic, no
matter how many times you reorganize the document.

When you create an index with Word, you generate entries in one of four ways:

■ Select a word or phrase and add it manually to the list of entries in the index.
This works well if an entry occurs only a few times, because you must mark
every occurrence of the entry, one at a time.

■ Select a word or phrase and have Word search the document for every
occurrence of that entry. This is fast, efficient, and accurate. It isn't,

however, foolproof. For example, sometimes a portion of the document contains a particular topic which doesn't use the exact phrase you selected for that topic.

- Move the insertion point to the location of an entry, and mark the item as an index entry.
- Select a range of pages, assign it a bookmark, and then mark the book-marked pages as an index entry. This would result in an entry such as "freelance authors, 4–6" (where the 4–6 refers to the bookmarked range of pages).

You'll use all these methods as you create the index for the Market Survey Report.

Marking Index Entries

Generally, it's more efficient to create an index after your document is in its final form. Albert asks you to create an index for the Market Survey Report, which is essentially completed.

REFERENCE WINDOW   **RW**

Marking Index Entries and Subentries

- Select the word or phrase you want to mark as an index entry.
- Press Alt+Shift+X to open the Mark Index Entry dialog box.
- Make sure the Current page option button in the Options section is selected.
- If necessary, type an index entry in the Main entry text box, and then, if desired, type an entry in the Subentry text box.
- Click the Mark button to mark this occurrence, or click the Mark All button to mark every occurrence in the document.
- Click the Close button.

You'll start creating the index by selecting the first occurrence of a word or phrase that you want as an index entry, and then telling Word to mark every occurrence of it throughout the document. The first entry you'll mark is "Committee," which in this document always refers to the Committee on Publications.

To mark every occurrence of a main index entry:

1. Press **Ctrl+Home** to move the insertion point to the beginning of the document, and then use the Find command on the Edit menu to move to and select the word **Committee**. Now you can add this word to the index.

2. With "Committee" selected, press **Alt+Shift+X** to open the Mark Index Entry dialog box. (You can also open it as follows: Click Insert on the menu bar, point to Reference, click Index and Tables, and then, if necessary, click the Index tab and click the Mark Entry button.) The word you selected, "Committee," appears in the Main entry text box.

3. If necessary, click the **Current page** option button (in the Options section of the dialog box) to select it. This ensures that the current page of this entry will appear in the index.

4. Click the **Mark All** button. Word searches your document for every occurrence of "Committee" and marks each as an index entry. Instead of marking more entries, you'll return to the document to see how Word marked the word "Committee."

5. Click the **Close** button to return to the document window, press the **right arrow** key to deselect the word "Committee," and then move the insertion point to the right of the index field code. See Figure 10-37.

Figure 10-37	DOCUMENT WITH MARKED INDEX ENTRY

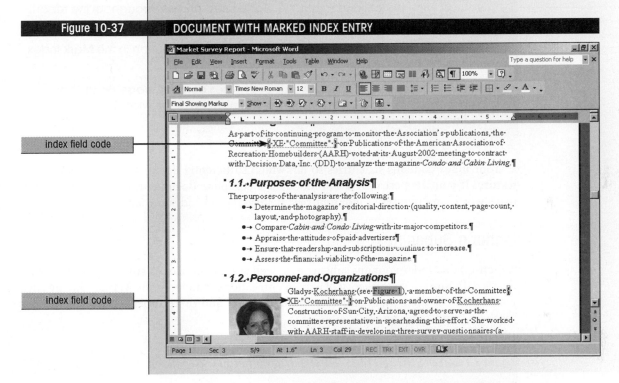

Throughout the report, Word marks "Committee" as an index entry, as indicated by the {XE "Committee"} field code to the right of each instance of the word. If you scroll to the paragraph below the heading "1.2. Personnel and Organizations," you'll see another "Committee" marked with the {XE "Committee"} field code. (Because Word inserts the {XE "Committee"} field code, you don't need to know much about it, except that "XE" stands for "index entry." If you do need to insert or modify the field, however, look up "XE field code" in Word online Help). You'll mark a few more index entries now.

To mark more index entries:

1. Scroll to display the first paragraph below the heading "1. Background."

2. Select the phrase **American Association of Recreation Homebuilders** in the first sentence of the paragraph.

3. Press **Alt+Shift+X** to open the Mark Index Entry dialog box, and then click the **Mark All** button. Word marks every occurrence of American Association of Recreation Homebuilders with the XE field code.

The Mark Index Entry dialog box is one of the few dialog boxes that you can leave open while you scroll through a document and select text.

4. Without closing the Mark Index Entry dialog box, click in the document window, and then select the phrase **Decision Data, Inc.** in the same paragraph. If necessary, drag the dialog box out of the way to see the phrase, but don't close the dialog box.

5. Click the **Mark All** button in the Mark Index Entry dialog box. Even though the button was dimmed (because the document window is active, rather than the dialog box), Word immediately activates the dialog box and the button when you click the button, and marks the highlighted phrase throughout the report.

6. Select the word **quality** in the first bulleted item below the heading "1.1. Purposes of the Analysis," and then click the **Mark All** button in the Mark Index Entry dialog box. Don't close the dialog box.

7. Repeat this procedure for the words or phrases **content**, **page count**, **layout**, and **photography**, all in the first bulleted item. Leave the Mark Index Entry dialog box open.

Your index contains six entries so far, which sufficiently demonstrates the power of this feature. If you were creating a full index for a complete document, you would continue to mark words and phrases as index entries. Instead, you'll add some subentries to the index.

Marking Subentries

A high-quality index contains subentries as well as main entries. A **subentry** is an index item that is a division or subcategory of a main entry. For example, in the Market Survey Report, you want to create a main entry for "respondents," and three subentries for "subscribers," "authors," and "advertisers."

To create subentries in an index:

1. Scroll down until you see the heading "1.3. Market Research Overview," and then select the word **subscribers** in the first sentence.

2. Click the title bar of the Mark Index Entry dialog box to make it active without marking an index entry.

3. Double-click the **Main** entry text box, type **respondents**, press the **Tab** key to move the insertion point to the Subentry text box, and then type **subscribers**. This creates a main entry for "respondents," with the subentry "subscribers."

4. Click the **Mark All** button. Word marks all occurrences of "subscribers" with the entry "respondents" and the subentry "subscribers."

5. Repeat Steps 1 through 4, except select the words **authors** and **advertisers** and create the index entries with "respondents" as the main entry and "authors" or "advertisers" as the subentries.

6. Select the word **respondents** at the end of the first sentence, and mark it as a main entry, without a subentry, and then mark all occurrences of the word throughout the text. Don't close the Mark Index Entry dialog box.

You have marked several subentries for a main index entry. Next you'll create a cross-reference index entry.

Creating Cross-Reference Index Entries

A **cross-reference index entry** is a phrase that tells readers to look at a different index entry to find the information they seek. For example, you've already marked "American Association of Recreation Homebuilders" as an index entry, but what if someone looks up AARH? You'd want the index to say: "AARH. *See* American Association of Recreation Homebuilders." You'll create the necessary cross-reference now.

To create a cross-reference index entry:

1. Select the abbreviation **AARH**, located in parentheses in the paragraph below the heading "1. Background."

2. Click the title bar in the Mark Index Entry dialog box.

3. With "AARH" as the main entry, click the **Cross-reference** option button (in the Options section of the dialog box), and, after the word "*See*" and the space, type **American Association of Recreation Homebuilders**.

4. Click the **Mark** button. You can't click the Mark All button, because this entry only has to appear once in the index, and doesn't carry a page number. Word inserts an XE field so the cross-reference will appear in the index. Now you'll create the "DDI" cross-reference that tells readers to look up "Data Decision, Inc." in the index.

5. In the paragraph below the heading "1. Background," select **DDI**, and mark it with a cross-reference to "Data Decision, Inc." Don't close the Mark Index Entry dialog box.

The index you're creating for the Market Survey Report includes two cross-references. Next you'll add an index entry that refers to a range of pages.

Creating an Index Entry for a Page Range

In addition to main entries and subentries that list individual pages, sometimes you'll want to include an index entry that refers to a range of pages, for example, the range of pages for the Freelance Authors section. This requires a more complicated procedure: you must select the pages of the section you want to mark as an index entry; create a bookmark for the selected pages; and then mark that bookmark name as the page-range entry.

REFERENCE WINDOW   **RW**

<u>Creating a Page Range Index Entry</u>
- Select a range of pages—for example, a section.
- Click Insert on the menu bar, and then click Bookmark.
- Type the name of the bookmark, and then click the Add button. The Bookmark dialog box closes.
- Make sure the Mark Index Entry dialog box is open, and then click the Page range option button, click the Bookmark list arrow, and click the bookmark name.
- Click the Mark button.

Next, you need to create an entry for "Freelance Authors." This entry will span a range of pages.

To create an index entry with a reference to a range of pages:

1. Scroll until you see the heading "4. Freelance Authors."

2. Switch to outline view and select the entire section by clicking the Expand icon ⊹ to the left of the heading. This highlights the section title and the three subtitles and their paragraphs.

3. Click **Insert** on the menu bar, and then click **Bookmark** to open the Bookmark dialog box.

4. Type **FreelanceAuthors** (all one word, with no spaces) as the bookmark name, and then click the **Add** button to create a bookmark for the selected range of pages.

5. With the text still selected, open the Mark Index Entry dialog box if necessary, click the **Page range** option button in the Mark Index Entry dialog box, click the **Bookmark** list arrow, and then click **FreelanceAuthors**.

6. Change the Main entry to **authors**. See Figure 10-38.

| Figure 10-38 | MARK INDEX ENTRY DIALOG BOX |

7. Click the **Mark** button to mark this index entry.

8. Using the same procedure, select the entire section titled "Subscribers," assign it the bookmark **Subscribers**, and then create a page range index entry, with the main entry **subscribers**. Do the same for the section titled "Advertisers."

   TROUBLE? If paragraph numbering disappears from some paragraphs, don't worry; you'll fix it later.

9. Click the **Close** button in the Mark Index Entry dialog box, and then save the document.

Although you have marked only a few words and phrases in the document, you have learned how to create all the different types of entries.

Compiling and Updating an Index

After you mark all the desired index entries, subentries, cross-references, and page-range references, you're ready to **compile the index**—that is, you're ready to tell Word to generate the index using the marked entries. Most often, indexes appear at the end of books, reports, or long documents. You'll compile the index on a new page at the end of the Market Survey Report.

REFERENCE WINDOW **RW**

Compiling an Index

- Hide nonprinting characters. This is necessary because the field codes take up extra space and change the pagination of the document.
- Click Insert on the menu bar, point to Reference, click Index and Tables, and then click the Index tab, if necessary.
- Select the desired options for how you want your index to appear in the document.
- Click the OK button. Word compiles the index.

You'll begin by hiding nonprinting characters.

To compile the index:

1. Switch to print layout view, press **Ctrl+End** to move the insertion point to the end of the document, and then click the **Show/Hide ¶** button ¶ on the Standard toolbar so nonprinting characters (including the XE codes) are not visible. This ensures that Word compiles accurate page numbers for the index entries.

   TROUBLE? If the index codes still appear in the text, click Tools on the menu bar, click Options, click the View tab, and then click the Formatting marks check box in the Nonprinting characters section of the dialog box.

2. Press **Ctrl+Enter** to insert a page break below the last paragraph, type **Index**, and then press **Enter** to insert a blank line below the heading.

3. Double-click **Index** to select it, and format it in **16-point**, **bold Arial**, the same format as the "Contents" heading.

4. Deselect the text and move the insertion point to the blank line below the heading. Make sure the blank line is formatted in Normal style, with the font set to 12-point Times New Roman. You're ready to compile the index.

5. Click **Insert** on the menu bar, point to **Reference**, click **Index and Tables**, and then click the **Index** tab, if necessary.

6. Make sure "From template" appears in the Formats list box to ensure that the index is formatted using the document's template styles.

7. Make sure "**2**" appears in the Columns text box, and that the "Right align page numbers" check box is not selected.

8. Click the **OK** button. Word compiles the index. Scroll to view the completed index. See Figure 10-39.

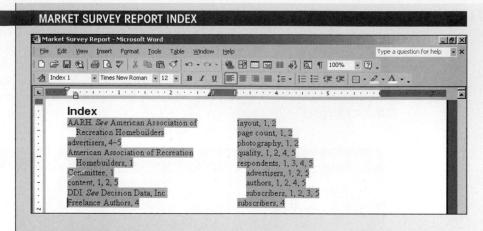

Figure 10-39   MARKET SURVEY REPORT INDEX

TROUBLE? If your page numbers aren't the same as those shown in Figure 10-39, make sure the nonprinting characters are hidden (by clicking ¶), and then go on to the next set of steps, where you'll regenerate the index. If the pages are still not the same, don't worry—differences in printers can cause page numbering differences.

Your index is short but representative of the entries that would appear in a full index. Albert asks you to add one more entry to the index. You'll mark the entry, and then update the index to include the new entry.

To update an index:

1. Select the term **e-business** in the last paragraph of the document, just above the index. You might need to scroll up to see it.

2. Mark all occurrences of "e-business" as main index entries.

3. Close the Mark Index Entry dialog box, and then hide the nonprinting characters.

4. Press **Ctrl+A** to select the entire document. Because the index is a field, you update it like you do any field—by pressing the F9 key.

5. Press the **F9** key to update the index (and all the fields in the document). Verify that the term "e-business" appears in the index.

Your next task is to create a table of contents and a table of figures.

Creating a Table of Contents and a Table of Figures

Creating a table of contents is similar to creating an index. As you know, a **table of contents** is a list that always appears in the front matter and includes all the headings in a document and the page numbers on which they appear. A table of contents should help readers locate specific topics or sections. A reader should be able to scan the table of contents to get a quick overview of the scope and range of topics covered.

To create a table of contents:

1. Move the insertion point to the blank line below the heading "Contents" on page i in the front matter. This is where you'll insert the table of contents. In the publishing industry, it's traditional for the table of contents heading to be the single word "Contents," not "Table of Contents."

2. Click **Insert** on the menu bar, point to **Reference**, click **Index and Tables**, and then click the **Table of Contents** tab. Make sure the **Show page numbers** checkbox is selected, that the **Right align page numbers** check box is selected, that the Tab leader list box is set to a dotted line, that the Formats list box is set to **From template**, and that Show levels is set to **3**. Click the **OK** button. Word generates the table of contents based on its predefined heading styles. See Figure 10-40.

Figure 10-40	TABLE OF CONTENTS

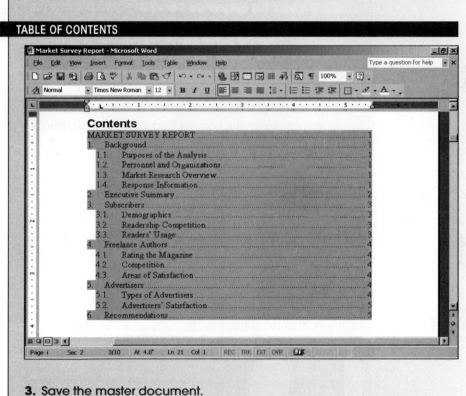

3. Save the master document.

You have completed the index and table of contents, and now you have one more task: creating a **table of figures**, which is a list of the captions for pictures, charts, graphs, slides, or other illustrations in a document, along with the page number on which they are found. Although a table of figures in a short report such as the Market Survey Report is unusual, it is not unusual in manuals, dissertations, technical documents, textbooks, and other long documents.

To create a table of figures:

1. Move the insertion point to the blank line below the heading "List of Figures" on page ii in the front matter. This is where you'll insert the list of figures.

2. Click **Insert** on the menu bar, point to **Reference**, click **Index and Tables**, and then click the **Table of Figures** tab. Make sure the **Show page numbers** checkbox is selected, that the **Right align page numbers** checkbox is selected, that the Tab leader list box is set to a dotted line, that the Formats list box is set to **From template**, and that the Caption label is set to **Figure**. Click the **OK** button. Word displays an error message in the document telling you that no table of figures entries was found.

This problem occurs because of text wrapping around figures. When you wrap text around a figure, Word makes the figure a floating object; then when you insert the caption, the caption becomes a text box, which is also a type of floating object, and not part of the main text of the document. When Word tries to generate the list of figures, it searches through the main text only, not through text in floating objects.

You can solve this problem by converting the text boxes to frames. (To learn more about the difference between frames and text boxes, use the Help Answer Wizard and ask the question "What is the difference between a text and a frame?") For the purposes of this tutorial, you only need to know that captions in text boxes are ignored when Word generates a list of figures; captions in frames are not ignored. You'll convert the text boxes to frames now.

3. Scroll so you can see the caption for "Figure 1. Gladys Kocherhans," click anywhere in the caption text box, right-click the edge of the text box to open a shortcut menu, click **Format Text Box**, click the **Text Box** tab, click the **Convert to Frame** button, and then click the **OK** button in the warning dialog box. The text box becomes a frame.

4. Right-click the edge of the caption frame, and then click **Format Frame** in the shortcut menu. The caption position undoubtedly changed before or after you converted it to a frame, so you'll reposition it now.

5. In the Horizontal section click the **Position** list arrow, click **Left**, click the **Relative to** list arrow, click **Margin**, and then click the **OK** button. The frame is now positioned as in Figure 10-41. You might have to move the caption so it is positioned below the photo.

Figure 10-41	CHANGING CAPTION TEXT BOXES TO FRAMES

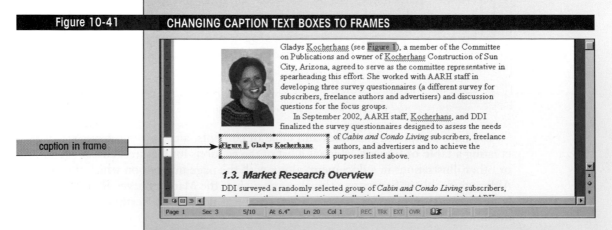

caption in frame

6. Repeat the procedure in Steps 3 through 5 to convert the other two captions to frames, and then reposition them. For Figure 2, set the Position to **Right**; for Figure 3, set the Position to **Left**.

7. Scroll up so you can see the "List of Figures" page, click anywhere in the text "Error! No table of figures entries found," press **F9**, and then save the master document. Word generates the table of figures based on its predefined heading styles. See Figure 10-42.

Figure 10-42   LIST OF FIGURES IN MASTER DOCUMENT

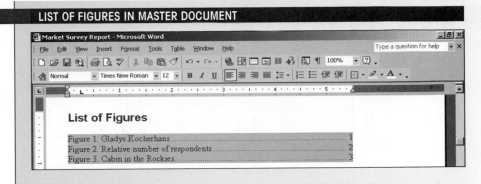

TROUBLE? If your table of figures doesn't look like Figure 10-42, select the table of figures (the area marked in gray), delete it, and then repeat Step 2 above.

Besides tables of contents and lists of figures, Word can also generate other lists, such as a **list of tables** (similar to a list of figures, but for the captioned tables in your document), and tables of authorities. A **table of authorities** is a list of the references in a legal document, such as references to cases, statutes, and rules. Similarly to other Word-generated lists, a table of authorities includes the page numbers on which the references appear. To create a table of authorities, you first have to mark all the citations (references). To mark a citation, select it, press Alt+Shift+I to display the Mark Citation dialog box, select the category (cases, statutes, rules, treatises, and so forth), and then click Mark or Mark All. To generate the table of authorities, you follow the same steps as when generating an index, except you use the Table of Authorities tab on the Index and Tables dialog box. You'll generate a table of authorities in Case Problem 3 at the end of the tutorial.

You have completed the report and are ready to print it. However, before printing, you have to make sure that Word is set up to update fields (caption numbers, cross-references, index, table of contents, and table of figures) whenever you print a document.

To print the completed report:

1. Click **Tools** on the menu bar, click **Options**, click the **Print** tab, in the Printing options section click the **Update fields** check box to select it if necessary, and then click the **OK** button. This ensures that the fields are always updated when you print the report.

2. Scroll through the report, and if any heading lacks a heading number, open the Styles and Formatting Task Pane, click anywhere in the heading (in the document), and double-click that heading's style in the Task Pane.

3. Print the Market Survey Report. When Word prompts you to update the table of contents and other tables, click the **Cancel** button because the tables don't need to be updated. Figure 10-43 shows the printed Market Survey Report.

| Figure 10-43 | PRINTED REPORT |

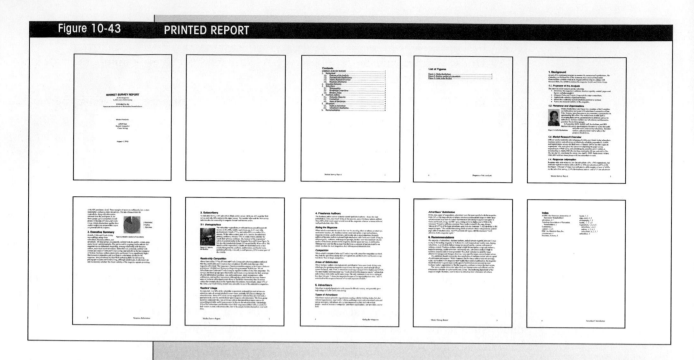

4. Close any open documents, click the **Yes** button to save the document if prompted to do so, and then exit Word.

As you can see, the report includes one blank page. This is because you specified different odd and even pages, and then set two consecutive pages (the title page and the contents) to be numbered as page 1. You can't have two odd-numbered pages in a row (or the margins, gutter spacing, and footer text would be off), so Word inserted a blank, even-numbered page.

Albert is pleased with your work on the report. He is sure that his client, the American Association of Recreation Homebuilders will be pleased with the results.

Session 10.3 QUICK CHECK

1. Under what circumstances might you want to change the page number format in a section of your document?

2. Briefly describe how you set the page number format to lowercase Roman numerals.

3. What is a gutter? Why would you change the gutter value from 0"?

4. How do you tell Word to insert the section name in a footer?

5. How do you mark a main index entry?

6. What does it mean to compile an index? How do you update an index?

7. How do you create a table of contents?

8. If you try to create a table of figures, and Word can't find any table of figures entries, what might be the problem?

REVIEW ASSIGNMENTS

The Decision Data, Inc. (DDI) team of Cindy Myrup, Bonnie Langarica, and Albert Kjar asks for your help with another project. This time the team has to prepare a market analysis report for a travel agency in Memphis, Tennessee. The travel agency, Northern European Tours (NET), wants to assess its effectiveness in planning and guiding tours to Norway, Sweden and Finland. To this end, the DDI team developed, administered, and analyzed print and Web surveys of former tour participants. Each member of the team wrote a section of the report. It's your job to manage the report as a master document, to help with necessary revisions, to format and otherwise prepare the report for printing, and then print the report.

1. If necessary, start Word, make sure Word is set up so that it won't apply built-in styles as you type, and make sure your Data Disk is in the appropriate drive. Open the file **NETRep** from the Review folder for Tutorial 10 on your Data Disk, and save it in the same folder using the filename **Northern European Tours Report**.

2. On the title page (page 1), below "Albert Kjar" in the list of market analysts (the "Prepared by" group), double-space and then type "Assisted by" followed by a space and your name.

3. Make copies of the three files **NETAnal1**, **NETAnal2**, and **NETIntro** and rename the copies **NET Analysis 1**, **NET Analysis 2**, and **NET Introduction**, respectively.

4. Switch to master document view, move the insertion point to the top of page 4 (which is blank), and then insert **NET Introduction** as a subdocument in the Northern European Tours Report.

5. Immediately after the first subdocument, insert the files **NET Analysis 1**, and **NET Analysis 2**, as additional subdocuments.

6. Merge the two subdocuments NET Analysis 1 (which begins with the heading "Survey Results and Analysis") and NET Analysis 2 (which begins with "Transportation"), and then delete both section breaks above the heading "Transportation."

7. Create a subdocument of the section that begins with the level-1 heading "Demographics of Respondents." The subdocument should end just before the next heading, "Executive Summary."

8. Make sure that the Normal style has Widow/Orphan control turned on. (It should be active in your documents already, but it's a good idea to double-check.)

9. For all heading styles in the document (Heading 1, Heading 2, and Heading 3), turn on the Keep with next option so that no heading becomes isolated at the bottom of the page, and change the "Spacing before" setting to 6 points.

Explore 10. Using the legal format, double-number all the section headings using the Word built-in section numbering system. The legal format is, for example, "1" for Heading 1, "1.1" for Heading 2, and "1.1.1" for Heading 3.

Explore 11. Add captions to all the tables. (*Hint*: You add table captions essentially the same way you add figure captions.) Position the table captions centered above the tables. (*Hint*: After creating the caption, and with the insertion point still in the caption text, center the caption as you would center any other line of text.) Don't wrap text around the tables. For the caption text (from the first caption to the last in the master document with all its subdocuments), use the following text (where the word "Table" and the table number are set automatically by Word): "Table 1. Demographics of Respondents," "Table 2. Rating System Used in Survey," "Table 3. Sample Ratings of Geographical and Geological Notes," "Table 4. Sample Ratings of Ground Transportation," "Table 5. Sample Ratings of Tour Managers," "Table 6. Rating System Used for Tour Sites," "Table 7. Ratings of Sample Tour Sites," and "Table 8. Sample Ratings of Overall Impressions."

Explore 12. Create a cross-reference to each of the eight tables. On the text lines just above each table, you'll see an incomplete phrase or sentence, with something like "as shown in." Complete each of these phrases or sentences so that they read, for example, "as shown in Table 1," with only the label and number, not the complete caption. Make sure you properly format the text, including (if applicable) a period at the end of the sentence. (*Hint*: Use the same method as when cross-referencing figures, except select Tables as the reference type.)

Explore 13. Turn on revision tracking, and then change the revision mark color so that inserted text is violet with double underlines. (*Hint*: Click the Show list arrow on the Reviewing Toolbar and then click Options. Note that sometimes, even when you set the feature to double-underlining, Word still only single underlines.)

14. Delete the word "corporation" from the first line under the "Background" heading, and insert at the same location the comment "The phrase 'agency corporation' seems awkward." In the same paragraph, after the phrase "to create a customer survey," insert the phrase "test the survey," (including the comma and necessary spaces), and then insert the comment "DDI also tested the survey before using it." In the same paragraph, change the phrase "holding a focus group" to "holding focus groups", and then insert the comment "DDI held three focus groups."

Explore 15. Switch to normal view, if necessary, and then click the Reviewing Pane button ▣. Click ▣ once or twice more to make sure the Reviewing Pane is open, and then scroll through and read all the revision marks and comments in the Reviewing Pane.

16. Print a copy of the markups (which include the revision marks and comments) in the document.

17. Turn off revision tracking and close the Reviewing Pane, but leave the Reviewing toolbar open.

Explore 18. Accept all the revisions at once. (*Hint*: Click the Accept Change list arrow, and then click the appropriate option.) Leave all the comments in the document.

19. Center the title page between its top and bottom margins.

20. Set the page numbering of the front matter to Roman numerals, with page i starting on the Contents page, and then set the remainder of the report to Arabic numerals, with page 1 starting on the page containing the heading "Background."

21. Set up the pages for back-to-back printing, with a 0.5-inch gutter.

22. Set up footers so that the odd-page footers (starting on page 1, which is Section 3) include the document title "Northern European Tours Report" at the left margin, and the page number at the right margin; and the even-page footers have the page number at the left margin, and the Heading 1 text at the right margin.

23. Create an index with index entries for every occurrence of "Decision Data, Inc.," "Northern European Tours," "return rate," "electronic surveys," "demographics," "Rating System," "cultural information," "transportation," "bus," "tour guides," and any other words or phrases you'd like to add.

24. Create a cross-reference for the abbreviations "DDI" and "NET" to "Decision Data, Inc.," and "Northern European Tours," respectively.

25. Select the entire section "4. Survey Results and Analysis," mark it with the bookmark "ResultsAndAnalysis" (all one word), and then mark that section with the index entry "Survey Results and Analysis."

26. Move the insertion point to the end of the document, below the heading "Index," and generate the index. Then, below the "Contents" heading in the front matter, insert a table of contents.

Explore 27. Below the "List of Tables" heading in the front matter, insert a list of all the tables. (*Hint*: Use the same procedure as when inserting a list of figures, but select Tables as the caption label.)

28. Save and then print the completed report. (*Note*: If the numbering in the Heading 2 and Heading 3 styles disappears, just print the document without that numbering. Sometimes, Word also automatically applies styles to the title lines and other headings to which you did *not* want styles applied. In those cases, go through and remove the styles, and then format them manually in bold Arial, with the appropriate font size.)

29. Close the master document, open and then attach your digital signature to the two sub-documents Demographics of Respondents and (NET Analysis 1 and NET Analysis 2), and then save each document. Close any open files and exit Word.

Case 1. Pierre Promotional Products   Janette Kracl of Pierre, South Dakota, has recently started a business named Pierre Promotional Products, which will manufacture and market promotional items—that is, items on which other companies imprint their name, logo, address, or other information for marketing purposes. Janette's company will make eye-glass retainers (colorful straps to keep eyeglasses and sunglasses from getting lost or scratched), name badges, name-badge lanyards (small straps that go around the neck for holding name badges), and luggage identification tags. She and her three partners have written part of a business plan. She asks you to help her put the document together and to format it for printing so she can see how the document looks. After that, she'll add the remaining sections.

1. If necessary, start Word, make sure Word is set up so that it won't apply built-in styles as you type, and make sure your Data Disk is in the appropriate drive. Open the file **PierreBP** from the Cases folder for Tutorial.10 on your Data Disk, and save it in the same folder using the filename **Pierre Business Plan**.

2. On the title page (page 1), below Janette Kracl's name, double-space and then type "Assisted by" followed by a space and your name.

3. In the Cases folder for Tutorial.10 on your Data Disk, make copies of the three files **PierreES**, **PierreBV**, and **PierreMA**, and rename the copies **Pierre Executive Summary**, **Pierre Business Venture**, and **Pierre Market Analysis**, respectively.

4. Move the insertion point to the blank line below "List of Tables," insert a section break that begins a new page, and then insert **Pierre Executive Summary** as a subdocument in the Pierre Business Plan. Immediately after the first subdocument, insert **Pierre Business Venture**, and then **Pierre Market Analysis** as additional subdocuments.

5. Merge the two subdocuments named "Pierre Executive Summary" and "Pierre Business Venture," and then delete both section breaks above the heading "The Business Venture." (After you delete the section breaks, you might have to reapply the heading format to "The Business Venture" and make other formatting adjustments.)

6. Split the new, larger subdocument "Pierre Executive Summary," at the heading "The Company" to create a new subdocument (from which Word will create a disk file titled **The Company**).

7. Make sure that the Normal style has Widow/Orphan control turned on. (It should be active in your documents already, but it's a good idea to double-check.)

Explore   8. Move the insertion point to the table in the section "Sales Forecast." Depending on the printer and fonts installed on your computer, this table might be divided between two pages. Force all the rows of the table to stay together on the same page. Do the same for the other tables in the document. (*Hint*: Select the rows and then set them to Keep with next. As you work with the document, if any of the tables become divided between two pages, use the same method to keep all the rows together.)

9. Number all the section headings using the Word built-in section numbering system. You may use any numbering system you'd like. Make sure that after you add the numbering, the heading paragraphs are flush against the left margin and not indented.

Explore   10. Add captions to all the tables. (*Hint*: Add table captions essentially the same way you add figure captions) Position the table captions centered above the tables. (*Hint*: After creating the caption and with the insertion point still in the caption text, center it as you would center any other line of text.) Don't wrap text around the tables. For the caption text (from the first caption to the last in the master document with all its subdocuments), use the following text (where the word "Table" and the table number are set automatically by Word): "Table 1. Principles of Pierre Promotion Products", "Table 2. Sample List of Companies Expressing Interest in P3", and "Table 3. First Three Years' Sales Forecast".

Explore   11. Below the "List of Tables" heading in the front matter, insert a list of all the tables. (*Hint*: Use the same procedure as when inserting a list of figures, but select Tables as the caption label.)

12. Save and close the master document, and then open the document **Pierce Executive Summary** from the Cases folder for Tutorial.10 on your Data Disk.

13. Change your User Information so the user name is "Helen Barkley". Make sure you write down the name of the original user (the one that was there before you started this Case) on the User Information tab of the Options toolbar.

Explore   14. Turn on revision tracking, and then change the revision mark color so that inserted text is green (not bright green). (*Hint*: Click Show on the Reviewing Toolbar and then click Options.)

15. Move the insertion point to the second paragraph below the "Executive Summary" heading in the document. After the phrase "Pierre Promotional Products," insert a comma, a space, and the abbreviation "Inc." (including the period). At the location of this correction, insert the comment (as if from Helen), "Let's use the company's entire name here."

16. After the phrase "high-quality, low-priced," insert a comma, a space, and the phrase "highly unique" (no punctuation after). Delete the word "unique" from the next sentence. At the location of this correction, insert the comment "Delete 'unique' here to avoid repetition."

17. Change your computer's user name to Janna Knuteson. Keep revision tracking turned on.

18. In the fourth paragraph below "Executive Summary," in the first line, change "could" to "can", and then on the second line, at the end of the first sentence, insert the phrase "as P3 can" (using proper spacing and punctuation).

19. In the fifth paragraph, change "company" to "Company." After this correction, insert the comment, "In referring to our Company, the word should always be capitalized."

20. Save this subdocument as a new version, with the version description "With Jana's and Helen's revisions". Turn off revision tracking but leave the Reviewing toolbar open.

21. Change the user name in the Options dialog box back to the name that appeared there before you started this Case.

22. Review the document one markup at a time. Don't delete any of the comments, but accept the addition of "Inc.," reject the added phrase "highly unique," reject the deletion of "unique," and accept all the other changes.

23. Save the document with your digital signature, and then close the document. Open the master document again, and expand the subdocuments.

24. Center the title page between its left and right margins, and between its top and bottom margins.

25. Set up the pages for back-to-back printing, with a 0.5-inch gutter.

26. Set the page numbering of the front matter to Roman numerals, with page i starting on the Contents page, and then start Arabic numeral numbering with page 1 on the Executive Summary page.

27. Set up the footers so that the odd page footers (starting on page 1, which is Section 3) include the text "P3 Business Plan" at the left margin and the page number at the right margin; the even page footers should have the page number at the left margin and the Heading 1 text at the right margin.

28. Create an index with entries for every occurrence of "Pierre Promotional Products," "marketing," "promotional products," "markets," "labor," "investment," "exhibitors," "prototypes," and any other words or phrases you'd like to add.

29. Mark the abbreviations "P3" as cross-references to "Pierre Promotional Products."

30. Select the section Market Analysis," mark it with the bookmark "MarketAnalysis" (all one word), and then mark that section with the index entry "Market Analysis."

31. Move the insertion point to the end of the document, below the heading "Index," and generate the index. Don't right-align page numbers.

32. Below the "Contents" heading in the front matter, insert a table of contents.

Explore ➤ 33. Sort the bulleted list located near the beginning of page 4, below the heading "D. Market Analysis." (*Hint*: To sort lines or paragraphs, you select the text that you want to sort, select Sort from the Table menu, set Sort by to Paragraphs, and Type to Text, select Ascending to sort from A to Z, or Descending to sort Z to A, and then click the OK button.

34. Save and then print the completed report. Make sure you set the user name in the Options dialog box back to the proper name. Close any open files and exit Word.

Case 2. IT Department, Wyoming State University Gabriela Crozier is information technology officer in the Information Technology Department at Wyoming State University in Rock Springs, Wyoming. She and her staff want to review the department's Computer Security Policy, which is currently in one Word file. She asks you to prepare front and back matter for the report and to create two subdocuments within the master document so her staff can review each section individually. You'll help Gabriela manage the various section of the report, format the document, and prepare it for printing.

1. If necessary, start Word, make sure Word is set so that it won't apply built-in styles as you type, and make sure your Data Disk is in the appropriate drive. Open the file **ITSecur** from the Cases folder for Tutorial.10 on your Data Disk, and save it in the same folder using the filename **IT Security Policy**.

2. Insert a section break that begins a new page at the beginning of the document to create a title page. Before typing the text of the title page, make sure the style is set to Normal.

3. On the title page, type each of the following words or phrases on separate lines with at least one blank line between each line of text: "Computer Security Policy", "Information Technology Department", "Wyoming State University", "Cheyenne, Wyoming", "Prepared by Gabriela Crozier, IT Officer", "Assisted by [Your Name]", and then today's date.

4. Format the title page with varying fonts and font styles to make it attractive and easy to read. Keep the appearance conservative to match the topic, security policies. Center the text on the title page between the left and right margins and between the top and bottom margins.

5. Insert a new section that begins a new page break after the title page, and insert the heading "Contents". This will become the table of contents page.

6. At the end of the document, insert a page break, and then insert the heading "Index", applying the Heading 1 style.

7. Create two subdocuments, the first starting with the heading "Introduction", and the second with the heading "Security Procedures". Don't include the title page, table of contents page, or the index page in the subdocuments.

8. Save the master document and its two subdocuments, and then close the document.

9. Open the Security Procedures subdocument, and change the user name in the User Information to "Gabriela Crozier", with the initials "CG". Make sure you note the real user name, so you can restore it later.

Explore ▶ 10. Protect the document for tracked changes and assign the document a password. Use the password "wyo4yshikes" (which you can remember because it stands for "Wyoming for Yellowstone Hikes"). Be extremely careful as you type the password (you have to type it twice) so that you can open the document later on.

11. Make sure the tracking color in the Track Changes options is set to "By author."

12. In the first paragraph under the "Security Procedures" heading, delete the phrase "and procedures," and then insert the comment "The policies include procedures, so this phrase is redundant."

13. In the same paragraph, change "to find a happy medium" to the phrase "to balance," and then insert the comment "To reduce wordiness."

14. In the second sentence of the paragraph, change "organization" to "computer system".

15. Replace all occurrences of "procedure" with "policy".

16. Below the heading "Security Organization," change the grammatical error "consists" to "consist".

17. Change the user name in the Options dialog box from Gabriela Crozier to "Paul Stott", with the initials "PS". Paul is one of Gabriela's assistants.

18. In the phrase just above the second set of bullets in the "Security Organization" paragraph, delete "are" and type "include the following:" in its place.

19. In the next paragraph, change "have" in the phrase "IT Officer will have one part-time employee" to "direct", and then change "who can spend" to "for".

Explore ▶ 20. Using the Security Tab on the Options dialog box, set the file encryption password to "w2002gabby". Now whenever someone tries to open the document, he or she must use the password.

21. Save the Security Procedures document, close it, and then open it again. Notice that you have to use the password to open it.

22. Unprotect the document. You'll have to use the password "wyo4yshikes".

Explore ▶ 23. Accept all the revisions at once. (*Hint*: Click the Accept Change list arrow.) Delete all the comments at once. (*Hint*: Click the Reject Change list arrow.)

24. Save the Security Procedures document, close it, and then open the IT Security Policy document.

25. Set the page numbering to start with page 1 on the Contents page.

Explore ▶ 26. Insert a header that begins on the Contents page and ends on the last page of the document. Type the phrase "Computer Security Policy" at the left margin and insert a page number at the right margin in the heading. Add a bottom border to the heading text. (*Hint*: Use the appropriate Border button after you select all the text of the header). Change the header font to 10-point Arial. Examine the header to make sure the bottom border spans the entire width of the page from left margin to right margin.

Explore ▶ 27. Replace all occurrences of "e-mail" (with a hyphen) with "e-mail" (with a nonbreaking hyphen). This prevents the word from being split between two lines. (*Hint*: In the Find and Replace dialog box, click the More button, and then click Special.)

Explore ▶ 28. Replace all occurrences of " . . ." (space, period, space, period, space, period, with normal spaces) with " . . ." (with nonbreaking spaces). (Use the Hint from Step 27 or insert the nonbreaking space by pressing Ctrl+Shift+Spacebar.)

29. Insert a table of contents below the "Contents" heading on page 1.

Explore 30. Modify the heading styles to use Roman numeral outline numbering (I, II, III, . . .) for level-1 headings, uppercase letters for level-2 headings (A, B, C, . . .), and Roman numerals for level-3 headings. Customize the numbering so that the number position of levels 2 and 3 is aligned at the left margin, with no indentation, and so that "Tab space after" (the amount of horizontal space between the heading number and the heading text) is set to 0.25 inch. (*Hint*: Click the Customize button on the Bullets and Numbering dialog box after you select the desired numbering style.)

31. Mark index entries for all occurrences of at least 10 words in the document. Make sure the entries include "Information Technology" and "password."

32. Mark "IT" as a cross-reference to "*See* Information Technology." Mark "passwords" as a cross-reference to "password."

33. Generate an index at the end of the document.

34. Save, print, and close the document. Change the user name in the Options dialog box back to the name that appeared there before you began this Case Problem. Exit Word.

Case 3. LifeGoals Recruiting Mario Valdivia of Columbia, Missouri, is the director of training for LifeGoals Recruiting, Inc., a job placement company. LifeGoals not only matches employment opportunities with potential employees, but also helps train job seekers on how to get good jobs. One of the training areas is "How to Write a Letter of Application and Resume." Mario and his staff have written the text for a document with that title and now he wants you to help him prepare the document for publication. In addition, the LifeGoals legal department recently brought a lawsuit against another job placement company and they want you to help them generate a table of authorities for a legal brief.

1. In the Cases folder for Tutorial 10 on your Data Disk, copy each of the three files **LGCovLet**, **LGProbs**, and **LGResume** using the filenames **LifeGoals Cover Letter Tips**, **LifeGoals Resume Problems**, and **LifeGoals Resume Tips**. Open and read each of these documents, and familiarize yourself with their contents.

2. Create a master document with an appropriate title page, contents page, and index page. The title on the title page should be "Job Application Tips". Include other information, as needed or desired, on the title page. Make sure you include the company name, the name of the director of training (Mario Valdivia), and the date. On one of the title page lines, type "Assisted by [your name]", to identify yourself as assisting with this document. At this point, include only headings on the contents and index pages.

3. Save the document to the Cases folder for Tutorial 10 using the filename **LifeGoals Job Application Tips**.

4. Create a new page in the master document, just after the Contents page, with the heading "Introduction", and then below the heading, type a one- to three-paragraph introduction based on the information in the three LifeGoals documents that you copied.

5. Insert the three LifeGoals documents as subdocuments in the LifeGoals Job Application Tips document. Use the following order: LifeGoals Resume Tips, LifeGoals Resume Problems, and LifeGoals Cover Letter Tips.

6. Add an appropriate header or footer, with odd-even page numbering. Include in the header or footer a style reference to the current section heading of the document.

7. Apply section numbers to the section headings. Use any format you desire.

8. Generate a table of contents on the Contents page of the document.

9. Mark at least 10 different words for the index. Include at least one cross-reference. Include at least one range of pages. Include at least two entries with subentries.

10. Generate an index on the last page of the document.

11. Protect the document, and then make any desired editing changes. Modify or correct any spelling, grammar, or stylistic problems you might find. Include at least five modifications to the document. Insert at least three comments, possibly explaining each of your modifications.

12. Save the document. Print it without displaying the markups. Close the document.

13. Open the document **LGLegal** from the Cases folder for Tutorial 10 (LGLegal includes the title page and only three pages of a 30-page legal brief). Save the document in the same folder using the filename **LifeGoals Legal Brief**. (This legal brief is part of a lawsuit brought by LifeGoals against Jobs4U for copyright infringement. Jobs4U was copying and distributing portions of LifeGoals Recruiting training materials.)

Explore 14. Go to page 3, the second paragraph, and select the phrase "Sheldon v. MGM Pictures, Corp., 81 F.2d 49, 56 (2d Cir. 1935)". Don't include the space before or the punctuation after this phrase, but include from the beginning of "Sheldon" to the close parenthesis after "(2d Cir. 1935)." Mark this citation for a table of authorities, using the category "Case."

15. Similarly, mark the other seven citations in this paragraph.

Explore ▶ 16. Move the insertion point to the blank line below the heading "Table of Authorities" on page 2, and then generate a table of authorities. Accept all the defaults on the Tables of Authorities tab of the Index and Tables dialog box.

17. Save the legal brief, print it, and then close it. Exit Word.

Case 4. Preparing an Information Brochure Your instructor will divide your class into work-groups of three to six students and appoint a workgroup leader or have each workgroup select one. Each workgroup will collaborate to prepare an information brochure. You can select from any of the following topics or choose your own topic. Your brochure topic should be approved by your instructor.

- A hobby, such as scrapbooking, horseback riding, computers, baseball card collecting, or chess
- An outdoor activity, such as fly-fishing, rock climbing, camping, hiking, gardening, or mountain biking
- A cultural activity, such as traveling through Europe, traveling to a national park or historic site, attending symphony concerts, going to the theater, or visiting an art museum
- A fitness or health activity, such as walking, running, Tae Bo, kickboxing, aerobic dancing, resistance training, or weight management

You might want to select a topic in which most of your workgroup has some interest and possibly one member of the group has expertise. On the other hand, you might want to select a topic on which no members have knowledge or experience, but one which all members are willing to investigate.

The workgroup leader should do the following:

1. Discuss in a pre-writing planning meeting how the workgroup will accomplish their goals and how they can make all the chapters consistent in style and format.

2. Assign each workgroup member a chapter to write for the information brochure. Coordinate topics for each chapter.

3. Ask each workgroup member to protect his or her completed document for revisions (without a password). Each member will then pass a copy of the file to at least two other workgroup members who should add edits and comments, and then save a new version of the file (using the Versions feature) with the description: "Edits and Comments made by [name]." (Each workgroup member should replace [name] with his or her first and last name.)

4. Ask the workgroup members to use built-in heading styles for the chapter name and other headings, and to insert at least one figure or a table (with a caption) into their chapters.

5. Collect the files of all the chapters, and then compare and merge (using the Compare and Merge command on the Tools menu) all the versions of each document into one document for each chapter.

6. Prepare a title page, write a brief preface or introduction, and set up headings for the table of contents, for the list of figures and/or list of tables, and for the index.

Explore   7. Set up the brochure for landscape-orientation, two-sided printing with two pages per sheet (each page will take up one-half of a folded sheet of paper). (*Hint*: Use Help to figure out how to do this, or go to the Page Setup dialog box, Margins tab, and choose the desired multiple pages option.) Because of the size of the paper, you might want to lower the font size to 8–10 points.

8. Create appropriate headers or footers for the odd and even pages. Make sure you include page numbers, the document name, and chapter names.

9. Insert all the chapters into the document with the title page and preface as subdocuments.

10. Mark appropriate index entries for the preface.

11. Print a list of all the markups (revisions and comments) created by the reviewers of each subdocument.

Explore   12. Review the edits and comments from within the master document by reviewer, one reviewer at a time. (*Hint*: On the Reviewing toolbar, click Show, point to Reviewers, and clear all the check boxes except one. Repeat this for each reviewer.) In this way you can find the contribution of each member of the workgroup who reviewed the subdocuments.

13. As you review the document, decide which revisions to accept and which to reject. The final document should have no revision marks or comments.

14. Compile the table of contents and the index.

15. Save the document in the Cases folder for Tutorial 10 on your Data Disk, using the filename **Information Brochure**, and then preview and print it. If possible, print it double-sided.

16. Distribute a copy of the final master document file along with all its subdocument files to each workgroup member.

Each workgroup member (other than the workgroup leader) should do the following:

1. Write a chapter that is at least two single-spaced pages long.

2. Begin the chapter with a level-1 heading. You may also include level-2 and level-3 headings if you desire.

3. Mark at least 10 index entries. If applicable, include cross-reference entries, subentries, and entries for a ranges of pages.

4. Include at least one figure or table in the chapter. The figure can be a graph, chart, table, or picture such as clip art.

5. Create a caption for each figure and table in the chapter.

6. Include a cross-reference to each figure and table within the text.

7. Attach your digital signature to the document.

8. Save the chapter to a disk, and give the disk to a workgroup member as assigned by the workgroup leader.

9. Open another workgroup member's document and check the digital signature.

10. Make revisions while tracking changes. Make at least five changes to the document.

11. Include at least three comments in the document you are editing. Most of the comments might include explanations of your revisions.

12. Save a new version (using the Versions feature) of the edited document with the description "Edits and Comments made by [name]". Be sure to replace [name] with your first and last name. (*Note*: When you save the edited chapter, the digital signature will be stripped from the document because you have modified it.)

13. Repeat Steps 8 through 12 for another document. Then give the file to your workgroup leader to insert into the master document.

14. Get a copy of the final master document file along with all its subdocument files from your workgroup leader.

15. Save copies of all the documents you worked on in the Cases folder for Tutorial 10 on your Data Disk.

16. Make sure your workgroup leader submits a copy of the master document to your instructor.

QUICK CHECK ANSWERS

Session 10.1

1. **a.** Word document divided into several smaller, individual files, to help you organize and maintain a lengthy document
   b. one of several small, separate files that are part of a master document
   c. divide one subdocument into two subdocument files
   d. combine two adjacent subdocuments into one subdocument
   e. convert the text of a subdocument into the text of the master document
   f. the last line of a paragraph appearing alone at the top of a page
   g. the first line of a paragraph appearing alone at the bottom of a page

2. consistent formatting elements; accurate numbering; accurate cross-referencing; complete table of contents and index; faster editing

3. False

4. Convert an existing document into a master document, and then divide it into subdocuments using built-in heading styles; insert existing disk files into a Word document.

5. It's useful to split a subdocument when one subdocument gets too long, or when several people need to work on different parts of one subdocument.

6. It's useful to merge subdocuments when the subdocuments are very short, or when one person is writing or editing both subdocuments.

7. a hyphen that won't allow the word or phrase it connects to break between two lines; a space that won't allow the words on either side to break between two lines; when you want to keep the two words on the same line of text

Session 10.2

1. Open the Bullets and Numbering dialog box, select the desired heading numbering style on the Outline Numbered tab, click Customize, and select the desired numbering form.

2. automatic sequential numbering; numbering across subdocuments; consistent numbering style

3. marks text you delete and add; marks two authors' revisions in different colors

4. so that no one can make revisions without your knowledge

5. notes written from one writer or editor to another that are not part of the printed document; to allow communication within a workgroup

6. by the color assigned to that author; by the name of the author on the ScreenTip of the comment

7. Before printing, select List of markup from the Print what list in the Print dialog box.

8. an attachment to a file that vouches for its authenticity

Session 10.3

1. to number front matter in a different format from the rest of the document

2. Change the Number format in the Page Numbers dialog box.

3. an extra blank space on the side of each page where the pages are bound together; to allow space for binding a document with pages printed back-to-back

4. Insert a Style Reference field to the section title in the footnotes.

5. Select the word or phrase, and then insert an Index mark using the Mark Entry feature on the Index tab.

6. to tell Word to generate the index from the marked entries at a certain location; select the index and press the F9 key

7. Move the insertion point where you want the table of contents, and then use the Table of Contents tab on the Index and Tables dialog box.

8. The problem is likely that the captions are floating text boxes rather than framed text.

OBJECTIVES

In this case you will:

- Use mail merge to create a form letter
- Use mail merge to create mailing labels
- Insert, resize, and position a graphic
- Insert and format a Word date field
- Change the font and font size
- Insert a tab stop with dot leader
- Insert a watermark
- Add paragraph borders

CREATING A FORM LETTER AND A PROGRAM

Evans Piano Studio

Garth Evans is owner of Evans Piano Studio, which provides private and group piano instruction, rents recital facilities, and sells discount sheet music and music books. He wants to send a letter to all of his private students notifying them of an upcoming recital in which each student is invited to play. He asks you to help him use mail merge to prepare the form letter and to print mailing labels. He also wants you to help him use mail merge to prepare the printed program for the recital.

1. Start Word (if necessary), make sure your Data Disk is in an appropriate drive, and then open **EPSLet** from the AddCases folder on your Data Disk, and save the file as **EPS Form Letter** in the same folder.

2. Begin a mail merge using the **EPS Form Letter** document as the main document.

3. Use the file **EPSData** from the AddCases folder on your Data Disk as the data source for the mail merge.

4. Switch to the main document so you can edit it.

5. At the top of document (on the blank line), insert the Evans Piano Studio logo (**Piano.jpg**) from the AddCases folder. Center the picture and scale its height and width to 50%.

6. Center the five lines of information about Evans Piano Studio below the logo, change the font of "Evans Piano Studio" to 16-point Arial Black. (If your computer doesn't have Arial Black, use Arial bold.)

7. Insert blank lines and a Word date field in the "11 Feb 2004" format so that the date appears two lines below the Evans Piano Studio phone number and two lines above the inside address fields. (You will have to edit the field code.)

8. Throughout the letter, delete all the text in brackets (including the brackets) and replace it with appropriate merge field codes, and then save the document.

9. Merge the EPS Form Letter main document with all records of the data source. Merge to a new document.

10. Save the merge document as **EPS Recital Letters** in the Add Cases folder on your Data Disk.

11. Print the last letter of the merged document, and then close all the documents.

12. Open a new blank document, set it up as a mail merge main document, of type Directory, so that you can print a list of students with their recital pieces. Use the file **EPSData** from the AddCases folder on your Data Disk as the data file.

13. At the left margin, insert the merge fields for the performer name (First Name, a space, and Last Name).

14. On the Word ruler, insert a right-align tab stop, and edit the tab stop to include a dot leader.

15. Click to the right of the the Last Name merge field for the performer's name, press the Tab key, and insert at the right margin the Piece Name, a space, the word "by," a space, and then the Piece Composer merge field. Press the Enter key to create a blank line below these merge fields.

16. Save the new main document in the AddCases folder using the filename **EPS Recital List Form**.

17. Merge to a new document.

18. At the top of the document, insert and center "Winter Recital" in 20-point Arial Black. (If your computer doesn't have Arial Black, use Arial bold.)

19. Centered below "Winter Recital," using normal font, type "Evans Piano Studio," and on a new line centered below that, type the date of the recital (February 11, 2004).

20. Insert two blank lines below the date of the recital and above the list of performers and their pieces, and then save the document in the AddCases folder using the filename **EPS Recital Program**.

21. Add a watermark, using the **Piano.jpg** file from the AddCases folder on your Data Disk, so that it appears behind the dot leaders in the program. Reduce the size of the graphic so that its top is positioned near the first performer name and its bottom is near the last performer name in the list.

22. Set the image control color of the watermark to Washout.

23. Select the first line in the list of performers, and then set its top border to a double line (with one line thicker than the other).

24. Repeat the previous step, *except* set the bottom border of the last line in the list of performers to the same double line.

25. Make any adjustments necessary to make the program look like Figure 1.

26. Save and print the recital program

Figure 1

Winter Recital

Evans Piano Studio
February 11, 2004

Kathy Poulson	Ballade No. 4 by Chopin
Ronda Crittendon	Moonlight Sonata by Beethoven
Darrell Harris	Sabre Dance by Khachaturian
Karen Shao	Pictures at an Exhibition by Mussorgsky
Steven Lundquist	Cantos de Espana by Albeniz
John Contreras	Serenade K374 by Mozart
Carl Marchesi	Tritsch Tratsch Polka by Johann Strauss
Renato Martinez	Waltz in E Flat Major by Chopin
Dell Scott	Miada by Rimsky-Korsakov
Byron Woolstenhulme	Melody in F by Rubinstein

27. Use the Mail Merge Wizard to create a new main document for creating Avery 5860 mailing labels (30 labels per page). (If the Avery 5860 style is not an option for you, choose another style.) For the data file, use the file **EPSData** from the AddCases folder on your Data Disk.

28. Following the steps of the Mail Merge Wizard, complete the merge, and then save the document as **EPS Labels** in the AddCases folder on your Data Disk.

29. Print the mailing labels (on a blank sheet of paper to simulate an Avery labels sheet), close any open documents, and exit Word.

OBJECTIVES

In this case you will:

- Adjust the margins of a document

- Change the text's font, size, color, and effect

- Import and modify digital pictures

- Create WordArt

- Modify the Normal style

- Adjust column widths in a Word table

- Change the border lines in a table

- Sort the rows of a table

- Center text and images in cells of a table

CREATING AN ADVERTISEMENT FLYER

CASE

The Chess Corner

Shridhar Kalavagunta owns and operates a small store called The Chess Corner, which sells chess sets, boards, clocks, software, and other supplies, in the greater Seattle area. Shridhar asks you to help him create an attractive flyer that he can hand out at chess tournaments and chess club meetings to advertise his store.

1. Start Word (if necessary), make sure your Data Disk is in an appropriate drive, and then open **CCFlyer** from the AddCases folder of your Data Disk, and then save the document back in the same folder using the filename **Chess Corner Flyer**.

2. Change the page setup so that the top and bottom margins are 0.5 inch and the left and right margins are 1 inch.

3. In the table, adjust the width of the Description column in the table so that the table spans the width of the page. (The page itself should be 6.5 inches wide.)

4. Sort the rows of the table so that the Categories in column 2 appear in alphabetical order.

5. In cell A2, delete the text "CCclock" and then insert the graphics file **CCclock**, that is, the file whose name you just deleted. Repeat this procedure in cells A3 through A10, that is, delete the name of the graphics file and then insert the graphics file (digital image) into the cell. All the image files are located in the AddCases folder of your Student disk. Adjust the width (with the aspect ratio fixed) of each of the pictures to ¾ inch to 1 inch.

6. Erase the left and top border lines (but not the gridlines) of cell A1.

7. Draw thick (2¼ points) line across the top of cells B1 and C1, and across the bottoms of cells A1, B1, and C1. Similarly, draw a 2¼-point line across all three cells at the bottom of the table.

8. Change the font of the text in cells B1 and C1 to brown, 14-point Impact. If your computer doesn't have the Impact font, use Arial.

9. At the top of the flyer, insert The Chess Corner logo, **CClogo.jpg**, located in the AddCases folder on your Data Disk.

10. Set the size of the logo to 1.5 inches in height (keeping the aspect ratio locked), set the text wrapping to Right Only, and set the picture position so that the horizontal alignment is centered. Note that you will have to use the Advanced button on one or more of the tabs in the Format Picture dialog box.

11. Change the font of the company name ("The Chess Corner") to 28-point Impact. (If your computer doesn't have Impact, use Arial bold.)

12. Change the font color to brown (you can pick any shade of brown you like), and change the font effects to Emboss.

13. Change the Normal style font to 11-point Arial.

14. Insert two WordArt boxes, one with the text "Largest inventory in the state!" and the other with the text "Lowest prices anywhere!" Use a font and styles to match those in Figure 2, the finished, printed flyer.

15. Set the lines and fills of WordArt text to blue in one of the WordArt boxes and red in the other.

16. Make each of the WordArt boxes a floating box with wrapping behind the text, and then move both boxes to the left of the company logo at the top of the page.

17. Compare your final document with Figure 2. Make any adjustments necessary so your document matches.

18. Save and print the Chess Corner Flyer, and then close any open documents.

Figure 2

The Chess Corner

Largest inventory in the state!

Lowest prices anywhere!

At the corner of Pike Street and 4th Avenue
408 East Pike Street
Seattle, WA 98101
(245) 555-4510

We provide everything you need to feed your chess hobby. Here is what we sell:

	Category	Description
	Chess clocks	Analog and digital clocks, FIDE approved
	Hand carved specialty chess sets	Imported sets from Africa and Ecuador
	Luxury chess sets	Chess sets in storage and display cases. True works of art. Staunton designs.
	Plastic chess sets	Low-priced sets for club and personal use.
	Rosewood chess sets	Rosewood chess sets from India. Beautifully carved knights. Triple weighted.
	Software and Chess Computers	A wide variety of chess engines, both commercial and shareware. Also, chess education software.
	Vinyl chess boards	Ideal for home and club play. Ranks and files labeled for algebraic notation.
	Wooden chess boards	Inlaid wood of natural colors.
	Wooden chess sets	Reasonably priced tournament Staunton boxwood sets. King 2.5 to 4.75 inches.

We stock the largest inventory of chess supplies of anyone in the entire state of Washington. Come in and see our beautiful chess sets, or see our Web site at www.thechesscorner.com. To request a catalog, e-mail us at catalog@chessc.com.

OBJECTIVES

In this case you will:

- Create a document template

- Customize a toolbar by adding buttons

- Assign shortcut keys to special symbols and insert symbols

- Create and use AutoText entries

- Automate parts of a document with field codes and a calculation form field

- Create a paragraph style with borders and shading

- Set a paragraph style to avoid improper page breaks

- Create bulleted lists

- Merge cells within a table

- Record, edit, and run a macro

- Use a document template to create a fitness report

CREATING A FITNESS TEST REPORT

CASE

Flab-To-Fit Personal Trainers

Kathi Banks is a personal trainer and manager for Flab-To-Fit Personal Trainers, a small private company located in Reno, Nevada. Kathi and the other four personal trainers employed by the company help clients set weight and fitness goals and provide them with personal training prescriptions based on their goals and on their current fitness level. To determine the current fitness level, Flab-To-Fit personnel administer fitness tests, and then provide fitness reports to the clients. Kathi asks you to help her set up a document template for preparing fitness test reports.

1. Start Word (if necessary), make sure your Data Disk is in the appropriate drive, open **FTReport** from the AddCases folder of your Data Disk, and then save the document as a document template in the same folder using the filename **Fitness Test Report Template**.

2. Add the View Field Codes button to a convenient place on the Standard toolbar. Make sure the change to the toolbar applies only to the current document template.

3. To the right of the View Field Codes button, add the Insert Field button, again making this change apply only to the current document template. Leave the text on the button as "Field . . .".

4. You can use keyboard shortcuts to have Word automatically insert special symbols in a document. Click Insert on the menu bar, click Symbol, click the Font list arrow, click Symbol, click ≤ (the less than or equal sign), click the Shortcut Key button, press Alt+, (the Alt key and the comma key), click the Assign button, and then close all open dialog boxes.

5. Move the insertion point to the left of "25" in cell D5 (the "Excellent" value for the Body Mass Index), and insert ≤ using the shortcut key.

6. Move the insertion point down one cell to D6, and insert ≤ in front of the "120," and do the same in cell D7, in front of the "70."

7. Move the insertion point down one cell to D8, and insert ≤ (using the shortcut key) in front of the "48." Also insert ≤ in front of "1.1" in cell D9, in front of "1.9" in cell D10, and in front of "16" in D11. Finally insert ≤ in front of "18" and "120" in cell D12.

8. Create the AutoText entries "Personal Trainer" with the abbreviation "pt" and "Flab-To-Fit" with the abbreviation "ftf." Make sure you assign these entries to the current document template.

9. Move the insertion point to the right of "Flab-To-Fit" on the second line from the top, insert a space, and then use AutoText to insert "Personal Trainer."

10. Move the insertion point to the left of the period after "your," located at the end of the first sentence below the heading "Understanding the Results," which is just below the table. Insert a space and then using AutoText, insert "Flab-To-Fit," insert another space, and insert "Fitness Trainer."

11. Move the insertion point to the left of the comma located in that same sentence, and insert a Fill-in Field (using the Field button on the customized Standard toolbar) with the prompt "Name of the customer's personal trainer" and with the default response "Kathi Banks."

12. Select this Fill-in Field, assign it the bookmark "PersonalTrainer," move the insertion point between "with" and the comma on the first line below the heading "Setting Your Goals," insert a space, and then insert a field that automatically inserts the name of the customer's personal trainer. Use the View Field Codes button to turn on and turn off the field code view, so that you can see either the name of the field codes or the results of the field codes ("Kathi Banks").

13. Create a paragraph style called "Report Heading" with 14-point bold Arial font, a box border (with 1-point weight solid lines), and a shading of Gray-20%. Also set the space before the paragraph to 12 points.

14. Modify the Report Heading style so that it always stays with the next paragraph and never appears alone at the bottom of a page.

15. Apply the Report Heading style to the headings "Your Test Results," "Understanding the Results," "Setting Your Goals," and "Receiving Your Personalized Training Program."

16. Select the four paragraphs (sentence fragments) below "set goals in the following areas" in the "Setting Your Goals" section of the template, and apply bullets to those paragraphs.

17. Similarly apply bullets to the six areas of fitness goals located in the "Receiving Your Personalized Training Program" section of the document template.

18. On the blank line just above "Your Test Results," insert a Date field so the date appears in the format "5 August 2004."

19. Merge cells A1 and B1 (so that "Last Name:" appears in the merged cell). Similarly, merge cells C1 and D1 (so that "First Name:" appears in the merged cell).

20. Insert a new row 4 above the headings "Fitness Factor," "Your Measurement," "Average," and "Excellent."

21. Remove all the vertical border lines in the new row 4. By so doing, the first three rows of the table will appear to be a separate table from the lower nine rows.

22. Change the font in row 5 (with the headings "Fitness Factor" and so forth) to 13-point bold Arial, center each heading within its cell, and set the vertical alignment to the bottom of the cell.

23. In that same row, set the shading color to Gray-20%.

24. Apply the built-in Title style to the first line of the document ("Fitness Test Report").

25. Center the second line of the document below the title, but don't change the font.

26. In the appropriate locations in the top part of the table, insert Fill-in fields with the prompts "Client last name," "Client first name," "Client age in years," "Client height in inches," "Client weight in pounds," "Client gender (M or F)." In the case of the last and first names, insert a space to the right of "Last Name:" and "First Name:," and then insert the Fill-in field in the same cell. In the other cases, insert the Fill-in field in the cell to the right of the label. For example, the Fill-in field for "Age:" (located in cell A2) goes in cell B2. You won't use Fill-in fields in the bottom part of the table.

27. Right-align all the labels except "Last Name" and First Name" in the top part of the table, and right-justify all the labels in column A below the heading "Fitness Factor."

28. In cell B6 (to the right of "Body Mass Index") insert a Text Form Field. Set its Type to Calculation. Set the number format to "0.0." Set the calculation expression to "=B3*0.4536/(D2*0.0254)^2," which takes the weight in kilograms and divides it by the square of the height in meters. (The number 0.4536 converts pounds to kilograms, and the number 0.0254 converts inches to meters.)

29. Create a footer with "Fitness Report for" followed by the client's name, properly formatted, at the left margin and the page number at the right margin. Use Ref field codes to automatically insert the client's first and last names from the document table.

30. Create an AutoNew macro for this template that moves the insertion point to the right of "BP Systolic" (where, when you create an actual report, you'll insert the systolic measurement of the blood pressure).

31. Compare your document template with the format of the sample document in Figure 3. Make any format adjustments necessary in your document so that, when it's used to start a new document, it will appear similar to Figure 3.

32. Save the document template in the AddCases folder on your Data Disk and in the Templates folder.

33. Start a new document using the **Fitness Test Report Template** in the Templates folder.

34. Fill in the report using the information shown in Figure 3.

35. Save the filled-in document as **Fitness Test Report** in the AddCases folder on your Data disk, print the document, and then close any open documents.

36. Delete the **Fitness Test Report Template** file from the Templates folder and exit Word.

Figure 3   **PAGE 1**

Fitness Test Report

Flab-To-Fit Personal Trainer

10 October 2001

Your Test Results

Last Name: Hogue		First Name: Sean	
Age:	32	Height (in):	69.5
Weight (lbs):	198	Gender:	M

Fitness Factor	Your Measurement	Average	Excellent
Body Mass Index:	28.8	28	≤25
BP Systolic:	128	135	≤120
BP Diastolic:	72	80	≤70
Treadmill VO2 (mL/kg/min)	44	40	≥48
Bench Press (lbs/body weight):	0.78	0.85	≥1.1
Leg Press (lbs/body weight):	1.47	1.6	≥1.9
Flexibility Sit & Reach (in):	12	12	≥16
%Body Fat:	23	28 (women) 20 (men)	≤18 ≤12

Understanding the Results

The above table gives the results of your recent fitness test administered by Kelli Jewkes, your Flab-To-Fit Personal Trainer. Please note that numbers labeled as "Average" and "Excellent" in each of the fitness factors are generalizations for our typical client with an average body build and in the age range of 20-40. These numbers might not apply to someone of your age and body build. Take the time to discuss each of these fitness factors with your Personal Trainer to understand how each applies to you.

Setting Your Goals

In consultation with Kelli Jewkes, you will set goals in the following areas:
- Body weight (based on your height and bone structure)
- Percent body fat (related to but not the same as your body weight)
- Treadmill VO2 (the volume of oxygen uptake per kg of body mass per minute, a measure of your cardiovascular fitness)
- Strength (as measured by your bench press and leg press or squat)

Fitness Report for Sean Hogue   1

Figure 3 **PAGE 2**

Receiving Your Personalized Training Program

Your training program will consist of six areas to help you achieve your fitness goals:

- Nutrition, including daily calorie and fat intake.
- Cardio Exercise, including regular aerobic exercise and auxiliary cross-training activities.
- Strength Training, including a regular weight lifting program.
- Flexibility Training, including a regular stretching routine.
- Stress Management, including relaxation techniques and time management.
- Cognitive Behavior Therapy, including attitude and thought management.

You'll receive weekly consultations from your Personal Trainer during the first six months on your Flab-To-Fit program, and monthly consultations thereafter. In this way, you'll quickly achieve your goals and receive the support over the long haul to maintain a high fitness level.

Fitness Report for Sean Hogue 2

CREATING AN ONSCREEN ORDER FORM

In this case you will:

- Change page orientation
- Design and create an on-screen form
- Merge and split cells and change column width in a table
- Shade cells in a table
- Change font effects and colors
- Rotate text within a table cell
- Insert form fields for text, drop-down lists, and check boxes
- Set up form for automatic calculations

CASE

Spanish Translation Services

Clara Carreras, who grew up bilingual in English and Spanish and graduated with a degree in Spanish from the University of Miami, owns a company called Spanish Translation Services (USTS), located in Fort Myers, Florida. She and her employees translate Spanish to English or English to Spanish and serve as interpreters. They translate a wide variety of documents, including advertising content, brochures, catalogs, contracts, legal documents, marketing materials, newsletters, press releases, reports, and speeches. They also serve as live interpreters for Spanish-speaking dignitaries, politicians, and religious leaders, and for English speakers at Spanish-speaking functions.

Clara asks you to help her design and implement an on-line (computerized) order form, so that as her employees receive requests for services, they can fill out a standard form.

1. Start Word (if necessary), make sure your Data Disk is in an appropriate drive, open **STSOrder** from the AddCases folder of your Data Disk, and then save the document as a document template in the same folder using the filename **STS Order Form**.

2. Change the page orientation from portrait to landscape orientation and set the top and bottom margins to 0.5 inch.

3. Increase the width of column B until the right edge of the table is at the right margin, about 1.25 inches from the right edge of the page.

4. Decrease the width of column A to about 2.1 inches. The width of column B should then be about 6.5 inches so the final table will all fit on one page.

5. Change the normal font to 12-point Arial, and then change the font of the company name (in cell b1) to 30-point bold Book Antiqua.

6. Center all the text in cell B1 (the company information), horizontally and vertically, and then apply the shading color Gray-20% to the cell.

7. Insert the picture file **STSLogo** into cell A1, and change its height to 1.5 inches while maintaining its aspect ratio.

8. Merge cells A2 and B2, center the text ("Billing Information") in the new merged cell, change its font to white, 16-point, bold Book Antiqua, and then apply a black shading to the cell.

9. Similarly, merge cells A12 and B2 (with the text "Translation Services), and apply the same formatting, so that rows 2 and 12 look the same (except for different text). Do the same for cells A17 and B17 (with the text "Interpretation Services").

10. Split cell B14 into two columns. In the new cell B14, insert a checkbox form field, with the default set to checked. To the right of the check box, insert a space and then the text "Spanish to English." In the new cell C14, insert a checkbox form field, with the default set to unchecked. To the right of the check box, insert a space and then the text "English to Spanish."

11. Split cell B19 into two columns, and then copy cells B14 and C14 to cells B19 and C19.

12. Insert the date/time field code into cell B3, so that the date and time appear in the form Aug 06 2004 4:42 PM. (Edit the field code if necessary.)

13. Using the following table as a guide, insert the indicated type of form fields into the indicated cells. Use default values, maximum lengths, formats, and status bar text, as indicated in the table. Do not include any Help (F1) text. (Edit the field codes as necessary.)

CELLS	TYPE	DEFAULT VALUE	MAXIMUM LENGTH	FORMAT	STATUS BAR TEXT
B4, B5, B6	Regular text	(none)	Unlimited	Uppercase	Customer's name, Customer's address, Customer's address
B7	Regular text	Miami	Unlimited	Uppercase	Customer's city
B8	Regular text	FL	2	Uppercase	Customer's state
B9	Number text	33101	5	0 (integer)	Customer's ZIP
B10	Regular text	303-	Unlimited	(none)	Customer's phone number, including area code
B11	Regular text	(none)	Unlimited	(none)	Customer's e-mail address
B13	Drop-down	Items: None Letter Brochure Catalog Contract Legal Doc Newsletter Report Speech Web page Other	(none)	(none)	(none)
B15	Number text	(none)	6	0	Approximate number of words in source document
B16	Date text	(none)	(none)	MMM dd, YYYY	Due date for translated document
B18	Drop-down	Items: None Business Religious Political Informal Other	(none)	(none)	(none)
B20	Regular text	(none)	Unlimited	(none)	Name of event (if any)
B21	Date text	(none)	(none)	MMM dd, YYYY	Starting date of event
B22	Date text	(none)	Unlimited	HH:mm	(none)
B23	Number text	(none)	3	0.0	Approximate duration in hours (use decimal number)
B24	Calculation	Formula: =B23*55	Unlimited	$#,##0.00	(none)

14. Compare your document template with the format of the sample document in Figure 4. Make any format adjustments necessary in your document so that, when it's used to start a new document, it will appear similar to Figure 4.

15. Protect the completed document template form, and then save it in the AddCases folder and in the Templates folder.

16. Start a new document using the STS Order Form in the Templates folder.

17. Fill in the report using the information shown in Figure 4.

18. Save the filled-in document as **STS Order**, print the document, and then close any open documents.

19. Delete the **STS Order Form** file from the Templates folder.

Figure 4

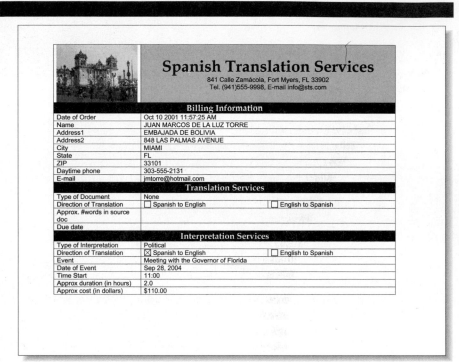

Spanish Translation Services
841 Calle Zamácola, Fort Myers, FL 33902
Tel. (941)555-9998, E-mail info@sts.com

Billing Information

Date of Order	Oct 10 2001 11:57:25 AM
Name	JUAN MARCOS DE LA LUZ TORRE
Address1	EMBAJADA DE BOLIVIA
Address2	848 LAS PALMAS AVENUE
City	MIAMI
State	FL
ZIP	33101
Daytime phone	303-555-2131
E-mail	jmtorre@hotmail.com

Translation Services

Type of Document	None	
Direction of Translation	☐ Spanish to English	☐ English to Spanish
Approx. #words in source doc		
Due date		

Interpretation Services

Type of Interpretation	Political	
Direction of Translation	☒ Spanish to English	☐ English to Spanish
Event	Meeting with the Governor of Florida	
Date of Event	Sep 28, 2004	
Time Start	11:00	
Approx duration (in hours)	2.0	
Approx cost (in dollars)	$110.00	

K

Key Paragraph, WD 8.10
keyboard shortcut
  macros, WD 8.44–8.45
  Office, OFF 13

L

letter. *See also* **form letter**
  preparing in Word, WD 1.14–1.16
  query letter, WD 8.04
line. *See also* **gridline**
  inserting horizontal lines,
    WD 7.42–7.43
line spacing. *See also* **spacing**
  changing, WD 2.23–2.24
  1.5 line spacing, WD 2.23
    double spacing, WD 2.23
line style, WD 3.28. *See also* **styles**
line weight, WD 3.28
link. *See* **hyperlinks**
linking. *See also* **hyperlinks**
  Excel chart
    in general, WD 7.17–7.19
    modifying, WD 7.19–7.21
    updating link, WD 7.21–7.24
  OLE. WD 7.10–7.11
    compared to embedding,
      WD 7.11–7.12
list
  adding bullets to, WD 2.28–2.30
  adding numbers to, WD 2.29
list box, using, WIN 2000 1.23–1.24

M

macros
  AutoMacro, recording,
    WD 8.45–8.46
  editing, with VBA editor,
    WD 8.42–8.44
  in general, WD 8.32–8.33
    ResizePictureLeft, WD 8.33
    ResizePictureRight, WD 8.33
  keyboard shortcut for,
    WD 8.44–8.45
  recording, WD 8.38
    to change field order,
      WD 9.37–9.42
    to draw border, WD 8.38–8.41
  running, WD 8.35–8.38,
    WD 8.50–8.52
  VBA macro, WD 8.34–8.35
Mail Merge Wizard. *See also*
  merge process
  editing data source, WD 6.24–6.26
  using, WD 6.05–6.06

mailing labels. *See also* **merge**
  process
  creating, WD 6.29–6.34
main document, WD 6.02. *See*
  also **document; merge process**
  editing, WD 6.16–6.20
    adding date field, WD 6.16–6.17
    revision marks, WD 7.02,
      WD 7.08
  merge process
    accepting and rejecting changes,
      WD 7.07–7.08
    changes in document,
      WD 7.03–7.05, WD 7.05–7.06
    inserting merge fields,
      WD 6.17–6.20
    previewing, WD 6.21–6.22
    selecting, WD 6.06–6.08
    with data source, WD 6.22–6.24
margins. *See also* **indenting;**
  ruler; text
  changing, WD 2.21–2.22
  paragraph indentation,
    WD 2.25–2.26
master document. *See also*
  document
  converting document into,
    WD 10.05–10.07
  creating, WD 10.04
  in general, WD 10.02–10.04
  planning, WD 10.02
  preparing to use, WD 10.04–10.05
    master document view, 10.04
  reopening, WD 10.19–10.20
  saving, WD 10.09
  subdocuments, WD 10.02
    collapsing, WD 10.19
    creating, WD 10.10
    expanding, WD 10.19
    inserting, WD 10.07–10.09
    merging, WD 10.12–10.13
    numbering, WD 10.20
    removing, WD 10.13–10.14
    splitting, WD 10.11–10.12
menu. *See also* **button; toolbar**
  clicking on, WIN 2000 1.07
  commands, WIN 2000 1.20
  menu options, WIN 2000 1.20
  Office, OFF 13–16
  personalized, OFF 13–14
  Personalized Menus,
    WIN 2000 1.10
  program menu
    in general, WIN 2000 1.20
    selecting options,
      WIN 2000 1.20–1.22
  shortcut menu, WIN 2000 1.09
  Start menu, WIN 2000 1.07

menu command, OFF 13
merge field, WD 6.02.
  See also **field**
  inserting, WD 6.17–6.20
merge process
  data fields and records, WD 6.05
  data source, WD 6.03, WD 6.08
    displaying records, WD 6.14
    entering data in, WD 6.11–6.14
    saving data source, WD 6.14–6.16
    selecting fields, WD 6.08–6.11
  in general, WD 6.02–6.04
  inserting merge fields,
    WD 6.17–6.20
  mail merge fields, WD 6.04
  Mail Merge Wizard, WD 6.05–6.06
  mailing labels, creating,
    WD 6.29–6.34
  main document
    accepting and rejecting changes,
      WD 7.07–7.08
    changes in document,
      WD 7.03–7.05, WD 7.05–7.06
    comparing, WD 7.02
    data source and, WD 6.22–6.24
    previewing, WD 6.21–6.22
    selecting, WD 6.06–6.08
  record selection, WD 6.28–6.29
merged document, WD 6.03. *See*
  also **document; main document**
Microsoft Access 2002. *See* **Access**
Microsoft Excel 2002. *See* **Excel**
Microsoft Front Page, WD 7.38
Microsoft Graph, chart creation,
  WD 10.26–10.29
Microsoft Internet Explorer,
  WD 7.26
Microsoft Office XP. *See* **Office**
Microsoft Outlook 2002.
  See **Outlook**
Microsoft PowerPoint 2002.
  See **PowerPoint**
Microsoft Word 2002. *See* **Word**
mouse, WIN 2000 1.05. *See also*
  pointing device
mouse pad, WIN 2000 1.06
MS–DOS, DOS text,
  WIN 2000 2.09
multitasking, WIN 2000 1.12
My Computer window,
  WIN 2000 2.02. *See also*
  desktop
  changing appearance of
    changing icon display,
      WIN 2000 2.18–2.20
    controlling toolbar display,
      WIN 2000 2.17–2.18
    in general, WIN 2000 2.17

TASK	PAGE #	RECOMMENDED METHOD
Action, redo most recent	WD 2.12	Click ↻
Action, undo most recent	WD 2.12	Click ↺
AutoCorrect, customize	WD 8.14	Click Tools, click AutoCorrect Options, click AutoCorrect tab, click Exceptions button, click INitial CAps tab, type word or acronym with two initial capital letters that you don't want Word to correct, click OK button twice
AutoCorrect, use	WD 1.28	Click AutoCorrect Options ⚡▾, click correct spelling
AutoText, create	WD 8.12	Select text or graphics, click Insert, point to AutoText, click AutoText, enter name, select desired template, click Add button.
AutoText, insert	WD 8.15	Type name of AutoText entry, press F3 key
AutoText, print list of entries	WD 8.16	Click File, click Print, click Print what list arrow, click AutoText entries, click OK button
Background, apply textured	WD 7.35	Click Format, point to Background, click Fill Effects, click Gradient tab, select colors and shading style, click OK button
Boldface, add to text	WD 2.34	Select text, click **B**
Bookmark, create	WD 7.29	Move insertion point to desired location, click Insert, click Bookmark, type bookmark name, click Add button
Border, change in table	WD 3.28, WD 3.32	See Reference Window: Altering Table Borders
Borders, draw	WD 9.05	Click ▦, click Line Weight list arrow, select a line weight, click Line Style list arrow, select a line style drag pointer along cell gridlines
Border, draw around page	WD 4.28, WD 4.34	Click Format, click Borders and Shading, click Page Border tab, click Box, click Apply to, click Whole document
Borders, remove from table	WD 9.05	Click ▦, click Line Style list arrow, click No Border, drag pointer along cell gridlines
Bullets, add to paragraphs	WD 2.31	Select paragraphs, click ☰
Captions, create double-numbered	WD 9.33	Select table or figure, click Insert, point to Reference, click Caption, click Label list arrow, click type of object, click Numbering button, select Include chapter number checkbox, click OK button twice
Character spacing, adjust	WD 5.37	Select text, click Format, click Font, click Character Spacing tab, click Spacing list arrow, click spacing style, change number of points between characters, click OK button

TASK	PAGE #	RECOMMENDED METHOD
Character spacing, expand or condense	WD 5.36	See Reference Window: Expanding or Condensing Spacing Between Characters
Chart, create	WD 9.51	Click Insert, click Object, click Create New tab, click Microsoft Graft Chart, click OK button, select entire data sheet, press Delete key, fill in datasheet, click outside of chart to deselect it (or if chart is in separate window, click File, click Exit and Return to…)
Check Box Form Field, insert	WD 9.33	Click ☑ on Forms toolbar, click 🗐, set options, click OK button
Click and Type, enable	WD 5.32	Click Tools, click Options, click Edit tab, select the Enable click and type check box, click OK button
Clip art, crop	WD 4.20, WD 4.25	Click clip art, click 🔲, drag picture border to crop
Clip art, find	WD 4.17, WD 4.20	Click 🔳 on Drawing toolbar, type search criteria, click Search
Clip art, insert in document	WD 4.17, WD 4.20	Click 🔳 on Drawing toolbar, click Clip Organizer, click picture, click Copy, click in document, click 🔲
Clip art, resize	WD 4.20, WD 4.24	Click clip art, drag resize handle
Clip art, rotate	WD 4.21, WD 4.26	Click clip art, click 🔲 on the Picture toolbar
Clip art, wrap text around	WD 4.22, WD 4.27	Click clip art, click 🔲 button on the Picture toolbar, click text wrapping option
Clipboard Task Pane, open	WD 2.18	Click Edit, click Office Clipboard
Clipboard Task Pane, use to cut, copy, and paste	WD 2.16	See Reference Window: Using the Clipboard Task Pane
Column, insert in table	WD 3.22, WD 3.25	Click Table, point to Insert, click Columns to the Right or Columns to the Left
Column width, change in table	WD 3.25, WD 3.28	Double-click or drag border between columns; to see measurements, press and hold Alt while dragging
Columns, balance	WD 4.27, WD 4.33	Click the end of the right-most column, click Insert, click Break, click Continuous, click OK button
Columns, format text in	WD 4.1,	Click where you want to insert columns, or select text to divide into columns, click Format, click Columns, select options, click OK button
Columns, newspaper-style, create	WD 4.15	Click where you want to insert columns, or select text to divide into columns, click Format, click Columns, select options, click OK button

TASK	PAGE #	RECOMMENDED METHOD
Comment, add or edit	WD 2.37	See Reference Window: Using Comments
Comment, display	WD 2.38	Point to comment
Comment, insert	WD 2.37	Click Insert, click Comment, type comment, click in document window
Comments, delete	WD 10.42	With insertion point in comment, click 🔲 on Reviewing toolbar
Comments, find and view	WD 10.42	Switch to Print Layout view, click 🔲 on Reviewing toolbar, read comments in right margin.
Comments, include your name in	WD 10.41	Click Tools, click Options, insert name and initials in User Information tab, click OK button, insert comments
Comments, protect a document for	WD 10.41	Click Tools, click Protect Document, click Comments option button, click OK button
Comments and revisions, print	WD 10.43	Click File, click Print, click Print what list arrow, click List of Markup, click OK button
Cross references, create	WD 10.29	Move insertion point to cross-reference location, type preceding text (such as "See"), click Insert, point to Reference, click Cross-reference, select reference type, select information to appear in cross-reference, click Insert button, and click Close button
Data source, attach	WD 6.16	Click Tools, point to Letters and Mailings, click Mail Merge Wizard; in Step 3 of the wizard, click Use an existing list, click Browse, select data source, click Open
Data source, create	WD 6.10	Click Tools, point to Letters and Mailings, click Mail Merge Wizard; in Step 3 of the wizard, click Type a new list, click Create, enter information, click OK button
Data source, sort	WD 6.27	See Reference Window: Sorting a Data Source
Date field, insert	WD 6.16	Click Insert, click Date and Time, select Update automatically checkbox, select date style, click OK button
Date, insert with AutoComplete	WD 1.32	Start typing date, press Enter
Digital signature, authenticate document with	WD 10.46	Open document, click Tools, click Options, click User Information tab, add your name and initials, click Security tab, click Digital Signature button, click Add button, click Yes button, if document has tracked changes click Yes button again, click name in list of issued certificates, click OK button three times, save document, close document

TASK	PAGE #	RECOMMENDED METHOD
Digital signature, create	WD 10.45	Click Start button on Task Bar, click Run, click Browse button, locate Microsoft\Office folder, double click SELFCERT, click OK button, type your name in Your nametext box, click OK, wait for acknowledgement, click OK button
Document, close	WD 1.39	Click ☒
Document, open	WD 2.03	Click ☞, select drive and folder, click filename, click Open button
Document, open new	WD 1.17	Click ☐
Document, preview	WD 1.36	Click ☖
Document, print	WD 1.37	Click ☷
Document, route to multiple recipients	WD 9.48	Log on to Internet, return to Word window, click File, point to Send To, click Routing Recipient, click Address button, click recipient name, click To button, continue until all recipients have been added to Message Recipients list box, click OK button, click Route button, switch to e-mail program (if necessary) and send e-mail
Document, route to next recipient	WD 9.48	Log on to Internet, return to Word window, click File, point to Send To, click Next Routing Recipient, switch to e-mail program and send e-mail
Document, save with new name	WD 2.04	Click File, click Save As, select drive and folder, enter new filename, click Save button
Document, save with same name	WD 1.21	Click ☐
Documents, compare and merge	WD 10.39	Open one document, click Tools, click Compare and Merge Documents, select document, click Merge button, repeat for other documents
Drawing toolbar, open	WD 4.07	Click ☖
Drop cap, insert	WD 4.24, WD 4.30	Click in paragraph, click Format, click Drop Cap, select options, click OK button
Drop-down Form Field, insert	WD 9.31	Click ☷ on Forms toolbar, click ☷, type item in Drop-down item text box, click Add button, repeat to complete list, click OK button
Embedded object, modify	WD 7.14	Double-click object, use commands and tools of source program to modify object, click outside embedded object

TASK	PAGE #	RECOMMENDED METHOD
Envelope, print	WD 1.38	Click Tools, point to Letters and Mailings, click Envelopes and Labels, click Envelopes tab, type delivery and return addresses, click Print button
Fax, create and send	WD 9.48	Create and save document, click File, point to Send To, click Fax Recipient, follow instructions in Fax Wizard
Field code, view	WD 9.22	Press Alt+F9 or click {a}
Field, edit	WD 8.26	Click field to edit, if necessary press Alt+F9 to view field code, change field information or switches
Field, insert	WD 8.25	Click Insert, click Field, click desired field, click OK button
Field, update	WD 8.27	Select field, press F9 key
Fill-In Field, insert	WD 8.27	Click Insert, click Field, click Mail Merge category, click Fill-in, click OK button
Find and replace text	WD 2.20	See Reference Window: Finding and Replacing Text
Folder, create new	WD 5.04	Click File, click Save As, click 📄, type folder name, click OK button
Font and font size, change	WD 2.33	See Reference Window: Changing the Font and Font Size
Font size, select	WD 1.14	Click Format, click Font, click font size
Font, select	WD 1.13	Click Format, click Font, click font name
Footer, add	WD 3.11, WD 3.13	Click View, click Header and Footer, click 📑, type footer text, click Close button
Footer, setup for odd/even pages	WD 10.51	Click File, click Page Setup, click Layout tab, select Different odd and even checkbox, click OK button, click View, click Header and Footer, click 📑, insert odd page footer text, click 📑, insert even page footer text, click Close button on Header and Footer toolbar
Footnote, add	WD 5.30	Switch to Normal view, click footnote reference location, click Insert, point to Reference, click Footnote, select note type and numbering method, set format, click Insert, type footnote, click Close button
Form Fields, perform calculations with	WD 9.35	Move insertion point to results cell, insert text form field, click 📋, click Type list arrow, click Calculations, type expression, click Number format list arrow, select format, click OK button
Format, copy	WD 2.30	Select text with desired format, double-click 🖌, click paragraphs to format, click 🖌

TASK	PAGE #	RECOMMENDED METHOD
Graph, create		See "Chart, create"
Graphic, crop	WD 4.20, WD 4.25	Click graphic, click 🔲, drag to crop
Graphic, find	WD 4.17, WD 4.20	Click 🔲 on Drawing toolbar, type search criteria, click Search
Graphic, resize	WD 4.20, WD 4.24	Click graphic, drag resize handle
Graphic, rotate	WD 4.21, WD 4.26	Click graphic, click 🔲 on the Picture toolbar
Graphic, wrap text around	WD 4.22, WD 4.27	Click graphic, click 🔲 button on the Picture toolbar, click text wrapping option
Graphic file, insert	WD 8.05, WD 8.06	Click at desired graphic location, click Insert, point to Picture, click From File, select graphic file, click Insert button
Header, add	WD 3.11, WD 3.13	Click View, click Header and Footer, type header text, click Close button
Heading styles, add numbers to	WD 10.21	Position insertion point in text formatted with heading style you want to number, click Format, click Bullets and Numbering, click Outline Numbering tab, select heading numbering style, click Customize to modify numbering style, click OK button twice
Horizontal line, insert	WD 7.42	Click Format, click Borders and Shading, click Borders tab, click Horizontal Line button, click a line style, click OK button
Hyperlink, add to document	WD 4.05	Type e-mail address or URL, press spacebar or Enter key
Hyperlink, edit	WD 7.45	Right-click the hyperlink, click Edit Hyperlink, edit filename or select a new file, click OK button
Hyperlink, remove	WD 4.06	Right-click hyperlink, click Remove Hyperlink
Hyperlink to another document, create	WD 7.31	Select text, click 🔲, click Existing File or Web Page, locate target document, click OK button
Hyperlink to same document, create	WD 7.28	Insert bookmark at target location, select hyperlink text or graphic, click 🔲, click Place in This Document, click bookmark name, click OK button twice
Hyperlink, use	WD 7.30	Hold down Ctrl and then click the underlined hyperlink; click 🔲 to return to original location
Hyphenation, change	WD 5.28	Click Tools, point to Language, click Hyphenation, ente size of Hyphenation Zone, set limit for consecutive hyphens, click Automatically hyphenate document, click OK button
Index, compile	WD 10.61	Move insertion point to desired location for index, click Insert, point to Reference, click Index and Tables, click Index tab, set desired options, click OK button

TASK	PAGE #	RECOMMENDED METHOD
Index, create cross reference entries	WD 10.59	Select cross-reference in document, press Alt+Shift+X, click Cross-reference option button, type main entry in Cross-reference text box, click Mark button
Index, create page range references	WD 10.59	Select range of pages, click Insert, click Bookmark, type name of bookmark, click Add button, press Alt+Shift+X, click Page Range option button, click Bookmark list arrow, click bookmark name, click Mark button
Index, mark main entries	WD 10.56	Select entry in document, press Alt+Shift+X, click Mark All button
Index, mark subentries	WD 10.58	Select subentry in document, press Alt+Shift+X, type main entry in Main entry text box, type subentry in Subentry text box, click Mark All button
Insertion point, position with Click and Type	WD 5.33	Point to location where you want to insert text, table, or graphic; double-click
Italics, add to text	WD 2.36	Select text, click I
Keyboard shortcut, assign to macro	WD 8.43	Click Tools, click Customize, click Keyboard button, click Macros in Categories list box, click macro name in Macros list box, click in Press new shortcut key text box, press desired key combination, click Assign button, Close button twice
Line spacing, change	WD 2.25	Select text, press Ctrl+1 for single spacing, Ctrl+5 for 1.5 line spacing, or Ctrl+2 for double spacing
Link, update	WD 7.22	Open destination file, click Edit, click Links, select filename, click Update Now, click OK button
Macro, edit	WD 8.41	Click Tools, point to Macro, click Macros, click name of macro, click Edit, edit macro, close Visual Basic Editor window
Macro, import	WD 8.33	Click Tools, point to Macro, click Visual Basic Editor, click File, click Import File, select macro file, click Open button, double-click Modules folder in Project pane, double-click name of imported macro, click ☒ in VBA Editor window
Macro, record	WD 8.37	Double-click REC on status bar, type macro name, type description, click Store Macro in list box, click template name, click Record button, record keystrokes, click Stop Recording button on Stop toolbar
Macro, run	WD 8.34	Click Tools, point to Macro, click Macros, click name of macro, click Run button

TASK	PAGE #	RECOMMENDED METHOD
Mail Merge, perform	WD 6.06	Click Tools, point to Letters and Mailings, click Mail Merge Wizard, follow wizard Steps 1-6
Mailing labels, create	WD 6.30	Click Tools, point to Letters and Mailings, click Mail Merge Wizard, click Labels, click Next: Starting document, click Label options, select label type, click OK, click Next: Select Recipients, select or create data source, click Next: Arrange your labels, insert merge fields, click Update all labels, click Next: Preview your labels, click Next: Complete the merge
Main Document, select	WD 6.07	Click Tools, point to Letters and Mailings, click Mail Merge Wizard, select document type, click Next: Starting document, select document
Margins, change	WD 2.23	Click File, click Page Setup, click Margins tab, enter margin values, click OK button
Master Document view, switch to	WD 10.06	Switch to Outline view, click 🗐 on Outlining toolbar to select it
Master Document, create	WD 10.04	Switch to Master Document view, insert a subdocument, click 🖫
Master Document, create subdocument from	WD 10.10	In Master Document view, select section to be transformed into subdocument, click 🖹 on Outlining toolbar
Master Document, insert subdocuments in	WD 10.07	Click 🖹 on Outlining toolbar, select document, click Open button
Master Document, merge adjacent subdocuments in	WD 10.12	Switch to Master Document view, click 🖾 for first subdocument, press and hold Shift key, click 🖾 for adjacent subdocument, click 🖹
Master Document, remove subdocument from	WD 10.14	Click 🖾 for desired subdocument, click 🖻 on Outlining toolbar
Master Document, split subdocument in	WD 10.11	Switch to Master Document view, click in heading of subdocument to be split, click 🖹 on Outlining toolbar
Merge fields, insert in main document	WD 6.18	Click Tools, point to Letters and Mailings, click Mail Merge Wizard; in Step 4, click More Items, click field name, click Insert, click Close button
Merged data, view in main document	WD 6.21	Click Tools, point to Letters and Mailings, click Mail Merge Wizard; on Step 5, click Next and Previous buttons in Task Panes, or click ⏮, ◀, ▶, and ⏭ the Mail Merge toolbar
Nonprinting characters, show	WD 1.14	Click ¶
Normal view, change to	WD 1.09	Click 🗏

TASK	PAGE #	RECOMMENDED METHOD
Number of Pages field, insert in header or footer		Switch to Header and Footer view, click 🔲 on Header and Footer toolbar
Numbered list, create	WD 2.32	Select paragraphs, click 🔢
Object, embed	WD 7.12	Click destination location, click Insert, click Object, click Create from File tab, click Browse, select file, click Insert, click OK button
Object, link	WD 7.17	Click destination location, click Insert, click Object, click Create from File tab, click Browse, select file, click Insert, click Link to File check box, click OK button
Object, modify linked	WD 7.20	Double-click linked object, use source program tools to modify object, click outside linked object; or open object in source program, modify, save, open destination program, and update links
On-screen form, protect	WD 9.42	Click 🔒 on Forms toolbar
On-screen form, save data in	WD 9.51	Click Tools, click Options, click Save tab, select Save data only in forms check box, click OK button, click 💾, type new filename if necessary, click Save button
Outline, create	WD 5.24	See Reference Window: Creating and Editing Outlines
Outline, edit	WD 5.24	See Reference Window: Creating and Editing Outlines
Page, preview more than one	WD 3.10	Click 🔍, click ⊞
Page, vertically align	WD 3.10, WD 3.11	Click File, click Page Setup, click Layout tab, click Vertical alignment list arrow, click Center, click OK button
Page, view whole	WD 4.14, WD 4.16	Click Zoom list arrow, click Whole Page
Page break, insert	WD 3.15, WD 3.17	Click where you want to break the page, press Ctrl+Enter
Page number, insert	WD 3.12, WD 3.14	Open header or footer, click 🔢 on Header/Footer toolbar
Page Number field, insert in header or footer	WD 10.53	Switch to Header and Footer view, switch to footer if necessary, click at location of page number, click 🔢 on Header and Footer toolbar
Page numbers, change format	WD 10.49	Click Insert, click Page Numbers, click Format, click Number format list arrow, select format, click OK button twice
Paragraph, decrease indent	WD 2.28	Click 🔳
Paragraph, indent	WD 2.28	Click 🔳
Paragraph spacing, adjust	WD 5.38	See Reference Window: Adjusting Spacing Between Paragraphs

TASK	PAGE #	RECOMMENDED METHOD
Picture, insert Clip Art	WD 4.17, WD 4.20	Click [image] on Drawing toolbar, click Clip Organizer, click picture, click list arrow, click Copy, click in document, click [image]
Print layout view, change to	WD 3.16, WD 3.18	Click [image]
Reference Field, insert	WD 8.28	Select reference, click Insert, click Bookmark, type bookmark name, click Add button, click at reference location, click Insert, click Field, click Categories list arrow, click Links and References, click Ref in Field names list box, click bookmark name in Bookmark name list box, select field options, click OK button
Replace text	WD 2.20	See Reference Window: Finding and Replacing Text
Reverse type, format characters in	WD 9.14	Select paragraph or table cell, click [image], click [image] on Tables and Borders toolbar, click dark tile, click [image], click white tile
Reviewing pane, open or close	WD 2.38	Click [image] on Reviewing toolbar
Revision marks, display	WD 10.34	Click Display for Review list arrow in Reviewing toolbar, click Final Showing Markup
Revision marks, display by individual reviewer	WD 10.37	Click Display for Review list arrow in Reviewing toolbar, click Original Showing Markup, click Show button in Reviewing toolbar, point to Reviews, click reviewer name
Revision marks, display for all reviewers	WD 10.37	Click Display for Review list arrow in Reviewing toolbar, click Original Showing Markup, click Show button in Reviewing toolbar, point to Reviews, click All Reviewers
Revision marks, edit a document with	WD 10.33	If document is protected for revision marks, edit document. If document is not protected for revision marks, double-click TRK button on status bar
Revision marks, hide	WD 10.34	Click Display for Review list arrow in Reviewing toolbar, click Final
Revision marks, include your name in	WD 10.33	Click Tools, click Options, insert name and initials in User Information tab, click OK button, insert comments
Revision marks, select different colors for different reviewers in	WD 10.35	Click Show button on Reviewing toolbar, click Options, click Color list arrow, click By author, click OK button
Revisions, accept and reject	WD 7.07, WD 10.37	Click [image] on Reviewing toolbar, click [image] to reject change or click [image] to accept change

TASK	PAGE #	RECOMMENDED METHOD
Revisions, protect a document for	WD 10.32	Click Tools, click Protect Document, click Tracked changes option button, click OK button
Row, delete from table	WD 3.24, WD 3.27	Select the rows you want to delete, click Table, point to Delete, click Rows
Row, insert in table	WD 3.23, WD 3.26	Click bottom-right cell, press Tab
Row height, change in table	WD 3.26, WD 3.29	Drag divider between rows; to see measurements, press and hold Alt while dragging
Ruler, display	WD 1.12	Click View, click Ruler
Section, insert in document	WD 3.08	Click where you want to insert a section break, click Insert, click Break, click Section break types option button, click OK
Section, vertically align	WD 3.09, WD 3.11	Click File, click Page Setup, click Layout tab, click Vertical alignment list arrow, click Center, click OK
Shading, apply to table	WD 3.29, WD 3.33	Select table area to shade, click Shading Color list arrow on Tables and Borders toolbar, click a color
Smart Tag, remove	WD 1.34	Click ⬚ ▾ , click Remove this Smart Tag
Smart Tags, select actions for	WD 8.17	Click within tagged text, click ⬚ , click desired action, complete action as directed
Smart Tags, turn on	WD 8.18	Click Tools, click AutoCorrect Options, click Smart Tags tab, select Label Text with Smart Tags check box, click OK button
Special character, insert	WD 4.26, WD 4.33	Click Insert, click Symbol, click Special Characters tab, click special character, click Insert, click Close button
Spelling and grammar, check	WD 2.05	See Reference Window: Checking a Document for Spelling and Grammatical Errors
Spelling and grammar, check document	WD 2.05	Click ⬚ , click Correction, click Change; click Ignore Once to skip an item
Spelling, correct individual words	WD 1.30	Right-click misspelled word (as indicated by a wavy red line), click correctly spelled word
Style, apply	WD 5.16	Select text, click Style list arrow, click style name
Style, define by example	WD 5.19	See Reference Window: Defining New Styles
Style, define new with style command	WD 5.19	See Reference Window: Defining New Styles
Style, modify	WD 5.16	See Reference Window: Modifying a Style

TASK	PAGE #	RECOMMENDED METHOD
Style Reference, insert in footer	WD 10.53	Switch to Header and Footer view, click Insert, click Field, click Categories list arrow, click Links and References, click StyleRef in Field names list box, click style in Style name list box, click OK button
Symbol, insert	WD 4.26, WD 4.33	Click Insert, click Symbol, click desired symbol, click Insert, click Close button
Tab stop, set	WD 3.05,	Click tab alignment selector, click ruler
Table, adjust column width	WD 9.17	Position ┼‖→ over column border, press and hold down Alt key, drag ┼‖→ while viewing column width in ruler
Table, align text in	WD 9.15	Click in cell or select multiple cells, click appropriate alignment button on formatting toolbar
Table, center on page	WD 3.30, WD 3.34	Click in table, click Table, click Table Properties, click Table tab, click Center alignment option, click OK button
Table, create	WD 3.15, WD 3.22	Click 🔲, drag to select columns and rows; or click ✏ on Tables and Borders toolbar, draw columns and rows
Table, insert blank	WD 3.18	Click 🔲
Table, merge cells in	WD 9.13	Select cells, click Table, click Merge Cells
Table, sort	WD 3.20, WD 3.24	Click in the column you want to sort, click ⬇ or ⬇ on Tables and Borders toolbar
Table, split cells in	WD 9.11	Select cells, click Table, click Split Cells, set number of rows and columns, click OK button
Table, sum values in	WD 9.37, WD 9.61	Click cell at bottom of column of numbers or on right of row of numbers, click Σ
Tables and Borders toolbar, display	WD 3.19, WD 3.22	Click 🔲
Table of Contents, create	WD 5.39	See Reference Window: Creating a Table of Contents
Table of figures, create	WD 10.63	Click at desired table location, click insert, point to References, click Index and Tables, click Table of Figures tab, select options, click OK button
Task Pane, close	WD 1.08	Click ✖
Telephone List, create	WD 6.35	Click Tools, point to Letters and Mailings, click Mail Merge Wizard, click Directory, click Next: Starting document, select or create telephone list document, click Next: Select Recipients, select or create data source, click Next: Arrange your directory, insert merge fields, click Next: Preview your directory, click Next: Complete the merge

TASK	PAGE #	RECOMMENDED METHOD
Template, create new	WD 5.22	See Reference Window: Creating and Using a New Template
Template, saved in any location, open	WD 5.13	Click Tools, click Templates and Add-Ins, click Attach, select template, click Open, select the Automatically update document styles check box, click OK button
Template, saved in Template folder, open	WD 5.12	Click File, click New, click General Templates on the New Document Task Pane, click icon for template in the General tab, click OK button
Text, align	WD 2.26	Select text, click ▤, ▤, ▤, or ▤
Text, align in table	WD 3.26, WD 3.30	Click Align list arrow on Tables and Borders toolbar, click alignment option
Text, animate	WD 7.34	Select text, click Format, click Font, click Text Effects tab, select animation style, click OK button
Text, bold	WD 2.34	Select text, click **B**
Text, copy and paste	WD 2.17	Select text, click 📋, move to target location, click 📋
Text, delete	WD 2.10	Press Backspace to delete character to left of insertion point; press Delete to delete character to the right; press Ctrl+Backspace to delete to beginning of word; press Ctrl+Delete to delete to end of word
Text, highlight	WD 5.35	Select text, click ✎
Text, import	WD 8.47	Click at location for new text, click insert, click File, select file containing text, click Insert button
Text, italic	WD 2.36	Select text, click *I*
Text, move by cut and paste	WD 2.17	Select text, click ✂, move to target location, click 📋
Text, move by drag and drop	WD 2.14	Select text, drag pointer to target location, release mouse button
Text, rotate in table	WD 9.09	Display Tables and Borders toolbar, select text, click ☐
Text, select a block of	WD 2.07	Click at beginning of block, press and hold Shift and click at end of block
Text, select entire document	WD 2.08	Press Ctrl and click in selection bar
Text, select multiple adjacent lines	WD 2.07	Click and drag in selection bar
Text, select multiple nonadjacent lines	WD 2.08	Select text, press and hold Ctrl, and select next text
Text, select multiple paragraphs	WD 2.08	Double-click and drag in selection bar

TASK	PAGE #	RECOMMENDED METHOD
Text, select paragraph	WD 2.07	Double-click in selection bar next to paragraph
Text, select sentence	WD 2.07	Press Ctrl and click in sentence
Text, underline	WD 2.36	Select text, click U
Text, wrap around WordArt	WD 4.22, WD 4.27	Click WordArt, click 🔲 on the WordArt toolbar, click text wrap option
Text Form Fields, add help text for	WD 9.23	Click text form field, click 🖆, click Add Help Text button, click Help Key (F1) tab, click Type Your Own option button, click OK button twice
Text Form Fields, add status bar prompt for	WD 9.23	Click text form field, click 🖆, click Add Help Text button, click Status Bar tab, click Type Your Own option button, click OK button twice
Text Form Fields for dates, insert	WD 9.28	Click abl on Forms toolbar, click 🖆, click Type list arrow, click Date (or click Current date), if necessary type default date, click Date format list arrow, select date format or type date-time picture, click OK button
Text Form Field for numbers, insert	WD 9.20	Click abl on Forms toolbar, click 🖆, click Type list arrow, click Number, if necessary type default number, click Number format list arrow, select number format or type number picture, click OK button
Text Form Fields for text, insert	WD 9.29	Click abl on Forms toolbar, click 🖆, click Type list arrow, click Regular text, if necessary type default text, if necessary click Text format list arrow and select text format, click OK button
Thesaurus, use	WD 5.05	See Reference Window: Using the Thesaurus
Toolbar, change location of buttons on	WD 8.22	Click Tools, click Customize, drag button to new location, click Close button
Toolbar, display	WD 1.10	Right-click any visible toolbar, click toolbar name
Toolbar, remove button from	WD 8.21	Click Tools, click Customize, drag button off toolbar, click Close button
Toolbars, add buttons to	WD 8.21	Click Tools, click Customize, click Commands tab, click category in Categories list box, drag button from Commands list box to toolbar, click Save in list arrow, click template, click Close button
Underline, add to text	WD 2.36	Select text, click U
Version of a document, retrieve	WD 10.39	Click File, click Versions, click version, click Open button

TASK	PAGE #	RECOMMENDED METHOD
Versions of a document, save	WD 10.39	Save the document, click File, click Versions, click Save Now, type comment about version, click OK button
Web layout view, change to	WD 7.33	Open document, click 🔲
Web page, create	WD 7.38	See Reference Window: Saving a Word Document as a Web Page
Web page, view in Web browser	WD 7.46	Click File, click Web Page Preview
Widow/orphan protection, turn on for entire document	WD 10.15	Display Styles and Formatting task pane, point to the Normal style, click the Normal Style's list arrow, click Modify, click Format button, click Paragraph, click Line and Page Breaks tab, select Keep with next checkbox, select Widow/Orphan control check box, click OK button twice
Widow/orphan protection, turn on for heading style	WD 10.17	Display Styles and Formatting task pane, point to style in task pane, click style's list arrow, click Modify, click Format button, click Paragraph, click Line and Page Breaks tab, select Keep with next checkbox, select Widow/Orphan control check box click OK button twice
Word, exit	WD 1.40	Click ⊠
Word, start	WD 1.05	Click 🏁Start, point to Programs, click Microsoft Word
WordArt, change shape	WD 4.10	Click WordArt, click 🔲 on the WordArt toolbar, click shape
WordArt, edit text	WD 4.09, WD 4.10	Click WordArt, click Edit Text button on WordArt toolbar, edit text, click OK button
WordArt, insert	WD 4.07,	Click ◢, click WordArt style, click OK button, type WordArt text, select font, size, and style, click OK button
WordArt, wrap text	WD 4.22, WD 4.27	Click WordArt, click 🔲 on the WordArt toolbar, click text wrap option
Zoom setting, change	WD 1.12	Click Zoom list arrow, click zoom percentage

Standardized Coding Number	Certification Skill Activity — Activity	Courseware Reqs	Tutorial Pages	End-of-Tutorial Practice — End-of-Tutorial Pages	Exercise	Step Number
W2002-1	**Inserting and Modifying Text**					
W2002-1-1	Insert, modify and move text and symbols	Insert, cut, copy, paste and paste special	1.16–1.18 (insert)	1.35	RA	1–9, 11
				1.36	CP1	3–7
				1.36–1.37	CP2	3–8
				1.37	CP3	2
				1.38	CP4	5–8
			2.14–2.17 (cut, copy, paste)	2.40	RA	14
				2.44	CP4	6
				7.55 (Paste Special)	CP2	3
		Finding and replacing text	2.17–2.19	2.38	RA	7
				2.41	CP1	8
				2.42	CP2	4
				2.43	CP3	11
				2.44	CP4	12
		Using AutoCorrect to insert frequently used text	1.23–1.25	1.35	RA	10
				1.36	CP1	4
W2002–1–2	Apply and modify text formats	Applying and modifying character formats	2.31–2.34	2.38	RA	7
				2.41	CP1	6, 13 15, 16
				2.42	CP2	9
				2.43	CP3	4, 11 14, 15
				2.44–2.45	CP4	13, 15 16
W2002–1–3	Correct spelling and grammar usage	Using Spelling and Grammar checks	1.24–1.26	1.35	RA	15
				1.36	CP1	10
			2.05–2.06	2.38	RA	3
				2.41	CP1	2
				2.42	CP2	2
				2.44	CP4	3
		Using the Thesaurus	5.05–5.06	5.45	RA	5
				5.48	CP1	8
				5.50	CP3	6

MOUS CERTIFICATION GRID

Standardized Coding Number	Certification Skill Activity — Activity	Courseware Reqs	Tutorial Pages	End-of-Tutorial Practice — End-of-Tutorial Pages	Exercise	Step Number
W2002–1–4	Apply font and text effects	Applying character effects (superscript, subscript, etc.) and text effects (animation)	5.36	5.45 5.48	RA CP1	8, 10
			7.34–7.35 (animation)	7.49	RA	15
		Applying highlights	2.08–2.09 (select)	2.40 2.41 2.43 2.44	RA CP1 CP3 CP4	13, 14 13, 15 15 11
			5.35–5.36 (color)	5.46	RA	16
				5.47 5.50	CP1 CP3	6 10
W2002–1–5	Enter and format Date and Time	Inserting date/time fields and modifying field formats	1.27–1.29 (Auto Complete)	1.35 1.36	RA CP1	10 4
			5.34–5.35	5.46 5.49 5.51	RA CP2 CP4	17 13 8
W2002–1–6	Apply character styles	Applying character styles	5.15	5.45	RA	9
W2002–2	**Creating and Modifying Paragraphs**					
W2002–2–1	Modify paragraph formats	Applying paragraph formats	2.23–2.25 2.27–2.28	2.38 2.41 2.42 2.43 2.44	RA CP1 CP2 CP3 CP4	7 5, 10 10 14 11
		Applying borders and shading to paragraphs	5.19 4.28–29	2.32	CP1	9
		Indenting paragraphs	2.25–2.26	2.38–2.40 2.42 2.44	RA CP3 CP4	6, 13 6 10

Standardized Coding Number	Certification Skill Activity — Activity	Courseware Reqs	Tutorial Pages	End-of-Tutorial Pages	Exercise	Step Number
W2002–2–2	Set and modify tabs	Setting and modifying tabs	3.04–3.07	3.33 3.35	RA CP1	3 7
W2002–2–3	Apply bullet, outline, and numbering format to paragraphs	Applying bullets and numbering	2.28–2.29	2.38 2.41 2.42 2.43 2.44	RA CP1 CP2 CP3 CP4	7 9 7 6 7
		Creating outlines	5.24–5.27	5.46 5.47 5.49 5.50 5.51	RA CP1 CP2 CP3 CP4	11–13 2 7 3–4 3–6
W2002–2–4	Apply paragraph styles	Applying paragraph styles (e.g.; Heading 1)	5.16	5.45 5.49	RA CP2	7 4, 6
W2002–3	**Formatting Documents**					
W2002–3–1	Create and modify a header and footer	Creating and modifying document headers and footers	3.11–3.13	3.33 3.35 3.36	RA CP1 CP2	7, 8 5, 6 6, 7
W2002–3–2	Apply and modify column settings	Applying columns and modifying text alignment	4.13–4.14 4.27–4.28	4.31 4.32 4.34 4.35	RA CP1 CP2 CP3	12, 21 10 8 6
		Creating newsletter columns	4.13–4.14	4.31 4.32	RA CP1	12 10
		Revising column layout	4.27–4.28	4.31 4.34 4.35	RA CP2 CP3	21 8 6
W2002–3–3	Modify document layout and Page Setup options	Inserting page breaks	3.14–3.15	3.34 3.35	RA CP1	8 8
		Inserting page numbers	3.12	3.33 3.35	RA CP1	8 6
		Modifying page margins, page orientation	2.20–2.22 (margins)	2.38 2.41 2.42 2.43	RA CP1 CP2 CP3	5, 6 4 5 12, 13
W2002–3–4	Create and modify tables	Creating and modifying tables	3.13–3.18 3.21–3.27	3.34 3.35 3.36 3.37 3.38	RA CP1 CP2 CP3 CP4	8, 10–12 10–12 8, 9 4, 7 6, 7

MOUS CERTIFICATION GRID

Standardized Coding Number	Certification Skill Activity — Activity	Courseware Reqs	Tutorial Pages	End-of-Tutorial Practice		
				End-of-Tutorial Pages	Exercise	Step Number
		Applying AutoFormats to tables	3.24	3.37	CP3	5
		Modifying table borders and shading	3.27–3.30	3.34	RA	12, 13
				3.35	CP1	13
				3.36	CP2	11
				3.38	CP4	6
		Revise tables (insert and delete rows and columns, modify cell formats)	3.21–3.27	3.34	RA	10–12 17,18
			3.35		CP1	12
			3.36		CP2	10
			3.37		CP3	4
W2002-3-5	Preview and Print documents, envelopes, and labels	Using Print Preview	1.30–1.31	1.35	RA	18
				1.36	CP1	14
				1.37	CP2	11
				1.37	CP3	4
				1.38	CP4	12
		Printing documents, envelopes, and labels	1.31–1.32 (documents)	1.35	RA	18
				1.36	CP1	14
				1.37	CP2	11
				1.37	CP3	4
				1.38	CP4	12
			1.32 (envelopes)	1.35	RA	20
				1.37	CP2	12
				1.37	CP3	5
W2002-4	**Managing Documents**					
W2002-4-1	Manage files and folders for documents	Creating folders for document storage	5.04–5.05	5.45	RA	3
				5.50	CP3	2
W2002-4-2	Create documents using templates	Creating a document from a template	5.22 5.47	5.47	RA	24
W2002-4-3	Save documents using different names and file formats	Using Save, Save As	1.18–1.19 (Save)	1.35	RA	13, 17 21
				1.36	CP1	8, 14
				1.37	CP2	9, 13
				1.37	CP3	3, 6
				1.38	CP4	10, 12

Standardized Coding Number	Certification Skill Activity		Courseware Reqs	Tutorial Pages	End-of-Tutorial Practice		
		Activity			End-of-Tutorial Pages	Exercise	Step Number
				2.04 (Save As)	2.38	RA	2, 18
					2.41	CP1	1
					2.42	CP2	1
					2.43	CP3	2
					2.44	CP4	2
W2002–5		**Working with Graphics**					
W2002–5–1		Insert images and graphics	Adding images to document	4.16–4.19	4.31	RA	14
					4.33	CP1	11
					4.34	CP2	9
					4.36	CP4	9
W2002–5–2		Create and modify diagrams and charts	Creating and modifying charts and diagrams	7.17–7.23	7.48 (charts)	RA	8
						CP1	3–5
					7.55 (diagrams)	CP4	18
W2002–6		**Workgroup Collaboration**					
W2002–6–1		Compare and Merge documents	Compare and Merge documents	7.2–7.6	7.48	RA	3–5
W2002–6–2		Insert, view and edit comments	Insert, view and edit comments	2.34–2.35	2.40	RA	17
					2.42	CP2	11
		Convert documents into Web pages	Previewing as documents as web pages	7.46–7.47	7.49, 7.50	RA	11, 21
					7.51	CP1	7
					7.52	CP2	9
			Saving documents as web pages	7.38–7.39	7.49	RA	17
					7.52	CP2	10
					7.53	CP3	7
					7.55	CP4	10

Standardized Coding Number	Certification Skill Activity — Activity	Courseware Reqs	Tutorial Pages	End-of-Tutorial Practice — End-of-Tutorial Pages	Exercise	Step Number
W2002e–1	**Customizing Paragraphs**					
W2002e–1–1	Control Pagination	Managing orphans and widows	10.14–10.17	10.68	RA	8–9
				10.71	CP1	7–8
		Setting line and page breaks	10.15–10.18	10.72	CP1	6
			3.08	3.33	RA	5
			3.14	3.35	CP1	8
				3.36	CP2	4
W2002e–1–2	Sort paragraphs in lists and tables	Using the Sort feature	3.20–3.21, 3.23	3.34	RA	10
				3.37	CP3	6
				10.114	CP1	32
W2002e–2	**Formatting documents**					
W2002e–2–1	Create and format document sections	Using Page Setup options to format sections	3.09–3.10	3.33	RA	5–6
				3.35	CP1	3–4
				3.36	CP2	4–5
		Verifying paragraph formats	5.10, 5.15	5.47	RA	23
				5.49–5.50	CP2	5, 15
			8.10–8.12	8.64	CP3	5
		Clearing Formats	5.33, 5.39	5.46	RA	16, 18
				5.49	CP2	11
W2002e–2–2	Create and apply character and paragraph styles	Creating and applying character and paragraph styles	8.10–8.13	8.58	RA	3–4
				8.60	CP1	8
				8.64	CP3	5
			5.09–5.11	5.45	RA	7–9
			5.15–5.16	5.49	CP2	4–6
			5.19–5–21	5.50	CP3	9
W2002e–2–3	Create and update document indexes and tables of contents, figures, and authorities	Inserting an index	10.55–10.62	10.70–10.71	RA	23–30
				10.74–10.77	CP2	6, 31, 33
				10.78	CP3	3, 9–10
		Inserting a table of contents, table of figures, or tables of authorities	5.39–5.41	5.47	RA	18
				5.48	CP1	12
				5.50	CP3	11
			10.62–10.65	10.70	RA	26–27
				10.74	CP1	31
				10.77	CP2	29
				10.78–10.79	CP3	8, 14–16
				10.80	CP4	14

Standardized Coding Number	Certification Skill Activity — Activity	Courseware Reqs	Tutorial Pages	End-of-Tutorial Practice — End-of-Tutorial Pages	Exercise	Step Number
W2002e–2–4	Create cross–references	Inserting cross–references	10.29–10.31	10.69–10.70 10.73 10.77 10.80	RA CP1 CP2 CP4	12, 24 28 32 6
W2002e–2–5	Add and revise endnotes and footnotes	Create, format, and edit footnotes and endnotes	5.29–5.31	5.48 5.48 5.50	RA CP1 CP3	14 9 7
W2002e–2–6	Create and manage master documents and subdocuments	Creating master documents with three or more subdocuments	10.02–10.14, 10.19–10.20	10.68–10.70 10.71 10.75 10.77–10.78	RA CP1 CP2 CP3	4–7, 29 3–6 7–8 1–5
W2002e–2–7	Move within documents	Using automation features for document navigation (bookmarks and Document Map)	7.27–7.30 8.45–8.46 9.37–9.42	7.49 8.61 8.63 8.65 9.54	RA CP1 CP2 CP3 RA	12, 14–15 15 11 15 11–20
W2002e–2–8	Create and modify forms using various form controls	Creating custom forms using two or more form controls	9.1–9.53	9.53–9.55 9.56 9.59–9.60 9.60–9.61	RA CP1 CP3 CP4	1–27 1–25 1–22 1–23
W2002e–2–9	Create forms and prepare forms for distribution	Protecting forms	9.26–9.27 9.42–9.44	9.54 9.56 9.58 9.60 9.61	RA CP1 CP2 CP3 CP4	23 21 21 22 19
		Distributing forms	9.48–9.50	9.58	CP2	22
W2002e–3	**Customizing Tables**					
W2002e–3–1	Use Excel data in tables	Using object linking to display Excel worksheet data as a Word table or worksheet object	7.17–7.18	7.52 7.57	RA CP2	8 3
W2002e–3–1	Perform calculations in Word tables	Use formulas in tables	 9.35–9.37	3.34 9.54 9.58 9.59 9.61	RA RA CP2 CP3 CP4	18, 19 17 17 8–9 11

Standardized Coding Number	Certification Skill Activity — Activity	Courseware Reqs	Tutorial Pages	End-of-Tutorial Practice — End-of-Tutorial Pages	Exercise	Step Number
		Modifying table formats by merging and/or splitting table cells	9.11–9.14	9.53	RA	7, 10
				9.56	CP1	9
				9.59–9.60	CP3	5, 13
				9.60	CP4	6
				3.34	RA	17
W2002e–4	**Creating and Modifying Graphics**					
W2002e–4–1	Create, modify, and position graphics	Creating and inserting graphics in documents	4.06–4.13 4.16–4.23	4.31	RA	5, 6, 14–16
				4.33	CP1	3–5, 11–13
				4.34	CP2	5, 6, 9–13
				4.36	CP3	8–10
				4.38	CP4	4, 9–10
			9.10–9.11	9.53	RA	3
		Modifying graphics	4.16–4.23	4.31	RA	5, 6, 14–16
				4.33	CP1	3–5, 11–13
				4.34	CP2	5, 6, 9–13
				4.36	CP3	8–10
					CP4	9–10
W2002e–4–2	Create and modify charts using data from other applications	Creating and revising charts using Excel or Access data	7.17–7.23	7.48	RA	7–8
				7.51	CP1	3–5
W2002e–4–3	Align text and graphics	Using advanced text wrapping and layout options with graphics	4.22	4.31	RA	18
				4.33	CP1	13
				4.34	CP2	13
				4.36	CP4	10
W2002e–5	**Customizing Word**					
W2002e–5–1	Create, edit, and run macros	Creating macros	8.32–8.46	8.59	RA	15, 16
				8.61	CP1	15
				8.63	CP2	11
			9.37–9.42	9.54	RA	19
				9.60	CP3	17
		Editing a macro using the Visual Basic Editor	8.42–8.44	8.59	RA	17
				8.63	CP2	12
		Running macros	8.50–8.52	8.59	RA	16, 17
				8.61	CP1	15
				8.63	CP2	11
			9.44–9.47	9.54	RA	19
				9.60	CP3	17

Standardized Coding Number	Certification Skill Activity — Activity	Courseware Reqs	Tutorial Pages	End-of-Tutorial Practice — End-of-Tutorial Pages	Exercise	Step Number
W2002e–5–2	Customize menus and toolbars	Creating a custom menu	8.4–8.5	8.60–8.62	CP1	4, 21
		Adding and removing buttons from a toolbar	8.22–8.24	8.58–59	RA	10–11 16, 22
W2002e–6	**Workgroup Collaboration**					
W2002e–6–1	Track, accept, and reject changes to documents	Tracking changes	7.07–7.08	7.50	RA	4–5
			10.31–10.36	10.69 10.72–10.73 10.75–10.76	RA CP1 CP2	13–18 13–21 11–23
		Reviewing changes by type and reviewer	10.37	10.80	CP4	12
		Responding to proposed changes	7.07–7.08	7.50	RA	4–5
			10.36–10.39	10.69 10.73 10.76	RA CP1 CP2	18 21 23
W2002e–6–2	Merge input from several reviewers	Distributing documents for revision via e–mail	7.25–7.26	7.50 7.51	RA CP1	24 13
			9.48–9.50			
			10. 41	10.80	CP4	16
		Merging three or more revisions of the same document	7.02–7.05	7.48	RA	3
			10.39	10.80	CP4	5
W2002e–6–3	Insert and modify hyperlinks to other documents and Web pages	Inserting and modifying hyperlinks	4.04–4.07	4.30 4.33 4.35	RA CP2 CP3	4 4 3
			7.27–7.32	7.49 7.51 7.52 7.53 7.54	RA CP1 CP2 CP3 CP4	12, 13, 14 9, 10 12 9 3, 5, 7, 11